THE SUBTLETY OF HOMER

The Subtlety of Homer

Richard J. Defouw

© 2018 Richard J. Defouw

All rights reserved.

No part of this publication may be reproduced, stored in a retrieval system, or transmitted, in any form or by any means, without the written permission of the author.

Published by Richard J. Defouw
4654 Harwich Street
Boulder, CO 80301
U.S.A.
rjdefouw@gmail.com

ISBN: 978-0-692-18543-8

CONTENTS

Chapter Contents vi
Preface viii
Conventions x
1. Wily Odysseus in Scheria 1
2. The Last Stratagem of Odysseus 15
3. The Humiliation of Agamemnon 56
4. Inconsistency and the Homeric Question 79
5. The Relationship between the *Iliad* and the *Odyssey* 84
6. Mysterious Inconsistency in the *Iliad* and the *Odyssey* 131
7. Mysterious Inconsistency in the Writings of Gurdjieff 189
8. Allusions to Homer in *Meetings with Remarkable Men* 200
9. Gurdjieff's Answer to the Homeric Question 227
Notes 253
Bibliography 337
Index of Homeric Passages 347

CHAPTER CONTENTS

1. WILY ODYSSEUS IN SCHERIA 1
   - 1.1 Critical stance 1
   - 1.2 The problem of the double weeping 3
   - 1.3 A solution 6
   - 1.4 Objections 9
   - 1.5 Associated narrative techniques 11
   - 1.6 Conclusion and transition 13

2. THE LAST STRATAGEM OF ODYSSEUS 15
   - 2.1 The contest of the bow 16
   - 2.2 Penelope's decision to hold the contest 16
   - 2.3 The removal of the arms 18
   - 2.4 The birth of the idea of the contest 20
   - 2.5 The motivation of Penelope 23
   - 2.6 Odysseus's reaction to Penelope's decision 27
   - 2.7 The wait for the contest 28
   - 2.8 The silencing of Telemachos 31
   - 2.9 Amphimedon's account 33
   - 2.10 Odysseus and Hephaistos 34
   - 2.11 The post-reunion conversation of Odysseus and Penelope 35
   - 2.12 Discussion and recapitulation 37
   - 2.13 The strategic contribution of Athene 38
   - 2.14 Athene in the Cyclops episode 46
   - 2.15 Behind the scenes on Olympos 49
   - 2.16 Implications 54

3. THE HUMILIATION OF AGAMEMNON 56
   - 3.1 The spurious reconciliation of Achilles and Agamemnon 56
   - 3.2 The spear-throwing event at the funeral games 60
   - 3.3 Agamemnon's failure to mention the games for Patroklos 68
   - 3.4 The other humiliation of Agamemnon 70
   - 3.5 The rapprochement of Achilles and Priam 72
   - 3.6 Achilles and Agamemnon at the end of the *Iliad* 74
   - 3.7 The chariot race 75

4. INCONSISTENCY AND THE HOMERIC QUESTION 79

5. THE RELATIONSHIP BETWEEN THE *ILIAD* AND THE *ODYSSEY* 84
   - 5.1 The Priority of the *Iliad* 84
   - 5.2 Comprehensible inconsistency in the *Odyssey* 88

5.3	Achilles in the *Odyssey* 92
5.4	The slaughter of the suitors 107
5.5	Chariots in warfare 116
5.6	Does the *Iliad* allude to the *Odyssey*? 118
5.7	Structural integration of the *Iliad* and the *Odyssey* 121
5.8	Monro's Law 128

6. Mysterious Inconsistency in the *Iliad* and the *Odyssey* 131

6.1	The embassy duals and associated problems 132
6.2	The embassy in the talk between Achilles and Patroklos 135
6.3	Agamemnon's test of the army 142
6.4	Divine interventions in the confrontation of Achilles and Aineias .. 153
6.5	The illogicality of the defensive ditch 163
6.6	Triadic inconsistencies involving Circe and Kalypso 167
6.7	Illogical instructions for Odysseus and Telemachos 173
6.8	The warning concerning the suitors 177
6.9	The absurd pretext for the removal of the arms 181
6.10	The shooting of Antinoös 182
6.11	Overview 186
6.12	One poet or two? 187

7. Mysterious Inconsistency in the Writings of Gurdjieff 189

7.1	The Lubovedsky triad 190
7.2	The triad of Ashiata Shiemash 191
7.3	A hub of inconsistency 194
7.4	Interleaved inconsistencies 195
7.5	Two properties of the inconsistencies 197
7.6	Reminder and overview 198

8. Allusions to Homer in *Meetings with Remarkable Men* 200

8.1	Singers of tales 200
8.2	Related inconsistencies 205
8.3	Odysseus as a remarkable man 207
8.4	The incident of the dogs 208
8.5	The substance of Odysseus 214
8.6	More inconsistencies 215
8.7	East and West in the writings of Gurdjieff 216
8.8	On the significance of the allusions 225

9. Gurdjieff's Answer to the Homeric Question 227

9.1	The Homeric epics as objective art 227
9.2	Generalized cognitive dissonance in Homer 233
9.3	The inconsistency of Aksharpanziar 239
9.4	Gurdjieff's implementation of Aksharpanziar's scheme 242
9.5	The origin of objective art 243
9.6	The unity of Homer the man 245
9.7	Extension of the East-West symmetry in *All and Everything* ... 249
9.8	Concluding remarks 251

PREFACE

This book discusses three levels of subtlety in the poems of Homer. On the first level, the poet clearly describes the actions of a character, but leaves it to the audience to infer the reasons or motivations for the actions from the character's psychology and situation. Examples are the weeping of Odysseus in front of the Phaiakians (chapter 1) and Achilles' treatment of Agamemnon in the funeral games for Patroklos (chapter 3). On the second level, important actions of a character go unmentioned but can be deduced from what is given. Examples are the devising by Odysseus of the contest of the bow, his communication of this idea to Athene, and her implanting of this idea in the mind of Penelope (chapter 2). On the third level, unexpected experiences are engendered in the audience by means of inconsistencies intentionally created by the poet without regard for ordinary dramatic considerations. This level represents a quantum jump in the subtlety of the poet's communication with his audience. It is poorly understood, but its existence is demonstrated by examples too numerous to mention here (see chapters 5 and 6).

The successive levels of subtlety deviate increasingly from conventional conceptions of Homeric poetry and for this reason become increasingly hard to credit. Although even the first level contradicts assertions of Homer's transparency that can be found in the scholarly literature, I don't believe that many readers will have trouble taking seriously the interpretations advanced in chapters 1 and 3. The second level (the idea that important actions take place below the surface of the poem) may be more difficult to accept. I urge readers of chapter 2 to put preconceptions aside and to consider the elegance of the solution to certain fundamental problems as well as the attractive corollaries (up to and including section 2.11) to the interpretation based on subtlety of the second level. If the second level invites skepticism, the third level would appear to be totally beyond belief. After all, what conceivable reason could the poet have for creating inconsistencies? Well, as a matter of fact, the existence of intentional inconsistencies in the *Iliad* and the *Odyssey* can be explained if these poems are specimens of what G. I. Gurdjieff called objective art, and I shall argue that Gurdjieff himself thought that they are. Unfortunately, my understanding of objective art, like that of others who have written on this subject (apart from Gurdjieff), is superficial, and the idea that the Homeric epics are objective art is merely a hypothesis. My hope is that the existence of a possible explanation for intentional inconsistency will lower resistance to the idea and help the reader to evaluate the evidence on its own merits.

Although I appeal to certain ideas of Gurdjieff in order to explain a mysterious phenomenon in Homer, it must be emphasized that my principal argument for the existence of this phenomenon is independent of Gurdjieff and rests entirely on the Homeric texts. To avoid any misunderstanding on this point, I have decided not to mention Gurdjieff in the title of this book. Nevertheless, the book may be of interest to students of Gurdjieff as well as to students of Homer. I have therefore written it in such a way that most of it should be accessible to readers with no prior knowledge of either Homer or Gurdjieff. The first two chapters do presuppose familiarity with the *Odyssey*, but they can be skipped by readers interested only in the (potentially) Gurdjieffian aspect of Homeric subtlety. Homerists who wish to understand the relevant ideas of Gurdjieff without going into the detailed arguments for their applicability to Homer should skip chapters 7 and 8 and read sections 9.1, 9.2, and 9.6; those who wish to ignore Gurdjieff entirely may still be interested in section 9.2.

Perhaps I should explain how I plan to make the existence of this book known to students of Gurdjieff. Two readers of my previous book, *The Enneagram in the Writings of Gurdjieff*, were generous enough to send me scans of typescripts of Gurdjieff's *Meetings with Remarkable Men* which show how he hid the true structure of this work from his pupils while he was alive in order to prevent them from seeing that this structure is based on the symbol known as the enneagram. The typescripts contain clear indications that their structure was meant to be temporary, presumably to be changed when the work was published after his death, and thus that the true structure possesses a hidden significance. This is another validation of the thesis of that earlier book, a thesis which already stood on a solid foundation. The typescripts also offer fascinating insight into Gurdjieff's long-range planning and the benevolent deceptions he carried out for the ultimate benefit of his followers. For both of these reasons, I intend to explain this material, as well as related material connected with another of his works, in a second edition of my previous book. This will afford a natural opportunity to refer to the present volume, because inconsistency in the writings of Gurdjieff, which I discuss in chapter 7 and in parts of chapters 8 and 9, also comes up in the earlier book, if only incidentally.

I am much indebted to Dr. Jon Thompson for a careful reading and a lengthy correspondence which led to significant improvements in my discussion of objective art. Dr. Thompson also kindly sent me a scan of Gurdjieff's Russian typescript of a chapter from *Meetings with Remarkable Men* so that I could resolve a conflict between the English and French translations. I wish to express my gratitude to Dr. Richard Rutherford for reading several chapters, sharing his varied reactions, and calling my attention to a useful reference. Finally, I thank my wife Laura for unearthing another useful reference and for her unfailing support.

Richard Defouw

Boulder, Colorado
September 2018

CONVENTIONS

Except where stated otherwise, all quotations from the *Iliad* and the *Odyssey* are from the translations by Richmond Lattimore. A few of the slight changes to Lattimore's *Iliad* made in the 2011 edition have not been adopted in the present volume; on the other hand, that edition's dieresis in "Danaäns" has been applied to the *Odyssey* as well.

Passages from prose translations are identified by Lattimore's line numbers, which are close to those of the Greek text.

In my own writing, I adopt Lattimore's spelling of all names except that of Achilles. To refer to the entity that leaves the body at death and goes to the underworld in Homeric eschatology, I use the term "shade" or "ghost" instead of the term "soul" favored by Lattimore and many other translators.

The word "Homer" is used for both the Homeric corpus (the *Iliad* and the *Odyssey*) and the poet(s) who composed it. I often write as if the two poems were composed by the same poet; this is what I believe, but no meaning should be read into this convention until I address the issue explicitly. I adopt a similarly cavalier attitude in referring to Homer's audience as either listeners or readers: consumers of Homer's poetry were originally listeners; now, of course, they tend to be readers.

"*Il*. 3.5" refers to line 5 of the third book of the *Iliad*. "*Il*. 24.339 = *Od*. 5.43" means that the indicated lines are identical in the Greek text given in the Loeb Classical Library (see bibliography under A. T. Murray) or The Chicago Homer (see bibliography under Ahuvia Kahane and Martin Mueller), an online database which, among other things, enables one to find all repetitions of a given phrase or passage in Homer. "*Il*. 11.403 = 17.90" is equivalent to "*Il*. 11.403 = *Il*. 17.90." (Another valuable online resource is the Perseus Digital Library at www.perseus.tufts.edu.)

<u>Homeric Name Equivalences and Conventions</u>
Achaeans = Achaians = Greeks
Aeneas = Aineias
Aias = the greater Aias (son of Telamon) except where stated otherwise; the lesser Aias = son of Oïleus
Achilleus = Akhilleus = Achilles
Antinous = Antinoös
Argeïphontes = Hermes

Argives = Greeks
Athena = Athene
Danaäns = Greeks
Demodocus = Demodokos
Ilion = Troy
Myrmidons = the people ruled by Peleus, the father of Achilles; at Troy: the contingent led by Achilles
son of Atreus = Agamemnon except where Menelaos is specified
son of Laertes = Odysseus
son of Menoitios = Patroklos
son of Peleus = Achilles
Phaiacian = Phaiakian
Menelaus = Menelaos
Ulysses = Odysseus

Bibliographical Abbreviations

Some references are specified by a combination of the author's name and an abbreviated title that is sufficient to identify the source in the bibliography. Other references are specified with an abbreviated title only. The abbreviations of this type (apart from *Il.* = the *Iliad* and *Od.* = the *Odyssey*) are shown below together with the information needed to locate each source in the bibliography.

Il. Comm. I = Kirk, *The Iliad: A Commentary*, vol. I
Il. Comm. II = Kirk, *The Iliad: A Commentary*, vol. II
Il. Comm. III = Hainsworth, *The Iliad: A Commentary*, vol. III
Il. Comm. IV = Janko, *The Iliad: A Commentary*, vol. IV
Il. Comm. V = Edwards, *The Iliad: A Commentary*, vol. V
Il. Comm. VI = Richardson, *The Iliad: A Commentary*, vol. VI
Herald = Gurdjieff, *The Herald of Coming Good*
BT = Gurdjieff, *Beelzebub's Tales to His Grandson* (1950 translation)
*BT*1992 = Gurdjieff, *Beelzebub's Tales to His Grandson* (1992 translation)
RM = Gurdjieff, *Meetings with Remarkable Men*
LIR = Gurdjieff, *Life Is Real Only Then, When "I Am"*
Fragments = Ouspensky, *In Search of the Miraculous: Fragments of an Unknown Teaching*
Views = Gurdjieff, *Views from the Real World: Early Talks of Gurdjieff*
EWG = Defouw, *The Enneagram in the Writings of Gurdjieff*

Chapter 1

Wily Odysseus in Scheria

How much meaning lies below the surface of the *Iliad* and the *Odyssey*? What sorts of things does Homer want the audience to understand even though they are not explicitly stated? Sharply contrasting answers to this question have been advanced either explicitly or implicitly. According to Erich Auerbach, "the basic impulse of the Homeric style" is "to represent phenomena in a fully externalized form, visible and palpable in all their parts." In a similar vein, Milman Parry says that "from every point of view the mark of Homeric style" is directness, so that one should "exclude any interpretation which does not instantly and easily come to mind."[1] At the opposite pole are theories of Penelope's "surrender" (her decision to hold the contest of the bow and to marry the winner of the contest) which posit a psychological subtext in conflict with the surface meaning of the text.[2] I regard these theories as desperate attempts to address a persistent problem of interpretation in the *Odyssey*. Bernard Fenik eschews such theories, but is led by the same problem to say of the *Odyssey* poet that "Clear, logical cause and effect, air-tight motivation or strict verisimilitude are not his concern. His interest is in emotion, irony, and pathos."[3] In the next chapter I will propose a solution to the problem of Penelope's surrender that preserves logical cause and effect and air-tight motivation without any loss of emotion, irony, or pathos—and without contradicting any part of the text. It does, however, require that significant developments in the poem take place below the surface. I now prepare the way for this solution and for the solution to the simpler problem discussed in the present chapter by addressing some possible objections, including the charge that these solutions are textbook examples of the documentary fallacy.

1.1. Critical Stance

Speaking of Penelope's mysterious "surrender" (or Penelope's "collapse," as he calls it), W. J. Woodhouse says the following:

> It would merely imply ignorance of his proper business for the poet to leave us to find our own reasons and explanations, from our general knowledge of human nature, or from some store of working maxims .... That will not do. We are shut up within what is given; in constructing his characters the maker is bound to equip them completely for their work, and has no right to expect

> his public to draw upon private stores in order to supply his deficiencies. The world into which at his invitation we follow him must be complete, so far as the story requires.
>
> Quote 1.1: Woodhouse, *Composition*, p. 89

According to Woodhouse, the *Odyssey* is incomplete because the poet provides no motivation for Penelope's surrender, and this incompleteness must be accepted as a flaw in the poem that is not to be rectified by the reader's speculations.

The principle articulated in quote 1.1 underlies what, thanks to A. J. A. Waldock, is now called the "documentary fallacy."[4] A work of fiction, observes Waldock, aims to achieve a carefully calculated effect, and in order to do this it must be complete; that is, everything needed to understand it must be provided by the author if the effect on the reader is to be under the author's control. By contrast, a factual text, or *document*, may well be incomplete and may reasonably be supplemented with outside sources. A critic who treats a work of literature as a document is guilty of the documentary fallacy.

The requirement that everything needed to understand a work of fiction must be provided by the author leaves open the question of how the author is required or permitted to provide the necessary information. Waldock asserts that in literature "*appearance* is everything, and there is no reality below the appearance" and that "in reading literature our impressions are everything and … outside them there is nothing to be found." If these assertions mean that everything must be explicitly stated by the author, then surely they are too restrictive. For example, Jasper Griffin has shown that it is sometimes legitimate to read into a passage from Homer psychology that the poet does not make explicit.[5] Parry's statement quoted above suggests that an interpretation of a Homeric passage is acceptable as long as it comes to mind "instantly and easily." This standard would allow the interpretations discussed by Griffin, and even Waldock seems to agree with it in practice.[6] I shall call it the Parry-Waldock criterion.

According to the Parry-Waldock criterion, all meaning in a work of literature is to be found on or very near the surface: "Literature operates on a thinnish crust, and there is nothing underneath this crust."[7] This description certainly fits some types of literature, including much of Homer, but I question its validity as a general rule that applies to all of Homer. Whereas Griffin showed that it is legitimate to use common sense to extrapolate from what is explicit, I submit that it can also be legitimate to extrapolate on the basis of logical inference, provided the inference is tightly constrained by what is explicit. What is inferred may lie far below the surface of the text. As long as the reader can be counted on to make the intended extrapolation, however, the effect of the work on the reader remains under the author's control, and this is what is important. Even if the inference is not made for some time, the effect will be achieved when it is made, and it may be that this delayed effect is what the author intends.

Two conditions are necessary for the author to be able to count on the reader making the intended extrapolation. First, the reader must be motivated to search for a solution to some problem of interpretation. And second, the solution obtained by logical inference must be completely determined by the explicitly given information; that is, it must be unique. The latter condition is sufficient to guarantee the completeness demanded by Woodhouse in quote 1.1 and to ensure that the reader does not run afoul of the documentary fallacy.

Some will undoubtedly object that this theorizing contemplates authorial behavior which is un-Homeric. But how does one know this? It is fair to believe that X is un-Homeric because one has not seen X in Homer and because X is very different from what one has seen. It is not fair, however, to use this belief to challenge a claim that X is found in Homer. It may be that this is the type of circular argument that Walter Burkert warned against in his remarks emphasizing that the fundamental question of "which categories of understanding, which criteria, are appropriate" in Homeric studies can be answered only from the text itself.[8]

Another likely objection is that this theorizing does not take into account the conditions of oral poetics. How can an oral poet compose so subtly? How can an audience listening to a performance be expected to make inferences like those contemplated here? I answer the first question by rejecting the strict oralist position and citing the attractive conjecture, to be discussed in chapter 4, that Homer made use of writing to compose poems in a style which had been developed by an oral tradition.[9] Even if this conjecture is correct, however, one still assumes that people in Homer's time were exposed to the *Iliad* and the *Odyssey* through oral performance. To not be able to refer to a written copy would have been a significant disadvantage in solving a deep problem of interpretation. Fortunately, people of Homer's time would have enjoyed a significant compensating advantage: they would have known that a solution exists (if it does), that the problem they were trying to solve was not merely a consequence of, say, the poet's lack of concern with logical cause and effect. For if members of an audience had complained that Penelope's surrender, for example, was not well motivated, Homer surely would have given them at least a knowing wink.

I have argued that it may be legitimate to search below the surface of a text for a solution to a problem of interpretation if the search is conducted on the basis of logical inference that is tightly constrained by what is said on the surface (which would include what we know about the psychology of a character). In chapter 2 I will discuss a set of related problems that includes the problem posed by Penelope's surrender. The uniqueness of the proposed solution is almost guaranteed by the large number of constraints imposed by the various problems. In the present chapter I discuss the single problem described in the following section. This problem is simple enough that one can convince oneself of the uniqueness of the solution by trying to come up with an alternative. The key in both cases will be to put ourselves in the position of Odysseus, relying only on what we know about him and about how he would react to the circumstances he faces.

1.2. The Problem of the Double Weeping

Odysseus spends three days in Scheria as a guest of the Phaiakians before they transport him to Ithaka, the beloved homeland he had left twenty years earlier to join the Greek expedition to Troy. The second day is a day of entertainment which includes three songs sung by the Phaiakian bard Demodokos. The middle song is a humorous tale which amuses everyone but has no bearing on the present discussion. The other two songs, each of which follows a meal, form a matching pair in important respects, and give rise to an interesting problem of interpretation.

The first song of Demodokos is about a quarrel between Odysseus and Achilles which Agamemnon believes to be connected with a prophecy concerning the outcome of the Trojan War. The Phaiakians do not yet know the identity of their guest, and will not know it until after the third song, so it is just by chance that the first song involves Odysseus. Our attention will be focused on his reaction to the song (the song itself will be discussed in a later chapter):

> These things the famous singer sang for them, but Odysseus,
> taking in his ponderous hands the great mantle dyed in
> sea-purple, drew it over his head and veiled his fine features,
> shamed for tears running down his face before the Phaiakians;
> and every time the divine singer would pause in his singing,
> he would take the mantle away from his head, and wipe the tears off,
> and taking up a two-handled goblet would pour a libation
> to the gods, but every time he began again, and the greatest
> of the Phaiakians would urge him to sing, since they joyed in his stories,
> Odysseus would cover his head again and make lamentation.
> There, shedding tears, he went unnoticed by all the others,
> but Alkinoös alone understood what he did and noticed,
> since he was sitting next him and heard him groaning heavily.
> <div align="right">Quote 1.2: <i>Od</i>. 8.83–95</div>

As no explanation is given for this reaction, it is up to the audience to guess or, if possible, to deduce why Odysseus weeps.

The third song is about the Wooden Horse and the sack of Troy. Like the first, then, it relates to Odysseus and the Trojan War. This time, however, the subject of the song to be sung by Demodokos is chosen by Odysseus, the anonymous guest of honor. Again Odysseus weeps:

> So the famous singer sang his tale, but Odysseus
> melted, and from under his eyes the tears ran down, drenching
> his cheeks. As a woman weeps, lying over the body
> of her dear husband, who fell fighting for her city and people
> as he tried to beat off the pitiless day from city and children;
> she sees him dying and gasping for breath, and winding her body
> about him she cries high and shrill, while the men behind her,
> hitting her with their spear butts on the back and the shoulders,
> force her up and lead her away into slavery, to have
> hard work and sorrow, and her cheeks are wracked with pitiful weeping.
> Such were the pitiful tears Odysseus shed from under
> his brows, but they went unnoticed by all the others,
> but Alkinoös alone understood what he did and noticed,
> since he was sitting next him and heard him groaning heavily.
> <div align="right">Quote 1.3: <i>Od</i>. 8.521–534</div>

Odysseus seems to weep with less restraint after this song than after the first. Unlike the woman to whom he is compared, however, he maintains at least

1.2. THE PROBLEM OF THE DOUBLE WEEPING

some self-control, inasmuch as he presumably covers his head as in quote 1.2 so that only Alkinoös notices (compare the last three lines of quotes 1.2 and 1.3). What is most important is that Odysseus again weeps in response to a song about himself and the Trojan War, and again Homer offers no explanation for this reaction.

The simile in quote 1.3 compares Odysseus, who led the sack of Troy according to the song that Demodokos has just sung, to a woman who is being taken into slavery as her husband lies dying during the sack of their city. Largely on the basis of this comparison, it is often suggested that the song moves Odysseus to empathize with his victims in the sack of Troy and to weep out of pity for them.[10] This interpretation is just speculation, inasmuch as the poet says only that Odysseus wept like the woman. Such speculation is natural since one wants to understand both why Odysseus weeps and why the poet makes such a strange comparison. I shall offer my own explanations for these things in due course (the latter in chapter 9, the former in the next section). Now I make two observations. First, the attempt to read meaning into the simile is dangerous since other similes in Homer make strange comparisons with no apparent meaning beyond the obvious point of contact between the things compared.[11] Second, the mentioned interpretation is difficult to reconcile with Odysseus's matter-of-fact account of his sack of Ismaros, the city of the Kikonians:

> "... I sacked their city and killed their people,
> and out of their city taking their wives and many possessions
> we shared them out, so none might go cheated of his proper
> portion. ..."
>
> Quote 1.4: *Od.* 9.40–43

This account, which follows closely upon quote 1.3, shows no sign of remorse and is unaccompanied by tears. If Odysseus does not pity the victims of his sack of Ismaros, it is unlikely that he pities the victims of his sack of Troy. We must look elsewhere for an explanation of why he weeps at the third song of Demodokos.

The weeping of Odysseus in Scheria is quite surprising. He wept a great deal on Kalypso's island, it is true, but there he wept out of desperate longing for home.[12] His situation is very different now. By the time he hears Demodokos sing, he has been promised conveyance home by the Phaiakians, and a ship has been made ready for his departure.[13] In addition, he has just heard his deeds at Troy celebrated in song, the dream of a Homeric hero. He should be overjoyed on both counts.[14] Another cause for surprise is his exceptional self-control, which we will have occasion to document in chapter 8. For now it suffices to recall the famous scene in which, disguised as a beggar, he brings Penelope to tears with a tale of how he met her husband twenty years earlier, when he was on his way to Troy:

> As she listened her tears ran and her body was melted,
> as the snow melts along the high places of the mountains
> when the West Wind has piled it there, but the South Wind melts it,
> and as it melts the rivers run full flood. It was even
> so that her beautiful cheeks were streaming tears, as Penelope

>   wept for her man, who was sitting there by her side. But Odysseus
>   in his heart had pity for his wife as she mourned him,
>   but his eyes stayed, as if they were made of horn or iron,
>   steady under his lids. He hid his tears and deceived her.
>
> Quote 1.5: Od. 19.204–212

If Odysseus can restrain himself as his wife weeps for him, not realizing that it is he who is sitting next to her, he is not likely to break down in front of the Phaiakians. But this is what he seems to do after both the first and third songs of Demodokos. His repeated weeping in response to songs about himself as a hero in the Trojan War demands an explanation.[15, 16]

1.3. A Solution

In trying to understand why Odysseus weeps in Scheria, we should prefer a single explanation that accounts for his weeping on two related occasions, that is, in response to both the first song of Demodokos and the third. I shall now propose such an explanation.

Let us suppose on the basis of his self-control that Odysseus would not weep involuntarily at a Phaiakian banquet even once, much less twice. We are then led to consider the possibility that his weeping is intentional. It is not difficult to construct a scenario in which this is the case. Once Odysseus has been assured of his return home, his attention undoubtedly turns to the problem of how he can extract the most gifts from his Phaiakian hosts to make up for the loss at sea of all the booty he won at Troy. As I shall explain, his weeping can be understood as a calculated maneuver designed to contribute to the solution of this problem.

When Demodokos begins to sing his first song, the song about a quarrel between Odysseus and Achilles, I assume that Odysseus quickly comes up with the idea of weeping to suggest a connection between himself and the subject of the song. His hope is that the Phaiakians will honor him with suitable gifts when they realize that their guest is a great hero. Presumably in deference to social convention (see section 1.4), he hides his tears by covering his head with a cloak, but he also groans so that Alkinoös, sitting next to him, will think that he is deeply affected by the song (quote 1.2). Alkinoös notices his groaning, and tactfully redirects the course of the festivities. But Odysseus now knows that Demodokos is aware of his exploits. At this point, we may suppose, he makes his plan: after the next meal he will ask Demodokos to sing about the Wooden Horse and the sack of Troy, and he will again weep so that his connection with the subject will be suspected, only this time he will weep more copiously in order to elicit a stronger reaction from Alkinoös (hence his apparently uncontrolled weeping in quote 1.3).

Before the next meal, the Phaiakians give Odysseus a guest gift,[17] the gift that a host is expected to give to a guest. This particular guest gift is actually a substantial collection of presents and is unusually generous, perhaps because the host, King Alkinoös, wishes to make up for the rude behavior of one of his young subjects towards Odysseus, or because of Odysseus's masterful response to this slight (including an impressive demonstration of athletic prowess), or because of the gracious compliments Odysseus has offered.[18]

Whatever the reason, the guest gift is lavish, and most guests would be more than satisfied with it. However, Odysseus's natural inclination is always to increase his fortune. Recall that the first thing he does after leaving Troy with all his plunder is to sack Ismaros (quote 1.4). And he insists on staying in the cave of the Cyclops—despite the pleas of his comrades and his own fear that the cave belongs to "someone clothed in enormous strength, a savage with no notion of justice or law"—partly because he is curious to see who lives there but also because he entertains hopes of receiving a guest gift.[19] Finally, his unquenchable thirst for riches is seen when, disguised as a beggar, he tells Penelope that Odysseus could have been home a long time ago but decided instead to travel in search of more treasure, even though the Phaiakians had already given him many gifts.[20] The beggar has invented much of this, but surely he has done so knowing that his story will ring true, that it will tally with Penelope's knowledge of her husband. There can be little doubt, then, that after receiving the guest gift Odysseus continues to be intent on accumulating as much wealth as possible.[21]

Although the Phaiakians do not yet know the identity of their guest, Odysseus has shown them that he is worthy of respect as an individual; their appreciation of this fact presumably accounts for the generosity of the guest gift. To show that he is worthy of even more honor and therefore even more gifts, he must establish his standing in the world. The plan he formulated after the first song of Demodokos therefore remains in effect.

Dinner is served soon after the giving of the guest gift. Calling the herald, Odysseus sends a choice piece of meat to Demodokos along with his compliments. When the meal is over, he addresses more compliments to the singer and requests that he sing about the sack of Troy and Odysseus's stratagem of the Wooden Horse. Demodokos obliges, and Odysseus responds with tears as described in quote 1.3. By showing particular respect to Demodokos beforehand, he has prepared everyone for the realization that the song he requests has a special significance for him. In any case, his plan works: Alkinoös infers from his weeping that he has a personal connection to the subject of the song.[22] The king communicates to all those present the fact that the song made the guest weep and (implicitly) his inference that there is some connection between the guest and the subject of the song.[23] With this preparation, when Odysseus identifies himself shortly afterwards at the urging of his host, he can do so with this announcement:

"I am Odysseus son of Laertes, known before all men
for the study of crafty designs, and my fame goes up to the heavens."
Quote 1.6: *Od.* 9.19–20

The connection between the guest and Demodokos's song becomes clear to all. There is no need for him to prove his fame since Demodokos has just done this for him by singing of his exploits, and there is no need for him to demonstrate his knowledge of crafty designs since the exploits included the stratagem of the Wooden Horse.[24] The guest has established his standing in the world, and he has done so in a way befitting his reputation.

After identifying himself, Odysseus embarks on a long narrative about what has happened to him since he left Troy. During a pause in this narrative,

Arete proposes that the Phaiakians give him a second round of gifts.[25] The Phaiakian elder Echeneos and Alkinoös both agree, and the latter takes responsibility for collecting the gifts. Odysseus responds with gratitude:

> "O great Alkinoös, pre-eminent among all people,
> if you urged me to stay here even for the length of a year,
> and still sped my conveyance home and gave me glorious
> presents, that would be what I wished, there would be much advantage
> in coming back with a fuller hand to my own dear country,
> and I would be more respected so and be more popular
> with all people who saw me make my return to Ithaka."
>
> Quote 1.7: *Od.* 11.355–361

His interest in gifts beyond those he received in the first round, forthrightly expressed here, is in accord with our expectations. The additional gifts are collected the next day and given to Odysseus.[26] They are so substantial that the kings who give them intend to reimburse themselves with a collection from their people. In fact, the Phaiakians give Odysseus more treasure, in the first and second rounds combined, than he won at Troy and then lost at sea.[27]

Why does Arete propose another round of gifts when Odysseus has already been given a generous guest gift? There have been two significant developments since someone other than Odysseus last spoke: Odysseus has identified himself, and he has recounted some of his adventures. After the first and third songs of Demodokos, one about a quarrel between Odysseus and Achilles and the other about Odysseus's leading role in the sack of Troy, the revelation that their guest is Odysseus himself must have impressed the Phaiakians. His stature in their eyes can only have grown further when they heard about his encounter with the Cyclops and his visit to the underworld. The second round of gifts is the inevitable result if the Phaiakians wish to honor their guest in proportion to the esteem in which they hold him.

For my final observations in this exposition of the theory that Odysseus's weeping is deliberate, it is necessary to view his weeping in the context of his behavior elsewhere in the Phaiakian books of the *Odyssey* (not including his past behavior in the tales of his adventures that he recounts to the Phaiakians). If we ignore the weeping scenes for the moment, it can be said with confidence that he never loses his self-possession in Scheria, even under trying circumstances. On the contrary, we are treated to several demonstrations of his cunning and presence of mind. When he must supplicate the princess Nausikaa under conditions where the contact involved in a conventional supplication is inadvisable, he does so and wins her support with a brilliant speech that the poet himself describes as crafty.[28] When he is challenged with a menacing question from Queen Arete, who holds his fate in her hands, his response is again both brilliant and crafty and completely satisfies the queen.[29] And when King Alkinoös points to his daughter's apparent breach of hospitality, Odysseus gallantly invents a white lie to take the blame himself, which (along with other considerations) moves the king to offer Odysseus Nausikaa's hand in marriage.[30] In short, the hero shows himself to be master of the situation in scene after scene. It would be strange if this hero succumbs to two bouts of involuntary weeping. It would also call into question his ability to meet the challenges waiting for him in Ithaka. I suggest that the poet has no incentive to undermine the unity of his poem in these ways, and would much prefer to have his hero continue in the weeping scenes to display the craft and self-possession that will be needed in Ithaka and that are shown in the other scenes in Scheria, especially in furtherance of an aim that we know he must have.

To recapitulate, the scenario described in this section explains the double weeping of Odysseus in a way that is fully consistent with his psychology. It explains why he weeps when he has more reason for optimism than he has had in many years and therefore should not be prone to weeping. And instead of appealing to repeated and uncharacteristic lapses in his self-control and to hypothetical pity that is contradicted by other evidence, the explanation is solidly based on his reputation for cunning (discussed at greater length in the next chapter) and his well-established appetite for riches.

1.4. Objections

I now discuss some possible objections to the proposed reading.

The conventional view that Odysseus's weeping in Scheria is sincere would seem to be supported by his often-gloomy remarks.[31] When he returns to Ithaka in disguise, however, Odysseus says things to Eumaios and Penelope that are just as gloomy as anything he says to the Phaiakians,[32] and yet we know that there he is pursuing an active campaign against the suitors and is not indulging in self-pity. Of course, his dispirited remarks in Ithaka are appropriate to a man who has fallen on hard times, and they support Odysseus's disguise as a beggar. But his gloomy remarks in Scheria are also functional. First, they highlight the hardships he has suffered and his resulting need for help, as when he supplicates Arete; and indeed Arete mentions his great need when she proposes the second round of gifts.[33] Second, they contrast his present sorry state with his true position as an aristocrat. Thus, Odysseus concludes a speech to Alkinoös on the theme of his suffering by requesting conveyance home and exclaiming, "let life leave me when I have once more seen my property, my serving people, and my great high-roofed house."[34] The Phaiakians must know his true status if they are eventually to accept him as the great hero Odysseus. These observations make clear the danger of inferring anything about his weeping from his gloomy remarks. What must be decisive is the objective fact that Odysseus weeps even though his fortunes have taken a dramatic turn for the better: he weeps after the first song of Demodokos when he has been granted conveyance home, and he weeps again when he has also been given a generous guest gift and has just heard his triumph at Troy celebrated in the third song. These positive developments must have dispelled the despair he felt in Ogygia, allowing his powers to be concentrated on extracting all possible benefit from his benefactors in Scheria.

Let us now consider a second objection. Before they give him the guest gift, the Phaiakians are told by Odysseus that he was one of the best Achaian archers at Troy, second only to Philoktetes.[35] Alkinoös presumably takes this information into account when he decides what to give the unnamed guest. Since the fact that the guest was a significant participant in the Trojan War has then been factored into the first round of gifts, one might argue that the revelation of Odysseus's identity plays no role in the second round of gifts (i.e., that Arete is moved to propose this round solely by Odysseus's tales of his adventures), in which case there would be no point to the stratagem attributed to him in the preceding section. This objection is easily addressed.

Odysseus tells Penelope that the Phaiakians honored him like a god,[36] and this assertion is justified by the wealth that they bestowed upon him. However, the greatest fighters at Troy were not archers. Although Odysseus's archery at Troy may earn him some respect from the Phaiakians and may even contribute to the generosity of the guest gift, it would not cause him to be honored like a god (all the more since he was only the second-best archer). Once Odysseus's identity becomes known, however, it is another matter entirely. The Phaiakians now realize that their guest is a great hero whose exploits are the subject of song. From the first song of Demodokos they realize that he is someone whose stature at Troy was comparable to that of Achilles, and from the third song they realize that he was key to the sack of Troy. Their guest, then, was not merely valuable to the Achaian effort, he was invaluable. He is worthy not only of respect but of glory, and this puts him on another level that calls for the second round of gifts.

Now a third objection. We are told that Odysseus covers his head with a cloak when he weeps in response to the first song of Demodokos, and the strong presumption is that he does the same during the third song. This is puzzling if, as I suppose, he wants the Phaiakians to be aware of his reaction to those songs. According to quote 1.2, Odysseus covers his head because he is ashamed to have the Phaiakians see him weeping. But surely he would not let a little embarrassment interfere with his scheme. I shall argue that Lattimore's translation here is wrong, even though it is in line with most other translations and is perfectly reasonable if the verses translated are considered in isolation. The basic point, made by Peter Jones, is that heroes in Homer are not usually ashamed to weep.[37] Let us examine some of the evidence Jones cites in support of this assertion.

In a scene to be discussed in more detail in the following section, Telemachos covers his face with a cloak when he weeps in front of Menelaos and Nestor's son Peisistratos. There is no indication that he does this because he is ashamed to be seen weeping. Indeed, it is unlikely that shame plays any role in this scene, for shortly afterwards Telemachos, Peisistratos, Menelaos, and Helen all weep openly in each other's company. Weeping in a social gathering seems to be acceptable if everyone joins in but impolite or intrusive if done by only one person. This understanding apparently informs Martin Hammond's nonstandard (but probably more accurate) translation of the text that corresponds to the fourth line in quote 1.2: "he [Odysseus] was shedding tears from his eyes, and out of politeness did not wish the Phaiacians to see them." On the basis of the evidence that supports this translation, I suggest that it is not shame but rather consideration for what is proper (i.e., socially acceptable) that prevents Odysseus from weeping openly in front of the Phaiakians[38] and forces him to communicate with them indirectly via Alkinoös.[39]

A fourth objection is prompted by the statement "Odysseus melted" in the opening lines of quote 1.3. This statement appears to describe Odysseus's emotional reaction to the third song of Demodokos and the resulting spontaneous flow of tears from his eyes. This would obviously mean that his weeping is sincere rather than premeditated as I believe. Here again, the problem may be one of translation. For comparison, let us consider the statement "her body was melted" in the first line of quote 1.5. The verb that is translated there as "was melted" is τηκετο, which is indeed in the passive voice. The same verb form is used in the second line of quote 1.3. This would seem to suggest that a more literal translation would be "Odysseus was melted [by the song]," which is essentially equivalent to Lattimore's translation "Odysseus melted." However, the verb τηκετο can be in either the passive voice or the middle voice—one can decide only from the context. While the passive voice is clearly indicated by the context in quote 1.5, I posit that τηκετο in the Greek source for quote 1.3 is in the middle voice. The middle voice is used when the subject acts reflexively in some sense. Thus, Οδυσσευς τηκετο could mean "Odysseus made himself melt [into tears]," a translation perfectly consistent with premeditated weeping.[40]

Let us now consider the "pitiful tears" that Odysseus is said to have shed near the end of quote 1.3. In Cunliffe's lexicon, the adjective translated as "pitiful" (ελεεινον) is said to refer in general to something "that is a fitting object of pity" and to refer in quote 1.3 to something "caused by feelings worthy of pity." In our context, these definitions imply that Odysseus's weeping was sincere. For the proposed reading to be valid, the adjective in question must be capable of referring to anything that would arouse pity in an observer, even if only by deception.

The last objection may be the most serious: we have no independent evidence that Odysseus is capable of acting well enough to fool Alkinoös with his weeping and groaning. He is, of course, a master of certain kinds of deception—he excels at false tales and is expert at playing the role of a beggar—but can he weep at will and convince others that his calculated weeping is actually sincere? The fact that he covers his head when he weeps may reduce the demand on his acting ability, but he still must produce those "pitiful tears." He is good at hiding emotion that he feels, but can he feign emotion that he does not feel? The need to *assume* a positive answer to this question is a weak point of my theory.

Although it has been possible to answer most of the objections, I must admit that some uncertainty remains. I leave it to the reader to weigh this uncertainty against the attractive features of the theory.

1.5. Associated Narrative Techniques

The material in this section has no bearing on the validity of the proposed reading, but it rounds out the discussion and introduces a concept that will be useful later.

(*a*) Unanswered Questions

When, after the third song of Demodokos, Alkinoös urges Odysseus to identify himself, he also asks him to explain why he weeps when he hears about the Trojan War.[41] This question is a natural one for Alkinoös to ask, but it would be awkward for Odysseus to answer it if his weeping was just part of a plan for wheedling gifts from his hosts. It is common in the *Odyssey* for a question to be ignored when the answer would be awkward or inconsistent with the poet's plans.[42] Let us see what happens in the present instance.

Alkinoös poses his question about Odysseus's weeping with great specificity in the last ten lines of his speech. Odysseus acknowledges the question,[43] but he does so in a way that robs it of its specificity:

> "But now your wish was inclined to ask me about my mournful
> sufferings, so that I must mourn and grieve even more. What then
> shall I recite to you first of all, what leave till later?
> Many are the sorrows the gods of the sky have given me."
>
> Quote 1.8: *Od.* 9.12–15

This generalized perspective allows him to shift attention to another question that Alkinoös has asked, the question about where his wanderings have taken him.[44] He smoothes the transition by emphasizing the troubles encountered during his travels:

> "But come, I will tell you of my voyage home with its many
> troubles, which Zeus inflicted on me as I came from Troy land."
>
> Quote 1.9: *Od.* 9.37–38

Odysseus has cleverly avoided the question about his weeping. Here, then, is an example of the poet's practice of allowing a question to be raised without being answered if the answer would be awkward or inconvenient. This is not further evidence for the scenario described in section 1.3, since one could argue that the answer would also be awkward in other scenarios. The example is noteworthy, however, because it departs from the poet's usual practice in one respect: instead of simply ignoring the question, Odysseus at first pretends that he is going to answer it. It is interesting to note that he employs the same strategy with Arete.

On his first day among the Phaiakians, Arete asks Odysseus who he is, where he is from, who gave him the clothes he is wearing, and how he came to Scheria.[45] Siegfried Besslich has pointed out that the beginning of his reply to the queen gives the impression that he is answering the second question and will presumably answer the first.[46] In fact, it turns out that he answers only the last two questions. Thus, Odysseus's response to multiple questions from Arete is analogous to his response to multiple questions from Alkinoös: he pretends that he is going to give a full answer, but actually answers only the questions that suit him.

(*b*) Fenik's Anticipation Pattern

Fenik has pointed out that the double weeping of Odysseus in Scheria is an instance of a common narrative pattern in the Homeric poems in which a scene is followed after some interval by a similar scene of greater importance.[47] Demodokos sings about Odysseus and Troy after two meals; each time Odysseus weeps but covers his face to hide his tears, and each time Alkinoös, sitting next to him, hears him groaning. The first bout of weeping has little effect on the course of events, as Alkinoös simply moves to the next item on the day's program of entertainment, but the second bout leads to the dramatic revelation of Odysseus's identity. The double weeping evidently fits the pattern nicely.[48] We now turn to a second example.

Several aspects of the weeping of Odysseus at the court of Alkinoös in response to the third song of Demodokos are anticipated by the earlier weeping of Telemachos in the palace of Menelaos.[49] Like his father, Telemachos has not yet identified himself to his host. Also like his father, he covers his face with a cloak when he weeps. He weeps when Menelaos speaks sorrowfully about the long absence and unknown fate of Odysseus, and this enables Menelaos to guess his identity. This scene, then, introduces the connection between weeping and identification that becomes the basis for Odysseus's scheme for revealing himself to the Phaiakians and that eventually manifests in the revelation of his identity after the third song of Demodokos.[50] The identification of Telemachos through his weeping is of little intrinsic importance, however, because at the same moment Helen enters the room and immediately identifies him from his physical resemblance to his father. It is also of little importance because it simply does not matter how Telemachos's identity is revealed: Menelaos and Helen will welcome him warmly regardless of how they learn who he is. It follows that this scene and the scene of Odysseus weeping at the third song of Demodokos form another pair of similar scenes, the second of which is more important than the first.

The scene in which Odysseus weeps at the third song of Demodokos is thus related by Fenik's pattern to two earlier scenes: the scene in which he weeps at the first song of Demodokos and the scene in which Telemachos first weeps in the presence of Menelaos. For the purposes of this paragraph, I refer to the resulting structure as a "V structure," where the two lines of the V represent the two instances of Fenik's pattern and the point where the two lines intersect represents the single scene that functions as the later, more important scene in both instances. There is also a V structure in the *Iliad*: the fatal encounter between Achilles and Hektor in book 22 is related by Fenik's pattern to both the preliminary encounter between them in book 20 and the encounter between Achilles and Agenor at the end of book 21.[51] The fact that both poems contain a V structure may be of no significance, but I mention it because later in this book I shall present evidence that the *Odyssey* poet intentionally replicated structure found in the *Iliad*.

Some interesting examples of Fenik's pattern, henceforth referred to as "Fenik's anticipation pattern," will be described in the next chapter.

1.6. Conclusion and Transition

We are never told why Odysseus weeps in Scheria, but a simple explanation fits his psychology and his circumstances: his weeping is part of a stratagem for extracting riches from the Phaiakians. This suggests that Homer created a mystery that he wanted us to solve. In the next chapter we will investigate a more subtle mystery which concerns a stratagem devised by Odysseus when he is back home in Ithaka. In the Scherian mystery, the poet relates the actions of a character without explaining the character's motivation; in the Ithakan mystery, I claim that even some of the actions are implicit and must be deduced from certain clues. Anyone who makes such a bold claim is obligated to supply correspondingly strong supporting evidence. In the present case, the claim of unusual subtlety for the Ithakan mystery will be justified by the explanatory power of the proposed solution.

The mystery discussed in this chapter and the main mystery discussed in the next chapter each involve a stratagem devised by Odysseus below the surface of the poem. The consequence of the Ithakan stratagem (the slaughter of the suitors) is far more significant than that of the Scherian stratagem (the winning of additional gifts from the Phaiakians). In addition, the development and execution of the Ithakan stratagem occupy six books of the *Odyssey* (books 16–21), while the Scherian stratagem occupies only one (book 8). The two implicit stratagems of Odysseus might therefore be regarded as another instance of Fenik's anticipation pattern. Indeed, the moderate subtlety of the Scherian stratagem prepares for the greater subtlety of the Ithakan stratagem "as if to familiarize the hearer with the concept before its most significant occurrence" (to quote from one description of Fenik's pattern[52]).

Chapter 2

The Last Stratagem of Odysseus

One of the theses of this book is that what appear to be flaws in the Homeric epics arising from difficulties of composition or transmission sometimes actually reflect the intentions of the poet. The specific form that this thesis will eventually take demands an expansion of our conception of what art can be and of the subtlety that is possible for the communication between the artist and the audience. This chapter introduces the thesis in a less challenging form that merely requires us to acknowledge in Homer a subtlety that is easily comprehended but not generally recognized. The need for a new interpretation is suggested by an unsatisfying aspect of the *Odyssey* as the poem is usually understood.

The attribute of Odysseus for which he is most famous is his resourcefulness. Helen says that Odysseus knew "every manner of shiftiness and crafty counsels"; Nestor says that "there was no man who wanted to be set up for cunning against great Odysseus; he far surpassed them in every kind of stratagem"; and Odysseus himself says that he is "known before all men for the study of crafty designs."[1] Of his distinctive epithets (that is, epithets that are used for him but for no other mortal), the most common ($πολυμητις$) characterizes him as a man of many counsels or devices, a man of extraordinary ingenuity.[2]

The *Odyssey* relates the crafty designs of Odysseus which made possible the sack of Troy[3] and the escape from the Cyclops.[4] And yet, according to conventional understanding, his resourcefulness contributes little to the solution of the central problem he faces in that poem: how to rid his palace of the 108 men who, in his absence, have been courting his wife against her will, consuming the substance of his estate, and threatening the welfare and even the life of his son. In this chapter I propose a reading in which the destruction of the suitors is actually another triumph of his craftiness.[5] In addition to showing how Homer fulfills what almost amounts to an artistic obligation, this reading shows that what appear to be some of the most glaring defects in the *Odyssey* give this impression only because of one's failure to appreciate the subtle development of the plot of the poem.

2.1. The Contest of the Bow

The key to the destruction of the suitors is that Odysseus is able to overcome their numerical advantage by using his bow. The contest set by Penelope to determine which of the suitors she will marry is an essential preliminary to the slaughter, for it is this contest which enables Odysseus to get his hands on the bow.

The contest of the bow has two parts: each contestant must attempt to string the great bow of Odysseus and then, if he is able to do this, must shoot an arrow through twelve axes set up in a row. As explained by W. J. Woodhouse, this is a cleverly designed scheme.[6] The stringing of the bow, although it represents an impressive feat of strength, is not sufficient for Odysseus's purpose, because it does not involve arrows and therefore will not bring him the arrows he needs to kill the suitors. The feat of marksmanship—the shooting of an arrow through twelve axes (whatever that may mean)—is also not sufficient, since each attempt will reduce the supply of arrows, with the probable result that none will be left by the time Odysseus can get the bow in his hands. The solution is to require each contestant to string the bow before he can attempt to shoot an arrow through the axes. Since few, if any, suitors will be able to accomplish the feat of strength, few arrows will be wasted on the feat of marksmanship, and Odysseus can expect to receive, along with the bow, a quiver that is full or nearly so. I submit that this twofold contest (to use Woodhouse's phrase) is a worthy candidate for a stratagem of the man of many wiles.[7]

2.2. Penelope's Decision to Hold the Contest

The contest of the bow is first mentioned near the end of the conversation between Penelope and her husband which takes place when Odysseus is disguised as an old beggar and has not revealed his true identity to anyone except Telemachos. The stranger has already won the confidence of the queen. Seemingly out of nowhere, she says to him:

> "This dawn will be a day of evil name, which will take me
> away from the house of Odysseus; for now I will set up a contest:
> those axes which, in his palace, he used to set up in order
> so that, twelve in all, they stood in a row, like timbers
> to hold a ship. He would stand far off, and send a shaft through them.
> Now I will set these up as a contest before my suitors,
> and the one who takes the bow in his hands, strings it with the greatest
> ease, and sends an arrow clean through all the twelve axes
> shall be the one I will go away with, forsaking this house
> where I was a bride, a lovely place and full of good living.
> I think that even in my dreams I shall never forget it."
>
> Quote 2.1: *Od.* 19.571–581

Here we have a description of the twofold contest[8] and a statement of Penelope's intention to hold it. Since the contest has not been mentioned earlier in the narrative, it is generally assumed that it was not conceived by Odysseus. The argument against this assumption presented in this chapter

2.2. PENELOPE'S DECISION

offers solutions to several well-known mysteries, one of which is the following.

Penelope's decision to hold the contest is perplexing given the circumstances in which it is made. On the very day of the decision, she hears from Telemachos, returned from his journey in search of news of his father, that Odysseus was still alive (although detained by Kalypso) two years ago;[9] she is told by the old beggar that Odysseus was in nearby Thesprotia quite recently and will certainly be home soon;[10] and she is assured by the prophet Theoklymenos that Odysseus is now in Ithaka.[11] Moreover, when she first hears the beggar's "news" from the loyal swineherd Eumaios earlier in the day, she receives a favorable omen which encourages her to believe that Odysseus may indeed return home soon and kill the suitors.[12] Surely she has never had so much cause for optimism at any previous time during the twenty-year absence of her husband. And indeed, optimism is evident in her reaction to the omen. On top of all this, she has had a dream that points clearly to the return of Odysseus and his destruction of the suitors.[13] After the old beggar confirms the obvious interpretation of the dream, however, she expresses doubt as to its reliability, and then abruptly makes the declaration in quote 2.1. In short, just when she has received multiple indications that she will soon be reunited with the husband she has longed for for so long, Penelope decides to marry one of the suitors whom she loathes. This decision is what is called Penelope's "surrender" or Penelope's "collapse."

The striking illogicality just described has exercised a number of scholars, but has never been resolved.[14] I will now discuss one of the various explanations that have been suggested in order to introduce some material that will be needed later in this chapter.

Penelope first announces that she has resigned herself to a new marriage in a speech that she gives to the suitors some hours before her conversation with the beggar.[15] The key part of this speech begins with an account of what Odysseus said to her upon his departure for Troy:

> "When he went and left me behind in the land of his fathers,
> he took me by the right hand at the wrist, and then said to me:
> 'Dear wife, since I do not think the strong-greaved Achaians
> will all come safely home from Troy without hurt, seeing
> that people say the Trojans are men who can fight in battle,
> ...
> I do not know if the god will spare me, or if I must be lost
> there in Troy; here let everything be in your charge.
> ...
> But when you see our son grown up and bearded, then
> marry whatever man you please, forsaking your household.'
> So he spoke then; and now all this is being accomplished.
> And there will come that night when a hateful marriage is given
> to wretched me, for Zeus has taken my happiness from me."[16]
>
> Quote 2.2: *Od.* 18.257–261, 265–266, 269–273

She goes on to complain that her suitors should be giving her gifts instead of feasting at her expense without offering anything in return. The suitors respond favorably, each sending his herald to fetch a generous present for the queen.

Uvo Hölscher has argued that Penelope's speech should be accepted at face value, that she does indeed decide to marry one of the suitors in order to obey the final instruction she says she received from Odysseus when he left for Troy.[17] Given the numerous signs, recognized by everyone, that Telemachos has recently reached adulthood, this instruction is admittedly sufficient to explain *to the suitors* her decision to remarry—they are unaware of the indications that Odysseus is alive and will soon be home. But the audience *is* aware of these indications and knows that Penelope is also,[18] and should therefore be surprised if she does not wait a little longer before taking a new husband, regardless of the instruction.[19] The simplest interpretation is that she is deceiving the suitors. In fact, contrary to what is often asserted or implied, it can be shown that Odysseus never gave the last instruction that Penelope attributes to him in quote 2.2.[20] This is demonstrated by several aspects of the conversation between the queen and the beggar.

At two points in the conversation, the queen relates to the beggar the considerations that have a bearing on whether she should remarry.[21] If Odysseus's parting instruction to Penelope were genuine, we would expect her to mention it on at least one of these occasions, but she does not.[22] Instead she says on the first occasion that, now that she has been forced to finish the shroud for Laertes, she cannot think of another subterfuge.[23] Since she clearly would like to come up with another delaying tactic, Odysseus cannot have told her to remarry when their son reached adulthood. These two arguments for the fictitiousness of Odysseus's instruction owe some of their force to the evident sincerity with which the queen speaks to the beggar. My last argument is based on a lie the beggar tells the queen, but its force is in no way diminished by the fact that what he says is false. The beggar says that Odysseus deliberately delayed his return in order to accumulate riches;[24] he obviously would not make up this lie if he did give the instruction upon his departure for Troy and therefore would know that the long delay entailed a risk that Penelope would remarry.[25]

Thus, Odysseus's final instruction is a fabrication and cannot be used to explain why Penelope decides to marry one of the suitors just when her husband may be about to return. The reason for the fabrication (and the question of whether the decision to remarry is genuine even though the instruction is not[26]) will be discussed later in this chapter. What is important now is the apparent lack of motivation for Penelope's decision to hold a contest for her hand in marriage. This apparently unmotivated decision, which plays such an important role in the poem, must either be explained or be accepted as a flaw in the development of the plot. Before suggesting a solution, I describe another well-known mystery that must be addressed.

2.3. The Removal of the Arms

It is evening in Ithaka, the suitors have just left the palace for the night, and Odysseus (disguised as an old beggar) and Telemachos (the only person who knows that the old beggar is his father) are alone in the great hall. The

2.3. THE REMOVAL OF THE ARMS

beggar's audience with the queen that was arranged earlier in the day—the audience that will become the extended conversation during which Penelope states her intention to hold the contest of the bow—is to take place soon, but first the hero and his son have important business to attend to:

> Now great Odysseus still remained in the hall, pondering
> how, with the help of Athene, he would murder the suitors.
> Presently he spoke in winged words to Telemachos:
> "Telemachos, we must have the weapons stored away inside
> the high chamber; and when the suitors miss them and ask you
> about them, answer and beguile them with soft words, saying
> 'I stored them away out of the smoke, since they are no longer
> like what Odysseus left behind when he went to Troy land,
> but are made foul, with all the smoke of the fire upon them.
> Also, some divinity put into my head this even
> greater thought, that with the wine in you, you might stand up
> and fight, and wound each other, and spoil the feast and the courting;
> since iron all of itself works on a man and attracts him.'"
> So he spoke, and Telemachos obeyed his dear father,
> and summoned out Eurykleia his nurse, and said to her:
> "Come, nurse, please detain the women inside the palace,
> while I put away my father's beautiful armor
> in the inner room; it is carelessly laid in the house, and darkened
> with smoke, in my father's absence, and I was a child all that time.
> Now I would put it away, where smoke from the fire will not reach it."
> ...
>   The two men, Odysseus and his glorious son, sprang up
> and began carrying helmets, shields massive in the middle,
> and pointed spears, and before them Pallas Athene, holding
> a golden lamp, gave them splendid illumination.
> Suddenly Telemachos spoke a word to his father:
> "Father, here is a great wonder that my eyes look on.
> Always it seems that the chamber walls, the handsome bases
> and roof timbers of fir and tall columns sustaining them,
> shine in my eyes as if a fire were blazing. There must be
> surely a god here, one of those who hold the high heaven."
> Then resourceful Odysseus spoke in turn and answered him:
> "Hush, and keep it in your own mind, and do not ask questions.
> For this is the very way of the gods, who hold Olympos.
> You should now go to bed, ..."
> ...
>   [Then Telemachos went to bed]
> while great Odysseus still remained in the hall, pondering
> how, with the help of Athene, he would murder the suitors.
>   Quote 2.3: *Od.* 19.1–20, 31–44, 51–52

A man with a spear and a shield is much more of a threat than a man with only the short sword worn by the suitors.[27] The removal of the arms from the hall is therefore necessary so that the suitors will not be able to defend themselves effectively when Odysseus launches his surprise attack. What is interesting is that the way the removal is carried out, as described in this passage, differs in one crucial respect from the way Odysseus intended it to be carried out just the day before.

When Odysseus and Telemachos return to Ithaka—Odysseus after twenty years, Telemachos after a month—Athene arranges their reunion by directing each of them to go to the hut of Eumaios. After the swineherd has been dispatched to the palace to tell Penelope of her son's safe return, Odysseus identifies himself, and eventually father and son settle down to the business of considering how to deal with the suitors. The instructions Odysseus gives Telemachos include a preliminary plan for removing the arms from the great hall of the palace:

> "When Athene, lady of many counsels, puts it into
> my mind, I will nod my head to you, and when you perceive it,
> take all the warlike weapons which are stored in the great hall,
> and carry them off and store them away in the inward corner
> of the high chamber; and when the suitors miss them and ask you
> about them, answer and beguile them with soft words, saying:
> 'I stored them away out of the smoke, since they are no longer
> like what Odysseus left behind when he went to Troy land,
> but are made foul, with all the smoke of the fire upon them.
> Also, the son of Kronos [Zeus] put into my head this even
> greater thought, that with the wine in you, you might stand up
> and fight, and wound each other, and spoil the feast and the courting,
> since iron all of itself works on a man and attracts him.'
> But leave behind, for you and me alone, a pair each
> of swords and spears, and a pair of oxhide shields, to take up
> in our hands, and wield them, and kill these men; and Zeus of the counsels
> and Pallas Athene will be there to maze the wits in them."
>
> Quote 2.4: *Od.* 16.282–298

Odysseus has no way of knowing, of course, that on the evening of the following day he and his son will be alone in the hall and will be able to remove the arms together as described in quote 2.3. The fact that the scenario reasonably envisaged in the first part of quote 2.4 never comes to pass is therefore not an inconsistency.[28] The middle part of the passage gives, almost exactly as they appear in quote 2.3, two explanations that Telemachos is to offer if the suitors notice that the arms are missing.[29] In the last part of the passage, Telemachos is told to leave in the hall two sets of arms, one for Odysseus and one for himself. There is no mention of this when the arms are actually removed (quote 2.3), and in fact we know from what happens later that no arms are left in the hall.[30] This unexplained departure from the original plan constitutes the well-known inconsistency associated with the removal of the arms.[31] The resolution of this inconsistency is one result of the reading that I now begin to expound.

2.4. The Birth of the Idea of the Contest

The instructions for the removal of the arms given in quote 2.4 imply that Odysseus has a plan for the destruction of the suitors: he and his son will kill them using the two sets of arms Telemachos is to leave in the hall.[32] This plan is very dangerous. Two men with swords, spears, and shields are not likely to be able to overcome 108 men with swords (the spears, of course, will be in the hands of the suitors once they have been thrown). In addition, leaving two sets

2.4. THE BIRTH OF THE IDEA OF THE CONTEST   21

of arms in the hall is risky because these arms, if noticed by the suitors, would arouse their suspicion and damage the credibility of the explanations they are to be given for the removal of the other arms (this point, made by Wilhelm Büchner and Harmut Erbse,[33] is not invalidated by the fact that one of the explanations has no credibility to begin with, as discussed in section 6.9). The plan has obviously been adopted out of desperation for lack of a better one. Fortunately, a new development has opened up the possibility of a more promising approach to dealing with the suitors.

Although Odysseus does not learn of Penelope's ruse of the shroud for Laertes until the conversation between the queen and the beggar, he does know that she has been putting off a new marriage for three years (see quote 6.42). This fact has inevitably constrained his thinking about how he might slay the suitors. But Penelope has just announced to the suitors that she has finally decided, albeit reluctantly, that the time has come for her to remarry (see quote 2.2). This decision would make it natural for her to arrange a contest for her hand in marriage. Indeed, a contest leaving the selection of her new husband to factors beyond her control would be appropriate given the distaste for the marriage which she expresses in her speech. We may surmise that these considerations prompt Odysseus to conceive the idea of a contest involving his great bow, a weapon that could enable him to overcome the numerical superiority of the suitors if he could somehow get it in his hands along with a sufficient number of arrows. The man of many wiles then devises the twofold contest as the means by which he will achieve this. He realizes that he and Telemachos will still need armor and spears, as he will not have enough arrows to kill all 108 suitors. But leaving behind two sets of arms is risky for the reasons already explained. This tactic was included in the original plan out of necessity, but the bow will enable Odysseus to deal with the suitors long enough for Telemachos to fetch armor from the storeroom. The prudent course now is to remove all the arms from the hall. Thus, the apparent inconsistency between quote 2.3 and quote 2.4 can be explained provided that Odysseus has time to devise the contest of the bow before the arms are removed from the hall.[34]

We may assume that Odysseus immediately realizes the importance of Penelope's speech to the suitors (he is in the audience disguised as a beggar) and begins to consider its implications at the first opportunity. This opportunity presents itself during the interval between the speech and the departure of the suitors from the palace at the end of the day. After Penelope announces her decision to remarry, extracts courtship presents, and returns to her chamber, the suitors entertain themselves with singing and dancing. When night falls, they build a few fires for light, and Odysseus occupies himself with the tending of these fires. This relatively relaxed period would give him the opportunity to think about the possibilities offered by the new situation. In fact, Homer tells us that while Odysseus was tending the fires "the heart within him was pondering other thoughts, which were not to go unaccomplished."[35] His pondering is interrupted by a bitter interaction with the suitor Eurymachos,[36] but the beginning of quote 2.3 shows that it has resumed by the time the suitors have gone home for the night. Since the arms are removed from the hall after the suitors leave, we see that Odysseus could in fact have devised the contest in time to account for the discrepancy between quote 2.3 and quote 2.4.

This solution to the problem of the removal of the arms is difficult to refine further owing to an ambiguity in the Greek. The word $αιψα$ which Lattimore translates as "presently" in the third line of quote 2.3 can mean either "immediately" or "soon." In this instance, it is not clear from the context which meaning is appropriate. Unlike Lattimore, most translators choose the first meaning (e.g., "at once" or "straightaway"). The reasoning behind this decision is easy to guess. The arms must be removed from the hall as quickly as possible because Penelope may come downstairs at any moment for the meeting with the beggar that was arranged earlier in the day. If we assume that the pondering mentioned at the beginning of quote 2.3 is of no particular significance, it follows that Odysseus will begin to remove the arms as soon as the suitors have left, in which case $αιψα$ should be translated here as "immediately." This translation is also appropriate in the reading I have proposed if Odysseus has finished devising the twofold contest by the time the suitors leave for the night. If his pondering has not yet gotten this far, however, he would delay the removal of the arms until he knows whether he should leave two panoplies in the hall, in which case $αιψα$ should be translated here as "soon" or "presently."

Even if Odysseus devises the twofold contest before the suitors leave the palace, there are still details for him to consider, such as how he can actually get the bow in his hands when he, disguised as an old beggar, is supposed to be merely an onlooker at a contest for the hand of Penelope. His pondering at the beginning of quote 2.3 therefore comes as no surprise. For the same reason, it is not surprising to see him pondering again at the end of the passage, when we know that he has devised the contest since he and Telemachos have removed the arms from the hall without leaving behind any for themselves. In addition, the pondering at the end of quote 2.3 may have the special significance that I shall attach to it in section 2.8.

One may object to the reading I have begun to explain in this section on the grounds that it takes Homer at his word when he says in quote 2.3 that Odysseus was pondering how he would murder the suitors and when he says that Odysseus "was pondering other thoughts, which were not to go unaccomplished" while he was tending the fires for the suitors. This is problematic because a number of superficially similar passages describe situations which clearly involve no productive thinking.[37] When Odysseus is hit by a footstool thrown by Antinoös, his first reaction is to shake his head in silence, "deeply devising evils." Telemachos reacts in the same way to the blow suffered by his father. Although both father and son are said to be devising evils, it is unlikely that either is engaged in strategizing at this moment; rather, they are both simply wishing evil for Antinoös and the other suitors (they are "filled with thoughts of revenge" is the formulation offered by Rieu). The same interpretation undoubtedly applies when Odysseus is said to devise evils while listening to Eumaios speak about the suitors and after being insulted by Melanthios. The question is whether it also applies to the passages where I maintain that the hero is considering the implications of

Penelope's speech to the suitors, devising the contest of the bow, and working out further details of his plan.

It could be significant that the repetition of the first two lines of quote 2.3 in the last two lines of the passage creates a pair of bookends surrounding the description of the removal of the arms. Although repetition of lines is common in Homer, bookends of this sort are not.[38] It is tempting to argue that these bookends link the pondering of Odysseus to the actual removal of the arms (as opposed to the plan for their removal in quote 2.4), which would fit my reading nicely. On the other hand, Richard Rutherford applies the usual interpretation which asserts that no productive thinking is involved: "the repetition emphasises further the hero's determination on revenge."[39] What one sees in these lines is evidently conditioned by how one understands the poem. All that can be said objectively is that the lines of Homer which I would take literally are more specific in their description than the ones which seem to express only a desire for revenge. This observation allows us to entertain the hypothesis that the former lines mean something different from the latter. The validity of this hypothesis should be judged on the basis of its explanatory power. So far we have seen that the hypothesis makes possible a reading which solves the problem associated with the removal of the arms. I will show next that this reading can be extended to account for Penelope's illogical decision to hold the contest of the bow.

2.5. The Motivation of Penelope

According to the proposed reading, the plan that emerges from Odysseus's pondering during the interval between Penelope's speech and the departure of the suitors at the end of the day is the stratagem of the twofold contest for Penelope's hand. This plan requires two preparatory steps: the arms must be removed from the hall so that the suitors will not be able to defend themselves, and Penelope must be motivated to hold the contest. Odysseus and Telemachos accomplish the first step when the suitors leave the palace. I suggest that the second step, the motivation of Penelope, is accomplished by Athene. We are told that Athene has Penelope actually begin the contest, announcing it to the suitors and setting before them the bow and the other necessary apparatus,[40] but this takes place on the day after Penelope has told the beggar of her decision to hold the contest. What I am suggesting is that Athene is also responsible for this otherwise inexplicable decision.

Athene does something very similar to what is required for the implementation of Odysseus's plan earlier on the same day that he conceives the plan and removes the arms from the hall:

> But now the goddess, gray-eyed Athene, put it in the mind
> of the daughter of Ikarios, circumspect Penelope,
> to show herself to the suitors, so that she might all the more
> open their hearts, and so that she might seem all the more precious
> in the eyes of her husband and son even than she had been before this.
>   Quote 2.5: *Od.* 18.158–162

So begins the scene in which Penelope appears before the suitors and announces her decision to remarry in quote 2.2. What is important now is simply that Athene implants in Penelope's mind an idea—the idea of showing herself to the suitors—that is alien to her own thoughts and inclinations, and that Penelope goes on to act in accordance with this idea even though she never would have done so on her own initiative.[41] In the same way, Athene could implant in Penelope's mind the idea of the contest and the decision, however reluctant, to marry the winner.[42] Moreover, Odysseus would know that Athene could do this since it is generally accepted (with justification) by Homer's characters that the gods can make mortals behave irrationally.[43]

The scenario I propose is the following. When Odysseus comes up with the idea of the twofold contest, he plans to inform Athene so that she can put the idea in Penelope's mind. Athene has undoubtedly also realized that Penelope's announcement of her intention to remarry has opened up new possibilities for dealing with the suitors (in the scenario contemplated in section 2.13, she would even have had advance knowledge of the significance of Penelope's announcement). As soon as Odysseus springs into action to remove the arms from the hall, she therefore joins him (see *Od.* 19.31–34 in quote 2.3) to learn what plan he has devised after hearing Penelope's speech. Sometime during the interval covered by quote 2.3, probably after Telemachos has gone to bed (see section 2.8), Odysseus tells her his plan. She apparently decides not to put the idea of holding the contest in Penelope's mind until after the awaited conversation between the queen and the beggar, because she would want Penelope to be able to express her true feelings when she speaks with her husband for the first time in twenty years. It is when the conversation between Penelope and the disguised Odysseus reaches a natural stopping point, and the queen instructs her attendants to prepare a bed for the stranger and to wash his feet, that Athene implants the idea of the contest in Penelope's mind. This can be seen as follows.

The woman who washes Odysseus's feet is Eurykleia, who was his nurse when he was a child. While attending to the beggar, Eurykleia recognizes Odysseus from a distinctive scar on his thigh, the result of an encounter with a boar in his youth. In her surprise she lets go of his foot and the basin of water gets knocked over. Penelope does not notice the disturbance or Eurykleia's excitement, because she has been distracted by Athene.[44] Lattimore's translation—"Athene turned aside her perception"—reflects the usual view that nothing else of significance is happening at this moment, but Murray's more accurate translation—"Athene had turned her thoughts aside"—implies that Penelope is distracted because Athene has given a new direction to her thinking, has made her preoccupied with an unexpected thought.[45] That unexpected thought, I suggest, is the idea of holding the contest of the bow for the purpose of selecting a new husband.[46]

After Odysseus has impressed upon Eurykleia the need for silence and she has finished washing his feet, Penelope indicates to the beggar that she wishes to talk with him a little more.[47] The resumption of the conversation is surprising in itself since Penelope seemed to have terminated it with her instructions to her attending women regarding the care of the stranger. Furthermore, for the first time she now expresses doubts as to what she should do, whether she should keep putting the suitors off or whether she should marry one of them. This is followed by her rejection of the dream that clearly

2.5. THE MOTIVATION OF PENELOPE

foretells the return of Odysseus and his destruction of the suitors and then by her abrupt statement that she will marry the winner of a contest that she intends to hold the next day (quote 2.1). All of this unexpected behavior makes sense if Athene suggested the idea of the contest to Penelope during the scene of the foot washing and Eurykleia's recognition.[48]

It is not difficult to understand why Athene must deceive Penelope about the purpose of the contest and have her accept the idea of remarriage as if under the power of hypnotic suggestion. The reason, of course, is that Odysseus's presence on Ithaka must be kept secret even from the queen. This was decided by Athene and agreed to by Odysseus[49] not because of doubts about Penelope's loyalty, but, I believe, from the fear that, after all she has endured, she will not be able to maintain her composure when she is told that Odysseus has returned: her emotional turmoil coincident with the arrival of the beggar will be noticed by her serving women, and the secret of Odysseus's return, which is so crucial to the possibility of overthrowing the suitors, will be in jeopardy.[50, 51] Thus, Penelope must be kept in the dark about the true purpose of the contest and must be influenced by Athene to accept an alternate purpose which she would ordinarily reject.

As mentioned at the beginning of this section, Athene "activates" Penelope when it is time to begin the contest. In a marked departure from her usual conduct, the queen has placed a chair just outside the door to her chamber and is listening to the suitors talk as they prepare their feast. She is presumably waiting for the right time to act, and Athene tells her when that time has come:[52]

> But now the goddess, gray-eyed Athene, put it in the mind
> of the daughter of Ikarios, circumspect Penelope,
> to set the bow before the suitors, and the grey iron,
> in the house of Odysseus: the contest, the beginning of the slaughter.
>
> Quote 2.6: *Od.* 21.1–4

Penelope then fetches Odysseus's bow and a quiver of arrows, goes to the suitors, and announces the contest just as she described it to the beggar in the last half of quote 2.1.[53] The first two lines of quote 2.6 are identical to the corresponding lines of quote 2.5. Woodhouse remarks, "These are the only places in which this formula is found in the Odyssey, and the only examples of humanly unmotived action in the poem."[54] This link between Penelope's actual initiation of the contest and her showing herself to the suitors is evident, but it is not precise. When Athene suggests that she show herself to the suitors (quote 2.5), Penelope gives an unnatural laugh and explains her intention to her attendant in a way that betrays her own confusion:[55]

> She [Penelope] laughed, in an idle way, and spoke to her nurse and named her:
> "Eurynome, my heart desires, though before it did not,
> to show myself to the suitors, although I still hate them. Also,
> I would speak a word to my son, and that would be for the better,
> that he should not always go among the insolent suitors,
> who speak him well, but are plotting evil things for the future."
>
> Quote 2.7: *Od.* 18.163–168

But when Athene suggests that she set the bow before the suitors (quote 2.6), she goes into action immediately, as the psychological adjustment to the foreign idea has already taken place during the interval between Eurykleia's recognition of Odysseus (when Athene suggests the idea of the contest to Penelope) and Penelope's declaration to the beggar of her decision to hold the contest and to remarry.

I am not the first to argue that Athene suggests the contest to Penelope. What has been argued before, however, is that Athene, not Odysseus, is the originator of the idea.[56] This approach assumes, of course, that Athene knows about Odysseus's great bow and his feat of shooting an arrow through the axes.[57] It does explain why Penelope suddenly decides to remarry despite the signs that her husband's return is imminent, but my approach explains this *and* offers a satisfying motivation for Odysseus's departure from his original plan for the removal of the arms.[58]

My theory for the motivation of Penelope has implications for the interpretation of quote 2.2. The demonstration in section 2.2 that Penelope is lying to the suitors when she tells them about Odysseus's final instruction justifies some suspicion that she may also be deceiving them when she indicates, in the context of the fabricated instruction, that she has resigned herself to a new marriage. Perhaps the main reason that has been cited for believing that her surrender at this stage is genuine is that just a few hours later she tells the beggar of her intention to hold the contest of the bow and to marry the winner.[59] In my theory, of course, her statement to the beggar is explained by Athene's intervention at a certain point during the few hours in question. This intervention decouples the real surrender in quote 2.1 from the professed surrender in quote 2.2 and eliminates what is probably the most compelling reason for believing that the latter surrender is also real. This is a desirable result, for there are several reasons to think that in quote 2.2 Penelope only pretends to have accepted the inevitability of a new marriage.

First, Athene's motives for having Penelope appear before the suitors (see quote 2.5 and discussion in section 2.13) may require Penelope to convince the suitors that she will take a new husband (so that she can wheedle courtship gifts out of them, for example), but they do not require her to actually intend to do so. Since she is quite capable of dissimulation (after all, she tells the suitors about an instruction from Odysseus that he never actually gave; recall also her ruse of the shroud for Laertes), Athene would have no reason at this point to implant such an intention in her mind. Second, Penelope's reaction to Athene's suggestion in quote 2.5 is not dismay at the prospect of a new marriage, but only perplexity at the impulse she feels to show herself to the suitors (see quote 2.7). Finally, the reading proposed here provides a nice example of Fenik's anticipation pattern (see section 1.5) if Penelope does not resign herself to a new marriage until Athene "suggests" to her the idea of the contest, for then Athene twice has Penelope do something that goes against her own inclinations, first in relatively minor way (showing herself to the suitors and pretending to be open to courtship) and then in a major way (holding what she thinks is a real contest for her hand in marriage).

I conclude this section with an interesting parallel between the destruction of the suitors and the sack of Troy. In both cases, Athene not only aids

Odysseus in the fighting,[60] but also contributes to the implementation of the stratagem that he devised to make the fighting possible: she helps with the construction of the Wooden Horse conceived by Odysseus,[61] and she implants in the mind of Penelope his idea of the contest of the bow. Note, however, that the parallel breaks down if, as I shall tentatively suggest in section 2.13, Athene makes a strategic contribution to the destruction of the suitors.

2.6. Odysseus's Reaction to Penelope's Decision

When Penelope declares to the beggar her intention to hold the contest of the bow and to marry the winner (quote 2.1), Odysseus responds as follows:

> "O respected wife of Odysseus, son of Laertes,
> do not put off this contest in your house any longer.
> Before these people can handle the well-wrought bow, and manage
> to hook the string and bend it, and send a shaft through the iron,
> Odysseus of the many designs will be back here with you."
>
> Quote 2.8: *Od.* 19.583–587

Odysseus reacts immediately by urging Penelope to hold the contest as soon as possible. This reaction makes perfect sense in the reading I propose since the idea of the contest originated with him and is the centerpiece of his plan for overthrowing the suitors. The final lines of this passage serve simply to reassure the queen that she need not fear the consequences of going forward.

Rutherford infers from this speech that Penelope's declaration of her intention to hold the contest is what prompts Odysseus to think of using the bow, obtained by means of the contest, to destroy his enemies.[62] For Erbse, the speech indicates that Athene has by this time communicated to Odysseus *her* idea of using the bow.[63] The scene that follows the conversation between Penelope and the beggar includes material that seems to contradict these interpretations as well as my own. This material and the reasons Rutherford and I discount it (it is not addressed by Erbse) are discussed in the following section.

In his conversation with Penelope, the beggar refers to Odysseus by name fourteen times in the Greek text (not including the several occurrences of the first line in quote 2.8). On only one of these fourteen occasions, shown in the last line of quote 2.8, does he characterize him as resourceful or crafty (πολυμητις, here translated by Lattimore as "of the many designs"). Is it just by chance that this description occurs in the context of the contest which I claim is the fruit of his resourcefulness? As mentioned at the beginning of this chapter, πολυμητις is the most common distinctive epithet used for Odysseus. The use of a particular epithet is usually determined not by its meaning but by the metrical utility of the formula in which it appears (see the second endnote to this chapter). However, the present usage of πολυμητις is not formulaic (the adjective is not even next to Odysseus's name). It is therefore legitimate to speculate that πολυμητις may be meaningful here.[64] The following argument shows that this speculation deserves to be taken seriously.

During his conversation with Eumaios in book 14, the beggar refers to Odysseus by name eight times, but characterizes him as resourceful only one of these times.[65] In this case the adjective meaning "resourceful" (this time πολυμηχανος) appears in a formula. It nevertheless seems meaningful, as the formula is used to introduce a (made-up) anecdote illustrating Odysseus's craftiness, the only such anecdote the beggar ever tells. If the description of Odysseus in the last line of quote 2.8 relates to the contest mentioned in the passage—that is, if the contest was devised by "Odysseus of the many designs"—we have an intriguing parallel between the beggar's conversations with Eumaios and Penelope. Another aspect of the parallelism is that in both conversations the beggar characterizes Odysseus as resourceful the last time he refers to him by name. But there is one respect in which the parallelism is strained: whereas the ruse described in the anecdote the beggar relates to Eumaios is of no significance, the contest of the bow is crucial to Odysseus's revenge and the success of his homecoming. The combination of this contrast and the general parallelism means that the beggar's conversations with Eumaios and Penelope together form one more example of Fenik's anticipation pattern—provided, of course, that the contest of the bow is the brainchild of Odysseus. What makes this especially noteworthy is that these conversations are already known as a fine example of this pattern.[66]

2.7. The Wait for the Contest

Once the arms have been removed from the hall and Penelope has been motivated to hold the contest of the bow, there is nothing for Odysseus to do but wait for the contest. Nevertheless, this interval is of great interest in connection with the reading proposed in this chapter, in part because it contains the main evidence *against* this reading. Here I discuss this evidence and show that it is nullified by other evidence from the same interval.

Odysseus spends the first part of the night after his conversation with Penelope tossing and turning with worry, "meditating how, though he was alone against many, he could lay hands on the shameless suitors."[67] This description is the conflicting evidence to which I was just referring. It gives the impression that Odysseus does not yet know how he is going to deal with the suitors, that he still has not thought of killing them with the bow obtained by means of the contest.[68] Since Penelope has brought the bow to mind by declaring her intention to hold the contest, this interpretation not only undermines my reading but also implies a mental slowness that one would not expect of Odysseus. I argue, on the contrary, that Odysseus knows very well how he *hopes* to dispose of the suitors; he is simply worried that his plan may not work against so many adversaries. The description of him being "alone against many," which is a little strange since it ignores Telemachos and any other allies that might be recruited, could actually refer to this plan: Odysseus will indeed be alone, in effect, during the first part of the battle, when arms have not yet been fetched from the storeroom and he is the only one with a weapon.[69] However that may be, my general interpretation receives support when Athene comes to reassure him and he expresses his concerns:

> "... here is something the heart inside me is pondering,
> how, when I am alone against many, I can lay hands on
> the shameless suitors. And they are always here in a body.
> And here is a still bigger problem that my heart is pondering.

2.7. THE WAIT FOR THE CONTEST

Even if, by grace of Zeus and yourself, I kill them,
how shall I make my escape? It is what I would have you think on."

Quote 2.9: *Od.* 20.38–43

According to my reading, Odysseus is apprehensive about facing 108 suitors with his bow. Although he has been tossing and turning in desperation to think of a less risky alternative, he is at a loss to do so since, as he notes here, the suitors are always together when they are in his palace. Significantly, he worries that, even if he succeeds in killing the suitors, he will have to escape the revenge of their relatives. The fact that this problem has come to the fore—Odysseus considers it to be bigger than the challenge of killing the suitors and more in need of Athene's attention—suggests that a plan for killing the suitors is indeed already in place.[70] This suggestion is confirmed by the following evidence.

Shortly before Odysseus starts to toss and turn with worry, he hears the slave women who have become mistresses of the suitors leaving the palace to join their lovers. Their disloyalty to his household infuriates him:

But the spirit deep in the heart of Odysseus was stirred by this,
and much he pondered in the division of mind and spirit,
whether to spring on them and kill each one, or rather
to let them lie this one more time with the insolent suitors,
for the last and latest time; but the heart was growling within him.

Quote 2.10: *Od.* 20.9–13

In his heart Odysseus wants to kill the disloyal women, but his mind knows that to do so before the suitors have been dealt with would be a strategic blunder of the highest order. The fact that the alternative to killing the women then and there is to let them have one last night with their lovers implies that he intends to kill the suitors the very next day. This is what my reading leads us to expect, of course, since the next day is the day of the contest (see quote 2.1). Even if we ignore the connection with the contest, quote 2.10 implies that Odysseus must have a plan for killing the suitors, as we inferred from the last three lines of quote 2.9. The description of Odysseus as "meditating how, though he was alone against many, he could lay hands on the shameless suitors" must reflect not the absence of a plan but understandable nervousness about whether his plan will work.

Odysseus is reassured by Athene and falls asleep, but he wants more reassurance when he wakes up in the morning. He prays to Zeus for two omens, one from somebody inside the house and an outside one directly from Zeus himself. Zeus immediately responds with thunder from a cloudless sky. A woman inside the house notices this omen and delivers a short speech which serves as the other omen. Here are two lines from her speech followed by the verses that conclude this scene:

"On this day let the suitors take, for the last and latest
time, their desirable feasting in the halls of Odysseus.
..."
　　So she spoke, and great Odysseus welcomed the ominous
speech, and the thunder of Zeus. He thought he would punish the sinners.

Quote 2.11: *Od.* 20.116–121

The excerpt from the speech quoted here supports the implication of quote 2.10 that Odysseus intends to kill the suitors on the day of the contest (although in the case of the speech it is possible, in principle, that he intends to kill them early on the following day).

The two omens have dispelled the hero's worry: "He thought he would punish the sinners." But how can he be confident that he will overcome the suitors that very day unless he already has a plan for accomplishing this? The omens cannot mean that a way to kill the suitors is about to fall into his lap. Rather, they must mean that the way he has already thought of, though apparently fraught with uncertainty and danger, will succeed. This is certainly the meaning of the omen that Zeus sends *after* the contest, when Odysseus has strung his bow and is about to launch his attack on the suitors:

> A great sorrow fell now upon the suitors, and all their color
> was changed, and Zeus showing forth his portents thundered mightily.
> Hearing this, long-suffering great Odysseus was happy
> that the son of devious-devising Kronos had sent him a portent.
> Quote 2.12: *Od.* 21.412–415

As Odysseus's plan is now well underway, the latest thunder sent by Zeus can only mean that the rest of his plan will also succeed. Quotes 2.11 and 2.12 show that Odysseus receives all three omens with the same welcoming attitude. I suggest that this is because the two omens sent earlier in the day have the same significance as the omen sent just as he is about to slaughter the suitors: they all foretell the success of the hero's plan.

The final proof of Odysseus's plan is found in the interval between the first two omens and Penelope's announcement of the contest to the suitors. The confidence he feels after those initial omens is evident in a declaration he makes a little later (in his disguise as an old beggar), when the oxherd Philoitios expresses the hope that Odysseus will come back and get rid of the suitors:

> "… I will tell you this, and swear a great oath upon it.
> Zeus be my witness, first of the gods, and the table of friendship,
> and the hearth of blameless Odysseus, to which I come as a suppliant;
> Odysseus will come home again, while you are still here
> in the house, and with your own eyes, if you desire to,
> you can watch him killing the suitors, who are supreme here."
> Quote 2.13: *Od.* 20.229–234

Since Philoitios lives on a neighboring island and will presumably be returning there at the end of the festival of Apollo being celebrated that day, this declaration amounts to a prediction that Odysseus will kill the suitors that very day. The specificity and certainty of this prediction are incompatible with the notion that Odysseus does not know how he is going to accomplish this. As there is no hint of a plan having been conceived during the time that has elapsed since he was tossing and turning with worry the night before, he must have been worrying about whether the plan he already had in mind was going to work, in the accordance with the reading proposed for quote 2.9.[71]

2.8. The Silencing of Telemachos

A curious feature of the scene in which Odysseus and Telemachos remove the arms from the great hall is how the father reacts when his son remarks that a god must be lighting their way (see *Od.* 19.35–44 in quote 2.3). Odysseus does give a response to the remark, saying "this is the very way of the gods," but he also tells Telemachos to keep quiet, not to ask questions, and to go to bed. It is easy to understand why the poet has Odysseus behave in this way. Telemachos is bound to ask why they are not leaving two panoplies in the hall as originally planned, but this question cannot be allowed if the plot is to be developed in the subtle manner described in the preceding sections. Odysseus's silencing of Telemachos is a satisfactory solution to this problem provided this measure also makes sense in terms of the plot. Let us see whether it does.

Once the contest of the bow has been conceived and the arms have been removed from the hall, the most pressing need for the implementation of Odysseus's plan is to arrange for Penelope to hold the contest. Odysseus must therefore inform Athene of his plan so that she can put the idea of the contest in Penelope's mind. The hero evidently communicates with the goddess sometime during the interval covered by quote 2.3 since there is no other opportunity for them to confer between the conception of Odysseus's plan and Penelope's statement of her intention to hold the contest in quote 2.1. I shall now pin down more precisely when the communication takes place.

At the beginning and end of quote 2.3 we find Odysseus "pondering how, with the help of Athene, he would murder the suitors." In Murray's translation, however, Odysseus is "planning with Athene's aid the slaying of the suitors." The variation regarding Athene's role seems to reflect ambiguity in the Greek text, since it is also found in other translations: some assert that Odysseus is pondering alone but has in mind the help that Athene can provide, some assert that Odysseus and Athene are planning together, and the rest are ambiguous on this point.[72] Any given translation applies the same interpretation to the beginning and end of the passage. This is natural since the Greek is the same in both places. If the ambiguity is intentional, however, it may be that we should apply one interpretation to the beginning of the passage and the other interpretation to the end. My preference would be to keep Lattimore's translation at the beginning of quote 2.3 so that Odysseus can be seen as having devised the contest of the bow on his own (like the stratagem of the Wooden Horse and the escape from the Cyclops), but to switch to Murray's interpretation at the end of the passage. The latter choice gives Odysseus the opportunity to communicate his plan to Athene, enabling her to suggest the contest to Penelope later in the evening.

The consultation with Athene is a matter of urgency for Odysseus since he expects Penelope to arrive at any moment for her meeting with the beggar. And indeed, Penelope descends from her chamber in the verse that immediately follows quote 2.3—that is, according to the interpretation just proposed, immediately after Odysseus and Athene confer. The urgency felt by Odysseus accounts for his silencing of Telemachos: he simply does not have time to explain his new plan to his son.

Since Odysseus has no further opportunity to speak with his son alone, Telemachos remains ignorant of his father's intention to exact revenge with the bow until Penelope announces the contest to the suitors. This is confirmed by the way he looks at his father for a signal that it is time to act, even when the bow is not at hand.[73] But Telemachos's ignorance of the plan is no argument against its existence. As I have explained, Odysseus has more pressing concerns on the one occasion he could communicate his plan to Telemachos. Fortunately, Telemachos is quick-witted enough to grasp the plan on his own—or at least to know what he must do (for he may not realize that the contest was planned by his father)—when the time to act has arrived.

To understand the story of the last stratagem of Odysseus, we do not need to know precisely when Telemachos realizes that the great bow is the instrument which will enable his father at least to attempt to destroy the mass of suitors. However, a discussion of this question is worthwhile because it will provide another example of the subtlety of Homer's account, in which important developments occur without being mentioned explicitly.

After Penelope announces the contest to the suitors and tells Eumaios to set the bow before them, both Eumaios and Philoitios begin to weep at the sight of their master's bow and, presumably, at the momentous step that Penelope is taking. Antinoös scolds the two herdsmen for their tears, and remarks that the bow of Odysseus will probably be difficult to string. The reaction of Telemachos to his mother's announcement is revealed in a speech to which we will return in a moment. He concludes this speech by urging the suitors not to put off their attempts to string the bow out of fear of failure, adding that he himself will try it. After setting up the axes in the configuration required for the test of marksmanship, he tries three times to string the bow, and only a warning nod from Odysseus prevents him from making a fourth attempt, which, we are told, would have been successful. According to the interpretation of Woodhouse, his father's signal to put down the bow is what makes Telemachos realize its significance.[74] But the following argument, due to Büchner,[75] shows that the significance of the bow is apparent to him before this.

There can be no doubt that Telemachos has been wondering how the suitors can possibly be eliminated, especially after he and his father have removed all the arms from the hall without leaving any behind for themselves. Given his preoccupation with this problem, he must realize as soon as the bow is introduced by Penelope that this weapon offers a possible solution, since it could enable his father to keep the suitors at a distance while picking them off one by one. The relief that comes with this realization explains why his first reaction to his mother's announcement, as we learn from his speech, is to laugh with joy.[76] His speech, which gives the impression of a confused reaction to his mother's unexpected announcement, is actually intended to hide from the suitors the reason for his spontaneous laughter. As it also hides this reason from most readers owing to the misleading impression it creates, we must be grateful to Büchner for his perceptive analysis, which has exposed another subtlety of the plot development in the second half of the *Odyssey*.[77]

2.9. Amphimedon's Account

At the end of the *Odyssey*, the shade of Amphimedon, one of the slaughtered suitors, relates to the shade of Agamemnon the story of the courting of Penelope and Odysseus's revenge. His story includes an account of three events he did not witness—the plotting of Odysseus and Telemachos against the suitors, the removal of the arms, and Penelope's decision to hold the contest of the bow:

> "... These two [Odysseus and Telemachos],
> after compacting their plot of a foul death for the suitors,
> made their way to the glorious town. ...
> ...
> [H]e [Odysseus], with Telemachos, took away the glorious armor,
> and stowed it away in the chamber, closing the doors upon it.
> Then, in the craftiness of his mind, he urged his lady
> to set the bow and the gray iron in front of the suitors,
> the contest for us ill-fated men, the start of our slaughter."
>
> Quote 2.14: *Od.* 24.152–154, 165–169

This account, which consists of plausible inferences based on what Amphimedon and the other suitors saw, accurately represents the first two events. Its portrayal of the third event, on the other hand, seems to be contradicted by the main narrative of the poem. I claim, however, that the contradiction disappears when the subtlety of the narrative is taken into account and that the portrayal of the third event is also essentially correct.

Amphimedon presumably believes that Penelope held the contest at the urging of Odysseus because it took place the day after the king's return to the palace and was ideally suited to pave the way for his revenge. This reasonable belief would appear to be inconsistent with the fact that the contest is not mentioned in the poem until Penelope declares her intention to hold it in quote 2.1.[78] According to the reading proposed in this chapter, however, Odysseus is the one who comes up with the idea of the contest, as Amphimedon assumes, and he uses Athene as an intermediary to "urge" Penelope to hold it. Amphimedon has no way of knowing Athene's role, of course, but he has correctly described the essence of what happened.

The proposed reading evidently enables us to regard quote 2.14 as a factual statement. With this excerpt validated, it becomes possible to regard the entirety of Amphimedon's story as an accurate report, provided only that reasonable allowance is made for his subjective point of view.[79] This is a satisfying result, for it means that Homer provides a summary of the *Odyssey* at the end of the poem by having Odysseus summarize the first half, his trials and adventures prior to his return to Ithaka, and Amphimedon summarize the second half, the events on Ithaka after the hero's return.[80]

Finally, let us observe the irony in quote 2.14. According to the usual interpretation of the last three lines of the passage, Amphimedon believes that Odysseus and Penelope conspired to kill the suitors.[81] This interpretation is almost certainly correct: Without using Athene as an intermediary, Odysseus could urge Penelope to hold the contest only if she knew his identity and was conspiring with him, since the beggar that he pretends to be would not know about Odysseus's great bow or his feat of archery. However, there cannot have been a conspiracy since Penelope does not recognize Odysseus until after the slaughter.[82] The audience knows this, but Amphimedon does not. We therefore have an ordinary dramatic irony. But the reading suggested here implies that there is also another sort of irony. The audience assumes at first that Amphimedon's statement that Odysseus urged Penelope to hold the contest is as erroneous as his belief in a conspiracy. There is a discrepancy between the appearance that Amphimedon is completely mistaken in this matter and the reality that his statement is a lot closer to the truth than the audience's belief that it was Penelope who introduced the idea of the contest to Odysseus, not vice versa. This is an irony that the audience does not see on its first exposure to the poem and will not see until it has perceived the subtle plot development described in this chapter.

2.10. Odysseus and Hephaistos

As in the preceding section, we now consider a passage which does not advance our understanding of the development or execution of Odysseus's last stratagem but which takes on a satisfying new significance when viewed in the light of the reading proposed here. The passage is the second song sung by Demodokos on the day that Odysseus is entertained by the Phaiakians. We begin by noting a key property shared by Odysseus and the protagonist of the song, the god Hephaistos.

At the beginning of this chapter I mentioned that a distinctive epithet of a mortal is defined to be an epithet that is used for him or her but for no other mortal. This definition allows the possibility that one or more of the distinctive epithets of a mortal may also be used for a god. In fact, two of the distinctive epithets that characterize Odysseus as resourceful and intelligent ($\pi o \lambda \upsilon \mu \eta \tau \iota \varsigma$ and $\pi o \lambda \upsilon \varphi \rho \omega \nu$) are also used for Hephaistos.[83]

The cunning intelligence of Hephaistos is on display in the second song of Demodokos. Learning that Aphrodite (his wife for the purposes of the song) is having an affair with Ares, the famed craftsman gets justice and revenge by making an ingenious trap which ensnares the lovers together in bed for all the other gods to see. This story can be regarded as a microcosm of the *Odyssey*. Although Aphrodite and Penelope behave entirely differently, the marriages of Hephaistos and Odysseus are both under threat from one or more wrongdoers (Ares, the suitors), and in both cases the wrongdoers are brought to justice by means of an ingenious device conceived by the protagonist. In the case of Odysseus, of course, the device is the contest of the bow. Some parallelism between Demodokos's song and the *Odyssey* is evident even in conventional readings of the poem owing to the cunning of Odysseus in his disguise as a beggar,[84] but the parallelism is much more complete and satisfying if he devised the contest, as argued here.

Walter Burkert has shown that "the song of Ares and Aphrodite" alludes to three scenes in the *Iliad*.[85] We have just seen that the same passage serves as a microcosm of the *Odyssey*. There is a sense, then, in which the two Homeric epics are united in the second song of Demodokos. The significance

2.11. The Post-Reunion Conversation of Odysseus and Penelope

The conversation between Odysseus and Penelope that follows Penelope's recognition of her husband, in particular the part between their weeping and their lovemaking, is surprising for both what it contains and what it does not contain. When Eurykleia wakes Penelope to tell her that Odysseus is home and has killed the suitors, Penelope asks her how he, just one man, was able to overcome the mass of suitors.[86] Since Eurykleia is unable to answer, we would expect Penelope to put the same question to Odysseus as soon as the initial excitement of their reunion has subsided enough for them to talk. However, the subject of how Odysseus liberated his palace never comes up. Instead, the first thing the husband says to his wife once she has recognized him after a separation of twenty years is that their troubles are not yet over:

> "Dear wife, we have not yet come to the limit of all our
> trials. There is unmeasured labor left for the future,
> both difficult and great, and all of it I must accomplish.
> So the soul of Teiresias prophesied to me, on that day
> when I went down inside the house of Hades, seeking
> to learn about homecoming, for myself and for my companions.
> But come, my wife, let us go to bed, so that at long last
> we can enjoy the sweetness of slumber, sleeping together."
>   Quote 2.15: *Od.* 23.248–255

When one thinks of all the tears Penelope has shed during those twenty years, it is incredible that Odysseus does not let her have at least a short period of untroubled joy. This speech is also strange in two other respects. After telling Penelope that he must perform a "difficult and great" labor, Odysseus expects her to put this out of her mind and to go to bed with no further explanation of what lies ahead. This expectation is obviously unrealistic; in fact, she asks for an explanation, and he obliges by recounting in its entirety the part of Teiresias's prophecy that remains to be fulfilled.[87] Also unrealistic is his apparent failure to realize that she will be filled with curiosity about his trip to the underworld and will want to ask him many questions about that.[88] In short, this is a speech that no man would ever give, and no woman would want to hear, just before reunion sex.[89]

The strangeness of quote 2.15 becomes even more striking when one realizes that all difficulties disappear if Odysseus simply tells Penelope about the remaining trial later in the night. After making love, they tell each other what happened during their separation, and then finally they fall asleep.[90] The natural time for Odysseus to speak of the labor he must perform is at the end of his story. At this point he has already spoken of his trip to the underworld and his consultation with Teiresias, so these things will not create distracting surprises when he describes the seer's instructions. At this point, as well, there is no reason for him to hold back the details of his task, as he tries to do in quote 2.15. Furthermore, his task can now be seen in the context of all the dangers he faced while he was away, a perspective which shows it to be more of an annoyance than an existential threat. And of course by waiting until this point to speak of the remaining trial, Odysseus will have given Penelope a much-needed interval of carefree joy. Finally, this timing makes possible an elegant transition to sleep: the last prophecy of Teiresias, that Odysseus will have a happy old age, causes Penelope to say, "If the gods are accomplishing a more prosperous old age, then there is hope that you shall have an escape from your troubles";[91] Homer has only to add, "At these words from his dear wife, the sweet sleep came to relax his limbs and slip the cares from his spirit."[92]

In view of the difficulties posed by quote 2.15 and the ease with which they could have been avoided, it is gratifying to discover that the theory proposed here for the origin of the contest of the bow enables us to account for the structure and content of the post-reunion conversation between Odysseus and Penelope, as I shall now explain.

As mentioned above, one would normally expect Penelope to begin the conversation by asking Odysseus how he managed to prevail over the suitors. He would, of course, reply that the contest gave him the opportunity to get his hands on the bow and that this weapon offset the numerical advantage of his adversaries. In addition, if Odysseus conceived the idea of the contest and had Athene implant in Penelope's mind the foreign thought that she should hold the contest and marry the winner, he certainly owes it to his wife to explain this to her. But the poet cannot let him do this since the explanation would bring to the surface information about events that occurred below the surface of the text, spoiling the mystery for an uninitiated audience. On the other hand, if the poet has Odysseus give an explanation that omits the hidden events, an initiated audience would rightly complain that Odysseus would never neglect to mention his brilliant stratagem and would never leave his wife wondering about the motivation for her own behavior. We understand, then, why Penelope cannot be allowed to ask him how he was able to dispatch the suitors.

Now let us consider why the poet strangely has Odysseus bring up the trial foretold by Teiresias instead of letting Penelope enjoy their reunion free of care and why he then compounds the strangeness by having the hero drop the subject of the trial as soon as he has raised it. To discern the poet's motive, it is natural to look at the consequence of his procedure, which is that Penelope's curiosity is aroused and she asks to be told about the trial:

"But since a god put this into your mind, and you understand it,
tell me what this trial is …"

Quote 2.16: *Od.* 23.260–261[93]

Penelope supposes in the first line of this fragment that Odysseus brought up the trial because a god had put the trial in his mind. According to the reading proposed in section 2.5, Penelope tells the disguised Odysseus of her intention to hold the contest of the bow because Athene has put the idea of the contest in her mind. The evident correspondence between these two situations is increased by the fact that the word for "trial" ($αεθλος$) is the same as the word for "contest." In both cases, then, a god puts an $αεθλος$ in the mind of someone (Penelope or Odysseus) who then describes the $αεθλος$ to someone else

(Odysseus or Penelope). I submit that quote 2.16, in conjunction with quote 2.15, alludes to the contest-related events in book 19, Athene giving Penelope the idea of the contest (below the surface of the poem during the foot-washing scene) and Penelope telling the beggar of her intention to hold the contest. If this is correct, the allusion is strategically placed, for it is found at just that place in the narrative where one would expect Odysseus to explain to his wife how he managed to kill the suitors and how she contributed to the victory through the contest "suggested" to her by Athene. These explanations cannot be allowed, as we have seen, but the poet makes up for this shortcoming by acknowledging it with this allusion placed just where the excluded explanations would have been. Of course, the allusion can be recognized only by those who are aware of what has happened below the surface of the poem; others will either rationalize the peculiarities of the post-reunion conversation between Odysseus and Penelope or perceive them as unfortunate lapses.

2.12. Discussion and Recapitulation

The problems discussed in some of the preceding sections have often been viewed as unfortunate consequences of a complex compositional history. Thus, Amphimedon's account and Penelope's decision to hold the contest for her hand in marriage have both suggested to some scholars that the *Odyssey* retains traces of an earlier story in which Penelope recognizes Odysseus soon after his return to the palace and the two conspire to undo the suitors.[94] It has also been claimed that the passages dealing with the removal of the arms, quotes 2.3 and 2.4, reflect different stages in the evolution of the poem.[95] An attractive feature of the reading proposed here is that it enables us to see the poem as a much more coherent composition.

It may be objected that the proposed reading is surprising because one would expect a more explicit treatment of a subject as important as the origin of the plan for the destruction of the suitors. However, the force of this objection is greatly diminished by the fact that we are never told explicitly when Odysseus gets the idea of using the bow to kill the suitors.

Odysseus certainly thinks of slaughtering the suitors with the bow by the time when, having revealed himself to Eumaios and Philoitios, he tells the swineherd to bring him the bow when the suitors are objecting to his having it and then to arrange for the doors of the hall to be barred (*Od.* 21.231–241). If the idea occurs to him before this, when he is watching Telemachos attempt to string the bow, we can understand why he signals his son to stop trying (*Od.* 21.128–130): he wants to avoid any disruption to his plan that might ensue if Telemachos were to succeed. If he gets the idea still earlier, when Penelope reveals to him her decision to hold the contest, we can understand why both he and Athene support this decision so firmly, he urging that the contest be held without delay (quote 2.8) and she activating Penelope when it is time to start the contest (quote 2.6). But we understand all this and much more if Odysseus thinks of using the bow during the interval between Penelope's speech to the suitors (quote 2.2) and the removal of the arms: we understand why two panoplies are not left in the hall as originally planned, and we understand Penelope's illogical decision to hold the contest and marry the winner. Earlier than this we cannot go, for the contest does not become a viable idea until the suitors are convinced that Penelope has resigned herself to taking a new husband. Thus, although Homer's treatment is indirect, it is also precise, enabling us to pinpoint when Odysseus thinks of the contest and, as explained in section 2.5, when Athene puts this idea in Penelope's mind.

The proposed reading merits attention not only for its unifying and explanatory power, but also because it allows the hero of the poem to live up to his reputation. That the *Odyssey* should be understood in a way that does justice to the wiles of Odysseus, besides being attractive as a matter of principle, is suggested by certain words and thoughts of various characters. In quote 2.14 Amphimedon credits the craftiness of Odysseus for the contest of the bow. I maintain that the poet would find it awkward to include this attribution if it were not accurate, since he would be drawing attention to his failure to fulfill his artistic obligation to the reputation of his hero. Now consider Telemachos. After killing the suitors, Odysseus calls his son's attention to the problem of how they are going to escape the vengeance of the relatives (a problem he raised previously with Athene in quote 2.9). Telemachos, who is not aware that the contest of the bow was a stratagem devised by Odysseus and assumes that his father simply took advantage of the opportunity provided by his mother's unexpected decision to hold the contest, replies that his father should supply the solution to this problem since he is "held to be the best man in the world for stratagems."[96] The latter remark, in which the son must rely on what he has heard about the craftiness of his father from Nestor and others,[97] evidently reflects his perception that the famous resourcefulness of Odysseus played no role in the destruction of the suitors. The poet would hardly make a point of this perception if it were accurate. Finally, consider Odysseus. While he is torn between killing the disloyal slave women and letting them spend one last night with their lovers (quote 2.10), Odysseus thinks back to one of the crafty designs for which he is famous and speaks to himself as follows:

> "Bear up, my heart. You have had worse to endure before this
> on that day when the irresistible Cyclops ate up
> my strong companions, but you endured it until intelligence
> got you out of the cave, though you expected to perish."
>
> Quote 2.17: *Od.* 20.18–21

The hero recalls that the escape from the Cyclops was an achievement of his resourcefulness. It would be disappointing if that resourcefulness were to fail him now and he had to depend on a whim of Penelope—her illogical decision to hold the contest—for the key to the destruction of the suitors. On the other hand, it is very satisfying if the twofold contest of the bow is his own invention and this passage signals that he is overcoming the present crisis through his wits, just as he overcame the crisis in the cave of the Cyclops.[98]

2.13. The Strategic Contribution of Athene

Having argued that the contest of the bow is devised by Odysseus, I now discuss the possibility that Athene also makes a strategic contribution to the destruction of the suitors, one that in fact paves the way for the stratagem of

2.13. THE STRATEGIC CONTRIBUTION OF ATHENE

the hero. We know that the goddess begins to help Odysseus in his struggle against the suitors as soon as he arrives back in Ithaka by disguising him as an old beggar and by arranging his reunion with Telemachos. But I will suggest that, in addition, she devises and implements a crucial ruse comparable in its cleverness to something we expect from Odysseus; like the latter's design of the contest of the bow, Athene's trickery is treated implicitly in the poem and must be inferred from what is said and what can be surmised. In part (*a*) I support the plausibility of this suggestion with a discussion of a conversation between Odysseus and Athene, but I also emphasize the limits of what can be inferred from this conversation. I discuss the ruse itself in part (*b*) and objections to the proposed interpretation in part (*c*). Although my rebuttal of these objections leaves room for doubt, I believe the speculations in this section offer an attractive complement to the reading proposed in the previous sections of this chapter.

(*a*) The Craftiness of Athene and Odysseus

So far in this chapter the emphasis has been on the craftiness of Odysseus. But in the long conversation between Athene and Odysseus that takes place upon the latter's return to Ithaka, the conversation in which they first conspire to murder the suitors, it becomes clear that craftiness is equally to be considered an attribute of the goddess. Athene says to Odysseus,

> "... both of us are skilled
> in shrewdness, since you are by far the best of mortals
> in plans and in stories, and I among all the gods
> am famed for planning and shrewdness ..."
> Quote 2.18: *Od.* 13.296–299 (Cook trans.[99])

The word which Cook here translates as "shrewdness" is translated by Murray as "craft" and by Lattimore as "sharp practice" and "sharpness." As one commentator remarks, "it is noteworthy that Athene sees *mētis* [cunning intelligence] as the quality which predominantly defines the sort of hero Odysseus is—and the sort of goddess she is."[100] Before developing this theme, I relate this discussion to the earlier part of this chapter.

According to quote 2.18, the shrewdness of Odysseus is manifested in plans and in stories. The latter manifestation is abundantly documented. In fact, not yet knowing with whom he is speaking, Odysseus has just told Athene an elaborate false tale explaining his background and how he has come to be in Ithaka, and such tales will figure prominently in his subsequent interactions, especially with Eumaios and Penelope. But how does shrewd planning contribute to the destruction of the suitors? Odysseus does formulate a plan for their destruction in quote 2.4, but that plan is never implemented. Only if the contest of the bow is a stratagem devised by Odysseus does Athene's description of him become fully relevant to the second half of the poem.

What is of interest now is Athene's statement that she also is noted for shrewd planning. The possibility that this relates to what is to come is indicated almost immediately afterwards, when she says to Odysseus, "I have come here to weave a plan with you."[101] Later in the conversation, she seems to place on him the entire burden of devising a plan for getting rid of the suitors (see quote 6.42), but he shifts the responsibility back to her when he says in reply, "Come then, weave the design, the way I shall take my vengeance upon them."[102] All this suggests that Odysseus and Athene will both contribute to the strategy that will undo the suitors. In my reading, of course, the contribution made by Odysseus is the contest of the bow. The contribution made by Athene will be discussed in part (*b*), but first I must caution the reader that the quotations in this paragraph are not as straightforward as they seem.

After Athene says to Odysseus, "I am here to help you in your devising of schemes," she says that she also will help him hide the possessions he has brought home with him and will tell him about the troubles he will meet when he gets back to his palace.[103] The three things that Athene says she will do are accomplished in reverse order, creating a typical Homeric ring structure (more precisely, a stack structure as defined in section 5.7): Athene tells Odysseus that he must silently endure indignities and acts of violence in his house; then (after some unrelated conversation) the two of them hide his possessions in a cave; and then they sit down against the trunk of an olive tree and are said to plot the destruction of the suitors.[104] While the said plotting consists of nothing more than some general statements (e.g., quotes 6.42, 6.43, and 2.17) and the simple preparatory steps described in the next paragraph, we can assume that this is the help in the "devising of schemes" that Athene promised, inasmuch as what she tells Odysseus about the troubles he will have is also very superficial.

The words of Odysseus which I first interpreted to indicate that Athene will make a strategic contribution to the destruction of the suitors form the beginning of this passage:

> "Come then, weave the design, the way I shall take my vengeance
> upon them; stand beside me, inspire me with strength and courage,
> as when together we brought down Troy's shining coronal.
> For if in your fury, O grey-eyed goddess, you stood beside me,
> I would fight, lady and goddess, with your help against three hundred
> men if you, freely and in full heart, would help me."
>
> Quote 2.19: *Od.* 13.386–391

Athene begins her reply by assuring Odysseus that she will indeed be at his side when the time comes to fight the suitors. She then takes the initial steps needed to prepare for Odysseus's revenge: she disguises him as an old and destitute man, and she tells him to go to the swineherd Eumaios while she goes to Sparta to fetch Telemachos (whom she will also send to Eumaios to be reunited with his father). Thus, quote 2.19 forms the first half of another ring composition if these initial steps are considered to fulfill Odysseus's request at the beginning of the passage. We are then left with no suggestion that Athene will make a further contribution to the strategy used to deal with the suitors.

This discussion of the two ring structures explains why, my earlier remarks notwithstanding, I do not place much weight on certain statements made by Athene and Odysseus during their first conversation in Ithaka. However, the assertion in quote 2.18 that Athene and Odysseus are equals in terms of shrewd planning is not called into question. Owing to this assertion alone, we should not be surprised if Athene makes a strategic contribution to the destruction of the suitors that is on a par with that of Odysseus. Furthermore, owing to the symmetry implied by the assertion, I believe we should also not be surprised if Homer treats a contribution of the goddess as subtly as he does that of the hero.

(*b*) Athene's Stratagem

Penelope's announcement to the suitors that she is ready to remarry is what makes them believe her subsequent announcement of a contest for her hand in marriage. The expectation of this result inspires Odysseus to devise such a contest (see section 2.4). For these reasons, the speech Penelope gives to the suitors when she appears before them at the prompting of Athene is crucial to their destruction by Odysseus. I now suggest that this speech may be the result of a strategic calculation made by Athene. To see this, let us consider what Homer tells us, and what can be surmised, about the motivations for the speech.

According to quote 2.5, Athene influences Penelope to show herself to the suitors so that "she might all the more open their hearts" and so that "she might seem all the more precious in the eyes of her husband and son." What it means to open the hearts of the suitors seems obvious enough when we read how they react when she enters the hall after Athene has enhanced her beauty:

> Their knees gave way, and the hearts within them were bemused with
>   passion,
> and each one prayed for the privilege of lying beside her[.]
>
> Quote 2.20: *Od.* 18.212–213

But is this all there is to it? If Athene just wants Penelope to fill the suitors with lust and to win more esteem from her husband and son, we must be disappointed both with the goddess, who occupies herself with such trivial things when she should be doing everything in her power to assist Odysseus, and with the poet who has her behave in this way. I propose to solve this problem by suggesting a broader interpretation of what it means for Penelope to open the hearts of the suitors. For this purpose we turn our attention to the core content of Penelope's speech: the last instruction supposedly given to her by Odysseus when he left for Troy and her announcement that she has resigned herself to the prospect of a new marriage (see quote 2.2).

We saw in section 2.2 that Odysseus's parting instruction is a fabrication. It is evidently fabricated in order to explain Penelope's professed decision to remarry and to make this decision credible.[105] For the suitors have two reasons to be suspicious of such a decision. First, they recently discovered that for three years she had been putting off a new marriage by pretending to weave a shroud for Laertes. Why would she suddenly switch from resistance to acceptance? Second, just the day before she shows herself to the suitors at Athene's suggestion, Penelope confronts them over their plotting against the life of Telemachos, whose increasing assertiveness they regard as a threat to their continued wooing of the queen. What could induce her to marry anyone who has been involved in a conspiracy to murder her son? The fabricated instruction that Penelope was to remarry when Telemachos reached maturity addresses both of these problems. The independence and maturity that he has shown of late (ever since Athene's visit at the beginning of the poem) and that have alarmed the suitors also trigger the execution of this instruction. Given this instruction, in other words, the sudden signs that Telemachos has reached adulthood provide a plausible explanation for Penelope's abrupt switch from putting off marriage to accepting it. Similarly, only Penelope's wish to be faithful to an instruction from Odysseus could explain her apparent willingness to marry one of the conspirators.

Returning to the question of what it means for Penelope to "open the hearts" of the suitors, we see that the lust she arouses in them is only part of the answer. Their hearts are also opened by her speech, which defuses the confrontational atmosphere that has been created by her ruse of the shroud and by their conspiracy to murder Telemachos. By convincing the suitors that Penelope is now open to being courted, the speech gives her a power to manipulate them that she would not have if they were to remain suspicious of her motives. This power, which is magnified by the lust she has aroused, is seen in her extraction of generous gifts. But I suggest that the real reason Athene has Penelope open the hearts of the suitors is strategic: she wishes to create conditions that are conducive to their destruction, and the ability to influence them through Penelope furthers this aim, even though she does not yet know how or whether she will use this ability. As it turns out, of course, the ability to influence the suitors is crucial to making the contest of the bow seem legitimate and indeed establishing its legitimacy so firmly that they do not balk when they are unable to string the bow.

The idea that Penelope's speech excerpted in quote 2.2 is motivated by strategic considerations of Athene implies that it is the goddess who fabricates Odysseus's parting instruction. This view is consistent with what we are told about her motives. One of Athene's stated goals in quote 2.5 is for Penelope to "seem all the more precious in the eyes of her husband," and we are told after Penelope gives her speech to the suitors that Odysseus "was happy because she beguiled gifts out of them" (see quote 2.24 below). Let us suppose, then, that Athene, who is well aware of Odysseus's love of riches, has Penelope solicit gifts from the suitors when she appears before them. Since Penelope must convince the suitors that she is open to being courted before she can extract courtship gifts from them, it is natural to suppose further that Athene invents Odysseus's parting instruction and shares this invention with Penelope. Athene thereby implements her stratagem for gaining influence over the suitors as she works toward her stated (but unnecessary) goal of increasing Penelope's value in the eyes of Odysseus. This does not require any greater influence of the goddess over the queen than what we have already assumed, for if Athene communicates to Penelope the details of the contest of the bow (as proposed in section 2.5), she could also supply Penelope with a speech to give to the suitors.

Some may see the idea that the speech is crafted by Athene as belittling Penelope by making her a puppet of the goddess.[106] I do not see it that way. First, it is indisputable that Penelope shows herself to the suitors only because of Athene's influence, and yet we surely are not to think less of her for this. My suggestion merely enlarges the domain of influence to include her speech to the suitors (and, of course, her decision to hold the contest of the bow). Second, Penelope is perfectly worthy and suited to be the wife of Odysseus. Their *homophrosyne* (likeness of mind), which Odysseus sees as the ideal for a married couple,[107] is evident: they both are able to endure much suffering, they both exercise unusual caution to avoid being deceived,[108] and they both excel in trickery. Notably, Penelope tricks not only the suitors (with the ruse of the shroud for Laertes) but Odysseus himself, making him lose his composure and involuntarily provide incontrovertible proof of his identity.[109] Her success in making Odysseus give himself away near the end of the poem, impressive enough in its own right, contrasts favorably with Athene's failure to do the same near the beginning of the Ithakan books.[110] Thus, Penelope's ability to act independently and indeed with cunning is not in question, and our appreciation of it is not diminished if Athene has her deliver a certain speech.

The character who must be defended is not Penelope but Athene. It is easy to understand why Woodhouse says that the goddess "for all her fussing is perhaps, upon the whole, somewhat futile."[111] A conventional reading of quote 2.5 would suggest that Athene's motives for having Penelope show herself to the suitors are rather frivolous in the context of the grave situation faced by Odysseus: she occupies herself with arranging for Penelope to fill the suitors with lust (the conventional interpretation of opening their hearts) and, also to no purpose, increasing the esteem in which Penelope is held by her husband and son when she should be doing everything possible to strengthen the position of Odysseus and weaken that of the suitors. If this is correct, the poet also should be criticized for having Penelope's consequential appearance before the suitors arise from what is little more than a whim of Athene. But if "opening the hearts" of the suitors means making the suitors more open and susceptible to the wishes of Penelope, then Athene intentionally makes a strategic contribution and a vital one at that: Odysseus designs the contest of the bow, but she creates the conditions needed for his breakthrough and its success.

(*c*) Discussion of Objections

The thesis that Athene devises the stratagem that I have just described would be undermined if Penelope is the one who fabricates Odysseus's parting instruction. The purpose of this subsection is to discuss several reasons for thinking that this might be the case.

By convincing the suitors that she is ready to remarry, Penelope could hope to regain some of the wealth lost to the suitors by wheedling gifts out of them,[112] and she might also hope to remove the threat they pose to her son.[113] This double motivation is not in itself a reason to prefer Penelope as the fabricator of the instruction since it also applies to Athene: we have just noted that the goddess could well have Penelope solicit gifts for the appreciation of Odysseus, and she has acted before to protect Telemachos against the suitors.[114] But we know from quote 2.7 that Penelope has her son's safety in mind shortly before she shows herself to the suitors. The fact that she does not proceed to warn Telemachos about the suitors as she says she will in quote 2.7

could be interpreted to mean that she decides instead to try to protect him by convincing the suitors that she will marry one of them. This interpretation is difficult to accept because it implies that Penelope takes advantage of Athene's suggestion in quote 2.5 to do something that is more important than what the goddess herself has in mind (on a superficial reading of the passage), but I must admit that it poses a difficulty for the thesis of this section.

Indications that Penelope might indeed have invented Odysseus's instruction are found in Eurynome's reply to her mistress's declaration of her intention to appear before the suitors (quote 2.7):

> Eurynome the housekeeper said to her in answer:
> "Now all this you have said, my child, was fair and orderly.
> .... Only
> first you should wash your body and anoint your face. Do not
> go down with a face so ravaged all over by tears, as it now is,
> since nothing is gained by indiscriminate sorrowing always.
> For now your son is come of age, and you know you always
> prayed the immortals, beyond all else, to see him bearded."
>
> Quote 2.21: *Od.* 18.169–176

In the reading advocated by Wilamowitz and supported by Fenik,[115] Eurynome interprets Penelope's declaration to mean that the queen has given up hope for Odysseus's return and has reluctantly decided to marry one of the suitors; she endorses this decision implicitly by suggesting that Penelope take care of her appearance before presenting herself to the suitors and by implying that the time has indeed come for Penelope to remarry since Telemachos is now a grown man. Fenik goes on to assert that Eurynome's last remark inspires Penelope to invent Odysseus's parting instruction.

The idea that Eurynome thinks Penelope should marry one of the suitors is difficult to reconcile with what she says earlier on the same day. When Penelope learns that the newly arrived stranger (Odysseus disguised as a beggar) has been struck by a footstool thrown by Antinoös, she is outraged at this breach of hospitality in her own house and exclaims, "Thus, I pray, may the archer Apollo strike at the striker." To this Eurynome adds,

> "If only some fulfillment befell our prayers. Then not one
> of these men would be alive to meet the Dawn in her splendor."
>
> Quote 2.22: *Od.* 17.496–497

Thus, the reading of Wilamowitz and Fenik requires that Eurynome change within a matter of hours from wishing that all the suitors were dead to wishing that Penelope would marry one of them. Such a change, if it actually occurred, would be all the more jarring because quotes 2.21 and 2.22 are the only places in the entire poem where Eurynome speaks and are separated from each other by fewer than 300 lines. Furthermore, the passages in which supposedly opposing attitudes are expressed are made to confront each other through a connection between the scene in which Penelope shows herself to the suitors and the scene in which Antinoös throws a footstool at Odysseus. This connection is worth describing in detail as it provides another example of the kind of subtlety that I claim for the *Odyssey* in this chapter and for the *Iliad* in chapter 3.

When Penelope appears before the suitors, but before she speaks to them, she admonishes her son for having allowed the stranger to be mistreated in their house. (Although Telemachos was deeply disturbed by the suffering inflicted on his father by Antinoös, his only external reaction was to shake his head in silence.[116]) Penelope's scolding of her son connects the scene in which she shows herself to the suitors with the scene in which Antinoös throws a footstool at Odysseus. This connection between the two scenes in turn ties Eurynome's words in quote 2.21 to those in quote 2.22 since the reactions of Penelope and Eurynome to the mistreatment of the stranger are described immediately after the reaction of Telemachos. The link between these passages makes the interpretation of the former passage advocated by Wilamowitz and Fenik even more difficult to defend.

The subtlety of the connection between the scene in which Penelope shows herself to the suitors and the scene in which Antinoös throws a footstool at Odysseus begins with the fact that Penelope does not refer explicitly to the latter scene when she admonishes her son. What she says is that

> "such a thing has been done now, here in our palace, and you
> permitted our stranger guest to be so outrageously handled.
> How must it be now, if the stranger who sits in our household
> is to be made to suffer so from bitter brutality?
> That must be your outrage and shame as people see it."
>
> Quote 2.23: *Od.* 18.221–225

Telemachos actually had a good reason for allowing the abuse of the stranger to pass in silence: his father had specifically told him not to come to his aid if the suitors should pelt him with missiles,[117] obviously so that they would not suspect a connection between them. But he cannot explain this to his mother because she is not to know that the stranger is Odysseus (and because the suitors may be listening to their conversation). Instead he acknowledges the justness of his mother's criticism and claims that he is simply overwhelmed by his situation. Finding himself unable to convincingly defend his passivity in the footstool incident, he then *pretends* (according to my interpretation) to believe that his mother's criticism referred to a subsequent incident in which his own behavior required less justification: the fight between the stranger and the genuine beggar Iros in which Odysseus was the one who delivered the punishment. Since this fight is the only incident that is explicitly mentioned in the conversation, some commentators assume that Penelope really did criticize Telemachos for allowing the fight to take place,[118] despite the fact that quote 2.23 clearly refers not to the fight in which the stranger thrashes Iros but to the rough treatment of the stranger by Antinoös.[119] These commentators do not appreciate a fundamental point of this chapter and chapter 3: a scene from the *Iliad* or the *Odyssey* may contain a key element that is not stated explicitly but must be inferred from what is given and from what may reasonably be surmised about the psychological state of the characters. Once this subtlety of Homer is accepted, Penelope's scolding of Telemachos reminds us of Antinoös's abuse of the stranger and Eurynome's wish for the death of the suitors (quote 2.22). We then realize that Eurynome does not hope that

Penelope will marry one of them. The reading of quote 2.21 advocated by Wilamowitz and Fenik is thereby excluded.

But quote 2.21 indicates in another, more direct way that it may be Penelope, not Athene, who fabricates Odysseus's parting instruction. Odysseus's instruction contains an echo of Eurynome's remarks which suggests that Penelope's speech to the suitors is influenced by her conversation with her maid.[120] In her account of Odysseus's instruction, Penelope uses Telemachos's beard as a sign that he has grown up, just as Eurynome did shortly before (the word γενειησαντα—bearded, i.e., having acquired a beard—is used in the penultimate line of quote 2.2 and the last line of quote 2.21 but nowhere else in Homer). Why would the poet create this echo if he did not intend to indicate that Eurynome's remark inspired Penelope to invent Odysseus's instruction? In fact, another explanation is possible.

According to Eurynome, Penelope always prayed that she would live long enough to see Telemachos with a beard. Combined with Odysseus's instruction, this implies that Penelope hoped to live long enough to remarry if Odysseus did not return. This inference goes against everything we know about Penelope's attitude toward taking a new husband. If Eurynome speaks accurately, and we must assume that she does, this incongruity is yet another indication that Odysseus's parting instruction is fictitious. This particular indication is strategically placed to inform the reader's understanding of both Penelope's speech and Odysseus's reaction to it:

> She spoke, and much-enduring great Odysseus was happy
> because she beguiled gifts out of them, and enchanted their spirits
> with blandishing words, while her own mind had other intentions.
>
> Quote 2.24: *Od.* 18.281–283

The poet's wish to indicate at this significant point that Odysseus's instruction is a fabrication could account for the echo of Eurynome's remark in the instruction attributed to Odysseus. In this reading, Eurynome's last remark to Penelope in quote 2.21 influences only the form in which Penelope expresses herself to the suitors in quote 2.2.

The above discussion is not sufficient to rule out the possibility that Penelope is the one who invents Odysseus's parting instruction. However, I think it does show that there is no evidence that compels us to believe this. It therefore remains attractive, for the reasons explained in part (*b*), to think that the instruction is fabricated by Athene and communicated to Penelope for use in her speech to the suitors.

2.14. Athene in the Cyclops Episode

I conclude the exposition of my reading of the Ithakan books of the *Odyssey* by asserting a deep analogy between Odysseus's confrontation with the suitors and the episode of the Cyclops. Certain parallels between these two parts of the poem are obvious and well known: the gross violations of the guest-host relationship, Odysseus's exacting of vengeance,[121] and his success against overwhelming force (a powerful monster or a small army of adversaries). My account of the last stratagem of Odysseus implies another significant correspondence: the confrontations with the suitors and the Cyclops are both showcases for the resourcefulness of the hero. Admittedly, the type of resourcefulness that is on open display in the Cyclops episode is below the surface of the Ithakan books and can be discerned there only by means of close reading. The analogy I am about to discuss is even deeper, as it emerges only when one looks below the surface of both parts of the poem. We have already done the necessary work for one part; now we turn to the other.

In the account of the Cyclops adventure that he gives to the Phaiakians, Odysseus mentions Athene only once. The Cyclops Polyphemos has just left the cave, having eaten four of the hero's companions by this time, and Odysseus says, "I was left there, devising evil in the depths of my heart, if in any way I might take vengeance on him, and Athene grant me glory."[122] The goddess herself plays no role in the episode as far as one can tell from the surface of the text. Nevertheless, I maintain that Athene provides crucial assistance to Odysseus in his encounter with the Cyclops. To defend this assertion, I must first show that it is consistent with the conversation between the goddess and the hero discussed in part (*a*) of the preceding section.

During the course of the mentioned conversation, Athene tells Odysseus that she will help him in Ithaka as she helped him in the land of the Phaiakians; he complains that she did not help him earlier in his wanderings, before he reached the Phaiakians; and in her reply she makes no mention of any assistance she gave him with the Cyclops, but only gives the excuse that she did not want to fight with Poseidon, who was holding a grudge against him because he had blinded Polyphemos.[123] Her failure to mention assistance that would have directly addressed his complaint could naturally be taken to mean that she provided no such assistance. However, Athene does not mention help we know she gave Odysseus: she does not mention that it was her efforts that led to his release by Kalypso,[124] and she does not tell him that she came to his aid (as soon as Poseidon had left the scene) when he was struggling in the storm-tossed sea before reaching the land of the Phaiakians.[125] We therefore cannot conclude from the conversation that she did not help him in his encounter with the Cyclops. On the contrary, if Athene's excuse is truthful, there is no reason she could not have helped Odysseus at any time before the conclusion of the Cyclops episode, the point at which Polyphemos prays to Poseidon for revenge against Odysseus.

Some scholars have argued that Athene's excuse is false on the grounds that she does not help Odysseus even before the onset of Poseidon's wrath.[126] However, it is precisely this premise that I am about to challenge. There is another reason one might doubt the truthfulness of the excuse, but I shall dispose of this difficulty in the following section. Given the absence of any objection and the fact that Athene helped Odysseus in the storm-tossed sea when, and only when, Poseidon had left the scene, it is only reasonable to take her at her word when she tells Odysseus that she did not help him more because she did not want to fight with Poseidon.[127]

Now that we have seen that Athene could have provided assistance to Odysseus in the Cyclops episode, a review of the relevant facts from the episode[128] will show that she actually did. Odysseus and his companions enter the cave of Polyphemos when he is away tending his flocks. When the Cyclops comes home at the end of the day, he drives into the cave only the female sheep and goats. After milking the animals and doing other chores, he lights a fire and sees Odysseus and his men for the first time. He eats two of the men for supper and another two for breakfast the next morning. When he leaves the cave after breakfast, he closes the door behind him—that is to say, he blocks the entrance to his cave with a huge boulder. This is obviously a departure from his normal pattern—we know the cave was open the previous day since Odysseus was able to enter it—but this change in his behavior is easily explained: he wants to prevent Odysseus and his remaining companions from escaping. When he comes home at the end of the second day, there is another change from the previous day: he drives into the cave all his animals, not just the females. This change has no natural explanation, so Odysseus tells the Phaiakians that Polyphemos drove all his animals into the cave on the second night "either from some foreboding or because a god so bade him."[129] The first explanation suggested by Odysseus, that the Cyclops had a foreboding of what lay in store for him, can be rejected. We know he had no such foreboding because, although a prophet had told him long ago that one day he would be blinded by someone named Odysseus, he is very surprised to learn that the puny weakling (from his point of view) who blinded him was the Odysseus mentioned by the prophet (Odysseus, of course, doesn't tell Polyphemos his real name until he has blinded him and made his escape).[130] In any case, even if he had a foreboding, what would be the point of bringing the male animals into the cave? The explanation we are left with is that the Cyclops drives all his animals into the cave at the prompting of some god. Since the only consequence of having the rams in the cave is that Odysseus and his men are provided with the means to make their escape, the god that prompts the Cyclops is almost certainly the patron deity of Odysseus, Athene.[131]

Although Athene presumably understands how the rams will enable Odysseus's party to leave the cave without being detected by the Cyclops, Odysseus comes up with the idea on his own.[132] It is part of the display of his craftiness which is key to a major theme of the whole episode, the triumph of resourcefulness over brute force. By having the Cyclops drive all his animals into the cave, Athene creates the conditions needed for Odysseus to devise his stratagem for escape and for this stratagem to work. In the preceding section I suggested that, by having Penelope convince the suitors that she is ready to remarry, Athene creates the conditions needed for Odysseus to devise his stratagem of the contest of the bow and for *this* stratagem to work. We thus begin to see a deep analogy between Odysseus's confrontation with the suitors and the episode of the Cyclops. It is to be noted that in both cases Athene acts by influencing someone to do something that he or she would not ordinarily do: she has Penelope show herself to the suitors, and she has Polyphemos drive all his animals into the cave.

Another aspect of the analogy between the confrontation with the suitors and the confrontation with the Cyclops is that in both cases the strategic assistance provided by Athene is not explicitly acknowledged. Of course, the implicitness of the Cyclops episode, the fact that Athene's role is not mentioned, is necessary since the episode is related by Odysseus and he does not know that the goddess helped him. Furthermore, it could not be otherwise:

Homer could not have had Athene appear during the episode since he wanted Odysseus to come up on his own with the idea of using the rams for his escape. Nevertheless, it is clear that the implicitness of the Cyclops episode was not only necessary but desired for its own sake. For Homer could have had Athene tell Odysseus that she made his escape possible when he complains to her that she did not help him in his wanderings prior to his arrival in the land of the Phaiakians. Telling him this would have answered his complaint, and it would also have supported her assertion that she did not help him more because she did not want to fight with Poseidon after his wrath had been ignited by the prayer of the blinded Cyclops. The fact that she does not tell him shows that Homer wanted her role in the Cyclops episode to remain below the surface of the text, just like her strategic role in the confrontation with the suitors.

Since Odysseus does not know that Athene helped him escape from the cave of the Cyclops, and since Athene does not enlighten him on this matter in response to his complaint, he presumably does not believe her when she claims that she did not help him early in his wanderings because she did not want to fight with Poseidon. But Homer cannot allow Odysseus to challenge her excuse since such a challenge would force Athene to bring her role in the Cyclops episode to the surface of the text. A challenge is neatly avoided by having Athene move instantly from her excuse to a demonstration that Odysseus is back home in Ithaka, a fact which causes him to rejoice and to temporarily forget any other concern.[133] However, Homer does reveal in a more subtle manner the state of Odysseus's knowledge and belief shortly before the end of the scene,[134] when the assistance that Athene has begun to give Odysseus in his approaching confrontation with the suitors has made it unnecessary for her to justify her behavior in the past.

Let us now observe that Homer could easily have given us a Cyclops episode in which help from Athene was unnecessary: he could have had Polyphemos drive all his animals into the cave every night instead of separating the females from the males. Indeed, this version would have been preferable from a superficial point of view since the action would not have depended on a poorly motivated departure from the Cyclops' routine. We therefore know two things: (1) Homer wanted Athene to help Odysseus in the Cyclops episode and (2) he did not want to make Athene's role explicit. The Cyclops episode is thus a model for that part of the confrontation with the suitors that I discussed in the preceding section. It also provides one more validation of the thesis that underlies this whole chapter, the thesis that important developments in Homer are sometimes left unsaid and must be inferred from clues supplied by the poet. Yet another illustration of this thesis is discussed in the following section.

2.15. Behind the Scenes on Olympos

According to the conventional view, Odysseus receives no help from his patron goddess Athene at any time during the Great Wanderings recounted in books 9–12 of the *Odyssey*. I depart from that view in claiming that Athene provides crucial assistance which makes it possible for Odysseus and his men to escape from the cave of the Cyclops. Nevertheless, it is certainly true that Athene provides no further assistance from the time Polyphemos prays to Poseidon for revenge against Odysseus until the council of the gods at the beginning of the poem, when Zeus gives her permission to initiate the hero's homecoming and declares that Poseidon will have to give up his anger. The history of her assistance inclines us to believe Athene when she tells Odysseus that she did not help him more during his return voyage from Troy because she did not want to fight with Poseidon. Before we can accept this excuse, however, we must explain how it is that Hermes can help Odysseus during the interval in which Athene is absent. For Hermes gives Odysseus guidance on how to deal with Circe and a medicine ("moly") to counteract the potion she will give him.[135] Without this assistance from Hermes, we can assume that Odysseus would never have left Circe's island (indeed, Hermes himself says as much[136]), just as he would never have escaped the cave of the Cyclops without the assistance of Athene. If Athene refrains from helping Odysseus in the Circe adventure out of respect for Poseidon, we must ask why the same consideration does not rule out the intervention of Hermes, especially since Athene and Hermes share the same relationship with Poseidon (as a brother of Zeus, he is an uncle of both).[137] My goal in this section is to offer a plausible answer to this question. Toward this end, I construct a hypothetical scenario for the period immediately following the triggering of Poseidon's wrath by the prayer of Polyphemos.

When Poseidon wishes to punish the Phaiakians for showering Odysseus with gifts and conveying him back to Ithaka, the first thing he does is consult Zeus.[138] It is reasonable to assume he does the same when he wishes to punish Odysseus for the blinding of Polyphemos, all the more so because he must ensure that the other gods, and Athene in particular, are prevented from intervening on Odysseus's behalf. I postulate that Zeus responds by convening an assembly of the gods analogous to the one in the *Iliad* in which he orders all the other deities not to interfere in the war between the Greeks and the Trojans.[139] In the present case I assume he orders them not to interfere with the plans of Poseidon. In the Iliadic assembly, Athene submits to the command of Zeus, but she also expresses concern for the Greeks and receives reassurance from her father. As the patron goddess of Odysseus, she presumably also voices a note of protest in the assembly that, according to my conjecture, takes place behind the scenes of the *Odyssey*. I postulate further that Zeus reconciles the wishes of Poseidon and Athene at this assembly by giving his brother free rein to inflict suffering on Odysseus as long as he does not kill him and assuring his daughter that he will look after the safety of Odysseus and will guarantee his homecoming.

The divine assembly envisaged in this scenario has two consequences for the Circe adventure. First, Zeus's order prevents Athene from taking action on her own initiative to protect Odysseus. Second, Zeus's promise to Athene that Odysseus will return home obliges him to intervene so that the hero will not be transformed into a pig like the companions who have preceded him. In principle, he could send whomever he wishes, even Athene,[140] to give Odysseus the moly and the guidance he will need to avoid Circe's enchantment. But the poet cannot let Athene play Hermes' role in the Circe episode because this would give us the impression that Athene defied Poseidon and would make one wonder why she did not help Odysseus in his subsequent adventures. Fortunately, the selection of Hermes as Zeus's emissary on this mission is perfectly natural, as I will explain in due course.

The scenario described above is plausible given what we know from Homer about how business is conducted on Olympos. It becomes even more plausible in the light of the following considerations.

A well-known scholar once wrote a paper pointing out that the first book of the *Odyssey* is of critical importance because it is in that book that Athene seeks and obtains Zeus's permission to go to the aid of Odysseus.[141] "Without the consent of Zeus obtained in Book 1 Athena could not have been an actor in the poem; hence without Book 1 there could have been no Odyssey." But left unaddressed in that paper was the question of *why* Athene must get Zeus's permission to help Odysseus. The proposed scenario offers a natural answer to that question.

At the beginning of the *Odyssey*, Odysseus has been held prisoner on a remote island for seven years by the nymph Kalypso. The hero's homecoming is set in motion when Zeus, at Athene's request,[142] sends Hermes to instruct Kalypso to release her prisoner:

> "Hermes, since you are our messenger in all things, tell the lovely-haired nymph of our infallible decree, that enduring Odysseus must start on his journey home — without help from gods or mortal men. But it will be on a raft tied together with many ropes, and a voyage of great hardship. On the twentieth day he will reach fertile Scheria, the land of the Phaiacians, who are a people close to the gods. They will honour him like a god with all their hearts, and bring him home in a ship to his own dear native land, giving him bronze and gold and clothing in plenty — many gifts, more than Odysseus would ever have brought out of Troy, if he had come home unharmed with his full share of the spoil. That is how he is fated to see his family again and return to his high-roofed house and his own native land."
>
> Quote 2.25: *Od.* 5.29–42 (Hammond trans.)

Here we see Zeus balancing the concerns of Athene and Poseidon, as postulated in the scenario. Although Odysseus is to return home, and moreover with great wealth, he will continue to suffer hardship until he reaches Scheria. Since Poseidon is not present during the deliberations which lead to Hermes' mission, it is evident that Zeus must have acceded to Poseidon's wish for the punishment of Odysseus before the divine council described at the beginning of the poem.

When Hermes communicates Zeus's directive to Kalypso, she has Odysseus build a raft and sends him on his way. Poseidon, returning from Ethiopia, catches sight of Odysseus on the open sea just as he is nearing Scheria, and says to himself, "For shame, surely the gods have rashly changed their intentions about Odysseus while I was away."[143] From this we see that the gods as a group, not Zeus alone, must have once agreed not to interfere with the plans of Poseidon. I suggest that this took place during the hypothesized assembly convened by Zeus at the prompting of Poseidon following the prayer of Polyphemos.

Turning from the wishes of Poseidon to those of Athene, we can see that Zeus first guaranteed the homecoming of Odysseus prior to the divine assembly at the beginning of the poem. When Odysseus has finally made it back to Ithaka, Poseidon says to Zeus, "I have never taken his homecoming altogether away, since first you nodded your head and assented to it."[144] Although Zeus supports Odysseus's return during both of the assemblies described in the poem,[145] he does not give his assent by nodding his head on either occasion (even if he did nod, Poseidon would not have seen him do it since he was not present at these assemblies). Poseidon's statement therefore shows that Zeus must have first agreed to the homecoming of Odysseus on some previous occasion, which I take to be the assembly convened shortly after the prayer of Polyphemos. The existence of some such occasion is also suggested by another aspect of Poseidon's statement. The divine assemblies described in the *Odyssey* take place shortly before Odysseus is released by Kalypso and transported home by the Phaiakians, after his return home has already been delayed for ten years. When Poseidon says that he has *never* taken away the homecoming of Odysseus, he surely is not referring to the brief period between the first of the reported assemblies and the hero's return to Ithaka. It follows that Zeus must have insisted upon the eventual homecoming of Odysseus long before this assembly.

Thus, Zeus must have reconciled the wishes of Poseidon and Athene before we see him do this in quote 2.25. The simplest explanation is that the reconciliation is first accomplished at an assembly of the gods convened shortly after the prayer of Polyphemos to Poseidon, as postulated in our scenario.

Let us now turn our attention from the divine assembly to the intervention of Hermes in the Circe adventure. His role in this adventure is similar in a number of ways to his role in the last book of the *Iliad*, where the Trojan king Priam goes to the shelter of Achilles to ransom the body of his son Hektor,[146] much as Odysseus goes to the house of Circe to secure the release of his companions.[147] In both cases, Hermes meets the mortal on his way to his adversary, takes his hand and asks him where he is going, tells him about his lost dear one(s), promises to help him and does so (in part by telling him how to interact with the adversary[148]), and then goes off to Olympos while the mortal proceeds to enter the adversary's dwelling, where he receives hospitality and is granted the release of his dear one(s). I shall argue that the similarities between the Iliadic and Odyssean scenes go beyond these surface parallels.

Odysseus begins his account of his encounter with Hermes as follows:

> "But as I went up through the lonely glens, and was coming
> near to the great house of Circe, skilled in medicines,
> there as I came up to the house, Hermes, of the golden
> staff, met me on my way, in the likeness of a young man
> with beard new grown, which is the most graceful time of young manhood."
>
> Quote 2.26: *Od.* 10.275–279

It is unusual for Odysseus or any other mortal to attribute a divine manifestation to a particular deity, because a character, unlike the poet, generally has no way of knowing which god has performed some act.[149] The passage just quoted is an exception to this rule: Odysseus names Hermes without ever explaining how he knows the identity of his benefactor. The mystery of Odysseus's knowledge of Hermes' identity is deepened by comparison with the corresponding scene from the *Iliad*. The description of the god given in the Iliadic scene is almost identical to the distinctive description in the last line and a half of quote 2.26,[150] and yet Priam doesn't know the identity of his helper until Hermes identifies himself at the end of the scene. Since Priam is unable to recognize Hermes, one must assume that Odysseus is not able to recognize him either.[151]

The solution to this problem, I believe, is that Hermes reveals his identity to Odysseus and that the latter simply neglects to mention this when he tells his story to the Phaiakians. It is possible to entertain this hypothesis because Odysseus omits from his narrative the last words spoken to him by Hermes. After quoting the speech in which Hermes greets him, promises to give him a medicine that will protect him from the enchantment of Circe, and tells him how to deal with her, Odysseus gives this account of the last part of their interaction:

> "So spoke Argeïphontes [Hermes], and he gave me the medicine,
> which he picked out of the ground, and he explained the nature
> of it to me. It was black at the root, but with a milky
> flower. The gods call it moly. It is hard for mortal
> men to dig up, but the gods have power to do all things."
>
> Quote 2.27: *Od.* 10.302–306

Hermes tells Odysseus the name the gods use for the medicine. Furthermore, having himself dug up some moly, he explains that it is hard for mortals to dig it up, but that the gods can do all things. This passage clearly implies that Hermes reveals that he is a god. This revelation is reported explicitly in the corresponding scene from the *Iliad*: Hermes tells Priam that he is a god when he has finished escorting him to the shelter of Achilles.[152] We therefore see another parallel between the two scenes: Hermes reveals his divine nature to the mortal at the end of both encounters. In fact, Hermes does more than this. When he tells Priam that he is a god, he also gives his name. Now that we realize that the account in quote 2.27 is incomplete, there can be no objection to the conclusion that Hermes likewise identifies himself to Odysseus. Indeed, this conclusion is most welcome, as it solves the mystery of how Odysseus knows the identity of his divine helper.[153, 154]

There is evidently more than surface parallelism between the two scenes. It is therefore of great interest that Hermes is sent to help Priam by Zeus following a divine council in which Zeus decides that Priam shall be able to ransom Hektor's body from Achilles. For parallelism would imply that Hermes is sent to help Odysseus by Zeus after a divine council in which Zeus makes a decision (e.g., that Odysseus shall return to Ithaka) that requires Odysseus to be protected from enchantment by Circe—a nice corroboration of the scenario proposed in this section. Of course, it is not possible to prove that this extrapolation from the established parallelism is valid. The fact remains, however, that a scenario constructed on the basis of analogies with other scenes in Homer (Poseidon's consultation with Zeus prior to the punishment of the Phaiakians; the assembly in which Zeus orders the other gods not to interfere in the Trojan War) receives a measure of validation from another such analogy.[155] Some may find it difficult to accept that the analogies which involve scenes from the *Iliad* could be significant. In chapter 5, however, I will present evidence for a surprisingly deep engagement of the *Odyssey* poet with the earlier poem.

Having emphasized the similarities between the scenes in which Hermes comes to the aid of Priam and Odysseus, I should also address certain important differences.[156] The selection of Hermes to guide Priam to the shelter of Achilles is natural since he acts as a guide elsewhere.[157] It is also natural to cast Hermes in this role because he puts the Greek sentries to sleep, and he is known for the wand "with which he mazes the eyes of those mortals whose eyes he would maze, or wakes again the sleepers."[158] Although the wand is mentioned in quote 2.26, it plays no part in the Circe episode. Moreover, Odysseus has no need of a guide to get to the house of Circe. Accordingly, it may seem that the choice of Hermes to help Odysseus in the Circe adventure is much more arbitrary than his selection as the helper of Priam. I believe, on the contrary, that the role of Hermes in the scenario proposed earlier in this section is perfectly natural. What makes it so is, in fact, the Priam scene: the last book of the *Iliad* has already presented Hermes as an emissary sent by Zeus to protect a man who is on a dangerous mission. The numerous parallels between the Iliadic and Odyssean scenes, especially the ones that are not obvious, support the relevance of the former as a precedent for the latter.[159]

I conclude that the scenario described in this section is consistent with the text of the *Odyssey* and is even supported by significant hints in that poem and by analogies with certain scenes in the *Iliad*.[160] If it is indeed correct, it has two important consequences for our earlier discussion. First, it shows that Hermes' intervention in the Circe episode does not undermine Athene's claim that she did not help Odysseus during much of his journey because she did not want to fight with Poseidon. Since her claim appears to be valid, she might well have helped Odysseus escape from the cave of the Cyclops (before Poseidon was roused to anger by the prayer of Polyphemos), as suggested in the preceding section. Second, the scenario reinforces with additional examples the conclusion from our analysis of the Cyclops episode that implied actions in the *Odyssey*—actions that are not mentioned explicitly but can be inferred from the text—are not limited to those associated with the last stratagem of Odysseus, but are also found in the first half of the poem.

2.16. Implications

The existence demonstrated in this chapter of a solution to a set of Odyssean problems suggests that at least one of the Homeric epics was less subject to disruptive forces during its composition and transmission than is generally realized. This conclusion is in harmony with the view advanced later in this book that some of the inconsistencies in Homer were deliberate constructs of the poet. Furthermore, some of the demonstrations in chapters 5 and 6 of intentional inconsistency in the *Iliad* and the *Odyssey* rely on textual connections and structures that could have survived and could have been created in the first place only in the relative absence of disturbing influences.

The cohesiveness of the text analyzed in this chapter bolsters the credibility of these demonstrations by supporting the judgment that the poems must have been created and passed on under such conditions.

Before we turn our attention to the question of intentional inconsistency in Homer and the possibility of even deeper subtlety than we have seen so far, it is necessary to consider another example of the kind of subtlety we observed in chapter 1. In this case it is a passage from the *Iliad* which relates the actions of a character without explaining the character's motivation.

Chapter 3

The Humiliation of Agamemnon

Referring mainly to the *Odyssey*, Ruth Scodel has written, "The narrator is omniscient, but sometimes stingy with his knowledge."[1] I have argued in the previous two chapters that the narrator of the *Odyssey* sometimes withholds crucial information in the expectation that the reader or listener will be able to make the necessary inferences on the basis of his or her understanding of the psychology of a character and the situation faced by that character. In the present chapter I argue that the narrator of the *Iliad* does the same thing in a passage that has usually (though not always) been completely misconstrued. The interpretation of that passage proposed here is intrinsically plausible and gains further credibility by integrating our understanding of several Homeric passages previously assumed to be unrelated.

This chapter plays a transitional role in the plan of this book. On one hand, it continues the discussion of the type of Homeric subtlety considered in the previous two chapters, especially chapter 1. On the other hand, it lays groundwork that will be useful when we begin to consider an entirely different kind of Homeric subtlety in chapter 5. I start by summarizing the background needed to understand the passage in question.

3.1. The Spurious Reconciliation of Achilles and Agamemnon

The *Iliad* begins with a public quarrel between Achilles, the greatest Greek warrior in the Trojan War, and Agamemnon, a lesser man but the leader of the Greek expedition to Troy. The Greeks have suffered greatly from a plague sent by Apollo in answer to the prayers of a priest whose daughter was captured during the sack of a town near Troy and taken as a prize by Agamemnon, who has refused to release her in return for ransom from her father. At a general assembly convened by Achilles, it is determined that the only way to escape the plague is for Agamemnon to return the girl to her father. But Agamemnon is an insecure leader and cannot accept what he perceives to be the indignity of being the only Greek leader to be deprived of his prize. Taking advantage of his position as the supreme leader, he declares that he will compensate himself for his loss by appropriating a girl who has been acquired as a prize by one of the other leaders. This threat infuriates Achilles, who objects that he always does most of the fighting but never gets a prize as good as Agamemnon's. When the quarrel ends after the exchange of many insults, Agamemnon has vowed to relieve Achilles of his prize (a vow that he soon carries out), and Achilles has withdrawn from the war effort with the prediction that everyone will see how much he is needed and realize what a great man has been dishonored by Agamemnon.

Achilles' unpatriotic but understandable wish to be sorely missed in battle is fulfilled: the military position of the Greeks begins to look untenable, and Agamemnon even proposes that they flee in their ships.[2] Nestor, the oldest and wisest of the Greek leaders, proposes instead that Agamemnon make up for the dishonor he has done to Achilles and try to persuade him to return to battle "with words of supplication and with the gifts of friendship."[3] Agamemnon appears to accept this proposal, offering to return Achilles' prize and to give him in addition an abundance of magnificent gifts if he will let go of his anger and rejoin the Greek cause.[4] But instead of offering "words of supplication," Agamemnon insists that Achilles will have to submit to him.[5] Realizing that no more can be expected from Agamemnon, who is simply incapable of the humility required by the situation, Nestor praises the offered gifts and makes a wise selection of three men to make the appeal to Achilles.[6] Of the three ambassadors, it is Odysseus who presents Agamemnon's offer. While he faithfully repeats the long list of magnificent gifts,[7] Odysseus omits Agamemnon's demand for submission from Achilles because he knows that the quarrel is a matter of pride for Achilles as much as it is for Agamemnon.[8] Instead he acknowledges that Achilles may despise Agamemnon's promised gifts, magnificent though they are, and entreats him to return to battle anyway for the good of his comrades and for the glory he might win by slaying the Trojan hero Hektor.[9] Achilles replies in the strongest possible terms that indeed all the gifts in the world would not change his mind unless Agamemnon were to make up for his "heartrending insolence"[10]—that is, unless he were to offer a genuine apology.

Without Achilles and his fellow Myrmidons in the fight, the Greeks continue to lose ground to the Trojans until finally Achilles' close friend Patroklos, acting on a suggestion from Nestor,[11] borrows Achilles' armor and, with his assent, leads the Myrmidons into battle.[12] Patroklos fights valiantly and averts a military catastrophe that had seemed imminent, but is ultimately killed by Hektor. The death of Patroklos is the turning point of the *Iliad*. The quarrel with Agamemnon, which has had such devastating consequences, ceases to be important to Achilles. His fury is now concentrated on Hektor, and all he wants is to return to battle in order to avenge the loss of his cherished friend.

As soon as he has acquired new armor (the armor borrowed by Patroklos was taken by Hektor), Achilles calls an assembly in order to effect a public reconciliation with Agamemnon so that he can rejoin the Greeks in battle and exact revenge against Hektor. Addressing Agamemnon in front of everyone, he briefly but forcefully acknowledges the disastrous consequences of their quarrel and his withdrawal from the fighting. Then he says,

> "Still, we will let all this be a thing of the past, though it hurts us,
> and beat down by constraint the anger that rises inside us.
> Now I am making an end of my anger. It does not become me
> unrelentingly to rage on. Come, then! The more quickly

>   drive on the flowing-haired Achaians into the fighting,
>   so that I may go up against the Trojans ..."
>
>   Quote 3.1: *Il.* 19.65–70

When Achilles says that "I am making an end of my anger," he clearly does not mean that he is somehow terminating his emotional response to the quarrel.[13] Rather, he will "beat down by constraint the anger" he still feels towards Agamemnon because now his overriding concern is for revenge against the killer of his dearest friend.[14] And the soldiers subsequently rejoice that Achilles has "unsaid his anger"[15] not because they have witnessed a moving scene of heartfelt reconciliation, but simply because they are relieved that their greatest warrior, who has been sorely missed, is returning to the fight.

Although the interpretation I have suggested for quote 3.1 is straightforward in my opinion and by no means original,[16] it is not supported by all Homeric scholars. For example, one commentator says that "Book 19 is an important stage in the dramatic plot of the Anger of Achilleus; it is the moment when he renounces the quarrel initiated in Book 1."[17] On the contrary, I argue that the assembly achieves no fundamental change in the status of the quarrel initiated in book 1: Achilles' anger towards Agamemnon has been pushed into the background by the tragic death of Patroklos, but will reassert itself when that death has been avenged and Patroklos has received a proper funeral.

An examination of what takes place after Achilles' brief opening speech reveals nothing that might defuse his anger and much that would intensify it if he were not preoccupied with taking revenge against Hektor. Agamemnon responds to Achilles' overture not by welcoming him back to the war effort but by attempting to save face with the assembled men, many of whom have hung back from the fighting out of anger at Agamemnon's treatment of Achilles and the resulting withdrawal of their most valuable warrior.[18] After asking for silence—it is clear that the men care more about Achilles' return than about anything that Agamemnon might have to say—the latter continues:

> "I shall address the son of Peleus; yet all you other
> Argives listen also, and give my word careful attention.
> This is the word the Achaians have spoken often against me
> and found fault with me in it, yet I am not responsible
> but Zeus is, and Destiny, and Erinys the mist-walking
> who in assembly caught my heart in the savage delusion
> on that day I myself stripped from him the prize of Achilleus.
> Yet what could I do? It is the god who accomplishes all things.
> Delusion is the elder daughter of Zeus, the accursed
> who deludes all; ..."
>
> Quote 3.2: *Il.* 19.83–92

Instead of apologizing, Agamemnon tries to excuse his behavior by attributing it to a delusion sent by Zeus. In subsequent lines he has the nerve to recite a lengthy myth about how even Zeus was once deluded. If Achilles were offering sincere reconciliation, this response would surely bring his wrath back to the boiling point. But he is interested only in avenging the death of Patroklos and will say anything that brings him closer to this goal. As soon as

3.1. THE SPURIOUS RECONCILIATION

the opportunity arises, he therefore brings the assembly to a close with the following words:

> "Father Zeus, great are the delusions with which you visit men.
> Without you, the son of Atreus could never have stirred so
> the heart inside my breast, nor taken the girl away from me
> against my will, and be in helplessness. No, but Zeus somehow
> wished that death should befall great numbers of the Achaians.
> Go now and take your dinner, so we may draw on the battle."
>
> Quote 3.3: *Il.* 19.270–275

Achilles allows Agamemnon to get away with his excuse, since to challenge it would only delay the return to battle. So that there will be no question, he even validates the excuse by using it to explain the vehemence of his own reaction to Agamemnon's insult.[19]

Achilles' wish to attack the Trojans right away is thwarted by the emergence of two issues. First, Agamemnon concludes his lengthy response to Achilles' opening remarks by saying that to make up for his delusion he will give Achilles the magnificent gifts he had offered previously and by suggesting that Achilles might wish to wait until he has received the gifts before going into battle. The need to respond again to the offer of gifts and—more importantly—to reject the idea of delaying battle until the gifts have been retrieved and given to him prevents Achilles from immediately accepting Agamemnon's excuse and breaking up the assembly. He replies that Agamemnon can do whatever he pleases with the gifts, but that what is important is to go into battle immediately. Odysseus raises the second issue when he interjects that the men cannot begin a day of fighting on an empty stomach and should first have a meal. Achilles insists—"I would now drive forward the sons of the Achaians into the fighting starving and unfed,"[20] he says—but Odysseus continues to press the more sensible course of action and artfully makes it more difficult for Achilles to object by saying that the men must report for battle immediately after the meal without waiting for any further summons.[21]

With support from Odysseus, Agamemnon's wishes prevail: the promised gifts are taken from his camp and brought back to the assembly. There follows an elaborate ceremony, involving the sacrifice of a boar, in which Agamemnon swears that he never touched Briseis, the girl he took from Achilles. These proceedings hold no interest for the hero impatient for battle, and as soon as they are over he terminates the assembly with the speech in quote 3.3. His last line—"Go now and take your dinner …"—reflects his resignation to the fact that the agenda is not in his hands. It also confirms that his closing words express not what he really wants and believes, but what is realistically necessary to minimize any further delay of his revenge against Hektor.

The assembly accomplishes a formal public reconciliation between the adversaries in the great quarrel with which the *Iliad* begins, but what are its real implications for the relationship between Achilles and Agamemnon and for the public perception of this relationship? It is necessary to ask this question because of Achilles' statement in quote 3.1 that "I am making an end of my anger." Although this statement does not mean that he no longer feels anger towards Agamemnon, it does obligate him, as a man of his word, not to give vent to his anger in the absence of any new provocation. A brief recapitulation will show, however, that the assembly itself supplies ample provocation and justification for some sort of retaliation.

Approximately 36 hours before the assembly, Odysseus and two other ambassadors had been sent to Achilles to offer him magnificent gifts if he would return to the fighting. Achilles emphatically rejected the petition because it was not a genuine apology but merely an attempt to buy his services with gifts whose magnificence would only highlight Agamemnon's dominant position.[22] But in the assembly, with Achilles desperate to avenge the death of Patroklos, Agamemnon has been able to accomplish what had been impossible shortly before: he has gotten Achilles to accept the gifts without anything approaching a real apology. Even if Achilles' anger had been subsiding, this affront to his dignity would surely have re-ignited it. Furthermore, since Achilles stressed repeatedly that he did not care about the gifts and that his one and only concern was to return to battle immediately, it is obvious to everyone that Agamemnon has gotten his way over the strenuous objections of the supreme warrior. The original quarrel has been given a new life: as in that quarrel, the better man has publicly been forced to submit. This time the lesser man has won (for the time being) by taking advantage of the other's grief and rage at the killing of his closest friend. The declaration that "I am making an end of my anger" can no longer be considered binding. Indeed, we should be surprised if Achilles does not exact retribution against Agamemnon once he has avenged his friend and given him a proper funeral.[23]

3.2. The Spear-Throwing Event at the Funeral Games

Despite the delay he is forced to endure, Achilles manages to kill Hektor on the day of his superficial reconciliation with Agamemnon, the day immediately following the death of Patroklos. Having avenged his friend, he can now turn his attention to the funeral. A huge pyre erected the next day, with the body of Patroklos at its peak, is consumed over the following night in a fire corresponding in its scale and intensity to the magnitude of Achilles' grief. After the remnants of the blaze have been extinguished, the cremated remains have been collected, and a fitting grave mound has been constructed, the rest of the second day following the spurious reconciliation is devoted to a series of athletic contests in honor of Patroklos.

The funeral games are characterized by a shift from lamentation to celebration. The competitors strive through their efforts to honor the deceased and to win honor for themselves. As the host, Achilles does not compete in the games, but honors Patroklos through the quality and spirit of the proceedings and through the lavishness of the prizes he awards the participants. The contests and the number of lines that Homer devotes to their description are listed in order in the table below.

3.2. THE SPEAR-THROWING EVENT

	CONTEST	NUMBER OF LINES
1	chariot race	393
2	boxing	47
3	wrestling	40
4	foot race	58
5	armed combat	28
6	weight throwing	24
7	archery	34
8	spear throwing	14

We see from the table that Homer gives the most space by far to the first event, the chariot race, and the least space to the last event, the spear throwing. The chariot race will be discussed later in this chapter insofar as it serves as a kind of preparation for the spear-throwing event. The latter event is our central concern because it is the single event in which Agamemnon participates. Here is how it is described by Homer:

> Then the son of Peleus carried into the circle and set down
> a far-shadowing spear and an unfired cauldron with patterns
> of flowers on it, the worth of an ox. And the spear-throwers rose up.
> The son of Atreus rose, wide-powerful Agamemnon,
> and Meriones rose up, Idomeneus' powerful henchman.
> But now among them spoke swift-footed brilliant Achilleus:
> "Son of Atreus, for we know how much you surpass all others,
> by how much you are the greatest for strength among the spear-throwers,
> therefore take this prize and keep it and go back to your hollow
> ships; but let us give the spear to the hero Meriones;
> if your own heart would have it this way, for so I invite you."
> He spoke, nor did Agamemnon lord of men disobey him.
> The hero gave the bronze spear to Meriones, and thereafter
> handed his prize, surpassingly lovely, to the herald Talthybios.
>
> Quote 3.4: *Il.* 23.884–897

The conventional interpretation of this passage is that Achilles acts graciously towards Agamemnon and thereby completes the reconciliation which he had initiated under tense conditions at the assembly where he announced his return to battle.[24] My interpretation is quite different and will require a close reading.

In six of the eight contests over which Achilles presides, every contestant receives his own prize.[25] This means, for example, that in a two-man contest such as boxing or wrestling, even the loser is given a prize. The key to understanding the spear-throwing event is to realize that the cauldron Achilles gives to Agamemnon is the prize intended for the loser. This assertion is contrary to what is generally assumed and to what is clearly implied by the first three lines of Achilles' speech in quote 3.4. However, the logic of these lines is obscure in the original Greek, and Lattimore, like other translators, has given them a meaning they do not necessarily possess. I postpone consideration of the ambiguous verses until the end of this section, and begin the discussion instead with evidence which is easier to understand.

In five of the six contests where everyone receives a prize, the prizes for first place, second place, and so on are all specified; it is only for the spear throwing that we are not told explicitly the ranking of the prizes. But there is a definite pattern: in all five cases where the ranking is given, the prizes are listed in descending order, that is, beginning with the prize for the winner. If we assume this pattern extends to the spear throwing, it follows that the cauldron is the prize for the loser. This inference is consistent with the limited information we are given on the valuation of the prizes. In the case of the wrestling match, we are told that the first prize is worth twelve oxen and the second prize is worth four oxen.[26] According to quote 3.4, the cauldron is valued at only one ox. Of course, the spear could be worth even less—we are not told its value—but it is clear that the cauldron reserved for the spear-throwing event is a relatively poor prize and could well be the prize for the loser. That it is called "surpassingly lovely" (line 897 in quote 3.4) is irrelevant because, whatever good qualities it may have, we know it is worth only one ox.

The behavior of the characters is also revealing. Achilles asks Agamemnon for his assent to the proposed distribution of prizes ("if your own heart would have it this way"). But it is Meriones' permission he should seek if he proposes to deprive him of the opportunity to compete for first prize by giving that prize to Agamemnon without a contest.[27] Achilles' *apparent* deference to Agamemnon therefore actually supports the view that the cauldron is the loser's prize. Now let us consider Agamemnon's reaction to Achilles' proposal.

The most remarkable and telling aspect of the spear-throwing event may be the silence of Agamemnon. If Achilles is proposing to honor him with first prize without the need to compete for it, we would expect Agamemnon to respond with a speech ostensibly expressing his gratitude for the honor but actually arising from his need to bask in the superiority of his position. We would feel confident in predicting such a speech since even in inappropriate circumstances Agamemnon has shown himself willing to speak in public about the honor he considers his due.[28] Furthermore, a superficially similar speech is delivered earlier in the games, when Achilles gives Nestor an honorary prize because the respected elder is too old to compete. Near the end of his acceptance speech, Nestor says, "I accept this from you gratefully, and my heart is happy ... that I am not forgotten for the honor that should be my honor among the Achaians."[29] The fact that Agamemnon says nothing in response to Achilles' proposal, despite his psychological needs and Nestor's precedent, indicates that he is not being honored with first prize after all but is being forced to accept second prize. And so we are not surprised when, without comment, he hands his prize to the herald as if the cauldron is not something he is proud to hold himself.[30]

The description of the spear-throwing event evidently contains several indications that the prize given to Agamemnon is the loser's prize. If this is correct, we must reject the conventional interpretation that Achilles' treatment of Agamemnon at the conclusion of the funeral games for Patroklos is deferential and magnanimous. Instead it becomes apparent that Achilles actually intends to humiliate the man who has consistently treated him in a high-handed fashion.[31] This view was first advanced by Norman Postlethwaite.[32] As I will show in the following sections of this chapter, it leads to readings of several passages in Homer that are more satisfying than those implied by the conventional interpretation. It also enables us to solve a fundamental problem of plot integrity.

The generous and forgiving behavior that is attributed to Achilles in the conventional interpretation of the spear-throwing event has no motivation and is actually contrary to what we should expect. His last significant interaction with Agamemnon before the funeral games takes place at the assembly where he announces his return to battle. As we saw in the preceding section, that interaction is anything but a genuine reconciliation; it is a one-sided transaction in which Agamemnon takes advantage of Achilles' need to avenge the death of Patroklos and Achilles must submit if he is to gratify his lust for revenge against Hektor. However, once Hektor has been killed, Patroklos has received his funeral rites, and games have been held in his honor, Achilles has fulfilled all his obligations to his friend and is dependent on Agamemnon for nothing. With the successful games coming to a close and Agamemnon entered in the final event, the time is finally ripe for the proud Achilles to exact revenge against the overbearing leader who has twice dominated him in public. Thus, understood as a humiliation of Agamemnon, the spear-throwing event is no longer an unmotivated reconciliation, but a retaliation that is amply motivated by the preceding action in the poem.

Besides being well motivated, Achilles' retaliation against Agamemnon is well suited to the latter's original offense. I begin with the obvious point that the initial offense and the retaliation both deprive someone of a prize: Agamemnon takes back a prize from Achilles, while Achilles withholds the winner's prize from Agamemnon.[33] Agamemnon is usually in charge of the distribution of prizes,[34] but Achilles is the host of the funeral games for Patroklos, he supplies the prizes for the games,[35] and he can distribute these prizes as he sees fit. He is therefore in a position to exercise over Agamemnon the same type of arbitrary authority that the latter previously exercised over him. This opportunity enables Achilles to pay back Agamemnon in kind for one of his specific grievances, which he expressed to Patroklos as follows:

> "but this thought comes as a bitter sorrow to my heart and my spirit
> when a man tries to foul one who is his equal, to take back
> a prize of honor, because he goes in greater authority."
>
> Quote 3.5: *Il.* 16.52–4

Achilles is also sensitive to the fact that Agamemnon has singled him out from everyone else:

> "All the other prizes of honor he gave the great men and the princes
> are held fast by them, but from me alone of all the Achaians
> he has taken and keeps the bride of my heart."
>
> Quote 3.6: *Il.* 9.334–336

Consider in this light Achilles' generosity during the games: he almost always gives a prize to every contestant in an event;[36] he upgrades the prize of the man who comes in last in the chariot race; he doubles the amount of gold Antilochos receives for last place in the foot race; and he gives an honorary prize to Nestor, who does not even compete. This pattern of generosity sets up

Agamemnon to be singled out for harsh treatment and serves to intensify his humiliation in the final event of the games.[37]

Achilles has made the pursuit of a hero's glory the aim of his life. In the ancient Greek heroic tradition, one's glory depends to a large extent on the prizes one has received as tangible expressions of honor. Agamemnon therefore diminishes Achilles' honor and undermines the aim of his life when he takes away his prize.[38] What makes this absolutely insupportable for Achilles is that he, more than any other Greek (or Trojan, for that matter), is worthy of heroic honor: he is indisputably the greatest warrior and, in his own words, "the best of the Achaians."[39] This injustice actually continues a pattern to which Achilles draws attention in his quarrel with Agamemnon:

> "Never, when the Achaians sack some well-founded citadel
> of the Trojans, do I have a prize that is equal to your prize.
> Always the greater part of the painful fighting is the work of
> my hands; but when the time comes to distribute the booty
> yours is far the greater reward, and I with some small thing
> yet dear to me go back to my ships when I am weary with fighting."
>
> Quote 3.7: *Il.* 1.163–168

The spear-throwing event gives Achilles the opportunity to pay Agamemnon back for this injustice, and this he does with surgical precision. His method is to put Agamemnon in a position analogous to his own. Whereas he himself is acknowledged to be the supreme warrior, he says in quote 3.4—whether truthfully or not, it does not matter—that Agamemnon is acknowledged to be the supreme spear-thrower. "But," he says in effect to Agamemnon (we will see below that the "therefore" in line 892 should be replaced by "but" or "nevertheless"), "you cannot have the prize that you deserve: I am taking advantage of my authority as host of these games to give the winner's prize to Meriones." Agamemnon is now on the receiving end of an injustice that closely parallels the one he inflicted on Achilles at the beginning of the *Iliad*.[40] Thus, Achilles' revenge is exquisitely tuned to Agamemnon's original offense.

We can now understand why Achilles intervenes to distribute the prizes without allowing the actual spear-throwing to proceed. There are two explanations. First, suppose that Agamemnon were to lose the contest, either because he is not really the best spear-thrower, as some have suggested,[41] or because an accident or outside agency produces an unexpected outcome. There is ample precedent for the latter possibility in the chariot race, where a strong contender who should have come in no worse than second actually finishes last in a field of five owing to divine intervention.[42] In either case, the loser's prize would go to Agamemnon automatically, depriving Achilles of the opportunity to dominate him by forcing it on him unjustly. The obvious explanation for Achilles' intervention is that he wishes to preempt this eventuality. The more subtle explanation has to do with the artistry of his revenge. The point he is making before the crowd is that Agamemnon is getting the loser's prize regardless of his merits. To allow the spear-throwing to take place would be to introduce an extraneous element that would only dilute the force of the humiliation.

Having shown that Achilles' revenge is designed to fit the abuse he received from Agamemnon at the beginning of the *Iliad*, in the assembly where he withdrew from the Greek cause, I now suggest that it is also a fitting response to what transpired at the assembly where he announced his return to battle. By giving Agamemnon the prize intended for the loser of the spear-throwing event, Achilles accomplishes two things: (*a*) he deprives Agamemnon of the winner's prize and (*b*) he forces Agamemnon to accept a prize in which he has no interest. The first result pays Agamemnon back for seizing Achilles' prize in the original quarrel; the second pays him back for forcing his unwanted gifts on Achilles at the second assembly.

A review of how Agamemnon first presses the unwanted gifts on Achilles will shed light on the latter's last line of speech in the funeral games. Achilles opens the second assembly with the announcement that he is putting the quarrel with Agamemnon behind him in order to return to the fighting. The urgency he feels for battle is clear in quote 3.1. Agamemnon acknowledges this urgency in the concluding words of his lengthy reply:

"Rise up, then, to the fighting and rouse the rest of the people.
...
Or if you will, hold back, though you lean hard into the battle,
while my followers take the gifts from my ship and bring them
to you, so you may see what I give to comfort your spirit."

Quote 3.8: *Il.* 19.139, 142–144

While acknowledging Achilles' wish, Agamemnon also suggests an alternative, that Achilles delay his return to the fighting in order to accept Agamemnon's gifts. This alternative is what Agamemnon wants, of course, but he prefaces his suggestion with the courteous "if you will," as if there were some chance that it is also what Achilles would prefer. Achilles forcefully rejects Agamemnon's suggestion, yet this "suggestion" eventually carries the day.

In quote 3.4 Achilles appears to make the allocation of prizes for the spear-throwing dependent on the consent of Agamemnon. His words "if your own heart would have it this way" in line 23.894 correspond to the "if you will" in line 142 of quote 3.8: although they seem courteous, they do not reflect a genuine concern for what the other wants. Just as Achilles' expressed wish to return to battle immediately is overruled, Agamemnon is powerless to affect how the host of the games will distribute the prizes; as I will discuss shortly, he is afraid to even try. All he can do is remain silent and attempt to distance himself from the proceedings by handing his relatively poor prize to the herald. The impossibility of any response to the highly ironic line 23.894 highlights his powerlessness and his inevitable submission, the crux of Achilles' retaliation for how he was treated at both assemblies.[43]

We are now in a position to fully appreciate one more aspect of Achilles' revenge. Just before the end of quote 3.4, we learn that it is Agamemnon who hands the spear to Meriones.[44] Thus, when Achilles says, "let us give the spear to the hero Meriones," he apparently gives the spear to Agamemnon for *him* to give to Meriones. This is puzzling indeed under the conventional interpretation: why would Achilles want Agamemnon to hand the consolation prize to Meriones? But all becomes clear if the spear is the first prize and Achilles is humiliating Agamemnon by arbitrarily awarding it to Meriones. By having Agamemnon give away the spear, Achilles makes him participate in his own humiliation and show the assembled army his complete submission to the warrior he had previously dishonored.

Before we can conclude that the proposed interpretation of the spear-throwing event provides a coherent reading that takes into account all the relevant circumstances, it is necessary to answer several questions. First, why does Agamemnon put up with the abuse from Achilles? Why does he not simply reject the proposed allocation of prizes on the basis of his superior social position, which he asserted so emphatically in the original quarrel? One answer may lie in the loss of prestige he has suffered since the beginning of the *Iliad*. But the main answer is surely that he fears for his life, and with good reason. Achilles came close to killing him in the original quarrel, going as far as taking his sword at least partly out of its scabbard.[45] Any restraint Achilles felt then will have vanished after the death of Patroklos,[46] a death whose ultimate cause was Agamemnon's outrageous behavior in book 1. Achilles' ferocity in avenging that death, showing a total disregard for normal conventions of human society,[47] will have left no doubt in Agamemnon's mind that he would be struck down instantly if he were to defy Achilles at the funeral games for his friend.

Since Agamemnon never apologized sincerely to Achilles and even took advantage of the latter's urgent need to avenge the death of Patroklos, he must suspect that Achilles will seek retribution at the first opportunity. Why then does he put himself at Achilles' mercy by entering the spear-throwing event? One possibility is that Achilles' generosity and goodwill in the preceding events have led Agamemnon to hope for forgiveness or at least leniency. It seems more likely, however, that he enters the contest with a great deal of trepidation and only because he has no real choice. If he does not enter the event, he will be the only major hero not to participate in the games (apart from the aged Nestor), and his failure to participate will be an open admission of guilt and fear. More important, it will also be a failure to show proper respect to Patroklos, a perfect pretext for Achilles to "invite" him to compete. Since refusal of this invitation would certainly cost him his life, Agamemnon might as well make it appear that he is entering the event of his own free will and then take what is coming to him, a humiliation that is as inevitable as it is artful.

It is sometimes argued that the quarrel at the beginning of the *Iliad* arouses in Achilles an animosity towards the entire Greek army for acquiescing in Agamemnon's seizure of his prize.[48] In a variation of this position, it is felt that Odysseus and Aias, whose prizes at first are also threatened by Agamemnon,[49] are especially culpable in Achilles' eyes for not having supported him.[50] If either scenario is correct, is it reasonable to claim that Achilles humiliates Agamemnon in the spear-throwing event when he behaves graciously towards everyone else in the funeral games? Perhaps he relented after all, and Agamemnon actually does have reason to hope for lenient treatment after seeing the generosity and courtesy Achilles has extended to other participants in the games.

Here is my answer: Only Agamemnon wishes to assert his superiority over Achilles, and therefore only Agamemnon is the object of Achilles' wrath. Those who do not make a stand with Achilles against Agamemnon may be guilty of spinelessness—as Achilles says to his adversary, "you rule over nobodies: otherwise, son of Atreus, this outrage would prove your last"[51]—but fear is not an offense against Achilles' honor and is something he can forgive. It is true that Achilles wants the Greeks to suffer as a result of his absence from combat, but even this is just an indication of his wrath against Agamemnon, for his motive is to have Agamemnon see that he blundered by dishonoring his greatest warrior[52] and to generate among the masses the resentment toward their leader that we see reflected in Agamemnon's need to save face at the assembly where Achilles announces his return to the fighting. By his genuinely courteous treatment of the heralds that Agamemnon sends to take his prize[53] and by his warm welcome of Agamemnon's ambassadors (two of whom are Odysseus and Aias),[54] Achilles shows that his anger against Agamemnon does not prevent him from having good relations with others. Therefore, we should not be fooled by his gracious hosting of the funeral games into thinking that he is being considerate towards Agamemnon as well.

Finally, it is necessary to address the problematic lines of Achilles' speech in quote 3.4 (lines 890–892). The difficulty that these lines pose for a translator arises from the presence of two words, $\gamma\alpha\rho$ ("since" or "for") and $\alpha\lambda\lambda\alpha$ ("but," "yet," or "nevertheless"), combined in a way that yields a strange construct equivalent to "Since we know you are the best spear-thrower, but take this prize." Some translators try to solve the problem by rendering $\alpha\lambda\lambda\alpha$ as "therefore" (Lattimore) or "so" (Hammond) instead of "but"; others (Murray and Rieu, for example) simply leave $\alpha\lambda\lambda\alpha$ (as well as $\gamma\alpha\rho$) untranslated, which has the same effect.[55] In an attempt to reconcile the sense of the lines in such translations with the adversative meaning of $\alpha\lambda\lambda\alpha$, one commentator suggests that "the implication [of $\alpha\lambda\lambda\alpha$ in line 892] is presumably 'but do not feel the need to display your supremacy'."[56] The verses in question evidently do not provide a solid basis for the conventional interpretation of the spear-throwing event. Whether they can be interpreted in a way that supports the reading proposed here is not clear, however. There is certainly no problem if we ignore the word $\gamma\alpha\rho$ (giving us, in effect, "We know you are the best spear-thrower, but take this prize"), but a justification for ignoring $\gamma\alpha\rho$ eludes me. Another solution would be the expansion "Since we know you are the best spear-thrower, you are entitled to first prize, but take this prize instead," but this is not what Homer says. I conclude that these lines cannot be used to decide between the conventional interpretation and my own. (This conclusion has not prevented me from explaining how I believe the lines relate to quote 3.7.) Fortunately, the latter interpretation, which I hope is already plausible, should be compelling by the end of this chapter.

The thrust of this section can be formulated as follows. The quarrel between Achilles and Agamemnon which begins the *Iliad* motivates directly or indirectly most of the action of the poem, but according to the conventional interpretation it eventually just fades away: in their last scene together, the spear-throwing event at the funeral games for Patroklos, Achilles treats Agamemnon with the utmost respect without ever having received an apology for the dishonor that set in motion the events that culminated in the tragic death of his friend. The funeral games themselves also seem to just fade away, both in terms of the lengths of the descriptions of the individual events (see the table at the beginning of this section) and in terms of dramatic tension.[57] The interpretation proposed in this section could not be more different: the games end with a bang, not a whimper, in a scene whose power is only accentuated by its compactness, a scene that also brings the Quarrel to a decisive conclusion with a humiliation of Agamemnon that he will never forget.

3.3. Agamemnon's Failure to Mention the Games for Patroklos

The interpretation of the spear-throwing event in the funeral games for Patroklos as an intense humiliation for Agamemnon that he will never forget provides a simple explanation for an otherwise mysterious passage in the *Odyssey*. The passage in question is found in the conversation between the shades of Achilles and Agamemnon in the underworld, the former having been killed in battle and the latter upon his return home from the war. The surprising friendliness of the conversation has often been remarked upon, and will be discussed in chapter 5. Here I focus on one anomaly. Agamemnon describes how the Greeks and even the gods honored Achilles following his death in a manner befitting his status as the preeminent hero. Let us consider just the description of the funeral games:

> "Then your mother, asking the gods for the gift of beautiful
> prizes, set them in the field for the best of the Achaians.
> I in my time have attended the funerals of many
> heroes, at those times when, because a king has perished,
> the young men gird themselves for sport and set up the prizes;
> but these your heart would have admired beyond any others,
> such beautiful prizes as were set up by the goddess, silver-footed
> Thetis, for your sake. You were very dear to the gods."
>
> Quote 3.9: *Od.* 24.85–92

It is strange that this passage does not mention the funeral games that Achilles held in honor of Patroklos. I say this for several reasons, one of which is based on the passage itself. After the first two lines, Agamemnon could simply have said, "The magnificence of the prizes showed everyone how dear you were to the gods," in which case there would have been no need to mention the games for Patroklos. Instead, he refers to the other funerals he had attended during his life,[58] and it suddenly seems peculiar that he does not mention the splendid games that had been hosted by his partner in the conversation, games that occupy over 600 lines of the *Iliad*.[59] Since Achilles had said that a fitting grave mound for Patroklos would not be very great in comparison with his own,[60] there would have been no harm in saying, "Magnificent as were the games you held for Patroklos, the games held in your honor were far greater still."

Our surprise that Agamemnon does not mention the funeral games for Patroklos is heightened by the fact that he refers to the death of Patroklos just a few lines before the passage just quoted:

> "But after the flame of Hephaistos had consumed you utterly,
> then at dawn we gathered your white bones, Achilleus,
> together with unmixed wine and unguents. Your mother gave you

3.3. FAILURE TO MENTION THE GAMES

a golden jar with handles. She said that it was a present
from Dionysos, and was the work of renowned Hephaistos.
In this your white bones are laid away, O shining Achilleus,
mixed with the bones of the dead Patroklos, son of Menoitios,
and apart from those of Antilochos, whom you prized above all
the rest of your companions after the death of Patroklos."

Quote 3.10: *Od.* 24.71–79

This passage alludes to a scene in the *Iliad* that immediately precedes Patroklos's funeral.[61] During the night following the day of Achilles' revenge against Hektor, the ghost of Patroklos appears to Achilles in his sleep and asks to be given his funeral rites as quickly as possible so that he may enter the underworld. The ghost concludes his appeal with a final request:

"And you, Achilleus like the gods, have your own destiny;
to be killed under the wall of the prospering Trojans. There is one
more thing I will say, and ask of you, if you will obey me:
do not have my bones laid apart from yours, Achilleus,
but with them, just as we grew up together in your house,
...
Therefore, let one single vessel, (the golden two-handled
urn the lady your mother gave you), hold both our ashes."

Quote 3.11: *Il.* 23.80–84, 91–92 (parentheses added[62])

Twice in this passage the ghost of Patroklos asks that his remains be buried with those of Achilles; the second formulation specifies that the remains of the two men should be put in the same vessel (which will itself be buried[63]). Achilles replies that he will do as he has been asked,[64] and when Patroklos's body has been cremated, he gives instructions preparing for the fulfillment of the request.[65] Quote 3.10 indicates that the request was indeed carried out when he died. Whether Agamemnon was aware of Achilles' vision of Patroklos's ghost is never explicitly addressed, but he did know of the related instructions issued by Achilles after the cremation of Patroklos's body. Thus, in his conversation with Achilles in the *Odyssey*, Agamemnon refers not only to the death of Patroklos, but also to events from Patroklos's funeral in the *Iliad*. His failure to mention the games that form such an important part of this funeral a few lines later, when the context practically demands that they be mentioned, is therefore even more of a mystery.

The mystery is further compounded by the reference at the end of quote 3.10 to Antilochos and his friendship with Achilles. Although Antilochos appears in many battle scenes in the *Iliad*, it is not until he is selected to be the one to give Achilles the news of Patroklos's death[66] that we realize there is a special relationship between the two men. This relationship is subsequently highlighted in the funeral games, during which Achilles' fondness for Antilochos is made clear on two occasions.[67] Of the 45 lines of speech attributed to Antilochos in the *Iliad*, 41 are delivered during the games[68] (the other four lines inform Achilles of the death of Patroklos). Thus, there is a strong association between Antilochos and his friendship with Achilles, on the one hand, and the funeral games. It is therefore reasonable to think that Agamemnon still has in mind the games for Patroklos when he utters the last lines of quote 3.10. Once again we are led to ask why he refrains from mentioning these particular games in his conversation with Achilles.

The absence of any reference to the funeral games for Patroklos in quote 3.9 becomes perfectly understandable when we take into account the analysis in the preceding section. What surely stands out in Agamemnon's memories of the games is his humiliation at the hands of Achilles in the final event. After all, he was willing to put the success of the entire Greek expedition at risk in order to avoid the perceived dishonor of being the only leader forced to give up a prize; he continued to insist on Achilles' submission even when the Greeks were in desperate need of their greatest warrior; and he remained preoccupied with his reputation when everyone else was heaving a collective sigh of relief that Achilles was finally returning to the war. For such a man, public humiliation at the hands of his adversary and the lack of any possible response to this humiliation—that is, the necessity of his own submission—could not have been more agonizing. It is no wonder, then, that Agamemnon does not bring up the funeral games for Patroklos in his conversation with Achilles in the *Odyssey*: the subject is simply too painful. Indeed, we may see in Agamemnon's avoidance of the topic an allusion to the *Iliad* that is somewhat more subtle than the allusions in quote 3.10 discussed above. The only question is why Agamemnon speaks in such a friendly way in the *Odyssey* to the man who caused him so much suffering in their last encounter in the *Iliad*. As I have already mentioned, this question will be addressed in chapter 5.

Readers who are acquainted with Monro's Law, an observation regarding the relationship between the *Iliad* and the *Odyssey*, may think that I read too much into Agamemnon's failure to mention the funeral games for Patroklos. I shall respond to this objection in the final section of chapter 5, when we will have gained a new perspective on the relationship between the two poems. Knowledgeable readers may also be concerned that the conversation between the shades of Achilles and Agamemnon is contained in part of the *Odyssey* whose authenticity has been questioned. I shall address this issue as well in chapter 5, which fortifies the case for authenticity with an entirely new argument.

3.4. The Other Humiliation of Agamemnon

To the proposed explanation for Agamemnon's failure to mention the funeral games for Patroklos when he speaks with Achilles in the underworld, one might object that he speaks without hesitation about another extremely painful subject: his ignominious death at the hands of his unfaithful wife and her lover.[69] However, this objection is easily answered: Agamemnon has no choice but to openly face the truth in this case because he is always surrounded by those who died with him.[70]

The humiliating circumstances of Agamemnon's death may also cause one to object to the title of this chapter, in which I refer to Achilles' humiliation of Agamemnon at the conclusion of the funeral games for Patroklos as *the* humiliation of Agamemnon. But in this title (unlike the title of this section) I am using the word "humiliation" in the sense of an intentional

3.4. THE OTHER HUMILIATION

humiliation of someone by someone else, as opposed to a humiliation that is incidental to the accomplishment of some other goal (such as self-preservation in the case of the murderers of Agamemnon[71]). This distinction is ignored in the present section, for my purpose here is to discuss the possibility of a connection between the two humiliations of Agamemnon, the intentional one by Achilles and the incidental one by Klytaimestra and Aigisthos.

It is often remarked that certain events supposed to have taken place after the period treated in the *Iliad* appear to be foreshadowed in the funeral games for Patroklos.[72] Those who make this observation have in mind events mentioned in the *Odyssey* as well as those described in the poems of the Epic Cycle. In the latter case, the idea is typically that Homer and the Cyclic poets drew on a shared oral tradition. Here, for simplicity, I cite only examples of possible foreshadowing that involve post-Iliadic events mentioned in the *Odyssey*.

When Achilles and Antilochos are killed (sometime after the end of the *Iliad*), their remains are buried in a way that reflects their friendship in life (see quote 3.10[73]); as mentioned in the preceding section, this friendship is highlighted in the funeral games for Patroklos. After the death of Achilles, a contest for his armor between Odysseus and Aias is decided in favor of Odysseus, to the bitter disappointment of Aias;[74] in the funeral games for Patroklos, a close wrestling match between Odysseus and Aias is eventually terminated by Achilles and called a draw, but a decision based on the incomplete results would presumably have gone to Odysseus.[75] On his way home from Troy, the lesser Aias is killed by Poseidon as a direct result of his inability to control his tongue;[76] this inability is displayed in the *Iliad* during the chariot race in the funeral games for Patroklos, when Aias showers verbal abuse on a fellow spectator and, in a blatant act of projection, unfairly accuses him of having a big mouth.[77]

If the proposed interpretation of the spear-throwing event is correct, we can add one more example: Agamemnon suffers a humiliating death upon his return home from Troy; Achilles' humiliation of Agamemnon is the whole point of the final event in the funeral games for Patroklos. Except for one interesting difference that I shall discuss in a moment, this new instance of possible foreshadowing fits well with the others.[78] We may take it as new evidence supporting the conjecture that post-Iliadic events are intentionally foreshadowed in the funeral games for Patroklos. Alternatively, if we believed the conjecture to be true even before this, the existence of a post-Iliadic humiliation of Agamemnon lends additional support to the view that Agamemnon is humiliated during the games honoring Patroklos.

The way in which the new instance of possible foreshadowing differs from other instances is interesting because it strengthens the connection between the two humiliations. Let me explain.

The burial of Antilochos is mentioned only once in the *Odyssey* (quote 3.10) and plays a minimal role in the poem. The same can be said about the contest for the armor of Achilles and the death of the lesser Aias. The murder of Agamemnon, on the other hand, is mentioned many times and serves several important functions in the *Odyssey*.[79] Similarly, while the friendly exchanges between Antilochos and Achilles in the funeral games, the wrestling match between Odysseus and Aias, and the lesser Aias's verbal abuse of a fellow spectator are not essential to the plot of the *Iliad*, what may foreshadow the humiliating death of Agamemnon—namely, his humiliation by Achilles in the spear-throwing event—is significant for the poem as a whole.

The larger significance of the spear-throwing event is twofold. First, Achilles' humiliation of Agamemnon brings to a decisive close the theme of Achilles' original wrath stated in the first lines of the poem, developed in the rest of book 1 (the Quarrel), and renewed most notably in books 9 (Agamemnon's attempt to win Achilles over with gifts without offering an apology) and 19 (the spurious reconciliation). Second, this conclusion to the story of Achilles' original wrath provides a counterpoint for the subsequent resolution of his second wrath, the wrath occasioned by the death of Patroklos. As the latter contribution deepens our appreciation of one of the highlights of the entire poem, the meeting between Achilles and Priam, I shall discuss it in a section of its own.

3.5. The Rapprochement of Achilles and Priam

When the funeral is over, Achilles is still far from accepting the death of Patroklos. He takes out his anger on the body of Hektor, each day dragging the corpse behind his chariot three times around Patroklos's tomb and then leaving it face down in the dust. After nine days of this abuse, the gods decide to intervene. Zeus sends a messenger to Priam, Hektor's father and the king of Troy, telling him to go to Achilles with ransom for the release of his son's body, and he sends the goddess Thetis, Achilles' mother, to instruct her son to accept the ransom. Priam and Achilles carry out their respective instructions, but what happens when the two men meet turns out to be much more than a simple ransom transaction. It will be instructive to compare their meeting with Agamemnon's attempt to persuade Achilles to return to the fighting.[80]

As the reader will recall, Agamemnon is advised by Nestor to repair his relationship with Achilles "with words of supplication and with the gifts of friendship." He enthusiastically embraces the idea of gift-giving, and takes 35 lines of the poem just to enumerate the magnificent gifts he is willing to give if Achilles will relent from his anger. Instead of offering these gifts in a spirit of supplication or friendship, however, he insists that his superior position be acknowledged. Odysseus wisely leaves out this condition when he relays the proposal to Achilles, but it is obvious that Agamemnon is using the gift-giving merely to show off his wealth and power and to demonstrate his dominance by securing Achilles' compliance with overwhelming riches. The proposed transaction therefore amounts to an insult, a proof of Agamemnon's unabated arrogance, and it is rejected forthwith by Achilles.

Unlike Agamemnon, Priam goes to Achilles in person, putting himself at the mercy of the fearsome Greek warrior whose almost superhuman rage at the death of Patroklos was directed not only at Hektor but also at all the other children of Priam[81] and presumably Priam himself. He immediately takes the position of a suppliant, grasping the knees and kissing the hands of an astonished Achilles. Whereas Agamemnon makes a show of his gifts, Priam mentions the generous ransom he has brought for Hektor's body only as a necessary formality. The essence of his supplication is an appeal to Achilles' pity, which he seeks to arouse through Achilles' feelings for his own father, Peleus, who like Priam finds himself in old age without the protection of his son.[82]

In their respective approaches to Achilles, attempting to overpower him with gifts or seeking to move him to pity so that he will grant a request of his own volition, Agamemnon corresponds to the wind in Aesop's fable of the wind and the sun, while Priam corresponds to the sun. It does not hurt Priam's cause that the parallel between himself and Peleus is even stronger than he realizes: as Achilles knows full well, he is destined to die at Troy and his father, like Priam, will never see his cherished son again. Achilles begins to weep for his father, as well as for Patroklos, while Priam sits at his feet weeping for Hektor. This shared lamentation is the first stage in the development of a bond between these two men whom fate has cast in the roles of enemies. Feeling pity for the old man, Achilles raises Priam to his feet, expresses wonder at his inner strength ("How could you dare to come alone to the ships of the Achaians and before my eyes ...? The heart in you is iron"[83]), and attempts to console him with a philosophical speech on human suffering.

Although Achilles' respect and compassion are genuine, there is still within him at this stage in the encounter an anger that could erupt at a single misstep by Priam and cause him to kill the old man.[84] Aware that this might well happen if Priam were to see his son's body, Achilles has him stay inside while he goes to have the corpse washed, anointed, and exchanged for the ransom in Priam's wagon. When Achilles returns, he tells Priam that his wishes have been granted and that he can see his son's body when he takes him away at dawn. He then recites a mythological precedent to persuade Priam to give up his mourning for a while and to join him in supper, the first food and drink Priam will have taken since the death of Hektor. With tensions dissipated by the successful completion of the difficult transaction followed by the sharing of a meal, the two men are liberated from their fated roles and gaze at each other in silent admiration.[85] These moments of silence and openness to the other constitute the spiritual climax of the poem. Afterwards, Achilles can address Priam as "friend,"[86] and Priam can sleep peacefully as Achilles' guest.[87] They have gone far beyond the instructions they received from Zeus. Indeed, the meeting of Achilles and Priam on the common ground of the human condition has brought them to an experience not available to the immortal gods.

It is sometimes said that Achilles' impeccable hosting of the funeral games for Patroklos signals his reintegration into society and his resumption of normal human relations that will culminate in the reconciliation with Priam. Speaking in particular of Achilles' supposedly generous treatment of Agamemnon in the spear-throwing event, one commentator remarks, "This courteous gesture sets the final seal on their reconciliation, and Akhilleus' moderation and sense of propriety prepare us for his change of heart when he receives Priam's supplication."[88] Since my interpretation of the spear-throwing event is quite different from that assumed by this commentator and others, I must address the impact of this interpretation on how we perceive the encounter between Achilles and Priam.

In my view, no advance preparation is needed for the reconciliation between Achilles and Priam, as it is fully motivated by the way Priam approaches Achilles and the psychological dynamics of their subsequent interaction. Moreover, the supposed reconciliation between Achilles and Agamemenon, which is not motivated by the preceding action of the poem and is even contrary to what one should expect, actually does harm by diluting the force of the psychologically well-motivated reconciliation between Achilles and Priam. By contrast, Achilles' harsh treatment of Agamemnon in my interpretation of the spear-throwing event reminds us of his intransigence and thereby highlights the uniqueness of what takes place between Achilles and Priam, a genuine contact between two human beings that transcends the roles in which they find themselves in life and that represents a breakthrough to a kind of experience not found anywhere else in the poem.[89]

According to the conventional interpretation, the quarrel between Achilles and Agamemnon eventually just fades away, and the encounter between Achilles and Priam represents the final stage of a relatively gradual development of Achilles' conciliatory attitude. When the spear-throwing event is interpreted as a humiliation of Agamemnon, however, the Quarrel is brought to a definite conclusion, and the scene between Achilles and Priam strikes us forcefully as a quantum jump in the spiritual level of the poem. To use a sculptural metaphor, the *Iliad* comes into focus as a more sharply chiseled work of art.

3.6. Achilles and Agamemnon at the End of the *Iliad*

After Achilles and Priam have shared a meal and gazed at each other in silent admiration, Priam asks for a place to sleep since he has not slept since the death of Hektor. Achilles gives orders for beds to be made on the porch for Priam and his herald, and then speaks to Priam as follows:

> "Sleep outside, aged sir and good friend, for fear some Achaian
> might come in here on a matter of counsel, since they keep coming
> and sitting by me and making plans; as they are supposed to.
> But if one of these come through the fleeting black night should notice you,
> he would go straight and tell Agamemnon, shepherd of the people,
> and there would be delay in the ransoming of the body.
> But come, tell me this and count off for me exactly
> how many days you intend for the burial of great Hektor.
> Tell me, so I myself shall stay still and hold back the people."
>
> Quote 3.12: *Il.* 24.650–658

Priam explains that the preparations for Hektor's funeral and the funeral itself would require eleven days. Achilles replies:

> "Then all this, aged Priam, shall be done as you ask it.
> I will hold off our attack for as much time as you bid me."
>
> Quote 3.13: *Il.* 24.669–670

These are the last words spoken by Achilles in the poem. Agamemnon is mentioned for the last time shortly afterwards, when the god Hermes wakes up

Priam by warning him that his remaining sons would have to pay a large ransom for him if he were caught in the Greek camp by Agamemnon.

The final exchange between Achilles and Priam, together with the warning from Hermes, says a great deal about how the relationship between Achilles and Agamemnon stands at the end of the *Iliad*. We know from Hermes that Agamemnon would have wanted to hold Priam for ransom, and it is clear from quote 3.12 that Achilles knows this too. When Agamemnon learns that Priam came to the Greek camp and was allowed to return to Troy with Hektor's body, he will be furious that he was deprived of the opportunity to profit from the situation. Yet Achilles shows no sign of being concerned about crossing the supposed leader of the Greeks. Furthermore, quote 3.13 and the last lines of quote 3.12 show that he has full confidence in his authority to commit the army to a truce regardless of what Agamemnon might have to say.[90] Something has evidently changed since the day before the funeral games for Patroklos, when Achilles said to Agamemnon, "Son of Atreus, beyond others the people of the Achaians will obey your words."[91] The change is inexplicable if Achilles behaved deferentially towards Agamemnon throughout the games, as posited in the conventional interpretation, but it makes perfect sense if Achilles dominated and humiliated Agamemnon during the spear-throwing event.[92]

3.7. The Chariot Race

The chariot race that begins the funeral games for Patroklos gives rise to two disputes which are of great interest for the present discussion.[93] Both disputes remind us of the Quarrel, and the second one reminds us in particular of the egregiousness of Agamemnon's behavior that arouses the wrath of Achilles. With the latter reminder still fresh in our minds when we reach the end of the games, we are practically forced to accept the interpretation of the spear-throwing event proposed in section 3.2.

As I have already had occasion to mention, divine interference causes a contestant who should have done well in the chariot race to come in last, with visible injuries and a damaged chariot that he has to drag behind him. Achilles takes pity on him and proposes to award him second prize. The man who actually comes in second, Antilochos, objects to this idea, saying

> "Achilleus, I shall be very angry with you if you accomplish
> what you have said. You mean to take my prize away from me[.]"
> Quote 3.14: *Il*. 23.543–544

Antilochos goes on to suggest that Achilles could give the loser something else from his personal riches, even something more valuable than the mare he has offered as second prize. "But," he says,

> "... the mare I will not give up, and the man who wants her
> must fight me for her with his hands before he can take her."
> Quote 3.15: *Il*. 23.553–554

Ordinarily it would be the height of folly to challenge Achilles in this way, but Antilochos and he are good friends. In fact, Achilles smiles and agrees to give the loser something else. This concludes the first "dispute."

Although the dispute between Achilles and Antilochos is inconsequential, it serves to remind us of the quarrel between Achilles and Agamemnon, with Antilochos playing the role of Achilles in that quarrel. For quote 3.14 is an obvious echo of Achilles' protest to Agamemnon:

> "And now my prize [the girl Briseis] you threaten in person to strip from me."
>
> Quote 3.16: *Il.* 1.161

In addition to this unmistakable parallel, one may detect in quote 3.15 an allusion to the last words of the Quarrel, where Achilles draws a line in the sand for Agamemnon:

> "With my hands I will not fight for the girl's sake, neither
> with you nor any other man, since you take her away who gave her.
> But of all the other things that are mine beside my fast black
> ship, you shall take nothing away against my pleasure.
> Come, then, only try it, that these others may see also;
> instantly your own black blood will stain my spearpoint."
>
> Quote 3.17: *Il.* 1.298–303

Although the correspondence between quotes 3.15 and 3.17 is not exact, the vehemence of Antilochos in the former passage seems to echo that of Achilles in the latter. Indeed, this may be part of the reason Achilles smiles after Antilochos's outburst.[94]

The second dispute following the chariot race is between Antilochos and Menelaos. The first dispute has established Antilochos in the role of Achilles in the Quarrel; in the second dispute, Menelaos takes the place of Agamemnon. This connection between Menelaos and Agamemnon is natural since they are brothers, not to mention the fact that one of the horses driven by Menelaos actually belongs to his brother.[95] The main basis for the connection, however, is the relationship between the behavior of Menelaos in his dispute with Antilochos and the behavior of Agamemnon in his quarrel with Achilles. Menelaos has a well-founded grievance against Antilochos, whereas Agamemnon's clash with Achilles is largely his own fault, and this difference sets the stage for a consistent divergence in the conduct of the two brothers.

Menelaos is justifiably angry after the race because he would certainly have taken second place if Antilochos had not resorted to a dirty trick to pull ahead of him. He scolds Antilochos and asks his fellow leaders to judge whether Antilochos should be disqualified:

> "You have defiled my horsemanship, you have fouled my horses
> by throwing your horses in their way, though yours were far slower.
> Come then, O leaders of the Argives and their men of counsel:
> judge between the two of us now; and without favor;
> so that no man of the bronze-armored Achaians shall say of us:
> 'Menelaos using lies and force against Antilochos
> went off with the mare he won, for his horses were far slower
> but he himself was greater in power and degree.' …"
>
> Quote 3.18: *Il.* 23.571–578

Here Menelaos calls for an impartial judgment, a judgment in which his superior political power would give him no advantage. We are again reminded of the quarrel between Achilles and Agamemnon, but this time it is the contrast that is striking. It is only by taking advantage of his position as the supreme political leader that Agamemnon is able to take the girl Briseis away from Achilles. Menelaos specifically does not want to be suspected of any such abuse of power (perhaps because he does not want the superiority of his horsemanship and his horses to be in doubt, but this does not matter).

Menelaos goes on to suggest a simpler way to reach a decision: if Antilochos is innocent, he should be willing to swear that he did not cheat. This approach actually occurs to Menelaos much earlier, immediately after Antilochos's questionable maneuver, at which time he yells to him, "you will not get this prize without having to take oath."[96] We are led to ask why Homer, in quote 3.18, has Menelaos request an impartial judgment before returning to his original idea of an oath. The reason, I believe, is that Homer wants to make explicit Menelaos's unwillingness to take advantage of his social position, and in so doing to contrast the dispute between Menelaos and Antilochos with the quarrel between Agamemnon and Achilles. As we shall see, this interpretation is supported by further points of contrast between the two interactions.

Unable to swear to his innocence and wishing to repair his relationship with Menelaos, Antilochos apologizes profusely for his youthful transgression and gives the mare to Menelaos. The latter readily accepts the apology, and concludes the interaction with the following explanation:

> "Any other man of the Achaians might not have appeased me.
> But you have suffered much for me, and done much hard work,
> and your noble father, too, and your brother for my sake. Therefore
> I will be ruled by your supplication. I will even give you
> the mare, though she is mine, so that these men too may be witnesses
> that the heart is never arrogant nor stubborn within me."
>
> Quote 3.19: *Il.* 23.606–611

This passage reveals more points of contrast between Menelaos and Agamemnon. Agamemnon mistreats Achilles even though the latter joined the war against Troy only as a favor to him. As this lack of gratitude is emphasized during the Quarrel,[97] Menelaos's expression of gratitude for the efforts of Antilochos on his behalf is further evidence that their dispute following the chariot race is intended as a foil to the quarrel that begins the *Iliad*. Agamemnon's arrogance and stubbornness were documented in section 3.1. When the Greeks desperately need Achilles to return to battle, Agamemnon is too arrogant to offer him "words of supplication" as advised by Nestor. When Achilles finally wants to return to battle of his own accord in order to avenge the death of Patroklos, Agamemnon's reaction is to defend his reputation and even to draw a parallel between himself and Zeus. As a consequence of his arrogance, he stubbornly forces on Achilles the ostentatious gifts which the hero has previously rejected and to which he remains indifferent. Agamemnon's stubbornness is also apparent in his original confrontation with Achilles, when he is simply unable to let matters rest after a speech by Nestor that gives him his due respect and the possibility of ending the quarrel without losing face.[98] Given all this background to quote

3.19, it is surely significant that Menelaos returns the mare to Antilochos specifically to demonstrate his freedom from arrogance and stubbornness.

The two disputes that follow the chariot race obviously differ from the quarrel between Achilles and Agamemnon in that they are resolved quickly and amicably. In the case of the second dispute, we have seen that the differences extend to a range of specific attributes—willingness to exercise authority arbitrarily, ingratitude, arrogance, and stubbornness—and are so pointed that Homer must want his audience to be conscious of the contrast.[99] Some scholars, recognizing the importance of the dispute between Menelaos and Antilochos for our understanding of the quarrel between Achilles and Agamemnon, believe that the purpose of the former is show how the latter could have been avoided or solved.[100] While this is certainly accomplished, I prefer to regard the dispute between Menelaos and Antilochos as preparation for the conclusion of the Quarrel. I have argued that the last event of the funeral games is the final manifestation of a vicious quarrel between two men who hate each other. On the other hand, the disputes that follow the first event of the games portray fair-minded men resolving their differences with respect and goodwill.[101] This contrast can only accentuate the harshness of the humiliation of Agamemnon at the end of the games. But the dispute between Menelaos and Antilochos also prepares us for the conclusion of the Quarrel in a more precise and calculated fashion.

In section 3.5 I noted that the respectful treatment of Agamemnon by Achilles that is assumed in the conventional interpretation of the spear-throwing event is sometimes considered to prefigure the reconciliation of Achilles and Priam. Someone who holds to the conventional interpretation might similarly argue that the friendly resolutions of the disputes following the chariot race prefigure Achilles' supposedly courteous treatment of Agamemnon at the end of the funeral games. But the disputes that follow the chariot race are so unlike the Quarrel—and here I emphasize above all Menelaos's unwillingness to be seen as prevailing by virtue of his political power and social position—that they cannot possibly be intended to prefigure a harmonious resolution of Achilles' wrath vis-à-vis Agamemnon. On the contrary, as reminders of the ugliness of the Quarrel and the egregiousness of Agamemnon's behavior, they signal that this wrath is still very much alive. It is to be appeased only by a retaliatory stroke that is so forceful and so well aimed that there is no possibility of a response from Agamemnon and no need for further action from Achilles. With the humiliation of Agamemnon, the Quarrel comes to a conclusion that is both just and decisive.

Chapter 4

Inconsistency and the Homeric Question

The poems of Homer present us with a well-known paradox. On one hand, the *Iliad* and the *Odyssey* are masterpieces of epic poetry, each of which forms an organic and artistic whole with a carefully conceived design and a basic structural unity.[1] On the other hand, each epic, when examined closely, displays a number of inconsistencies which seem to imply a degree of *disunity* in the construction of the poem. The central aim of the rest of this book is to suggest a novel resolution of this paradox based on a new understanding of some of the most notorious inconsistencies as well as others that are not so well known. This new understanding reveals an entirely new dimension of Homeric subtlety. To place the argument in context, this short chapter reviews how inconsistencies in Homer have been explained in the past.

The Roman poet Horace attributed inconsistencies in Homer's poems to momentary lapses of attention: "I even feel aggrieved, when good Homer nods; but when a work is long, a drowsy mood is understandable."[2] This formulation gave rise to the dictum "Even Homer sometimes nods," meaning, of course, that even Homer sometimes makes careless errors. For Aristotle, impossibilities in a poem, presumably including inconsistencies,[3] need not be oversights; they may actually be tolerated by the poet if they enable him to create a desired impression. Alexander Pope sided with Aristotle over Horace in *An Essay on Criticism* (1711):[4]

> Those oft are stratagems which errors seem,
> Nor is it Homer nods, but we that dream.

However, both positions survive in modern scholarship. An interpretation of the Homeric "nod" that is currently popular will be described later in this chapter. The Aristotelian view is seen, for example, when Stephanie West observes in relation to the *Odyssey* that "many of the difficulties to which critics have adverted arise from the poet's tendency to sacrifice overall consistency for short-term effect by combining striking elements from different versions of his story."[5]

In the modern era, inconsistency in the *Iliad* and the *Odyssey* has often been regarded not merely as something to be explained, but as an important source of insight into the process of their composition. For example, the students of Homer known as the analysts considered each of the Homeric epics to be the work of multiple authors and the inconsistencies in these epics to reflect the multiplicity of their sources. Analysis of the inconsistencies, it was thought, would make it possible to reconstruct the process by which the epics were assembled from the contributions of the various authors. Although the analysts dominated Homeric scholarship in the nineteenth and early twentieth centuries, they were unable, in the end, to explain the origin of the *Iliad* and the *Odyssey* in a way that could win general assent even among themselves.

In opposition to the analysts, the unitarians asserted what had been assumed in antiquity, that each of the Homeric epics was the work of a single poet. (Whether the two epics were composed by the same poet is a separate question, one on which unitarians could, and continue to, disagree with one another.) The unitarians and the analysts naturally emphasized opposite sides of the paradox mentioned above: "unitarianism put much more emphasis on the artistic unity of the epics and played down the inconsistencies and incoherences that the analysts had made the basis of their arguments."[6] Thus, referring to the time when the efforts of the analysts had lost much of their momentum and the unitarians had begun to assert themselves, E. R. Dodds could write, "it is now [1954] more than thirty years since the old logical game of discovering inconsistencies in Homer was replaced in public esteem by the new and equally enjoyable aesthetic game of explaining them away."[7]

Cedric Whitman had in mind the dispute between the analysts and the unitarians when he remarked concerning the poems of Homer that "few things outside the realm of theology have occasioned more controversy than the circumstances of their creation."[8] In fact, the subject of the controversy was so central to Homeric scholarship that it had long since come to be known as the Homeric Question. While at first, and for a long time, this referred to the question of whether each of the Homeric epics was the work of one poet or of more than one, the issues which have seemed most pressing have evolved over time.[9] Now one prefers to give the Homeric Question a more general formulation such as this: how and by whom were the *Iliad* and *Odyssey* composed and preserved?[10] Nevertheless, it is still possible to say, as Jenny Strauss Clay did in 1983, that "the history of the Homeric Question could well be written by focusing on the way scholars have dealt with contradictions within the Homeric texts."[11]

A key advance which broadened the scope of the Homeric Question was the demonstration by Milman Parry around 1930 that the Homeric epics employ a system of verbal formulas designed to facilitate versification under the pressures of live performance.[12] If we infer from this observation that the *Iliad* and the *Odyssey* were composed during performance (that is, improvised), we can easily understand how inconsistencies could have arisen and, indeed, would have been virtually inevitable, even taking into account planning of a performance and refinement over a succession of performances. C. M. Bowra stressed that the oral poet concentrates on one episode at a time, and may create contradictions when his focus on the current episode causes him to forget something that has already happened or that is to happen in the future.[13] Albert Lord pointed out that the susceptibility of oral poetry to inconsistencies generated in this way is amplified by the role of the *theme*, a group of ideas connected with a given subject that acquires something of the character of a fixed unit of exposition: "[I]t is not difficult to see how inconsistencies may arise in a type of composition which is based on the rapid handling of these units. ... [T]wo of these units may be put together in the same poem because they are fitting, and yet they contain details which are incongruous [that is, a detail of one theme may be inconsistent with a detail of another theme]. This, of course, does not upset the singer, intent as he is on the theme on which he is working at the moment."[14] William Hansen argued for a mechanism in which inconsistency results when the expression of a theme in one context is distorted by confusion with its expression in another context elsewhere in the poem; the confusion occurs because the theme in question belongs to a larger narrative pattern, a sequence of themes, that is used at both places in the poem.[15]

Even if details of the mechanism(s) involved remain to be settled, the inconsistencies in the Homeric epics are now often attributed to the difficulties of oral improvisation: a slip made during live performance is the modern interpretation of a Homeric "nod." This explanation, which has undermined the case for multiple authorship made by the analysts,[16] obviously assumes that errors made during the oral composition of the poems were not corrected when the poems were committed to writing. This requirement suggests the hypothesis, first put forward by Milman Parry and subsequently championed by Albert Lord and Richard Janko, that the *Iliad* and the *Odyssey* came to be written down when someone took dictation from Homer as he composed (or re-composed) them orally.[17]

The view of the Homeric epics as oral dictated texts, while accepted by many, is a significant extrapolation from what has actually been established. Adam Parry, the son of Milman Parry and an important scholar in his own right, pointed out more than once that what his father proved is that the style of the *Iliad* and the *Odyssey* is typical of oral poetry, not that these poems were composed orally. "It is still quite conceivable," said the son, "that Homer made use of writing to compose a poem in a style which had been developed by an oral tradition."[18] Martin Mueller concurs: "It remains a tempting speculation that 'Homer' is the result of a highly consequential encounter of two language technologies during the transition from an 'oral' to a 'literate' culture—a transition in which, as in other major cultural shifts, the 'old' is never completely replaced but lives on in different ways and shapes the ways of the 'new'."[19]

Part of the attraction of the belief that writing played a role in the composition of the Homeric epics, not just in their preservation, lies in the recognition that new ideas must have occurred to the poet during the extended period that was undoubtedly required to put the poems in writing.[20] More important, perhaps, is the conviction that poems of such sophistication on all scales, from exquisite detail to overall design, can only have been created with the aid of writing.[21] But if Homer composed with the aid of writing, the inconsistencies in his poems can no longer be blamed on the pressures of live performance. Instead one postulates that limitations of early writing technology (e.g., the laboriousness of writing or the scarcity of papyrus) gave the process of composition a certain kind of inertia, namely, a resistance to revision: "a text once written represented an investment one would touch only with reluctance."[22] The expansion of a poem subject to this inertia resulted in narrative discontinuities when the incorporation of new material was not accompanied by necessary revisions to the old material. Advocates of this scenario of "progressive fixation" use observed anomalies to reconstruct the stages of composition, much as the analysts did but without the assumption of multiple authorship.[23]

A critical survey of explanations for inconsistencies in Homer would consider the strengths and weaknesses of the different approaches in relation to inconsistencies of various kinds, from short-range illogicalities to large-scale structural anomalies. I have sought instead merely to highlight the attention that has been devoted to inconsistency in the *Iliad* and the *Odyssey* and to illustrate the relevance of this subject to the Homeric Question. This background provides the context for the argument of the following chapters.

In the following chapters I propose a new answer to the Homeric Question that is motivated by a fresh look at inconsistencies within and between the two poems of Homer. What this fresh look suggests can be explained with terminology that will also be useful later. The inconsistencies in the poems can be divided into those that are inadvertent and those that are intentional. An inadvertent inconsistency is one caused by a "nod" of Homer or by distortion over the centuries of transmission that preceded the emergence of a more or less stable text for each poem around 150 BCE.[24] An intentional inconsistency is one introduced by the poet knowingly, whether reluctantly or not. For example, an inconsistency may be introduced reluctantly if it is a necessary consequence of a compositional process such as progressive fixation; at the other extreme, an inconsistency may be introduced enthusiastically if it contributes to the story line (e.g., by illuminating the psychology of a character). A comprehensible inconsistency, in my terminology, is any inconsistency that lies somewhere on this spectrum—that is, any intentional inconsistency for which there is a plausible explanation. But an intentional inconsistency need not, in principle, be comprehensible, at least from an ordinary point of view. The following two chapters discuss Homeric inconsistencies that are mysterious: the poet seems to go out of his way to create them, but his reason for doing this is a mystery. The discussion concentrates on indications of intentionality, which can be surprisingly compelling. The impossibility of explaining the motivation for a given inconsistency cannot be proven, of course, but the variety of apparently intentional inconsistencies for which no convincing explanation seems to be available suggests that we are dealing with a real phenomenon in which the poet creates inconsistencies for their own sake, because inconsistency itself is desired. I call this phenomenon either *mysterious inconsistency* or *perverse inconsistency*.

The hypothesis of perverse inconsistency has not been entertained before in relation to the Homeric epics because it is so counterintuitive; one naturally tends to overlook or to shrug off indications of intentionality when inconsistencies can so easily have been generated inadvertently by one

4. INCONSISTENCY AND THE HOMERIC QUESTION

mechanism or another.[25] When one drops the understandable prejudice against the hypothesis, however, the evidence for it becomes too substantial to ignore. Furthermore, despite its counterintuitiveness, perverse inconsistency does have a rationale (and so could more accurately be termed *apparently perverse inconsistency*). That there must be such a rationale is evident from the fact that the writings of G. I. Gurdjieff, a spiritual teacher who worked in the first half of the twentieth century,[26] are full of inconsistencies that are clearly intentional but have no obvious explanation. Like the inconsistencies in the poems of Homer, the inconsistencies in the writings of Gurdjieff generally go unnoticed by the casual reader and do not affect the reader's engagement with the material, which gives the impression of great unity. The combination of inconsistency and unity in Gurdjieff's books recalls the paradox described at the beginning of this chapter. In the case of Gurdjieff, however, there is no paradox, as the inconsistencies were certainly created intentionally by the same author who was responsible for the overall unity. Perverse inconsistency may also be the key to resolving the paradox in the case of Homer.

Gurdjieff's use of inconsistency in his writings can be understood in terms of his concept of *objective art*. Objective art is the only art that he regards as authentic. It is largely, although not entirely, a phenomenon of the distant past. In this kind of art, the artist may make use of inconsistencies to provoke certain experiences in the viewer, experiences which (for the viewer able to understand them) communicate ideas or feelings that are too subtle to be transmitted by ordinary means, as, for instance, by narratives using words whose precise meaning varies from one person to another and hence is subjective.

It follows from the ideas of Gurdjieff to be explained in chapter 9 that the most fundamental question we can ask about Homer is whether the *Iliad* and the *Odyssey* are works of objective art. Gurdjieff himself thought that they are. I say this because, although he never mentions Homer, he alludes to the *Odyssey* in his *Meetings with Remarkable Men*, and he would not do this unless he considered the *Odyssey* to be a work of objective art. (I shall be arguing that his allusions to the *Odyssey* are intended to be taken as allusions to the Homeric corpus as a whole.) If correct, Gurdjieff's assessment would do more than explain the origin of apparently perverse inconsistencies in the Homeric epics: it would also throw an entirely new light on the poet himself. For objective art, Gurdjieff tells us, can be created only by someone who has achieved an inner unity that is not possessed by an ordinary person. Thus, Gurdjieff's answer to the Homeric Question is more unitarian than that of the unitarians. It is ironic indeed that such an answer should be motivated by the inconsistencies which fueled the efforts of the analysts for so long.

Chapter 5

The Relationship between the *Iliad* and the *Odyssey*

The literature on Homer contains a number of excellent observations concerning the relationship between the *Iliad* and the *Odyssey*.[1] In this chapter I venture to suggest that this relationship is even deeper and more sophisticated than has previously been supposed. The most striking aspect of the relationship is the existence of perverse inconsistency between the poems, inconsistency introduced by the poet apparently for its own sake. In the next chapter I show that perverse inconsistencies are also found in each poem considered by itself. Thus, perverse inconsistency is a property of the Homeric corpus as a whole, not merely an aspect of the relationship between the two Homeric epics. In this chapter and the next I seek only to document this counterintuitive phenomenon, not to explain it. In chapter 7 I begin a line of reasoning that leads, in chapter 9, to a possible rationale for perverse inconsistency in terms of Gurdjieff's concept of objective art.

Our investigation of the relationship between the two poems of Homer focuses on the parts of the *Odyssey* which have a particularly strong connection with the *Iliad*: the passages in which the protagonist of the *Iliad* plays an active role and the passages that remind one of an Iliadic battle scene. For these parts of the *Odyssey* to be intentionally inconsistent with the *Iliad*, the latter must have been composed before the former. The priority of the *Iliad* is, in fact, accepted by a majority of Homeric scholars,[2] and for good reasons. In the opening section of this chapter, I quickly review the principal reasons for this conclusion and then discuss in detail a specimen from one line of evidence. In addition to making the priority of the *Iliad* plausible to the general reader, this discussion prepares the way for a first look at intentional inconsistency in Homer.

5.1. The Priority of the *Iliad*

Since the story of Odysseus's return home from the Trojan War presupposes the existence of a story of the war itself, it is natural to assume that the *Odyssey* was composed after the *Iliad*. A later date for the *Odyssey* seems even more likely when we realize that it serves as an effective sequel to the *Iliad*, telling us not only how the war was eventually won by means of Odysseus's

5.1. THE PRIORITY OF THE *ILIAD*

stratagem of the Wooden Horse, but also what happened to all the major Greek characters of the *Iliad* who were alive at the end of the poem (Achilles, Agamemnon, Menelaos, Helen, both Aiases, Nestor, Antilochos, Diomedes, and Idomeneus, not to mention Odysseus) as well as to the bones of the only one who had been killed (Patroklos).[3] A (slightly) later date for the *Odyssey* is also indicated by linguistic comparison of the two poems.[4] Furthermore, apparent allusions to the *Iliad* can be found in the *Odyssey*.[5] Finally, the *Iliad* and the *Odyssey* share a number of verses that are perfectly appropriate in the *Iliad* but are less well suited to their Odyssean contexts; the natural assumption is that these verses were composed by the poet of the *Iliad* and borrowed by the poet of the *Odyssey*.[6] The present section describes a well-known specimen from this last line of evidence in preparation for a first look at intentional inconsistency.

The Greeks dominate the Trojans on the first day of battle described in the *Iliad*. Although Achilles is absent from the fighting, the formidable Diomedes has risen to the occasion and has essentially taken his place. In desperation, Hektor rallies his troops and then goes back to the city to tell his mother to make appeals to the goddess Athene. Before returning to battle, he goes to his house to see his wife Andromache and their baby boy. But they are not at home: alarmed by news of the Greek onslaught, Andromache has rushed to the gate of the city from which she can watch the events that will determine the future of her family. This is the same gate through which Hektor must pass to rejoin the fighting, and when he gets there, the family is united in a famously touching scene. Husband and wife share their fears of the expected fall of Troy, death of Hektor, and enslavement of Andromache, although the sexual aspect of Andromache's enslavement goes unmentioned and the probable fate of their son is also too painful to be confronted. Hektor's last words to Andromache are:

> "Go therefore back to our house, and take up your own work,
> the loom and the distaff, and see to it that your handmaidens
> ply their work also; but the men must see to the fighting,
> all men who are the people of Ilion, but I beyond others."
>
> Quote 5.1: *Il.* 6.490–493

Perhaps an attempt at normalcy, working with the loom and the distaff, will give his wife a measure of calm and a sense of continued communion with the husband who gave her this instruction. When Andromache returns home, she is joined by her handmaidens in lamentation over the anticipated death of Hektor. When we see her next, however, she is indeed working at the loom.[7] But the sound of shrieks and groans causes her to drop her work and to run frantically to the wall of the city, from which she sees, on the plain below, the body of her husband being dragged behind the chariot of Achilles.

The *Odyssey* contains two passages with a strong resemblance to quote 5.1:

> "Go therefore back in the house, and take up your own work,
> the loom and the distaff, and see to it that your handmaidens
> ply their work also; but the men must see to discussion,
> all men, but I most of all. For mine is the power in this household."
>
> Quote 5.2: *Od.* 1.356–359

"Go therefore back into the house, and take up your own work,
the loom and the distaff, and see to it that your handmaidens
ply their work also; but the men must see to the bow,
all men, but I most of all. For mine is the power in this household."
                Quote 5.3: *Od.* 21.350–353 (modified from Lattimore[8])

We can ignore the slight variability of the first half-line of quotes 5.1–5.3 since it is an artifact of translation (the underlying Greek is the same in all three cases). Quotes 5.2 and 5.3 are then identical except for the ending of the third line ("discussion" vs. "the bow"). In the Iliadic passage, quote 5.1, "discussion" of quote 5.2 and "the bow" of quote 5.3 are replaced by "the fighting," but the agreement with the Odyssean passages is otherwise perfect until we reach the middle of the last line (the phrase of *Il.* 6.493 that has no parallel in the Odyssean passages ["who are the people of Ilion"] occurs at the end of the Greek line where in the Odyssean passages is found the clause ["For mine is the power in this household"] that has no parallel in the Iliadic passage). It is unlikely that the detailed agreement between the Iliadic and Odyssean passages covering multiple unrelated concepts (going back to the house; working with the loom and the distaff; the province of men; the uniqueness of the speaker in relation to other men) can be explained by Homer's use of set phrases ("formulas") and type scenes.[9] We must conclude that the *Odyssey* is quoting the *Iliad* or vice versa. In fact, it is easy to ascertain which is quoting which.

As years have gone by since the end of the Trojan War and it has seemed increasingly likely that Odysseus would not be coming home, his wife Penelope has become besieged with more than a hundred unwelcome suitors who treat the palace of Odysseus as their own and feast on his livestock on a regular basis. For three years Penelope has put off the suitors by means of a ruse, weaving a shroud for her father-in-law Laertes during the day but undoing the work at night in order to prolong the task she says she must complete before she can remarry. But the suitors have recently learned of the trick and forced Penelope to finish the shroud,[10] so it seems that the time is not far off when she will have to choose one of them. Adding to the pressure is the fact that Telemachos, the son of Penelope and Odysseus born shortly before the latter's departure for Troy twenty years ago, is now reaching manhood. He bitterly resents that the suitors are consuming his inheritance, but is powerless to do anything about it. This is the context in which we must consider quotes 5.2 and 5.3, for in both passages Telemachos is addressing his mother in the presence of the suitors.

As we read quotes 5.2 and 5.3 in conjunction with quote 5.1, we repeatedly find that what is quite appropriate in the passage from the *Iliad* seems somewhat suspect or even entirely out of place in the passages from the *Odyssey*. Thus, the first half-line of quote 5.1, "Go therefore back to our house," is perfectly natural since Andromache left the house to view the battle from the Skaian gates, where Hektor met up with her and spoke these words as their encounter was drawing to a close. But the first half-line of quotes 5.2 and 5.3, "Go therefore back in/into the house," is a little disturbing since Penelope was already in the house![11] There may actually be no problem here, because the word that Lattimore translates as "house" can sometimes mean a part of a house[12] and in quotes 5.2 and 5.3 may refer to Penelope's quarters.[13] Indeed, this solution is adopted in some translations. Nevertheless, there is at least a certain tension, because, as mentioned above, the first half-line of quotes 5.2 and 5.3 is identical in the Greek to the first half-line of quote 5.1.

Similarly, it is perfectly natural for Hektor to tell Andromache to take up her work with the loom and the distaff as a means of keeping her occupied for her own peace of mind when everything she holds dear is threatened by forces beyond her control. But what inevitably comes to mind when one thinks of Penelope in the context of weaving is how she tricked the suitors with her ruse of the shroud for Laertes.[14] This is also very much on the mind of the suitors: when Telemachos airs his grievances against them at a public assembly, one of their leaders deflects blame by recounting the story of Penelope's ruse; after the suitors have been slaughtered by Odysseus, the shade of one of them tells the same story almost as if the suitors had been victimized by Penelope. Accordingly, one would think that Telemachos commits a glaring faux pas and risks rousing the ire of the suitors by bringing up his mother's weaving in their presence.

Next, no one in the *Iliad* would disagree with Hektor's statement in quote 5.1 that "the men must see to the fighting." On the other hand, Telemachos's assertion in quote 5.2 that "the men must see to discussion" is contrary to Homeric custom,[15] for Helen and Arete, women of Penelope's status, are full participants in the conversation elsewhere in the *Odyssey*.[16] His assertion in quote 5.3 that "the men must see to the bow" is also difficult to justify since it is Penelope who brings the bow of Odysseus to the suitors and specifies how it is to be used to determine whom she will marry.[17] These questionable claims by Telemachos are just the beginning of remarks that are totally unsuited to the circumstances in which he finds himself. For comparison, I shall once again begin with the contrasting situation of Hektor.

When Hektor says that "the men must see to the fighting, all men who are the people of Ilion, but I beyond others," he affirms his solidarity with the other men of Troy, but at the same time sets himself apart from them. The solidarity with the other men and the uniqueness of Hektor are both real: the other men are allied with Hektor in the war, but, as the mightiest warrior of Troy, he is looked up to as its chief defender.[18] By contrast, Telemachos's statement that "the men must see to discussion [quote 5.2]/the bow [quote 5.3], all men, but I most of all. For mine is the power in this household" is divorced from reality in relation to two corresponding considerations. First, the gratuitous amplification "all men" includes the suitors since they make up the majority of those present. Why should Telemachos align himself with them? After all, the suitors are his enemies, usurping his household in open defiance of his wishes. Second, although he claims that "mine is the power in this household," it is precisely because of his *lack* of power that the suitors have been able to take over.

It could be argued that one should be more forgiving in the analysis of quote 5.3. In that passage Telemachos is simply trying to remove his mother from the scene where he knows that violent combat is imminent, and he will evidently say whatever is necessary to accomplish this goal most expeditiously. Indeed, this may be one reason that Aristarchus, the most distinguished Homeric scholar of antiquity, spared quote 5.3 at the same time that he cast doubt on the authenticity of quote 5.2.[19] But quote 5.3 is not well designed even for its intended purpose. A number of the suitors, including one of their leaders, have already shown themselves incapable of stringing Odysseus's bow, the first feat that Penelope requires of the man who will win her hand; the task looks so daunting that the suitors have decided not to make any more attempts until the next day. By bringing up Penelope's weaving, and thereby recalling her ruse of the shroud for Laertes, Telemachos opens the way for the suitors to charge that the contest of the bow is another trick she has devised to put off her marriage; it is fortunate that they do not take advantage of this opportunity, since otherwise Penelope would have to delay her departure from the scene in order to deny the charge.

Even if we are indulgent in our interpretation of some of the incongruities in quotes 5.2 and 5.3, there are so many of them, and some of them are so blatant, that we cannot possibly believe that these passages were created from scratch for their respective contexts in the *Odyssey*. Quote 5.1, by contrast, forms an ideal ending, fitting in every respect, to the meeting of Hektor and Andromache at the Skaian gates. The only reasonable conclusion is that quote 5.1 was composed expressly for this scene, while quotes 5.2 and 5.3 were based on this Iliadic model.[20] Thus, the *Odyssey* quotes the *Iliad* and must be the later of the two poems.

5.2. Comprehensible Inconsistency in the *Odyssey*

Before proceeding to the heart of this chapter, I wish to dwell a little longer on the two passages from the *Odyssey* discussed in the preceding section. The following discussion of these passages sheds no direct light on the relationship between the *Iliad* and the *Odyssey*, but it provides a gentle introduction to a phenomenon that plays a crucial role in the next section and in parts of chapter 6 as well: the repetition of distinctive patterns of apparently intentional inconsistency in Homer. I call this introduction "gentle" because the inconsistencies I am about to describe, unlike most of the inconsistencies discussed in this book, are comprehensible rather than perverse, which is to say that they are well motivated from an ordinary point of view.

We have seen that two almost identical passages in the *Odyssey*, quotes 5.2 and 5.3, are unsuited to their context in the poem. We now focus on one of the anomalies associated with these passages, the contradiction between the concluding assertion of Telemachos that "mine is the power in this household" and the reality that the unwelcome suitors of his mother have been able to take over the household because he does not have the power to resist them. This reality is a recurrent theme for which extensive documentation would be superfluous. What is interesting, however, is that the powerlessness of Telemachos is given special expression by Telemachos himself shortly after each of the two passages in which he claims to possess the power in the household.

After Telemachos speaks to his mother in quote 5.2, he addresses the suitors as follows:

"... tomorrow let us all go to the place of assembly,
and hold a session, where I will give you my forthright statement,
that you go out of my palace and do your feasting elsewhere,
eating up your own possessions, taking turns, household by household.
But if you decide it is more profitable and better
to go on, eating up one man's livelihood, without payment,
then spoil my house. I will cry out to the gods everlasting
in the hope that Zeus might somehow grant a reversal of fortunes.
Then you may perish in this house, with no payment given."

Quote 5.4: *Od.* 1.372–380

In other words, Telemachos will argue in a public forum that the suitors should leave his household, but he recognizes that the decision is in their hands. If they reject his plea, the only recourse open to him will be to beg the gods to intervene. These admissions are not what we would expect from someone who has just declared that he wields the power in his household. And in fact the contradiction is made explicit shortly afterwards, when Telemachos, responding to a suitor's surprised reaction to quote 5.4, voices his determination to become the master of his own household.[21]

After the suitors put off further attempts to string the bow in Penelope's contest and Telemachos concludes his speech to his mother with quote 5.3, the loyal swineherd begins to carry the bow to the disguised Odysseus so that he can try to string it, as he has requested.[22] Strong objections from the suitors cause the swineherd to put back the bow in fear, but Telemachos good-naturedly orders him to continue:

"Keep on with the bow, old fellow. You cannot do what everyone
tells you. Take care, or, younger though I am, I might chase you
out to the fields with a shower of stones. I am stronger than you are.
I only wish I were as much stronger, and more of a fighter
with my hands, than all these suitors who are here in my household.
So I could hatefully speed any man of them on his journey
out of our house, where they are contriving evils against us."

Quote 5.5: *Od.* 21.369–375

Here again, shortly after claiming that he holds the power in his household, Telemachos contradicts himself by highlighting his helplessness: although he is strong, he does not have the strength that would be required to expel the suitors.[23] Apart from the question of strength, of course, the implicit acknowledgment that the suitors could be removed only by force underlines the fact that they are in his household against his will.

The proximity of the contradictory passages is worth emphasizing: only 12 lines separate the beginning of quote 5.4 from the end of quote 5.2, and only 15 lines separate the beginning of quote 5.5 from the end of quote 5.3. The intervals of interest are actually even shorter, since quotes 5.2 and 5.3 are immediately followed by identical passages of fives lines describing Penelope's reaction to the words of her son.[24] Thus, the special expressions of the powerlessness of Telemachos in quotes 5.4 and 5.5 are closely associated with his perplexing claim of power at the end of quotes 5.2 and 5.3. Homer apparently goes out of his way to create the same juxtaposition twice.

One's impression that Homer goes out of his way to juxtapose an expression of the powerlessness of Telemachos with each of the latter's assertions that he holds the power in his household is reinforced by the fact that quote 5.4 itself constitutes an anomaly that calls for an explanation. The *Odyssey* opens with a council of the gods in which Athene urges that steps be taken to facilitate the long-delayed homecoming of Odysseus. She gives herself the mission of going to Ithaka to raise the spirit of Telemachos and to give him certain instructions.[25] His execution of her instructions is described in books 2–4. At the beginning of book 2, for example, he carries out her instruction to call an assembly of the Ithakans and to tell the suitors in this public forum to leave his palace.[26] But there is one respect in which Telemachos deviates from the instructions given by Athene: he gives the suitors advance notice of his intention to call the assembly and to tell them to leave, and he even gives them a preview of a crucial part of the speech that he will deliver at the assembly the next day.[27] This departure from Athene's instructions, which he otherwise executes quite faithfully, is what we see in quote 5.4. While other explanations have been proposed[28] and cannot be ruled out, the fact that this anomalous passage serves the same function in relation to quote 5.2 that quote 5.5 serves in relation to quote 5.3 raises the possibility that Telemachos's sole deviation from Athene's instructions is introduced specifically for the purpose of this duplication.

Regardless of the validity of this interpretation, the existence of two contradictions that are closely related in both form and content is a strong indication that they are intentional and not the result of Homer nodding. Unlike other intentional inconsistencies discussed in this book, these two make sense in terms of the story line of the poem, as I shall now explain.

When we first see him in the *Odyssey*, Telemachos understandably feels disheartened and helpless, with his home overrun by a crowd of insolent men who are always feasting at his expense and courting his mother against her wishes. Athene, disguised as a mortal, pays him a visit and gives a long speech in which she encourages him to be bold and to take steps to expel the suitors and assume his rightful position in the household.[29] We are told that her visit has the intended effect on him—"she left in his spirit determination and courage"[30]—and we see this effect almost immediately after her departure as he asserts himself for the first time. His assertiveness is initially directed not at the suitors but at his mother, whom he addresses sternly in a speech that concludes with quote 5.2 and his declaration that "mine is the power in this household." After he has dismissed his amazed mother from the hall, he announces to the suitors in quote 5.4 that he intends to confront them the next day in a public assembly, and they are amazed by his new daring and spirit. As noted at the beginning of this section, his announcement acknowledges the reality of his powerlessness and therefore contradicts his claim that "mine is the power in this household." The contradiction is perfectly understandable, however, as his unrealistic claim of power is merely a clumsy expression of the boldness that he now feels for the first time thanks to the influence of Athene.

The psychological state of Telemachos is entirely different the next time he declares to his mother that "mine is the power in this household" (quote

5.3). During the interval, he has gained experience and self-confidence from his travels to Nestor and Menelaos in search of news of his father, and he has gained a powerful ally against the suitors with the return of Odysseus to Ithaka. Now when he says that "mine is the power in this household," it is no longer an awkward, emotionally driven assertion of his rightful position, but a statement calculated to help get the bow to his father and thereby to advance his father's plan for the destruction of the suitors. And when he goes on to contradict himself by highlighting his helplessness (quote 5.5), he is actually deflecting attention from the fact that he is defying the suitors by telling the swineherd to take the bow to the disguised Odysseus.

Thus, the two inconsistencies discussed in this section both make sense, one (between quotes 5.2 and 5.4) from a psychological standpoint and the other (between quotes 5.3 and 5.5) from the standpoint of strategy. These inconsistencies are comprehensible, not perverse. Moreover, they make sense not only individually but also as a pair since comparison of the two highlights the change in the psychological state of Telemachos over the course of the poem.

Although the self-contradictions of Telemachos do not contribute directly to the case I shall be making for perverse inconsistency in Homer, they do contribute indirectly as a precedent for inferring the intentionality of inconsistencies that form a matching pair. This is one of the methods I shall use to argue for the intentionality of inconsistencies that are clearly perverse if they are intentional. In fact, this method is applied in the next section to a set of three analogous inconsistencies. Before turning to this application, however, I argue that a departure from the pattern described in the present section is harmless and has no bearing on the proposed approach.

Referring to Odysseus, who has stopped in the middle of the account of his adventures to ask to be allowed to sleep and to remind his Phaiakian hosts that he is relying on them for conveyance home, King Alkinoös makes the following pronouncement:

"But let our guest, much though he longs for the homeward journey,
still endure to wait till tomorrow, until I have raised all
the contribution; but the men must see to his convoy home,
all men, but I most of all. For mine is the power in this district."
Quote 5.6: *Od.* 11.350–353 (modified from Lattimore[31])

There is a clear correspondence between the last two lines of this passage and those of quotes 5.2 and 5.3, as is well known.[32] Furthermore, Alkinoös, like Telemachos, does not actually wield the power he claims.[33] It may therefore be disturbing that the pattern observed earlier in this section is not sustained: quotes 5.4 and 5.5, the passages following quotes 5.2 and 5.3 in which Telemachos expresses his powerlessness, have no analogue in the case of Alkinoös. However, the situations of Alkinoös and Telemachos are fundamentally different even though neither man possesses the power he claims to have. The power that rightfully belongs to Telemachos has been usurped by ruffians who threaten his livelihood and even his life; on the other hand, the power that ordinarily would belong to Alkinoös, the king, is exercised benevolently by Arete, his queen, in a way that enhances the welfare of his people and the stature of his court. Telemachos is desperate for change and therefore stresses the injustice of his situation; Alkinoös, by contrast, holds his wife in great esteem, realizes that the status quo is best for everyone, and therefore has no wish to call attention to his relatively subservient position. The absence of a Phaiakian analogue to quotes 5.4 and 5.5 is thus to be expected, and in no way weakens the case for intentionality of the inconsistencies associated with these passages.

5.3. Achilles in the *Odyssey*

We now get to the main business of this chapter. In this section I discuss the three passages in the *Odyssey* in which Achilles, the protagonist of the *Iliad*, plays an active role. I discuss these passages together in one section because they all share a certain complex relationship with the *Iliad*, one aspect of which is apparently perverse inconsistency.

(*a*) The Conversation between the Shades of Achilles and Agamemnon

The last passage in the *Odyssey* in which Achilles appears recounts the conversation that takes place in the underworld between his shade and that of Agamemnon.[34] In section 3.3 I referred to well-known allusions to the *Iliad* in the excerpt from that conversation reproduced in quote 3.10.[35] It is fair to say on the basis of those allusions that the conversation reported in the *Odyssey* exhibits an awareness of the *Iliad*. What is strange is that the same conversation also seems to deny the very existence of the earlier epic.

If Achilles humiliates Agamemnon in the spear-throwing event of the funeral games for Patroklos, as argued in chapter 3, it is clear that the two are never reconciled after the Quarrel and remain bitter enemies to the end of the *Iliad*. But the conversation between their shades near the end of the *Odyssey*, the only interaction between Achilles and Agamemnon after the spear-throwing event that is recorded in Homer, is perfectly cordial, showing both respect and sympathy. In quote 3.9, for example, Agamemnon dwells on how dear Achilles was to the gods. He then goes on to declare the everlasting glory of Achilles among men:

> "even now you have died, you have not lost your name, but always
> in the sight of all mankind your fame shall be great, Achilleus;"
>
> Quote 5.7: *Od.* 24.93–94

Agamemnon also praises Achilles implicitly in his description of the struggle with the Trojans over his corpse and of the grief over his death among both gods and men. Achilles, for his part, appears to express genuine sympathy for Agamemnon's pitiful death at the hands of his wife's lover. He also emphasizes the respect accorded to Agamemnon during his life:

> "Son of Atreus, we thought that all your days you were favored
> beyond all other heroes by Zeus who delights in the thunder,
> because you were lord over numerous people, and strong ones,
> in the land of the Trojans, where we Achaians suffered hardships."
>
> Quote 5.8: *Od.* 24.24–27

Even apart from its friendly tone, this passage is striking when we think back to the Quarrel, for it was precisely Agamemnon's position as supreme commander at Troy that gave him the power and, in his opinion, the right to confiscate Achilles' prize. Nestor made reference to this in his attempt to placate the two adversaries. To Achilles he said,

> "... [Do not] think to match your strength with
> the king, since never equal with the rest is the portion of honor
> of the sceptred king to whom Zeus gives magnificence. Even
> though you are the stronger man, and the mother who bore you was
>   immortal,
> yet is this man greater who is lord over more than you rule."
>
> Quote 5.9: *Il.* 1.277–281

When speaking to Agamemnon in the underworld (quote 5.8), Achilles affirms the principle articulated by Nestor in the last line of this passage, the very principle he flouted by standing up to Agamemnon in the Quarrel. Thus, in their conversation in the underworld that Homer relates in the last book of the *Odyssey*, both Agamemnon and Achilles speak as if the quarrel between them in the first book of the *Iliad* had never taken place.

Citing quote 5.8, but referring to the entire conversation between the shades of Achilles and Agamemnon, one commentator observes, "It is tempting to look for irony in this exchange between Agamemnon and Achilleus, but both appear to speak with great politeness towards each other."[36] Another remarks, "The very friendly conversation between Agamemnon and Achilles comes as a considerable surprise, or should, to anyone who knows the *Iliad*. In that poem Achilles and Agamemnon can scarcely tolerate one another, exchange some extremely bitter insults, and are never reconciled."[37] One possible explanation is that the pettiness of earthly grudges dissipates in the hopelessness of the underworld, but this is ruled out by the interaction between Odysseus and the shade of Aias, who continues to harbor resentment over his loss of the arms of Achilles.[38] Another possibility is that Agamemnon's overweening pride, which has always stood in the way of his reconciliation with Achilles, has finally been extinguished by the pitiful circumstances of his death. But if this were so, his humiliation by Achilles in the funeral games for Patroklos would no longer be so painful that he could not bear to mention these games when the context of the conversation in question practically demanded that they be mentioned (see section 3.3). In any case, it is Achilles, not Agamemnon, who begins this conversation, and he begins it with the surprisingly friendly words reproduced in quote 5.8.

In principle it would be possible to solve this problem by supposing that Achilles and Agamemnon become reconciled between the time frame of the *Iliad* and that of the *Odyssey*. In fact, support for this idea can be found in the surviving summary of the *Returns* (one of the poems of the Epic Cycle), according to which "when Agamemnon's party is preparing to sail [home after the sack of Troy], Achilles' ghost appears and tries to prevent them by foretelling what will happen."[39] But the warning of Agamemnon by the ghost of Achilles is never mentioned in the *Odyssey*, despite the fact that his murder by Aigisthos upon his return home is recalled many times in that poem, with details provided on the background of the murder, its aftermath, and the murder itself.[40] Furthermore, the *Odyssey* says specifically that Agamemnon suspects nothing when he reaches his homeland and is invited to a feast by Aigisthos.[41] This shows that Homer did not consider Agamemnon to have been warned by the ghost of Achilles,[42] negating the support from the *Returns* for the hypothetical solution to the problem in the *Odyssey*.

I think we must conclude that the underworld conversation between Achilles and Agamemnon simply ignores the Quarrel. Furthermore, it makes a point of ignoring the Quarrel by having Achilles acknowledge the basis for Agamemnon's former claim to superiority (quote 5.8). In so doing, it pointedly ignores the *Iliad* itself, for the Quarrel is the foundation of the entire epic. This apparent denial of the existence of the *Iliad* is the first of two strange properties that are shared by all three passages that I discuss in this section. The other is that the apparent denial of the *Iliad* is combined in the same passage with an affirmation of that poem; in the case of the underworld conversation between Achilles and Agamemnon, the affirmation of the *Iliad* is accomplished by the allusions mentioned at the beginning of this subsection.[43] We shall now identify these properties in the first passage of the *Odyssey* in which Achilles plays an important role, Homer's much-discussed account of a song sung by the Phaiakian bard Demodokos.

(b) The First Song of Demodokos

During the course of a day of entertainment provided by his Phaiakian hosts shortly before they facilitate the last leg of his journey home to Ithaka after the Trojan War, Odysseus hears three songs sung by Demodokos. The first and last songs deal with events associated with the war, while the middle song is a comedy revolving around an adulterous affair between the god of war (Ares) and the goddess of love (Aphrodite).[44] The first song concerns a quarrel between Achilles and Odysseus. Homer's account of this song is the shortest of the three and goes as follows:

> [T]he Muse stirred the singer to sing the famous actions
> of men on that venture, whose fame goes up into the wide heaven,
> the quarrel between Odysseus and Peleus' son, Achilleus,
> how these once contended, at the gods' generous festival,
> with words of violence, so that the lord of men, Agamemnon,
> was happy in his heart that the best of the Achaians were quarreling;
> for so in prophecy Phoibos Apollo had spoken to him
> in sacred Pytho, when he had stepped across the stone doorstep
> to consult; for now the beginning of evil rolled on, descending
> on Trojans, and on Danaäns, through the designs of great Zeus.
>
> Quote 5.10: *Od.* 8.73–82

This passage refers to a violent quarrel between Odysseus and Achilles that is said to be famous.[45] However, this quarrel is mentioned nowhere else in the *Odyssey*, nowhere at all in the *Iliad*, and nowhere in any of the other literature that has survived from ancient Greece.[46] By ignoring the quarrel that really is famous, the quarrel between Achilles and Agamemnon that forms the foundation of the *Iliad*, the first song of Demodokos seems almost to deny the existence of the earlier poem. This impression is strengthened upon further

5.3. ACHILLES IN THE *ODYSSEY*

scrutiny, for it will become clear that the quarrel mentioned in quote 5.10 is difficult to reconcile with the *Iliad*.

The quarrel between Achilles and Odysseus is said to have caused Agamemnon to rejoice because it fulfilled Apollo's prophecy of a quarrel between the best of the Achaians (which presumably was a good omen). It follows that the quarrel between Achilles and Odysseus occurred, if it occurred at all, before the quarrel between Achilles and Agamemnon; otherwise, Agamemnon would have taken the latter quarrel to be the fulfillment of the prophecy,[47] inasmuch as he considered himself "the best of the Achaians."[48] Even if he did not immediately connect his own quarrel with Apollo's prophecy, he would surely have made the connection shortly afterwards, when he received another divine prophecy of victory in the form of a dream sent by Zeus (which I discuss below).[49] Of course, one might argue that Agamemnon does not remember the prophecy at the time of his quarrel with Achilles simply because he consulted the oracle at Pytho (Delphi[50]) so long ago, presumably just before he went to Troy. But since he does remember the prophecy at the time of the supposed quarrel between Achilles and Odysseus, we are still forced to conclude that the latter quarrel occurred first.

A violent quarrel between Achilles and Odysseus that precedes the quarrel between Achilles and Agamemnon and therefore the time frame of the *Iliad* would appear to be inconsistent with the Embassy scene, the scene in which Odysseus and his fellow ambassadors visit Achilles to plead for his return to battle. It would be difficult to understand, first of all, how Nestor could select Odysseus to be one of the ambassadors on this delicate mission[51] and how Odysseus could agree to participate in a mission that could be jeopardized by any lingering hostility between Achilles and himself. It would also be difficult to understand how Achilles could greet the ambassadors in the warmest possible terms:

> "Welcome. You are my friends who have come, and greatly I need you,
> who even to this my anger are dearest of all the Achaians."
> So brilliant Achilleus spoke, and guided them forward,
> and caused them to sit down on couches with purple coverlets
> and at once called over to Patroklos who was not far from him:
> "Son of Menoitios, set up a mixing-bowl that is bigger,
> and mix us stronger drink, and make ready a cup for each man,
> since these who have come beneath my roof are the men that I love best."
>
> Quote 5.11: *Il.* 9.197–204

The sincerity of Achilles cannot be doubted, not only because of his forthright nature, but also because the sentiment he expresses in the last line of this passage is corroborated by one of the ambassadors.[52] It is possible, of course, since the supposed quarrel between Achilles and Odysseus may have occurred a long time ago, that good relations between the two men have subsequently been restored. But surely the reconciliation would be mentioned in order to explain how Odysseus could serve as ambassador to Achilles after the two had famously quarreled. Regardless, by having Demodokos sing about a quarrel that is difficult to reconcile with the *Iliad*, Homer intensifies one's impression that the very existence of the *Iliad* is being denied.

Here a digression is necessary to address the belief of some scholars that the Embassy scene contains evidence of hostility between Achilles and Odysseus, a hostility that would go some way towards reconciling this scene with the first song of Demodokos. The alleged evidence is found in Achilles' response to the speech in which Odysseus tries to persuade him to return to the fighting, the first of the speeches by the three ambassadors. Achilles begins his reply as follows:

> "Son of Laertes and seed of Zeus, resourceful Odysseus:
> without consideration for you I must make my answer,
> the way I think, and the way it will be accomplished, that you may not
> come one after another, and sit by me, and speak softly.
> **For as I detest the doorways of Death, I detest that man, who**
> **hides one thing in the depths of his heart, and speaks forth another.**
> But I will speak to you the way it seems best to me: neither
> do I think the son of Atreus, Agamemnon, will persuade me,
> nor the rest of the Danaäns, since there was no gratitude given
> for fighting incessantly forever against your enemies."
> <div align="right">Quote 5.12: <i>Il.</i> 9.308–317 (boldface added)</div>

In his appeal to Achilles, as I mentioned in section 3.1, Odysseus accurately reports the magnificent gifts that Agamemnon is offering for Achilles' return, but he wisely leaves out Agamemnon's demand for Achilles' submission. It is claimed by some that Achilles somehow detects a lack of complete candor and is referring to Odysseus in the part of quote 5.12 that I have put in boldface.[53] If one accepts this interpretation, it is easy to sense in those two lines a vehemence possibly indicative of a long-standing hostility. However, I believe that those lines cannot refer to Odysseus for two reasons: (*a*) they are not a reasonable response to his speech as a whole and (*b*) more plausible interpretations can be (and have been) proposed. Let us consider these points in turn.

Although Odysseus deliberately leaves out of his speech Agamemnon's demand for Achilles' submission, he is perfectly candid in communicating his own thoughts. After relaying Agamemnon's lengthy offer of gifts, he concludes his speech as follows:

> "But if the son of Atreus is too much hated in your heart,
> himself and his gifts, at least take pity on all the other
> Achaians, who are afflicted along the host, and will honor you
> as a god. You may win very great glory among them.
> For now you might kill Hektor, since he would come very close to you
> with the wicked fury upon him, since he thinks there is not his equal
> among the rest of the Danaäns the ships carried hither."
> <div align="right">Quote 5.13: <i>Il.</i> 9.300–306</div>

By acknowledging that Achilles' hatred for Agamemnon may be such that he will spurn the gifts, Odysseus signals that he is here expressing his own views. (The possibility that these concluding appeals were first suggested by Nestor [see *Il.* 9.179–181] does not mean that they are not endorsed and put forward sincerely by Odysseus.) Given his evident forthrightness, Achilles has no reason to accuse him of hiding one thing "in the depths of his heart" and saying another.

A more plausible interpretation is that it is Agamemnon whom Achilles is accusing of being two-faced. The offer of gifts is more than generous, but it comes with no apology. It is evident to Achilles that Agamemnon continues to harbor only animosity towards him and feels no remorse for the dishonor he has done to his greatest warrior. Achilles can only assume that Agamemnon is hiding his true feelings behind the extravagant offer of material goods, an offer that comes easily to him as it displays his wealth and, if accepted, will demonstrate his dominance while securing Achilles' return to the fighting.

Another plausible interpretation is that Achilles is not referring in the boldfaced part of quote 5.12 to either Odysseus or Agamemnon, but is expressing the principle of forthrightness that will guide his response to Odysseus's speech. This explanation shares with the previous one the advantage that it does not attribute to Achilles an uncanny ability to detect the omission of something (Agamemnon's demand for his submission) that one would not even have expected. It has the additional advantage of affirming the continuity of Achilles' thought. This can be seen in Lattimore's translation given in quote 5.12, but is even more apparent in the prose translation of Murray:

> "Zeus-born son of Laertes, Odysseus of many wiles, I must speak my words outright, exactly as I think, and as it will come to pass, so that you will not sit by me here on this side and on that and prate endlessly. **For hateful in my eyes as the gates of Hades is that man who hides one thing in his mind and says another.** So I will speak what seems to me to be best. Not me, I think, will Atreus' son, Agamemnon, persuade, nor yet will the other Danaäns, since it is clear there was to be no thanks for warring against the foe without respite."
>
> Quote 5.14: *Il.* 9.308–317 (Murray trans.; boldface added)

Both before and after the words that some interpret as a reference to Odysseus's speech (words here shown again in boldface), Achilles describes how he intends to respond. The simplest interpretation of the intervening words is that they refer to the same thing, and indeed they can be read as a fitting elaboration of Achilles' initial statement that "I must speak my words outright, exactly as I think." It is only at the end of this passage ("it is clear there was to be no thanks for warring against the foe without respite") that Achilles begins to address the contents of Odysseus's speech.

The literature contains a variety of views on which interpretation of *Il.* 9.312–313 (the boldfaced part of quote 5.12 or 5.14), or which combination of interpretations, is most plausible.[54] For the reasons given in this digression, I reject the interpretation that these lines refer to Odysseus. The Embassy scene then contains no suggestion of hostility between him and Achilles, and there is no reason to question either the selection of Odysseus as one of the ambassadors or the warm welcome from Achilles in quote 5.11.[55, 56] All this is difficult to reconcile with a violent quarrel between Achilles and Odysseus that precedes the time frame of the *Iliad*. The song of Demodokos that presupposes such a quarrel and, what is more, elevates this quarrel to legendary status while ignoring the quarrel between Achilles and Agamemnon effectively ignores the *Iliad* itself.

Having considered the apparent denial of the *Iliad* by the first song of Demodokos, we now turn to the other side of the coin: the affirmation of the *Iliad* by means of certain allusions in the same passage that appears to deny it.

It is widely accepted that the first song of Demodokos alludes to the beginning of the *Iliad*.[57] For example, one commentator says, "The language [of the first song of Demodokos] pointedly recalls the opening lines of the *Iliad* and the very bitter, indeed deadly, quarrel between Agamemnon and Achilles";[58] another says, "[*Od.* 8.] 75–82 look suspiciously like *Iliad* 1.1–7!";[59] and yet another says, "The verbal and thematic similarities between the beginning of the *Iliad* and the tale of Demodocus are most striking, and I do not believe them to be coincidental."[60] Let us consider the connections between quote 5.10 and the *Iliad* that elicit these reactions.

Most obviously, the first song of Demodokos and the first lines of the *Iliad* share the motif of a quarrel between two leading Greek heroes as the beginning of a series of troubles.[61] In both cases, furthermore, one of the quarreling heroes is the preeminent warrior Achilles, and the ensuing troubles are willed by the preeminent god Zeus. Additional correspondences arise on closer inspection. Apart from Achilles and Zeus, Demodokos's song has a cast of three characters: Odysseus, Agamemnon, and Apollo. Except for the addition of Odysseus, these are the same characters that appear in the *Iliad* in the description of the quarrel between Achilles and Agamemnon (Apollo is mentioned almost immediately as the god who started that quarrel[62]). Furthermore, in quote 5.10 there is a special relationship between Agamemnon and Apollo, and this is true of the Iliadic account as well, because in that account Apollo acts when one of his priests is spurned by Agamemnon.[63] Thus, quote 5.10 places the quarrel between Achilles and Odysseus in a context that recalls the beginning of the *Iliad*. This set of allusions has a dual result: it suggests an awareness of the *Iliad*, and it strengthens one's sense that the quarrel between Achilles and Agamemnon has been deliberately ignored.

Notwithstanding the mentioned parallels, there is one significant difference between the first song of Demodokos and the beginning of the *Iliad* besides the identity of the hero who quarrels with Achilles. Zeus's plans cause great suffering for both the Trojans and the Greeks in Homer's account of the song (see the last two lines of quote 5.10), but only for the Greeks in the opening lines of the *Iliad*. We can eliminate this difference by extending the scope of the song's allusion to the *Iliad* as follows.

During his quarrel with Agamemnon, after he has vowed to withdraw from the war, Achilles predicts that the day will come when the Greeks will miss him sorely in battle. After the quarrel, he asks his mother, the goddess Thetis, to persuade Zeus to help the Trojans so that their success will demonstrate his indispensability to the Greeks. Zeus is beholden to Thetis and agrees to her request. In a first attempt to help the Trojans, he sends to Agamemnon a delusive dream which assures him in the name of Zeus that the time is ripe for an attack on the Trojans. Having delivered the message, the dream

> ... went away, and left Agamemnon
> there, believing things in his heart that were not to be accomplished.
> For he thought that on that very day he would take Priam's city;

fool, who knew nothing of all the things Zeus planned to accomplish,
Zeus, who yet was minded to visit tears and sufferings
on Trojans and Danaäns alike in the strong encounters.

Quote 5.15: *Il.* 2.35–40

This is the first statement in the *Iliad* that Zeus planned to cause suffering for both the Trojans and the Greeks.[64] To increase the correspondence between the first song of Demodokos and the *Iliad*, we postulate that the Iliadic material to which the song alludes extends to quote 5.15. This postulate is surprisingly effective, for it enlarges the correspondence between the song and the *Iliad* in other ways as well.

The first song of Demodokos refers implicitly to a divine prophecy of Greek success in the war. But the dream sent to Agamemnon by Zeus is also such a prophecy, albeit a deceitful one. Furthermore, Agamemnon, the recipient of both prophecies, errs in both cases when he assumes that a Greek victory is imminent (compare the first three lines of quote 5.15 with what is implied by Agamemnon's happiness in quote 5.10). These connections seem significant and have in fact led some scholars to assert that the scope of the song's allusion reaches into the second book of the *Iliad*.[65]

The expanded scope of the allusion in the first song of Demodokos receives further support from two facts that I will demonstrate in the next chapter (see part (*d*) of section 6.3): (*a*) the Iliadic text from the beginning of the quarrel between Achilles and Agamemnon to the completion of the discussion of Agamemnon's delusive dream forms an intentional structural unit and (*b*) an important phrase in quote 5.10 ("the best of the Achaians") plays a key role in the definition of this structural unit. Since the *Iliad* was composed before the *Odyssey*, Homer was presumably motivated to create the mentioned structural unit by purely Iliadic considerations. Although created for another reason (also explained in chapter 6), the structural unit was then available as a target for allusion in the *Odyssey*.

It is apparent that the first song of Demodokos, like the conversation between the shades of Achilles and Agamemnon, both affirms and denies the *Iliad*. It affirms the *Iliad* by means of the various parallels we have just reviewed, but at the same time it effectively denies the very existence of that poem by replacing the quarrel between Achilles and Agamemnon with an otherwise unknown quarrel between Achilles and Odysseus, a quarrel which, moreover, does not seem to be compatible with the *Iliad*. In the next subsection we shall see this strange combination of affirmation and denial of the *Iliad* in a third passage from the *Odyssey*. But first I wish to discuss briefly a passage that displays only a minor inconsistency with the *Iliad*, but nevertheless is of some interest in connection with the first song of Demodokos.

In the second song of Demodokos,[66] the humorous song about an adulterous affair between Ares and Aphrodite, the lame and misshapen Hephaistos is said to be married to the famously beautiful Aphrodite. This unlikely pairing has no foundation in mythology.[67] It also contradicts the *Iliad*, in which Hephaistos is said to be married to one Charis.[68] This discrepancy between the *Iliad* and the *Odyssey* was cited in antiquity by those who believed in separate authorship for the two poems; others have tried to explain it away by one means or another.[69] Most likely, however, it is simply a matter of artistic license. It is well known that Homer will modify a myth, sometimes drastically, to fit a situation in which it is used as a paradigm. For example, he has Achilles refer to the supposed precedent of Niobe in order to persuade Priam to take supper,[70] but the "real" Niobe of mythology is inconsolable and never eats after the death of her children.[71] We should not be surprised, then, if Homer has us imagine that Hephaistos is married to Aphrodite when it suits his purpose. This conceit suits his purpose in the second song of Demodokos for several reasons: the implausible pairing of Hephaistos with Aphrodite, besides being amusing in itself, provides a natural context for adultery; she has a logical partner in Ares owing to their friendship in the *Iliad*;[72] and her great beauty offers further opportunity for humor.[73] To recall a distinction made in chapter 4, the contradiction with the *Iliad* is not a perverse inconsistency but a comprehensible one: it was introduced knowingly, to be sure, but for reasons such as those just enumerated and not because the inconsistency itself was desired.

The second song of Demodokos is similar in several respects to the first. First, both songs allude to the beginning of the *Iliad*, one to the Quarrel and the delusive dream and the other to the scene on Olympos between those two episodes.[74] Second, both songs are inconsistent with the *Iliad*. Finally, the inconsistency in both cases arises from a fabricated interaction or relationship between two characters, the otherwise unknown quarrel between Achilles and Odysseus or the otherwise unknown marriage of Hephaistos and Aphrodite.[75] It is the last similarity—the confirmation that the poet of the *Odyssey* feels free to invent a fictitious relationship between characters from the *Iliad* when it suits him—that makes the second song relevant to our discussion of the first, even if its inconsistency with the *Iliad* is perfectly comprehensible and concerns only an unimportant detail of that poem.

(c) The Conversation between Odysseus and the Shade of Achilles

In the preceding subsections we saw that two scenes in the *Odyssey* which feature Achilles both appear to deny the existence of the *Iliad* by calling into question, in one way or another, the foundation stone of that poem, the quarrel between Achilles and Agamemnon. I shall now argue that the only other Odyssean scene in which the protagonist of the *Iliad* plays a prominent role, the conversation between Odysseus and the shade of Achilles that takes place during the former's visit to the underworld, denies the *Iliad* in a different way, by calling into question the heroic tradition that is fundamental to that poem.

In the heroic tradition embodied in the *Iliad*, the only consolation for mortality is the sort of immortality that can be earned through heroic deeds, namely, the "imperishable glory" manifested in what is said about a hero after his death. This concern with a glory that survives death is expressed twice by Hektor.[76] When he challenges any of the Greeks to confront him in single combat, he says that, should he prevail, he will return the corpse of his opponent so that the Greeks can bury it and build a memorial mound over it; the memorial for his victim will then bring him, Hektor, undying glory:

5.3. ACHILLES IN THE *ODYSSEY*

"And some day one of the men to come will say, as he sees it,
...
'This is the mound of a man who died long ago in battle,
who was one of the bravest, and glorious Hektor killed him.'
So he will speak some day, and my glory will not be forgotten."

Quote 5.16: *Il.* 7.87–91

Imperishable glory can also be won in defeat. When he realizes that he is about to be killed by Achilles, Hektor says,

"Let me at least not die without a struggle, inglorious,
but do some big thing first, that men to come shall know of it."

Quote 5.17: *Il.* 22.304–305

For his part, Achilles relates what his mother, the goddess Thetis, has told him:

"I carry two sorts of destiny toward the day of my death. Either,
if I stay here and fight beside the city of the Trojans,
my return home is gone, but my glory shall be everlasting;
but if I return home to the beloved land of my fathers,
the excellence of my glory is gone, but there will be a long life
left for me, and my end in death will not come to me quickly."

Quote 5.18: *Il.* 9.411–416

A short life ("my return home is gone") with glory ever after is to be weighed against a long life without glory. Essentially the same dichotomy is expressed in Achilles' anguished lament uttered when he fears he is about to die ingloriously during his struggle with the river Skamandros:

"I wish now Hektor had killed me, the greatest man grown in this place.
A brave man would have been the slayer, as the slain was a brave man.
But now this is a dismal death I am doomed to be caught in,
trapped in a big river as if I were a boy and a swineherd
swept away by a torrent when he tries to cross in a rainstorm."

Quote 5.19: *Il.* 21.279–283

Thus, the chief heroes on both sides of the conflict express the idea that glory won by a man in battle, whether in victory or defeat, outlives the man and serves as at least a partial compensation for his death.

A variation on this heroic ideal is found in the words of the Trojan ally Sarpedon to his friend Glaukos:

"Man, supposing you and I, escaping this battle,
would be able to live on forever, ageless, immortal,
so neither would I myself go on fighting in the foremost
nor would I urge you into the fighting where men win glory.
But now, seeing that the spirits of death stand close about us
in their thousands, no man can turn aside nor escape them,
let us go on and win glory for ourselves, or yield it to others."

Quote 5.20: *Il.* 12.322–328

The last line of this passage, unlike quotes 5.17 and 5.19, suggests that glory goes only to the victor. Nevertheless, the passage clearly affirms the heroic ethos for mortal man. If there were no death, says Sarpedon, there would be no point in striving for glory. It follows that glory derives its significance from mortality, and the winning of glory must provide some consolation for one's inevitable death.

Although the heroic ideal of the *Iliad* is not central to the plot of the *Odyssey*, it nevertheless finds expression at several points in the later poem.[77] We have already seen one example in quote 5.7, where the shade of Agamemnon assures the shade of Achilles of his undying fame. Of particular interest for the present discussion are the thoughts of Odysseus as he and his raft are tossed about during a violent storm at sea:

> "... My sheer destruction is certain.
> Three times and four times happy those Danaäns were who died then
> in wide Troy land, bringing favor to the sons of Atreus,
> as I wish I too had died at that time and met my destiny
> on the day when the greatest number of Trojans threw their bronze-headed
> weapons upon me, over the body of perished Achilleus,
> and I would have had my rites and the Achaians given me glory.
> Now it is by a dismal death that I must be taken."
>
> Quote 5.21: *Od.* 5.305–312

There are a number of correspondences between this passage and quote 5.19.[78] All that is important for us, however, is that Odysseus in the *Odyssey* shares the heroic ethos of the *Iliad*. He would prefer to have died winning glory in battle than to have lived ten years longer (including seven years as the lover of a goddess[79]), only to die a "dismal death" without glory.

Having reviewed the heroic ideal of the *Iliad* and its reaffirmation in the *Odyssey*, we now turn to the conversation between Odysseus and the shade of Achilles. Odysseus is visiting the underworld to obtain information that will help him return home to Ithaka. The conversation begins with the hero of the *Iliad* addressing the hero of the *Odyssey*:

> "Son of Laertes and seed of Zeus, resourceful Odysseus,
> hard man, what made you think of this bigger endeavor, how could you
> endure to come down here to Hades' place, where the senseless
> dead men dwell, mere imitations of perished mortals?"
>
> Quote 5.22: *Od.* 11.473–476

After explaining the purpose of his visit, Odysseus tries to console Achilles:

> "... Achilleus,
> no man before has been more blessed than you, nor ever
> will be. Before, when you were alive, we Argives honored you
> as we did the gods, and now in this place you have great authority
> over the dead. Do not grieve, even in death, Achilleus."
>
> Quote 5.23: *Od.* 11.482–486

This passage comes as a shock because Odysseus does not mention the consolation for death that is actually available to the Homeric hero: the imperishable glory he has won by his heroic deeds. We have seen the shade of Agamemnon offering this consolation to the shade of Achilles in quote 5.7. We also know from quote 5.21 that Odysseus's failure to mention it cannot be attributed to a lack of adherence to the heroic ideal on his part. Rather, just as the conversation between the shades of Agamemnon and Achilles and the first song of Demodokos both essentially deny the *Iliad* by ignoring the Quarrel, quote 5.23 denies the *Iliad* by ignoring the heroic ethos that is so important in that poem.

Odysseus's words to Achilles are also surprising for another reason: the consolation of "great authority over the dead" that he offers in place of the generally accepted consolation of imperishable glory is really no consolation at all. In the Homeric view of the afterlife, the shades of the dead are hardly conscious, so authority over them would be meaningless, and all the more so because this authority would be possessed by another shade that is hardly conscious. The obliviousness of the dead is stated by Achilles in the *Iliad*: "the dead forget the dead in the house of Hades."[80] This belief is confirmed by actual knowledge and experience in the *Odyssey*. Consider how Circe explains to Odysseus that he must go to the underworld before he can go to Ithaka:

"... first there is another journey you must accomplish
and reach the house of Hades and of revered Persephone,
there to consult with the soul of Teiresias the Theban,
the blind prophet, whose senses stay unshaken within him,
to whom alone Persephone has granted intelligence
even after death, but the rest of them are flittering shadows."

Quote 5.24: *Od.* 10.490–495

With the single exception of Teiresias, people lose their sense and their intelligence when they die, becoming nothing more than "flittering shadows." Odysseus learns this firsthand when the shade of his mother does not recognize him until she has drunk from the blood of the sheep[81] he has brought with him and killed according to Circe's instructions. Thus, Odysseus knows full well, from what Circe has told him and from his own experience, that the consolation of "great authority over the dead" that he offers Achilles in quote 5.23 makes no sense. Why then does he offer this spurious consolation? The answer, I suggest, is that Homer wants to accentuate the absence of the valid consolation Odysseus could have offered, the consolation of the hero's imperishable glory. Thus, quote 5.23 disregards the heroic tradition of the *Iliad* in a way that is evidently meant to be perceived as intentional.

It is necessary to address two possible objections to this conclusion. The first is that the *Odyssey* does not present a consistent view of the afterlife. The underworld portrayed in the final part of Odysseus's visit is very different from what I have just described: it is "a Hades in which the ghosts of the dead retain their faculties unimpaired, able to think and speak, to seek pleasure and to suffer punishment; a busy, noisy underworld, not very unlike the world above."[82] Likewise, in the *Odyssey*'s other scene in the land of the dead, the so-called second Nekuia (the first Nekuia being Odysseus's visit to the underworld), shades are able to speak to each other (as in the conversation between the shades of Achilles and Agamemnon discussed in part (*a*) of this section) without having to revive their faculties by drinking blood imported from the land of the living. This inconsistency is an important problem, one whose solution may or may not involve the perverse inconsistency that is a central theme of the present volume. This problem does not affect the present discussion, however, because the conversation between Odysseus and the shade of Achilles is firmly rooted in the part of the *Odyssey* where the inhabitants of the underworld are presumed to be essentially unconscious. This is established directly by Achilles' characterization of the dead in quote 5.22 (where Achilles has presumably had his own consciousness temporarily restored by drinking from the blood of the sheep). It follows from this characterization alone that the consolation attempted shortly afterwards by Odysseus is worthless. And in fact the futility of the consolation in quote 5.23 is confirmed by Achilles' famous response:

> "O shining Odysseus, never try to console me for dying.
> I would rather follow the plow as thrall to another
> man, one with no land allotted to him and not much to live on,
> than be a king over all the perished dead. ..."
>
> Quote 5.25: *Od.* 11.488–491

It has been claimed that this response signals the *Odyssey*'s rejection of the heroic ideal of the *Iliad*: "they would sing a very different tune, the poet suggests, when they really faced the facts of death."[83] But the Achilles of the *Iliad* is already well aware of the emptiness of the afterlife, as we see from his above-mentioned statement that "the dead forget the dead in the house of Hades." Indeed, the importance of the glory won by heroic deeds lies precisely in the fact that essentially all that survives death is one's reputation. Furthermore, the heroic ideal of the *Iliad* is reaffirmed in the *Odyssey* by Odysseus after he has personally witnessed the nature of existence in the underworld (quote 5.21 is taken from a scene that really occurs after the visit to the underworld even though it appears earlier in the *Odyssey*).[84] Finally, Achilles' preference for a life without material goods or social status over a total absence of life is not inconsistent with anything we know from the *Iliad* about his character.[85] These considerations show that there is nothing remarkable about quote 5.25. It is quote 5.23 that should be the focus of our attention: the absence from the consolation offered by Odysseus of any mention of glory among the living as compensation for death makes *this* passage a repudiation of the heroic ideal of the *Iliad* that is unique in all of Homer; the accentuation of the absence of glory by the substitution of meaningless authority over the unconscious shades of the dead shows that this repudiation is intentional but is not meant to be taken seriously.

I have just said that quote 5.23 is unique in all of Homer in repudiating the heroic ideal of the *Iliad*. It can be argued, however, that the heroic ideal is repudiated in the *Iliad* itself when Achilles replies to Odysseus in the Embassy scene.[86] In that scene, Odysseus concludes his appeal by emphasizing that Achilles might win great glory if he were to return to battle, for he now has a unique opportunity to kill Hektor, who has been venturing farther from the safety of the walls of Troy with Achilles out of the fight (quote 5.13). Achilles acknowledges this opportunity, but says that he is no longer interested in fighting Hektor and will return home instead.[87] This apparent rejection of the heroic ideal is reinforced soon afterwards when Achilles explicitly links his return home with the loss of glory (quote 5.18). In this apparent rejection lies the second possible objection to my interpretation of quote 5.23: perhaps Odysseus does not mention glory to the shade of Achilles because he remembers the disregard for glory seemingly implied by Achilles' reaction to his appeal in the Embassy scene. But it is not true that Achilles rejects the ideal of glory. Rather, as Bernard Knox has pointed out,[88] he has abandoned his pursuit of glory only because the dishonor done to him by Agamemnon in the Quarrel (which, in the absence of an apology, is not rectified by the offer of gifts in the Embassy) has convinced him that the path of glory is not available at Troy. As he explains to Odysseus and the other ambassadors, Agamemnon's attempt to induce him to return to battle will not succeed

> "... since there was no gratitude given
> for fighting incessantly forever against your enemies.
> Fate is the same for the man who holds back, the same if he fights hard.
> We are all held in a single honor, the brave with the weaklings.
> A man dies still if he has done nothing, as one who has done much.[89]
> Nothing is won for me, now that my heart has gone through its afflictions
> in forever setting my life on the hazard of battle."
>
> Quote 5.26: *Il.* 9.316–322

Since this explanation would certainly not have been lost on Odysseus, he would have no reason to believe that Achilles ever repudiated the heroic ideal. On the contrary, from having heard Achilles' description of his two destinies (quote 5.18) and having witnessed Achilles' death on the battlefield (see quote 5.21), it would have been obvious to Odysseus that Achilles had chosen the destiny of a short life with everlasting glory.[90] It follows that Odysseus would have had no reason not to mention glory in his attempted consolation of the shade of Achilles. His substitution in quote 5.23 of a nonsensical authority over the dead for the valid consolation of imperishable glory therefore has no logical explanation.

To recapitulate, Odysseus could have consoled the shade of Achilles by assuring him that his fame will endure forever among the living, as Agamemnon does in quote 5.7. Instead of offering the one consolation with a strong foundation in the *Iliad*, however, Odysseus offers a consolation with no foundation whatsoever. By pointedly ignoring the heroic consolation of imperishable glory, the conversation between Odysseus and the shade of Achilles denies something that is so fundamental to the *Iliad* that it seems to deny the *Iliad* itself. This is the same kind of treatment of the *Iliad* that we have previously seen in the first song of Demodokos and in the conversation between the shades of Achilles and Agamemnon. We shall now find that, like each of those episodes, the conversation between Odysseus and the shade of Achilles combines its denial of the *Iliad* with an affirmation in the form of a clear allusion to the earlier poem.

Immediately after rejecting in quote 5.25 Odysseus's attempted consolation in quote 5.23, Achilles goes on to ask for news of his son and father. This could be regarded as an allusion to the passage in the *Iliad* where Achilles says that not even the death of either of these would be harder to bear than the death of Patroklos.[91] The request for news of his son and father is so natural, however, that this can hardly be considered a convincing allusion. On the other hand, the *manner* in which Achilles asks Odysseus for news of his father is full of meaning:

> "and tell me anything you have heard about stately Peleus,
> whether he still keeps his position among the Myrmidon
> hordes, or whether in Hellas and Phthia they have diminished
> his state, because old age constrains his hands and feet, and I
> am no longer there under the light of the sun to help him,
> not the man I used to be once, when in the wide Troad
> I killed the best of their people fighting for the Argives. If only
> for a little while I could come like that to the house of my father,
> my force and my invincible hands would terrify such men
> as use force on him and keep him away from his rightful honors."
>
> Quote 5.27: *Od.* 11.494–503

Here Achilles shows the same concern for his old father and the same regret for his own inability to protect him that he shows near the end of the *Iliad*. Priam awakens these emotions at the beginning of his supplication for Hektor's body:

> "Achilleus like the gods, remember your father, one who
> is of years like mine, and on the door-sill of sorrowful old age.
> And they who dwell nearby encompass him and afflict him,
> nor is there any to defend him against the wrath, the destruction."
>
> Quote 5.28: *Il.* 24.486–489

Achilles weeps for his father and acknowledges Priam's point explicitly:

> " ... I give him [Peleus]
> no care as he grows old, since far from the land of my fathers
> I sit here in Troy, and bring nothing but sorrow to you and your children."
>
> Quote 5.29: *Il.* 24.540–542

Given the importance of the scene of reconciliation between Achilles and Priam and the prominent role played in this scene by Achilles' regrets concerning his father, the repetition of the same regrets in the underworld constitutes a significant allusion.[92] Thus, the conversation between Odysseus and the shade of Achilles displays an awareness of the *Iliad* just moments after it has seemed oblivious to the heroic ethos of that poem.

(*d*) Remarks

Each of the three primary passages from the *Odyssey* discussed in this section—the first song of Demodokos and the two conversations involving the shade of Achilles—is inconsistent with the *Iliad* at a fundamental level but also makes one or more ordinary allusions to the poem, as if to indicate that the inconsistency is deliberate. However counterintuitive, intentional inconsistency with no apparent motivation (i.e., perverse inconsistency) is difficult to deny when inconsistency manifests in such a distinctive fashion in three passages that already form a well-defined set: the set of all the interactions between the protagonist of the *Iliad* and another individual that are related directly or indirectly in the *Odyssey*.[93, 94] In addition, the fact that all the members of this set exhibit the same strange combination of affirmation and denial of the *Iliad* has an important consequence for a long-standing question in Homeric scholarship.

The authenticity of the part of the *Odyssey* from 23.297 to the end of the poem was questioned in antiquity and continues to be debated to the present day.[95] The conversation between the shades of Achilles and Agamemnon belongs to this contested part of the poem, but the other two passages discussed in this section are generally accepted as authentic.[96] I assume from the depth of the connections among all three passages that these passages are the work of a single poet. The authenticity of two of them therefore implies the authenticity of the third. It follows that the concluding part of the *Odyssey*, if it can be judged as a unit, is also authentic. This is the argument I promised at the end of section 3.3.

5.4. The Slaughter of the Suitors

The most fruitful places to look for evidence of perverse inconsistency between the two Homeric epics are presumably those passages in the *Odyssey* which have the strongest connection with the *Iliad* based on their subject matter. We have already found that three such passages, those in which the protagonist of the *Iliad* plays an active role, all contain strong indications of perverse inconsistency. Another natural place to look would be the scene in which Odysseus, aided by Telemachos and two loyal herdsmen, slaughters the suitors of Penelope, for this part of the *Odyssey* is comparable to the battle scenes that occupy a full third of the *Iliad*.[97] In the slaughter of the suitors, there is much that is reminiscent of an Iliadic battle scene but also, inevitably, much that is different.[98] My concern is not with a comparison of general properties, however, but with allusions in the account of the slaughter (the so-called Mnesterophonia) to specific scenes in the *Iliad*. In part (*a*) I review some well-known allusions to the *Iliad* found at various stages of the slaughter. The purpose of this review is merely to show that we should not be surprised to find allusions to the *Iliad* in the immediate aftermath of the slaughter. In part (*b*) I identify such allusions in a passage which is remarkable for its striking inconsistency with the *Iliad* and for signs that this inconsistency is intentional. In part (*c*) I explain how a certain passage in the *Iliad* virtually confirms the already strong case for intentional (and indeed perverse) inconsistency presented in part (*b*). Finally, in part (*d*) I argue that the Odyssean passage that is discussed in parts (*b*) and (*c*) is noteworthy not only for its apparently intentional inconsistency with the *Iliad* but also for its equally intentional inconsistency with the rest of the *Odyssey*.

(*a*) Allusions to the *Iliad* in the Mnesterophonia

After the suitors have postponed further attempts to string the bow (see section 5.1), Odysseus manages to get hold of it, to string it with ease, and to perform the feat of archery—an old trick of his—specified by Penelope as the second part of the contest for her hand in marriage. He then turns his bow on the suitors. His first victim is Antinoös, one of their leaders. When he identifies himself to the stunned suitors, their other leader, Eurymachos, places all the blame on Antinoös and promises Odysseus ample reparations for all the food and drink they have consumed if he will spare the rest of them. Odysseus rejects this offer in terms and syntax that unmistakably recall two scenes in the

Iliad: Achilles' rejection of the gifts promised by Agamemnon in return for his rejoining the fighting and his rejection of dying Hektor's plea that Achilles allow his body to be ransomed.[99] In calling attention to this double allusion, Richard Rutherford says that "the parallelism could be coincidental, simply the traditional formulae for an angry speech in epic, but ... I doubt if that is a sufficient explanation; indeed, here above all I am convinced that the *Odyssey* imitates the *Iliad*"; likewise, Seth Schein asserts that the effect of the double allusion (I use this term even though Schein is careful to note that the *Odyssey* could simply be drawing on a tradition shared with the *Iliad*) is "to represent Odysseus, at a particular point in the narrative, as uncharacteristically and significantly Iliadic," "a representation that is strengthened by the subsequent description of the Iliadic combat in which he kills all the suitors."[100]

With his offer rejected and Odysseus clearly intent on revenge, Eurymachos calls on his fellow suitors to attack. He himself is quickly dispatched, however, with an arrow from Odysseus. Another suitor, Amphinomos, then rushes Odysseus, but is killed by a spear thrown by Telemachos:

> Telemachos
> was too quick with a cast of the brazen spear from behind him
>   [Amphinomos]
> between the shoulders, and drove it through to the chest beyond it.
> He fell, thunderously, and took the earth full on his forehead.
>
> Quote 5.30: *Od.* 22.91–94

The details of Amphinomos's death match those of four killings in the *Iliad*.[101] Paradoxically, it is probably for this reason that quote 5.30 is not usually mentioned as a significant allusion to the *Iliad*. The reasoning presumably is that the four instances of this manner of killing in the *Iliad* testify to the existence of a corresponding pattern in the poetic tradition that gave rise to that poem, and that the poet of the *Odyssey* is simply drawing on the same tradition. I take the contrary view that quote 5.30 alludes specifically to one of its four analogues in the *Iliad*, and will explain why in part (*b*) of this section.

After killing Amphinomos, Telemachos hurries to the storeroom to fetch shields, helmets, and spears for himself, his father, and the two herdsmen who will join them in battle against the numerous suitors. Odysseus meanwhile uses his bow efficiently to kill one suitor after another. When he runs out of arrows, he dons the armor brought by Telemachos and switches from the bow to the spear. The *Iliad* contains a very similar scene in which an archer is forced to exchange his bow for a spear, this time because of a broken bowstring.[102] Knut Usener's discussion of the two scenes, the only re-arming scenes in all of Homer, leaves little doubt that they constitute a significant (i.e., non-coincidental) connection between the poems.[103]

Although it is during the spear fighting that we find in the slaughter of the suitors certain characteristics of Iliadic battle scenes,[104] the account of the slaughter does not allude to another specific scene in the *Iliad* until only one suitor is left alive. This suitor, Leodes, rushes to Odysseus, assumes the standard posture of supplication, and begs for mercy. He argues that he is not like the other suitors in that he never forced himself on any of Odysseus's women servants and, in fact, always tried to dissuade the others from doing so.[105] We know he is speaking the truth from what Homer has told us in the only other scene in which Leodes appears, the scene in which he is (by chance) the first to attempt to string the bow in the contest set by Penelope.[106] But Odysseus has three reasons for seeking revenge against the suitors: they despoiled his household, they forced themselves on his serving women, and they sought to win his wife while he was still alive.[107] Leodes is well aware of these grievances since Odysseus announced them after killing Antinoös. Since he is innocent of only one of the three offenses, his attempt to distance himself from the other suitors falls short, and he must die, as he himself senses.[108] All this is strongly reminiscent of the scene in the *Iliad* in which another minor character, Lykaon, begs the hero of the poem for his life.[109] Like Odysseus, Achilles is bent on revenge and is not in a forgiving mood. Like Leodes, Lykaon senses that he will not be spared. He nevertheless attempts to distance himself from the main object of Achilles' fury by pointing out that he did not come from the same womb as the man who killed Patroklos (although, as a son of Priam, he is a half brother of Hektor). This desperate attempt, like that of Leodes, is doomed to fail.

(*b*) Inconsistency with the *Iliad* in the Aftermath of the Slaughter

Having seen allusions to the *Iliad* at various stages of the destruction of the suitors, we now examine several Iliadic allusions in a passage from the immediate aftermath of the slaughter. The allusions we are about to consider all relate, directly or indirectly, to a certain inconsistency between the two epics. Even more interesting than this common focus is the fact that at least one of the allusions seems designed to call attention to this inconsistency.

Surveying the scene of the slaughter, Odysseus satisfies himself that all the suitors have been killed. He then directs Telemachos to fetch the aged nurse Eurykleia. Her arrival on the scene is described as follows:

> There she found Odysseus among the slaughtered dead men,
> spattered over with gore and battle filth, like a lion
> who has been feeding on an ox of the fields, and goes off
> covered with blood, all his chest and his flanks on either
> side bloody, a terrible thing to look in the face; so
> now Odysseus' feet and the hands above them were spattered.
> She, when she saw the dead men and the endless blood, began then
> to raise the cry of triumph, having seen it was monstrous
> work, but Odysseus checked her and held her, for all her eagerness,
> and spoke to her and addressed her in winged words, saying:
> "Keep your joy in your heart, old dame; stop, do not raise up
> the cry. **It is not piety to glory so over slain men.**
> These were destroyed by the doom of the gods and their own hard actions,
> for these men paid no attention at all to any man on earth
> who came their way, no matter if he were base or noble.
> So by their own recklessness they have found a shameful
> death. ..."

Quote 5.31: *Od.* 22.401–417 (boldface added)

Odysseus's declaration that "it is not piety to glory so over slain men" (or, in Murray's translation, "an unholy thing is it to boast over slain men") is as un-

Iliadic as his failure to acknowledge the heroic ethos of the *Iliad* in quote 5.23. Boasting over the body of an enemy one has just killed is common in that poem, there being 16 gloating speeches according to Martin Mueller.[110] Moreover, there is no indication that the gods are displeased by such boasting.[111] Finally, whereas Odysseus prevents Eurykleia from expressing her joy over the death of the suitors, Achilles incites his comrades-in-arms to sing a song of victory after he has killed Hektor.[112] I shall argue that the deviation of quote 5.31 from the *Iliad* is intentional and meant to be perceived as such.

Odysseus, who condemns boasting over slain men in the *Odyssey*, is himself guilty of such boasting in the *Iliad*. Here is Homer's account of Odysseus killing the Trojan Sokos and boasting over his body:

> ... Sokos turning from him [Odysseus] was striding in flight
> but in his back even as he was turning the spear fixed
> between the shoulders and was driven on through the chest beyond it.
> He fell, thunderously, and great Odysseus boasted over him:
> "Sokos, son of wise Hippasos the breaker of horses,
> death was too quick for you and ran you down; you could not
> avoid it. Wretch, since now your father and your honored mother
> will not be able to close your eyes in death, but the tearing
> birds will get you, with their wings close-beating about you.
> If I die, the brilliant Achaians will bury me in honor."
>
> Quote 5.32: *Il.* 11.446–455

It is difficult to reconcile Odysseus's boasting here with his declaration in quote 5.31 that "it is not piety to glory so over slain men."[113] Furthermore, Homer seems to have taken steps to force us to confront this discrepancy. Notice that the killing that marks Telemachos's initiation into battle, the only killing by spear in the archery phase of the slaughter of the suitors, is identical to the killing of Sokos by Odysseus (compare quote 5.30 with the first lines of quote 5.32). As I have already indicated, three men besides Sokos are killed in the same manner in the *Iliad*, so perhaps I should not make too much of this correspondence.[114] But there is also another parallel. In the *Iliad*, just before the encounter with Sokos, Odysseus finds himself in the unusual position of being the only Greek surrounded by Trojans.[115] In the *Odyssey*, he does not face the suitors by himself, but he does find himself in a battle where he is the chief combatant and his side is vastly outnumbered. Thus, there are two parallels between the Iliadic and Odyssean scenes. To these possibly significant parallels I will now add a confrontation between the two scenes that is really striking.

When Odysseus is the only Greek in the midst of the Trojans, he manages to kill several of them, including a brother of Sokos. Sokos steps in to avenge his brother, but first addresses his adversary as follows:

> "Honored Odysseus, insatiable of guile and endeavor,
> today you will have two sons of Hippasos to vaunt over
> for having killed two such men as we and stripping our armor,
> or else, stricken underneath my spear, you might lose your own life."
>
> Quote 5.33: *Il.* 11.430–433

This speech is remarkable because it is the only place in the *Iliad* where someone who is about to be killed refers to the boasting that his killer will be entitled to. In fact, this is the only place in the *Iliad* where someone who is about to fight refers to the boasting that the victor will be entitled to. This boasting is, of course, at the heart of the contradiction between the Iliadic and Odyssean scenes under discussion. That it receives a unique kind of emphasis in just that scene of the *Iliad* where the warrior who in the *Odyssey* condemns boasting over slain men is himself guilty of such boasting suggests that Homer wants his audience to take note of the inconsistency between the two poems.[116]

Quote 5.31 contains another allusion to the *Iliad*. The key to this allusion is the lion simile that occupies the first half of the passage. Lion similes form "by far the largest and most complex family of similes in the *Iliad*,"[117] and they are "the commonest of all similes used in the *Iliad* to depict triumphant warriors."[118] In fact, the simile in quote 5.31 has a close parallel in the *Iliad*. It is found when Automedon has exacted partial revenge for the death of Patroklos by killing a lesser Trojan:

> Then Automedon, a match for the running god of battles,
> stripped the armor, and spoke a word of boasting above him:
> "Now I have put a little sorrow from my heart for Patroklos'
> death, although the man I killed was not as great as he was."
>   So he spoke, and took up the bloody war spoils and laid them
> inside the chariot, and himself mounted it, the blood running
> from hands and feet, as on some lion who has eaten a bullock.
>   Quote 5.34: *Il*. 17.536–542

Quotes 5.31 and 5.34 are clearly linked together by the comparison of the victorious warrior whose hands and feet are bloody to a lion bloodied by feeding on a farm animal. These are the only places in Homer where this comparison is made.[119] It is noteworthy that the passage in the *Odyssey* that condemns boasting over slain men again alludes to a passage in the *Iliad* that contains an instance of such boasting.

To summarize the argument up to this point, the passage in the *Odyssey* in which Odysseus condemns boasting over slain men alludes to two passages in the *Iliad* in which a warrior who has just killed someone boasts over his victim. In one of the Iliadic passages, the boasting is done by Odysseus himself, and the act of boasting over slain enemies is highlighted in a way that is unique in Homer. In the other Iliadic passage, the boasting is done by someone who is described with a simile whose only close analogue elsewhere in Homer is the simile used for Odysseus in the mentioned passage from the *Odyssey*. It is difficult to escape the conclusion that the inconsistency between the two poems is intentional and meant to be noticed.

(*c*) Confirmation

That Homer wants us to connect the boldfaced part of quote 5.31 with the Sokos episode is confirmed by the passage in the *Iliad* that describes the confrontation between Menelaos and the Trojan Euphorbos over the corpse of Patroklos. After Apollo stuns Patroklos and knocks the divine and presumably impenetrable armor of Achilles off him, it is Euphorbos who first takes advantage of Patroklos's vulnerability, hitting him with a spear in the back, between the shoulders.[120] Euphorbos then retreats, but Hektor sees the wounded Patroklos and finishes him off. As Hektor goes in pursuit of another victim, Menelaos comes and stands over the corpse to protect it from capture and abuse. At this point Euphorbos returns and addresses Menelaos as follows (to understand this exchange, it is necessary to know that Euphorbos and Hyperenor were brothers, sons of Panthoös):

> "Son of Atreus, Menelaos, illustrious, leader of armies:
> give way, let the bloody spoils be, get back from this body,
> since before me no one of the Trojans, or renowned companions,
> struck Patroklos down with the spear in the strong encounter.
> Thereby let me win this great glory among the Trojans
> before I hit you and strip the sweetness of life away from you."
>   Deeply stirred, Menelaos of the fair hair answered him:
> "Father Zeus, **it is not well for the proud man to glory.**
> Neither the fury of the leopard is such, not such is the lion's,
> nor the fury of the devastating wild boar, within whose breast
> the spirit is biggest and vaunts in the pride of his strength, is so great
> as goes the pride in these sons of Panthoös of the strong ash spear.
> Yet even the strength of Hyperenor, breaker of horses,
> had no joy of his youth when he stood against me and taunted me
> and said that among all the Danaäns I was the weakest
> in battle. Yet I think that his feet shall no more carry him
> back, to pleasure his beloved wife and his honored parents.
> So I think I can break your strength as well, if you only
> stand against me. No, but I myself tell you to get back
> into the multitude, not stand to face me, before you
> take some harm. Once a thing has been done, the fool sees it."
>   He spoke so, but did not persuade Euphorbos, who answered:
> "Then, lordly Menelaos, you must now pay the penalty
> for my brother, whom you killed, and **boast that you did it**,
> and made his wife a widow in the depth of a young bride chamber
> and left to his parents the curse of lamentation and sorrow."
>   Quote 5.35: *Il.* 17.12–37 (boldface added)

This passage is concerned with two kinds of boasting: boasting about having killed someone (or, in the case of Euphorbos, having played a major role in a killing) and boasting that one can kill the person one is speaking to. Since Euphorbos is guilty of both kinds of boasting in his opening speech, it is not immediately clear in which sense Menelaos uses the verb "to glory" in the first line I have put in boldface (*Il.* 17.19). However, it becomes evident from the story about Hyperenor, who taunted Menelaos but then was killed by him, that Menelaos is referring to the second kind of boasting. Menelaos himself is guilty of this kind of boasting when he asserts that he can kill Euphorbos as he did his brother. In fact, Menelaos is guilty of both kinds of boasting, since he also boasts about killing Hyperenor, as Euphorbos observes in the second fragment in boldface.[121]

Since Menelaos is guilty of the boasting that he criticizes in *Il.* 17.19, quote 5.35 encapsulates the contradiction between Odysseus's condemnation of boasting over slain men in the *Odyssey* (quote 5.31) and his own such boasting in the *Iliad* (quote 5.32), with only a change in the identity of the hero and the kind of boasting involved. But that is not all. In addition to encapsulating the contradiction between quote 5.31 and quote 5.32, quote 5.35 serves as a link between these passages by virtue of strong connections it has with both of them, as I shall now explain.

In quote 5.35 Menelaos says that "it is not well for the proud man to glory"; in quote 5.31 Odysseus says that "it is not piety to glory so over slain men."[122] These are the only places in Homer where boasting is condemned.[123] It may or may not be significant that, although there are three verbs that Homer uses to refer to boasting, the same one is used in both of these condemnations despite the fact that this one is used (with this meaning) far less frequently than the other two.[124] Either way, the connection between quote 5.35 and quote 5.31 is clear.[125]

Quotes 5.35 and 5.32 are connected with each other via closely associated passages that I must now review. The verbal exchange between Menelaos and Euphorbos is followed by a fight in which the Trojan is quickly dispatched. As Menelaos is stripping the armor from the corpse, he becomes aware that Hektor is approaching. He debates whether to stand his ground or to temporarily abandon the body of Patroklos and go in search of Aias for reinforcement. He decides to take the prudent course, but returns with Aias in time to force Hektor to retreat before he can decapitate the corpse of Patroklos.

The scene in which Menelaos debates what to do as Hektor approaches is one of four similar scenes in the *Iliad*.[126] In each case, a lone warrior in a dangerous situation begins a deliberation that is introduced with the words "Deeply troubled, he spoke to his own great-hearted spirit:" (*Il.* 11.403 = 17.90 = 21.552 = 22.98). After considering his options, the warrior says to himself, "Yet still, why does the heart within me debate on these things?" (*Il.* 11.407 = 17.97 = 21.562 = 22.122), and then proceeds to state his decision and the reasoning behind it.[127] The deliberating warrior is Greek in two of the four scenes of this type. The other Greek besides Menelaos is Odysseus. Whereas Menelaos takes the prudent course, Odysseus makes a heroic stand, and it is during this stand that he has the encounter with Sokos. Although Odysseus is victorious in this encounter, he is wounded fairly seriously and still must face an onslaught of Trojans. Fortunately, Aias and Menelaos come to the rescue. The verse used to describe how Aias disperses the Trojans is identical to the verse that describes how he, again accompanied by Menelaos, causes Hektor to draw back from the body of Patroklos: "Aias came near him, carrying like a wall his shield" (*Il.* 11.485 = 17.128), a verse that appears in only one other place in the poem (*Il.* 7.219) and then in a very different context (the duel between Aias and Hektor).

Thus, the encounter between Odysseus and Sokos is sandwiched between two distinctive passages, Odysseus's deliberation and his rescue by Aias and Menelaos, which have close parallels shortly after the encounter between Menelaos and Euphorbos. This is the promised connection between quote 5.35 (from the latter encounter) and quote 5.32 (from the former).[128] Since we have already seen a strong connection between quote 5.35 and quote 5.31, it follows that Odysseus's condemnation of boasting over slain men (quote 5.31) is linked to his own boasting over the body of Sokos (quote 5.32) via the encounter between Menelaos and Euphorbos (quote 5.35) and associated text.

This link between the two contradictory passages reinforces the connection between them that we already suspected in the preceding subsection. That Homer wants us to confront the contradiction becomes undeniable when we recall that the passage at the center of the new link contains within itself a contradiction of the same sort, with Odysseus replaced by Menelaos.

A strong case can evidently be made that Odysseus's condemnation of boasting over slain men in the *Odyssey* is intentionally and perversely inconsistent with the *Iliad*. The contribution to this case made in this subsection revolves around parallels between Odysseus and Menelaos. These are the only men in Homer to be critical of boasting, and their criticism is inconsistent with their own behavior. They are also the only Greek heroes who are shown deliberating with themselves while facing grave danger alone. The assumption that these parallels are significant is supported by the existence of equally strong parallels between the two men in the *Odyssey*. The latter parallels are reviewed and exploited in sections 6.7 and 6.8.

(*d*) An Anomaly in the *Odyssey*

I have been arguing that the poet took special measures to draw attention to the inconsistency between the Odyssean passage quote 5.31 and the *Iliad*. Now I add that he also took special measures to create the inconsistency in the first place, in that the passage in question is an anomaly within the context of the *Odyssey* itself.

One reason quote 5.31, with its injunction against boasting over slain men, seems out of touch with the rest of the *Odyssey* is that the poem contains a scene in which the loyal herdsman Philoitios vaunts over the body of a suitor he has just killed, the nasty Ktesippos, without being reprimanded by Odysseus.[129] However, this observation is not sufficient to establish the anomalous character of quote 5.31 since it could be argued that Odysseus would not rebuke one of his allies in the heat of battle.

A more fundamental reason to regard quote 5.31 as an anomaly in the *Odyssey* is that it implies an interpretation of events which does not accord with the narrative of the poem. Thus, one commentator attempts to explain the passage by saying that "it is a major theme of the *Odyssey* that Odysseus is the instrument by which the *gods* punish the suitors" and that Odysseus restrains Eurykleia because the death of the suitors is the gods' doing, not his.[130] But the only divine interest in the punishment of the suitors that we ever see is that of Athene, and she helps Odysseus get revenge simply because that is what he needs (he has to kill the suitors since they certainly would not leave his palace peacefully) and what he naturally wants (there is no indication that his desire for revenge must be awakened by the gods[131]). The two divine councils described in the poem[132] are concerned mainly with his longing for home and the planning of his homecoming. The punishment of the suitors comes up only once and then just briefly, as something that he would obviously want to accomplish when he gets back to Ithaka.[133] Significantly, then, Zeus implies at the end of the poem that the deliberations of the gods related to the punishment of the suitors were limited to Athene's advocacy for Odysseus in the councils.[134]

5.4. THE SLAUGHTER OF THE SUITORS

It is possible to see an exception to my claim that Athene is the only deity to show an interest in the punishment of the suitors, but the discussion of this apparent exception will only strengthen my case. As anticipated in quote 5.4, Telemachos calls a public assembly in which he tells the suitors to leave his house and says that, if they do not, he will "cry out to the gods everlasting in the hope that Zeus might somehow grant a reversal of fortunes [resulting in the suitors' destruction]."[135] Immediately afterwards, Zeus sends a dramatic bird sign to show his support for Telemachos. Since Telemachos has just expressed a wish for the destruction of the suitors, the omen sent by Zeus might be taken to indicate that divine interest in the punishment of the suitors is not limited to Athene. However, the true significance of this scene for my argument can be inferred from the well-known parallel between the fate of the suitors and that of Aigisthos, the murderer of Agamemnon.[136] The story of Aigisthos, first related by Zeus at the beginning of the *Odyssey*,[137] serves as a paradigm for the story of the suitors that unfolds over the course of the poem. According to his own account, Zeus sent Hermes to warn Aigisthos that he would suffer the vengeance of Orestes if he were to murder Agamemnon. Similarly, as the interpretation by Halitherses makes explicit, the bird sign sent by Zeus serves as a warning to the suitors.[138] They, like Aigisthos, do not heed Zeus's warning and thereby bring about their own well-deserved destruction. What is important for this discussion is that there is no indication that Orestes was acting for the gods when he avenged the murder of his father. By analogy, then, there is no reason to suppose that Odysseus is acting for the gods when he takes his revenge against the suitors. (The applicability of the analogy, incidentally, is reinforced by the fact that the vengeance of Orestes was to come when he "longed for his own country,"[139] inasmuch as the revenge of Odysseus is a consequence of *his* longing for his country, the longing stressed by Athene in her reply to Zeus's story of Aigisthos and Orestes.) Zeus does grant the reversal of fortunes wished for by Telemachos, but only by enabling the homecoming of Odysseus; the subsequent destruction of the suitors, although facilitated by Athene, is fully motivated by the natural drives of the hero for self-preservation, protection of his family, restoration of his kingship, and revenge.[140] The basis for condemning boasting over the slain suitors cited in quote 5.31 is therefore spurious.

The Aigisthos/Orestes paradigm provides another route to the same conclusion. Orestes is said repeatedly to have earned fame and glory by killing his father's murderer.[141] If the story of Aigisthos is truly a model for the story of the suitors (and in fact Athene urges Telemachos to kill the suitors so that he, like Orestes, will be praised for generations to come[142]), he who kills the suitors should likewise win glory and therefore, presumably, the right to vaunt over their corpses.[143] Odysseus's prohibition of vaunting over the slain suitors violates this expectation.

The anomalous nature of quote 5.31 in its Odyssean context is underlined by a speech made by Penelope when Eurykleia wakes her up and announces that Odysseus is home and has slain the suitors. The queen cannot believe the wonderful news of Odysseus's return and thinks instead that the suitors must have been killed by a god:

> "Dear nurse, do not yet laugh aloud in triumph. You know
> how welcome he would be if he appeared in the palace:
> to all, but above all to me and the son we gave birth to.
> No, but this story is not true as you tell it; rather,
> some one of the immortals has killed the haughty suitors
> in anger over their wicked deeds and heart-hurting violence;
> for these men paid no attention at all to any man on earth
> who came their way, no matter if he were base or noble.
> So they suffered for their own recklessness. But Odysseus
> has lost his homecoming and lost his life, far from Achaia."
>
> Quote 5.36: *Od.* 23.59–68

The parallelism between this passage and the second half of quote 5.31 is remarkable. Penelope, like Odysseus, tells Eurykleia not to express her jubilation; husband and wife both attribute the destruction of the suitors to divine displeasure at their wicked acts; both note that the suitors "paid no attention at all to any man on earth who came their way, no matter if he were base or noble"; and both remark that it was the recklessness of the suitors that led to their destruction. Furthermore, these shared properties appear in the same order in the two passages.[144] Despite all these similarities, however, the two passages are fundamentally different. Whereas Odysseus's speech seems out of place in the *Odyssey*, Penelope's makes perfect sense. First, it seems strange that Odysseus credits the gods for the slaughter of the suitors (even when the crucial assistance he receives from Athene is taken into account), but it is obvious why Penelope thinks the suitors must have been killed by a god: she cannot believe that so many men were killed by a single mortal,[145] and in any case she thinks Odysseus is dead. Second, it seems strange that Odysseus tells Eurykleia not to give a cry of triumph, but it is obvious why Penelope tells Eurykleia not to "laugh aloud in triumph": she believes that the "triumph" of Odysseus's return has not occurred (quote 5.36 may be paraphrased as follows: "Nurse, do not rejoice. I too would rejoice if Odysseus were back home, but he is not. The suitors must have been killed by some god angered by their wicked deeds, for Odysseus is dead.").[146] Thus, the relationship between quotes 5.31 and 5.36 is complex, combining similarity and contrast, somewhat like the relationship to the *Iliad* of the three main Odyssean passages discussed in section 5.3. The contrast between the straightforwardness of Penelope's speech and the absurdities in the speech of Odysseus drives home the message that the latter speech is a conscious anomaly. This anomaly disturbs the reader both in its Odyssean context and through its evidently intentional contradiction of the *Iliad*. A framework for understanding why the poet might want to create these disturbing effects will be proposed in the last chapter of this book.

5.5. Chariots in Warfare

The slaughter of the suitors is not the only scene in the *Odyssey* that is reminiscent of an Iliadic battle scene. After Odysseus recounts to the

5.5. CHARIOTS IN WARFARE

Phaiakians his sack of the city of the Kikonians (see quote 1.4) and the refusal of his men to make a quick departure after the sack, he gives a summary description of the costly battle that ensues:

> "... [T]he Kikonians went and summoned the other
> Kikonians, who were their neighbors living in the inland country,
> more numerous and better men, **well skilled in fighting
> their foes from chariots and, where necessary,
> on foot**. They came at early morning, like flowers in season
> or leaves, and the luck that came our way from Zeus was evil,
> to make us unfortunate, so we must have hard pains to suffer.
> <u>Both sides stood and fought their battle there by the running
> ships</u>, and with bronze-headed spears they cast at each other,
> and *as long as it was early and the sacred daylight increasing,
> so long we stood fast and fought them off, though there were more of them;
> but when the sun had gone to the time for unyoking of cattle,
> then at last the Kikonians turned the Achaians back and beat them,*
> and out of each ship six of my strong-greaved companions
> were killed, but the rest of us fled away from death and destruction."
>
> Quote 5.37: *Od.* 9.47–61 (boldface, underlining, and italics added)[147]

Although this description of a day-long battle is highly compressed, it contains several features that remind us of the *Iliad*, two of which I note here. First, the fact that the Kikonians fight Odysseus and his men by the ships (see the underlined part of quote 5.37) must resonate with anyone familiar with the *Iliad*, where there is intense fighting by the ships which has a special significance owing to Hektor's determination to set them on fire. And second, the italicized part of the passage, which describes a balance of forces early in the day giving way to the dominance of one side, replicates a structure that is found three times in the *Iliad*.[148]

Despite its Iliadic feel, quote 5.37 is strikingly un-Iliadic in the role it assigns to chariots in warfare. According to the boldfaced part of the passage, the Kikonians are skilled in fighting from chariots and apparently even prefer this type of fighting to fighting on foot. In the *Iliad*, by contrast, chariots are used almost exclusively for transportation: once a hero has been conveyed to the front, he descends from his chariot in order to fight while the driver keeps the chariot nearby.[149] Since the Kikonians fought at Troy (they were allies of the Trojans[150]), and since the Trojan plain would have been a good place for fighting from chariots, quote 5.37 is inconsistent with the *Iliad*. Moreover, the fact that the passage makes a point of saying that the Kikonians fight from chariots where possible suggests that the inconsistency is intentional.

On the few occasions in the *Iliad* when a warrior does fight from a chariot, as often as not he does so by throwing a spear,[151] something he could not do again unless he dismounted from his chariot to retrieve his spear or to fetch another. A sustainable way to fight from a chariot, where the spear is used for thrusting instead of throwing, is described by Nestor in these instructions to his men:

> "Let no man in the pride of his horsemanship and his manhood
> dare to fight alone with the Trojans in front of the rest of us,
> neither let him give ground, since that way you will be weaker.

> When a man from his own car encounters the enemy chariots
> let him stab with his spear, since this is the stronger fighting.
> So the men before your time sacked tower and city,
> keeping a spirit like this in their hearts, and like this their purpose."
>
> Quote 5.38: *Il.* 4.303–309

Note, however, that Nestor says that this method of fighting is a thing of the past. In fact, we never see these instructions carried out. It is as if the poet included this passage to emphasize that true chariot fighting is foreign to the *Iliad*, thereby underlining the inconsistency between this poem and the Odyssean passage reproduced in quote 5.37.

5.6. Does the *Iliad* Allude to the *Odyssey*?

As discussed in section 5.1, there are several indications that the *Odyssey* was composed after the *Iliad*. And indeed, most of this chapter makes sense only if we assume this sequence. But some of the connections between the two poems that I discussed in the preceding two sections suggest that either the *Iliad* was composed with incredible foresight or it was revised from time to time as Homer was composing the *Odyssey*. Are we to suppose that it was just by chance that the poet of the *Iliad* gave special attention to boasting over slain enemies (quote 5.33) in the scene where Odysseus performs such boasting and thereby enabled the poet of the *Odyssey* to create a particularly striking inconsistency by means of quote 5.31? Was it just by chance that the encounter between Menelaos and Euphorbos turned out to be a model for that same inconsistency while at the same time serving as a link connecting the inconsistent passages? And finally, was it just by chance that the *Iliad* poet accentuated the inconsistency between his poem and a passage from the *Odyssey* (quote 5.37) by calling attention to chariot fighting as a thing of the past and, what is more, doing this in a passage which has no apparent purpose since it communicates instructions that are never carried out (quote 5.38)? My own tentative conclusion from the observations to be made in this section is that the assumption of the priority of the *Iliad* is broadly correct, but that relatively minor modifications of that poem may have been made during the composition of the *Odyssey*.

The idea that the *Iliad* was influenced by, and perhaps even refers to, the *Odyssey*, while not new,[152] is usually rejected implicitly. To illustrate this attitude and to argue for the opposite position, I discuss the two places in the *Iliad* where Odysseus refers to himself as the father of Telemachos. At one place, Odysseus says that if he does not fulfill a certain vow, then

> "nevermore let the head of Odysseus sit on his shoulders,
> let me nevermore be called Telemachos' father[.]"
>
> Quote 5.39: *Il.* 2.259–260

At the other, he responds to an accusation that he is hanging back from the fighting by saying,

> "... Only watch, if you care to and if it concerns you,
> the very father of Telemachos locked with the champion
> Trojans, breakers of horses. Your talk is wind, and no meaning."
>
> Quote 5.40: *Il.* 4.353–355

5.6. DOES THE *ILIAD* ALLUDE TO THE *ODYSSEY*?

Peter Jones and Stephanie West both infer from these passages that Telemachos was not invented by the poet of the *Odyssey*.[153] To Richard Rutherford, these passages seem to imply that the connection between Odysseus and Telemachos was important even before the *Iliad*.[154] Similarly, Jasper Griffin asserts that pre-Homeric poetic tradition must have included a formulaic phrase that characterized Odysseus as the father of Telemachos.[155] W. J. Woodhouse, who considers Telemachos to be fundamental to the *Odyssey*, suggests that Odysseus was selected to be the hero of the poem because he was the only candidate who had a son.[156] All these inferences and suppositions presume that quotes 5.39 and 5.40 were included in the *Iliad* without any thought of the *Odyssey*. The same can be said of the more detailed suggestions made by Ruth Scodel,[157] which I shall review because they illustrate how difficult it is to account for these passages.

Quote 5.39 is taken from Odysseus's rebuke of Thersites, a common soldier who has the temerity to speak against Agamemnon during an assembly of the army. Although most of his abuse is directed at Agamemnon, Thersites also insults all the soldiers by calling them "women, not men" for their submission to Agamemnon. Scodel suggests that Odysseus refers to himself as the father of Telemachos in quote 5.39 to assert his virility in defense against Thersites' insult. But Odysseus surely has no need to defend himself against this insult, as he has just given a most convincing demonstration of his manliness by single-handedly halting what was virtually a stampede of the entire Greek army (see section 6.3). In any case, fatherhood would not be much of a defense against an accusation of weakness in the face of Agamemnon.

We are told that the *Cypria*, one of the poems of the Epic Cycle, contained a story of Odysseus feigning madness in an attempt to avoid having to join the expedition to Troy.[158] In this story, which may have belonged to the tradition that Homer inherited, Odysseus is compelled to drop his pretense of madness by a ruse in which Telemachos is placed in harm's way so that the father will have to protect his baby son. Scodel suggests that quote 5.40 alludes to this story by mentioning Telemachos in the context of a charge that Odysseus is reluctant to fight. Yet she acknowledges that such an allusion would bring up an aspect of the traditional Odysseus that is otherwise suppressed in the *Iliad*, a poem which portrays Odysseus as a forceful and reliable champion of the Greek cause (the accusation that he is hanging back from the fighting is not meant to be taken seriously and is withdrawn immediately after his angry response).

Scodel attempts to account for Odysseus's two references to himself as the father of Telemachos with two unrelated explanations, neither of which is persuasive. Nevertheless, it cannot be denied that these references are puzzling and call for an explanation. Odysseus is the only character in the *Iliad* who refers to himself as the father of his son.[159] It is especially incongruous for a great hero to refer to himself like this, and with evident pride,[160] when the son is a little boy and cannot possibly have made a name for himself.[161] We are led to ask whether it is just by chance that the character who does this is the one whose return home after the war is the subject of another epic, an epic in which the son reaches manhood and shows himself to be worthy of his father.

I suggest that the answer is no and that Odysseus's references to himself as the father of Telemachos are intentional forward references to the later poem.[162] This hypothesis is supported by the following considerations.

The children of many Homeric heroes have names that connect them with their fathers. "Telemachos" means "fighter at a distance," and presumably refers to Odysseus's skill as an archer and to his use of the bow as a weapon.[163] But Odysseus fights with a spear in the *Iliad*, never with a bow,[164] and he doesn't even enter the archery contest in the funeral games for Patroklos. By contrast, his accuracy with the bow and his effective use of it in battle are highlighted in the *Odyssey*,[165] which could almost be considered a vehicle for showing off these talents. Again, quotes 5.39 and 5.40 seem out of place in the *Iliad*, but make sense as forward references to the *Odyssey*.[166]

Quotes 5.39 and 5.40 make effective references to the *Odyssey* in part because it is this poem that justifies two features of these passages: the evident pride of Odysseus in Telemachos and the name "Telemachos" itself. These references also owe part of their effectiveness simply to the importance of Telemachos in the *Odyssey*. The sense of crisis on Ithaka is intensified by his reaching the age where he should assert the rights to his property. His emerging confrontation with the suitors leads to their attempt to murder him, which magnifies their guilt and the justification for their slaughter.[167] His journey in search of news of his father establishes the stature of Odysseus through the reminiscences of Nestor, Menelaos, and Helen (and also brings the reader up to date on what happened after the war to these and other characters from the *Iliad*).[168] From a structural standpoint, the attention given to Telemachos makes two significant contributions. First, it gives a nice balance to the poem, which begins and ends on Ithaka and has the Wanderings of Odysseus as a centerpiece.[169] Second, it makes possible what Alfred Heubeck calls the "virtuosity in construction" of two strands of narrative, the stories of Telemachos and Odysseus, which run parallel until they merge at the reunion of father and son on Ithaka.[170] At the same time, the parallel between Telemachos and Orestes, the son of Agamemnon who also performs a heroic deed connected with the homecoming of his father, enhances the cohesiveness of the *Odyssey* by increasing the number and variety of opportunities to recall the leitmotif of Agamemnon's tragic return.[171] Woodhouse goes so far as to say that "the *Odyssey* was born into the world" when Homer (with the story of Agamemnon in mind) conceived "the brilliant idea of retarding the return of Odysseus until Telemachos should be of an age to take part in the action"; in other words, "Without Telemachos, no *Odyssey*."[172] For Woodhouse, "Son standing shoulder to shoulder with Father, both of them instruments of divine Nemesis in upholding the sanctities of Home and asserting the triumph of Right over Wrong [the slaughter of the suitors]—that is the essential element, the very heart's core, of the *Odyssey*." To this reading I would add the following observations.

By delaying the return of Odysseus until Telemachos has reached manhood, Homer gives their separation a special poignancy: the son has grown up without a father, and the father has missed the childhood and youth of his son. But the same tactic enables the poet to create a compelling reunion in which father and son make up for the time they lost. As Telemachos joins with Odysseus in the plotting against the suitors, the acting (deception) in their presence,[173] and the fighting, the father gets to see the mettle of his son and the son gets to witness the greatness of his father. Although deprived of a normal father-son experience, Odysseus and Telemachos are given the gift of another kind of experience together, a formidable test from which they emerge triumphant and united. Moreover, this triumphant reunion extends to another generation, to Odysseus's father Laertes, who rejoices when he sees his son and grandson "contending over their courage" as the three of them prepare to fight the fathers and brothers of the slain suitors.[174]

When the considerations of the preceding two paragraphs are combined, we are forced to acknowledge that much of the interest and power of the *Odyssey* can be attributed to the poet's exploitation of the character of Telemachos. It is unlikely that Telemachos played a role of such importance in any other part of the tradition that Homer helped to propagate. If Homer inserted quotes 5.39 and 5.40 in the *Iliad* during or after the composition of the generally later *Odyssey*, as I am tentatively suggesting, he evidently could have counted on these passages to act as forward references to the later poem.[175]

In the next section I suggest a possible motive for the references to the *Odyssey* in quotes 5.39 and 5.40. What is important now is that if the *Iliad* was modified to include these references, it could also have been modified to enable the startling connections between the two poems that I discussed in section 5.4.

5.7. Structural Integration of the *Iliad* and the *Odyssey*

I now show that our understanding of Achilles' treatment of Agamemnon in the funeral games for Patroklos enables us to see in the plot of the *Iliad* a simple structure that can also be recognized in the Homeric corpus as a whole, beginning in the first book of the *Iliad* and ending in the last book of the *Odyssey*. What is particularly interesting is that the Odyssean components of the corpus-level structure are the three passages I discussed in section 5.3, namely, the three passages in the *Odyssey* in which the protagonist of the *Iliad* plays an active role. In my discussion of these passages, I showed that they all share an unusual relationship to the *Iliad*. The affinity of these passages seen in this shared relationship is reaffirmed by their common membership in the corpus-level structure described below. This reaffirmation reinforces the argument given in part (*d*) of section 5.3 for the authenticity of the last book of the *Odyssey*. It also indirectly strengthens the case for perverse inconsistency since this unexpected property is key to the unusual relationship of the three passages to the *Iliad*.

Part (*a*) of this section lays the groundwork for the main discussion in part (*b*) by describing a well-known generic structure that is often found in ancient literature and introducing a term for a particular kind of this structure.

(a) Ring and Stack Structures

I wish to distinguish between two structures that appear frequently in Homer and are generally treated together under the heading of "ring composition." Let us first review the meaning of this term.

Consider, for example, three concentric circles (or rings) labeled A, B, and C from the largest to the smallest, with a straight line passing through all three circles. As we move from one end of the line to the other, we encounter circles A, B, C, C, B, and A. The resulting ABCCBA pattern, or the equally symmetric pattern ABCDCBA, is called a ring structure.[176] It can be given a literary form, as in the following excerpt from the meeting between Achilles and Priam (in which the A, B, and C parts are indicated by underlining, italics, and boldface, respectively):

> "Your son is given back to you, aged sir, as you asked it.
> He lies on a bier. When dawn shows you yourself shall see him
> as you take him away. *Now you and I must remember our supper.*
> **For even Niobe, she of the lovely tresses, remembered
> to eat**, whose twelve children were destroyed in her palace,
> ... [lines 604–612: the story of Niobe]
> **But she remembered to eat when she was worn out with weeping.**
> ... [lines 614–617: postscript to the story of Niobe]
> *Come then, we also, aged magnificent sir, must remember
> to eat*, and afterward you may take your beloved son back
> to Ilion, and mourn for him; and he will be much lamented."
>
> Quote 5.41: *Il.* 24.599–620 (underlining, italics, and boldface added)

This instance of Homeric ring composition is usually regarded as an example of the ABCDCBA pattern,[177] with the story of Niobe related in lines 604–612 representing the central element (D) and the postscript in lines 614–617 representing a relatively minor blemish on the otherwise clear symmetry characteristic of the ring structure. As is well known, quote 5.41 belongs to a class of passages that Homer typically renders in ring composition, namely, passages in which the speaker supports his position with a mythological paradigm (which is often modified to fit the circumstances, as it is in the case of the story of Niobe).[178] I shall now describe two other common applications of ring composition because they illustrate a special kind of ring structure that deserves separate consideration.[179]

The first class of instances of the special kind of ring structure consists of passages in which someone asks a series of questions which someone else then answers in reverse order. The most striking member of this class, found in the account of Odysseus's interaction with the shade of his mother during his visit to the underworld, contains seven rings (that is, Odysseus asks seven questions which his mother then answers in reverse order).[180] Examples with only two rings[181] may be less impressive, but are also respectable members of the class. The second class whose members exhibit the same special ring structure consists of passages in which two actions, A and B, are proposed or commanded in the order AB and then executed in the order BA. The most striking member of this class is Athene's plan for securing the homecoming of Odysseus: she begins to execute the second part of her plan (going to Ithaka to put some spirit into his son) immediately, but the first part (sending Hermes to tell Kalypso "with all speed" that she must release Odysseus) is not acted on until four books later.[182]

The ring structures in which questions are answered or actions are executed in reverse order possess a characteristic that is not part of the definition of a ring structure and that is not found in quote 5.41 or in many other examples of ring composition: the elements of the first half of the structure all refer to one act (the asking of a question or the proposal of an action), while the elements of the second half all refer to another act (the answering of a question or the execution of an action) which is opposite or complementary to the first. If the two opposite or complementary acts are denoted by X and Y, and if we continue to use the letters A and B to refer to rings, then a two-ring instance of this kind of structure can be described by the formula $X_A X_B Y_B Y_A$. Consider, for example, the passage from Odysseus's visit to the underworld in which the shade of Achilles asks for news of his son and father.[183] The structure of this passage conforms to the mentioned formula if X denotes a question, Y denotes an answer, A represents Achilles' son, and B represents his father (so that X_A = Achilles' question about his son, X_B = Achilles' question about his father, Y_B = Odysseus's response to Achilles' question about his father, and Y_A = Odysseus's response to Achilles' question about his son).

Just as it is convenient to have the generic term "ring composition" or "ring structure" based on a simple mental model, it will be convenient to have a generic term and a simple mental model for the type of structure just described. Suppose someone builds a stack of blocks by adding one block at a time and then destroys the stack by removing the blocks one at a time until they are all gone. If X represents the addition of a block to the stack, Y represents the removal of a block from the stack, and letters from the beginning of the alphabet are used to identify different blocks, then the process of creating and then destroying a stack of three blocks is represented by the formula $X_A X_B X_C Y_C Y_B Y_A$. I shall refer to any structure that can be described by a formula of this type as a "stack structure."

A ring structure and a stack structure are both one-dimensional in the sense that they are both linear sequences of elements. When we consider the number of parameters needed to describe an individual element, a ring structure is still one-dimensional but a stack structure is two-dimensional (it is necessary to specify not only the ring to which an element belongs, but also whether it is an element that refers to act X or act Y). Owing to this two-dimensionality, a stack structure possesses two properties that would otherwise be contradictory: symmetry (the symmetry of a ring structure) and polarity (the structure has an X end and a Y end).

At this point, the distinction between a ring structure and a stack structure may not seem useful. For in the examples discussed so far, a textual element X_A is almost certain to be followed, sooner or later, by the corresponding element Y_A: a question will usually be answered, and an action that is planned or commanded will usually be executed. In such cases, what is interesting about the structure $X_A X_B Y_B Y_A$, given that it begins with $X_A X_B$, is simply the reversal in the order of the subscripts (AB is followed by BA), so there is no harm in regarding the stack structure as nothing more than a ring structure. But these examples have been discussed only to introduce the concept of a stack structure and to acknowledge the logical precursors of the structures to be discussed in the next subsection. In the structures we are about to consider, the very existence of Y_A and Y_B is an interesting fact, the result of conscious decisions on Homer's part, and to reduce the $X_A X_B Y_B Y_A$ structure to an ABBA structure would be to lose critical information.

(b) Large-Scale Stack Structures in Homer

While many instances of ring composition in Homer are found in brief passages such as quote 5.41, this type of structure is also evident on much larger scales. Indeed, a ring structure spans essentially the entire *Iliad*.[184] I shall now describe a stack structure of almost the same scale. After that, I describe a stack structure of even greater extent: a structure that spans the entire Homeric corpus.

The *Iliad* is the story of the wrath of Achilles and its consequences. Achilles' wrath is aroused by two distinct outrages: his dishonor by Agamemnon in the quarrel that begins the poem and the killing of his friend Patroklos by Hektor. Although the death of Patroklos is the indirect result of the Quarrel (since it is Achilles' withdrawal from the fighting as a result of the Quarrel that leads to the deterioration in the military position of the Greeks and the need for Patroklos to join the fighting), the second outrage is so devastating to Achilles that for him it eclipses the first, as we saw in the discussion of the spurious reconciliation between him and Agamemnon (section 3.1). It is only after Achilles has taken revenge for the second outrage by killing Hektor that he exacts revenge for the first outrage by humiliating Agamemnon at the end of the funeral games for Patroklos (section 3.2). Thus, the story of the wrath of Achilles and his acts of retaliation takes the form of the stack structure $X_A X_B Y_B Y_A$, where X represents an outrage that arouses the wrath of Achilles and Y represents his revenge for the outrage, while the subscripts A and B identify the outrage in question (the dishonor done to Achilles by Agamemnon or the killing of Patroklos by Hektor, respectively). I shall call this the Iliadic stack structure.

In the conventional interpretation of the spear-throwing event in the funeral games for Patroklos, there is no Y_A (Achilles never takes revenge on Agamemnon) and so what I call the Iliadic stack structure does not exist. With the interpretation proposed in chapter 3, the structure certainly exists, but it appears at first glance to be very lopsided, since three of its four "legs" are major plot elements (the Quarrel, the killing of Patroklos, and the killing of Hektor) while the fourth consists of a 14-line account of an athletic event that does not even take place (quote 3.4). It is doubtful whether an argument can legitimately be based on a structure that is as lopsided as this one appears to be. I shall argue, however, that the Iliadic stack structure is not as lopsided as it appears and is, on the contrary, nicely balanced when judged by the criterion that matters most.

It should first be pointed out that the fourth component of the Iliadic stack structure is not actually limited to the 14 lines of the spear-throwing event. For after we have read those 14 lines and given them the interpretation suggested in chapter 3, we realize that Homer set us up to experience the full force of Agamemnon's humiliation by means of Achilles' exemplary behavior in the earlier events, most notably in the chariot race with which the games begin. Let us consider the qualities displayed by Achilles in connection with that contest. As I mentioned near the end of chapter 3, he takes pity on the man who came in last in the race and proposes to award him second prize.[185] He then yields to the objection of the man who came in second and generously supplies a different prize for the loser.[186] The prize that had originally been intended for whomever should come in last he gives to the aged Nestor, who did not participate in the race and is very grateful for the honor.[187] Thus, in his handling of the outcome of the chariot race, Achilles exhibits sympathy, willingness to yield to a just demand, generosity, kindness, and respect for his elders. In the course of the race itself he exhibits tact and diplomatic skill when he defuses a nasty quarrel between two spectators with the following words:

> "No longer now, Aias [son of Oïleus] and Idomeneus, continue
> to exchange this bitter and evil talk. It is not becoming.
> If another acted so, you yourselves would be angry.
> Rather sit down again among those assembled ..."
>
> Quote 5.42: *Il.* 23.492–495

Note, in addition, how he condemns "bitter and evil talk," a description which would also apply to his quarrel with Agamemnon. But the differences between the Achilles of the Quarrel and the Achilles of the chariot race are fully accounted for by the change in circumstances and do not imply any change in Achilles himself. In the Quarrel, Achilles is defending his honor, the measure of his worth in the heroic tradition, against an unjust assault, whereas quote 5.42 refers to a minor irritation that has escalated into an ugly confrontation that threatens to spoil the atmosphere of the funeral games for no good reason. When Achilles and Agamemnon meet for the last time in the spear-throwing event, one as host and the other as contestant, Achilles maintains the self-possession he has exhibited throughout the games. That this man who has been shown to be sympathetic, yielding, generous, kind, respectful, tactful, and diplomatic under appropriate circumstances goes on to subject Agamemnon to a searing humiliation underscores, for both the audience of the funeral games and the audience of the *Iliad*, the egregiousness of Agamemnon's offense and the depth of his shame.

The amount of text that relates to the fourth component of the Iliadic stack structure is only one factor that bears on the balance of this structure. The primary consideration must be whether the revenge Y_A (Achilles' humiliation of Agamemnon in the spear-throwing event) is proportionate to the outrage X_A (the dishonor done to Achilles by Agamemnon). The answer to this question is clear from the analysis of the spear-throwing event which I summarized in chapter 3 as follows: the games end with a bang, not a whimper, in a scene whose power is only accentuated by its compactness, a scene that also brings the Quarrel to a decisive conclusion with a humiliation of Agamemnon that he will never forget.

The large-scale structure of the *Iliad* is generally considered to be based on two principles: (*a*) the symmetry manifested in the grand ring composition mentioned at the beginning of this subsection and (*b*) the forward advance of the plot (which is often divided into three phases or "movements").[188] It may be worth noting, if only as a curiosity, that the same two principles are clearly visible in the stack structure $X_A X_B Y_B Y_A$: the symmetry of ring composition is visible in the subscripts (ABBA), and the forward advance of the plot is visible in the main symbols (XXYY, which in this case represents the progression from outrage, in the sense of a transgression, to revenge for the transgression). I do not mean to suggest that Homer deliberately set out to create a large-scale stack structure in the plot of the *Iliad*. Unlike the ring structure of the poem as a whole, which seems to have been intentional (although how far it extends from the beginning and end of the poem into its middle books is a matter of opinion), the Iliadic stack structure is simply a natural structure for the development of the theme of Achilles' wrath.

The story of the wrath of Achilles does not end with his humiliation of Agamemnon, which is described at the end of book 23, for we learn at the beginning of book 24 that Achilles continues to abuse Hektor's corpse after the funeral games for Patroklos. The wrath story really ends only when we see Achilles finally freed from his wrath in the moments of silence and openness to the other that constitute the spiritual climax of the poem (see section 3.5). Nevertheless, and despite the fact that the meeting of Achilles and Priam is more important to the plot than the humiliation of Agamemnon (which is not even recognized in the conventional interpretation of the spear-throwing event), I shall sometimes write in what follows that the Iliadic stack structure reflects the plot structure of the poem. Although this is an oversimplification, it is justified by the pattern of outrage and revenge that is so clear and so clearly fundamental to the plot (provided one accepts the interpretation of the spear-throwing event advanced in chapter 3).

The Iliadic stack structure extends over most of the length of the *Iliad*. As promised at the beginning of this subsection, I shall now describe a stack structure of even greater extent. I shall refer to this second large-scale stack structure as the corpus stack structure because it is made up of elements from both poems of the Homeric corpus.

The corpus stack structure, like the Iliadic, revolves around Achilles. Only two violent quarrels between Achilles and another Greek hero are described in Homer: the quarrel between Achilles and Agamemnon related at the beginning of the *Iliad* and the quarrel between Achilles and Odysseus that is the subject of the first song of Demodokos (see part (*b*) of section 5.3). Likewise, the shade of Achilles participates in only two conversations: one with the shade of Agamemnon (see part (*a*) of section 5.3) and one with Odysseus during the latter's visit to the underworld (see part (*c*) of section 5.3). Thus, the heroes with whom Achilles converses in the underworld are the same as the ones with whom he has a violent quarrel while alive. If X represents a fierce quarrel between Achilles and another Greek hero, Y represents an underworld conversation in which Achilles participates, and the subscripts A and B identify the man with whom Achilles quarrels or converses (with A = Agamemnon and B = Odysseus), then the two quarrels and the two conversations are arranged in the sequence $X_A X_B Y_B Y_A$ (given that the *Odyssey* follows the *Iliad*). This is the corpus stack structure.[189] Since X_A is in the first book of the *Iliad* and Y_A is in the last book of the *Odyssey*, it is fair to say that this structure spans the Homeric corpus.

The corpus stack structure is composed of one element from the *Iliad* and three from the *Odyssey*. The Odyssean components form a well-defined set, namely, the set of all passages in the *Odyssey* that feature the protagonist of the *Iliad*.[190] In section 5.3 we found that these three passages all bear a certain strange relationship to the *Iliad*. Now we find that the same three passages in conjunction with the foundational scene of the *Iliad* form a structure that replicates the structure of the plot of that poem. Either of these findings pointing to the specialness of the three passages and their mutual affinity can be considered to reinforce the other.

What suggests that the corpus stack structure was intentionally created by the poet is that it duplicates the structure of the *Iliad* as described by the Iliadic stack structure. In addition, there is a special relationship between corresponding components of the two stack structures, namely, between their initial components (the X_A's) and between their final components (the Y_A's). The relationship between the initial components is obvious: they are the same (X_A = the Quarrel for both the Iliadic and corpus stack structures) except for a difference in emphasis (what is important in the corpus-level structure is simply the occurrence of a violent quarrel involving Achilles, regardless of any moral injury he may have sustained). The relationship between the final components is more subtle, but even so it is clear from the discussion in section 3.3. There I argued that Agamemnon's mysterious failure to mention the funeral games for Patroklos in his underworld conversation with Achilles is explained by his wish to avoid an extremely painful topic, his humiliation by Achilles in the final event of those games. Since the humiliation of Agamemnon by Achilles in the funeral games for Patroklos is the Y_A of the Iliadic stack structure and the underworld conversation between the Achilles and Agamemnon is the Y_A of the corpus stack structure, there is a significant connection between the final components of these two structures. We should be open to the possibility that the significance of the corpus stack structure is signaled by its relationship with the Iliadic stack structure, which encompasses both their structural equivalence and the connections between corresponding elements of the two structures.

If the corpus stack structure was constructed intentionally by Homer, it would seem that he used it to bind his two epics into one whole. There have been indications before this that the two poems are to be regarded as a single whole. First and foremost is the way the *Odyssey* brings the story of the Trojan War to a close, telling us not only about the Wooden Horse and the sack of Troy, but also what finally happened to all the major Greek heroes of the *Iliad*.[191] In addition, the last book of the *Iliad* seems to provide a smooth transition to the *Odyssey*.[192] After reviewing the parallels between *Iliad* book 24 and the *Odyssey*, one scholar offers his assessment that the *Iliad* is "dovetailed thematically with the *Odyssey*, as if the two works could really almost be regarded as one great epic *continuum*, stretching from the Wrath of Akhilleus to the safe homecoming and triumph of the last of the heroes,

Odysseus."[193] Although these links between the poems have long been recognized, the corpus stack structure provides the strongest indication that Homer wanted his two poems to be regarded as parts of one whole. I suggest that the allusions to the *Odyssey* in the *Iliad* discussed in the preceding section, balancing to some extent the allusions to the *Iliad* in the *Odyssey* mentioned in an early note to this chapter, are to be understood in this context. It is tempting to infer from all this that the two epics were composed by the same poet, as my language has already implied. This proposition will be considered at greater length in section 6.12.

5.8. Monro's Law

The relationship between the *Iliad* and the *Odyssey* described in this chapter is undeniably strange owing to the role of perverse inconsistency. In this concluding section of the chapter, I compare this relationship with another strange relationship between the two epics, one that was first noted in modern times by D. B. Monro and is now often referred to as Monro's Law.

The *Odyssey*, observed Monro, "never repeats or refers to any incident related in the *Iliad*."[194] Asserting on this basis that "the *Odyssey* shows no awareness of the existence of the *Iliad*," Denys Page concluded that the poet of the *Odyssey* simply had no knowledge of the *Iliad*,[195] a position that has since been refuted.[196] The generally accepted interpretation of Monro's Law is that the *Odyssey* poet was familiar with the *Iliad*, but took care not to duplicate material from the earlier poem.[197] Gregory Nagy puts it this way: contrary to Page, "the *Odyssey* displays an awareness of the *Iliad* by steering clear of it."[198] But this is strange, because "traditional poetry," in the words of Jenny Strauss Clay, "is notoriously promiscuous,"[199] meaning that one would expect the poet of the *Odyssey* to incorporate Iliadic elements. My own position, of course, is that the *Odyssey* does *not* steer clear of *Iliad*, but engages with it in a very sophisticated fashion. It displays an awareness of the *Iliad* by feigning lack of awareness in a calculated manner that is meant to be noticed. As a result, the *Odyssey* sometimes gives the impression that it is avoiding an episode from the *Iliad* when actually there is much more that is going on. For an illustration, let us return to one of the passages discussed in section 5.3.

The conversation between the shades of Achilles and Agamemnon in the underworld is the only interaction between these heroes in the *Odyssey* and the first in Homer since Achilles' humiliation of Agamemnon in the funeral games for Patroklos. For the friendliness of this conversation to seem natural in this context, it would be necessary for these men to explicitly put the Quarrel behind them, perhaps by expressing their regret for all the harm it caused.[200] One might wish to explain their failure to do so in terms of Monro's Law, which forbids any reference to the Quarrel. But this "explanation" would be inadequate. The underworld conversation does not merely avoid referring to the Quarrel as required by Monro's Law: it conveys a mutual respect between Achilles and Agamemnon which virtually denies that the Quarrel ever occurred. Moreover, this denial is accentuated by Achilles' acknowledgment in quote 5.8 of the basis for Agamemnon's claim to superiority in that confrontation. And quite apart from its relationship to the

Quarrel, the conversation between the shades of Achilles and Agamemnon contains unmistakable allusions to the *Iliad*. The excerpt shown in quote 3.10 mentions the special burial of Patroklos, whose bones were to be mixed with those of Achilles upon the latter's death, and the special friendship between Achilles and Antilochos, which is evident in the funeral games for Patroklos and in the selection of Antilochos to be the one to inform Achilles of his death. Thus, the relationship of the conversation to the *Iliad* is far richer than that envisaged by Monro's Law: it not merely ignores the Quarrel, but denies it pointedly while alluding to other aspects of the poem.

The rich relationship between the *Iliad* and the *Odyssey* seen in the latter's conversation between Achilles and Agamemnon is also seen in the other two passages discussed in section 5.3. The first song of Demodokos is similar to the conversation between the shades of Achilles and Agamemnon in that it also seems to make a point of denying the Quarrel, and it also makes allusions to the *Iliad*. But the underworld conversation between Odysseus and the shade of Achilles is different in that what is conspicuous by its absence from this conversation is not an incident from the *Iliad* (such as the Quarrel) but the heroic ethos of that poem (which, significantly, is affirmed elsewhere in the *Odyssey*). For this reason, Monro's Law in this case is not merely inadequate but irrelevant.[201] By contrast, the conversation between Odysseus and the shade of Achilles harmonizes nicely with the other two passages discussed in section 5.3 in its combination of apparently perverse inconsistency with the *Iliad* (its denial of the heroic ethos) and ordinary allusion to that poem.

Monro's Law is also irrelevant to the relationship between the *Iliad* and the *Odyssey* as seen in the aftermath of the slaughter of the suitors (see section 5.4). No episode from the *Iliad* is conspicuous by its absence from this scene, but again there is a significant change in attitude. Odysseus's condemnation in quote 5.31 of boasting over slain men contradicts his own behavior in the *Iliad*, and Homer appears to have gone to great lengths to call one's attention to this contradiction.

Even with the limitations that I have just discussed, there is debate as to whether Monro's Law claims too much. Seth Schein believes that the references to the death and burial of Patroklos in quote 3.10 constitute a violation of the law.[202] Gregory Nagy and Douglas Cairns, on the other hand, assert that there is no violation since the mixing of the bones of Achilles and Patroklos, although predicted in the *Iliad*, does not actually take place until after the time frame of the poem.[203] Another response is to explicitly limit the range of validity of the law, as in this formulation: "The *Odyssey* never refers to the main narrative events of the *Iliad*, the wrath of Achilles over Briseis, the fresh anger against Hector, the death of Troy's noblest defender."[204]

Regardless of the approach, I question whether the effort to save Monro's Law is worthwhile. For no matter how it is formulated, this law fails to capture much that is strange in the relationship between the *Iliad* and the *Odyssey*. In particular, it overlooks the peculiar combination of affirmation and denial of the earlier poem by the later one that we have observed in several passages, and it sheds no light whatever on Odyssean passages that, without excluding

Iliadic episodes, seem to deliberately deviate from Iliadic norms. This composite objection is the first of two criticisms.

What I sometimes call a "denial" of some aspect of the *Iliad* by the *Odyssey* is manifested in an apparently perverse inconsistency between the poems. This inconsistency is obviously the strangest aspect of their relationship. In the next chapter, I argue that perverse inconsistency is also evident in each poem considered separately from the other. It is thus a property of the Homeric corpus as a whole and not just an aspect of the relationship between the two poems that make up the corpus. My second criticism of any formulation of Monro's Law is that a greater unification can be achieved if we expand the domain of discourse to include not only the relationship between the *Iliad* and the *Odyssey* but also the illogicalities within each poem. That is what we now proceed to do.

Chapter 6

Mysterious Inconsistency in the *Iliad* and the *Odyssey*

The primary aim of chapter 5 was to show that certain passages in the *Odyssey* are perversely inconsistent with the *Iliad*—that is, for some mysterious reason they were designed to be inconsistent with the *Iliad*. Having argued for perverse inconsistency between the two epics, I now make a case for perverse inconsistency within each one. It follows from the persuasiveness of this case that the inconsistencies discussed in the preceding chapter should not be interpreted as some kind of statement by the poet of the *Odyssey* concerning the relationship between his poem and the *Iliad*. Rather, as I have mentioned before, perverse inconsistency is a property of Homer in general, where "Homer" is simply a collective term for the two epics.

The reader will observe that a few of the anomalies discussed in this chapter are not really inconsistencies but rather are illogicalities of another sort. This distinction is not important: these other illogicalities are just as disturbing and apparently inexplicable as the inconsistencies, and the illogicalities of both kinds fall within the theoretical framework introduced later in this book. Although the more inclusive term "illogicality" would be more precise, I will continue to use the term "inconsistency" when speaking in general, partly because of the historical background covered in chapter 4 and partly because the vast majority of illogicalities discussed in this chapter and chapter 5 are, in fact, inconsistencies. In addition, the illogicalities to which I have been referring (which are those discussed in sections 6.5 and 6.7) can be regarded as inconsistencies with common sense.

The claim that a given inconsistency is perverse is based on one or more indications that it was intentional together with an intuitive judgment that it cannot be understood in terms of any ordinary motivation of the poet. As it is not possible to provide evidence for the absence of an ordinary motivation, the discussion focuses on the indications of intentionality (as in chapter 5). When I claim that an inconsistency must have been intentional, it should be understood that I consider it to be perverse (the only exceptions to this rule are the inconsistencies discussed in section 5.2). This judgment is supported in retrospect by the number and variety of apparently intentional inconsistencies and the implausibility of the proposition that there is an explanation for each one.

6.1. The Embassy Duals and Associated Problems

One of the most notorious inconsistencies in Homer is found in the Embassy scene of the *Iliad*. Three ambassadors—Phoinix, Aias, and Odysseus—are selected to try to persuade Achilles to return to battle. Each of the three makes an appeal to Achilles and receives a reply from him. Yet the intervening passage which describes the walk of the ambassadors to Achilles' camp, their arrival, and their welcome[1] repeatedly refers to the three ambassadors in the dual, the grammatical form used in early Greek for precisely two subjects and their actions or attributes.[2] A number of attempts have been made to explain this anomaly,[3] but no approach has been entirely successful. The idea that the anomaly is intentional, on the other hand, has the virtue of disposing of other problems at the same time. To lay the foundation for this thesis, I now review in broad outline the progression of Achilles' responses to the three appeals.

In his reply to the first appeal, that of Odysseus, Achilles states his intention to return home with his fellow Myrmidons the next day; Odysseus and Aias are to report the failure of the embassy, while Phoinix (who had helped raise Achilles like a second father) is to spend the night in Achilles' shelter so that he can return home with him if he wishes. After the second appeal, that of Phoinix, Achilles remains firm in his rejection of Agamemnon's offer, but says that he will wait until dawn to decide whether he is going to return home; Odysseus and Aias are still to carry back the message of the embassy's failure, and Phoinix is still to spend the night in Achilles' shelter. In his reply to the last appeal, that of Aias, Achilles relents to some extent: he will return to battle, but only if and when the Trojans threaten the ships and shelters of the Myrmidons. He tells Odysseus and Aias to deliver this message to Agamemnon. Without further discussion, these two ambassadors return to make their report, while Phoinix stays with Achilles.

We are now confronted with a second problem: why does Phoinix end up staying with Achilles? As long as Achilles is contemplating leaving Troy the morning after the embassy, it makes sense for Phoinix to spend the night in Achilles' shelter so that he can go home with the Myrmidons if he so chooses. By the end of the embassy, however, Achilles no longer intends to leave Troy in the morning, and there is no reason Phoinix should not return with Aias and Odysseus to the shelter of Agamemnon. This is a serious problem that demands an explanation. Its seriousness is underscored by what Odysseus tells Agamemnon and the other leaders upon his return, or rather by what he does *not* tell them. Odysseus reports only what Achilles said in response to his own speech. He says that Achilles threatened to leave Troy at dawn, and neglects to mention that this threat was subsequently retracted. This omission, which ignores Achilles' instruction that his final response be communicated to Agamemnon, goes unchallenged by Aias and the heralds who accompanied the ambassadors. The incompleteness of Odysseus's report would be mysterious even in the absence of Achilles' instruction and constitutes a problem in its own right. The rationalizations that have been offered for this

6.1. THE EMBASSY DUALS

third problem[4] are not at all convincing, but I believe the solution is clear. It is obviously necessary for the returning ambassadors to explain why Phoinix did not return with them, and in fact Odysseus concludes his report by saying that Phoinix stayed with Achilles at the latter's urging so that he would be able to go home with the Myrmidons if he chose to do so.[5] If Agamemnon knew that Achilles had taken back his threat to leave Troy, no explanation would have been possible. Thus, Homer's decision to have Phoinix stay with Achilles even when the latter no longer intends to leave Troy forces the poet to have Odysseus give an incomplete report. This contrived set of circumstances—or, at a minimum, the poet's willingness to tolerate this awkward situation—shows that Homer must have had some reason for keeping Phoinix in Achilles' shelter. There is no such reason in the story line, but an interesting possibility emerges if we examine the immediate consequences of Homer's decision.

By having Phoinix stay behind with Achilles, separating him from the other two ambassadors, Homer gives himself the opportunity to refer to Odysseus and Aias as a pair and therefore the opportunity to use the dual form appropriately. He does in fact refer to the pair five times: once in Achilles' response to each of the three appeals (when the subject is the message to be delivered to Agamemnon), once when Odysseus and Aias leave Achilles, and once when they arrive back at the shelter of Agamemnon.[6] On each of these five occasions where the dual would be appropriate, however, the plural is used instead.[7] This is not a grammatical error, as the plural may be used for two subjects as well as for more than two.[8] But it does seem strange that the dual is avoided where it could be used, when previously it was used where it should have been avoided. The oddness of this combination is emphasized by J. B. Hainsworth: "There can be no plausible reason why Akhilleus should receive his visitors in the dual and dismiss them ... in the plural, nor why they should arrive in the dual and depart ... in the plural, especially when Akhilleus has subtracted Phoinix from their number."[9] The situation becomes odder still when we reflect that the separation of Phoinix from the other two ambassadors is achieved by transparently fraudulent means. Homer seems to go out of his way to be able to use duals and to be seen as having done this. The fact that he goes on to use plurals instead must therefore be significant. Since, by itself, the use of the plural for two of a thing is unremarkable, the significance of Homer's use of plurals for the two remaining ambassadors must lie in the contrast with his earlier failure to use them when they were required. But this explanation is available only if that earlier failure—that is, the use of the infamous duals—was intentional.[10] Thus, a unified solution to four mysteries—the use of duals to refer to the three ambassadors (grammatically incorrect), the subsequent use of plurals to refer to just two of them (not incorrect, but odd in combination with the first mystery), the overnight stay of Phoinix in the shelter of Achilles (unmotivated after Achilles has withdrawn his threat to leave Troy), and the incomplete report of Odysseus to Agamemnon (implausible on its face, but needed to accommodate the third mystery)—becomes possible if we accept the idea of intentional inconsistency.

Stated otherwise, my thesis is that the set of four mysteries can be regarded as a web of intentional inconsistencies. To see the attraction of this thesis from a slightly different point of view, let us suppose that it is wrong. Let us suppose, in particular, that the notorious duals were not intentional but rather, say, were carried over carelessly from an earlier version of the scene in which they were grammatically appropriate (to select one class of explanations that have been suggested). There would then be nothing remarkable in the use of plurals to refer to Odysseus and Aias since these plurals are noteworthy only in conjunction with the duals. If these plurals have no particular significance, there is no reason to separate Phoinix from the other two ambassadors. But the extraordinary measures taken to effect this separation—Phoinix's unmotivated stay with Achilles and Odysseus's incomplete report to Agamemnon—show that Homer must have had such a reason. This contradiction leads us to reject our starting assumption that the inappropriate duals were accidental and to conclude instead that the inconsistency between the actual number of ambassadors and the number implied by the duals must have been intentional and meant to be perceived as such. The intentional inconsistency in the Embassy evidently includes not only the infamous duals, but also the use of plurals to refer to Odysseus and Aias, which is inconsistent with one's expectations after duals were used earlier in the scene (one asks, "Why does Homer stop using duals when they would actually be appropriate?"), and it certainly also includes Phoinix's stay with Achilles and Odysseus's report to Agamemnon, both of which are inconsistent with Achilles' retraction of his threat to leave Troy.

I take it to be self-evident that no ordinary explanation is possible for the intentional inconsistency in the Embassy. It then follows that this inconsistency is perverse. Having presented the essence of my case for perverse inconsistency in the Embassy, I now address some issues that I have ignored for simplicity up to this point.

The first issue concerns my statement that "as long as Achilles is contemplating leaving Troy the morning after the embassy, it makes sense for Phoinix to spend the night in Achilles' shelter so that he can go home with the Myrmidons if he so chooses." This obviously assumes that Phoinix does not reside near Achilles, for if he did he would be well positioned to leave Troy with the Myrmidons the morning after the embassy if he spent the night in his own shelter. This poses a problem because one would expect Phoinix to live with the Myrmidons: (*a*) he has a strong, quasi-familial relationship with Achilles, and in fact he was sent to Troy by his benefactor Peleus as a sort of tutor to Achilles, who was quite young and inexperienced at the beginning of the war, and (*b*) he commands one of the Myrmidon battalions.[11]

A second issue is the unexplained presence of Phoinix at the council of Greek leaders at which the three ambassadors are selected for the mission to Achilles.[12] His presence at the council is surprising for two reasons: (*a*) as commander of just one of the five Myrmidon battalions, he presumably does not have the requisite rank, and (*b*) as a subordinate of Achilles, who has withdrawn himself and his men from the Greek cause, he would have no business participating in a Greek strategy session.

These two issues might be addressed as follows. Let us assume that Phoinix originally lived among the Myrmidons for the reasons given above. Achilles no longer needs a tutor, however, and Phoinix's position as commander of one of the Myrmidon battalions no longer obliges him to live near his men since they have been withdrawn from the fighting. It is therefore possible that Phoinix is living outside the Myrmidon camp at the time of the Embassy. How this change could have come about is not difficult to imagine. When Peleus sent Achilles and Phoinix to join Agamemnon's forces, the father advised his son to control his pride and temper and to avoid quarrels.[13] Phoinix may therefore consider it his duty to do what he can to smooth over the quarrel between Achilles and Agamemnon (as he attempts to do during the Embassy). With this in mind, and knowing that his attachment to Achilles would not be questioned, he may have moved his shelter closer to Agamemnon's after the Quarrel to show some solidarity with the Greek leader. We know that Achilles respects Phoinix's independence, and presumably would not have prevented such a move, since he accepts his role as one of Agamemnon's ambassadors[14] and since he states explicitly that he would not force Phoinix to leave Troy against his will.[15] For his part, Agamemnon would surely have welcomed Phoinix's move since it would lend much-needed legitimacy to his position in the Quarrel, and he may have gone on to invite Phoinix's participation in the council of the Greek leaders for the same reason. This scenario is admittedly speculative, but it shows that the two issues under discussion need not affect the case for perverse inconsistency presented earlier in this section. The alternative scenario of a fixed location for Phoinix's shelter (whether inside or outside the Myrmidon camp) only increases the number of inconsistencies that must be explained.

To recapitulate, the central inconsistency discussed in this section is between the number of ambassadors and the grammatical form used to refer to them. Later in this chapter I will argue more than once that some type of inconsistency appears to be intentional because it possesses distinctive features which are found in two separate instances of the inconsistency. In the present case, instead of a simple duplication, the second instance (the use of plurals when duals would have worked) is an inversion of the first (the use of duals when plurals were required). The inversion is not precise (the second instance is not actually an inconsistency since the plural can refer to two people), but Homer's artificial preparation for it (the contrived separation of Phoinix from the other two ambassadors) makes up for this, with the result that the infamous duals of the Embassy scene constitute a serious candidate for intentional, and indeed perverse, inconsistency.

6.2. The Embassy in the Talk between Achilles and Patroklos

Despite the importance to the *Iliad* of the friendship between Achilles and Patroklos, these two characters speak to each other more than briefly only once, when the Trojans have forced their way to the Greek ships and are attempting to set them on fire. Patroklos tries to get Achilles to go to the rescue, but he also has a backup plan, suggested to him by Nestor,[16] should Achilles refuse: to get Achilles' permission to lead the Myrmidons into battle himself. Adhering to Nestor's formulation, he proposes this alternative as follows:

> "But if you are drawing back from some prophecy known in your own heart
> and by Zeus' will your honored mother has told you of something,
> then send me out at least, let the rest of the Myrmidon people
> follow me, and I may be a light given to the Danaäns.
> Give me your armor to wear on my shoulders into the fighting;
> so perhaps the Trojans might think I am you, and give way"
>
> Quote 6.1: *Il.* 16.36–41

Achilles replies:

> "Ah, Patroklos, illustrious, what is this you are saying?
> I have not any prophecy in mind that I know of;
> there is no word from Zeus my honored mother has told me,
> but this thought comes as a bitter sorrow to my heart and my spirit
> when a man tries to foul one who is his equal, to take back
> a prize of honor, because he goes in greater authority.
> This is a bitter thought to me; my desire has been dealt with
> roughly. The girl the sons of the Achaians chose out for my honor,
> and I won her with my own spear, and stormed a strong-fenced city,
> is taken back out of my hands by powerful Agamemnon,
> the son of Atreus, as if I were some dishonored vagabond.
> Still, we will let all this be a thing of the past; and it was not
> in my heart to be angry forever; and yet I have said
> I would not give over my anger until that time came
> when the fighting with all its clamor came up to my own ships.
> So do you draw my glorious armor about your shoulders;
> lead the Myrmidons whose delight is battle into the fighting,"
>
> Quote 6.2: *Il.* 16.49–65

After expressing his bitterness at the way he was treated by Agamemnon, Achilles indicates that he would put the Quarrel behind him except for the fact that he has vowed to stay out of the fighting until it has reached his own ships. Since he made this vow in his reply to Aias during the Embassy,[17] we have here a clear reference to this scene. Achilles reinforces this already clear reference when he says in quote 6.2 that Agamemnon treated him "as if I were some dishonored vagabond," a description that is also found just before his vow to Aias (*Il.* 9.648 = 16.59) but otherwise appears nowhere else in Homer.[18]

While the reference in quote 6.2 to Achilles' vow to Aias is widely accepted,[19] it is rejected by Denys Page and Richard Janko. These two apparently make a valid technical point, but I shall argue that their point does little to discredit the reference seen by others. The observation made by Page and Janko, and also by the Alexandrian scholar Aristarchus, is that what is sometimes translated as "I said" in *Il.* 16.61 and what Lattimore renders as "I have said" (see quote 6.2) actually means "I meant" or "I intended."[20] In quote 6.2, therefore, Achilles is not referring directly to his reply to Aias's appeal in the Embassy. This conclusion also follows from the fact that the Greek verb in question, εφην, is the imperfect of the verb φημι ("to say"), and therefore does not signify a completed action such as the vow made to Aias. But this observation loses its force when we consider the context. Achilles is saying that he will not join the fighting now, although he will let Patroklos take his place, because he *intended* to stay out of the fighting until it reached his own

6.2. THE TALK BETWEEN ACHILLES AND PATROKLOS 137

ships. If "intended" here refers merely to a decision that he has kept to himself until now, this stance makes no sense since there is no reason Achilles should be bound by a private decision. Rather, Achilles' stance implies that he has made his decision known to others and feels bound by it because he does not want to be seen as having given in and gone against his word. Since he came to his decision over the course of the Embassy and communicated it in his reply to Aias (which he wished to be made public[21]), quote 6.2 must refer to this reply after all: Achilles intended to stay out of the fighting until it reached his own ships ever since he made this decision at the conclusion of the Embassy.

As the reader will recall from the preceding section, Aias made the last of the three appeals to Achilles during the Embassy. In his reply to the first appeal, that of Odysseus, Achilles stated that he intended to return home with his fellow Myrmidons the next day. In explanation of this decision, he told the ambassadors that his mother had told him that he faced one of two possible destinies: if he were to stay and fight at Troy, he would die young but with everlasting glory, but if he were to return home, he would live long but without glory (see quote 5.18). Patroklos must be referring to this contingent prediction at the beginning of quote 6.1: it would be strange if he were to inquire out of the blue about a prophecy Achilles might have been told by his mother if Achilles had not previously spoken of such a prophecy. (That Patroklos mentions the prophecy only as a hypothetical possibility is necessary for Achilles' subsequent denial of it, to be discussed presently.) We therefore have here another reference to the Embassy.[22] This conclusion holds even though Patroklos in quote 6.1 is simply following the lead of Nestor (*Il.* 11.793–798). Since the reason for Achilles' refusal to fight is well known, it would be strange if, without knowing about the prophecy, Nestor suggested that Achilles might continue to refuse because of some prophecy from his mother. But he does know about Achilles' two possible destinies, as there can be little doubt, despite the fact that the relevant text is not self-consistent,[23] that he asked Odysseus for a report of what transpired during the Embassy. And since Patroklos was present at the Embassy, *he* is well aware of the prophecy to which Nestor refers.

I maintain, then, that the conversation between Achilles and Patroklos alludes to several elements from the Embassy scene: Achilles' vow to Aias, his reference to himself as having been treated by Agamemnon "as if I were some dishonored vagabond," and the prophecy he received from his mother. But the same conversation also displays what seems to be willful ignorance of the earlier scene.

Since the Embassy took place just the night before the conversation in question, Achilles must know what prophecy Patroklos is referring to in quote 6.1. But in quote 6.2 he says he has received no prophecy from his mother. Malcolm Willcock proposes to explain this contradiction by postulating that the prophecy Achilles is said to have received from his mother (quote 5.18) was just a momentary invention by the poet for the speech in which it appears and was not meant to influence the *Iliad* to any wider extent.[24] But if this idea is correct, what is Patroklos referring to at the beginning of quote 6.1? Alternatively, Norman Postlethwaite accepts that the contradiction is real, but suggests that Achilles denies having received the prophecy so that his refusal to join the battle will not be construed as cowardice.[25] But the idea that Achilles would be vulnerable to a charge of cowardice flies in the face of everything we know about him.[26] In any case, why would he be more concerned about such a charge when he is speaking with Patroklos than he was the night before? The weakness of the proposed explanations forces us to acknowledge that the beginning of quote 6.2 is simply inconsistent with the Embassy.

The talk between Achilles and Patroklos contains another passage that is difficult to reconcile with the Embassy. The instructions that Achilles begins to give Patroklos in the last two lines of quote 6.2 include the following:

> "... beat the bane [the Trojans] aside from our ships; fall
> upon them with all of your strength; let them not with fire's blazing
> inflame our ships, and take away our desired homecoming.
> But obey to the end this word I put upon your attention
> **so that you can win, for me, great honor and glory**
> **in the sight of all the Danaäns, so they will bring back to me**
> **the lovely girl, and give me shining gifts in addition.**
> When you have driven them from the ships, come back; although later
> the thunderous lord of Hera might grant you the winning of glory,
> you must not set your mind on fighting the Trojans, whose delight
> is in battle, without me. So you will diminish my honor."
>
> Quote 6.3: *Il.* 16.80–90 (boldface added)

The part of this passage I have put in boldface is incongruous after the Embassy because here Achilles expresses great interest in things to which he was indifferent the night before. What strikes one first is his interest in gifts and the return of the girl Briseis. Agamemnon had hoped to secure Achilles' return to the war effort by offering to give back Briseis and to give him in addition an abundance of magnificent gifts. Quote 6.3 appears to allude to this offer. But Achilles had rejected Agamemnon's offer, communicated to him by Odysseus during the Embassy, in the strongest possible terms:

> "I hate his gifts. I hold him light as the strip of a splinter.
> Not if he gave me ten times as much, and twenty times over
> as he possesses now, not if more should come to him from elsewhere,
> or gave all that is brought in to Orchomenos, all that is brought in
> to Thebes of Egypt, where the greatest possessions lie up in the houses,
> ...
> not if he gave me gifts as many as the sand or the dust is,
> not even so would Agamemnon have his way with my spirit
> until he had made good to me all this heartrending insolence."
>
> Quote 6.4: *Il.* 9.378–387

The lavishness of Agamemnon's offer and the vehemence of Achilles' rejection of the offer make such a strong impression that the offer and its rejection inevitably come to mind when one reads the boldfaced part of quote 6.3; the awareness or sensation of a contradiction must follow.

Attempts have been made to minimize the significance of this contradiction. G. S. Kirk and Wolfgang Schadewaldt, for example, have both argued that it is not inconsistent for Achilles to be interested in gifts after rejecting them during the Embassy because the situation has changed: now that the ships are in imminent danger of being set on fire, he has authorized Patroklos to repel the Trojan attack, something that was not considered the night before.[27] This rationalization will not do, however, since Achilles sends Patroklos into battle in his place only because he wants to be seen as sticking to a position he staked out during the Embassy, that he himself will stay out of the fighting until it has reached his own ships. His rejection of Agamemnon's offer is another such strongly stated position. Given his unwillingness to back down from the stance he took during the Embassy as expressed in his vow to Aias, it is unthinkable after the diatribe in quote 6.4 that Achilles would express an interest in gifts without first receiving a genuine apology.

It has also been suggested that there is no inconsistency between quote 6.3 and the Embassy because Achilles might welcome from the Greek army as a whole what he would not accept from Agamemnon.[28] This brings us to the second incongruous feature of quote 6.3: Achilles' interest in receiving "great honor and glory in the sight of all the Danaäns." At the end of his speech in the Embassy, Odysseus anticipates the rejection of Agamemnon's offer and switches his appeal to one based on the honor and glory that Achilles can expect from the rest of the Greeks if he comes to their rescue (see quote 5.13). Achilles does not even refer to this new appeal when he replies. For him, evidently, honor and glory in the sight of all the Danaäns are not worth considering in the absence of an apology from Agamemnon. In quote 6.3 his attitude has changed completely even though he still has not received an apology. The contradiction with the Embassy that we sense immediately upon reading quote 6.3 is confirmed.

The hope Achilles expresses in quote 6.3 for honor and gifts from the Greeks and for the return of Briseis raises two difficult questions. So far I have concentrated on the first: Why would Achilles reverse his attitude towards these things when he has just made a point of his resolve by reaffirming the vow he made to Aias during the Embassy? The second is equally perplexing: What makes Achilles think that the Greeks would honor with gifts someone who has vowed not to join them in fighting the Trojans until his own ships are in danger? The difficulty presented by this question is evident in the variety of answers that have been proposed.[29] The ease with which both difficulties could have been avoided by leaving out the boldfaced lines in quote 6.3 suggests that they are intentional. This observation may be considered a footnote to my main argument for intentional inconsistency. To introduce that argument, I now review a popular idea concerning the composition of the *Iliad*.

We have observed two inconsistencies with the Embassy in the conversation between Achilles and Patroklos: Achilles' denial at the beginning of quote 6.2 that he has received a prophecy from his mother and his eagerness in quote 6.3 for honor and gifts from the Greeks and for the return of Briseis. The main theory that has been proposed in the past to explain such inconsistencies is that the Embassy was not yet part of the *Iliad* when the conversation in question (as well as the rest of the Patrokleia [book 16]) was composed. This suggestion has been made both by analysts arguing for multiple authorship and by those unitarians who argue that their single poet composed the *Iliad* in a process of progressive fixation.[30] But this theory cannot be correct if the conversation also refers to the Embassy.[31] I have pointed to two such references: the allusion in quote 6.1 to the prophecy Achilles received from his mother and the allusion in quote 6.2 to the vow Achilles made to Aias (from now on I consider the repetition of *Il.* 9.648 at 16.59 simply as a device used to strengthen the latter allusion). To support the claim that the conversation between Achilles and Patroklos actually alludes to the Embassy, I repeat and extend an argument due to Schadewaldt.

Achilles' decision to stay out of the fighting until it has reached his own ships is carefully developed in the succession of his responses to the three ambassadors (see section 6.1). Without the Embassy, his decision would simply appear out of nowhere in the conversation between Achilles and Patroklos (quote 6.2). Schadewaldt plausibly infers from this that book 16 (containing the conversation) alludes to book 9 (the Embassy) and that book 9 was not created on the basis of book 16.[32] To this I would add a similar argument based on Patroklos's allusion in quote 6.1 to the prophecy received by Achilles from his mother: as I said before, it would be strange if Patroklos were to inquire out of the blue in book 16 about such a prophecy if Achilles had not previously made it known in book 9 that he had in fact received one.

As this critique of a popular theory illustrates, the coexistence of inconsistencies with and allusions to the Embassy in the conversation between Achilles and Patroklos presents a dilemma for conventional interpretations. This dilemma has not been acknowledged by most scholars, who typically see inconsistencies *or* allusions but not both.[33] From the standpoint of the present study, of course, there is no dilemma: nothing prevents inconsistencies from coexisting with allusions if the inconsistencies are intentional. Indeed, we have seen the same phenomenon before: the combination of affirmation and denial of the Embassy that we see in the conversation between Achilles and Patroklos (in the allusions and the inconsistencies, respectively) is analogous to the affirmation and denial of the *Iliad* we observed in each of the three passages from the *Odyssey* discussed in section 5.3.

The difficulty of explaining the coexistence of inconsistencies and allusions in any other way constitutes my main argument for intentional inconsistency with the Embassy in the conversation between Achilles and Patroklos. In the remainder of this section I refine this argument slightly by suggesting that the inconsistencies are related in a certain way to the allusions. This suggestion would be undermined if the conversation between Achilles and Patroklos contained more inconsistencies with the Embassy than I have already discussed. The next order of business, therefore, is to dispose of some supposed inconsistencies that have been claimed by a number of scholars. I concentrate on the formulation of these claims by Denys Page because he makes their weakness most explicit.

In the part of his speech between quotes 6.2 and 6.3, Achilles says, "Soon the Trojans would be filling the ditches with their dead, *if Lord Agamemnon were well-disposed to me*" (Page's italics; I use his translation for consistency with his subsequent comment).[34] Page remarks, "There is only one way in which Agamemnon could show himself 'well-disposed' towards Achilles, and that is by apologizing and offering compensation: that is just what he did in the embassy, yet Achilles here complains that there has been no change in Agamemnon's disposition towards him." He adds that in the Embassy "Agamemnon has gone to the extremist possible lengths to show a change of heart towards Achilles." "The only possible judgement," concludes Page, is that Achilles' speech "was composed by a poet who knew nothing of any embassy."

The fatal flaw in this argument is the premise that Agamemnon apologizes to Achilles in the Embassy. Page apparently confuses Agamemnon's lavish offer of gifts with an apology. But the distinction is clear in the preliminaries to the Embassy and in the Embassy itself. The idea of an embassy is introduced when Nestor advises Agamemnon to repair his relationship with Achilles "with words of supplication and with the gifts of friendship" (see sections 3.1 and 3.5). The distinction between the two components comes to the fore when Agamemnon agrees to offer gifts, indeed far more than necessary, but fails to offer a single word of supplication, instead showing his true feelings by insisting that Achilles will have to submit to him. It is then reinforced by the lack of parallelism between Nestor's reply, which refers only to the enumerated gifts, and what he had suggested, the combination words of supplication and gifts of friendship.[35] In the Embassy itself, although Agamemnon's demand for submission is not mentioned, the absence of an apology is obvious. And it is obvious from his response to Agamemnon's offer—see the last lines of quote 6.4 in particular—that Achilles feels this absence and that all the gifts in the world could not make up for it.[36] Thus, the condition for his return that he states to Patroklos, "if Lord Agamemnon were well-disposed to me," is perfectly consistent with the Embassy.

Another claim of inconsistency with the Embassy which I dispute refers to a remark made by Achilles to Patroklos shortly before the main conversation discussed in this section (although substantially earlier in the *Iliad* owing to the retardation in the flow of time that characterizes this part of the poem). It is during the interval of perhaps a couple of hours between the remark and the conversation that Patroklos, who has gone to see Nestor on an errand for Achilles, is advised by Nestor to try to enlist Achilles' aid in the fighting or, failing that, to get his permission to lead the Myrmidons himself. The remark in question contains Achilles' first words since the Embassy of the night before and expresses his reaction to the even more desperate position that the Greeks now find themselves in:

> "[N]ow I think the Achaians will come to my knees and stay there
> in supplication, for a need past endurance has come to them."
>
> Quote 6.5: *Il.* 11.608–609

Page believes that these verses could not have been composed by a poet who was aware of the Embassy: "Now it seems very obvious that these words were not spoken by an Achilles about whose knees the Achaeans were in fact standing in supplication on the previous evening; an Achilles who had rejected their prayers, who had made it clear that he would never accept apology or compensation ...." And again: "It is absurd to say that the conduct of the ambassadors in the Ninth Book could not fairly be described as 'standing about the knees of Achilles in supplication'; a humbler apology, a more earnest prayer, could hardly be made."[37] Page fails to take into account that what matters to Achilles is what the conduct of the ambassadors reveals about the attitude of Agamemnon. Although Odysseus, Phoinix, and Aias implore Achilles to return to the fighting as earnestly as they can *as individuals*, it is clear to Achilles that they have not been authorized to offer an apology from Agamemnon. Quote 6.5 simply expresses his hope that the rapidly deteriorating situation will force a true supplication.

My rejection of two common claims of inconsistency echoes views that have been expressed by others.[38] Its significance for our discussion is that it leaves us with two real inconsistencies, each of which is in tension with one of the allusions to the Embassy in the conversation between Achilles and Patroklos. First, Achilles' denial that he has received a prophecy from his mother obviously contradicts Patroklos's allusion to the prophecy. Second, Achilles' eagerness for gifts and the return of Briseis conflicts with his insistence that he will stay out of the fighting until it reaches his own ships in that the latter is motivated by a wish to hold, as a matter of principle, to the stance he took during the Embassy while the former represents an about-face from the Embassy and therefore violates that wish. Since a sample of only two inconsistency/allusion pairs is not very convincing, I should reiterate the main point of this section: the conversation between Achilles and Patroklos contains both inconsistencies with and allusions to the Embassy, the sort of combination we saw repeatedly in section 5.3 and interpreted as evidence that the inconsistencies are intentional.

Achilles' loss of memory of the Embassy suggested by the real or perceived inconsistencies with that scene later in the poem has been called "the most violent contradiction in the *Iliad*."[39] Some authors give this distinction to the inappropriate duals in the Embassy itself.[40] Both problems have frequently been interpreted as clues to the compositional history of the poem.[41] According to this approach, the duals are remnants of an earlier version of the Embassy in which there were only two ambassadors, while Achilles' apparent loss of memory of the Embassy reveals a still earlier version of the poem in which there was no Embassy at all (as I mentioned earlier). This theory is attractive, but it is undermined by the indications of intentional inconsistency discussed in this section and section 6.1. The case for intentional inconsistency in the *Iliad* receives independent support in the next section from an analysis of a well-known problem that does not involve the Embassy.

6.3. Agamemnon's Test of the Army

From the standpoint of plot coherence, the most troubling episode in the *Iliad* is surely Agamemnon's test of the army. This affair has long been notorious, but I find it even more disturbing than previous commentaries would suggest. In part (*a*) of this section I provide the background needed to understand this reaction by revisiting some material outlined in part (*b*) of section 5.3. In part (*b*) I discuss the principal difficulties posed by the Test, which take the form of inconsistencies between this affair and earlier episodes in the poem. Finally, in parts (*c*) and (*d*) I show that the Test is the nucleus of an elaborate apparatus created by Homer with a great deal of premeditation. This apparatus, particularly the use of formal structures uniting the Test with the earlier episodes, demonstrates that the inconsistencies described in part (*b*) must have been intentional.

(*a*) Background

During the Quarrel, having vowed to withdraw from the war, Achilles declares to Agamemnon in front of the assembled army,

> "... And this shall be a great oath before you:
> some day longing for Achilleus will come to the sons of the Achaians,
> all of them. Then stricken at heart though you be, you will be able
> to do nothing, when in their numbers before man-slaughtering Hektor
> they drop and die. And then you will eat out the heart within you
> in sorrow, that you did no honor to the best of the Achaians."
>
> Quote 6.6: *Il.* 1.239–244

Achilles gives this dire prediction added emphasis by dashing the speaker's staff to the ground at the end. After the Quarrel, he asks his mother, the goddess Thetis, to persuade Zeus to help the Trojans so that their success during his absence from the fighting will prove his indispensability to the Greeks. Zeus is beholden to Thetis and agrees to her request. In a first attempt to help the Trojans, he sends to Agamemnon a delusive dream which says to him,

> "Listen quickly to what I say, since I am a messenger
> of Zeus, who far away cares much for you and is pitiful.
> Zeus bids you arm the flowing-haired Achaians for battle
> in all haste; since now you might take the wide-wayed city
> of the Trojans. ..."
>
> Quote 6.7: *Il.* 2.26–30

Agamemnon wakes up believing the dream (see quote 5.15), and has the heralds assemble the men while he holds a council of the princes. He relates the dream accurately to the princes, and then adds

> "Come then, let us see if we can arm the sons of the Achaians.
> Yet first, since it is the right way, I will make trial of them
> by words, and tell them even to flee in their benched vessels.
> Do you take stations here and there, to check them with orders."
>
> Quote 6.8: *Il.* 2.72–75

Agamemnon's speech elicits this response from Nestor:

> "Friends, who are leaders of the Argives and keep their counsel,
> had it been any other Achaian who told of this dream
> we should have called it a lie and we might rather have turned from it.
> Now he who claims to be far the best of the Achaians has seen it.[42]
> Come then, let us see if we can arm the sons of the Achaians."
>
> Quote 6.9: *Il.* 2.79–83

The council then breaks up and the princes proceed to the general assembly, where Agamemnon addresses the army as follows:

> "Fighting men and friends, O Danaäns, henchmen of Ares:
> Zeus son of Kronos has caught me fast in bitter futility.
> He is hard; who before this time promised me and consented
> that I might sack strong-walled Ilion and sail homeward.
> Now he has devised a vile deception, and bids me go back
> to Argos in dishonor having lost many of my people.
> ...
> Come then, do as I say, let us all be won over; let us
> run away with our ships to the beloved land of our fathers
> since no longer now shall we capture Troy of the wide ways."
>
> Quote 6.10: *Il.* 2.110–141

This is the test of the army which Agamemnon promised to the princes in quote 6.8. There are several reasons to expect that the men will not have to be told twice to "run away with [their] ships to the beloved land of [their] fathers." First, the lines I have omitted for brevity from quote 6.10 contain some very demoralizing observations, including references to the families waiting at home for the men and the deteriorating condition of the ships that must take them home. Second, Achilles' prediction of disaster in quote 6.6 is probably believable. Finally, even if disaster can be avoided, Agamemnon's pessimism in quote 6.10 seems justified: if the Greeks have been unable to take Troy in over nine years with their greatest warrior, how can they hope ever to be victorious without him? Indeed, the latter reasoning presumably lies behind Nestor's skepticism in quote 6.9. It comes as no surprise, then, that the temptation to run away proves impossible to resist; in fact, the men probably feel that they are responding to a sensible suggestion, not that they are succumbing to a temptation. Pandemonium reigns as they rush to the ships to make their departure. Even quick Odysseus is stunned at first, but he takes charge and restores order after being galvanized into action by Athene.

(*b*) The Inconsistency of the Test with the Dream and the Quarrel

Agamemnon must surely already have been aware that the loss of Achilles had eroded morale. This is confirmed by his words to the princes in quote 6.8 when he expresses uncertainty as to whether he will be able to arm the men[43] and when he anticipates that they might have to be restrained from fleeing. His speech to the army partially reproduced in quote 6.10 will just lower morale more. But the Dream told Agamemnon to arm his men "in all haste" (quote 6.7). To do this, he should obviously try to boost morale rather than lower it. He has two means at his disposal for this purpose. First, instead of saying falsely that Zeus wants him to return home in dishonor (*Il.* 2.114–115 in quote 6.10), he can tell the truth: Zeus has just told him (via the Dream) that the time has come to take Troy (quote 6.7). Second, he can back this up by citing the prediction witnessed by everyone when the expedition to Troy was about to set out from Aulis, the prediction that Troy would be captured after nine years—the nine years that have gone by since then.[44] As it is, it is left to Odysseus to recall this prediction for the men—it constitutes the climax of his appeal and succeeds in restoring their morale[45]—but there is no reason that Agamemnon could not have made use of it in a morale-boosting speech befitting a true leader.

6.3. AGAMEMNON'S TEST OF THE ARMY

Thus, the test of the army makes no sense on tactical grounds or as a response to the dream sent by Zeus. A logical course of action is available to Agamemnon, but he chooses the counterproductive Test instead. The remarks of one commentator reflect the assessment of many: "Agamemnon's conduct can only point to a disordered mind. No sane man would behave like that."[46] It is true that Agamemnon has shown unsound judgment before and will do so again,[47] and up to this point in our discussion the Test could be regarded simply as a particularly egregious example of his erratic leadership. But we have yet to consider what I think is the most important problem: the Test is not only contrary to reason, it is contrary to Agamemnon's nature. In particular, it is inconsistent with his deeply rooted pride, a driving force of the Quarrel.

In quote 6.6 Achilles says to Agamemnon, in effect, "You'll be sorry you dishonored me when, without me, your men are slaughtered by Hektor." If Achilles is indispensable to the Greek cause, as he implies, his alienation by Agamemnon is inexcusable and is bound to embitter the men whose sacrifices over almost ten years will have been in vain and who are now at risk of being slaughtered.[48] So it is not surprising that Agamemnon refuses to acknowledge what is at stake during the Quarrel. When Achilles first threatens to return home, Agamemnon deflects attention from the military implications with a twofold response: (*a*) he asserts that he does not need Achilles because there are others who will honor him and (*b*) he escalates the quarrel by saying that he will teach Achilles a lesson by taking away his prize (previously he had said only that he would compensate himself for the loss of his own prize by taking that of Achilles, Aias, or Odysseus). But the indispensability of Achilles, which Agamemnon will not and cannot admit during the Quarrel, is precisely what he seems to concede in the Test. For the only explanation he offers in quote 6.10 is that Zeus bids him go back to Argos; since nothing has happened since the Quarrel that might account for his change of heart, the army is bound to interpret this "explanation" as an admission that victory is impossible without Achilles. This implicit admission by Agamemnon, which puts him in a bad light at the same time that it vindicates his adversary, is a startling reversal from his arrogant stand in the Quarrel. In fact, given that Agamemnon is never able to overcome his pride in a public forum—recall his spurious reconciliation with Achilles in book 19 (see section 3.1)—it is fair to say that this reversal amounts to a psychological impossibility.

Agamemnon's inability to overcome his pride in a public forum is demonstrated not only by the spurious reconciliation in book 19 but also by the deliberations that culminate in the embassy to Achilles. Agamemnon sets these deliberations in motion by expressing despair at the deterioration of the military situation. In due course Nestor rebukes him for having alienated Achilles during the Quarrel, and then goes on to suggest an embassy seeking the return of the foremost Greek warrior. Here are the end of Nestor's speech and the beginning of Agamemnon's reply:

> "... [Y]ou, giving way to your proud heart's anger, dishonored a great man, one whom the immortals honor, since you have taken his prize and keep it. But let us even now think how we can make this good and persuade him with words of supplication and with the gifts of friendship."

> Then in turn the lord of men Agamemnon spoke to him:
> "Aged sir, this was no lie when you spoke of my madness.
> I was mad, I myself will not deny it. Worth many
> fighters is that man whom Zeus in his heart loves, as now
> he has honored this man and beaten down the Achaian people.
> But since I was mad, in the persuasion of my heart's evil,
> I am willing to make all good, and give back gifts in abundance."
>
> Quote 6.11: *Il.* 9.109–120

Confronted by the reality of the military situation and Nestor's rebuke, Agamemnon admits he was wrong to dishonor the man whom Zeus has now honored by helping the Trojans. If he were to make this admission in a sincere public apology to Achilles, he would likely secure the latter's return to battle. But he is psychologically incapable of this. Instead, after naming all the gifts he would offer Achilles, he concludes the speech begun in this passage by insisting that Achilles would still have to submit to him. Thus, even when he knows he is in the wrong and is willing to accept responsibility in private discussion with close associates, Agamemnon cannot bring himself to swallow his pride in public.[49] How unlike him, then, even implicitly to accept blame and to vindicate Achilles before the army in quote 6.10.

After setting the Test in quote 6.10 and thereby creating an upheaval in the army, Agamemnon does not speak again until order and morale have been restored by Odysseus and the troops have been prepared for war by Nestor. The speech he gives at this time, which concludes the episode of the Test, contains the following discussion of the Quarrel:

> "Zeus of the aegis, son of Kronos, has given me bitterness,
> who drives me into unprofitable abuse and quarrels.
> For I and Achilleus fought together for a girl's sake
> in words' violent encounter, and I was the first to be angry."
>
> Quote 6.12: *Il.* 2.375–378

Agamemnon first minimizes his role in the Quarrel by blaming Zeus. He then minimizes the Quarrel itself by saying that it was over a girl, when it was really a matter of honor, the chief concern of a Homeric hero. He also deflects attention from this chief concern by admitting only that he was the first to be angry, when his real transgression was to dishonor Achilles and thereby to put the Greek cause at risk merely for the sake of his own greed and ego.[50] From all this, it is obvious that he is sensitive on the subject of the Quarrel and realizes that he is vulnerable to criticism, condemnation even, with regard to his behavior in that episode. Such a man would never have contemplated a test that can reasonably be interpreted as an admission that his alienation of Achilles had lost the war.[51]

The Agamemnon that we see in quote 6.12, with his pride in the driver's seat, is the same man we see in the other relevant places of the *Iliad*: the Quarrel, the Embassy, and the spurious reconciliation in book 19. For this man the most fitting hell is the humiliation by Achilles at the conclusion of the funeral games for Patroklos (see section 3.2). I maintain that he could not rise above his pride, the one constant of his psyche, to save his own soul (to use an anachronistic expression), let alone for the nonsensical Test. The Test is therefore an aberration. Furthermore, it is not a casual aberration that could be explained by something like the nodding of Homer, the difficulty of oral composition-in-performance, or the influence of alternate versions of the story.[52] It is, rather, an intentional aberration, illogicality, or inconsistency— call it what you will—and I will now show this by describing how the episode of the Test is integrated into the fabric of the *Iliad*.

Homer integrates the Test with the rest of the *Iliad* by two different means: the repetition or echoing of parts of the Test later in the poem and the use of formal structures to unite the Test with the earlier parts of the poem. The latter method is the more important for the argument of this section since it confirms that the clashing episodes of the Test and the Quarrel are to be considered together as a unit. However, I shall begin with the former method because it lays a useful foundation for the thesis that a great deal of thought lies behind the place of the Test in the *Iliad*.

(c) Echoes of the Test

As is well known, Agamemnon repeats much of his Test speech in the prelude to the embassy to Achilles.[53] Specifically, his speech of despair at the deterioration of the military situation (*Il.* 9.17–28), the speech which eventually leads to Nestor's suggestion of the Embassy, is taken word for word (except for the opening line of salutation) from the speech excerpted in quote 6.10 (*Il.* 9.18–28 = *Il.* 2.111–118 + 139–141). Although this partial replication ("partial" because the block of lines *Il.* 2.119–138 is omitted in the later instance of the speech) is often mentioned, its significance has not been properly appreciated. For example, one author expresses the view of many when he says that "the reuse of blocks of verses in widely different contexts is part of the Homeric technique of scene building."[54] This statement, while true as far as it goes, does not do justice to the duplication of Agamemnon's "let us run away" speech in that it fails to acknowledge two phenomena associated with this duplication. First, the fact that one instance of the speech (the one in the prelude to the Embassy) is appropriate, or at least logical, while the other (the Test of the army) is illogical appears to be part of a pattern, for we saw in section 5.1 that a block of verses that fits beautifully at a certain point in the *Iliad* is reused in the *Odyssey* in places where it is inappropriate. Second, the repetition of the Test speech is just one of six echoes of the Test later in the *Iliad*;[55] the sheer number of these echoes suggests that Homer sometimes has more in mind than the efficient (or easily remembered) construction of a poem when he reuses a block of verses. The next echo we consider, which is also connected with the Embassy, sheds a new light on Homeric repetition, as what is repeated is not a block of verses but a meaningful silence under very specific conditions.

After Agamemnon relates the Dream to the princes and mentions his idea of the Test, Nestor expresses skepticism regarding the Dream but makes no reference at all to the Test (see quote 6.9). His decision not to comment on the proposed test surprises some commentators.[56] Why does Nestor not point out that the trial of the army proposed in quote 6.8 is bound to fail, that the men will surely agree to "flee in their benched vessels"? Or if Agamemnon has contrived the ruse of the Test so that the other leaders will be put in the position of having to support what he really wants (since he has undermined his own credibility and authority by alienating Achilles), why does Nestor not point out that there are much less risky ways to have the princes demonstrate their support to the assembled army? Actually, Nestor's silence in regard to the Test should come as no surprise. In book 1 Agamemnon amply demonstrated his unreasonableness and stubbornness by refusing to release the daughter of a priest of Apollo, contrary to the wish of all the other Greeks,[57] and by rejecting Nestor's attempt to reconcile him with Achilles.[58] It is no wonder, then, that in book 2 Nestor decides there is no use protesting the ridiculous idea of the Test.[59] (He does, however, give a nonverbal indication of his displeasure by leaving the meeting of the princes—presumably in disgust—before it has been adjourned by Agamemnon.[60]) The same explanation undoubtedly applies to the analogous situation that is found in book 9. Recall from section 3.1 or from the above discussion of quote 6.11 that Agamemnon follows only part of Nestor's advice to try to persuade Achilles to return to battle "with words of supplication and with the gifts of friendship": he gives a long speech detailing the gifts he will offer Achilles, but he ends this speech not with supplication but with a demand for Achilles' submission. In reply, Nestor praises the gifts but ignores the absurd demand for submission, which would doom the Embassy to certain failure if it were transmitted to Achilles. Thus, there are two situations in which Nestor does not react verbally to a foolish intention with which Agamemnon concludes a speech: the intention to test the army in book 2 and the intention to demand Achilles' submission in book 9. The situations are so similar that I consider the one in book 9 to be a "silent echo" of the one in book 2. (In book 9 Nestor cannot express his displeasure nonverbally by walking out of the meeting, as he did in book 2, because he must attend to the important business of selecting the ambassadors and giving them instructions.)

To return to conventional (i.e., non-silent) echoes, we saw in quote 6.12 that Agamemnon minimizes his role in the Quarrel by blaming Zeus at the end of the episode of the Test. He does exactly the same thing much later in the poem, during his spurious reconciliation with Achilles (see quote 3.2). It would be easy to dismiss this duplication as nothing more than an indication of either a tactic or a defense mechanism typical of Agamemnon. However, there are two other echoes of quote 6.12 in the spurious reconciliation that are more difficult to explain away. Consider how Achilles begins the episode of the spurious reconciliation with an earnest attempt to put the Quarrel in the past:

> "Son of Atreus, was this after all the better way for
> both, for you and me, that we, for all our hearts' sorrow,
> quarreled together for the sake of a girl in soul-perishing hatred?"
>
> Quote 6.13: *Il.* 19.56–58

Achilles wants to play down the Quarrel so that he can get on with what has recently become his most urgent business, avenging the death of Patroklos. To do this, he adopts the same approach used by Agamemnon in quote 6.12: he characterizes the Quarrel as a dispute over a girl and ignores its greater significance as a struggle over honor. Later in the episode, Odysseus continues the masquerade by gently admonishing Agamemnon to be more conciliatory,

> "... [f]or there is no fault when even one who is a king
> appeases a man, when the king was the first one to be angry."
>
> Quote 6.14: *Il.* 19.182–183

For Agamemnon's serious transgression of dishonoring Achilles during the Quarrel, Odysseus substitutes the comparatively trifling offense of being the first to be angry, just as Agamemnon himself had done in quote 6.12.

The last echo of the Test that I shall discuss was first pointed out by Karl Reinhardt.[61] Just as Agamemnon in book 2 proposes that the Greeks return home when what he actually wants is a renewal of warfare, Zeus in book 4 suggests that a reconciliation of the Greeks and the Trojans (with Troy spared and the Greeks returning home with Helen) might be an agreeable outcome for the inconclusive duel between Paris and Menelaos[62] when what he (Zeus) really wants is also a renewal of warfare. Whereas the Greek army eagerly accepts Agamemnon's proposal, however, the goddesses Hera and Athene rebel at Zeus's suggestion because of their thirst for revenge against Troy (commonly attributed to the judgment of Paris). The result is that Zeus gets exactly what he wants by his deception, whereas Agamemnon's deception is an abysmal failure.

Besides the divine echo of the Test, there is a divine echo of the Quarrel. And the same contrast between Agamemnon's leadership of the Greeks and Zeus's leadership of the gods that is emphasized in Reinhardt's comparison of Agamemnon's test of the army with Zeus's test of the gods is presented by the human and divine quarrels in book 1.[63] Just as Agamemnon asserts his authority over Achilles, Zeus asserts his power and his right to act arbitrarily and independently of his wife Hera.[64] Whereas Achilles remains bitterly defiant, however, Hera is forced to back down. And whereas a peace-making attempt by Nestor fails, leaving the Greek army in a state of tension and uncertainty, Hephaistos succeeds (in part by illustrating the power of Zeus at his own expense[65]) in calming his mother (Hera) and in restoring a convivial atmosphere on Olympos. Once again, Zeus is seen to be master of the divine realm, while Agamemnon's leadership leaves much to be desired.[66]

These parallel contrasts between Agamemnon and Zeus derived from the Test and the Quarrel combine to yield a possible indication that these two episodes are to be considered in relation to each other or, more precisely, that the Test is to be viewed in the context of the Quarrel, as I argued in the preceding subsection. As such, this pair of contrasts provides a transition from the discussion of echoes of the Test to the discussion of the second method used by Homer to integrate the Test with the rest of the *Iliad*: the use of formal structures linking the Test with the Quarrel.

(*d*) Structures Uniting Test-Related Episodes

The confrontation between Achilles and Agamemnon begins as follows. On the tenth day of the plague sent by Apollo when one of his priests is treated roughly by Agamemnon and not allowed to ransom his daughter, Achilles convenes an assembly and opens it with the following words:

"Son of Atreus, I believe now that straggling backward
we must make our way home if we can even escape death,
if fighting now must crush the Achaians and the plague likewise.
No, come, let us ask some holy man, some prophet,
even an interpreter of dreams, since a dream also
comes from Zeus, who can tell why Phoibos Apollo is so angry[.]"

Quote 6.15: *Il*. 1.59–64

The prophet Kalchas agrees to respond to this appeal, but asks for Achilles' protection because he is afraid that his answer will anger a powerful ruler of the Greeks. Achilles vows that he will not let *anyone* harm Kalchas,

"not one of all the Danaäns, even if you mean Agamemnon,
who now claims to be far the best of the Achaians."[67]

Quote 6.16: *Il*. 1.90–91

Thus reassured, Kalchas explains that Apollo is punishing the Greeks for Agamemnon's treatment of the priest and that the plague will end only when the Greeks give the girl back to her father and do so without demanding ransom. This answer does indeed anger Agamemnon, who addresses Kalchas with bitterness:

"Seer of evil: never yet have you told me a good thing.
Always the evil things are dear to your heart to prophesy,
but nothing excellent have you said nor ever accomplished."

Quote 6.17: *Il*. 1.106–108

Agamemnon realizes that he must give up the girl, but he insists on being compensated for the loss of his prize. When Achilles replies that all the other prizes have been distributed, Agamemnon reacts with a threat to confiscate the prize of Achilles or one of the other Greek leaders. The Quarrel escalates from there.

Achilles' mention of dreams and his assertion that they come from Zeus are superfluous in their immediate context, for dreams play no part in the explanation that Kalchas will provide. These elements of quote 6.15 make perfect sense, however, as a forward reference to the Dream.[68] This is unlikely to be a mere coincidence: while a number of dreams are described in Homer,[69] the only one that is sent by Zeus is the delusive dream he sends to Agamemnon. I suggest that the purpose of this forward reference is to create a pair of bookends (quote 6.15 and the Dream) enclosing the two episodes that are inconsistent with the Test: the Quarrel and the Dream. I shall now support this interpretation by showing how Homer reinforces the proposed bookends.

Near the end of part (*b*) of section 5.3, I mentioned that in the present subsection I would be describing an Iliadic structure connected with the phrase "the best of the Achaians." This phrase is used somewhat promiscuously by Homer,[70] but two occurrences of it stand out by virtue of their similarity to each other and their difference from all the rest. In both quote 6.9 and quote 6.16, someone says that Agamemnon "claims to be far the best of the Achaians."[71] Nowhere else in the *Iliad* or the *Odyssey* does someone say that someone else claims to be the best of the Achaians. In quote 6.9, Nestor does this just as he makes the final reference to the Dream in the *Iliad*; in quote 6.16, Achilles does the same shortly after he makes the forward reference to the Dream in quote 6.15. Thus, the dream bookends are accompanied by distinctive assertions regarding "the best of the Achaians," which together form a second pair of bookends reinforcing the first.

The phrase "the best of the Achaians" is generally used in Homer as a description of one character by another or by Homer himself. However, there are four exceptions to this rule. As we have already noted, someone says that someone else *claims to be* the best of the Achaians in quotes 6.9 and 6.16. The other two exceptions occur when Achilles makes that claim for himself. This he does in quote 6.6 and, in essentially identical terms, when he asks Thetis to persuade Zeus to help the Trojans,

> "that Atreus' son wide-ruling Agamemnon may recognize
> his madness, that he did no honor to the best of the Achaians."
>
> Quote 6.18: *Il.* 1.411–412[72]

In order of their appearance in the poem, the four exceptional references to "the best of the Achaians" are quotes 6.16, 6.6, 6.18, and 6.9. In the first and last of these references, someone (Achilles or Nestor) says that Agamemnon claims to be the best of the Achaians; in the middle two references, Achilles refers to himself as the best of the Achaians. Thus, the four references form an ABBA pattern, a simple ring structure. Moreover, this ring structure, beginning at *Il.* 1.91 and ending at *Il.* 2.82, is virtually coextensive with the section of the poem enclosed by the dream bookends. In other words, the Iliadic text framed by occurrences of the motif of dreams sent by Zeus is spanned by a ring composition based on the motif of "the best of the Achaians."

Like the section of the poem enclosed by the dream bookends, the section spanned by the ring composition includes the Quarrel and the Dream, the two episodes that are inconsistent with the Test. But it also includes a reference to the Test itself, in the form of Agamemnon's statement to the princes in quote 6.8. The ring composition based on the motif of "the best of the Achaians" could therefore be said to unite the Test with the two episodes that are inconsistent with it. In fact, since the ring composition ends with the line in which Nestor makes the last reference to the dream (the penultimate line of quote 6.9), the same could be said of the dream bookends, provided we identify the second of these bookends with the last reference to the dream and not, for example, with Agamemnon's actual experience of it (quote 6.7). Whether this point of view is correct is not important, however, for we shall now see that Homer takes special measures to create a structural unit ranging from the beginning of the Quarrel to the end of the Test.

The end of the episode of the Test is not sharply defined. In part (*b*) of this section I identified it with Agamemnon's speech from which quote 6.12 is taken. But before Agamemnon gives this speech, Odysseus has already repaired the damage done by the Test and revived the fighting spirit of the troops. The conclusion of his speech and the response of the army are related by Homer as follows:

> "Come then, you strong-greaved Achaians, let every man stay
> here, until we have taken the great citadel of Priam."
> So he spoke, and the Argives shouted aloud, and about them

> the ships echoed terribly to the roaring Achaians
> as they cried out applause to the word of godlike Odysseus.
>
> Quote 6.19: *Il.* 2.331–335

Since morale is undoubtedly higher now than it was before the Test, it is not unreasonable to consider this the end of the Test fiasco. What has Odysseus said to generate this enthusiastic response? He has recalled the prophecy made at Aulis nine years before, the prophecy that Troy would be captured after nine years, implying that victory should now be within reach at last. And who made this prophecy? Kalchas, the same man whose explanation of what must be done to propitiate Apollo triggered the quarrel between Achilles and Agamemnon.

Thus, a prophecy by Kalchas marks both the beginning of the Quarrel and the end of the episode of the Test. This would be insignificant if prophecies by Kalchas were plentiful in the *Iliad*, but they are not: these are the only ones in the entire poem.[73] Furthermore, the prophecy at Aulis and the passage containing the prophecy that leads to the Quarrel are connected in a second way, more subtle but still unmistakable. We can be sure that Agamemnon was not happy when Kalchas made his prophecy at Aulis, since it foretold nine years of fighting before the fall of Troy. Agamemnon's attitude in quote 6.17 is therefore understandable. But with the passage of those nine years, what was once a dismal prophecy has become a source of hope, which Odysseus uses to boost the morale of the troops. It is a great irony that the prophecies of Kalchas are condemned by Agamemnon at the beginning of the Quarrel when one of those prophecies plays a key role in the recovery from the near disaster of his ill-conceived Test.

There is clearly a strong connection between the passages that begin the Quarrel and end the episode of the Test: these passages contain the only prophecies by Kalchas in the *Iliad*, and each passage can be fully appreciated only with the other in mind owing to their ironical relationship. I suggest that Homer created this double bond to indicate that the episodes enclosed by these bookend passages—the episodes of the Quarrel, the Dream, and the Test—together form a meaningful unit and that the relationships between these episodes are therefore meaningful. It is commonly realized that the Test is inconsistent with the Dream, and I have added that, from a psychological point of view, it is equally inconsistent with the Quarrel. The bookends surrounding the episodes and combining them into a single unit therefore indicate that these inconsistencies are intentional.

This analysis offers a new perspective on an old observation: in both the Quarrel and the Test, Hera sends Athene to forestall a crisis in the nick of time.[74] In the Quarrel, Achilles is about to kill Agamemnon when Athene arrives to dissuade him; in the Test, the men are rushing to leave Troy when Athene prompts Odysseus to bring them back to their senses. Again we are dealing with a possibly significant pair of passages, as these are the only places in the *Iliad* where the goddesses act together in this way and under such circumstances.[75] If A denotes one of the Kalchas passages and B denotes one of the Hera/Athene passages, the passages in question occur in the sequence ABBA, where the initial AB is found in the Quarrel and the final BA is found in the episode of the Test. Thus, the Quarrel and the Test are united by a simple ring structure,[76] which supports my points that (*a*) the relationship between these episodes (which happens to be one of inconsistency) is significant and (*b*) the episodes spanned by this structure (which also include the Dream) form a meaningful unit.

In part (*b*) of this section we saw that Agamemnon's test of the army is an aberration in the context of the Dream and in the context of the Quarrel as well. We have now identified two ring structures (the one based on "the best of the Achaians" and the one that begins and ends with Kalchas) that, in one way or another, link the Test to the two episodes with which it is inconsistent. These structures suggest that Homer wants us to consider the Test in relation to those two episodes. Furthermore, we have seen that the ring structures are just two aspects of an elaborate apparatus constructed around the episode of the Test. With so much care and thought having gone into the integration of the Test with the rest of the poem, it is difficult to believe that the Test itself survives as some sort of oversight and that the inconsistencies associated with this episode are anything but intentional.

6.4. Divine Interventions in the Confrontation of Achilles and Aineias

In the inconsistencies discussed so far, gods play either supporting roles or no role at all. We now consider a scene in which the behavior of certain gods is inconsistent with our expectations and with their behavior elsewhere in the *Iliad*. This scene constitutes a significant part of book 20, the book in which Achilles returns to battle after his spurious reconciliation with Agamemnon in book 19. This is the first we see of Achilles in combat since he withdrew from the war as a result of the Quarrel at the beginning of the poem. In book 20 he slays fourteen named Trojans and an unspecified number of unnamed victims. He also takes part in duels with the foremost Trojans Hektor and Aineias, but these encounters are inconclusive because his opponents are both rescued by a god. We are primarily interested in the confrontation between Achilles and Aineias, but the subsequent meeting of Achilles and Hektor will provide a useful basis for comparison.

Aineias and Hektor are the most worthy opponents for Achilles, and are paired together from time to time elsewhere in the poem. The Trojan Helenos says to them, "You are our greatest in every course we take, whether it be in thought or in fighting." Ares, speaking to the Trojans in disguise as one of their allies, refers to Aineias as a man "honored as we honor Hektor the brilliant." The Greek Automedon calls Hektor and Aineias "the greatest men of the Trojans," and there is a scene in which the Greeks flee in terror from the pair.[77] It is clearly fitting that the two face Achilles in roughly parallel scenes, Aineias in his last appearance in the poem, Hektor in an anticipation of his fatal meeting with Achilles in book 22.[78]

(*a*) Role Reversals of Apollo and Poseidon

Apollo is a staunch supporter of the Trojans in almost all of the *Iliad*, and his pro-Trojan stance is evident in how he treats Hektor in book 20.[79] At first Hektor is intent on fighting Achilles, but Apollo warns him not to do so alone and urges him to stay with his men. Hektor takes this advice (which we know is sound, although this is not stated) and withdraws back into the crowd in fear. Achilles then goes on a killing spree that culminates in the gruesome death of Polydoros, a half brother of Hektor. With the death of Polydoros, Hektor's fear turns to rage, and he goes out to face Achilles. After a brief verbal exchange, Hektor throws his spear at Achilles, but the spear is deflected by the pro-Greek goddess Athene. Apollo saves Hektor from Achilles' ferocious counterattack by covering him with a thick mist and snatching him away. In the Hektor episode, therefore, Apollo acts as a strong defender of the Trojan, as we would expect: he tries to prevent Hektor from meeting Achilles, and comes to his rescue when that turns out to be necessary.

Apollo behaves very differently towards Aineias in *his* encounter with Achilles.[80] Instead of warning him to avoid Achilles, he persuades him, against his better judgment, to seek out and fight the mighty Greek warrior. Then, when Aineias is about to be killed by Achilles, it is not Apollo who shows concern for him, but the pro-Greek god Poseidon, who says,

> "Ah me; I am full of sorrow for great-hearted Aineias
> who must presently go down to death, overpowered by Achilleus,
> because he believed the words of Apollo, the far ranging;
> poor fool, since Apollo will do nothing to keep the grim death from him."
> Quote 6.20: *Il.* 20.293–296

Poseidon somehow knows that Apollo will not save Aineias.[81] After providing some justifications and gaining the grudging assent of the pro-Greek goddess Hera, Poseidon proceeds to rescue Aineias himself. This is extraordinary.[82] Nowhere else in the *Iliad* does a god without a strong personal motive help a fighter from the side he opposes.[83] Furthermore, after rescuing Aineias, Poseidon tells him to be sure to avoid Achilles in the future. Thus, a pro-Greek god takes Apollo's place as the protector of the Trojan: he rescues Aineias and instructs him to back down if he should face Achilles again. For his part, Apollo actually seems hostile to Aineias. One commentator, noting that "Apollo persuades Aeneas to attack Achilles, even though he must know that the Trojan has no chance," likens this to a situation in which Ares stirs up the fighting spirit of Menelaos in the hope that he will be killed in battle.[84] The difference, of course, is that it is natural for a pro-Trojan god (such as Ares or Apollo) to want the death of a Greek but not the death of a Trojan. The strangeness of Apollo's behavior is understated in another commentator's remark that "Apollo's motive in endangering Aineias is not made clear."[85] Poseidon expresses appropriate disbelief when, after rescuing Aineias, he asks him, "Which one of the gods is it who urges you to such madness that you fight in the face of Peleus' son, against his high courage though he is both stronger than you and dearer to the immortals?" We conclude, then, that both Apollo and Poseidon reverse their usual roles in the Aineias episode: the pro-Greek god assists the Trojan, while the pro-Trojan god acts against him.

The unexpected behavior of the gods in the Aineias episode stands in stark contrast with their normal behavior in the Hektor episode. I argue in the next subsection that Homer wanted us to make this comparison and therefore wanted to make the unexpected behavior stand out even more than it would on its own. Now I point out another aspect of the context of the Aineias episode that has the same effect.

In book 8 of the *Iliad*, Zeus orders the other gods not to interfere in the war. Although this order is disobeyed by certain gods from time to time, it remains in effect until the beginning of book 20, when Zeus rescinds the order and tells the gods that they are free, even encouraged, to intervene on behalf of either side. The gods then separate into their pro-Greek and pro-Trojan factions, and prepare not only to participate in the war but also to fight each other. Gods from the opposing factions are paired against each other, but the implied duels are not described until book 21. Instead, the action switches abruptly from conflict between gods to Apollo persuading Aineias to seek out and fight Achilles. Thus, the Aineias scene, in which Apollo and Poseidon inexplicably abandon their loyalties to the Trojans and the Greeks (respectively), is placed immediately after a scene in which the fierce loyalties of the gods to one side or the other receive special emphasis (and in which, by the way, Apollo and Poseidon are explicitly paired against each other[86]). This juxtaposition throws a spotlight on the unexpected nature of the divine interventions in the later scene.

These considerations suggest that the behavior of Apollo and Poseidon in relation to Aineias may be intentionally inconsistent with their usual behavior and with their roles as backers of the Trojans or the Greeks. I now challenge previous explanations for why Aineias is rescued by Poseidon instead of Apollo in order to make room for the view that this anomaly is a manifestation of the perverseness of Homer.

When Aineias goes in search of Achilles after having been urged to do so by Apollo, Hera worries that Achilles will be intimidated by an adversary who has the force of a god behind him. She suggests to Athene and Poseidon that the three of them should turn Aineias back or that one of them should stand by Achilles. Poseidon decides that they will interfere only if Ares or Apollo begins to fight or if they hold Achilles back and will not let him fight, in which case the pro-Greek gods will engage the pro-Trojan gods in battle.[87] It has been argued that this makes it impossible for Homer to have Apollo rescue Aineias: if Apollo were to intervene, the pro-Greek gods would have to respond and the Theomachy, the battle of the gods in book 21, would begin prematurely.[88] I do not accept this argument. Recall that Hera considers turning Aineias back; she presumably would be just as happy if Apollo were to remove him from the scene. Indeed, her concern is simply to protect Achilles, and this concern is reflected in Poseidon's condition for intervening, which would not be triggered by a rescue of Aineias.[89] Thus, the threat of a premature Theomachy is not real and does not prevent Homer from having Apollo rescue Aineias.

Apollo's failure to intervene to save Aineias from Achilles is surprising when we consider the rescues he does make in the *Iliad*. First, he saves Aineias himself from Diomedes earlier in the poem.[90] Second, shortly after Poseidon has to save Aineias from Achilles in his stead, Apollo saves Hektor from the same hero. And finally, he saves Agenor from Achilles in a situation similar to the one in which he declines to save Aineias, for it is thanks to him that both Agenor and Aineias face Achilles.[91] Scheibner attempts to reconcile

Apollo's failure to rescue Aineias from Achilles with his rescues of Hektor and Agenor.[92] He argues that if Apollo were to rescue Aineias, he would be acknowledging that he made a false step when he sent Aineias to fight Achilles, and we would ask why he did this in the first place. The Hektor and Agenor episodes do not fit this pattern. Apollo does not send Hektor to fight Achilles, but rather tries to prevent the meeting of these two. Apollo does have Agenor stand against Achilles, but only as part of a larger plan in which he takes on the appearance of Agenor after rescuing him in order to deceive Achilles. Thus, Scheibner's reasoning distinguishes the Aineias episode from the corresponding scenes with Hektor and Agenor. But this does not mean that Apollo's failure to rescue Aineias has been explained. Why Apollo sends Aineias to fight Achilles is a mystery regardless of whether Apollo then rescues Aineias from that fight. Indeed, when it turns out that Apollo will not rescue Aineias, we get the impression that Apollo intentionally put Aineias in danger, but are at a loss to explain why a pro-Trojan god would do this.

It has been suggested that Homer wished to elevate Aineias above all the other Trojans, perhaps in order to honor a royal family claiming descent from him.[93] Since there would be nothing special about a rescue of a Trojan by a pro-Trojan god such as Apollo, Homer has Aineias rescued by Poseidon, a pro-Greek god, instead.[94] However, the choice is not binary (pro-Trojan or pro-Greek). A rescue by Zeus, who stands above the two factions, would also glorify Aineias. In fact, a review of the circumstances will show that such a rescue would be quite natural.[95]

Poseidon rescues Aineias mainly out of fear that Zeus will be angry if Aineias is killed. For Aineias is destined to survive, and his survival will save from extinction the family line of Dardanos, who was dearest to Zeus of all his children by mortal women.[96] Scodel argues that Poseidon implausibly assumes a role that properly belongs to Zeus.[97] Whereas she emphasizes the strangeness of Poseidon's action, I would emphasize the strangeness of Zeus's failure to act. Two times in the *Iliad* Zeus wants to save the life of a Trojan and seriously considers doing so, but decides not to only because the man (Sarpedon or Hektor) is destined to die.[98] Saving Aineias, by contrast, would not be going against destiny but fulfilling it. Zeus's failure to save him, as well as Poseidon's implicit assumption that Zeus will not intervene himself, is therefore a great mystery. Homer seems to go out of his way to have Aineias rescued by a pro-Greek god.

Poseidon offers several reasons for saving Aineias besides acting in Zeus's interest and helping destiny be fulfilled.[99] All his reasons justify concern for the personal well-being of Aineias, nothing more. But after rescuing him and telling him to avoid Achilles in the future, Poseidon instructs Aineias to fight the Greeks with confidence once Achilles is dead because no other Greek will be able to kill him.[100] This goes well beyond looking after the safety of Aineias. Poseidon here acts as a partisan of the Trojans, the role that Apollo abandons in this episode.

Besides casting doubt on the usual explanations for the strange behavior of Apollo and Poseidon in the Aineias scene in book 20, this discussion has revealed several signs that this strange behavior is not incidental but has been carefully orchestrated. Two gods behave contrary to our expectations, and each of them does so in two ways. A pro-Trojan god (Apollo) puts a Trojan (Aineias) in danger by convincing him to fight Achilles, and then does not come to his rescue when he is about to be killed. On the other hand, a pro-Greek god (Poseidon) sees to the safety of the Trojan for no reason (Aineias should be rescued by Zeus), and—also for no reason—tells him that he can fight the Greeks without fear once Achilles is dead.

One's sense that this unexpected behavior has been carefully orchestrated is heightened by the combination of (1) the contrast between the strange conduct of Apollo in the Aineias episode and his normal conduct in the Hektor episode that follows and (2) certain indications that Homer wanted us to view these two episodes together. The latter indications are discussed in the next subsection.

(b) Links between the Aineias and Hektor Episodes

Although the Aineias episode in book 20 is much longer than the Hektor episode in the same book, there are enough similarities to suggest that the two episodes should be regarded as coequal members of a pair. The first similarity is that both episodes contain the following sequence of events: (1) Achilles begins a verbal exchange with his adversary, (2) the Trojan replies, (3) the Trojan initiates the fighting, (4) the Trojan is rescued by a god, and (5) Achilles gives a speech in which he comments on the rescue, speculates about a future encounter (or lack thereof) with the same adversary, and then turns his attention to other adversaries.[101] In addition, each episode is followed, either immediately (in the case of the Hektor episode) or eventually (in the case of the Aineias episode), by Achilles' slaughter of a number of lesser Trojans in a series of briefly described encounters.

The next similarity I shall discuss is that component (2), the reply of the Trojan to the speech of Achilles, begins with the same three verses in both episodes. As we shall see, the combination of this well-known fact with the fact that Achilles gives very different speeches to Aineias and Hektor invites a critical comparison of the two episodes.

The last thing Apollo says to Aineias when he sends him to fight Achilles is "do not let him turn you back with words of contempt and threats,"[102] and that is precisely what Achilles tries to do. He attributes to Aineias motives unworthy of a Homeric hero; he reminds Aineias of how he (Aineias) ran away from him the last time they met; and he concludes his withering speech by suggesting that Aineias retreat before he gets hurt.[103] Aineias begins his reply very appropriately: "Son of Peleus, never hope by words to frighten me as if I were a baby. I myself understand well enough how to speak in vituperation and how to make insults."[104] What is striking is that Hektor begins *his* reply to Achilles in exactly the same way,[105] despite the fact that Achilles' speech to him consists of an unremarkable challenge with no gratuitous insults. Given the generally acknowledged might of Achilles, his challenge to Hektor—"Come nearer, so that sooner you may reach your appointed destruction"[106]—merely expresses a reasonable expectation. In the continuation of his reply following the words borrowed from Aineias, Hektor acknowledges that he is weaker than Achilles, but points out that he may be victorious nevertheless. This by itself would be an appropriate response to Achilles' challenge. But the preceding lines taken from the Aineias episode are not appropriate in the Hektor episode.[107] The appearance of the same verses at corresponding places of the two episodes invites us to compare these episodes, and the inappropriateness of these verses in one of the episodes warns us to make this comparison critically. This context supports the significance of the observation that Apollo's behavior is normal in one episode but inappropriate (that is, contrary to all our expectations) in the other.

A further indication that the Aineias and Hektor episodes in book 20 should be considered coequal members of a pair is that each of these episodes is linked independently of the other to the Lykaon episode in book 21. Apollo gives himself the voice and appearance of Lykaon when he urges Aineias to fight Achilles.[108] Since the only previous mention of Lykaon is much earlier in the poem and quite unimportant,[109] it is safe to say that Lykaon is brought up here in anticipation of his major scene in book 21.[110] The link of the Hektor episode to the Lykaon episode is just as clear, even if it is less direct. The link is formed not by any passage within the Hektor episode, but by two framing passages just before and after that episode, in neither of which is Lykaon himself mentioned. In book 21 Lykaon recalls the killing of Polydoros by Achilles when he himself is about to be killed by the same man.[111] Polydoros was Lykaon's only full brother, but he was also a half brother of Hektor, and it was his gruesome death that drove Hektor to confront Achilles. The passage that describes the killing of Polydoros[112] is the first of the two framing passages that link the Hektor and Lykaon episodes. The other is found in the slaughter of lesser Trojans that immediately follows the Hektor episode. One of the victims attempts to beg Achilles for his life in a passage that is generally considered to be an anticipation of Lykaon's supplication of Achilles in book 21.[113] In summary, a passage in the Aineias episode links that episode to the Lykaon episode, while passages that surround the Hektor episode link *that* episode to the Lykaon episode. The independent linking of the Aineias and Hektor episodes to the Lykaon episode is another indication that the former two passages are to be regarded as comparable units even though one is much longer than the other.

It begins to appear that Homer took some trouble to show that he wanted us to think of the Aineias and Hektor episodes as a matched pair. I now make one more argument for this interpretation of Homer's intention.

There is an obvious connection between two passages that have already been mentioned: Aineias's reply to Achilles and the slaughter of lesser Trojans that immediately follows the Hektor episode. Aineias's speech famously contains a lengthy account of his genealogy.[114] This begins with Dardanos, son of Zeus, and includes Tros, the grandson of Dardanos and the eponymous founder of the Trojan people.[115] What is striking is that Dardanos and Tros are also the names of two of Achilles' victims in the slaughter following the Hektor episode (they are, in fact, essentially consecutive victims).[116] The effect of this connection is that our minds are brought back to the Aineias episode right after the Hektor episode.

It must be admitted that the use of the same name for different characters is common in the *Iliad*. Indeed, seven of the ten men killed by Achilles immediately after the Hektor episode share their names with other men in the poem.[117] Moreover, Dardanos and Tros are not the only two of the seven whose names appear together in an earlier passage: the names of Moulios and Echeklos (also killed one after the other by Achilles) also appear in a list of nine victims of Patroklos.[118] Nevertheless, Homer could reasonably have expected his reuse of the names Dardanos and Tros for victims of Achilles to recall the ancestors of Aineias. One reason is that the reuse occurs so soon (about 240 verses) after Aineias's account of his genealogy. Another is that Dardanos and Tros are important figures in the history of Troy whose names are familiar to an attentive audience. Each of them appears in a passage that is logically connected with Aineias's recitation of his genealogy. The continuation of the family line of Dardanos figures prominently in Poseidon's explanation of why Aineias should be rescued from Achilles.[119] Early in the poem we are told that Zeus gave some special horses to Tros as "recompense for his son Ganymedes";[120] why Zeus compensated Tros for Ganymedes is not explained until Aineias's recitation of his genealogy, when we learn that Ganymedes "was the loveliest born of the race of mortals, and therefore the gods caught him away to themselves, to be Zeus' wine-pourer, for the sake of his beauty, so he might be among the immortals."[121] On top of all this, the name of Dardanos appears in the form of a patronymic that is often applied to Priam[122] (the separate lines of descent that produced Priam and Aineias originated with two sons of Tros). In the light of these considerations, I regard the invention of doubles for Dardanos and Tros in the slaying catalogue that immediately follows the Hektor episode as yet another invitation to compare this episode with the one in which Aineias recounts his genealogy.

We have now seen several indications that Homer was preoccupied with the relationship between the Aineias and Hektor episodes. This preoccupation suggests that there is insight to be obtained from an examination of this relationship. Let us recall in this light the contrast between Apollo's solicitude for Hektor in book 20 and his apparent indifference or even hostility towards Aineias in the same book. Whereas Apollo warns Hektor to stay away from Achilles, he urges Aineias to face Achilles against his will, and whereas Apollo rescues Hektor from Achilles, he fails to rescue Aineias under similar circumstances. We now have reason to believe that Homer wanted us to make these comparisons. This completes the argument begun in subsection (*a*) for the claim that Apollo's behavior in the Aineias episode is an intentional anomaly, a manifestation of the perverseness of Homer. A separate argument for the same claim is presented in the next subsection.

(*c*) Achilles' Conflict with the River Skamandros

We have just observed a few connections between the Aineias and Hektor episodes in book 20. We now consider some remarkable connections between the former episode and a certain section of book 21. To define this section and to argue in advance for the plausibility of the connections to be considered, it is convenient first to summarize the relevant part of the story line.

Achilles' inconclusive encounters with Aineias and Hektor and his slaughter of lesser Trojans in book 20 all take place on the Trojan plain. At the beginning of book 21, Achilles has driven the Trojans to the river Skamandros.[123] For this phase of the slaughter, Homer describes in detail the deaths of two of Achilles' victims. The first is Lykaon, who begs for his life but is cut down without mercy and thrown into the river. The pro-Trojan river god Skamandros becomes angry and emboldens the Trojan ally Asteropaios to face Achilles. Asteropaios is a worthy opponent, but he is killed along with seven of his compatriots. When Achilles jumps into the river to claim still more victims, he is attacked by the river itself. Even mighty Achilles is no match for Skamandros, but eventually he is saved when Hera sends the fire god Hephaistos to subdue the river god.

The section of book 21 that I will be linking to the Aineias episode in book 20 consists of the duel between Achilles and Asteropaios together with the river's attack on Achilles. For simplicity I refer to the combination of these two scenes as Achilles' conflict with the river, with the justification that Asteropaios is incited to fight Achilles by Skamandros.

We should not be surprised if we find a strong linkage between the Aineias episode and Achilles' conflict with the river. First, these two sections of the poem are both part of a well-defined structural unit. And second, a strong linkage between them would be expected if this structural unit conforms to the principle of ring composition. Recall from subsection (*a*) that a march towards conflict between gods early in book 20 is interrupted by the Aineias episode just as the conflict is about to begin. This thread of the story is not picked up again until Hephaistos attacks Skamandros at the instigation of Hera in book 21. This attack clearly relates back to the divine conflict that seems imminent just prior to the Aineias episode, since Hephaistos and Skamandros stand opposed to each other at that point and the other pairs of opposed gods that are mentioned there fight (or, in some cases, explicitly decide not to fight) after Skamandros is defeated by Hephaistos.[124] The material that separates the introduction to the battle of the gods from the battle itself begins with the Aineias episode and ends with Achilles' conflict with the river. This material together with the framing material that relates to the battle of the gods forms a well-defined structural unit. If Achilles' duel with Aineias and his conflict with the river are related, this structural unit has an *ABCBA* structure, where *A* denotes material related to the battle of the gods, *B* denotes either of the two related conflicts (Achilles vs. Aineias or Achilles vs. the river), and *C* represents intervening material (including the Hektor episode in book 20 and the Lykaon episode in book 21).[125] We now consider the relationships that collectively justify the use of the same symbol (*B*) for the Aineias episode and Achilles' conflict with the river.

Our point of departure is the concern that Hera expresses to Poseidon and Athene when Aineias, emboldened by Apollo, goes in search of Achilles: "he [Achilles] will be terrified when he finds himself confronted by a god. The gods are difficult for any man to deal with, when they face him openly."[126] This concern turns out not to be justified in the Aineias episode, for Apollo abandons Aineias once he has convinced him to fight Achilles. Similarly, the river god gives Asteropaios the nerve to face Achilles, but does not help him in the actual fighting. It is not until Skamandros himself attacks that Achilles finds himself confronted by a god. He is then indeed seized with fear,[127] as

Hera said he would be. It appears that Hera's first speech in the Aineias episode anticipates the river god's assault on Achilles. This becomes even clearer when we consider another part of her speech.

One course of action that Hera proposes to Poseidon and Athene as Aineias seeks out Achilles is the following:

> "... one of us must stand by Achilleus
> and put enormous strength upon him, and let him not come short
> in courage, but *let him know that they love him who are the highest
> of the immortals*, but those who before now fended the fury
> of war, as now, from the Trojans are as wind and nothing."
>
> Quote 6.21: *Il.* 20.120–124 (italics added)

Nothing comes of this suggestion in the Aineias episode. However, this is what happens immediately after Achilles speaks despairingly of what he believes is his imminent death in the river (see quote 5.19):

> ... Poseidon and Athene came swiftly near him
> [Achilles]
> and stood beside him with their shapes in the likeness of mortals
> and caught him hand by hand and spoke to him in assurance.
> First of them to speak was the shaker of the earth, Poseidon.
> "Do not be afraid, son of Peleus, nor be so anxious,
> *such are we two of the gods who stand beside you to help you,
> by the consent of Zeus, myself and Pallas Athene.*
> Thereby it is not your destiny to be killed by the river,
> but he shall be presently stopped, and you yourself shall behold it."
>
> Quote 6.22: *Il.* 21.284–292 (italics added)

Shortly after this, Achilles is given great strength by Athene.[128] Thus, Hera's first speech in the Aineias episode anticipates not only Achilles' struggle with the river god, but also the support he receives from Poseidon and Athene during this struggle. Notable in the latter connection is the correspondence between the fragments I have italicized in quotes 6.21 and 6.22.

Let us now turn to the indirect part of Achilles' conflict with the river, the part where Asteropaios confronts Achilles at the prompting of Skamandros. While both Aineias and Asteropaios are inspired to fight Achilles by a god, we are told the god's motivation only in the latter case. The river god is angry at Achilles for his viciousness towards the Trojans and wants to bring his rampage to a halt.[129] While one would normally assume that Apollo also wants to protect the Trojans, this is not stated, and his abnormal behavior in the Aineias episode suggests that he actually wants to put Aineias in danger (see part (*a*)). Despite this fundamental difference, there are some noteworthy correspondences between Achilles' confrontations with Aineias and Asteropaios.

Achilles' duel with Aineias is his first combat in the *Iliad* and also the first occasion on which he uses the armor made for him by Hephaistos to replace the armor that was borrowed by Patroklos and then taken by Hektor. The great shield, whose elaborate decoration is famously described in a lengthy passage that forms the bulk of the poet's account of the forging of the armor by Hephaistos,[130] also plays a central role in the account of the duel. In 14 verses we hear how the shield absorbs the impact of Aineias's spear and does not allow the spear to pass through.[131] We also learn more about how the shield is constructed. We know from the description of the making of the armor that the shield consists of five layers.[132] Now we are told that the outer two layers are made of bronze, the inner two layers are made of tin, and the middle layer is made of gold. It is the gold layer that finally stops Aineias's spear.

The use of soft metals such as tin and gold for protective layers of a shield makes no sense, and the gold layer should be on the outside, not buried in the middle, if it is meant to be ornamental.[133] The authenticity of the verses describing the layers of the shield has therefore been questioned since antiquity.[134] Let us suppose, however, that the verses are both genuine and well considered. It remains true, of course, that they make us pause to ponder the illogicality of the construction of the divine shield. The significance of this becomes evident when we learn that a spear thrown by Asteropaios is also stopped by the gold in Achilles' shield.[135] Having puzzled over the construction of the shield when we were told that Aineias's spear was stopped by the gold layer, we naturally think back to the Aineias episode when we come to this part of the Asteropaios episode. Indeed, while it is possible for a bronze-headed spear to come to rest with its tip in the gold layer, this is not an intuitively plausible scenario, and the mere fact that the spears of Aineias and Asteropaios are both stopped by the gold is enough for us to connect the two episodes.[136]

A striking connection of another sort follows from the genealogical information provided in the Aineias and Asteropaios episodes: we learn in these episodes that the major warriors on the two sides of the war, Hektor and Achilles, are both descended from Zeus. The descent of the two heroes from Zeus is not mentioned anywhere else in the poem. We are reminded innumerable times that Achilles is the son of Peleus, and his relationship to Aiakos (the father of Peleus) is also familiar, but the fact that Zeus was the father of Aiakos comes up only when Achilles vaunts over the body of Asteropaios.[137] That Achilles has a relationship to the divine is a constant refrain, but the only aspect of this relationship that is mentioned elsewhere is that he is the son of Thetis. The revelation in the Asteropaios episode that he is also related to Zeus recalls the fact, buried in the extensive genealogy recited by Aineias, that the chief hero of the Trojans (like his third cousin Aineias) is also descended from Zeus.

It is possible to see another connection between the Aineias and Asteropaios episodes that is based on the descent of heroes from divinities. When Achilles proclaims his descent from Zeus, he does so to assert his superiority over Asteropaios, who claimed descent from the river god Axios.[138] "It is hard," says Achilles, "even for those sprung of a river to fight against the children of Kronos [e.g., Zeus], whose strength is almighty."[139] Although genealogies are common in the *Iliad*, the inference of relative strength in combat from a comparison of genealogies is not. Yet that is at least close to what Apollo does to convince Aineias, son of Aphrodite, that he can face Achilles, son of the lesser goddess Thetis.[140]

We have now seen a number of parallels between the Aineias episode in book 20 and Achilles' conflict with the river Skamandros in book 21, both the direct part of this conflict (the river's assault on Achilles) and the indirect part (the duel between Achilles and Asteropaios instigated by Skamandros). We have also seen that the existence of these parallels is not surprising from a structural point of view, in that the Aineias episode immediately follows the introduction to the battle of the gods, while Achilles' conflict with the river immediately precedes the resumption of this battle (the Theomachy). The purpose of all this discussion becomes clear when we consider the transition from the indirect part of Achilles' conflict with the river to the direct part.

After Achilles kills Asteropaios and some of his countrymen, the river angrily calls on him to desist. When Achilles refuses to stop slaughtering the Trojans, the river calls out to Apollo:

"Shame, lord of the silver bow, Zeus' son; you have not kept
the counsels of Kronion [Zeus], who very strongly ordered you
to stand by the Trojans and defend them, until the sun setting
at last goes down and darkens all the generous ploughland."

Quote 6.23: *Il.* 21.229–232

This elicits no response from Apollo. Instead, Achilles jumps into the river to resume his rampage, and the river surges violently to overpower him. The river's direct assault on Achilles, thus begun, continues until Hera sends Hephaistos to put an end to it.

The river god's rebuke of Apollo for not standing by the Trojans is the last exhibit in my case for the claim that the strange behavior of Apollo and Poseidon in the Aineias episode has been carefully orchestrated (see subsection (*a*)) and that Apollo's behavior, in particular, represents an intentional anomaly and a manifestation of the perverseness of Homer (see subsection (*b*)). If this claim is valid, we should not be surprised, in view of all the parallels noted in the present subsection, if Apollo's (temporary) neglect of the Trojans (first seen in his abandonment of Aineias) is mentioned somewhere in the course of Achilles' conflict with the river. This is, of course, just what we see in quote 6.23.[141, 142]

It must be admitted that the exclamation of the river god in quote 6.23 may be poetically justified as a device used to express his emotion and to build dramatic intensity.[143] It is also true, however, that these ends are achieved with some awkwardness: Apollo's failure to defend the Trojans is highlighted but given no explanation. This is very similar to what happens in the Aineias episode: Poseidon says that Apollo will not rescue Aineias from Achilles (quote 6.20) and goes on to rescue Aineias himself, but Apollo's failure to protect the Trojan is never explained. If the poet wished to avoid the subject of Apollo's inexplicable behavior in relation to Aineias, he would not have alluded to this subject in his account of Achilles' conflict with the river. That he did so in quote 6.23 demonstrates once again the perverseness of Homer.

6.5. The Illogicality of the Defensive Ditch

Relatively early in the *Iliad*, after the first of the four battles recounted in the poem, the Greeks fortify their camp with a gated wall, a deep and wide ditch just outside the wall, and sharp stakes planted along the ditch.[144] While the ditch and the stakes would make sense in the fortification of a city under siege, they are not suitable for protecting the camp of an army. Should the Greeks fighting out on the plain have to retreat, the ditch and the stakes would hinder their reaching safety behind the wall.[145] The danger that the Trojans might catch up to retreating Greeks while they are crossing the ditch is especially high for the chariots, since the ditch is a far greater hindrance to them than to men on foot. This danger is compounded by the fact that the Greeks must bring their chariots inside the camp whereas the Trojans are free to leave their chariots at the edge of the ditch and to pursue the Greek chariots on foot.

The illogicality of the ditch and the stakes—the fact that these elements of the Greek defenses pose a serious problem for the Greek themselves—is not explicitly acknowledged by Homer, but the poet shows indirectly that he is well aware of the problem. To see how he does this, consider what happens at the beginning of book 12. The Greeks withdraw to their camp under pressure from the Trojans. Their retreat across the ditch is ignored in the narration. Instead, Homer focuses our attention on the consequences of the ditch for the Trojan pursuit:

> ... **Hektor** ... went through the battle and rallied his companions
> and **drove them on to cross over the ditch, but now the fast-footed
> horses balked at the edge of the lip, and dared not cross, whinnying
> loud, since the ditch in its great width frightened them from it,
> being not easy for them to overleap, nor to walk through,
> since along the whole length the jut of the overhangs stood
> on both sides, and the surface of the floor was thickset with pointed
> palisades, which the sons of the Achaians had paled there
> dense and huge, so as to hold off the rage of attackers.
> And a horse straining at the strong-wheeled chariot might not easily
> enter there**, but the dismounted were strong in their effort.
> And now Poulydamas stood by bold Hektor, and spoke to him:
> "Hektor, and other lords of the Trojans and companions in battle,
> **we are senseless trying to drive our fast-footed horses over
> this ditch. It is hard indeed to cross, and sharp stakes are planted
> inside it**, and across from these the wall of the Achaians.
> There, there is no way to get down, no way again to do battle
> from horses, for the passage is narrow and I think they must be hurt there.
> ...
>   ... *if they [the Achaians] turn again and a backrush comes on us
> out of the ships, and we are driven against the deep ditch,
> then I think no longer could one man to carry a message
> get clear to the city, once the Achaians have turned back upon us.*
> Come then, do as I say, let us all be persuaded; **let us
> tell our henchmen to check our horses here by the ditch, then
> let ourselves, all of us dismounted and armed in our war gear,
> follow Hektor in mass formation**. As for the Achaians,
> they will not hold, if the bonds of death are fastened upon them."
>   So spoke Poulydamas, and this counsel of safety pleased Hektor.
> **And at once in all his armor he leapt to the ground from his chariot,
> and the rest of the Trojans assembled, not mounted behind their horses,
> but all sprang to the ground, when they saw brilliant Hektor had done it.
> Then each man gave orders to his own charioteer
> to check the horses in good order at the edge of the ditch**,
> and the fighters formed apart into groups ...
>   Quote 6.24: *Il.* 12.49–86 (boldface and italics added)

6.5. THE ILLOGICALITY OF THE DITCH

A large portion of this passage, shown in boldface, describes or reflects the great difficulty of crossing the ditch in a chariot. This difficulty is addressed by the narrator, by one of the characters, and then again by the narrator.[146] Of course, the obstacle presented by the ditch to retreating Greeks attempting to reach the safety of their camp with their enemy in hot pursuit is the same as the obstacle presented to the advancing Trojans, as described in this passage—except the Greeks do not have the option of leaving their chariots behind![147] How then, we are led to ask, did the Greeks manage to cross the ditch with such ease and so little adverse effect that this phase of their retreat could be ignored by the poet? Even if it is only implicit in this passage, the danger that the ditch poses to retreating Greeks in their chariots could not be more clear.

The italicized part of quote 6.24 does not mention chariots, but we may infer from the text that follows it that Poulydamas is describing the calamity that could be expected if the Trojans somehow managed to enter the camp with their chariots and the Greeks were to rally and drive them back against the ditch.[148] This emphasizes once again, from a new point of view, the difficulty of crossing the ditch in a chariot. In fact, the scenario envisaged by Poulydamas comes to pass later in the poem. The Trojans are able to enter the Greek camp with their chariots because Apollo makes a path for them by flattening part of the ditch and the wall.[149] When the Myrmidons led by Patroklos join the battle, however, the Trojans are forced to flee and are driven against the ditch as anticipated in the italicized part of quote 6.24:

> ... [The Trojans] were trapped by the deep-dug ditch unwilling,
> and in the ditch many fast horses who pulled the chariots
> left, broken short at the joining of the pole, their masters' chariots
>
> Quote 6.25: *Il.* 16.369–371

When a pair of horses tries to pull a chariot up the side of the ditch, the chariot pole snaps at the weak point behind the yoke and the chariot is left behind.[150]

Given the difficulty experienced by the fleeing Trojans, we may well ask how the Greeks are able to leave their camp with their chariots.[151] The description of the problem in quote 6.25 shows that it is important to make the chariot as light as possible. It is evidently for this reason that the Greek warriors dismount before crossing the ditch and rejoin their chariots on the other side:

> Then each gave instructions to his charioteer to pull in the horses in proper order right by the ditch's edge, and they themselves swarmed over on foot, dressed in all their armour: and their shouts rose ceaseless in the early morning. They made formation along the other side of the ditch well before the chariot-drivers, who came some way behind.
>
> Quote 6.26: *Il.* 11.47–52 (Hammond trans.)[152]

The same procedure is obviously necessary when the Greeks return to camp.[153] If the Trojans are in pursuit, however, the chariots, horses, and drivers will still be vulnerable to attack inasmuch as this passage indicates that the chariots are slowed down by the ditch even when carrying only one passenger.

Crossings of the ditch can be divided into four categories defined by which army is crossing and the direction of the crossing. So far we have considered Homer's descriptions of the obstacle presented by the ditch for three of the categories: the Trojans entering the camp, the Trojans leaving the camp, and the Greeks leaving the camp. But the category that relates to the illogicality of the Greek defenses is the fourth: the Greeks crossing the ditch to return to their camp. This occurs five times in the *Iliad*, with the Greeks pursued by the Trojans each time, but only three of these crossings are actually described in the poem.[154] I call the reader's attention to the fact that there is no mention of chariots in any of Homer's descriptions of the Greeks retreating across the ditch. This fact is remarkable, inasmuch as the particular difficulty that the ditch poses for chariots is emphasized for all three of the other categories of ditch crossing, as we have seen. I suggest that the poet's avoidance of the subject of chariots when the Greeks retreat across the ditch is one of the measures he takes to downplay the importance of the ditch in this situation. Let us now look at other measures that contribute to the same goal.

Here is Homer's first description of a Greek retreat across the ditch:

> Then the Olympian once more spurred strength into the Trojans, and they drove the Achaians back straight towards the deep ditch: and Hektor went among the first of them, revelling in his strength. ... Hektor pressed close on the long-haired Achaians, constantly killing the hindmost: and they fled in terror. When they had crossed the stakes and the ditch in their flight, and many had been brought down at the Trojans' hands, they came to a halt alongside the ships ...
>
> Quote 6.27: *Il.* 8.335–345 (Hammond trans.)

The last sentence of this passage implicitly blames the ditch and the stakes for the Greek casualties. What is interesting is that this sentence corresponds closely with the description of a Trojan retreat across the ditch in which chariots play no role because the Trojans left their chariots at the outer edge of the ditch before they entered the Greek camp (as anticipated in quote 6.24).[155] In other words, quote 6.27 fails to acknowledge that the Greeks are especially vulnerable since they cannot abandon their chariots when they reach the ditch. Now consider the second description of a Greek retreat across the ditch:

> [T]he Achaians were running in panic this way and that, fouled in the ditch they had dug and its stakes, and they were forced behind their wall.
>
> Quote 6.28: *Il.* 15.343–345 (Hammond trans.)

This passage makes explicit the obstacle that the ditch presents to the Greeks in retreat, even if there is no mention of chariots. Homer nevertheless minimizes the impact of this obstacle, for it turns out that the Trojans are busy stripping armor from men they have already killed, and fail to take advantage of the disorder of the ditch crossing to inflict additional casualties on the Greeks.[156] Finally, on the occasion of the last Greek retreat, we are told only that "many pieces of fine armour were dropped all around the ditch as the Danaäns ran."[157] Once again, the consequences of the ditch and the stakes for the retreating Greeks are relatively minor.

We see, then, that Homer downplays the importance of the ditch whenever the Greeks must cross it to escape their enemies. The reason for this special treatment is evident: the poet obviously does not want to draw too much attention to the fact that the ditch that is supposed to protect the Greeks actually endangers them in a situation that is encountered with some frequency. That the significance of the ditch is minimized repeatedly in this situation but not in others shows that the poet was aware of the illogicality of the Greek fortifications. Since the illogical elements of the fortifications—the ditch and the stakes—do not play an important role in the poem comparable to that of the wall and could easily have been left out, we infer not only that the illogicality was introduced knowingly, but that it was desired: in current parlance, it was "a feature, not a bug."

This concludes the discussion of perverse inconsistencies and other illogicalities in the *Iliad*. We now turn our attention to the *Odyssey*.

6.6. Triadic Inconsistencies Involving Circe and Kalypso

A much-discussed problem in the *Odyssey* takes the form of a blatant inconsistency that is part of a certain pattern of logical relationships in which the goddess Circe plays a central role. In this section I describe this pattern and then identify an instance of the same pattern in which the central role is played by the goddess Kalypso. As there are already a number of well-known parallels between Circe and Kalypso, the additional parallel of a shared pattern that revolves around an inconsistency of some sort is evidence for intentional inconsistency within the *Odyssey*. We have already seen intentional inconsistency within the *Odyssey* in section 5.2, but the inconsistencies discussed in that section are comprehensible. The inconsistencies that we are about to consider, on the other hand, have no apparent explanation and should therefore be classified as perverse.

After Odysseus has spent a year with Circe, his men persuade him that it is time to resume the journey home. Circe consents to their departure, but tells Odysseus that he must start by going to the underworld to consult with the shade of the prophet Teiresias. The prophet, says Circe to Odysseus,

> "... will tell you the way to go, the stages of your journey,
> and tell you how to make your way home on the sea where the fish swarm."
> Quote 6.29: *Od*. 10.539–540

Odysseus follows Circe's instructions, and Teiresias prophesies as follows:

> "*Glorious Odysseus, what you are after is sweet homecoming,*
> *but the god will make it hard for you. I think you will not*
> *escape the Shaker of the Earth [Poseidon], who holds a grudge against you*
> *in his heart, and because you blinded his dear son [the Cyclops Polyphemos],*
>   *hates you.*
> **But even so and still you might come back, after much suffering,**
> **if you can contain your own desire, and contain your companions',**
> **at that time when you first put in your well-made vessel**
> **at the island Thrinakia, escaping the sea's blue water,**
> **and there discover pasturing the cattle and fat sheep**
> **of Helios, who sees all things, and listens to all things.**
> **Then, if you keep your mind on homecoming, and leave these unharmed,**
> **you might all make your way to Ithaka, after much suffering;**
> **but if you do harm them, then I testify to the destruction**
> **of your ship and your companions, but if you yourself get clear,**
> **you will come home in bad case, with the loss of all your companions,**

> in someone else's ship, <u>and find troubles in your household,</u>
> <u>insolent men, who are eating away your livelihood</u>
> <u>and courting your godlike wife and offering gifts to win her.</u>
> <u>You may punish the violences of these men, when you come home.</u>
> <u>But after you have killed these suitors in your own palace,</u>
> <u>either by treachery, or openly with the sharp bronze,</u>
> *then you must take up your well-shaped oar and go on a journey*
> *until you come where there are men living who know nothing*
> *of the sea ...*
> ...
> *[T]hen you must plant your well-shaped oar in the ground, and render*
> *ceremonious sacrifice to the lord Poseidon,*
> ..."
>
> Quote 6.30: excerpts from *Od.* 11.100–137 (100–123, 129–130;
boldface, italics, and underlining added)

At first glance, the part of the prophecy that is shown in boldface, which is the only part that concerns us now (the italicized and underlined parts will be discussed in the following two sections), appears to support quote 6.29 since Teiresias does indeed give Odysseus information of importance for his journey home, namely, the information that he and his men must not harm the cattle on the island of Thrinakia. On the other hand, the statement that Odysseus will have to endure much suffering suggests that Teiresias has left out a good deal. In fact, when Odysseus returns from the underworld, Circe gives him a far more complete account of the challenges he will face on his journey back to Ithaka.[158] In addition to the information concerning Thrinakia already provided by Teiresias, Circe's account includes warnings about the Sirens, the Roving Rocks, Skylla, and Charybdis; our suspicion that Teiresias has left out a good deal is confirmed. In addition, Circe describes the challenges in their proper sequence, and tells Odysseus how to meet the ones that Teiresias does not even mention. Evidently it is she, not Teiresias, who tells Odysseus the stages of his journey and how he should make his way home on the sea.[159]

That Circe is the one who actually gives Odysseus the information that she earlier says will be given by Teiresias is a well-known problem.[160] The problem is compounded by her first words to Odysseus and his companions upon their return from the underworld:

> "Unhappy men, who went alive to the house of Hades,
> so dying twice, when all the rest of mankind die only
> once, come then eat what is there and drink your wine, staying
> here all the rest of the day, and then tomorrow, when dawn shows,
> you shall sail, and I will show you the way and make plain
> all details, so that neither by land nor on the salt water
> you may suffer and come to grief by unhappy bad designing."
>
> Quote 6.31: *Od.* 12.21–27

In the last three lines of this greeting, Circe promises to do what she had said Teiresias would do in quote 6.29. But it is only after this greeting and after Odysseus and his men have feasted all day that Circe learns from Odysseus what happened during his visit to the underworld. It follows that either Circe assumes in quote 6.31 that her prediction in quote 6.29 was false or else the poet is, in effect, denying the existence of quote 6.29. In either interpretation,

6.6. TRIADS INVOLVING CIRCE AND KALYPSO

quote 6.29 is contradicted by quote 6.31 in addition to Circe's actual explanation of the stages of Odysseus's journey home.

The material reviewed so far forms a logical structure in which an inconsistency emerges in three steps:

(*a*) a statement that will eventually turn out to be false (quote 6.29);

(*b*) information that appears to support the statement in part (*a*) but also hints that the latter statement may not be true (the part of quote 6.30 shown in boldface);

(*c*) information that is consistent with the information in part (*b*) but demonstrates conclusively that the statement in part (*a*) is false (Circe's explanation to Odysseus of the stages of his journey home, with quote 6.31 playing a supporting role).

I shall refer to this structure as a triadic inconsistency, with the understanding that its third component contains some structure of its own.

It is tempting to minimize the significance of the structure that I have just described, and there are at least two ways to do this. One may argue that the poet so wants to give his poem and its hero the stature and the connection with the larger tradition that come with a descent to the underworld and a consultation with Teiresias that he is even willing to give the descent a motivation (quote 6.29) that is unsuited to the prophetic powers of Teiresias.[161] Alternatively, one may assert that quote 6.29 simply illustrates the poet's willingness to use verses from his repertoire even when they are not strictly appropriate.[162] That such explanations may be misguided is suggested by the existence of a triadic inconsistency that is intimately connected with the one we have just considered.

The beginning of the *Odyssey* finds Odysseus longing for home and his wife Penelope while being held prisoner on the island of Ogygia by Kalypso, the nymph who wants him to be her husband.[163] The second triadic inconsistency is formed from three accounts of the disaster that brought him to Ogygia and caused the death of his last remaining companions. The first two accounts are found in the conversation between Kalypso and Hermes, who has been sent to Ogygia by Zeus (at the urging of Athene)[164] to tell Kalypso to release Odysseus. Before relaying the command from Zeus, Hermes says to Kalypso,

> "[Y]ou have with you the man who is wretched beyond all the other
> men of all those who fought around the city of Priam
> for nine years, and in the tenth they sacked the city and set sail
> for home, but on the voyage home they offended Athene,
> who let loose an evil tempest and tall waves against them.
> Then all the rest of his excellent companions perished,
> but the wind and the current carried him here and here they drove him."
>
> Quote 6.32: *Od.* 5.105–111

Thus, in the first of the three accounts, Hermes blames the disaster on Athene. The a priori plausibility of this attribution is debatable[165] but not relevant to the analysis of the triadic inconsistency. In her reply, Kalypso gives the second account:

> "... I keep beside me
> a man, the one I saved when he clung astride of the keel board
> all alone, since Zeus with a cast of the shining thunderbolt
> had shattered his fast ship midway on the wine-blue water.
> Then all the rest of his excellent companions perished,
> but the wind and the current carried him here and here they drove him,"
>
> Quote 6.33: *Od.* 5.129–134

We see that Kalypso blames Zeus instead of Athene. In spite of the apparent contradiction, Kalypso's account may actually support that of Hermes, for earlier in the poem Nestor blames the difficult return home from Troy on the joint action of Zeus and Athene:

> "But after we had sacked the sheer citadel of Priam,
> and were going away in our ships, and the god scattered the Achaians,
> then Zeus in his mind devised a sorry homecoming
> for the Argives, since not all were considerate nor righteous;
> therefore many of them found a bad way home, because of
> the ruinous anger of the Gray-eyed One [Athene], whose father is mighty.
> It was she who made a quarrel between the two sons of Atreus.
> ...
>   ... Zeus, hard-hearted, was not yet devising
> homecoming for us, but again inspired yet another quarrel."
>
> Quote 6.34: *Od.* 3.130–136, 160–161

In addition, we see Athene and Zeus working closely together, with Zeus supplying a thunderbolt, at the very end of the poem.[166] On the other hand, we would certainly be justified by the differences between quotes 6.32 and 6.33 in entertaining the possibility that only one of the first two accounts is correct.[167] As it happens, the latter possibility is confirmed by the third account, which is delivered by Odysseus in his tales to the Phaiakians.

After describing how his companions slaughtered the cattle of Helios while he was asleep, Odysseus relates to the Phaiakians that

> "Lampetia of the light robes ran swift with the message
> to Hyperion [Helios] the Sun God, that we had killed his cattle,
> and angered at the heart he spoke forth among the immortals:
> 'Father Zeus, and you other everlasting and blessed
> gods, punish the companions of Odysseus, son of Laertes;
> for they outrageously killed my cattle, in whom I always
> delighted, on my way up into the starry heaven,
> or when I turned back again from heaven toward earth. Unless
> these are made to give me just recompense for my cattle,
> I will go down to Hades' and give my light to the dead men.'
>   "Then in turn Zeus who gathers the clouds answered him:
> 'Helios, shine as you do, among the immortals
> and mortal men, all over the grain-giving earth. For my part
> I will strike these men's fast ship midway on the open
> wine-blue sea with a shining bolt and dash it to pieces.'
>   "All this I heard afterward from fair-haired Kalypso,
> and she told me she herself had heard it from the guide, Hermes."
>
> Quote 6.35: *Od.* 12.374–390

Odysseus's description of the subsequent events (*Od.* 12.391–449) includes the destruction of his ship by a thunderbolt from Zeus, the loss of his companions, his use of the keel and mast of the ship as a life raft, and his eventual arrival at Kalypso's island. Thus, the third account (quote 6.35 in combination with *Od.* 12.391–449) is fully compatible with the second (quote 6.33), but elaborates on it by explaining that Zeus struck Odysseus's ship with a thunderbolt in order to avenge the destruction of the cattle of Helios. This account is undoubtedly correct, given that Teiresias and Circe warned Odysseus that his ship and his companions would be destroyed if the cattle of Helios were harmed.[168] In fact, we know from the words of the poet himself (as opposed to one of his characters) at the very beginning of the poem that the companions of Odysseus lost their homecoming because they devoured the cattle of Helios.[169] Besides being correct, the third account gives every indication of being complete. Since it does not mention Athene, it follows that the account given by Hermes in quote 6.32 is wrong.[170]

Once again we have an inconsistency that emerges in three steps. The statement that eventually proves to be false is quote 6.32; the equivocal statement is quote 6.33; and the information that is consistent with the equivocal statement but demonstrates that the original statement is false is found in *Od.* 12.374–449, the first part of which is shown in quote 6.35.[171] The existence of two instances of the pattern that I call triadic inconsistency suggests that the pattern is intentional. This evidence for intentional inconsistency within the *Odyssey* is reinforced by special relationships that can be discerned between the two instances of the triadic pattern. Before describing these special relationships, however, I discuss a feature of the second instance that we have ignored so far.

The last two lines of quote 6.35 have been called "the greatest blemish in the whole narrative art of Homer."[172] Although other contenders for this distinction are discussed in this chapter, it is not difficult to see why these particular lines are considered a blemish. First, Homer's description of what happened on Ogygia gives no hint that Kalypso ever told Odysseus of her conversation with Hermes and actually implies that she did not.[173] Second, and even more disturbing, the explanation of the disaster that Hermes is said to have given Kalypso in quote 6.35 contradicts what Hermes says to Kalypso in quote 6.32.[174] However, I believe that what we are confronted with here is not a blemish but intentional inconsistency. The last two lines of quote 6.35 play a role in the second triadic inconsistency that is similar to the role played by quote 6.31 in the first. Each of the two passages can be read as a denial by the poet of the existence of the first part of the triad (quotes 6.32 and 6.29, respectively). Each passage (the last two lines of quote 6.35 or the last three lines of quote 6.31) reinforces the demonstration by the third part of the triad that the first part is false, but neither is essential to the demonstration. With this added similarity of the two triadic inconsistencies, we can say with even greater confidence than before that the existence of two instances of the triadic pattern suggests that this pattern is intentional.

The two triadic inconsistencies are related to each other not only in form, but also in content. As we have seen, the second triad is concerned with the disaster that brought Odysseus to Kalypso and caused the death of his last remaining companions, namely, the destruction of his ship by Zeus in retaliation for the destruction of the cattle of Helios on the island of Thrinakia. The possibility of precisely this disaster is foreseen by Teiresias in the second part of the first triad (indeed, this is the main part of his prophecy that actually relates to Odysseus's journey home) and by Circe in the third part of that triad. Furthermore, Odysseus's account of the disaster in the third part of the second triad fills in the main gap in Circe's account of Odysseus's journey in the third part of the first triad, which leaves out his arrival at Ogygia and his immediately preceding encounter with Charybdis. But perhaps more important than all of this is the fact that the first triad revolves around Circe, while the second triad revolves around Kalypso (Circe is the source of the first and third components of the first triad, and the indirect source of the second component since it is owing to Circe that Odysseus consults Teiresias; Kalypso, besides receiving Odysseus after the destruction of his ship, is a participant in the conversation that provides the first two components of the second triad and is said in *Od.* 12.389–390 to be the source of the third component). The connection of the two triadic inconsistencies with Circe and Kalypso is striking since it is well known that these two figures have a number of other things in common.

Circe and Kalypso are both minor goddesses who dwell on remote islands and who are described in unmistakably similar terms.[175] They both enjoy extended sexual relationships with Odysseus, who links them together explicitly at the beginning of his tales to the Phaiakians:

> "… Kalypso, shining among divinities, kept me
> with her in her hollow caverns, desiring me for her husband,
> and so likewise Aiaian Circe the guileful detained me
> beside her in her halls, desiring me for her husband,"[176]
>
> Quote 6.36: *Od.* 9.29–32

In addition to their intrinsic similarities, Circe and Kalypso play parallel roles in the poem.[177] Circe gives Odysseus refuge after he has lost all the ships of his fleet except his own; Kalypso gives him refuge after he has lost his own ship and his last remaining companions (as we saw in the second triad). After a substantial delay (one year in the case of Circe, upwards of seven years in the case of Kalypso), Circe and Kalypso both give Odysseus the directions he needs to make his way home,[178] as well as a suitable wind to speed him on his way.[179] Besides the many correspondences in their properties and in their roles, it is remarkable that the poet goes out of his way to mention them both in one of the few passages where he refers in his own voice to adventures related by Odysseus to the Phaiakians.[180] In view of all this, it is surely significant that Circe and Kalypso are both central figures in a triadic inconsistency. That two instances of a pattern that is already somewhat remarkable in itself are connected in such a special way is another indication that the pattern—and therefore some of the inconsistency in the *Odyssey*—is intentional.

6.7. Illogical Instructions for Odysseus and Telemachos

Let us now consider the parts of the prophecy of Teiresias that I have italicized in quote 6.30. In the part at the beginning of the passage, Teiresias tells Odysseus that Poseidon will make his homecoming difficult; in the part at the end, the seer instructs Odysseus to offer sacrifices to Poseidon *after* he has accomplished his homecoming and dealt with the suitors. This makes no sense: instead of offering sacrifices after enduring the hardships inflicted on him by Poseidon, Odysseus should obviously try to appease the god before his return home, when it is not too late for mercy.[181] Thus, the two italicized parts of quote 6.30 are inconsistent with each other.

The inconsistency of the two italicized parts of quote 6.30 is reinforced by explicit indications elsewhere in the poem that the wrath of Poseidon is to end upon Odysseus's return,[182] which proves that the sacrifices recommended by Teiresias are pointless. Of course we suspect this even without the mentioned explicit indications or the first italicized part of quote 6.30: the threat to Odysseus from the god of the sea can probably be assumed to be specific to the hero's voyage home.[183] What is important, therefore, is not really the inconsistency between the two italicized parts of quote 6.30 but rather the illogicality of Teiresias's instruction given in the second of these parts. The illogicality lies in the fact that someone is instructed to perform a certain act, but only when the act no longer makes sense. My argument that this is intentional begins with the fact that the *Odyssey* contains another instance of just this kind of illogicality.

Near the beginning of the poem, Athene (in disguise) advises Telemachos to go to Nestor and Menelaos in search of news of his father. What Telemachos should do when he gets back home will depend on what he finds out:

> "Thus if you hear your father is alive and on his way home,
> then, hard pressed though you are, you should still hold out for another year. But if you hear he has died and lives no longer,
> then make your way home to the beloved land of your fathers,
> and pile up a tomb in his honor, and there make sacrifices
> in great amount, as is fitting. And give your mother to a husband.
> Then, after you have made an end of these matters, and done them,
> next you must consider well in your heart and spirit
> some means by which you can kill the suitors who are in your household,
> by treachery or open attack. ..."
>
> Quote 6.37: Od. 1.287–296

If Odysseus has died or does not return to Ithaka within a year, Penelope is to remarry and *then* Telemachos is to slay the suitors in his household. Of the numerous observations that have been made in relation to Athene's instructions,[184] I shall repeat only one. After Penelope has remarried, she will no longer have any suitors, and the men who had been her suitors will presumably have dispersed. It will therefore be too late for Telemachos to kill the suitors, just as it will be too late for Odysseus to appease Poseidon once his homecoming has been accomplished.

Teiresias's instructions to Odysseus and Athene's instructions to Telemachos evidently contain analogous illogicalities. That there are two instances of this type of illogicality is just the first indication that they are intentional. The case for intentionality is reinforced by the existence of certain connections between the two illogical instructions and the two triadic inconsistencies discussed in the preceding section. Before describing these surprising connections, which link a member of one pair with a member of the other, I shall point out a simple property that is shared by the two pairs themselves.

It will be recalled from the end of the preceding section that the two triadic inconsistencies are associated with two figures, Circe and Kalypso, who are already known for having a lot in common. The same is true of the two illogical instructions, for the recipients of these instructions also have a great deal in common. To begin with, there is a strong physical resemblance between Odysseus and Telemachos, both in appearance (Helen and Menelaos recognize Telemachos as the son of Odysseus before he has identified himself) and in strength (Telemachos, unlike any of the suitors, is said to be capable of stringing Odysseus's bow).[185] Of course, such a resemblance is not surprising for a father and son. But there are also a number of parallels between the stories of these two characters before their reunion.[186] Here I shall mention only one, chosen because it seems to hint that the parallelism is intentional.

Athene urges Telemachos to be bold when he speaks with Nestor, and she likewise urges Odysseus to be bold when he speaks with the king and queen of the Phaiakians.[187] Such encouragement is entirely fitting in the case of the inexperienced Telemachos, but it is surely unnecessary in the case of the seasoned Odysseus, whose boldness in addressing both the lowly and the exalted is well known from the *Iliad* and whose ability to adjust his boldness to the situation at hand has just been demonstrated in his exquisite encounter with the Phaiakian princess Nausicaa.[188] Athene's advice to the great Odysseus that he should have no fear, but rather be bold, when he enters the royal residence is all the more strange because in this scene she has disguised herself as a little girl. The resulting incongruousness of this advice suggests that Homer included it expressly for the parallel with Athene's earlier advice to Telemachos.

My discussion of the pair of triadic inconsistencies and the pair of illogical instructions has referred to the doublet of Circe and Kalypso and the doublet of Odysseus and Telemachos, respectively. The following discussion connecting individual members of one pair with individual members of the other pair will make use of two other well-known doublets.

Besides Odysseus, Menelaos is the only Greek hero who returns home safely after the Trojan War but takes a long time to do so: Odysseus reaches Ithaka ten years after the war, Menelaos arrives in Sparta after eight.[189] During the course of their returns, both men are urged by a goddess to consult a seer concerning the way home: Odysseus consults Teiresias at the behest of Circe, and Menelaos consults Proteus at the advice of Eidothea. Thus, Odysseus + Circe + Teiresias and Menelaos + Eidothea + Proteus form a doublet. This doublet has been much discussed by others[190] and will be considered further in

6.7. ILLOGICAL INSTRUCTIONS

the next section. Now we want to compare the guidance that Proteus gives to Menelaos with the guidance that Teiresias gives to Odysseus.

When he finally sets out for home from Egypt, Menelaos does not get far on his first attempt. Owing to the absence of favorable winds, he and his men become stranded on an island a day's sail from Egypt. After twenty days on the island, he consults Proteus to learn the source of his trouble and how he can make his way home. Proteus explains as follows:

> "... you should have made grand sacrifices to Zeus and the other
> immortal gods, and so gone on board, so most quickly
> to reach your own country, sailing over the wine-blue water.
> It is not your destiny now to see your own people and come back
> to your strong-founded house and to the land of your fathers,
> until you have gone back once again to the water of Egypt,
> the sky-fallen river, and there have accomplished holy hecatombs
> in honor of all the immortal gods who hold wide heaven.
> Then the gods will grant you that journey that you so long for."
>
> Quote 6.38: *Od.* 4.472–480

Menelaos has offended the gods by not offering them appropriate sacrifices before embarking for home, much as Odysseus incurred the wrath of Poseidon by blinding Polyphemos (quote 6.30). Like Odysseus, Menelaos is advised by a seer to offer sacrifices to the offended god(s). Whereas Teiresias tells Odysseus to offer sacrifices after his return home, however, Proteus tells Menelaos that he can return home only after he has performed the necessary sacrifices. The latter sacrifices are perfectly logical, unlike the sacrifices that Odysseus is supposed to make after his return (when propitiation of Poseidon will be too late to do Odysseus any good). Thus, the advice of Proteus bears a special relationship, one of contrast, to one of the two illogical instructions discussed earlier in this section. I shall now argue that it bears a similar relationship to one of the two triadic inconsistencies discussed in the preceding section.

One of the interesting properties of the doublet formed by Odysseus + Circe + Teiresias and Menelaos + Eidothea + Proteus is that Circe and Eidothea use the same words to characterize the information the seer will provide,[191] namely, the words reproduced in quote 6.29. In the preceding section we saw that quote 6.29 is not an accurate description of the information that Teiresias provides Odysseus. Is it also an inaccurate description of the information that Proteus provides Menelaos? There is no scholarly consensus on this question.[192] Nevertheless, I maintain that Proteus fulfills the expectations raised by quote 6.29. In quote 6.38 he tells Menelaos to go back to Egypt to perform hecatombs (grand sacrifices) and then to set out again for home. Thus, Proteus, unlike Teiresias, does tell his questioner the stages of his journey. One may object that the voyage from Egypt to Sparta is not broken into stages, but the fact is that Proteus provides all the information necessary for Menelaos's journey home, which is accomplished expeditiously once the sacrifices have been performed.[193] There is consequently a significant contrast between the guidance that Proteus offers Menelaos and the guidance that Teiresias offers Odysseus.

In the preceding section we saw that quote 6.29 is the first component of a triadic inconsistency, the statement that is eventually shown to be false. I have just argued that the same statement is true in the context of Proteus's advice to Menelaos. This advice therefore bears the same relationship of contrast to the triadic inconsistency involving Circe that it bears to the illogical instruction to Odysseus. By virtue of this common relationship, the advice of Proteus in quote 6.38 can be said to link one of the two triads discussed in the preceding section to one of the two illogical instructions discussed in the present section. I shall now demonstrate that the other triad can be linked to the other illogical instruction in a roughly analogous fashion.

The action of the *Odyssey* is set in motion by two divine missions: Athene's mission to Ithaka to get Telemachos to begin to assert himself and Hermes' mission to Ogygia to tell Kalypso to free Odysseus. These two missions form another well-known doublet.[194] Each mission is occasioned by an assembly of the gods in which Athene calls attention to the plight of Odysseus on Ogygia.[195] The parallelism is accentuated by the fact that the outcome of the second assembly, the dispatching of Hermes to Kalypso, has already been suggested by Athene in the first assembly.[196, 197] The parallels continue as Athene and Hermes set out on their missions:[198]

> ... [S]he [Athene] bound upon her feet the fair sandals,
> golden and immortal, that carried her over the water
> as over the dry boundless earth abreast of the wind's blast.
> Then she caught up a powerful spear, edged with sharp bronze,
> heavy, huge, thick, wherewith she beats down the battalions of fighting
> men, against whom she of the mighty father is angered,
> and descended in a flash of speed from the peaks of Olympos,
>
> Quote 6.39: *Od.* 1.96–102

> Immediately he [Hermes] bound upon his feet the fair sandals,
> golden and immortal, that carried him over the water
> as over the dry boundless earth abreast of the wind's blast.
> He caught up the staff, with which he mazes the eyes of those mortals
> whose eyes he would maze, or wakes again the sleepers. Holding
> this in his hands, strong Argeïphontes winged his way onward.
>
> Quote 6.40: *Od.* 5.44–49

Central to each of the divine missions is a conversation. It is during her conversation with Telemachos that Athene gives the instructions from which I have taken quote 6.37. This conversation therefore includes the illogical instruction that Telemachos should kill his mother's suitors after she has remarried. The conversation between Hermes and Kalypso includes two components, quotes 6.32 and 6.33, of the second triadic inconsistency discussed in the preceding section. Thus, the parallels between the missions of Athene and Hermes link the triadic inconsistency involving Kalypso to the illogical instruction to Telemachos.

In this section and the preceding one, we have discovered a highly structured system of four inconsistencies in the *Odyssey*. Two of the inconsistencies are of the distinctive type that I call a triadic inconsistency, an inconsistency that emerges in three steps, and the other two belong to the distinctive type that I call an illogical instruction, an instruction near the end of a speech that is incompatible with what has gone before. The two members of each pair are bound together not only by their common form, but also by their association with the two members of a well-known character doublet. In addition, the two pairs of related inconsistencies are linked to each other via two other well-known doublets. The doubling of each type of inconsistency in combination with the links made possible by well-known doublets strongly suggests that the four inconsistencies composing the resulting system are intentional.

6.8. The Warning Concerning the Suitors

The prophecy of Teiresias played a key role in the preceding two sections, providing one of the illogical instructions as well as a component of one of the triadic inconsistencies, but we have not yet exhausted what this passage has to offer. In the underlined part of quote 6.30, Teiresias warns Odysseus that, if he makes it back to Ithaka, he will find insolent suitors courting his wife. This warning is, of course, perfectly valid, but it is inconsistent with two later passages in which Odysseus speaks as if Teiresias has not told him about the suitors.

Immediately after his consultation with the seer, Odysseus speaks with the shade of his mother Antikleia, who died from longing for him during his absence and has therefore been on Ithaka more recently than he has. The last of a series of questions he asks her (and the first question she answers, in accordance with the ring structure mentioned in part (*a*) of section 5.7) concerns Penelope:

> "... Tell me
> about the wife I married, what she wants, what she is thinking,
> and whether she stays fast by my son, and guards everything,
> or if she has married the best man among the Achaians."
> Quote 6.41: *Od.* 11.176–179

Odysseus seems to have forgotten what Teiresias just told him. For if he recalled that upon his return to Ithaka he will find his wife being courted by suitors, he would know that Penelope cannot have remarried.

When Odysseus finally gets back to Ithaka, his first encounter is with Athene, who summarizes for him the current state of affairs in his palace:

> "Son of Laertes and seed of Zeus, resourceful Odysseus,
> consider how you can lay your hands on these shameless suitors,
> who for three years now have been as lords in your palace,
> and courting your godlike wife, and offering gifts to win her.
> And she, though her heart forever grieves over your homecoming,
> holds out some hope for all, and makes promises to each man,
> sending them messages, but her mind has other intentions."
> Quote 6.42: *Od.* 13.375–381

Odysseus begins his reply with the following remark:

> "Surely I was on the point of perishing by an evil
> fate in my palace, like Atreus' son Agamemnon, unless
> you had told me, goddess, the very truth of all that has happened."
> Quote 6.43: *Od.* 13.383–385

Odysseus is saying that he surely would have been killed in his own palace if Athene had not warned him about the suitors. Again he seems to have forgotten the same warning from Teiresias.[199]

Quotes 6.41 and 6.43 are both inconsistent with Teiresias's warning concerning the suitors. The first of these inconsistencies is striking since it is found immediately after Odysseus receives this warning. The second inconsistency is also striking even though it occurs more than seven years later, for there are several reasons to believe that Odysseus remembers his meeting with Teiresias in the underworld while he is speaking with Athene in Ithaka. First, quote 6.43 shows that Odysseus must be thinking of his visit to the underworld since he knows about the fate of Agamemnon only through the conversation he had with him during this visit.[200] Second, in the conversation from which quotes 6.42 and 6.43 are taken, Athene refers to Poseidon's grudge against Odysseus in terms virtually identical to those used by Teiresias.[201] Last, and most important, it is during this conversation that Odysseus realizes that he is finally back in Ithaka.[202] As he has been transported there on a ship of the Phaiakians, it is fair to assume that he recalls Teiresias's prediction in quote 6.30 that he will come home in someone else's ship, especially since the unique seafaring ability of the Phaiakians and their pride in providing conveyance to all men have been impressed upon him repeatedly.[203]

In the two preceding sections (and section 5.1 as well), I have argued that when a strange phenomenon, such as an inconsistency, is encountered at one place in Homer and then found again at another place, the duplication (if it is sufficiently precise) is evidence that the strange phenomenon was created intentionally by the poet. I shall use this argument in this section as well. However, it does not apply at this point in the discussion since the two inconsistencies I have mentioned can be dispatched with a single stroke. Consider the simple explanation proposed by Denys Page. According to Page, the warning concerning the suitors was originally not part of Teiresias's prophecy, and the poet who added the warning to the prophecy neglected to make the adjustments needed to avoid the contradictions posed by quotes 6.41 and 6.43.[204] I shall argue that this explanation is untenable because the poet inserted peculiar allusions to Teiresias's warning elsewhere in the poem; if he went to the trouble of making these allusions, it is difficult to believe that he would not have removed the contradictions—unless, of course, the contradictions were intentional.[205]

To appreciate the first allusion to Teiresias's warning concerning the suitors, we must consider more of the parallels between Odysseus + Circe + Teiresias and Menelaos + Eidothea + Proteus, one of the doublets discussed in the preceding section. As I mentioned there, Odysseus and Menelaos are the only heroes whose return home from the Trojan War is greatly delayed. Furthermore, during the course of their returns, both men are urged by a goddess to consult a seer concerning the way home. The parallels extend to what they are told by their respective seers. They are both told that they have angered one or more gods and must offer sacrifices.[206] They are also both told how their lives will end: Odysseus will die in "sleek old age" with his people prosperous; Menelaos, as son-in-law of Zeus, will be conveyed to the Elysian

6.8. THE WARNING CONCERNING THE SUITORS

Field. Furthermore, Menelaos hears from Proteus what happened to three of the other Greek leaders after the war, while Odysseus actually encounters three former leaders in the underworld after his meeting with Teiresias; Agamemnon is the only leader common to the two groups of three, and it is here that Menelaos and Odysseus learn that he was murdered upon his return home. The parallels also extend to how the information to be received from each seer is characterized by the corresponding goddess. As I mentioned in the preceding section, Circe and Eidothea use the same words to give a (very incomplete) description of what Odysseus and Menelaos will be told by Teiresias and Proteus, respectively. This statement of mine is actually inaccurate or incomplete, depending on how it is interpreted; it is now necessary to clarify it.

Here is how Eidothea explains to Menelaos what he might hear from Proteus:

"[H]e could tell you the way to go, the stages of your journey,
and tell you how to make your way home on the sea where the fish swarm.
And he could tell you too, illustrious one, if you wish it,
what evil and what good has been done in your palace
while you have been gone away on your long and arduous voyage."
                                                    Quote 6.44: *Od.* 4.389–393

In the Greek, the first two lines of this passage are identical to what Circe tells Odysseus about Teiresias in quote 6.29. However, the last three lines have no parallel in what Circe says to Odysseus. The placement of the latter lines is very strange. Since they have no bearing on the situation of Menelaos (Proteus does not tell him about anything that happened in his palace during his absence[207]) but are highly relevant to Odysseus (Teiresias tells him about the unruly suitors who will be in his palace consuming his wealth and courting his wife),[208] they appear to have been transferred inappropriately from the mouth of Circe to the mouth of Eidothea. It is not difficult to see a possible motive for this transfer.

We know that Odysseus + Circe + Teiresias and Menelaos + Eidothea + Proteus form a doublet, and can say with some confidence that the doubling is intentional. I suggest that the purpose of the last three lines of quote 6.44 is to extend the correspondence between the two components of the doublet. Since Teiresias is to tell Odysseus what happened in his palace during his absence (more precisely, what will have happened by the time Odysseus returns home), the poet has Eidothea mention the possibility that Proteus might do this for Menelaos. One might object that this correspondence connects different phases of the two episodes, the prophecy of one seer as opposed to what is said about the prophecy of the other seer. But this objection carries little weight since this sort of looseness is seen in some of the other parallels. I have already mentioned that Menelaos hears about three Greek leaders from Proteus, while Odysseus encounters three leaders *after* his meeting with Teiresias. Similarly, Proteus's instruction that Menelaos offer sacrifices to the gods comes at the beginning of their exchange, while Teiresias's corresponding instruction to Odysseus comes near the end of his prophecy, where it makes no sense (as discussed in the preceding section). A parallel not mentioned above displays a different kind of looseness, as it involves noncorresponding members of the triplets Odysseus + Circe + Teiresias and Menelaos + Eidothea + Proteus: virtually the same four lines are used to describe the reaction of Menelaos to something said by Proteus and the reaction of Odysseus to something said by Circe, not Teiresias.[209] It seems fair to say, then, that what is said about the expected revelations of Proteus in the last three lines of quote 6.44 is in correspondence with the warning concerning the suitors in the prophecy of Teiresias. These three lines constitute the first allusion to Teiresias's warning.

As Odysseus is making his escape after blinding Polyphemos, the Cyclops utters the following prayer:

> "Hear me, Poseidon who circle the earth, dark-haired. If truly
> I am your son, and you acknowledge yourself as my father,
> grant that Odysseus, sacker of cities, son of Laertes,
> who makes his home in Ithaka, may never reach that home;
> but if it is decided that he shall see his own people,
> and come home to his strong-founded house and to his own country,
> let him come home late, in bad case, with the loss of all his companions,
> in someone else's ship, and find troubles in his household."
>
> Quote 6.45: *Od.* 9.528–535

The correspondence between the last two lines of this passage and two lines of quote 6.30 (*Od.* 11.114–115) is obvious and well known. Karl Reinhardt even declares that "the curse of Polyphemos and the speech of Teiresias refer to each other."[210] I will now suggest a slightly different view.

At the end of his prayer, Polyphemos asks Poseidon to cause troubles in the household of Odysseus. As Reinhardt notes, the idea that the scourge of the suitors was caused by Poseidon is not stated or implied anywhere else in the *Odyssey* and is "unthinkable."[211] Similarly, nowhere else is the loss of Odysseus's companions attributed to Poseidon; indeed, we know specifically that his last companions were lost owing to acts of Zeus motivated by the complaint of Helios (see section 6.6). Furthermore, it was on this occasion that Zeus destroyed Odysseus's last ship, with the consequence that any return to Ithaka would have to be made in someone else's ship. In short, the last two lines of quote 6.45 do not belong in a prayer to Poseidon. The corresponding lines in quote 6.30, on the other hand, are entirely appropriate. Following the principle that if a repeated passage is fitting in one instance but unsuitable in another, then the latter instance must refer to the former rather than vice versa (see section 5.1), we conclude that Polyphemos's prayer refers to Teiresias's prophecy. And since Teiresias elaborates the last half-line of the shared passage into the warning concerning the suitors (*Od.* 11.116–117 in quote 6.30), the prayer of Polyphemos alludes to the warning of Teiresias.[212]

Quotes 6.44 and 6.45 show that Homer went to some trouble to allude to Teiresias's warning concerning the suitors. Both allusions sit uncomfortably in their respective contexts, one because Eidothea mentions a subject that Proteus does not pursue and the other because Polyphemos prays for things that will come to pass without Poseidon's intervention. It is difficult to believe that a poet who made two such forced allusions to Teiresias's warning would have simply neglected to make the adjustments needed to avoid the contradictions with Teiresias's warning in quotes 6.41 and 6.43. I conclude that the contradictions were intentional.

Our route to the inference of intentional inconsistency also leads to another interesting observation. Quotes 6.41 and 6.43 essentially deny the existence of Teiresias's warning about the suitors since Odysseus speaks in these passages as if the seer has not told him about them. On the other hand, quotes 6.44 and 6.45 affirm the existence of Teiresias's warning by alluding to it. We have seen this strange combination of affirmation and denial before, in the relationship of the *Odyssey* to the *Iliad* (see sections 5.3 and 5.5) and in the relationship between two scenes in the *Iliad* (see section 6.2). What distinguishes the present instance of this combination is merely that the affirmation and denial are not confined to an individual passage (such as the talk between Achilles and Patroklos), but are distributed over a large part of the poem (in books 4, 9, 11, and 13).

6.9. The Absurd Pretext for the Removal of the Arms

A well-known inconsistency in the *Odyssey*, mentioned already in section 2.3, concerns the removal of the arms from the great hall of the palace: when the removal of the arms is planned (quote 2.4), Odysseus tells Telemachos to leave two sets of arms in the hall, but this is neither done nor even mentioned when the arms are actually removed (quote 2.3). This inconsistency turns out to be superficial, not a real inconsistency at all, if one accepts the explanation offered in chapter 2. But there is an inconsistency associated with the removal of the arms which is genuine and, I believe, clearly intentional.

During the planning and execution of the removal of the arms, Odysseus supplies Telemachos with two explanations he should give to the suitors if and when they notice that the arms are gone. The suggested explanations are the same, and are given in almost identical form, on the two occasions. Concerning the missing arms, Telemachos is to say this to the suitors:

> "I stored them away out of the smoke, since they are no longer
> like what Odysseus left behind when he went to Troy land,
> but are made foul, with all the smoke of the fire upon them.
> Also, some divinity put into my head this even
> greater thought, that with the wine in you, you might stand up
> and fight, and wound each other, and spoil the feast and the courting;
> since iron all of itself works on a man and attracts him."
> Quote 6.46: *Od.* 19.7–13 (cf. 16.288–294 in quote 2.4)

The first pretext, that Telemachos wants to save the arms from further blackening in the smoke from the fireplace, is perfectly reasonable, and we see in quote 2.3 that Telemachos uses it with Eurykleia. However, the second pretext is absurd. The idea that Telemachos would not want to spoil the suitors' feasting and courting is contrary to the basic story line of the *Odyssey*. One could cite what Telemachos himself says separately to Athene (disguised as Mentes), Nestor, Menelaos, Odysseus (before the latter has identified himself), an assembly of the Ithakans and the suitors, and the suitors alone.[213] I will quote only what he says to the assembly:

> "... my mother, against her will, is beset by suitors,
> own sons to the men who are greatest hereabouts. These
> shrink from making the journey to the house of her father
> Ikarios, so that he might take bride gifts for his daughter
> and bestow her on the one he wished, who came as his favorite;
> rather, all their days, they come and loiter in our house
> and sacrifice our oxen and our sheep and our fat goats
> and make a holiday feast of it and drink the bright wine
> recklessly. Most of our substance is wasted. We have no man here
> such as Odysseus was, to drive this curse from the household."
>
> Quote 6.47: *Od.* 2.50–59

Telemachos wants to shame the suitors into leaving his household. It may enhance one's appreciation of the contradiction posed by the second explanation to know that what Lattimore renders as "spoil the feast and the courting" in the penultimate line of quote 6.46 is better translated as "bring shame upon your feast and upon your suit."[214] That is exactly what Telemachos would like to do. And since the suitors are well aware of this, they would find the second explanation proposed by Odysseus simply unbelievable, as indeed it is.

The second explanation is inconsistent with the entire thrust of the *Odyssey*. I maintain that this inconsistency is perverse: it was introduced by the poet for its own sake. It is difficult to escape this conclusion when one considers that the inconsistency is not only blatant but gratuitous, inasmuch as the first explanation would have been sufficient on its own. Furthermore, the second explanation could be deleted with no adverse consequences for the passage (except that the phrase "beguile them with soft words" in quote 2.3 might no longer be appropriate) or for the poem as a whole (the second explanation is never used since the suitors do not notice that the arms are missing until it is too late).[215]

6.10. The Shooting of Antinoös

After Odysseus has accomplished both feats required in the contest of the bow (he has strung the bow and shot an arrow through the twelve axes), but before he has identified himself to the suitors, he begins his surprise attack by shooting an arrow through the neck of Antinoös. Here is how Homer describes the reactions of the other suitors:

> ... [A]ll the suitors
> clamored about the house when they saw that the man was fallen,
> sprang up from their seats and ranged about the room, throwing
> their glances every way along the well-built walls,
> but there was never a shield there nor any spear for them.
> But they scolded Odysseus in words full of anger, saying:
> "Stranger, it is badly done to hit men. You will never
> achieve any more trials. Now your sudden destruction is certain,
> for now you have struck down the man who was far the greatest
> of the youth of Ithaka. For that the vultures shall eat you."
> Each spoke at random, for **they thought he had not intended to kill the man, poor fools**, and they had not yet realized
> how over all of them the terms of death were now hanging.
>
> Quote 6.48: *Od.* 22.21–33 (italics and boldface added)

6.10. THE SHOOTING OF ANTINOÖS

The first part of this passage (shown in italics) is important because it confirms our impression from quote 2.3 that Odysseus and Telemachos left no arms in the hall, contrary to the original plan in quote 2.4. But what will engage our attention in this section is the apparent inconsistency between this part and the boldfaced part: if the suitors think that the shooting of Antinoös was accidental, why do they first react by searching the walls for shields and spears?[216] Some commentators seek to reconcile the action with the thought by interpreting it as a kind of mechanical reflex;[217] this approach seems desperate to me, and will not be considered further. Critics who acknowledge the existence of an inconsistency assume that it was caused by interpolation or some other modification of an earlier version of the *Odyssey* which did not include one part of the passage. In the scenario suggested by G. P. Goold, for example, the removal of the arms did not figure at all in the original version of the poem; when it was added, the italicized part of quote 6.48 was inserted as well, and the inconsistency resulted because the insertion was made without any change to the rest of the passage,[218] in accordance with Goold's theory of progressive fixation. (He explains the inconsistency between quotes 2.3 and 2.4 similarly, by supposing that the removal of the arms was added in two stages, each of which involved only addition of material, with no deletion or alteration of material that had previously been fixed in writing.)

In the reading proposed in chapter 2, the removal of the arms is essential to the development of the plot: the deviation of the execution of the removal (quote 2.3) from the original plan (quote 2.4) signals the birth of the idea of the contest of the bow, whose transmission to Penelope by Athene when Eurykleia recognizes Odysseus explains Penelope's subsequent behavior, including her strange decision to hold the contest and marry the winner. This reading is incompatible with the existence, postulated by Goold, of a version of the *Odyssey* without quotes 2.3 and 2.4. We therefore require another explanation for the inconsistency in quote 6.48. I begin by arguing that the boldfaced portion of this passage is simply false, a position also held by Büchner.[219]

That the suitors cannot possibly think that Odysseus shot Antinoös by accident is demonstrated by the collective force of a number of observations. First, by shooting an arrow through the twelve axes, Odysseus has shown that he is a highly skilled archer. Second, he prefaces his shooting of Antinoös with a dramatic announcement that he is about to make another shot, and his behavior immediately preceding this announcement, as well as the terms of the announcement itself, can leave no doubt in the suitors that this shot is a serious matter:[220]

> Now resourceful Odysseus stripped his rags from him, and sprang
> up atop the great threshold, holding his bow and the quiver
> filled with arrows, and scattered out the swift shafts before him
> on the ground next his feet, and spoke his word to the suitors:
> "Here is a task that has been achieved, without any deception.
> Now I shall shoot at another mark, one that no man yet
> has struck, if I can hit it and Apollo grants me the glory."
>   He spoke, and steered a bitter arrow against Antinoös.
> ...

> ... [I]n his [Antinoös's] heart there was no thought
> of death. For who would think that one man, alone in a company
> of many men at their feasting, though he were a very strong one,
> would ever inflict death upon him and dark doom? But Odysseus,
> aiming at this man, struck him in the throat with an arrow[.]
>
> Quote 6.49: *Od.* 22.1–8, 11–15

It is true that this passage portrays Antinoös himself as unsuspecting, for "Who at a banquet with many friends would ever expect a single adversary, however strong he might be, to court his own death (by taking them all on single-handed, to his own certain defeat)?"[221] But he is lifting a goblet of wine to his mouth, not looking at Odysseus. Surely, however, some suitors *are* looking at Odysseus, who, after all, has just stunned them with his success in the contest and is now behaving so dramatically. These suitors would see the expert archer take aim at Antinoös, and would know for a fact that the shooting was deliberate. And even the suitors who do not start paying attention until after the killing of Antinoös would observe Odysseus giving no indication that he has just made a grievous mistake. Finally, there is the fact that on the previous day Odysseus declared to all the suitors his wish for the death of Antinoös![222] In view of all this, it is clear that the suitors cannot fail to realize that the shooting of Antinoös was intentional, and it is no wonder that their first reaction is to search the walls for shields and spears.

Thus, a combination of textual evidence and common-sense inferences vindicates the italicized part of quote 6.48 but discredits the boldfaced part. How are we to account for the existence of the latter part? Büchner's view is that the last three lines of the passage must have been added by someone to whom the intervening lines in quote 6.48 (in normal type) seemed too weak if the suitors attribute an evil intention to the archer but understandable if they believe he simply made a mistake.[223] A review of the circumstances in which Odysseus declares his wish for the death of Antinoös will suggest another explanation.[224]

Between Odysseus's return to his palace (in his disguise as a beggar) and the massacre on the next day, three suitors throw something at him.[225] The first of these occasions, when Antinoös throws a footstool, stands out from the other two in that this is the only time Odysseus is struck by the thrown object and the only time he utters a response. It is at the end of this response, which is addressed to all the suitors, that he declares his wish for the death of Antinoös. The scene is strange in at least two ways. First, while Homer does much in the rest of the poem to put the suitors in a bad light, justifying their eventual destruction by Odysseus, in this scene all the suitors behave well with the single exception of Antinoös. At the instruction of Telemachos (who, of course, pretends not to know the beggar) and the urging of Athene, Odysseus makes the rounds of the suitors, begging each for food, and Antinoös is the only one who doesn't give him any. Also, when the beggar complains about this and Antinoös gets angry and throws the footstool, all the other suitors rebuke him for this violence. Second, the begging is pointless. Along with the instruction to beg from all the suitors, Telemachos sends the beggar (via the swineherd) plenty of food—indeed, "as much food as both arms could hold in their compass." A motivation for the begging does seem to appear when it is said that Athene urges Odysseus to beg so that he can learn which suitors are righteous and which are not, but this motivation evaporates when it is said immediately afterwards that she has no intention of sparing any of them. Thus, not only is the begging pointless, but its pointlessness is communicated in two different ways.

The emphasis on the pointlessness of the begging suggests that this scene has some ulterior purpose. This purpose presumably has to do with the other unique property of the scene, its focus on Antinoös and Odysseus's publicly stated wish for his death. The significance of this remains a mystery until the beggar shoots an arrow through Antinoös's neck, and the suitors are said to believe that the shooting was an accident. There is an obvious tension between this assertion and the beggar's declared wish for the death of Antinoös. When the latter is considered in combination with the immediate circumstances of the shooting, it becomes clear that the suitors cannot possibly believe that the shooting was accidental. Given the trouble Homer has taken to establish the falseness of the boldfaced part of quote 6.48, it seems likely that the inconsistency between this part of the passage and the italicized part is intentional.[226] And given that this inconsistency serves no ordinary purpose in the narrative, we must also classify it as perverse.

The perverse inconsistency I have just described differs from the one discussed in the preceding section in that it is compact, confined to a single passage, while the absurd pretext for the removal of the arms is inconsistent with the overall context provided by the poem. This difference is superficial, however. We could just as well ignore the italicized part of quote 6.48 and focus on the evidently intentional inconsistency between the boldfaced part and all the indications available to the suitors that the beggar must have shot Antinoös deliberately, including the declaration of his wish for the death of Antinoös five books prior to the shooting. What is important, as we shall see in chapter 9, is that some statement or passage has a jarring effect on the audience owing to its inconsistency with one or more other elements of the poem.

Thus, the explanation proposed here for the existence of the boldfaced part of quote 6.48 is that this statement was included by the poet specifically to create an inconsistency and the resulting jarring effect on the audience. Other parts of the passage may have been included in a supporting role, to give the appearance of a coherent narrative. I do not propose to analyze the entire passage from this point of view. It is sufficient to note that the poem would flow logically and forcefully if the italicized part of quote 6.48, the part that relates to the removal of the arms, were followed immediately by Odysseus's announcement of his identity, his grievances against the suitors, and his intention to destroy them.[227]

One more remark on quote 6.48 is needed to clarify the evolution of the suitors' state of mind following the shooting of Antinoös. The last three lines of the passage make two assertions: (*a*) the suitors thought that the beggar did not intend to kill Antinoös, and (*b*) they did not realize that they were all about to die. Büchner takes the position that both of these assertions are false. While I agree with him about the first, I am not so sure about the second. The intentional shooting of Antinoös is bound to alarm the suitors, of course, and this is why they immediately look to the walls for shields and spears. But the idea that the beggar on his own would be able to kill more than a hundred men, or even a fraction of this number, would probably not occur to them. It is another matter altogether when, immediately after quote 6.48, the beggar announces that he is Odysseus and declares his intention to kill them all. It would be immediately apparent that Odysseus must have prepared everything, must have arranged the contest of the bow, must have removed the arms from the hall. He is certainly working with Telemachos and may have recruited other allies as well. Above all, Odysseus is Odysseus, and he can be expected to unleash on the suitors the full force of his wrath for their mistreatment of his household. It is *now* that they realize they are about to die, and the alarm described indirectly at the beginning of quote 6.48 is replaced by terror: "the green fear took hold of all of them, and each man looked about him for a way to escape sheer death."[228]

6.11. Overview

The case for perverse inconsistency in Homer that I began to make in chapter 5 is now complete. The evidence that has been presented includes simple contradictions where the poet appears to have gone out of his way to supply inconsistent information (sections 5.5, 6.9, and 6.10) or to call attention to the inconsistency (sections 5.4*b* and 6.4), elaborate structures that seem to have been created in accordance with a grand plan (sections 5.4*c*, 6.1, 6.3, and 6.7), inconsistencies that are emphasized by contrast with ordinary allusions (sections 5.3, 6.2, and 6.8), and the repetition of distinctive types of inconsistency in related contexts (sections 5.3, 6.6, and 6.7). Even without the illogicalities that are not inconsistencies (sections 6.5 and 6.7), this evidence cannot be explained by the mechanisms for generating inconsistencies that have been suggested in the past (the pressures of oral performance, progressive fixation of a written text, etc.), and I believe it constitutes a strong case for intentional inconsistency. And since there is no apparent motivation for the inconsistencies in question (I have excluded the comprehensible inconsistencies discussed in section 5.2), this translates to a case for perverse inconsistency, inconsistency created apparently for its own sake.

Even though a sizable body of evidence points to the existence of perverse inconsistency in Homer, one is naturally reluctant to accept the reality of this phenomenon owing to its strangeness and the presumed lack of any motivation for it. The last three chapters of this book address these concerns by showing that the books of G. I. Gurdjieff are filled with unexplained inconsistencies that are certainly intentional (chapter 7), that Gurdjieff appears to have thought there was a deep connection between his work and that of Homer (chapter 8), and that the nature of this connection supplies a motivation and context for perverse inconsistency (chapter 9). Before we embark on this new phase of the argument, let us consider the implications of our findings so far for a fundamental question in Homeric studies.

6.12. One Poet or Two?

In antiquity most people, although not all, assumed that the *Iliad* and the *Odyssey* were composed by the same poet. This view is now a minority opinion in scholarly circles,[229] but it receives fresh support from the discussion in this chapter and chapter 5. Let us begin by reviewing two well-known points.

First, the *Iliad* and the *Odyssey* were composed around the same time. According to a leader in the study of Homeric diction, "The linguistic gap between the two Homeric epics is small, smaller than that between the two poems generally agreed to be by Hesiod; there is no linguistic evidence against the ancient view—and some in favour—that the *Iliad* and *Odyssey* are likewise the work of a single poet whose diction evolved with his years."[230] This first point merely shows that a necessary condition for common authorship is satisfied.

Second, the poet who composed the *Odyssey* possessed a detailed and wide-ranging knowledge of the *Iliad*. Quotations from virtually every part of the latter poem have been identified in the former.[231] These quotations obviously do not prove that the two poems were composed by the same person.[232] However, the *Odyssey*-poet's detailed knowledge of the *Iliad* is another necessary condition for common authorship that we know is satisfied. Referring to this detailed knowledge, M. L. West declares that "the implication is more momentous than is generally realized. Either P^{Od} [the *Odyssey* poet] had access to the complete written text of the *Iliad* and studied it, or he had opportunities to hear the whole of it recited by others."[233] A third possibility, of course, is that the *Odyssey* poet was so familiar with the *Iliad* because he had composed that poem as well. This natural explanation is not mentioned by West because he has previously inferred separate authorship from other considerations without taking this obviously relevant point into account. But if one poet was responsible for both epics, it is to be expected that he would use lines from the *Iliad* in the *Odyssey* just as he uses certain lines more than once in the earlier poem and other lines more than once in the later poem.[234]

Let us now consider perverse inconsistency. The existence of this strange phenomenon in both poems reveals an entirely new dimension of the *Odyssey* poet's knowledge of the *Iliad*: it was not only detailed and wide-ranging, it was also deep. He must have been aware of the perverse inconsistency in the *Iliad*, and he must have understood the reason for it, since it is almost inconceivable that he engaged in this mysterious practice independently or without understanding its purpose. Note further a striking similarity in implementation: the peculiar combination of allusion and inconsistency ("affirmation and denial") is found in both the *Iliad* (see section 6.2) and the *Odyssey* (see sections 5.3, 5.5, and 6.8). The shared logical contortions of the two poems, which make commonly noted differences in outlook seem superficial by comparison, constitute a strong argument for unity of authorship.

This argument will have to be revisited when a motivation for perverse inconsistency is proposed in chapter 9. In the light of this motivation, perverse inconsistency will seem less strange than it does now. On the other hand, two poets who shared this motivation would both have to have been very unusual in a certain respect. The argument given here, suitably modified, will therefore retain much of its original force.

It is necessary to acknowledge that earlier in this book I have also provided new ammunition for those who believe that the two poems were composed by different people. For it seems unlikely that the type of subtlety I attributed to the *Odyssey* in chapter 2, the subtlety of implied action, is also found in the *Iliad*. However, it is well known that the narrative technique of the *Odyssey* is more sophisticated than that of the *Iliad*.[235] Implied action could be just another innovation of a poet who wanted to explore new directions in his second monumental work (and who perhaps wanted this work to reflect the wiliness of its hero[236]).

The conclusion that the *Iliad* and the *Odyssey* were composed by the same poet enables us to give the corpus stack structure discussed in section 5.7 its most natural interpretation: Homer wished to combine his two monumental masterpieces into a grand edifice spanned by a structure that uses specially created components in the second poem to mirror the structure of the first poem (as captured in the Iliadic stack structure).[237] A second attractive consequence is that the *Iliad* could have been revised with the *Odyssey* in mind, as posited at the beginning of section 5.6. Finally, common authorship enables us to understand an otherwise mysterious symmetry. On one hand, we saw in sections 5.3 and 5.4 that the *Odyssey* poet went to great lengths to allude to the *Iliad*.[238] On the other hand, a reasonable inference from section 5.6 is that the *Iliad* poet was so determined to allude to the *Odyssey* that he was willing on two occasions to have Odysseus refer to himself somewhat ridiculously as the father of his little boy. The natural explanation for this symmetry is that the *Iliad* poet and the *Odyssey* poet were one and the same.

Chapter 7

Mysterious Inconsistency in the Writings of Gurdjieff

The main thesis of chapters 5 and 6 is that some of the many inconsistencies in the Homeric epics should not be attributed to the difficulties of composition in performance, to progressive fixation of the text, or to any of the other mechanisms that have previously been proposed, but are best understood as having been introduced intentionally during the composition of the poems. Moreover, these inconsistencies can be considered perverse because they were introduced for the sake of inconsistency itself, not in furtherance of some narrative aim. This conclusion is so counterintuitive that it is likely to generate vigorous opposition, regardless of the strength of the supporting evidence. In the present chapter I hope to soften the resistance by drawing attention to a body of literature filled with inconsistencies that are certainly perverse. The existence of this literature shows that the possibility of perverse inconsistency cannot simply be dismissed out of hand. This demonstration is a modest achievement, but it represents only the beginning of an argument that will eventually lead to a possible framework for understanding perverse inconsistency in Homer.

The literature that forms the basis for the remaining chapters of this book comprises the writings of G. I. Gurdjieff (c. 1866–1949), a spiritual teacher who dedicated his life to developing his being and consciousness and to assisting others in their own development. His written works consist of a booklet entitled *The Herald of Coming Good* and a trilogy entitled *All and Everything*. The three parts of *All and Everything*, each of which is referred to as a series of books, are: *Beelzebub's Tales to His Grandson* (the First Series), *Meetings with Remarkable Men* (the Second Series), and *Life is Real Only Then, When "I Am"* (the Third Series).

Like the epics of Homer, the writings of Gurdjieff convey an overall impression of unity despite the fact that they contain numerous inconsistencies. In the case of Gurdjieff, however, it is clear from the outset that the inconsistencies cannot possibly be explained by recourse to the mechanisms that have previously been suggested for Homer. First, unity of authorship is beyond doubt: the writings of Gurdjieff were written by him and no one else. Second, they were, indeed, written, not composed under the pressure of oral performance. In fact, with the exception of *Herald*, they were written and reworked by Gurdjieff and read aloud in his presence over a period of many years before he finally began the process of their publication. In short, there is no Gurdjieffian analogue of the Homeric Question. We are forced to conclude either that Gurdjieff was extraordinarily incompetent, careless, and oblivious or that the inconsistencies in his writings were intentional. The latter conclusion is inescapable because the former is simply out of the question for anyone who knows anything about Gurdjieff. Accordingly, I feel no need to select examples of inconsistency in the writings of Gurdjieff on the basis of their apparent intentionality. Instead, the examples discussed in this chapter have been selected because they resemble, to a greater or lesser extent, one or more of the Homeric inconsistencies discussed in the preceding chapters. I am not claiming that Gurdjieff modeled the inconsistencies described below after their Homeric counterparts, although that is possible in certain cases; I am merely illustrating the prevalence of inconsistencies in his writings by showing how many can be found that share a fairly arbitrary property. Similarly, although the next two chapters will be concerned primarily with other matters, we shall discover inconsistencies associated with these matters as well. I hope this approach will give the reader a sense of the pervasiveness of inconsistency in the writings of Gurdjieff and will leave little room for doubt that this inconsistency is intentional and indeed "perverse."

In the remainder of this book, for the reason just given, I generally do not bother to make explicit my claim that a given inconsistency is intentional and perverse; this claim should be taken for granted.

7.1. The Lubovedsky Triad

In the chapter of *Meetings with Remarkable Men* devoted to the Russian prince Yuri Lubovedsky, Gurdjieff writes that

> [the prince] was much older than I and for almost forty years was my elder comrade and closest friend.
>
> ...
>
> When I first met him, he was already middle-aged, while I was still a young man. From then on until his death we always kept in touch with each other.
>
> Quote 7.1: *RM*, pp. 118–119

After describing their first meeting, Gurdjieff goes on to say that

> from then on, owing to our common interests, a real bond was established between us; we met often, and our correspondence continued uninterruptedly for almost thirty-five years.
>
> Quote 7.2: *RM*, p. 121

Quote 7.1 says that Gurdjieff and Lubovedsky kept in touch with each other until the latter's death, and quote 7.2 says that their correspondence continued uninterruptedly for almost thirty-five years. The second quotation therefore seems to confirm the first. And yet there are grounds for doubt: quote 7.1 says they were friends for almost forty years, while quote 7.2 says that their correspondence continued for almost thirty-five years.¹ Is the second figure a more accurate restatement of the first, or is there a real discrepancy?

In fact, the discrepancy is real. It is simply not true that Gurdjieff and Lubovedsky kept in touch with each other until the latter's death:

> ... he [Lubovedsky] wrote to me at various times from Afghanistan, from Baluchistan, from Kafiristan, until our correspondence suddenly ceased; and from then on there was neither news nor rumour of him.
>
> I was convinced that he had perished on one of his journeys, and little by little I had become accustomed to the thought that I had lost for ever the man nearest to me, when suddenly, quite unexpectedly, I ran across him again in exceptional circumstances in the very heart of Asia.
>
> Quote 7.3: *RM*, p. 134

When the friends finally meet again, Gurdjieff says,

> I ... asked him why he had disappeared from sight so suddenly, why I had had no news from him all this time, and why he had let me worry over the uncertainty about him until finally, with grief in my heart, I had resigned myself to the thought of having lost him for ever. And I told him how, in case by any chance they might be useful to him, I had had requiems held for him, regardless of expense and even though I did not fully believe in their efficacy.
>
> Quote 7.4: *RM*, p. 155

Quotes 7.3 and 7.4 demonstrate unequivocally the falseness of the last sentence in quote 7.1.

The logical structure formed by Gurdjieff's statements regarding his correspondence with Prince Lubovedsky consists of three parts:

(*a*) a statement that will eventually turn out to be false (the last sentence of quote 7.1);

(*b*) information that appears to support the statement in part (*a*) but also hints that the latter statement may not be true (quote 7.2);

(*c*) information that is consistent with the information in part (*b*) but demonstrates conclusively that the statement in part (*a*) is false (quotes 7.3 and 7.4).

Apart from the specifics of the cited quotations, this structure is that of a triadic inconsistency as defined in section 6.6. In that section I described two instances of this structure in the *Odyssey*, one associated with Circe and the other with Kalypso. As far as I know, the Lubovedsky triad is the only exact parallel in the writings of Gurdjieff.² Although we cannot be sure that this triad is an intentional construct, the likelihood that it is is increased by the existence in the First Series of the closely related pattern described in the next section.

7.2. The Triad of Ashiata Shiemash

What may be the most stunning inconsistency in the entire Gurdjieffian corpus is found in *Beelzebub's Tales to His Grandson*. According to Beelzebub, the "Messenger from Above" Ashiata Shiemash once succeeded in guiding the lives of people on Earth in such a way that their existence became more normal. This "sacred Individual" recorded the deliberations which led him to his method in a legominism entitled "The Terror of the Situation" (the term "legominism" will be defined in section 9.3). According to this legominism, Ashiata Shiemash discovered that the "being-impulses" of faith, love, and hope have so degenerated in people that the three ways for self-perfection based on these impulses are no longer suitable for them. On the other hand, he also discovered that the impulse of objective conscience remains in people almost in its original state. This impulse, however, has become embedded in their subconsciousness and takes no part in the functioning of their ordinary consciousness. Ashiata Shiemash concluded that it would still be possible to save people, but only if the data in their subconsciousness for the impulse of objective conscience were to participate in the functioning of their ordinary "waking consciousness":

> "It was just then that I indubitably understood ... that if the functioning of that being-factor [objective conscience] still surviving in their common presences were to participate in the general functioning of that consciousness of theirs in which they pass their daily, as they here say, 'waking existence,' only then would it still be possible to save the contemporary three-brained beings here [the people of the Earth] ..."
>
> Quote 7.5: *BT*, p. 359

The legominism then closes with Ashiata Shiemash's decision to create the conditions that would allow this to happen.

The role of objective conscience in self-perfection is central to *Beelzebub's Tales*. Yet 700 pages after the chapters that deal with the deliberations of Ashiata Shiemash and the measures he took to implement his decision, Beelzebub says to his grandson,

> "You remember the Very Saintly Ashiata Shiemash, then in his deliberations, under the title 'The Terror of the Situation' said:
>
> "'If it is still possible to save the beings of the Earth, then Time alone can do it.'"
>
> Quote 7.6: *BT*, p. 1118

Beelzebub's supposed quotation from "The Terror of the Situation" actually appears nowhere in the legominism and is clearly at odds with Ashiata Shiemash's real conclusion in quote 7.5. The contradiction could not be more complete: According to quote 7.6, Ashiata Shiemash concluded there was nothing one could do to save people—one could only wait and hope—when in fact he concluded that there was something very definite that could be done and he resolved to do it.

The starkness of the contradiction does not, by itself, explain why it is so dramatic. For this we must consider the chapter of *Beelzebub's Tales* entitled "The Organization for Man's Existence Created by the Very Saintly Ashiata Shiemash." This chapter, which follows the chapter that quotes "The Terror of the Situation" in its entirety, describes the measures taken by Ashiata Shiemash to implement the decision announced at the end of the legominism. It is unique in *Beelzebub's Tales* for its unceasing repetition of a few ideas, namely, the idea that the impulse of objective conscience exists in the subconsciousness of people and the idea that this impulse could take part in the functioning of their ordinary consciousness. It is the sheer number of times these ideas are mentioned—especially in this chapter, but also in the chapter on the legominism and elsewhere in the book[3]—that causes the contradictory idea in quote 7.6 to hit the reader with such force. The reader knows without a moment's thought that this idea is false, but is struck by the casual and apparently senseless denial of what he knows to be true.

Quote 7.6 is somewhat analogous to quote 5.10. Just as Homer seems practically to deny the existence of the *Iliad* by having Demodokos sing about a fictitious famous quarrel between Achilles and Odysseus instead of the actual famous quarrel between Achilles and Agamemnon, Gurdjieff seems to repudiate his entire account of Ashiata Shiemash (which comprises three chapters, not counting those that address the undoing of his work) by having Beelzebub falsely attribute to him a conclusion contrary to the one which led him to undertake his activities for the welfare of mankind. Further examination of Gurdjieff's portrayal of Ashiata Shiemash will reveal what I believe are its closest parallels in Homer.

Well after the section of *Beelzebub's Tales* that is devoted to Ashiata Shiemash, but well before the discordant note sounded in quote 7.6, his name comes up again in the following passage (in which Beelzebub is speaking to his grandson):

> "There will never proceed in the presences of the three-brained beings of this ill-fated planet Earth of yours what is called the sacred 'Antkooano,' upon which, among other things, the Very Saintly Ashiata Shiemash also counted.
>
> "About this 'essence-loving-hope' of his, I chanced to learn during my investigations concerning His Very Saintly Activities there.
>
> "You, my boy, perhaps still do not know in what, namely, the cosmic process of the sacred Antkooano consists?
>
> "The sacred Antkooano is the name of that process of perfecting the Objective-Reason in the three-centered beings, which process proceeds by itself simply from the 'flow of time.'"

Quote 7.7: BT, pp. 562–563

By asserting that Ashiata Shiemash counted on a process that depends only on the flow of time, this passage paves the way for quote 7.6, in which Time is said to be the crucial element. It also smoothes the transition from the truth of quote 7.5 to the falseness of quote 7.6 by saying that the process depending only on the flow of time was among the things upon which Ashiata Shiemash *also* counted, where the "also" apparently means "in addition to the central role of objective conscience described in quote 7.5."

Quotes 7.5–7.7, when arranged in their order in *Beelzebub's Tales*, form a structure with the following three components:

(*a*) a true statement (quote 7.5);

(*b*) a statement that gives at least the appearance of being consistent with the statement in part (*a*) but suggests (correctly or not) that that statement may not be the whole truth (quote 7.7);

(*c*) an extension of the statement in part (*b*) that is definitely false and inconsistent with the statement in part (*a*) (quote 7.6).

This structure is an inversion of the triadic inconsistencies described in sections 6.6 and 7.1: an inconsistency emerges in three steps as before, but this time we begin with the true information and end with the false. Despite its uniqueness resulting from this inversion, the triadic inconsistency described in this section is the most clearly intentional triad we have seen, owing to the blatancy of the contradiction between parts (*a*) and (*c*) together with the transparently transitional role of part (*b*).

7.3. A Hub of Inconsistency

In chapter 6 we saw that the prophecy of Teiresias (quote 6.30) is connected with multiple inconsistencies. I shall now discuss a surprisingly similar "hub of inconsistency" in *Beelzebub's Tales*. After his grandson has despaired over the unjust plight of the people of the Earth, and the phenomenon of war in particular, Beelzebub replies:

> "Certainly there is something not quite right here.
>
> "But if nothing could be done for the beings of that planet by that Being who now already has the Reason of the sacred 'Podkoolad' and is one of the first assistants of our ENDLESSNESS in the government of the World, namely, the Very Saintly Ashiata Shiemash—if He could do nothing, what then can we expect, we, beings with the Reason of almost ordinary beings?
>
> **"You remember the Very Saintly Ashiata Shiemash, then in his deliberations, under the title 'The Terror of the Situation' said:**
>
> **"'If it is still possible to save the beings of the Earth, then Time alone can do it.'**
>
> "We can now only repeat the same in regard to this terrible property of theirs, of which we have just been speaking, namely, their periodic processes of the destruction of each other's existence.
>
> "We can only say now, that if this property of terrestrial beings is to disappear from that unfortunate planet, then *it will be with Time alone, thanks either to the guidance of a certain Being with very high Reason or to certain exceptional cosmic events.*"
>
> Quote 7.8: *BT*, p. 1118 (boldface, italics, and underlining added)

The parts of this passage that I have highlighted in various ways are analogous to the corresponding parts of quote 6.30. First, the boldfaced part of quote 7.8 is just quote 7.6 and is therefore one component of a triadic inconsistency, like the boldfaced part of quote 6.30 (see section 6.6). Second, the italicized part of quote 7.8 is not self-consistent: if war were to disappear owing to the guidance of someone with high Reason, it would obviously not be through Time alone (and in fact war largely disappeared as a result of the labors of Ashiata Shiemash and not merely through the passage of time[4]). Similarly, the italicized parts of quote 6.30 also form an internal inconsistency, an inconsistency that is completely defined within the passage (see section 6.7). Third, the underlined part of quote 7.8 forms part of yet another inconsistency: it implies that the Reason of Beelzebub is far below that of Ashiata Shiemash, whereas we later learn that Beelzebub has likewise attained the Reason of the sacred Podkoolad.[5] Once again, the corresponding part of quote 6.30 plays a similar formal role (see section 6.8). Actually, we saw in section 6.8 that the underlined part of quote 6.30, Teiresias's warning concerning the suitors, gives rise to two inconsistencies (one each involving Athene and Antikleia), and in fact the underlined part of quote 7.8 also creates a second inconsistency since it is definitely *not* true that Ashiata Shiemash could do nothing for the beings of the Earth (although admittedly the dramatic results of his labors were ultimately destroyed).

7.4. Interleaved Inconsistencies

In the preceding section I analyzed a passage from *Beelzebub's Tales* that exhibits a number of parallels with the passage from the *Odyssey* reproduced in quote 6.30. I shall now discuss a passage from *Meetings with Remarkable Men* that is formally similar to an extension of the same Odyssean passage and, in addition, provides the basis for some suggestive comparisons with the *Iliad*. The passage of interest is the following:

> Once, when <u>Ekim Bey and I with several of our comrades were in the town of Yangishar in Kashgar, having one of our usual long rests</u>, intending to go next into the valleys of the Hindu Kush Mountains, Ekim Bey received news from his uncle in Turkey that his father was failing rapidly and would probably not live long.
>
> **This news disturbed Ekim Bey so much that he decided to interrupt his journey and return to Turkey as quickly as possible, in order to spend what little time remained with his beloved father.**
>
> As <u>these incessant wanderings from place to place under constant nervous strain had begun to weary me</u>, and as I also wished to go and see my parents, I decided to break off my journey and travel as far as Russia with Ekim Bey.
>
> Taking leave of our comrades, we went through Irkeshtam towards Russia. After many adventures and a host of great difficulties, without following the usual roads from Kashgar, all of which went to Osh, we managed to reach the town of Andijan in the Ferghana region.
>
> **We had decided to go through this once great region, because we wished to take advantage of the opportunity to inspect the ruins of several ancient towns, about which we had heard a great deal and which we expected to find chiefly by means of logical deductions from certain historical data.**
>
> **We had thus greatly lengthened our journey** before we came out on to the main road near Andijan.
>
> Quote 7.9: *RM*, pp. 195–196 (boldface and underlining added)

Let us consider first the boldfaced parts of this passage. Learning that his father does not have long to live, Ekim Bey decides to go to him as quickly as possible. But then he greatly lengthens his journey in order to indulge his curiosity about the ruins of some ancient towns. These two fragments from the passage are obviously inconsistent with each other. Now let us consider the two underlined parts. If Gurdjieff is weary from incessant wanderings, why would he want to cut short his long rest? And if he and his comrades are accustomed to taking long rests, how could their wanderings be incessant? Thus, the two underlined parts are also inconsistent with each other.

The logical structure of the relatively short passage reproduced in quote 7.9 is captured in the formula $AB(\neg A)(\neg B)$, where A (the first underlined part) and B (the first boldfaced part) are independent statements, and $\neg A$ (the second underlined part) and $\neg B$ (the second boldfaced part) are statements that contradict A and B, respectively. A review of pertinent observations from chapter 6 will show that a relatively short passage from the *Odyssey* has the same structure. At the beginning of section 6.7 I pointed out the contradiction between the two italicized parts of quote 6.30; let us denote these two contradictory fragments by A and ¬A. At the beginning of section 6.8 I pointed out the contradiction between the underlined part of quote 6.30 and quote 6.41; let us denote these two fragments by B and ¬B, respectively. Arranging these fragments in their order in the *Odyssey*, we again arrive at the structure AB(¬A)(¬B), this time for a passage that spans only 80 lines from the beginning of A to the end of ¬B.

There are also parallels between quote 7.9 and the *Iliad*. Ekim Bey's willingness to greatly lengthen his journey in order to inspect the ruins of ancient towns, which comes as quite a surprise since he wants to get to his dying father as quickly as possible, recalls the illogicality of Agamemnon's notorious test of the army, in which he suggests that the Greeks return home (quote 6.10) just when he has been told that Zeus wants him to get his men ready for battle "in all haste" (quote 6.7). In both cases, something urgent is delayed for a reason that, in the given context, verges on the inexplicable.

As discussed in section 6.3, Agamemnon's test of the army is inconsistent not only with Zeus's instruction but also with the psychology of the Quarrel, since it seems to concede the indispensability of Achilles. Here the suggested comparison with quote 7.9 appears to fall short, inasmuch as the inspection of ruins by Ekim Bey and Gurdjieff is inconsistent only with Ekim Bey's wish to return to Turkey as quickly as possible. In reality, what has happened is that the direction of the doubling has been reversed. Gurdjieff goes on to describe how in Tashkent he and Ekim Bey made use of the latter's deep knowledge of the human psyche to earn money for their travels by means of public demonstrations of "supernatural phenomena." These demonstrations brought in more money than they needed, but also attracted much meaningless admiration, so the two "left without delay to escape from [their] burdensome admirers."[6] This concludes the account that begins with quote 7.9. Ekim Bey's decision to return to Turkey as quickly as possible, mentioned at the beginning of the account, is subsequently contradicted twice, first by the voluntary lengthening of the journey to inspect the ruins of ancient towns and then by the reason given for leaving Tashkent without delay.

The twofold contradiction of Ekim Bey's decision to return to Turkey as quickly as possible roughly parallels the grammatical treatment of the ambassadors in the Embassy scene of the *Iliad*. As we saw in section 6.1, duals are used to refer to three ambassadors in the first part of the scene, while plurals are used to refer to two ambassadors in the second part of the scene. The former usage is grammatically incorrect; the latter, while not incorrect, is awkward given the prior use of duals. Similarly, Ekim Bey's willingness to greatly lengthen his journey in order to inspect some ruins directly contradicts his decision to return to Turkey as quickly as possible; the reason given for his quick departure from Tashkent, while not strictly a contradiction since it does not lengthen his journey, is nevertheless awkward since the approaching death of his father is presumably uppermost in his mind.

7.5. Two Properties of the Inconsistencies

In chapter 9 I will offer a possible explanation for the perverse inconsistencies in the writings of Gurdjieff in terms of his concept of objective art, and I will suggest that the same explanation applies to the perverse inconsistencies in the poems of Homer. In this section I make two observations that begin to lend some plausibility to the weaker proposition that the role played by perverse inconsistencies in Homer is the same as the role played by perverse inconsistencies in Gurdjieff, whatever that role may be.

The first observation is that many of the inconsistencies in *All and Everything*, such as those discussed in sections 7.1 and 7.4, have nothing to do with the ideas of Gurdjieff but are simply ordinary narrative inconsistencies. We can infer that inconsistency itself has some significance independent of the subject matter. This point is crucial because it makes it possible for intentional inconsistencies in Homer to have the same significance as the inconsistencies in Gurdjieff.

The important conclusion just stated is not invalidated by the existence of inconsistencies that involve specifically Gurdjieffian content, such as those discussed in sections 7.2 and 7.3.[7] In any case, I do not see how the latter inconsistencies might convey any additional insight into the Gurdjieffian subject matter. It is true that a few inconsistencies in the writings of Gurdjieff serve as hints that the reader should look below the surface.[8] However, such inconsistencies are unusual and are easily distinguished from the vast majority of inconsistencies in Gurdjieff's writings.

To introduce the second observation, I ask the reader to consider a hypothetical situation. Suppose that the two contradictory components of an inconsistency (A and ¬A in the notation of the preceding section) are always found close together (e.g., within a page or two of each other) in the writings of Gurdjieff but are always far apart (e.g., separated by at least 2000 verses) in the poems of Homer. Such a situation could be awkward for the hypothesis that inconsistencies play the same role in the two bodies of work. However, the following discussion will show that the actual situation is quite different.

Let us first consider the inconsistencies in the writings of Gurdjieff discussed in this chapter. The boldfaced part of quote 7.8 is inconsistent with a passage that appears 759 pages earlier in *Beelzebub's Tales* (quote 7.5); the underlined part of quote 7.8 is inconsistent with a passage 59 pages away; and the italicized part of quote 7.8 is a complete inconsistency within the confines of a single sentence. Turning to *Meetings with Remarkable Men* (a work only one-fourth as long as *Beelzebub's Tales*), we saw that quote 7.1 is inconsistent with quotes 7.3 and 7.4, passages that are found 15 and 36 pages after quote 7.1, whereas quote 7.9 contains two inconsistencies in a single passage of a few paragraphs. Thus, the contradictory components of an inconsistency may be physically near each other, far apart, or separated by some intermediate distance. I shall use the term "scale-free inconsistency" to describe such a collection of inconsistencies with no characteristic or typical scale.

Let us now consider the inconsistencies in the Homeric epics discussed in chapter 6. The duals in the Embassy scene of the *Iliad* appear shortly after the selection of the three ambassadors (see section 6.1), and therefore create a small-scale inconsistency. Small-scale inconsistencies in the *Odyssey* (besides the comprehensible ones discussed in section 5.2) were noted in section 6.7 (quotes 6.30 and 6.37 each contain an instruction that doesn't make sense in the context of the passage). Sometimes a passage is inconsistent both with a passage that is nearby and with one that is farther away: Agamemnon's test of the army, discussed in section 6.3, is inconsistent with the delusive dream described in the same book and with the quarrel described in the previous book; Apollo's failure to rescue Aineias from Achilles, discussed in section 6.4, is behaviorally inconsistent with his rescue of Hektor shortly afterwards and with his rescue of Aineias from Diomedes much earlier in the poem; Teiresias's warning concerning the suitors, discussed in section 6.8, is inconsistent with Odysseus's questioning of his mother shortly afterwards and with his conversation with Athene upon his return to Ithaka; and the assertion that the suitors thought the beggar's shooting of Antinoös was accidental is inconsistent both with the immediate circumstances of the shooting and with the beggar's declaration of his wish for the death of Antinoös five books earlier (see section 6.10). Large-scale inconsistencies are also found by themselves in both poems, as described in sections 6.2 (between books 9 and 16 of the *Iliad*) and 6.6 (between books 5 and 12 of the *Odyssey* [the Kalypso triad], as well as between books 10 and 12 [the Circe triad]). Thus, no single scale characterizes the collection of inconsistencies discussed in chapter 6.

This discussion leads to the second main observation of this section: The writings of Gurdjieff and the poems of Homer both possess the property of scale-free inconsistency.[9] This observation does not prove anything, but, like the first observation, it prepares the ground for my argument that the role played by perverse inconsistencies in Homer is the same as the role played by perverse inconsistencies in Gurdjieff. That argument begins in earnest in the following chapter.

7.6. Reminder and Overview

I have chosen to document intentional inconsistency in the writings of Gurdjieff not with an exhaustive list of inconsistencies, but with selections of inconsistencies inspired by other topics. Since previous chapters have discussed inconsistencies in the poems of Homer, I have devoted this chapter to inconsistencies in the writings of Gurdjieff that are reminiscent of the Homeric inconsistencies already considered. As mentioned in the opening remarks of this chapter, additional inconsistencies in Gurdjieff will be encountered in the next two chapters as well. Yet another selection can be found in my study of the enneagram symbol as it appears in the writings of Gurdjieff.[10]

In chapters 5 and 6 I described a number of inconsistencies in the poems of Homer that give some indication of having been intentional and indeed perverse. No matter how suggestive these specimens might be, however, it is difficult to believe that their inconsistency was deliberate unless one can think of a goal that Homer might have been attempting to achieve with their help. The existence in the writings of Gurdjieff of inconsistencies whose deliberateness cannot be doubted demonstrates that, for Gurdjieff at least, such a goal did exist. The following chapter presents the first step in an argument that Homer was pursuing the same general goal as Gurdjieff, or at least that Gurdjieff thought he was. The concluding chapter of this book will complete that argument and at the same time will explain the purpose of perverse inconsistency in terms of Gurdjieff's concept of objective art.

Chapter 8

Allusions to Homer in *Meetings with Remarkable Men*

I hope to have shown in the preceding chapters that the poems of Homer and the writings of Gurdjieff share an unusual and mysterious property: perverse inconsistency. The thrust of the present chapter and the next is that the sharing of this property is not an accident. In this chapter I argue that Gurdjieff believed there is a connection between his works and those of Homer. In the next I argue that this connection relates to Gurdjieff's profound concept of objective art and would likely involve perverse inconsistency.

It may seem awkward for the thesis of this chapter that Homer is not mentioned anywhere in the writings of Gurdjieff. This fact is of little consequence, however, for Gurdjieff would often take an indirect approach in his spoken and written teaching. A striking example of such an approach is documented in my book *The Enneagram in the Writings of Gurdjieff*, where I show that Gurdjieff transmitted an understanding of the enneagram through his writings without ever mentioning it by name. Admittedly, the enneagram and Homer present very different situations. The connection between Gurdjieff and the enneagram is multifaceted and well known: in addition to serving as the emblem of Gurdjieff's teaching, the symbol received significant attention (although only a partial explanation) in his talks, and it also underlies some of the sacred dances and movement exercises that he taught. The existence of a connection between Gurdjieff and Homer, on the other hand, comes as a complete surprise. My argument that Gurdjieff saw such a connection is based mainly on what appear to be allusions to the *Odyssey* in *Meetings with Remarkable Men* (together with the symmetry consideration explained in section 8.7), but it begins with Gurdjieff's description in the same work of modern bards who might remind one of Homer.

8.1. Singers of Tales

The chapter of *Meetings with Remarkable Men* that Gurdjieff devotes to his father begins with a passage that is of interest in connection with Homer from several points of view:

> My father was widely known, during the final decades of the last century and the beginning of this one, as an *ashokh*, that is, a poet and narrator, under the nickname of "Adash"; and although he was not a professional *ashokh* but only an amateur, he was in his day very popular among the inhabitants of many countries of Transcaucasia and Asia Minor.
>
> *Ashokh* was the name given everywhere in Asia and the Balkan peninsula to the local bards, who composed, recited or sang poems, songs, legends, folk-tales and all sorts of stories.
>
> In spite of the fact that these people of the past who devoted themselves to such a career were in most cases illiterate, having not even been to an elementary school in their childhood, they possessed such a memory and such alertness of mind as would now be considered remarkable and even phenomenal.
>
> They not only knew by heart innumerable and often very lengthy narratives and poems, and sang from memory all their various melodies, but when improvising in their own, so to say, subjective way, they hit upon the appropriate rhymes and changes of rhythm for their verses with astounding rapidity.
>
> At the present time men with such abilities are no longer to be found anywhere.
>
> Even when I was very young, it was being said that they were becoming scarcer and scarcer.
>
> I personally saw a number of these *ashokhs* who were considered famous in those days, and their faces were strongly impressed on my memory.
>
> I happened to see them because my father used to take me as a child to the contests where these poet *ashokhs*, coming from various countries, such as Persia, Turkey, the Caucasus and even parts of Turkestan, competed before a great throng of people in improvising and singing.
>
> ...
>
> In Alexandropol and Kars, the towns where my family lived during my childhood, my father was often invited to evening gatherings to which many people who knew him came in order to hear his stories and songs.
>
> At these gatherings he would recite one of the many legends or poems he knew, according to the choice of those present, or he would render in song the dialogues between the different characters.
>
> The whole night would sometimes not be long enough for finishing a story and the audience would meet again on the following evening.
>
> Quote 8.1: *RM*, pp. 32–34

Two things can be said about this passage with confidence. First, it is based on fact: a pupil of Gurdjieff who met his parents and other members of his family during a visit to Alexandropol reported that "G.'s [Gurdjieff's] father was an amateur of local tales, legends, and traditions, something in the nature of a 'bard'; and he knew by heart thousands and thousands of verses in the local idioms."[1] Second, although it is at least partly factual (and may be entirely factual), there is more to it than meets the eye: the nickname Adash mentioned at the beginning is a deeply significant allusion to two passages in *Beelzebub's Tales*.[2] Later in this section I will suggest that this passage may also allude to Homer, or at least that it may serve as a support for Homeric allusions found elsewhere in *Meetings with Remarkable Men*. But first I would like to place this passage, as a matter of general interest, in the context of studies of oral narrative poetry.

Quote 8.1 will resonate with students of Homer and oral poetry for a number of reasons. One is the mention of the Balkan peninsula. For it was to the Balkans that Milman Parry, the most influential Homeric scholar of the twentieth century, went to collect field data on the form of oral narrative poetry, data that might confirm the oral character of the *Iliad* and the *Odyssey* which he strongly suspected on the basis of his foundational work on the use of formulas in those poems.[3] Another reason is Gurdjieff's emphasis on the illiteracy of the bards. All the singers interviewed and recorded by Parry and by his continuator Albert Lord were illiterate.[4] Yet another reason is Gurdjieff's assertion that the most accomplished bards were becoming increasingly scarce even when he was very young. Parry remarked in a similar vein,

> The old life and the old ways of song and speech are quickly going. I have found by experience that I risk obtaining poor material, both from a literary point of view and for my own purposes of study of oral processes, if I collect from anyone under fifty years of age. The old men are my best subjects, and four of those from whom I collected songs last year have already died. It is likely that the collection [of recordings] which I am making at present will remain as the one great collection of Southslavic oral material.
>
> Quote 8.2: M. Parry in an application for research funding (1934)[5]

Although the general thrust of these remarks is consistent with quote 8.1, there is a possibly significant discrepancy in detail. Whereas Parry's best subjects were dying off in 1934, quote 8.1 indicates that the most accomplished bards were already becoming scarce half a century earlier and were not to be found anywhere by 1930. We must draw one of three conclusions: (1) Gurdjieff intentionally exaggerated the rate of decline of the oral tradition in the Balkans, (2) he was unaware that this tradition continued to have full-strength representatives into his mature years, or (3) even Parry's best subjects were inferior to the most accomplished bards of half a century before.

Although the work of Parry and Lord in the Balkans is the best known to Homeric scholars, field studies of oral poetry have also been performed in many other parts of the world. Some observations from these studies were summarized by Oliver Taplin for their potential relevance to the performance of the Homeric epics in antiquity:

> It is a striking feature of the comparative evidence that in many parts of the world the long performances of heroic narrative take place not by day but at night, sometimes even for three or more successive nights. It is normal for such a performance to start some time towards sunset and to go on into the small hours, or even till dawn.
>
> Quote 8.3: Taplin, *Soundings*, p. 29

These observations agree with three aspects of Gurdjieff's account in the last paragraphs of quote 8.1: the performances of Gurdjieff's father would begin in the evening, they could last the entire night, and they could extend over more than one night.

The role attributed to memorization in *ashokh* performances deserves special consideration as it may seem to conflict with the thrust of modern research on oral narrative poetry. Although Gurdjieff makes clear that *ashokhs* would improvise, he strongly suggests that they would also recite from memory. In quote 8.1 he says that the illiterate bards of the past "possessed such a memory ... as would now be considered remarkable and even phenomenal" and that they "knew by heart innumerable and often very lengthy narratives and poems." Several pages after the passage reproduced in quote 8.1, he recounts how he once read in a magazine the deciphered text of inscriptions on tablets that had been found among the ruins of Babylon. The text was taken from the legend of Gilgamesh and included an excerpt from the legend with which he was particularly well acquainted from the singing of his father. Gurdjieff describes the excitement he felt when he realized that the excerpt had almost the same form of exposition as the song he was familiar with from his father, and adds: "I was struck by the fact, at first inexplicable to me, that this legend had been handed down by *ashokhs* from generation to generation for thousands of years, and yet had reached our day almost unchanged."[6]

It would appear that Lord could just as well have been targeting Gurdjieff when he criticized scholars who appealed to

> the "fantastic memories" so "well attested" of illiterate people. They felt that a text could remain from one generation to another unaltered, or altered only by inconsequential lapses of memory. This myth has remained strong even to the present day.
>
> Quote 8.4: Lord, *Singer of Tales*, p. 9

The error of such scholars, Lord goes on to say, lay in "the belief that in oral tradition there is a fixed text which is transmitted unchanged from one generation to another." In reality,

> fluidity and constant reconstitution of its materials are characteristic of oral heroic poetry, and the extraordinary powers of memorization demonstrated by those who have mastered its traditional techniques are accompanied by a facility in improvisation fatal to the accurate transmission of a work of any length or elaboration.
>
> Quote 8.5: S. West, "Transmission," p. 33

The facility in improvisation mentioned by West is made possible not only by the alertness of mind cited by Gurdjieff in quote 8.1, but also by the traditional techniques mentioned by West. These techniques include the use of verbal formulas that enable the bard to effortlessly refer to a particular person or thing in the desired grammatical case and at the desired position in a verse.[7] It was, in part, Parry's demonstration of the elaborateness and elegance of this formulaic system in ancient Greek epic that brought home the realization that Homeric diction was not the invention of a single poet but rather the product of a long tradition. There soon followed the realization that this tradition was an oral one and that the formulas served as an aid to rapid composition, that is, to composition during performance: "the bard who recites a poem composes it in the act of recitation," so that "to some extent each performance is a new creation."[8] Hence the "fluidity and constant reconstitution" of materials and the fallaciousness of a belief in "a fixed text which is transmitted unchanged from one generation to another."

The fact that much heroic poetry is being composed as it is being performed (i.e., that it is improvised[9]) was discovered before the work of Parry and Lord,[10] but their rediscovery of this fact after Parry's elucidation of the linguistic apparatus that would make such rapid composition possible gave rise, in time, to considerable excitement. It does not often happen in the humanities that a theoretical prediction is confirmed by observation. The ensuing enthusiasm led in some quarters to a dogmatic equation of oral performance with improvisation or recomposition. Among those who did not succumb to this dogma was C. M. Bowra:

> It is of course possible that some poems have reached a kind of finality, and no one would dare to give them a new form. But that is because they have been written down and circulated and become widely known. Their texts have been fixed, and they have passed into a national heritage.
>
> Quote 8.6: Bowra, *Heroic Poetry*, p. 218

Lord himself was to acknowledge that the writing down of an epic could give rise to the concept of a fixed text, of *the* text, and with that concept would arise "the need for memorization rather than recomposition as a means of transmission."[11] It is evidently appropriate that Gurdjieff should give equal attention in quote 8.1 to memorization and improvisation. This observation concludes my digression.

One cannot claim that the bards described in quote 8.1 remind one of Homer, for the simple reason that different people have, and long have had, different conceptions of Homer. It *is* fair to say, however, that the bards described by Gurdjieff remind one of a conception of Homer of which everyone is aware, namely, Homer as the illiterate creator of monumental poetry that was passed down faithfully over generations by other illiterate poets. This view, characterized as a myth by Lord in quote 8.4, was advocated as recently as 1962 by no less a scholar than G. S. Kirk.[12] Although it is considered to have been refuted by Adam Parry,[13] it could well have provided the basis for an allusion to Homer at the time when Gurdjieff wrote *Meetings with Remarkable Men*.

The idea that quote 8.1, which highlights the capacities and popularity of oral bards, may allude to Homer receives support from the fact that singers of tales figure prominently in the *Odyssey* and are always treated by Homer with the greatest respect. The esteem that is accorded to bards in the *Odyssey* is well known,[14] and will be illustrated here with only two short passages. As a guest at the dinner table of Alkinoös, Odysseus gives the following explanation when he honors Demodokos with a choice cut of meat:

> "For with all peoples upon the earth singers are entitled
> to be cherished and to their share of respect, since the Muse has taught them
> her own way, and since she loves all the company of singers."
>
> Quote 8.7: *Od.* 8.479–481

Speaking to Penelope, the swineherd Eumaios praises the story-telling ability of Odysseus himself (who has not yet revealed his identity) by comparing him to a singer:

> "But as when a man looks to a singer, who has been given
> from the gods the skill with which he sings for delight of mortals,
> and they are impassioned and strain to hear it when he sings to them,
> so he enchanted me in the halls as he sat beside me."
>
> Quote 8.8: *Od.* 17.518–521

In addition to consistently expressing respect for singers of tales, the poet of the *Odyssey* keeps the theme of bardic performance before his audience with periodic references to a bard, either Demodokos in the court of Alkinoös or Phemios at the palace of Odysseus.[15] Phemios is introduced in book 1 with the explanation that the suitors of Penelope forced him to sing for them. Later in the same book, his singing about the "bitter homecoming" of the Greeks from Troy causes Penelope to descend from her chamber to request that he sing about a less painful subject, a request that is opposed by Telemachos. After that, Phemios is not mentioned again until book 17, when his singing is heard by Odysseus and Eumaios as they stand outside the palace. Phemios appears for the last time in book 22, begging Odysseus to spare his life after the slaughter of the suitors. His successful supplication begins with a declaration of his worth as a singer and ends with his insistence that he sang for the suitors only because they forced him to, which makes a nice bookend to his introduction in book 1. In the large gap between the references to Phemios in books 1 and 17, we find a whole book, book 8, that is essentially built around three songs of Demodokos. The song near the beginning of the book and the song near the end form another pair of bookends, as both deal with the Trojan War and both cause Odysseus to weep (as discussed in chapter 1). As we saw in part (*b*) of section 5.3, the first song bears a rather sophisticated relationship to the *Iliad*. The song in the middle of book 8, a comedy about an adulterous affair between Ares and Aphrodite, is superficially very different, but it also contains clear allusions to the *Iliad* and to the story of the *Odyssey* as well.[16]

I have intended in this section only to motivate the hypothesis that Gurdjieff alludes to Homer. Quote 8.1 serves this function since it recalls both a familiar image of Homer himself and the attention given in the *Odyssey* to singers of tales and the tales they sing. Corroboration of the hypothesis will come later in this chapter with the identification of certain passages in *Meetings with Remarkable Men* that are best understood as allusions to the *Odyssey*.

8.2. Related Inconsistencies

In the preceding chapter I indicated that I would return to the subject of intentional inconsistency in the writings of Gurdjieff whenever new examples of this phenomenon came up naturally in the course of the discussion. I now interrupt the exposition of our present theme to describe two inconsistencies connected with the discussion in the preceding section. Although the blatancy of these inconsistencies is sufficient to make them seem intentional even when considered in isolation, they are presented here mainly to support a cumulative argument for intentional inconsistency based on the claim that inconsistencies can be found almost anywhere one looks in the writings of Gurdjieff.

We are told in quote 8.1 that Gurdjieff's father would sometimes stay up all night reciting a legend or poem. The fact that he would sometimes stay up all night is reinforced when, in connection with a certain friend of his father, Gurdjieff relates that

> This friend of his often dropped in to see him at his workshop, and sometimes they would sit all night long pondering on the meaning of the ancient legends and sayings.
>
> Quote 8.9: *RM*, p. 34

It was while listening to one of these discussions in his father's workshop that Gurdjieff became familiar with the excerpt from the Gilgamesh epic mentioned in the preceding section, and we are told specifically that this particular discussion between Gurdjieff's father and his friend lasted until daybreak. Given all these explicit statements, it comes as a shock when Gurdjieff says of his father that

> He himself led an almost pedantically regular life, and was merciless to himself in conforming to this regularity.
>
> For instance, he was accustomed to going to bed early so as to begin early the next morning whatever he had decided upon beforehand, and he made no exception to this even on the night of his daughter's wedding.
>
> Quote 8.10: *RM*, p. 45

The contradiction is blatant and clearly intentional.

Concerning the friend mentioned in quote 8.9, who happened to be the dean of the Kars Military Cathedral, Gurdjieff writes that

> the old dean often came to see my father in the workshop, where, sitting on the soft shavings at the back of the shop and drinking coffee made there by my father, they would converse for hours on all sorts of religious and historical subjects.
>
> Quote 8.11: *RM*, p. 51

We therefore know from both quote 8.9 and quote 8.11 that the dean often paid visits to Gurdjieff's father in his workshop. The dean's visits are mentioned again one page after quote 8.11:

> The dean often came to see my father, usually in the evenings when they were both free from their duties.
>
> In order, as he said, "not to lead others into temptation," he tried to make these visits inconspicuously, since he occupied a very eminent position in the town and almost everyone knew him by sight, whereas my father was only a simple carpenter.
>
> Quote 8.12: *RM*, p. 52

We now have three explicit statements that the dean often visited Gurdjieff's father. Yet midway between the last two of these statements, the ones which are separated from each other by a single page, Gurdjieff also writes of the dean that

> He led a very secluded life, mixing very little with those round him and paying no visits to acquaintances.
>
> Quote 8.13: *RM*, p. 51

Another blatant contradiction.

8.3. Odysseus as a Remarkable Man

I now resume the discussion of possible allusions to Homer in *Meetings with Remarkable Men*. At the end of the introduction to this work, Gurdjieff explains what he means by the term "remarkable man":

> [H]e can be called a remarkable man who stands out from those around him by the resourcefulness of his mind, and who knows how to be restrained in the manifestations which proceed from his nature, at the same time conducting himself justly and tolerantly towards the weaknesses of others.
>
> Quote 8.14: *RM*, p. 31

Surprisingly, Gurdjieff makes no attempt to show that this definition actually applies to the characters in the Second Series. To be sure, one of the three mentioned properties of a remarkable man may come to the fore on occasion—the main example is the resourcefulness of mind of three characters in the section entitled "The Death of Soloviev"[17]—but there is nothing approaching a systematic demonstration of the definition's applicability. The irrelevance of quote 8.14 to the rest of *Meetings with Remarkable Men* is evident from this description of the book's characters which has appeared on its back cover in some printings: "Although these men have no particular claim to fame, Gurdjieff calls them remarkable because they all shared a consuming desire to understand the deepest mysteries of life and were not dismayed by the obstacles encountered during the course of their search."

The fact that quote 8.14 seems almost out of place in *Meetings with Remarkable Men* suggests that it serves some hidden purpose. It may therefore be significant that this passage highlights some of the most distinguishing features of the hero of Homer's *Odyssey*, as the following discussion will show.

Concerning the resourcefulness of Odysseus, it suffices to refer to the second paragraph of chapter 2 and to the first sentence of its third paragraph. However, I cannot resist adding that most of that chapter is based on the premise that the association of Odysseus with resourcefulness is so strong that an important part of the plot of the *Odyssey* could rely on it implicitly.

The ability to be restrained in the manifestations which proceed from his nature is just as characteristic of Odysseus as the resourcefulness of his mind. When he first sees his son Telemachos after twenty years, he calmly plays the role of a stranger and guest, taking a meal and engaging in conversation. This is all the more remarkable juxtaposed, as it is, with the emotional reunion of Telemachos and the swineherd Eumaios, who during Odysseus's long absence have come to feel for each other as father and son.[18] Odysseus's calm indicates not a lack of feeling, but an unusual degree of self-restraint, for when Eumaios has left, Odysseus has identified himself, and Telemachos has overcome his initial disbelief, father and son experience their own emotional reunion whose intensity is emphasized in a well-known simile.[19] Odysseus also exhibits remarkable restraint in front of his wife before it is time to reveal his identity (see, for example, quote 1.5). Furthermore, he is able to control the expression of his anger as well as the expression of his love. On several occasions strategic considerations force him to suffer in silence the abuse hurled at him by the suitors, or their minions, who are like a plague on his palace. One example will suffice: After receiving a volley of insults and a blow to the hip from Melanthios, Odysseus "pondered within him whether to go for him with his cudgel, and take the life from him, or pick him up like a jug and break his head on the ground. Yet still he stood it, and kept it all inside him."[20]

The evidence that Odysseus conducts himself justly and tolerantly towards the weaknesses of others is not as strong as the incontrovertible evidence that he possesses the first two properties mentioned in quote 8.14. On one hand, Homer does make a point of Odysseus's fairness as a ruler. Mentor and Athene, in identical passages of five lines, describe him as a kind and gentle king, "one whose thought is schooled in justice." Penelope says, "he did no act and spoke no word in his own country that was unfair; and that is a way divine kings have, one will be hateful to a certain man, and favor another, but Odysseus was never outrageous at all to any man."[21] Furthermore, there are two episodes in the *Odyssey* in which Odysseus refrains from punishing his men for ruinous behavior that is clearly attributable to some weakness of theirs (greed in the first episode, inability to resist hunger in the second).[22] On the other hand, these episodes do not necessarily reveal a characteristic feature of Odysseus, because he really has no choice but to tolerate the weaknesses of his companions on these occasions: he would be one man against the many members of his crew,[23] he needs the cooperation of his crew in order to proceed, and in any event his men are as much victims of their behavior as he is.

If Gurdjieff's objective in quote 8.14 were simply to draw a portrait of Odysseus, he would have done better to mention firmness of purpose instead of just and tolerant conduct towards the weaknesses of others.[24] Indeed, without lengthening the definition, it would be difficult to improve upon the combination of resourcefulness, self-restraint, and determination as a thumbnail sketch of the protagonist of the *Odyssey*.[25] But the determined pursuit of a goal is such a central theme of the Second Series that this modification of the passage would have strengthened its connection to the rest of the book to such an extent that its connection to Odysseus would have been obscured. After all, what leads us to suspect a hidden purpose behind quote 8.14 is the fact that Gurdjieff's definition of a remarkable man does not play the thematic role in *Meetings with Remarkable Men* that we would expect. Only after we have noticed the apparent irrelevance of the definition are we likely to realize that it is a rather apt description of Odysseus. Our growing suspicion that Gurdjieff had Odysseus in mind when he formulated his definition is reinforced by the Homeric and Odyssean resonances of quote 8.1, which is the passage encountered by the reader of the Second Series immediately after quote 8.14 and a sentence that supplies a smooth transition from the definition to the chapter on Gurdjieff's father.

8.4. The Incident of the Dogs

The view that Gurdjieff alludes to Homer, and to the *Odyssey* in particular, in *Meetings with Remarkable Men* receives substantial corroboration from his

8.4. THE INCIDENT OF THE DOGS

description in that work of an incident that supposedly occurred during a journey that he made with one of his comrades:

> Pogossian and I were calmly walking along. He was humming some march and swinging his stick. Suddenly, as if from nowhere, a dog appeared, then another, and another, and still another—in all about fifteen sheep-dogs, who began barking at us. Pogossian imprudently flung a stone at them and they immediately sprang at us.
>
> They were Kurd sheep-dogs, very vicious, and in another moment they would have torn us to pieces if I had not instinctively pulled Pogossian down and made him sit beside me on the road. Just because we sat down the dogs stopped barking and springing at us; surrounding us, they also sat down.
>
> Quote 8.15: *RM*, p. 94

This incident recalls the scene from the *Odyssey* in which Odysseus, returning to his estate after an absence of twenty years, is threatened by fierce dogs and responds by sitting down on the ground.[26] This scene was undoubtedly familiar to Gurdjieff, whose father came from a Greek family and would tell stories to his children "about ancient great peoples and wonderful men" and who went on himself to develop a great interest in the literature and legends of antiquity.[27] I shall now suggest that during Gurdjieff's formative years the scene was very much in the awareness of anyone interested in Homer, so that, when he came to write *Meetings with Remarkable Men*, Gurdjieff could reasonably have expected quote 8.15 to be recognized as an allusion to the *Odyssey*.

The episode of Odysseus and the dogs was echoed by Heinrich Schliemann, the pioneering archaeologist of Troy and Mycenae, in *Ithaque, le Péloponnèse et Troie*, an account of his travels published in 1869:

> On that day, wishing to approach the farmyard of a peasant at the south end of the island, I was furiously attacked by four large dogs, that were not frightened by the stones or threats I hurled at them. I cried out for help; but my guide had remained behind and it seems that there was nobody in the peasant's house. In this terrible predicament, I fortunately recalled what Ulysses had done in a similar danger (*Od.* 14.29–31): "Suddenly the barking dogs saw Odysseus and ran up to him howling; but Odysseus prudently sat down and his stick fell from his hand." So I followed the example of the wise king, bravely sitting down on the ground, and remaining immobile, and at once the four dogs, who seemed ready to devour me, formed a circle around me and continued barking but did not touch me.
>
> Quote 8.16: Schliemann quoted by Traill, *Schliemann of Troy*, p. 46

David Traill argues plausibly that this incident was invented by Schliemann, probably with inspiration from Murray's *Handbook for Travellers in Greece* (1854), which advised travelers in Ithaca encountering fierce dogs to remember Odysseus's experience and to sit down and remain still.[28] What is important for us, however, is simply that the *Odyssey* scene was recalled both in Murray's *Handbook* (the most widely used guidebook of the day) and in Schliemann's first archaeological work. In addition, Schliemann's subsequent fame may have led to the diffusion of his story into one or more languages that Gurdjieff knew (which included Greek and Turkish).

Another traveler in Greece refers explicitly and repeatedly to the scene from the *Odyssey* while providing anecdotal evidence for the efficacy of Odysseus's response to the dogs in that scene. Writing in 1842, William Mure recounts how he first came to appreciate the value of Odysseus's tactic during a conversation concerning the fierceness of Greek dogs. One of his fellow guests at a dinner party had once been attacked by dogs and rescued by an old shepherd, who explained in the aftermath of the incident

> that he ought to have stopped and sat down, until some person whom the animals knew came to protect him. ... [The shepherd went on to explain] that, if any person in such a predicament will simply seat himself on the ground, laying aside his weapon of defence, the dogs will also squat in a circle round him; that as long as he remains quiet, they will follow his example; but that as soon as he rises and moves forward they will renew their assault.
>
> Quote 8.17: Mure, *Journal of a Tour*, vol. 1, p. 100

After restating the connection with the *Odyssey*, Mure says that the shepherd's explanation was confirmed by others present at the dinner from their own observation or experience. Apart from its support for the efficacy of Odysseus's response, this report is of particular interest because it furnishes additional material which can be correlated with Gurdjieff's account. The narrative begun in quote 8.15 continues as follows:

> Some time passed before we came to ourselves; and when we were able to take stock of the situation we burst out laughing. As long as we remained sitting the dogs also sat, peaceably and still, and when we threw them bread from our knapsacks, they ate it with great pleasure, some of them even wagging their tails in gratitude. But when, reassured by their friendliness, we tried to stand up, then, "Oh no, you don't!"—for they instantly jumped up and, baring their teeth, made ready to spring at us; so we were compelled to sit down once more. When we again tried to get up, the dogs showed themselves so viciously hostile that we did not risk trying a third time.
>
> In this situation we remained sitting for about three hours. I do not know how much longer we would have had to sit there if a young Kurd girl had not chanced to appear ...
>
> Quote 8.18: *RM*, pp. 94–95

Gurdjieff and Pogossian are finally rescued from their predicament when the young Kurd girl fetches the owners of the dogs. Thus, the incident related by Gurdjieff corresponds nicely to the explanation of the shepherd in quote 8.17.

Sitting down is such an unexpected and counterintuitive reaction to an attack by fierce dogs that anyone familiar with the *Odyssey* is bound to think of Odysseus when he reads Gurdjieff's account in quotes 8.15 and 8.18. By the same token, it is difficult not to believe that Gurdjieff was thinking of Odysseus when he wrote about his experience with Pogossian, especially since the Odyssean counterpart of this experience seems to have been very much "in the air" during his youth. Furthermore, since he would obviously have realized that his account could be taken as an allusion to Homer, this must have been his intention. To show this most clearly, I draw on a result to be established later in this chapter.

8.4. THE INCIDENT OF THE DOGS

In section 8.7 I demonstrate that a well-known connection between *Beelzebub's Tales* and the *Katha Upanishad* is, in fact, an intentional allusion. Since Gurdjieff definitely alludes to the *Katha Upanishad* and since he would not want to muddy the waters, it is safe to assume that he would not include a passage that could be interpreted as an allusion to the *Odyssey* unless that is what he intended.

I believe that the above argument is robust and able to withstand what at first sight would appear to be some rather strong objections. Why this is important becomes clear when we look closely at Homer's description of Odysseus's encounter with the fierce dogs. Disguised as an old beggar, Odysseus is nearing the shelter of his loyal swineherd, Eumaios, when he is intercepted by the four savage dogs who guard the pigs:

> Suddenly the wild-baying dogs caught sight of Odysseus.
> They ran at him with a great outcry, and Odysseus prudently
> sat down on the ground, and the staff fell out of his hand. But there,
> beside his own steading, he might have endured a shameful mauling,
> but the swineherd, quick and light on his feet, came hurrying to him
> across the porch, and let fall from his hand the shoe he was holding.
> He shouted at the dogs and scared them in every direction
> with volleyed showers of stones, and spoke then to his own master:
> "Old sir, the dogs were suddenly on you and would have savaged you
> badly; so you would have covered me with shame ..."
>
> Quote 8.19: *Od.* 14.29–38

The references to this scene discussed above—the explicit ones by Schliemann, Murray, and Mure and what I take to be the implicit one by Gurdjieff—all presume that the tactic of sitting down in the face of an attack by ferocious dogs actually works. While this position is supported early in quote 8.19, where it is said that "Odysseus *prudently* sat down on the ground" (emphasis added), Homer subsequently makes clear, both in his own voice and in the words of the swineherd, that Odysseus would have been mauled had Eumaios not come to his rescue. It is thus something of a mystery why the mentioned authors assume that Odysseus's tactic would work. Furthermore, a review by J. B. Hainsworth shows that a number of other authors, ancient and modern, make the same assumption.[29] Hainsworth himself cites observations of wolf behavior to support the efficacy of Odysseus's tactic. He explains the apparent ambivalence of Homer's narrative concerning this point as simply an illustration of the tolerance for inconsistency in archaic epic, where "the loss in logic, which in recitation may often escape notice, is counterbalanced by a gain in liveliness, interest, and wealth of detail" (the Aristotelian position discussed in chapter 4). Peter Jones suggests instead that although sitting down on the ground is "apparently a recognized method of dealing with an assault from wild dogs," it could evidently not be guaranteed to succeed.[30] For the present discussion it is not important to explain either Homer's apparent inconsistency or the willingness of so many authors to interpret quote 8.19 as an affirmation of the efficacy of Odysseus's tactic. All that matters is that this interpretation has prevailed over the centuries and therefore provides a sufficient basis for Gurdjieff's allusion to the *Odyssey* in quote 8.15.

It is possible that the disconnect between quote 8.19 and its common interpretation has to do with the aim of Odysseus's tactic rather than its efficacy. How we are to understand his behavior depends on the precise meaning of the word κερδοσύνη in the Greek text of *Od.* 14.31. The definition given by Cunliffe—"cunning, craft"—allows some flexibility. On one hand, the translations by W. H. D. Rouse and Robert Fagles construe "cunning" simply as shrewdness when they explain Odysseus's behavior by saying that he "knew the trick." And if sitting down is an effective trick for pacifying aggressive dogs, Lattimore (in quote 8.19) can reasonably say that Odysseus acted prudently when he used this trick. Likewise, when Mure quotes Homer as saying that Odysseus "sat down cunningly, dropping the stick from his hand," he also must mean that Odysseus hoped to pacify the dogs, since he connects quote 8.17 with the Odyssean passage. On the other hand, "cunning" may connote guile and deceitfulness, and there is no doubt that κερδοσύνη in *Il.* 22.247 (cited by Cunliffe) is intended to convey this meaning since it is used to describe how Athene tricked Hektor into standing his ground against Achilles by impersonating his brother Deïphobos. George Dimock has this sense of the word in mind when he translates *Od.* 14.31 as "he sat down with guileful intent, and let fall his staff."[31] But what does this mean? Surely Odysseus was not trying to deceive the dogs! Well, we know that Odysseus intends to pass himself off as a beggar. Dimock, following a remark by W. B. Stanford,[32] suggests that Odysseus's reaction to the dogs is the beginning of his deception of Eumaios. By sitting down and dropping his staff, Odysseus is feigning helplessness in the face of the attack. "Actually," says Dimock, "he is so confident of Eumaios's response that he takes what would seem to anyone else a serious risk of wounds or death in order to arouse his sympathy, such sympathy as only comes with the consciousness of having saved someone else's life." Erwin Cook expresses a similar view: "Rather than reveal his true stature by cudgeling the dogs, Odysseus 'cunningly' throws his staff to the ground, thereby compelling Eumaios to adopt the role of his protector."[33] According to Dimock and Cook, then, Odysseus is not trying to pacify the dogs when he puts himself in a defenseless position; he knows that he is exposing himself to danger, but trusts that Eumaios will come to his rescue. This interpretation avoids the inconsistency in quote 8.19 (and many other translations) regarding the efficacy of Odysseus's tactic.[34] It is also supported by the following argument.

Odysseus's response to the attacking dogs is twofold: he sits down and he drops his staff. The sitting down is the part that is relevant to Gurdjieff's allusion in quotes 8.15 and 8.18 and that tends to be emphasized in the explicit references to the *Odyssey* that I have reviewed in this section. Cook, however, concentrates on the dropping of the staff because this allows him to draw an interesting parallel between the incident of the dogs at the beginning of book 14 (quote 8.19) and a passage that appears later in the same book. After Odysseus has been rescued from the dogs and given a meal by Eumaios, the guest and his host have a long talk. When the time comes for Odysseus, who is disguised as a beggar, to explain who he is and where he comes from, he claims to be a wealthy and powerful man from Crete who has fallen on hard times after two narrow escapes from slavery. He says that his troubles can be traced to an expedition he made to Egypt with nine ships of companions. When his companions, against his express wishes, began plundering the Egyptian countryside, an Egyptian army responded with overwhelming force. Here is his account of what he did while his companions were panicking and being killed in large numbers:

> "At once I put the well-wrought helm from my head, the great shield
> off my shoulders, and from my hand I let the spear drop,
> and went out into the way of the king and up to his chariot,
> and kissed his knees and clasped them; he rescued me and took pity
> and seated me in his chariot and took me, weeping, homeward
> with him; and indeed many swept in on me with ash spears
> straining to kill me, for they were all too angered, but the king
> held them off from me ..."
>
> Quote 8.20: *Od.* 14.276–283

In this story invented by Odysseus, he was able to gain the protection of a king against those intent on killing him by dropping his spear (among other measures). Cook suggests that we are supposed to see an analogy with the incident at the beginning of the book in which Odysseus gains the protection of Eumaios against the attacking dogs by dropping his staff (and sitting down).

The general idea that there can be an intentional connection between a story made up by the disguised Odysseus and actual events at the swineherd's shelter is confirmed when Odysseus explicitly makes such a connection near the end of book 14. Night is falling, it is cold, and Odysseus is in need of a mantle with which to cover himself when he goes to bed. He gets Eumaios to give him one by (*a*) fabricating a story about how he (as the powerful man from Crete) once found himself in need of a mantle on a cold night at Troy and Odysseus secured one for him by means of a certain ruse and then (*b*) adding that he wished he was as young and strong as he was at Troy so that Eumaios or one of his helpers would give him a mantle out of respect. The explicit link between the false tale and actual situation at the swineherd's shelter supports the hypothesis of an implicit link between the false tale of the Cretan's expedition to Egypt and the incident of the dogs. The latter link receives additional support from what happens next. After giving a mantle to Odysseus the beggar, Eumaios goes outside to spend the night with the pigs, taking with him a javelin for protection against dogs and men. This closing scene of book 14 recalls the incident of the dogs at the beginning of the book and, in particular, the part played in this incident by the staff which Odysseus could have used to defend himself against the dogs. In other words, book 14 ends with a reminder of that part of the incident of the dogs which has a parallel in Odysseus's story of the Cretan's expedition to Egypt. In view of all this, it seems likely that this parallel is intentional and therefore that Odysseus's aim in sitting down and dropping his staff is not to pacify the dogs but to win the protection of Eumaios.

If the interpretation proposed by Dimock and Cook is correct, the allusion in *Meetings with Remarkable Men* to the incident of the dogs in the *Odyssey* is based on a misunderstanding. That is worth noting, as it suggests that Gurdjieff—along with many others—misconstrued Odysseus's actions in that incident. However, the misunderstanding does not undermine my claim that

8.5. The Substance of Odysseus

A constant refrain in the *Odyssey* is that the suitors of Penelope are consuming the wealth of Odysseus with their endless feasting. The substance of Odysseus is thus equated with his livestock.[35] There is one place in the poem where Homer elaborates on this equation. After rescuing the disguised Odysseus from the dogs and preparing him a meal, Eumaios voices and amplifies on the usual refrain concerning the suitors and then proceeds to enumerate the holdings of his master:

> "He [Odysseus] had an endlessly abundant livelihood. Not one
> of the heroes over on the black mainland had so much, no one
> here on Ithaka, no twenty men together had such
> quantity of substance as he. I will count it for you.
> Twelve herds of cattle on the mainland. As many sheepflocks.
> As many troops of pigs and again as many wide goatflocks,
> and friends over there, and his own herdsmen, pasture them for him.
> And here again, at the end of the island, eleven wide flocks
> of goats in all are pastured, good men have these in their keeping."
>
> Quote 8.21: *Od.* 14.96–104

Great wealth in the form of flocks and herds is also mentioned in *Meetings with Remarkable Men*:

> In former times the word "shepherd" did not have the same meaning as it has now. Formerly a shepherd himself was the owner of the flocks he grazed; and shepherds were considered among the richest people of the country; some of them even possessed several flocks and herds.
>
> Quote 8.22: *RM*, p. 88

Whereas the incidents of the dogs in the *Odyssey* and *Meetings with Remarkable Men* are unmistakably linked by the unexpected actions of the men under attack, quotes 8.21 and 8.22 share content that is rather ordinary in comparison and that does not necessarily lead one to suspect that the second alludes to the first. There may be a hint of an allusion, however, in the existence of a relationship involving all four passages. Gurdjieff's remark concerning the wealth of shepherds (quote 8.22) appears in a historical digression concerning an ancient city where Pogossian and Gurdjieff discovered an intriguing parchment that led them to undertake the journey in which they had their encounter with the vicious sheep-dogs (quotes 8.15 and 8.18). I have already mentioned that Eumaios enumerates the holdings of Odysseus (quote 8.21) shortly after rescuing him from the dogs (quote 8.19). Thus, in both the *Odyssey* and *Meetings with Remarkable Men*, the equation of wealth with large holdings of livestock enters the narrative in association with the incident of the dogs.

Wealth in the form of livestock is mentioned at one place in *Meetings with Remarkable Men* besides quote 8.22. In the chapter on his father, Gurdjieff says that his ancestors possessed enormous riches consisting in part of herds of cattle and that several herds were among the great riches inherited by his father.³⁶ If the book contained many such references to livestock as wealth, we could not take too seriously the association of quote 8.22 with the incident of the dogs. It follows that even the two references which appear together in the chapter on Gurdjieff's father must diminish the perceived significance of this association. On the other hand, it may be worth noting that both chapters that refer to wealth in the form of livestock, the chapter on Gurdjieff's father and the chapter on Pogossian, are chapters that already have a significant association with Homer via the attention given to oral bards (discussed in section 8.1) and the incident of the dogs (discussed in section 8.4).

It is only because fairly clear allusions to the *Odyssey* have been documented earlier in this chapter that the idea occurs to us that Gurdjieff might be alluding to the wealth of Odysseus when he mentions riches in the form of flocks and herds. Whether he is or not is therefore not important for my argument. The significant conclusion of this section is that the wealth inherited by Gurdjieff's father deserves to be mentioned in a discussion of possible allusions to the *Odyssey* in *Meetings with Remarkable Men*, for this fact is what justifies the inclusion of much of the material in the following section.

8.6. More Inconsistencies

As in section 8.2, I now interrupt the argument of this chapter to point out some inconsistencies in *Meetings with Remarkable Men* that can be linked, directly or indirectly, to the preceding discussion.

The herds of cattle inherited by Gurdjieff's father were wiped out by a plague, so that this once-rich man suddenly became a pauper forced to go into some kind of business to support his family. Gurdjieff tells us that his father's start in business was not auspicious:

> [H]e began by opening a lumber-yard and with it, according to local custom, a carpenter's shop for making all kinds of wooden articles.
>
> But from the very first year, owing to the fact that my father had never before in his life been engaged in commerce and had in consequence no business experience, the lumber-yard was a failure.
>
> He was finally compelled to liquidate it and to limit himself to the workshop, specializing in the production of small wooden articles.
>
> Quote 8.23: *RM*, p. 41

This account of his father's business failure is contradicted later in the chapter by an explanation in terms of a certain tendency of his father:

> It was chiefly on account of this tendency that from the very beginning, when he became poor and had to go into business, his affairs went so badly that his friends and those who had business dealings with him considered him unpractical and even not clever in this domain.
>
> And indeed, every business that my father carried on for the purpose of making money always went wrong and brought none of the results obtained by others. However, this was not because he was unpractical or lacked mental ability in this field, but only because of this tendency.

> This tendency of his nature, apparently acquired by him when still a child, I would define thus: "an instinctive aversion to deriving personal advantage for himself from the naïveté and bad luck of others."
>
> In other words, being highly honourable and honest, my father could never consciously build his own welfare on the misfortune of his neighbour. But most of those round him, being typical contemporary people, took advantage of his honesty and deliberately tried to cheat him ...
>
> Quote 8.24: RM, pp. 47–48

That the two explanations—lack of business experience in quote 8.23, honesty in quote 8.24—are really in conflict is demonstrated by the first sentence of the second passage, which leaves no doubt that the explanation in terms of honesty is supposed to apply to the lumber-yard whose failure was originally attributed to lack of business experience.

Quote 8.24 is also key to a second inconsistency. Referring to his friend Pogossian, Gurdjieff says that

> although he did not go into serious business until the year 1908, he is now one of the richest men on earth. As for his honesty in earning his wealth, that cannot be questioned.
>
> Quote 8.25: RM, pp. 107–108

Whereas Gurdjieff's father is said to have had no success in business because of his honesty, Pogossian's unquestioned honesty did not prevent him from becoming one of the richest men on earth. The mere existence of this inconsistency is all that is important since we can take for granted that the numerous inconsistencies in the writings of Gurdjieff are intentional. In this case, however, I would add that the mention of Pogossian's honesty in quote 8.25 seems gratuitous, which itself suggests that Gurdjieff included it specifically to create the inconsistency.[37]

8.7. East and West in the Writings of Gurdjieff

Returning to the main thesis of this chapter, I now conclude my case for allusions to the *Odyssey* in *Meetings with Remarkable Men* with an argument that makes no further reference to either work. The argument is based on the assumption that Gurdjieff would not have given special treatment in his writings to the West over the East. If his writings allude to Homer, and therefore to the beginning of Western literature, we would expect them also to allude to ancient Eastern literature. The identification of at least one clearly intentional allusion to the literature of ancient India confirms this prediction made on the basis of the premise that Gurdjieff alludes to Homer, and therefore makes this premise more credible.[38, 39]

Arguing that *Beelzebub's Tales* should be included among the 100 most influential books ever written, Martin Seymour-Smith says that the teaching of Gurdjieff is "the most convincing fusion of Eastern and Western thought that has yet been seen."[40] He adds that "elements of Zoroastrianism, Buddhism, Christianity (especially Eastern Orthodox), the KABBALAH, Sufism, Pythagorianism, and other religions and systems are present in the doctrine." Indeed, whole books have been written on some of these elements in Gurdjieff's writings.[41] Gurdjieff himself was explicit that both East and West have important contributions to make. Fritz Peters reports him saying that "unless the 'wisdom' of the East and the 'energy' of the West could be harnessed and used harmoniously, the world would be destroyed."[42] One of the aphorisms inscribed in a special script above the walls of the Study House at Gurdjieff's institute in France was "Take the understanding of the East and the knowledge of the West—and then seek."[43] These are the indications that lead me to assume that Gurdjieff would not have given a special place in his writings to Western civilization by alluding to Homer without also alluding to some work of ancient Eastern literature. I shall now provide the background needed to vindicate this assumption.

In *Beelzebub's Tales* Gurdjieff discusses a model of a human being in terms of a horse-drawn carriage.[44] In this model, the carriage corresponds to the person's body, the horse harnessed to the carriage corresponds to the person's feeling, and the coachman directing the horse corresponds to the person's mentation; the passenger sitting in the carriage and commanding the coachman is what Gurdjieff calls "I." A real "I" is represented in the model by a passenger who is the owner of the carriage. The development of such an "I" is the overarching goal of Gurdjieff's teaching: most people do not have a real "I" and can be modeled by a hackney carriage whose course is dictated by a succession of unrelated passengers.

Gurdjieff claims no originality for this model. In *Beelzebub's Tales* he says that it has been "worn threadbare by contemporary what are called spiritualists, occultists, theosophists, and other specialists in 'catching fish in muddy waters'." Elsewhere he attributes it to "certain Eastern teachings."[45] A connection with the literature of ancient India—the *Katha Upanishad* in particular—is now well known.[46] To show that this connection reflects an intentional allusion, I first review how the carriage model is introduced in *Beelzebub's Tales*.

Gurdjieff begins his preparation for the carriage model by saying that one's potential as a human being can be actualized only if one's individuality comprises four "personalities." The first of these "personalities" is the automatic functioning which people, in their ignorance, call "consciousness" or "mentation." The second "personality" consists of the data obtained through "the six organs called 'receivers of vibrations of different qualities'."[47] The third "personality" is the basic functioning of the organism together with its "motor-reflex-reciprocally-affecting-manifestations." Finally, the fourth "personality" is a genuine "I." Having given these definitions, Gurdjieff then goes on to say that someone who possesses all four "personalities" is "almost exactly comparable to that organization for conveying a passenger, which consists of a carriage, a horse, and a coachman":

> The body of a man with all its motor reflex manifestations corresponds simply to the carriage itself; all the functionings and manifestations of feeling of a man correspond to the horse harnessed to the carriage and drawing it; the coachman sitting on the box and directing the horse corresponds to that in a man which people call consciousness or mentation; and finally, the passenger seated in the carriage and commanding the coachman is that which is called "I."

Quote 8.26: *BT*, p. 1192

Three of the four components of the carriage model are clearly associated with three of the four "personalities" defined previously: the carriage corresponds to the third "personality," the coachman to the first "personality," and the passenger to the fourth "personality." But what about the horse? According to quote 8.26, the horse represents feeling, but feeling is not mentioned anywhere in the definitions of the four "personalities." The only "personality" not yet accounted for in the carriage model is the second one, which is said to consist of the data obtained through "the six organs called 'receivers of vibrations of different qualities'." It would be tempting to interpret the "receivers of vibrations of different qualities" as the senses were it not for the fact that Gurdjieff says that there are six of them. But the latter objection is nullified by the following sentence from elsewhere in *Beelzebub's Tales*:

> [A]ll the impressions inevitably perceived by means of the six "being-skernalitsioniks" or, in their terminology, "sense organs," existing in their presence specifically for the perception of externals—which, by the way, they count as five—come to be localized and, acquiring their independent functioning, gradually become predominant in the whole of their common presence.
>
> Quote 8.27: *BT*1992, p. 517 (cf. *BT*, p. 566)

Thus, if each component of the carriage model is associated with one of the four "personalities," as Gurdjieff implies, the horse must correspond to, or somehow be closely connected with, the senses. This is very strange. Everywhere else he discusses the carriage model, both in the remainder of his discussion of the model in *Beelzebub's Tales* (beginning with quote 8.26) and elsewhere,[48] Gurdjieff *always* equates the horse with feeling. Why does he imply at this one place that the horse corresponds to the senses? The answer, I suggest, is found in the following excerpt from the *Katha Upanishad*:

> Know the self as a rider in a chariot,
>   and the body, as simply the chariot.
> Know the intellect as the charioteer,
>   and the mind, as simply the reins.
>
> The senses, they say, are the horses,
>   and sense objects are the paths around them;
> ...
>
> Quote 8.28: *Katha Upanishad* 3.3–4 (Olivelle trans.)

If we draw a parallel between the "I" of Gurdjieff's teaching and the "self" (Sanskrit *ātman*) of Hindu philosophy (and it is no more than a parallel, for these are actually rather different concepts), there is an unmistakable connection between the carriage model of Gurdjieff and the chariot model of the Upanishad. In particular, if the horse in the former is considered to represent the senses, the two models give corresponding interpretations for the vehicle, the horse(s), the driver, and the passenger.[49] Other connections to Hindu philosophy can be seen in *Beelzebub's Tales*, as I will discuss later in this section, but this one stands out from the others in that it is the only one where we can see Gurdjieff deliberately changing something (the meaning of the horse) in order to strengthen the connection. Given the real differences between the carriage model and the chariot model, Gurdjieff's purpose in connecting the two cannot have been to suggest that a deeper understanding of the former can be reached through a study of the latter. Rather, his purpose must have been simply to create an allusion to the *Katha Upanishad*. This fulfills our expectation of an allusion to ancient Eastern literature, and therefore supports our basis for this expectation, the allusions to Homer identified earlier in this chapter.

To present my argument as simply as possible, I have so far used abbreviated versions of Gurdjieff's definitions of the first two "personalities." I now show that the gist of the argument survives when the full definitions are taken into account. Consider first the complete description of the first "personality":

> The first of these four independent personalities is nothing else than the totality of that automatic functioning which is proper to man as well as to all animals, the data for which are composed in them firstly of the sum total of the results of impressions previously perceived from all the surrounding reality as well as from everything intentionally artificially implanted in them from outside, and, secondly, from the result of the process also inherent in every animal called "daydreaming." And this totality of automatic functioning most people ignorantly name "consciousness," or, at best, "mentation."
>
> Quote 8.29: *BT*, pp. 1189–1190

As stated before, the first "personality" is the automatic functioning which is usually called "consciousness" or "mentation." Quote 8.29 adds that the data required for this "personality" comes from previously perceived impressions of external reality together with the results of daydreaming. This makes sense in that previously perceived impressions are necessary for the associations which are the "stuff" of mentation. Now consider Gurdjieff's description of the second "personality":

> The second of the four personalities, functioning in most cases entirely independently of the first, is the sum of the results of data deposited and fixed in the common presence of every man, as of every animal, through the six organs called "receivers of vibrations of different qualities"—organs that function in accordance with the new impressions perceived, and whose sensitivity depends upon heredity and upon the conditions of the preparatory formation for responsible existence of the given individual.
>
> Quote 8.30: *BT*1992, p. 1090 (cf. *BT*, p. 1190)

Analysis of this passage will show that it describes something that is hardly distinguishable from the first "personality." First, we have already identified the six organs here called "receivers of vibrations of different qualities" as the sense organs on the basis of quote 8.27. That quotation notes that the sense organs exist "specifically for the perception of externals." The data supplied by these organs therefore correspond to the impressions of external reality that are required for what is usually called "consciousness" or "mentation" according to quote 8.29. Second, whereas before I said that the second "personality" consists of the data obtained through "the six organs called 'receivers of vibrations of different qualities'," quote 8.30 actually says that it consists of "the sum of the results" of these data. Quote 8.27 indicates that the impressions perceived by the sense organs produce something with its own independent functioning which becomes predominant in the presence of a person. The text in which quote 8.27 is embedded in *Beelzebub's Tales*[50] makes clear that this predominant something is what Gurdjieff calls "false consciousness" and what most other people, in their ignorance, call simply "consciousness." The second "personality" must evidently be identified as what is commonly called "consciousness"; in other words, it is the same as the first "personality," described in quote 8.29. Thus, we can see that Gurdjieff is up to one of his tricks in his definitions of the "personalities" even before we come to quote 8.26 and its incomplete correspondence between the four "personalities" and the four components of the carriage model. Our only recourse is to abandon our attempt at strict literal interpretation and to pay attention instead to what Gurdjieff emphasizes. In quote 8.29 he emphasizes "consciousness" or "mentation," with impressions of external reality playing only a supporting role; in quote 8.30 he emphasizes the impressions themselves—that is, the senses—without specifying the nature of their results. In order to distinguish between the first and second "personalities," we are forced to associate the second with the senses. We therefore perceive Gurdjieff's allusion to the *Katha Upanishad* once again, this time with a clearer grasp of the mechanics of the allusion.

In Gurdjieff's carriage model, the passenger who is the owner of the carriage will seem mysterious because one typically has no idea what it would mean to have something higher than, and in control of, one's ordinary consciousness. Apart from this, the other components of the model present no problem. In particular, the idea that one's consciousness or mentation (the coachman) is in control of one's feelings (the horse) is at least understandable as an ideal, even if that ideal seems out of reach more often than not. The dichotomy between the actual and the ideal is, of course, fully recognized by Gurdjieff:[51]

> The wrong system of education existing at the present time has led to the coachman's ceasing to have any effect whatever on his horse, unless we allow the fact that he is merely able by means of the reins to engender in the consciousness of the horse just three ideas—right, left, and stop.
>
> Strictly speaking he cannot always do even this, because the reins in general are made of materials that react to various atmospheric phenomena ...
>
> The same proceeds in the general organization of the average man whenever ..., when his thoughts entirely lose all possibility of affecting his feeling-organization.
>
> <div align="right">Quote 8.31: <i>BT</i>, pp. 1200–1201</div>

The chariot model of the *Katha Upanishad* exhibits the same dichotomy in the relationship between the horses and the charioteer:

> When a man lacks understanding,
>   and his mind is never controlled;
> His senses do not obey him,
>   as bad horses, a charioteer.

> But when a man has understanding,
>   and his mind is ever controlled;
> His senses do obey him,
>   as good horses, a charioteer.
>   Quote 8.32: *Katha Upanishad* 3.5–6 (Olivelle trans.)

However, whereas there is nothing mysterious in the idea of feeling being subordinate to mentation, one may well ask what it would mean for the senses to obey the intellect. As we have already seen, one need not understand this in order to recognize Gurdjieff's allusion to the Upanishad. Nevertheless, the following explanation, taken from Mircea Eliade's treatise on Yoga,[52] may interest the reader who is coming to this material for the first time.

In the ordinary state of consciousness, one is constantly distracted, swept hither and thither (to use the phraseology of Eliade or his translator) by associations which are activated by sensations as well as by subconscious processes. Yoga seeks to replace this dispersed consciousness with a concentrated, unified consciousness. Towards this aim, Yoga meditation begins with concentration on a single object or thought; that is, the practitioner "reins in" his senses by concentrating on a single point. Thus, as Eliade points out, the chariot model in the *Katha Upanishad* is a yogic metaphor. The Upanishad itself makes this explicit:

> When senses are firmly reined in,
>   that is Yoga, so people think.
> From distractions a man is then free,
>   for Yoga is the coming-into-being,
>   as well as the ceasing-to-be.
>   Quote 8.33: *Katha Upanishad* 6.11 (Olivelle trans.)

The allusion in *Beelzebub's Tales* to the chariot model in the *Katha Upanishad* corresponds to the allusion in *Meetings with Remarkable Men* to the incident of the dogs in the *Odyssey* in that each of these allusions refers to a single passage. Just as *Meetings with Remarkable Men* contains, in addition, a much more sweeping allusion to the *Odyssey* (its definition of a remarkable man recalls the behavior or characterization of Odysseus at many points in the *Odyssey*), I shall now suggest that *Beelzebub's Tales* also contains a much more comprehensive allusion, only not to the *Katha Upanishad* but to the broader corpus of the Vedic Upanishads.

The Upanishads repeatedly affirm the equivalence of the innermost essence of a human being (*ātman*, usually translated in this context as "self") and the underlying essence or foundation of everything in the universe (*brahman*, the ultimate reality). The importance of this equivalence in the Upanishads is indicated by the remarks of three commentators: "The great discovery of the Upanishads was, of course, the systematic statement of the identity between the *ātman* and the *brahman*"; "This tremendous equation—'the Self is Brahman'—is the central discovery of the Upanishads"; and finally, the telling admonition that "it is incorrect to think that the single aim of all the Upanishads is to enunciate this simple truth."[53] The following demonstration that *Beelzebub's Tales* alludes to the equivalence of *ātman* and *brahman* therefore shows, in effect, that *Beelzebub's Tales* alludes to the Upanishads.

Gurdjieff's allusion to "the central discovery of the Upanishads" begins with a teaching that Beelzebub attributes to the Buddha:

> "It transpired that in His explanations to them about cosmic truths, Saint Buddha had, among other things, told them also that in general the three-centered beings existing on various planets of our Great Universe—and of course the three-centered beings of the Earth [i.e., human beings] also—were nothing else but part of that Most Great Greatness which is the All-embracing of all that exists; and that the foundation of this Most Great Greatness is there Above, for the convenience of the embracing of the essence of everything existing.
>
> "This Most Great Foundation of the All-embracing of everything that exists constantly emanates throughout the whole of the Universe and coats itself from its particles upon planets—in certain three-centered beings ...—into a definite unit in which alone Objective Divine Reason acquires the possibility of becoming concentrated and fixed."
>
> Quote 8.34: *BT*, p. 244

What Beelzebub calls the "Most Great Foundation of the All-embracing of everything that exists," which he relates to the essence of everything existing, can reasonably be regarded as the *brahman*. Indeed, the formulation is so apt that the addition that this Most Great Foundation "constantly emanates throughout the whole of the Universe" should not threaten the identification. To continue the interpretation of this passage, it is necessary to know that in the teaching of Gurdjieff "Objective Divine Reason" (elsewhere called simply objective Reason or objective consciousness), to which we will return in the next chapter, is a property that can be acquired only by the soul of a person.[54] The "definite unit in which alone Objective Divine Reason acquires the possibility of becoming concentrated and fixed" is therefore the soul. Thus, quote 8.34 asserts a direct connection between the *brahman* and an individual's soul. It is therefore of great interest that the word *ātman*, in contexts where it might be translated as the Self, is sometimes translated as the soul,[55] for this suggests that quote 8.34 relates *ātman* and *brahman* and thereby alludes to the Upanishads.[56]

I have just proposed a correspondence between the *ātman* of the Upanishads and the soul in the teaching of Gurdjieff. This correspondence is compelling, but only up to a certain point. It is compelling in that both the *ātman* and the soul represent the innermost and highest part of a person, the part that is said to be immortal. But there is also a fundamental difference. The *ātman* is found in every person (indeed, in every creature), and it is present at birth. By contrast, Gurdjieff insists that no one is born with a soul and that a soul can be created in oneself only by one's own efforts. This distinction means that quote 8.34 is, at best, an inexact statement of the equivalence of *ātman* and *brahman*. Quote 8.34 is just the beginning of an allusion to this equivalence, however, for Gurdjieff goes on to compensate for the mentioned inexactitude. The way he does this could be explained quickly, but I will lengthen the explanation a little in order to discuss his terminology, which is instructive in itself.

According to Beelzebub, the Buddha said that the "Great All-embracing of all that is embraced" is called "Holy Prana."[57] *Prāna* is a key term in the Upanishads with a cluster of related meanings which includes "breath" and "vital energy" (or "life energy"). My identification of the "Great All-embracing of all that is embraced" as *brahman* is consistent with the terminology that Beelzebub attributes to the Buddha, for several Upanishads state that *brahman* is *prāna*.[58]

Having introduced the suggestively Upanishadic term "Prana," Beelzebub then makes use of this term in his description of the fate of the Buddha's teaching:

> "This quite definite explanation of Saint Buddha was well understood by his contemporaries and many of them began ... to strive with eagerness, first to absorb and to coat in their presences the particle of this Most Great Greatness and afterwards to 'make-inherent' to it Divine Objective Reason.
>
> "But when the second and third generations of the contemporaries of Saint Buddha began wiseacring with His explanations of cosmic truths, they just wiseacred with their peculiar Reason and fixed—for its transmission—a very definite notion to the effect that that same 'Mister Prana' already begins to be in them immediately upon their arising.
>
> "Thanks to this misunderstanding, the beings of that period and of all subsequent generations including the contemporary, have imagined and still imagine that without any being-Partkdolg duty [i.e., without the efforts necessary to create and perfect a soul] they are already parts of that Most Great Greatness ...."
>
> Quote 8.35: *BT*, p. 245

In short, the Buddha's teaching was ultimately distorted in such a way as to bring it in line with the Upanishadic view that the *ātman* is present in a person at birth. When this distortion is taken into account, quote 8.34 is seen to form an effective allusion to the Upanishadic equivalence of *ātman* and *brahman*.

According to Beelzebub, the Buddha's teaching summarized in quote 8.34 was subjected to two distortions, the one described in quote 8.35 and a later one intentionally introduced by Beelzebub himself in order to combat the custom of animal sacrifice:

> "I began to spread there in Pearl-land [India] that that 'Most-Sacred-Prana,' about which our Divine Teacher Saint Buddha had explained, is already present not only in people, but also in all the other beings that arise and exist on our planet Earth.
>
> "A particle of that fundamental Most Great Great All-embracing, namely, the Most-Sacred-Prana, has already from the very beginning settled in every form of being of every scale, breeding on the surface of the planet, in the water, and also in the atmosphere.
>
> "I regret to have to say here, my boy, that I was then constrained more than once to emphasize that these words had been uttered by the very lips of Saint Buddha Himself."
>
> Quote 8.36: *BT*, p. 247

Beelzebub goes on to tell his grandson that his invention was adopted enthusiastically by the followers of the Buddha's teaching and that it so changed their attitude towards beings of other forms that they stopped using these beings for sacrificial offerings. As a result, animal sacrifice ceased to be practiced in India.

My contention that the teaching given in quote 8.34 and refined in quotes 8.35 and 8.36 constitutes an allusion to the Upanishads rests on two observations. The first is the affinity of this teaching with the doctrine concerning *ātman* and *brahman* that is so closely identified with the Upanishads (not to mention the use of the term *prāna*, which also figures prominently in these documents). The second observation is that Gurdjieff seems to go out of his way in these passages not to mention Hindu philosophy, much less the Upanishads themselves. I say this because the attribution of the teaching to the Buddha is inappropriate in three respects. First, the Buddha was not given to metaphysical speculation, which might distract people from the business of awakening, and accordingly had no use for the Upanishadic postulates of *ātman*, *brahman*, and their equivalence.[59] Second, even if it were philosophically reasonable to attribute the teaching to the Buddha (quote 8.34) and to those who came after him (quotes 8.35 and 8.36), this attribution would be anachronistic, as the equivalence of *ātman* and *brahman* is asserted in the earliest Upanishads, which predate the Buddha.[60] Finally, it is bizarre of Beelzebub to claim that an alteration to a teaching of the Buddha brought about the abolition of animal sacrifice in India. Animal sacrifice has never been a Buddhist practice, but it *was* central to the Brahmanism that was to evolve into classical Hinduism. And in fact two vedic rituals that involve animal sacrifice—the horse sacrifice and the Soma sacrifice—are much discussed in the Upanishads.[61] It is difficult not to get the impression from all this that the function of the Buddha in quotes 8.34–8.36 is to disguise the fact that these passages form an allusion to the Upanishads, but to do so in such a way that the disguise is transparent.

Much of the chapter of *Beelzebub's Tales* entitled "The First Visit of Beelzebub to India" is devoted to the Buddha and to teachings attributed to him, such as the material in quotes 8.34–8.36. By contrast, the only explicit reference to Hinduism in the entire chapter is found in a single sentence near the end of the chapter, following a transparently false etymology of the word 'kundalina' (i.e., kundalini):

> "Today the whole of so-called 'Hindu philosophy' is based on this famous 'kundalina,' and around the word itself exist thousands of occult 'sciences,' secret and revealed, which explain absolutely nothing."
> Quote 8.37: *BT*1992, p. 231 (cf. *BT*, p. 247)[62]

It can fairly be said that Hinduism is conspicuous by its virtual absence from Beelzebub's tales concerning India. The same can be said of the chapter on religion. Beelzebub lists five religions—Buddhism, Judaism, Christianity, Islam, and Lamaism[63]—and then, noting that he has already discussed the first (in the chapter on India), proceeds to discuss the other four. Of course, many religions are missing from Beelzebub's list, but by far the most egregious omission, based on the size of its following, is Hinduism. This omission is accentuated when the list is repeated with one surprising addition in *Meetings with Remarkable Men*:

[A]mong the adepts of this monastery there were former Christians, Jews, Mohammedans, Buddhists, Lamaists, and even one Shamanist.

Quote 8.38: *RM*, p. 239

A closer look at the chapter on religion in *Beelzebub's Tales* will confirm that Gurdjieff's failure to mention Hinduism in that chapter is intentional.[64]

Beelzebub explains that, over the course of time, a number of Sacred Individuals were sent to the Earth for the salvation of people and that, with only one exception (the Sacred Individual Ashiata Shiemash), the death of each Sacred Individual was followed by the invention of a religion based on the explanations of that Individual (or rather, a distortion of those explanations). In this way, the explanations of Saint Buddha in India gave rise to Buddhism, and those of "Saint Lama" in Tibet gave rise to Lamaism. The explanations and instructions of Saint Lama were based to a large extent on those of Saint Buddha (Lamaism is a term that is sometimes used for Tibetan Buddhism). Similarly, the explanations and instructions of Saint Buddha included many that had been provided by "Saint Krishnatkharna," a Sacred Individual who had supposedly been sent to the people of India before the Buddha. We know from Beelzebub's explanation of the origin of religions that the teaching of Saint Krishnatkharna must have given rise to a religion. From the chronology, the geography, and the name Krishnatkharna (Krishna being the name of a revered avatar of the Hindu god Vishnu), it is obvious that that religion was Hinduism. The failure to mention Hinduism has to be intentional.[65] I suggest that this blatant omission serves to support the allusions discussed above by removing any doubt that Gurdjieff might refer to Hindu scriptures without mentioning them.

Although this discussion is by no means complete,[66] I have said enough to confirm the prediction that the writings of Gurdjieff contain allusions to ancient literature of the East. The allusions to the Upanishads discussed in this section and the allusions to the *Odyssey* discussed earlier in this chapter combine to form a symmetric treatment of East and West in *All and Everything*. The failure to discover such a symmetry would have presented a serious objection to my claim that Gurdjieff alludes to Homer; the verification of the symmetry, on the other hand, provides an independent source of support for this claim. It is worth adding that the allusions to the East are found in *Beelzebub's Tales*, while the allusions to the West are found in *Meetings with Remarkable Men*, as this separation of duties extends the complementary relationship between the two works that I have demonstrated elsewhere.[67]

8.8. On the Significance of the Allusions

Since the allusions considered in this chapter—those to the *Odyssey* in *Meetings with Remarkable Men* and those to the Upanishads in *Beelzebub's Tales*—are not instructive in themselves, they must serve some other purpose. It is natural to ask whether this purpose is to call attention to themes that the ancient texts share with the writings of Gurdjieff. Such themes do exist. In the next chapter I discuss one that is shared by *Beelzebub's Tales* and the Upanishads. Odysseus's unflagging determination to return home matches the perseverance of Gurdjieff in his search for truth described in *Meetings with*

Remarkable Men. Anna Challenger argues that the contrast between Odysseus and the men with whom he must deal in the *Odyssey*, his crewmen and the suitors of Penelope, mirrors the contrast that Gurdjieff emphasizes between a person who possesses a real "I" (a concept touched on in the preceding section that is explained more fully in section 9.6) and the masses of those who do not.[68] Nevertheless, I do not feel that shared themes provide a satisfying explanation for Gurdjieff's allusions to the ancient texts. First, although it is in *Meetings with Remarkable Men* that Gurdjieff alludes to the *Odyssey*, it is only in *Beelzebub's Tales* that he speaks about the real "I." Second, Challenger shows that the ideas of Gurdjieff have parallels in the epic of Gilgamesh that are at least as strong as those in the *Odyssey*.[69] Yet Gurdjieff does not *allude* to the Gilgamesh legend, he refers to it explicitly.[70] Finally, if Gurdjieff made a practice of alluding to ancient literature that shares themes with his own work, he would certainly have alluded to the Gospels.[71] I therefore suggest that the special act of allusion indicates that Gurdjieff sees a hidden connection between his work and the work to which he alludes, a connection so deep that it is not revealed by a mere comparison of ideas. In the next chapter I propose one such connection for the Homeric epics and another for the Upanishads, and show that these two connections are themselves connected, thus extending the symmetry between East and West discussed in the preceding section.

I have just mentioned the Homeric epics, referring to both the *Iliad* and the *Odyssey*, despite the fact that I have made no case for allusions to the *Iliad* in the writings of Gurdjieff. It is possible to cite possible candidates for such allusions, but they are not convincing.[72] This is a weakness in my argument, for I do claim to see a deep connection between Gurdjieff and Homer that includes the *Iliad* as well as the *Odyssey*. Whether this weakness is serious will have to be judged on the basis of the rest of my argument. In the meantime, I ask the reader to entertain the possibility that the allusions discussed in this chapter were intended to bring to mind the idea of Homer as a whole.

Chapter 9

Gurdjieff's Answer to the Homeric Question

The observations made in the preceding chapter point to the conclusion that Gurdjieff must have seen a connection between his ideas and the *Odyssey* or even the Homeric corpus as a whole. This is intriguing in the light of our realization that the writings of Gurdjieff and the poems of Homer share a strange and unusual property. In fact, I shall now argue that this shared property—perverse inconsistency—enables us to identify a deep connection that Gurdjieff perceived between himself and Homer, a connection that implies a novel answer to the Homeric Question.

9.1. The Homeric Epics as Objective Art

We are indebted to P. D. Ouspensky for an invaluable record of the early phase of Gurdjieff's oral teaching that is published with the title *In Search of the Miraculous: Fragments of an Unknown Teaching,* a title which I abbreviate to *Fragments* for reasons explained elsewhere.[1] In two extended passages from this record, Gurdjieff distinguishes two kinds of art.[2] Here I quote briefly from both passages:

> "I do not call art all that you call art, which is simply mechanical reproduction, imitation of nature or other people, or simply fantasy, or an attempt to be original. Real art is something quite different. Among works of art, especially works of ancient art, you meet with many things you cannot explain and which contain a certain something you do not feel in modern works of art. But as you do not realize what this difference is you very soon forget it and continue to take everything as one kind of art. And yet there is an enormous difference between your art and the art of which I speak."
>
> Quote 9.1: *Fragments,* p. 26

> "[T]here are two kinds of art, one quite different from the other—objective art and subjective art. All that you know, all that you call art, is subjective art, that is, something that I do not call art at all because it is only objective art that I call art.
>
> "To define what I call objective art is difficult first of all because you ascribe to subjective art the characteristics of objective art, and secondly

because when you happen upon objective works of art you take them as being on the same level as subjective works of art."

Quote 9.2: *Fragments*, pp. 295–296

From his lack of regard for subjective art and his insistence that only objective art is real art I conclude that if, as I argued in chapter 8, Gurdjieff saw a connection between his ideas and one or both of the Homeric epics that was strong enough to motivate him to allude to Homer in his own writings, then he must have regarded the Homeric corpus, in whole or in part, as objective art.[3] I will support this conclusion with an argument which strongly suggests that it is, in fact, the entirety of the Homeric corpus—that is, both the *Iliad* and the *Odyssey*—that he considered to be objective art. But first let us examine the distinction between the two kinds of art.

A work of art inevitably evokes associations in an observer. In the case of ordinary art, these associations shape the observer's response. Different observers respond differently to a work of this kind of art since their associative mechanisms, conditioned by their experiences and predispositions, generate different associations. Since the response depends upon the observer (that is, since it varies from one observer to another), this kind of art is called subjective. Furthermore, not only is the response subjective, but so is the act of "creation," which depends upon the personal associations of the artist. Indeed, the term "creation" is not even appropriate since it implies intentionality, whereas an ordinary artist "creates" under the influence of associations that he does not control.

Objective art is another matter entirely. A work of this kind of art produces the same impression on every observer, and this is the impression that the artist intended to convey. While observers and artist alike experience their own associations, objective art works on another level. Consider two examples described by Gurdjieff:

> I saw some examples of architecture in Persia and Turkey—for instance, one building of two rooms. Everyone who entered these rooms, whether old or young, whether English or Persian, wept. This happened with people of different backgrounds and education. We continued this experiment for two or three weeks and observed everyone's reactions. The result was always the same. We specifically chose cheerful people. With these architectural combinations, the mathematically calculated vibrations contained in the building could not produce any other effect. We are under certain laws and cannot withstand external influences. Because the architect of this building had a different understanding and built mathematically, the result was always the same.
>
> ...
>
> You come to a monastery. You are not a religious man, but what is played and sung there evokes in you a desire to pray. Later you will be surprised by this. And so it is with everyone.
>
> This objective art is based on laws, whereas modern music is entirely subjective.

Quote 9.3: *Views*, p. 184–185

As indicated here, objective art is possible because we are all subject to external influences whose action on us conforms to certain laws. An understanding of these laws enables one to create a work that will have a predictable effect on those who observe it.

The ability to produce a predictable effect on all observers implies the ability to communicate. It should be possible, then, to encode a message in the impressions produced by a work of objective art, and it should be possible to transmit knowledge by this means. This idea helps explain the following claim made by Gurdjieff:

> In the past, art served the same purpose as is served today by books—the purpose of preserving and transmitting certain knowledge. In ancient times they did not write books but expressed knowledge in works of art.
>
> Quote 9.4: *Views*, p. 182–183

It also underlies his remark that "in the legend of Orpheus there are hints of objective music, for Orpheus used to impart knowledge by music."[4] This does not mean that all objective art is intended to impart knowledge. For example, the works of objective architecture and music described in quote 9.3 create definite impressions, but do not necessarily convey any knowledge. Nevertheless, we shall be concerned mainly with objective art that is intended to communicate knowledge.

It is actually an oversimplification to say that a work of objective art produces the same impression on every observer. Gurdjieff distinguishes different levels of consciousness (see section 9.6), and people may be considered to belong to different levels corresponding to their respective levels of consciousness. A work of objective art will produce different impressions on people of different levels,[5] who will nevertheless, "each according to his own level, receive the same ideas and the same feelings that the artist wanted to transmit to them."[6] Perhaps we may suppose that the "picture" (the collection of ideas and feelings) that the artist wanted to transmit is received in clearer focus by people with higher levels of consciousness. The picture may be just a blur for people on the lowest levels: "people of lower levels will never receive from it what people of higher levels receive."[7] Gurdjieff offers this analogy:

> "Imagine some scientific work—a book on astronomy or chemistry. It is impossible that one person should understand it in one way and another in another way. Everyone who is sufficiently prepared and who is able to read this book will understand what the author means, and precisely as the author means it. An objective work of art is just such a book, except that it affects the emotional and not only the intellectual side of man."
>
> Quote 9.5: *Fragments*, p. 27

Like a scientific book, a work of objective art has a definite meaning, but can be understood only by someone with the necessary preparation. Gurdjieff elaborates on this in relation to his own writings:

> [I]n Beelzebub [*Beelzebub's Tales*] ... there is everything one must know. It is a very interesting book. Everything is there. ... But one must understand, and to understand depends on one's individuality. The more man has been instructed in a certain way, the more he can see. Subjectively, everyone is able to understand according to the level he occupies, for it is an objective

book, and everyone should understand something in it. One person understands one part, another a thousand times more.

Quote 9.6: Gurdjieff, *Transcripts*, p. 69

Gurdjieff's pupil A. R. Orage asserts that *Beelzebub's Tales* is an objective work of art,[8] and Gurdjieff seems to confirm this assessment here by calling it an objective book. Indeed, it would be surprising if it were otherwise, given his attitude towards subjective art expressed in quotes 9.1 and 9.2. As a work of objective art, it communicates knowledge to readers in proportion to their ability to understand.

The terms "objective art" and "subjective art" do not appear anywhere in the writings of Gurdjieff, not even in the chapter on art in *Beelzebub's Tales*. This is not surprising, as in his writing Gurdjieff avoids, or uses very sparingly, much of the terminology from the early phase of his oral teaching. The art chapter of *Beelzebub's Tales* does discuss two kinds of art, however, and they correspond to objective art and subjective art. According to Beelzebub, the word "art" was coined in antiquity to designate a means for transmitting knowledge to future generations through sculpture, painting, music, theater, and so on.[9] This clearly refers to objective art (more precisely, to objective art that is used to transmit knowledge). Beelzebub tells his grandson that the principles of art, in the original sense of the word, were gradually forgotten, and that this art was almost completely replaced by a degenerate form which, although it also goes by the name "art," contributes nothing to the lofty aim of the original art but, on the contrary, exerts an insidious influence on man's psyche.[10] This degenerate form, which includes almost all of contemporary art, is surely to be identified as subjective art.

The crucial contribution of the art chapter of *Beelzebub's Tales* to the present discussion concerns the method by which knowledge was to be transmitted to future generations through works of genuine (objective) art. The basic idea was that a work of art would produce in the observer unexpected and unusual experiences which would convey in coded form the knowledge that one wishes to transmit.[11] An architect, for example, would design the interior of a building to produce definite impressions on an observer in accordance with the law called "Daivibrizkar," which describes how the vibrations arising in the atmosphere of enclosed spaces influence beings in particular ways (this is clearly what is spoken of in quote 9.3). But the interior would be designed in such a way that someone who entered the building would experience the impressions not in the anticipated order usual for the given type of building but in some other order, and it was in the deviations from the expected order that the architect would somehow place the information he wished to transmit to future generations.[12]

Thus, Gurdjieff asserts that knowledge can be communicated to someone observing a work of art through deviations from what the observer expects. Here we see a possible framework for understanding the significance of perverse inconsistency. For I submit that a perverse inconsistency is a quintessential deviation from what is expected: one is inevitably taken aback if, for example, one sees a previous assertion contradicted for no apparent reason. The idea that this is at least part of what Gurdjieff has in mind would seem to be confirmed by *Beelzebub's Tales*, itself an objective work of art intended to communicate knowledge and characterized by the presence of perverse inconsistencies. Perverse inconsistency in a work that is said to be objective strongly suggests that these two highly unusual properties are connected, in which case *Beelzebub's Tales* would seem to have been written in accordance with the ideas explained in its own chapter on art.[13] If this rationale accounts for the perverse inconsistencies in *Beelzebub's Tales*, it is safe to assume that it also applies to the inconsistencies in *Meetings with Remarkable Men*, which must also be a work of objective art.

Let us look at Homer in this light. Since Gurdjieff considered only objective art to be worthy of the name "art," he would never have alluded to the *Odyssey*, hinting that it possesses an unsuspected significance, if he did not consider the poem to be a work of objective art. Therefore, as noted at the beginning of this section, the allusions to the *Odyssey* in *Meetings with Remarkable Men* discussed in chapter 8 suggest that he regarded the *Odyssey* as objective art. We now see that this conclusion offers a possible explanation for the perverse inconsistency in the poem. Unless an alternative explanation for this strange phenomenon can be supplied, the existence of perverse inconsistencies in the *Odyssey* provides another reason for regarding that poem as objective art. Since the *Iliad* also contains perverse inconsistencies, I believe that this poem also is a work of objective art and that Gurdjieff's allusions to the *Odyssey* were intended to refer to the Homeric corpus as a whole.

In section 7.5 I made two general observations consistent with the idea that perverse inconsistencies play the same role in Homer and Gurdjieff. Nevertheless, in the absence of a detailed understanding of the principles of objective art, which I do not possess and which others who have commented on this subject (apart from Gurdjieff, of course)[14] probably would not claim either, the idea that the Homeric epics are objective art can be no more than a hypothesis. It is a very attractive hypothesis, however, as it accounts for Gurdjieff's treatment of the *Odyssey* in *Meetings with Remarkable Men* and, more importantly, for the extraordinary phenomenon of perverse inconsistency in Homer. I shall discuss the implications of this hypothesis for the Homeric Question in section 9.6.

It is important that there be no confusion regarding a certain elementary point. Beelzebub recounts the origin of the idea of transmitting knowledge to future generations by encoding it in works of sculpture, painting, architecture, music, theater, and so on. It was this idea that was new, not the various vehicles or technologies (sculpture, painting, etc.) used to implement it.[15] This distinction is crucial to my thesis that the Homeric epics may be works of objective art, for it is well known that these epics employ poetic techniques and language that must have been developed over the course of many generations.[16] It is universally recognized that Homer drew on a long tradition; I am suggesting that what he created with the material and techniques provided by this tradition was even more unique than is generally realized.

In order to focus attention on what I believe is important, I have simplified my discussion of the art chapter of *Beelzebub's Tales* in one respect. When referring to the encoding of knowledge in a work of art by means of deviations from what the observer expects, I have concentrated on one easily grasped basis for the expectations of a reader: if, for example, an assertion *A* is followed at some point by a contradictory assertion *B*, then *A* is obviously the basis for the expectation that is violated by *B*. In Beelzebub's account, however, the observer's expectations are said to be based on a fundamental cosmic law called the Law of Sevenfoldness.[17] It is necessary to mention this because familiarity with this terminology will be needed later in this chapter. I have felt justified in ignoring this esoteric element in the present section for two reasons. First, in the architectural illustration that I paraphrased earlier, Beelzebub makes clear that the observer's expectations are based not only on the Law of Sevenfoldness but also simply on what is familiar from "the mechanical practice of centuries."[18] Second, at one point he seems to characterize the deviations from the Law of Sevenfoldness as "illogicality,"[19] which is in line with my emphasis on logical inconsistency.

I now address several other potential difficulties.

The overview of *All and Everything* in the front matter of *Beelzebub's Tales* states that all three parts of the trilogy were written "according to entirely new principles of logical reasoning." This presumably refers, at least in part, to the use of logical inconsistencies. If Homer's use of such inconsistencies is related to their use by Gurdjieff, then the principles of logical reasoning employed in *All and Everything* cannot be entirely new. While this objection to my hypothesis must be acknowledged, I do not take it too seriously, as Gurdjieff may mean only that the method of exposition in *All and Everything* will be new to the reader, a warning which he goes on to repeat in the first chapter of *Beelzebub's Tales*.[20]

According to the art chapter of *Beelzebub's Tales*, the method for using art to transmit knowledge to future generations was devised at a conference of learned men who had been brought by coercion to Babylon from Egypt by a Persian king.[21] This account is properly situated with respect to the life of Pythagoras, who, according to Beelzebub, was instrumental in the organization of the conference and who, according to Iamblichus, was brought forcibly to Babylon from Egypt by the Persian king Cambyses.[22] The historical setting places the conference late in the sixth century BCE, more than a century after Homer. Beelzebub's account therefore contradicts the hypothesis that the said method for transmitting knowledge is implemented in the Homeric epics. Fortunately, the contradiction need not be taken seriously, since Beelzebub's account combines fact and fiction. What can be said for sure, as we shall see in section 9.5, is that in *Meetings with Remarkable Men* Gurdjieff indicates that the transmission of knowledge through objective art was conceived long before Pythagoras and long before Homer.

In a question-and-answer session with the public from which I have already quoted,[23] Gurdjieff associated objective art with Eastern ancient art. When asked "Does this mean that all Western art has no significance?" he replied, "I studied Western art after studying the ancient art of the East. To tell you the truth, I found nothing in the West to compare with Eastern art." This answer is the strongest evidence I know of against my thesis that Gurdjieff considered the Homeric epics to be objective art. However, when the questioner went on to ask specifically, "Haven't you found something similar [to the ancient art of the East] in the ancient art of the West?" Gurdjieff gave a lengthy response that did not answer the question. We cannot know whether this disconnect indicates deliberate evasion by Gurdjieff, an inaccurate reconstruction of the exchange, or something else. We do know that Gurdjieff would withhold information from his talks that he later divulged indirectly in his writings. My book on the enneagram documents one example of this, but the parallel is not exact since Gurdjieff explicitly acknowledged that he was withholding information concerning the enneagram in his talks with his pupils.

I conclude this section with a note on terminology. I have defined objective art as art that produces the same impression(s) on all observers. A special kind of objective art is used to preserve and transmit knowledge, which is encoded in the automatic impressions in a form which must be deciphered. This kind of objective art is the focus of the chapter on art in *Beelzebub's Tales* and is what I have in mind when I claim that Gurdjieff considered the *Iliad* and the *Odyssey* to be examples of objective art. In what follows, the term *objective art* will often refer to this kind of objective art, but will sometimes be used in its more general sense; where the meaning is not clear from the context, the more general meaning can be assumed.[24]

9.2. Generalized Cognitive Dissonance in Homer

In the preceding section I offered two arguments for the thesis that the Homeric epics are works of objective art. First, Gurdjieff alludes to the *Odyssey*, and he would not do this unless he considered that poem to be objective art. Second, the *Iliad* and the *Odyssey* exhibit a strange phenomenon—perverse inconsistency—that is explicable if they are objective art and that is actually observed in known works of such art (the writings of Gurdjieff in particular). The first argument requires some refinement (see section 9.7), but this is postponed until we have the necessary background in Gurdjieff's philosophy. In this section I expand the second argument by pointing to another strange phenomenon in the Homeric poems that makes sense within the framework of the art chapter of *Beelzebub's Tales*.

We recall that objective art transmits knowledge through unexpected experiences engendered in the observer. Perverse inconsistency is one method that can be used to produce unexpected experiences. In this book I have focused our attention on this method because an inconsistency is relatively easy to detect, and its perverseness can be inferred from indications of intentionality together with the absence of any apparent reason for its existence. But there are, of course, other ways to produce unexpected and unusual experiences in the observer. Let us return to the art chapter of *Beelzebub's Tales* for an illustration of another method.

Beelzebub explains how musicians in antiquity produced unusual experiences in their listeners:

> "Owing to these sequences of sounds which they combined simultaneously in the presences of beings, different kinds of impulses arose, which evoked various quite opposite sensations, and these sensations in their turn produced unusual experiencings in them and reflex movements not proper to them."
>
> Quote 9.7: *BT*, p. 490

He then gives an example based on his own experience:

"[T]he localization of my consciousness, or ... my 'thinking center,' engendered in my common presence, let us suppose, the impulse of joy; the second localization in me, or my 'feeling center,' engendered the impulse called 'sorrow'; and the localization of the body itself, or ... my 'moving center,' engendered the impulse of 'religiousness.'

"And it was just in these unusual impulses engendered in the beings by their musical and vocal melodies that they indicated what they wished."

Quote 9.8: *BT*, p. 491

Here we are concerned not with logical inconsistencies, impossibilities, but with conflicting experiences which produce another kind of cognitive dissonance. An unusual combination of concurrent experiencings is itself an unexpected experience and therefore provides another tool for the transmission of knowledge through objective art. I believe that Homer makes use of this technique as well.

In the famous scene at the Skaian gates, Hektor says to Andromache,

"*For I know this thing well in my heart, and my mind knows it: there will come a day when sacred Ilion shall perish, and Priam, and the people of Priam of the strong ash spear.*
But it is not so much the pain to come of the Trojans
that troubles me, not even of Priam the king nor Hekabe,
not the thought of my brothers who in their numbers and valor
shall drop in the dust under the hands of men who hate them,
as troubles me the thought of you, when some bronze-armored
Achaian leads you off, taking away your day of liberty,
in tears; ..."

Quote 9.9: *Il.* 6.447–456 (italics added)

The meeting of Hektor and Andromache is the most poignant scene in all of Homer. Yet the poignancy is mixed with a dissonant element that will be felt by the attentive reader or listener, for Hektor's prediction of the fall of Troy is an echo of the prediction made by a furious Agamemnon when the Trojan Pandaros breaks a truce between the Greeks and the Trojans by wounding Menelaos with an arrow:

"... [The Trojans] must pay a great penalty,
with their own heads, and with their women, and with their children.
*For I know this thing well in my heart, and my mind knows it:
there will come a day when sacred Ilion shall perish,
and Priam, and the people of Priam of the strong ash spear*[.]"

Quote 9.10: *Il.* 4.161–165 (italics added)

The same words are uttered by the man who is eager for the sack of Troy and the man who dreads it, by the pitiless man hungry for vengeance and the blameless man whose world will be destroyed. Martin Mueller remarks, "Most modern readers will find the echo disturbing and wish the words had been reserved for Hektor, in whose mouth they resonate with pathos and irony, an effect that is undercut by the vindictive certainty of the hysterical Agamemnon."[25] This disturbing effect, achieved without logical inconsistency, is an example of what I am calling generalized cognitive dissonance. A. R. Orage may have had this kind of effect in mind when, in his commentary on the art chapter of *Beelzebub's Tales*, he refers to "the artist's wish to disturb the beholders, not just to please."[26]

Was Homer insensitive to the interaction between quotes 9.9 and 9.10, or did he consciously repeat the italicized verses in order to unsettle the reader by means of the resulting interaction? Some scholars will claim that no significance can be attached to the repetition of the three italicized lines since the reuse of verse fragments, entire verses, and even multiple verses is a well-known characteristic of oral poetry.[27] However, other students of Homer realize that some repetitions serve a recognizable literary function. A prime example is the use of the same passage of 3.5 lines for the two most important deaths in the *Iliad*, those of Patroklos and Hektor.[28] But this clear example of meaningful repetition is very different from the specimen under discussion, where a passage of three lines appears in entirely different contexts in quotes 9.9 and 9.10. Nevertheless, there is evidence to suggest that the latter repetition is also intentional, that is, done for effect and not for economy of effort.

What is strange about quotes 9.9 and 9.10, of course, is that the same words concerning the expected fall of Troy are spoken by the victor and the victim. Although it may seem unlikely that Homer would intentionally forge a link between the conqueror and the conquered, he unmistakably does precisely this in the *Odyssey*. When Demodokos sings about the Wooden Horse and the sack of Troy, the reaction of Odysseus, who devised the stratagem of the Wooden Horse and led the sack of Troy, is to weep like a woman who is being led away into slavery as her husband lies dying during the sack of their city:

> So the famous singer sang his tale, but Odysseus
> melted, and from under his eyes the tears ran down, drenching
> his cheeks. As a woman weeps, lying over the body
> of her dear husband, who fell fighting for her city and people
> as he tried to beat off the pitiless day from city and children;
> she sees him dying and gasping for breath, and winding her body
> about him she cries high and shrill, while the men behind her,
> hitting her with their spear butts on the back and the shoulders,
> force her up and lead her away into slavery, to have
> hard work and sorrow, and her cheeks are wracked with pitiful weeping.
> Such were the pitiful tears Odysseus shed ...
>
> Quote 9.11: *Od.* 8.521–531

It is not difficult to imagine that the poet who composed this passage comparing the victor to the victim deliberately created the surprising correspondence between the italicized portions of quotes 9.9 and 9.10.

In addition to supporting the notion of a deliberate correspondence between quotes 9.9 and 9.10, quote 9.11 may itself be an instance of Homer intentionally giving his audience an experience of cognitive dissonance. Coming immediately after an account of Odysseus's participation in the sack of Troy, the simile likening his weeping to that of a devastated woman being widowed during the sack of her city has a jarring effect. In the words of one critic, "the power of this utterly 'untypical' simile derives from its shock value."[29] Another aspect of the simile's dissonance becomes apparent when we understand why Odysseus weeps in response to the song of Demodokos.

Whereas the woman who is wrenched from her dying husband to be led away into slavery wails involuntarily from the heart, I argued in chapter 1 that Odysseus weeps in accordance with a premeditated scheme devised by his calculating mind. One arouses in us the emotion of pity, the other elicits mental admiration. The simile thus produces in us an unusual combination of concurrent experiencings, much like the conflicting experiences evoked by quote 9.9 with the recall of quote 9.10 triggered by the common lines in these two passages.

This analysis enables us to see a close connection between the simile in quote 9.11 and another notorious simile in the *Odyssey*. Menelaos is indignant when he hears from Telemachos about the suitors of Penelope and their outrageous behavior, and he uses a simile to describe what will happen to them when mighty Odysseus returns home:

> "Just as when a deer leaves her two new-born suckling fawns to sleep in a mighty lion's den, while she goes looking for pasture over the mountain spurs and grassy glens, and then the lion comes back to his lair and brings a horrible fate on both the fawns — so Odysseus will bring a horrible fate on those men."
>
> Quote 9.12: *Od.* 4.335–340 (Hammond trans.[30])

The problem with the simile is that, unlike the suitors, the fawns do not deserve their fate.[31] Just as we feel pity for the distraught woman in quote 9.11 but not for cunning Odysseus, we feel pity for the innocent fawns but not for the lawless suitors. Once again Homer creates an experience of dissonance, as satisfaction at the anticipated destruction of the suitors is combined in us with pity for the fawns to whom the suitors are compared.

We now consider another unexpected experience that the poet produces in the reader or listener without the aid of logical inconsistency. When Deïphobos goes in search of Aineias for help in his confrontation with the Greek hero Idomeneus, he finds him

> ... at the uttermost edge of the battle
> standing, since he was forever angry with brilliant Priam
> because great as he was he did him no honor among his people.
>
> Quote 9.13: *Il.* 13.459–461

This passage is startling in two respects. First, one immediately recognizes in these few lines a condensation of the foundational circumstances of the *Iliad*: a hero has withdrawn from the fighting in anger at the king for the latter's failure to show him the respect he deserves.[32] Second, the transfer of the roles of Achilles and Agamemnon to Aineias and Priam is contrived and fleeting, without either motivation or consequence in the story line: nowhere else in the poem do we see Aineias hanging back from the fighting, nowhere else is there any hint that he is angry at Priam, and nowhere else are we told that he has been dishonored by him.[33] One is taken aback to see the circumstances of the Quarrel reproduced in a context of such diminished scale and significance. It is as if these lines, which serve no narrative function,[34] were designed specifically to deliver a jolt to the audience. In the lines that follow, Deïphobos appeals to Aineias for help, and Aineias springs into action, as our previous acquaintance with the character would lead us to expect: once the jolt has been delivered, everything goes back to normal as if nothing had happened, and in relation to quote 9.13 one is left to wonder, "What was *that*?"

Previously we saw that Homer jarringly links the conqueror and the conquered both in the *Iliad* (quotes 9.9 and 9.10) and in the *Odyssey*, in Odysseus's reaction (quote 9.11) to the third song of Demodokos. Now we see another striking parallel between the two poems: both quote 9.13 and the first song of Demodokos (quote 5.10; see discussion in section 5.3*b*) allude to the Quarrel and surprise the reader or listener by reframing it in an unexpected context.[35] I suggest in passing that these two parallels add to the case made for unity of authorship in section 6.12, as they are more subtle than what one would expect from an *Odyssey* poet imitating another poet's *Iliad*.

My last example requires a longer discussion. The reader should feel free to skip this and go directly to the concluding paragraph of this section.

The simile in quote 9.11, which describes the sack of a city from the viewpoint of the conquered, appears in the context of a description of the sack of Troy from the viewpoint of the conquerors (the third song of Demodokos). We now examine another simile which inverts the main narrative.[36] When Priam enters the dwelling of Achilles to ransom the body of Hektor, the amazement of Achilles and his companions at the sight of Priam is compared to the reaction of a household to the arrival of a fugitive from another country:

… As when dense disaster closes on one who has murdered
a man in his own land, and he comes to the country of others,
to a man of substance, and wonder seizes on those who behold him,
so Achilleus wondered as he looked on Priam, a godlike
man, and the rest of them wondered also, and looked at each other.

Quote 9.14: *Il.* 24.480–484

Priam is represented in the simile by a man who has gone into exile after killing someone. It is understood that this man intends to supplicate the "man of substance" for his protection (we know that Peleus received two such suppliants, and Telemachos also gives his protection to a fugitive who has killed someone[37]). Priam himself has already adopted the position of a suppliant, grasping the knees of the man who killed his son.[38] The most obvious of several inversions that are typically mentioned[39] is that the killer in the simile is the suppliant, while the killer in the main narrative is the man who is supplicated. The most important inversion, however, is that the suppliant in the simile seeks the protection of the man he supplicates, while the suppliant in the main narrative approaches the man he supplicates at great risk to his own life. The latter reversal is the most important because it relates directly to the comparison made by the simile, as I shall now discuss.

When Priam tells his wife that he is going to the Greek ships to ransom the body of their son from Achilles, she tries to dissuade him:

"How can you wish to go alone to the ships of the Achaians
before the eyes of a man who has slaughtered in such numbers
such brave sons of yours? The heart in you is iron. For if
he has you within his grasp and lays eyes upon you, that man
who is savage and not to be trusted will not take pity upon you
nor have respect for your rights."

Quote 9.15: *Il.* 24.203–208

Indeed, Achilles' unquenchable thirst for revenge against the Trojans after the death of Patroklos and the continued expression of his rage in his ruthless treatment of Hektor's body leave little doubt in the mind of any onlooker that he would kill the man who is both the king of Troy and the father of his companion's killer. Priam acknowledges the obvious danger in his reply. Although he has been assured by a messenger from Zeus that Achilles will not kill him, he indicates that his decision to go does not depend on this assurance:

> "If it is my destiny
> to die there by the ships of the bronze-armored Achaians,
> then I wish that. Achilleus can slay me at once, with my own son
> caught in my arms, once I have my fill of mourning above him."
>
> Quote 9.16: *Il.* 24.224–227

It is because Priam seems to be courting almost certain death at the hands of Achilles that Achilles and his companions are amazed at his arrival. In fact, even after he has been supplicated by Priam and the two have wept together over their respective losses, Achilles expresses his astonishment in words that closely parallel the first lines of quote 9.15:[40]

> "How could you dare to come alone to the ships of the Achaians
> and before my eyes, when I am one who have killed in such numbers
> such brave sons of yours? The heart in you is iron."
>
> Quote 9.17: *Il.* 24.519–521

A little later we are told that Achilles must control himself to obey Zeus and not to kill Priam.[41] It is clear from all this that Priam has taken a great risk by going to Achilles, a risk that fully accounts for the wonder that Achilles and his companions feel at his arrival.

By contrast, there is nothing surprising, either psychologically or socially, about a fugitive seeking refuge and therefore little to motivate the wonder that the fugitive is said to arouse in quote 9.14. C. W. Macleod comments that "the bystanders are amazed simply at the unexpectedness of the arrival [of the fugitive]."[42] This motivation is so feeble in comparison with the ample motivation for the astonishment of Achilles and his companions that it undermines the point of the simile, which is to equate the wonder evoked by Priam with that evoked by the fugitive.[43] I suggest that the flimsy motivation and its unsettling effect on the reader may have been intentional. Closer examination of the simile will support this suggestion by showing that Homer acknowledges the disparity between the wonder evoked by Priam and that evoked by the fugitive.

The Greek word that Lattimore translates as "disaster" in quote 9.14 is $\alpha\tau\eta$. It means delusion, folly, blindness of mind, and Lattimore correctly translates it as "delusion" in quote 3.2 (*Il.* 19.88 and 91). Why he chooses to give it a different meaning in quote 9.14 can be understood as follows. Macleod declares that, while one would expect the $\alpha\tau\eta$ of the murderer in quote 9.14 to refer to the impulse which made him commit murder, the phrasing actually "suggests that $\alpha\tau\eta$ causes what the man does *after* the murder."[44] This reading is surprising—where is the folly in a murderer's flight to safety in exile?—and not everyone agrees with it.[45] But consider this alternative to Lattimore's translation:

> As a thick cloud of delusion possesses a man who, after murdering someone in his own country, seeks refuge abroad in the home of a wealthy man, and the onlookers are astounded, so Achilles was astounded when he saw godlike Priam. The others were astounded too and exchanged glances.
> Quote 9.18: *Il.* 24.480–484 (Rieu, Jones, and Rieu trans.)

The translators here, in accordance with Macleod's reading, associate $ατη$ with what the man does after the murder. Lattimore does the same in quote 9.14. Unable to see folly in a murderer's flight to safety, however, he renders $ατη$ as "disaster" since disaster closing in on a murderer might well impel him to seek refuge in another country.[46] Let us agree with Macleod, then, that Homer transfers the action of $ατη$ from the act of murder to what the man does after the murder. Why does he do this?

Macleod's answer is that Homer wishes to fit the simile to the main narrative: since it seems crazy and reckless for Priam to go to Achilles, the simile can be shaped to the narrative if the fugitive is said to be under the influence of $ατη$.[47] Furthermore, the result of this supposed influence of $ατη$ is that the wonder evoked by the fugitive becomes comparable to the wonder evoked by Priam, as asserted by the simile. But since there is no basis for blaming the murderer's flight to safety on $ατη$, Homer is essentially acknowledging that the wonder evoked by the fugitive is *not* comparable to that evoked by Priam. The poet has supplied a simile that is clearly fraudulent, and this must have a disturbing effect on the attentive reader or listener.

The *Iliad* and the *Odyssey* both contain numerous dissonant elements. Many of these are probably Homeric "nods" or the consequences of formulaic composition (or both).[48] In this section and in chapters 5 and 6, however, I have called attention to passages where the dissonant effect seems to be intentional. The existence of these intentional dissonances demands an explanation. My suggestion, of course, is that the explanation is to be found in the chapter on art in *Beelzebub's Tales*.

9.3. The Inconsistency of Aksharpanziar

I now interrupt the argument of this chapter to provide more evidence of perverse inconsistency in the writings of Gurdjieff. As in chapter 7 and in sections 8.2 and 8.6, my approach is to document inconsistency within the context of whatever I happen to be discussing, the idea being that the ability to do this repeatedly will give the reader a sense of its pervasiveness and hence (one must assume in the case of Gurdjieff) its intentionality. And in fact a fine specimen lies at the heart of Beelzebub's tale concerning the origin of art that is used to transmit knowledge to future generations. I begin with some terminology.

According to Beelzebub, an *initiate* is someone who, thanks to suitable work on himself or herself, has acquired certain merits that can be sensed by others and that evoke in them trust and respect. The term *legominism* refers to a method for transmitting information from generation to generation through a chain of initiates.[49] In a closely related usage of the term, *a legominism* is an instance of the vehicle used to transmit information by this method. The legominism concerning the deliberations of Ashiata Shiemash (see section 7.2) is an example of the latter usage.

The probable derivation of *legominism* from the Greek verb λεγω (I say, I tell) and, in particular, from the passive participle λεγομενον (as in "hapax legomenon," something said only once) implies that the term denotes an oral communication.[50] That a legominism is not merely a written document that is passed along a chain of initiates is confirmed by the assertion that the transmission of knowledge by means of a legominism is accomplished by initiates through their "ableness-to-be."[51] A document may contain the contents of a legominism in the form of words on a page (this is what we have in the chapter of *Beelzebub's Tales* on the legominism concerning the deliberations of Ashiata Shiemash), but the full meaning of a legominism can only be transmitted directly from one initiate to another, somewhat as the voices, postures, and movements of actors on a stage add to the meaning of their written dialogue. For this reason, it may be said in passing, the common practice of referring to *Beelzebub's Tales* as Gurdjieff's legominism is, at best, an oversimplification.[52]

Beelzebub recounts how Pythagoras and another man, themselves both initiates, came to realize that for some reason wars cause the death of a disproportionate number of initiates and the corresponding loss of many legominisms. They decided to take advantage of the presence in Babylon of many learned beings to convene a conference that would address this worrisome situation. Early in this conference, a well-known learned being, the great Aksharpanziar, gave a speech that set the course for the remainder of the proceedings. In his speech, Aksharpanziar explained why many initiates lose their lives in times of war and what he thought should be done to deal with this problem.[53] His advice was to continue without change the transmission of knowledge through initiates by means of legominisms, but to supplement this approach with a new method in which the knowledge to be transmitted would be encoded in works of "art" (a term coined by Aksharpanziar to be explained in a moment) by means of deviations from the Law of Sevenfoldness, that is, by means of inexactitudes in this law intentionally embedded in these works of art. The key needed to interpret the inexactitudes employed in a given branch of art would be provided in a legominism which would be transmitted from generation to generation through initiates. These initiates would be called initiates of art, because the transmission of knowledge by this method would not be natural but artificial.

The inconsistency is obvious: in order to overcome a flaw inherent in the transmission of knowledge through initiates by means of legominisms, Aksharpanziar suggests a method of transmission that also relies on legominisms and their transmission through initiates. I have simplified my summary of Aksharpanziar's presentation to make this inconsistency as plain as possible. Let us now take a closer look.

When Aksharpanziar proposes his idea, he suggests that, for the key to the inexactitudes, "we shall further make in our productions *something like* a Legominism" (italics added). Thus, the key to the inexactitudes is not actually a legominism: it is not an oral communication, but something made in the same medium as the works of art ("productions").[54] What the key shares with

9.3. THE INCONSISTENCY OF AKSHARPANZIAR

true legominisms is the essential property that it is transmitted through initiates, and these initiates, though they are of a special kind, would presumably also be prone to die in wars in disproportionate numbers. In fact, by the end of the art chapter, we know without a doubt that Aksharpanziar's method suffers from the flaw that was to be corrected or something similar to it.

After illustrating at length the application of Aksharpanziar's idea to various branches of art, Beelzebub explains to his grandson what eventually became of this idea as a result of the propensity of human beings for "reciprocal destruction" (Beelzebub's term for war):

> "Thanks to their chief particularity, namely, to the 'periodic-process-of-reciprocal-destruction,' there almost wholly disappeared from amongst the ordinary beings there, soon after the period of the 'Babylonian-magnificence,' not only the Legominisms[55] concerning the keys to the lawful inexactitudes in the Law of Sevenfoldness ..., but, as I have already told you, there gradually also disappeared even the very notion of ... the Law of Sevenfoldness.
>
> "Every kind of conscious production of the beings of the Babylonian period was gradually destroyed, partly owing to decay from time and partly owing to the processes of 'reciprocal destruction,' ...
>
> ...
>
> "...[T]hanks to the second mentioned cause, there also gradually diminished and finally almost entirely ceased the employment of that new form—which had been established since Babylonian times—for the transmission of information and various fragments of knowledge to subsequent generations, through the beings they called 'Initiates-of-Art.'
>
> "About the disappearance there of just that practice of certain beings becoming Initiates-of-Art I know very well, because just before my departure forever from that planet I had to elucidate this very carefully for another aim of mine.
>
> ...
>
> "So then, I made it clear that there in most recent times only four of such beings, Initiates-of-Art, still remained by means of whose what is called 'immediate-line-of-inheritance' the keys to the understanding of the ancient art still continue to be transmitted, and this transmission by inheritance now proceeds there under very complex and arcane conditions."
>
> Quote 9.19: *BT*, pp. 517–518

Thus, Aksharpanziar's scheme did turn out to have the same vulnerability as the method of transmission it was intended to supplement: the keys to the inexactitudes (here called legominisms without qualification) and the initiates needed to pass these keys to future generations almost entirely disappeared as a consequence of war. Although there are possible hints in this passage that the flaw in Aksharpanziar's scheme may not be identical to that in the original method (the disappearance of the practice of certain beings becoming initiates of art; the role of inheritance), the strong parallels that do exist show at a minimum that Gurdjieff flirts with an inconsistency between the problem identified by Pythagoras and the solution proposed by Aksharpanziar.

We are now finished with "the inconsistency of Aksharpanziar" referred to in the title of this section, but there is another inconsistency I wish to point out. When he proposes the transmission of knowledge by means of the Law of

Sevenfoldness in works of art, Aksharpanziar asserts that it can "boldly be said that the knowledge indicated in this manner in the mentioned productions will exist ... forever on the Earth" because the Law of Sevenfoldness "will be seen and understood by men in all times as long as human thought exists on the Earth."[56] According to the first paragraph of quote 9.19, however, the notion of the Law of Sevenfoldness gradually disappeared as a consequence of war. Aksharpanziar was evidently mistaken. This is *not* the inconsistency I wish to point out, however; it is simply an error, and I mention it only to make this distinction clear. Rather, the inconsistency I have in mind concerns the reason given for the disappearance of awareness of the Law of Sevenfoldness. In quote 9.19, where this disappearance is blamed on war, Beelzebub reminds his grandson that he has mentioned it before. In fact, earlier in the art chapter, Beelzebub did say that human beings no longer even suspect the existence of the Law of Sevenfoldness, but that time he blamed a deterioration in the quality of human "being-rumination" that took place in the interval between the Babylonian civilization and the present day.[57] Beelzebub offers yet another explanation in a later chapter: at one time, he asserts, the action of a certain cosmic law caused a temporary loss of judgment on the part of the initiates who transmitted the knowledge of the Law of Sevenfoldness from generation to generation, as a consequence of which these initiates shared their knowledge with beings who distorted it with their speculations and ultimately almost destroyed it.[58] Thus, Beelzebub gives three mutually exclusive explanations for the disappearance of the awareness of the Law of Sevenfoldness. As these explanations give rise to inconsistencies on two scales (the explanation given in quote 9.19 is inconsistent with the explanations given 24 pages earlier and 325 pages later), this illustrates in a small way the idea of scale-free inconsistency discussed in section 7.5.

9.4. Gurdjieff's Implementation of Aksharpanziar's Scheme

In section 9.1 I pointed out a connection between *Beelzebub's Tales* as a work of art and the kind of art whose description occupies the bulk of its own chapter on art. The basic idea behind the latter kind of art, which falls under the rubric "objective art," is to transmit knowledge by means of unexpected experiences deliberately engendered in the observer. The connection with *Beelzebub's Tales* is that the perverse inconsistencies in that work inevitably give rise to unexpected experiences in the reader. The same connection obviously applies to *Meetings with Remarkable Men*, which has its own share of perverse inconsistencies. I now support my suggestion that *Beelzebub's Tales* and *Meetings with Remarkable Men* are instances of the kind of art described in the art chapter of the former work by pointing to other connections with that chapter.

According to the scheme of Aksharpanziar described in the art chapter, unexpected experiences engendered by a work of objective art are produced by deviations from the Law of Sevenfoldness, and these deviations are to be understood with the aid of a specially prepared key. As I intend to explain elsewhere,[59] the First and Second Series contain deviations from the Law of Sevenfoldness, and the booklet entitled *The Herald of Coming Good* was intended to serve as the key to these deviations (among other functions). These parallels with the art chapter of *Beelzebub's Tales* reinforce the case for believing that *Beelzebub's Tales* and *Meetings with Remarkable Men* should be considered works of objective art. The latter conclusion strengthens the link between perverse inconsistency and objective art proposed in section 9.1 and with it the claim that the *Iliad* and the *Odyssey* are also works of objective art.

9.5. The Origin of Objective Art

I now interrupt my argument one last time to illustrate perverse inconsistency in the writings of Gurdjieff. This final example differs from the ones considered earlier in that it involves not inconsistency within *Beelzebub's Tales* or *Meetings with Remarkable Men* but inconsistency between these two works.[60] Whereas in section 9.3 we examined a perverse inconsistency within Beelzebub's tale concerning the origin of art that is used to transmit knowledge to future generations, we will discover that this tale is contradicted by information concerning this kind of art that Gurdjieff gives in the Second Series. In the last paragraph of this section, I will return to the main argument and show that the mentioned information from the Second Series resolves an historical issue raised in section 9.1.

According to Beelzebub, sacred dances constituted one of the vehicles used to transmit knowledge to posterity since the time of the Babylonian conference organized by Pythagoras.[61] In fact, says Beelzebub, this is the only branch of art from the Babylonian conference that has survived to the present day. In *Meetings with Remarkable Men*, Gurdjieff reports having witnessed sacred dances at a monastery in Central Asia,[62] and there can be no question that these sacred dances correspond in their nature to those mentioned by Beelzebub. To establish the correspondence, I must first supply a fact that I omitted in my previous discussion of legominisms.

In section 9.3 I defined a legominism as a vehicle for transmitting information from generation to generation through a chain of initiates. When he introduces the concept, Beelzebub states that the information transmitted via legominisms concerns events that have occurred on Earth in the distant past.[63] Without, for the moment, trying to understand what this might really mean, we may derive a simple consequence of this fact. Since Aksharpanziar's scheme for the transmission of knowledge through art was devised to compensate for the loss of legominisms, works of art implementing this scheme must have been intended to serve the same function as legominisms; that is, they must have been intended to transmit information about long-past events. However, this is not stated anywhere in *Beelzebub's Tales*. It may be worth pausing to note how this obvious conclusion is sidestepped (the present argument resumes after the next two paragraphs).

In the speech in which he proposes his scheme, Aksharpanziar twice characterizes legominisms as vehicles for the transmission of information about past events, but he goes on to characterize them more generally as vehicles for the transmission of true knowledge,[64] and he sticks with this more general formulation, or variants of it, when the subject turns to art as an alternative or supplement to legominisms. In particular, what he proposes to transmit to future generations through works of art is characterized as "useful information and true knowledge," knowledge that is "useful for our remote descendants," and "true knowledge."[65]

The reader will notice that Aksharpanziar wished to transmit knowledge that is useful. In fact, Beelzebub later refers to "the hidden knowledge and useful information" in the works of art produced at the time of the Babylonian conference.[66] But in what way is the information useful? Beelzebub tells his grandson that hidden in sacred dances is information that is useful for one's Being (i.e., for the development of one's Being).[67] This accords nicely with our inference that works of art were to transmit information about long-past events, for we learn in *Meetings with Remarkable Men* that a certain spiritual authority asserted that one can acquire a soul "only through voluntary and involuntary experiencings and information intentionally learned about real events which [have] taken place in the past."[68] In this connection I simply mention in passing the common and reasonable assumption that the events which supposedly occurred on Earth in the distant past and which are described in *Beelzebub's Tales* (an objective work of art) have a symbolic significance, the understanding of which presumably could assist the growth of one's Being.

Referring to the sacred dances that he witnessed at a monastery in Central Asia, Gurdjieff says that "the brethren may read in these dances one or another truth which men have placed there thousands of years before." He continues:

> These dances correspond precisely to our books. Just as is now done on paper, so, once, certain information about long past events was recorded in dances and transmitted from century to century to people of subsequent generations. And these dances are called sacred.
>
> Quote 9.20: *RM*, pp. 162–163

What is striking about this passage, apart from its correspondence with quote 9.4, is that here, in the Second Series, Gurdjieff finally makes explicit what is implicit in the First Series, that works of art were used to transmit information about long-past events.

This discussion demonstrates that the sacred dances of *Meetings with Remarkable Men* must correspond in their nature to those of *Beelzebub's Tales*. Further evidence for this correspondence will be cited in the next paragraph. Now we come to the crucial point: whereas Beelzebub traces the origin of sacred dances to late in the sixth century BCE, Gurdjieff indicates that the sacred dances he saw at the chief monastery of the Sarmoung Brotherhood originated at least 4500 years ago. Thus, the First and Second Series give conflicting accounts for the origin of the idea and practice of transmitting knowledge to future generations through works of art,[69] yet another illustration of intentional inconsistency in the writings of Gurdjieff.[70]

The date assigned to the origin of the sacred dances that Gurdjieff witnessed in Central Asia has particular significance for the argument of this book. If the practice of transmitting knowledge to future generations through works of art originated at the time of Pythagoras, as described in *Beelzebub's Tales*, this practice cannot be used to account for the perverse inconsistency we have observed in the poems of Homer, who lived at least a century before

Pythagoras. The much earlier date given for the sacred dances in *Meetings with Remarkable Men* solves this problem. For the solution to be complete, however, it is necessary to show that knowledge was encoded in the sacred dances witnessed by Gurdjieff by means of deviations from what the observer expects, as in the method devised by Aksharpanziar. While this cannot be proven, there are enough correspondences to suggest that this is what Gurdjieff meant to imply. First, he tells us that knowledge was encoded in the sacred dances he observed by means of an "alphabet" of postures; the use of an alphabet of postures to encode knowledge is also mentioned in the context of Aksharpanziar's method.[71] And second, the postures assumed by the dancers were in both cases based on the Law of Sevenfoldness.[72] It is difficult to escape the conclusion, stated somewhat prematurely in the preceding paragraph, that the sacred dances of *Meetings with Remarkable Men* were intended by Gurdjieff to correspond in their nature to those of *Beelzebub's Tales*. The passage on sacred dances in *Meetings with Remarkable Men* therefore removes the "historical" objection to the hypothesis that the Homeric epics are objective art which implements the principles explained in the chapter on art in *Beelzebub's Tales*. This is important not because we are dealing with actual history but because I can hardly claim that Gurdjieff suggests the mentioned hypothesis by alluding to Homer if that hypothesis cannot be reconciled with his own historical account. It may be significant, then, that the passage on sacred dances which makes the reconciliation possible is found in the work that alludes to the *Odyssey*.

9.6. The Unity of Homer the Man

If the Homeric epics are objective art, what does this tell us about Homer himself? This question is best approached from the standpoint of Gurdjieff's views on the nature of man, which encompass both what a human being *is* and what he or she *could be*. Referring to the latter, Gurdjieff says, "Man is a being who can do," where "'to do' means to act consciously and by one's own initiative."[73] Our conviction that we can *do* in this sense is, according to Gurdjieff, our chief delusion.[74] The reality is that

> everything without exception from beginning to end does itself in contemporary man, and there is nothing which a contemporary man himself does.
>
> In personal, family, and communal life, in politics, science, art, philosophy, and religion, in short, in everything entering into the process of the ordinary life of a contemporary man, everything from beginning to end does itself, and not a single one of these "victims of contemporary civilization" can "do" anything.
>
> Quote 9.21: *BT*, pp. 1202–1203

To see what this means, let us take the example of art. In the case of subjective art,

> "The artist ... does not create; with him 'it creates itself.' This means that he is in the power of ideas, thoughts, and moods which he himself does not understand and over which he has no control whatever. They rule him and they express themselves in one form or another."
>
> Quote 9.22: *Fragments*, p. 296

In other words, a work of subjective art is created by a process in which the artist plays only a passive role. Unaware of the forces acting on him, much less controlling them, the artist inevitably reacts to these forces, which thereby create *through him* something that he mistakenly goes on to attribute to himself. By contrast,

> "in objective art the artist really does 'create,' that is, he makes what he intended, he puts into his work whatever ideas and feelings he wants to put into it."
>
> Quote 9.23: *Fragments*, p. 296

The creation of a work of objective art proceeds from the initiative of the artist, who is conscious of the forces acting within him and is able to express what he intends and not what these forces would dictate. Such an artist lives on a much higher level than that of an ordinary person. He is what Gurdjieff would call a real man, someone who can *do*. If the Homeric epics are objective art, Homer was such a man.

The delusion that we can *do* is just one of a number of misconceptions we have about ourselves. Another is the illusion of "I."[75] Each of us is constantly saying or thinking "I," as if there were some permanent entity called "I." But instead of a single permanent I, an ordinary person has many small I's, each of which is activated under specific circumstances.[76] Some of these I's may be incompatible with others, as when a person has one I that always tells the truth and another I that will lie. Such a person may not see this contradiction in himself because the I's in question are set in motion under different conditions. Or he may interpret the contradiction in terms of a single individuality that adapts its behavior appropriately to changing circumstances. But this is a rationalization that will not withstand scrutiny. It is true that our behavior is governed by the conditions in which we find ourselves and, in particular, by the associations triggered by these conditions. Related associations, by their very nature, are linked together, whereas dissimilar associations are separate. Each of the small I's that jointly make up one's personality consists of a group of related associations and the behaviors to which they give rise.[77] The unique I or individuality in which we believe implicitly has no corresponding reality.

And yet Gurdjieff tells us that it is possible to create a single, permanent I. Indeed, the creation of a real I is the overarching aim of his teaching, as I mentioned in section 8.7. In the carriage model described in that section, the random stream of passengers who hire the carriage one after another is replaced by a single, permanent passenger, the owner of the carriage. The multiplicity that characterizes an ordinary person is replaced by the inner unity of a real man. I use the same term, "real man," that I have previously used for someone who can *do*, because the possession of a real I and inner unity goes hand in hand with the ability to *do*.[78] It follows that if the Homeric epics are objective art, then one of the fundamental characteristics that distinguishes Homer from most other people is unity.

Of all the properties of Gurdjieff's "real man," unity deserves special emphasis in the case of Homer since the issue of unity has played an important role in the history of the Homeric Question. As I observed in chapter 4, it is ironic that the inconsistencies in the poems of Homer which have given rise to vigorous and extended questioning of their unity of authorship can be used to argue that these poems were composed by someone who possessed an inner unity that is beyond the experience of Homeric scholars themselves as well as all other ordinary men and women.

That objective art requires an unusual unity is stated explicitly by Gurdjieff:

> "Objective art requires at least flashes of objective consciousness; in order to understand these flashes properly and to make proper use of them a great inner unity is necessary and a great control of oneself."
>
> Quote 9.24: *Fragments*, p. 298

By implication, these remarks elaborate on Gurdjieff's answer to the Homeric Question. In addition to confirming that Homer must have possessed inner unity, they tell us that he must have experienced at least flashes of objective consciousness. What Gurdjieff calls "objective consciousness" is what is sometimes called "enlightenment." It is a state in which "a man can see things *as they are*."[79] To understand this formulation, it is necessary to examine Gurdjieff's conception of an ordinary person in greater depth.

The properties of an ordinary person that we have considered so far, his lack of unity and a permanent I and his inability to *do*, can be traced to a level of consciousness akin to sleep:

> "Taken in itself, a man's being has many different sides. The most characteristic feature of a modern man is the *absence of unity in him* and, further, the absence in him of even traces of those properties which he most likes to ascribe to himself, that is, 'lucid consciousness,' 'free will,' a 'permanent ego or I,' and the 'ability to do.' It may surprise you if I say that the chief feature of a modern man's being which explains *everything else that is lacking in him* is *sleep*."
>
> Quote 9.25: *Fragments*, p. 66 (italics in original)

One's psychic life consists of the flow of various series of associations; this passive, associative existence is what Gurdjieff means by "sleep."[80] And indeed one is always caught up in associations as in a dream; any knowledge acquired in this state is mixed with dreams and is therefore subjective.[81] Thus, we begin to understand why Gurdjieff says that one can see things as they are only in a higher state of consciousness, the state that he calls objective consciousness.

We have seen that objective art can be created only by someone who can *do*. If it is impossible to *do* in sleep (quote 9.25[82]), why does objective art require only flashes of objective consciousness (quote 9.24)? The answer to this question lies in the existence of a well-defined state of consciousness between ordinary consciousness ("sleep") and objective consciousness. Gurdjieff calls this state *self-consciousness* or *self-remembering*.[83] The chief obstacle to the development of self-consciousness, which is a prerequisite for the attainment of objective consciousness, is our assumption that we are already in this state, or that we can be whenever we want to. The reality is that, while we may know what we are doing at a given moment, we do not feel ourselves doing it; we are out of touch with ourselves and consequently unaware of forces acting on us and within us, and do not realize all this because we are lost in our associations, our dreams. The development of self-consciousness is a significant achievement and is accompanied by the acquisition of inner unity, a permanent I, and the ability to *do*. Furthermore, in the state of self-consciousness one can have flashes of objective consciousness and remember them, something that is not possible in the ordinary state of consciousness. It follows that, in addition to experiencing at least flashes of objective consciousness, Homer must have achieved the state of self-consciousness or, perhaps more accurately, the ability to enter this state. This completes my explanation of Gurdjieff's answer to the Homeric Question.

My thesis that Homer was not only an extraordinary poet but an awakened individual and a remarkable man in the deepest sense depends to a large extent on the indications that some, perhaps many, of the inconsistencies in the *Iliad* and the *Odyssey* were intentional. To summarize the thesis and its empirical motivation, I take the liberty of appropriating Pope's couplet quoted in chapter 4:

> Those oft are stratagems which errors seem,
> Nor is it Homer nods, but we that dream.
> Quote 9.26: Pope, *An Essay on Criticism*, lines 179–180

Of course, Pope had in mind stratagems understandable to someone in an ordinary state of consciousness, stratagems involving intentional inconsistencies that I call comprehensible, whereas I have in mind stratagems of objective art employing intentional inconsistencies that are perverse from the viewpoint of our usual state of consciousness because their function cannot be understood or *felt* in this state.

Let us now return to the subject discussed in section 6.12: the question of common versus separate authorship for the *Iliad* and the *Odyssey*. According to the view of Homer just proposed, each poem was composed by someone with a level of consciousness that is extremely rare today and that must always have been unusual. It would seem unlikely that two gifted and innovative poets working in the same tradition around the same time happen to have both reached the required level of consciousness. This line of thinking leads us as before to infer that the two poems were composed by the same person. However, the scenario of two exceptional poets who lived around the same time and who both attained enlightenment becomes somewhat plausible if we suppose that the *Odyssey* poet was both the poetic apprentice and the spiritual pupil of the *Iliad* poet. We must take this possibility seriously because Gurdjieff, who was himself a teacher of sacred dances, mentions spiritual teachers who specialize in some art.[84] On balance, the difficulty of achieving objective consciousness inclines me to believe that one poet was responsible for both poems, but the alternative cannot be excluded.

Fortunately, the question of common versus separate authorship for the *Iliad* and the *Odyssey* is of secondary importance if the conception of Homer proposed here is valid. For this conception implies that even if the two poems were the work of different poets, these poets shared something more fundamental than poetic virtuosity, something which set them apart at deep level from the vast majority of other people.

9.7. Extension of the East-West Symmetry in *All and Everything*

Once it has been decided that the poems of Homer are objective art, the most important implications of this conclusion for the Homeric Question follow immediately from the ideas of Gurdjieff, as explained in the preceding section. The crucial step of the argument of this chapter, therefore, is the identification of the Homeric epics as works of objective art. In this section I show how a check on this identification is made possible by an extension of the symmetry argument used in section 8.7. There I argued that the existence in the writings of Gurdjieff of allusions to the ancient literature of the West is supported by the existence in those writings of allusions to the ancient literature of the East. Now I show that the symmetry between East and West extends to the significance of the mentioned allusions: whereas the allusions to the *Odyssey* can be understood (that is, justified) in terms of Gurdjieff's concept of objective art, the allusions to the Upanishads can be understood in terms of his related concept of objective knowledge.

Just as Gurdjieff distinguishes between subjective and objective art, he also distinguishes between subjective and objective knowledge.[85] The two distinctions parallel each other in that objective knowledge, like objective art, is possible only in the state of objective consciousness;[86] that is, objective knowledge can be discovered or understood only by someone in the state of objective consciousness, just as objective art can be created or fully understood only by someone in this state. Besides this parallel between them, objective knowledge and objective art are connected to each other:

> "In antiquity that which is now called art served the aim of objective knowledge. And ... works of art represented an exposition and a record of the eternal laws of the structure of the universe. Those who devoted themselves to research and thus acquired a knowledge of important laws, embodied them in works of art, just as is done in books today."
>
> Quote 9.27: *Views*, p. 32[87]

In view of the interrelationship between objective knowledge and objective art, together with the East-West symmetry discussed in section 8.7, the identification of the Homeric epics as works of objective art would be reinforced if we could establish a fundamental connection between the Upanishads and objective knowledge. In fact, this is easily done.

The key to recognizing objective knowledge in the Upanishads is found in these remarks of Gurdjieff:

> "One of the most central of the ideas of objective knowledge," said G. [Gurdjieff], "is the idea of the unity of everything, of unity in diversity. From ancient times people who have understood the content and the meaning of this idea, and have seen in it the basis of objective knowledge, have endeavored to find a way of transmitting this idea in a form comprehensible to others. The successive transmission of the ideas of objective knowledge has always been a part of the task of those possessing this knowledge. In such cases the idea of the unity of everything, as the fundamental and central

idea of this knowledge, had to be transmitted first and transmitted with adequate completeness and exactitude. ... [T]he idea itself was put either into a logical form, as for instance in philosophical systems which endeavored to give a definition of the 'fundamental principle' or αρχή from which everything else was derived, or into religious teachings which endeavored to create an element of faith and to evoke a wave of emotion carrying people up to the level of 'objective consciousness.'"

Quote 9.28: *Fragments*, pp. 278–279

Although it would be an oversimplification to claim that the Vedic Upanishads present a self-consistent philosophical system, it is no exaggeration to say that these documents show a preoccupation with what Gurdjieff calls the fundamental and central idea of objective knowledge, namely, the idea of the unity of everything. Joel Brereton devotes the greater part of his overview of the Upanishads to their persistent attempts to create an "integrative vision" of the world and of human experience.[88] He notes:

> The Upanishads often create such an integrative vision by identifying a single, comprehensive and fundamental principle which shapes the world. One term by which the Upanishads designate that fundamental principle is "*brahman*."

Quote 9.29: Brereton, "The Upanishads," p. 118

The Upanishads contain innumerable statements and discussions concerning the nature of the fundamental principle called *brahman*; indeed, it is partly owing to the importance given to this concept that the philosophy of the Upanishads (if we use the term "philosophy" for a body of related affirmations) is sometimes called Brahmanism.[89] These documents evidently represent just the kind of effort to transmit the idea of unity that Gurdjieff describes in quote 9.28.

To illustrate the unity of everything that exists, Gurdjieff quotes the formula "As above, so below," which he attributes to the Emerald Tablets of Hermes Trismegistus.[90] This formula asserts, among other things, that there is a correspondence between man (the "microcosm") and the universe (the "macrocosm").[91] Gurdjieff offers an original and majestic conception of this correspondence in *Beelzebub's Tales*,[92] but the details need not concern us. The important point is that the correspondence between the microcosm and the macrocosm is a recurring theme in the Upanishads. For example, one such correspondence (or, rather, set of correspondences) is given in one Upanishad in the context of a creation myth and in another Upanishad in the context of what happens when a person dies.[93] "One means of demonstrating unity behind apparent diversity," says Brereton, "is by displaying correspondences among things belonging to different domains."[94] Thus, the attention given in the Upanishads to the correspondence between the microcosm and the macrocosm is another manifestation of their preoccupation with the unity of everything existing.[95]

According to Gurdjieff, "people who have possessed objective knowledge have tried to express the idea of unity in 'myths,' in 'symbols,' and in particular 'verbal formulas' which, having been transmitted without alteration, have carried on the idea from one school to another, often from one epoch to another."[96] The preceding discussion suggests that the Upanishads belong to this stream of transmission. The connection between these documents and objective knowledge accounts for the allusions to them in *Beelzebub's Tales*, just as the identification of the Homeric epics as works of objective art explains the allusions to the *Odyssey* in *Meetings with Remarkable Men*. This extension of the East-West symmetry discussed in section 8.7 completes my argument for the proposition that Gurdjieff made the latter identification and therefore must have held the conception of Homer explained in the preceding section.

9.8. Concluding Remarks

Ordinary communication using words is necessarily subjective since a given word can evoke different associations in different people. Special measures—perhaps including inconsistencies such as those discussed in this book—must therefore be necessary for objective communication, whether written or spoken. Consider what Gurdjieff once said in a talk to pupils:

> In order to be understood by another man, it is not only necessary for the speaker to know how to speak but for the listener to know how to listen. This is why I can say that if I were to speak in a way I consider exact, everybody here, with very few exceptions, would think I was crazy.
>
> Quote 9.30: *Views*, p. 41

The impression of craziness would of course be created by someone whose spoken thoughts were filled with intentional inconsistencies, even if the nature and combination of the inconsistencies were actually informed by a high level of reason. But Gurdjieff indicates that such speech can be understood by someone who knows how to listen. Similarly, objective literature can be fully understood by someone who knows how to read it. Gurdjieff asserts that "the exact sense of all writing" must be perceived by means of a specific kind of mentation that is distinct from "thought, in which words, always possessing a relative sense, are employed."[97] The reference to "all writing" notwithstanding, I assume he has in mind objective writing since only this kind of writing (apart from technical descriptions) has an exact sense, the same for all readers of a given level. It then follows that the meaning of objective literature can be perceived only with the other kind of mentation, which he calls "mentation by form."[98] A clue to what this entails is found in Gurdjieff's statement that this kind of mentation is proper to both people and animals, although only the former are capable of the development of "mechanical instinct" that leads to the attainment of objective consciousness.[99]

If the *Iliad* and the *Odyssey* are works of objective art, anomalies that are usually regarded as signs of disunity are actually intentional devices that are meant to be understood with one's instinct and feeling (see quote 9.5 as well as Gurdjieff's account of the decipherment of a certain statue[100]) and presumably do not undermine the unity of the epics at a deep level whose existence has not previously been suspected. This is the explanation promised at the beginning of chapter 4 for the paradoxical combination of unity and apparent disunity in the poems of Homer.

Notes

CHAPTER 1: Wily Odysseus in Scheria

1. Auerbach, *Mimesis*, p. 6; M. Parry, "Traditional Epithet," p. 156. Similarly, on the more specific question of whether one can ever detect psychological motivation that is not made explicit by the poet, see the remarks of von der Mühll, Kakridis, Kirk, and Kirchhoff quoted in Griffin, *Life and Death*, pp. 51, 62.

2. Overviews of such theories are given by Emlyn-Jones ("Reunion," pp. 210–213) and Rutherford (*Books XIX and XX*, pp. 34–35).

3. Fenik, *Studies*, p. 47. The quotation is Fenik's response to the question of verisimilitude of Penelope's "surrender" that he raises on p. 46.

4. Waldock, *Sophocles*, pp. 11–24, esp. pp. 15–16, 18.

5. Griffin, *Life and Death*, pp. 61–65.

6. Waldock, *Sophocles*, pp. 211–214. See also ibid., p. 18, where Waldock allows impressions to be supplemented "in restrained and cautious ways."

7. Ibid., p. 15.

8. Burkert, "Ares and Aphrodite," p. 29.

9. I have slightly adapted a formulation due to A. Parry ("Introduction," p. lxi, n. 1). See chapter 4 for the exact quotation and related references.

10. Macleod, "Homer on Poetry," p. 305; Rutherford, "Philosophy," pp. 173–175; Rutherford, *Books XIX and XX*, pp. 76–77; Podlecki, "Similes," p. 86; Foley, "Sex Roles," p. 206; Buxton, "Similes," p. 149; Nagy, *Achaeans*, p. 101; Pucci, *Odysseus Polutropos*, p. 222.

11. Nice examples are the similes at *Il.* 4.141–147 (Rutherford, *Books XIX and XX*, p. 76; the attempt in *Il. Comm.* I to see deeper meaning in this simile is not convincing), *Od.* 4.335–340 (discussed in section 9.2), and *Od.* 16.213–219 (Foley, "Sex Roles," p. 190; Podlecki, "Similes," p. 85).

12. *Od.* 4.555–560, 5.149–158 (also 5.81–84, 7.259–260).

13. *Od.* 7.317–328, 8.30–55. Demodokos first sings at 8.73.

14. In connection with quote 1.3, Jones (*Homer's Odyssey*, p. 75) comments: "One may care to ask — what is Odysseus weeping for/at? After all, his greatest triumph is being publicly rehearsed." See also Rutherford, "Philosophy," p. 173.

15. I am guilty of phrasing this challenge in a way that fits the answer to the challenge that I go on to propose. It is possible in principle that Odysseus would have wept at any song about himself or at any song about the war.

16. Rutherford ("Philosophy," pp. 173–175) suggests that the first song of Demodokos causes Odysseus to weep for himself and his comrades and that the third song causes him to weep for the Trojans. The first suggestion is just speculation, and the second is undermined by quote 1.4. In any case, it is difficult to understand why Odysseus should be so prone to weeping just when things are beginning to look up for him. Rutherford (ibid., p. 177) believes that Odysseus realizes the value of self-control only when he is back in Ithaka, but this belief depends on his interpretation of Odysseus's weeping in Scheria.

17. *Od.* 8.385–395, 417–448.

18. What makes the generosity possible is that Alkinoös obtains contributions from twelve other kings; it is not clear whether he would have done this for a less worthy guest.

19. *Od.* 9.213–215, 224–229 (see also 266–268). The quotation is from Hammond's translation.

20. *Od.* 19.272–295.

21. Other Homeric heroes may be just as eager for gifts as Odysseus (Stanford, *Ulysses Theme*, p. 76), but this is irrelevant to my argument.

22. *Od.* 8.577–586; Saïd, *Homer and the* Odyssey, p. 129.

23. *Od.* 8.539–541, 577–586.

24. Strictly speaking, the lines which credit Odysseus with the stratagem of the Wooden Horse (*Od.* 8.492–495) are spoken by Odysseus himself, but I think it is fair to say that Demodokos endorses them implicitly.

25. *Od.* 11.335–341.

26. *Od.* 13.13–21.

27. *Od.* 5.36–40, 13.134–138.

28. *Od.* 6.141–185, on which see Jones, *Homer's Odyssey*, pp. 58–59.

29. *Od.* 7.236–297. The craftiness of Odysseus's speech is discussed in Besslich, *Schweigen*; I have not seen this book, but Besslich's discussion is summarized by Fenik, *Studies*, pp. 16–18 (see also pp. 128–129).

30. *Od.* 7.298–315. On Odysseus's white lie, see Griffin, *Life and Death*, pp. 61–62. For the idea that Odysseus's gallantry towards Nausikaa causes Alkinoös to consider him as a possible son-in-law, see Fenik, *Studies*, p. 56. We know that Alkinoös is aware of his daughter's preoccupation with marriage and her embarrassment on the subject (*Od.* 6.66–67). Since she has been well brought up (as evidenced by her response to Odysseus's supplication), he must realize that her failure to accompany Odysseus to the palace must be due to this embarrassment, indicating that she thinks of the stranger as a possible husband. He also thinks this might be a suitable match when he sees that Odysseus's protective instinct towards her mirrors his own (could this be what he is referring to when he characterizes Odysseus as "thinking the way I do" in line 312?).

31. See Rutherford, "Philosophy," pp. 172–173.

32. *Od.* 14.196–198; 19.115–122, 165–170.

33. In supplication: *Od.* 7.151–152; in proposal of more gifts: *Od.* 11.340.

34. *Od.* 7.208–225.

35. Odysseus as archer at Troy: *Od.* 8.219–220; guest gift: *Od.* 8.385–395.

36. *Od.* 23.339.

37. Jones, *Homer's Odyssey*, pp. 37, 71.

38. Similarly, it is not shame but consideration for what is proper that prevents Penelope from appearing alone before the suitors. The same verb (αιδεομαι) is used in both contexts (*Od.* 8.86 and 18.184).

39. A second translation problem in quote 1.2 is more straightforward. The statement at *Od.* 8.92 that Odysseus would "make lamentation" assumes unnecessarily that what appears to be lamentation is sincere, contrary to my reading; the underlying Greek verb actually means "to weep, wail, show signs of grief" (Cunliffe, *Lexicon*, entry for γοαω), and this is reflected in most translations. I should perhaps also comment on the expression "pitiful tears" in quote 1.3. Cunliffe (entry for ελεεινος) suggests that this refers to tears "caused by feelings worthy of pity." This interpretation also ignores the possibility that Odysseus is only acting. I suggest instead that pitiful tears are simply tears that would arouse pity in an observer, seeming to be genuine even if they are not.

40. Another example of middle/passive ambiguity in the *Odyssey* is discussed by Rutherford, "Philosophy," p. 177, n. 65.

41. *Od.* 8.577–586.

42. Fenik, *Studies*, pp. 56–59.

43. It may be worth noting that the verbal connection between *Od.* 8.577 and 9.13, both of which contain a form of the verb οδυρομαι (to lament, grieve, weep), is stronger than shown in Lattimore's translation, although not as strong as in Cook's translation.

44. *Od.* 8.573–576.

45. Arete's questions and Odysseus's reply: *Od.* 7.236–297.

46. See discussion of *Od.* 7.244 in Fenik, *Studies*, pp. 16–17, based on Besslich, *Schweigen*, pp. 60 ff.

47. Fenik, *Studies*, pp. 101–103, 155. Fenik first discussed the Iliadic examples of this pattern in *Battle Scenes*, pp. 213–214; see also *Il. Comm.* V, pp. 19–21.

48. The double weeping is an atypical example of Fenik's pattern in one respect. Usually the two scenes that make up the pattern are independent of each other. For example, two warriors meet in battle on two separate occasions, the first encounter ending inconclusively, the second with a fatal outcome (this applies to the two most important deaths in the *Iliad*, those of Patroklos and Hektor [Fenik, *Battle Scenes*, p. 213; Fenik, *Studies*, pp. 101–102]). If the reading proposed in section 1.3 is correct, however, the second bout of weeping is causally connected to the first: after Demodokos's first song, Odysseus decides that later he will request and weep at a song about the Wooden Horse and the sack of Troy.

49. *Od.* 4.113–119, 151–154.

50. The prefiguring of the identification of Odysseus after he weeps at the third song of Demodokos by the identification of Telemachos by Menelaos is well known (Fenik, *Studies*, pp. 26, 155; S. West, "Books I–IV," p. 200). However, it is usually assumed that the weeping of Odysseus, like that of Telemachos, is sincere (Fenik, *Studies*, pp. 26, 43–45). If his weeping is premeditated, as I believe, the parallelism between the two scenes is somewhat less but still unmistakable.

51. These two instances of the pattern are described by Fenik (*Battle Scenes*, pp. 213–214; *Studies*, pp. 101–102) and Edwards (*Il. Comm.* V, p. 19).
52. *Il. Comm.* V, p. 19.

CHAPTER 2: The Last Stratagem of Odysseus

1. Helen: *Il.* 3.200–202; Nestor: *Od.* 3.120–122; Odysseus: *Od.* 9.19–20 (quote 1.6). See also Agamemnon at *Il.* 4.339 (Lattimore's translation is inadequate here), Diomedes at *Il.* 10.246–247, Sokos at *Il.* 11.430, Athene at *Od.* 13.291–299, and Telemachos at *Od.* 23.124–126.

2. Cunliffe, *Lexicon*; M. Parry, "Traditional Epithet," pp. 92, 145. My remark is a little misleading because, as Parry's analysis makes clear, the frequency with which Homer uses a given epithet for a person is a function of its usefulness in verse construction (its "metrical utility") and therefore should not be used as an indicator of that person's character. However, the meaning of a distinctive epithet does reflect the character of the person to whom it is applied, and three of the seven distinctive epithets for Odysseus in Parry's list (πολυμητις, πολυφρων, and ποικιλομητις) indicate resourcefulness. In addition, Odysseus has three related distinctive epithets not included in Parry's list. One, πολυμηχανος, appears most frequently in a whole-line formula that Parry quotes on pp. 63 and 140, and is commonly translated as "of many devices," "of many wiles," or "resourceful." The other two are not found in formulas at all: πολυκερδης means "very shrewd, astute, or cunning"; πολυτροπος, "of many turns," is ambiguous (see Clay, *Wrath*, pp. 29–31), but one possible meaning is that given by Cunliffe ("of many devices, resourceful"). See also Clay, *Wrath*, p. 31; Saïd, *Homer and the* Odyssey, p. 228.

3. The episode of the Wooden Horse is the subject of three passages in Homer: *Od.* 4.271–289, 8.492–520, and 11.523–532. The stratagem is attributed to Odysseus explicitly at *Od.* 8.492–495 (Saïd, *Homer and the* Odyssey, p. 226), implicitly at *Od.* 22.230 (where Athene indicates that Odysseus was responsible for the plan that led to the sack of Troy), and obliquely at *Od.* 1.2 (where he is simply credited with the sack of Troy).

Zeus's prediction in the *Iliad* that the Greeks will capture Troy "through the designs of Athene" (*Il.* 15.70–71) seems to deny that Odysseus devised the stratagem. This prediction is consistent with Proclus's summary of the *Little Iliad*, which states that Epeios built the Wooden Horse "at Athena's suggestion" (Burgess, *Tradition of the Trojan War*, p. 179) or "following an initiative of Athena's" (M. L. West, *Greek Epic Fragments*, p. 123). Thus, the attribution of the idea of the Wooden Horse to Odysseus may have been an innovation of the *Odyssey* poet (whether or not he also composed the *Iliad*). This tentative conclusion comes with the following caveat.

Zeus's predictions in the *Iliad* do not always bear close scrutiny (see *Il. Comm.* IV, p. 234). The *Odyssey* tells us that Athene's role in the scheme was to assist Epeios in the construction of the horse (*Od.* 8.493), a role which is consistent with the beginning of a simile in the *Iliad*: "But as a chalkline straightens the cutting of a ship's timber in the hands of an expert carpenter, who by Athene's inspiration is well versed in all his craft's subtlety …" (*Il.* 15.410–412). Hainsworth ("Books V–VIII," p. 379), who quotes these lines, explains that Athene is credited at *Od.* 8.493 "because the horse was an ingenious creation." This interpretation may go some way toward reconciling Zeus's prediction with the account in the *Odyssey*.

4. *Od.* 9.345–479.

5. In the title of the chapter I refer to the crafty design that leads to the destruction of the suitors as the last stratagem of Odysseus. I have in mind, of course, only the Odysseus of the Homeric epics. Even with this restriction, it is not the hero's last ruse—he also contrives to delay the public's discovery that the suitors have been slaughtered (*Od.* 23.117–152)—but it is the last stratagem worthy of the fame accorded to the Wooden Horse and the escape from the Cyclops.

6. Woodhouse (*Composition*, pp. 92–97, esp. 96–97) expounds the logic of the twofold contest in the context of what Homer had to consider, but the reading I propose requires Odysseus to work through the same considerations. Although Woodhouse asserts that the idea of using the bow is "entirely a happy thought of the man of 'many wiles'" (ibid., p. 110), he believes that the inspiration does not come to Odysseus until he signals to Telemachos not to string the bow (ibid., p. 112), that is, until the contest has already begun.

7. Archery contests for a woman's hand which combine feats of strength and marksmanship are found in the stories of various peoples (M. L. West, *Making of the Odyssey*, pp. 16–17). What distinguishes the twofold contest of the *Odyssey* is its brilliance as a solution to the problem of getting into the hands of Odysseus the equipment needed for him to kill a number of enemies.

8. That Penelope apparently does not fully appreciate the difficulty of stringing the bow (Woodhouse, *Composition*, p. 93) is of no consequence for the implementation of the contest.

9. *Od.* 17.142–146. Telemachos's news is two years old because Menelaos questioned Proteus two years before Odysseus returned to Ithaka.

10. *Od.* 19.270–307.

11. *Od.* 17.155–161.

12. *Od.* 17.525–547. Penelope first hears from Eumaios's account of his talks with the beggar that Odysseus has recently been in Thesprotia and is on his way home. When she then remarks that, if Odysseus were to return, he and Telemachos would soon take vengeance on the suitors, Telemachos (who is in the great hall with the suitors) sneezes so loudly that his mother hears it upstairs in her chamber. Following the practice of attributing unexplained phenomena to supernatural causes (see Dodds, *Irrational*, p. 13 and p. 24, n. 87), Penelope regards his sneeze as an omen and says to Eumaios, "Do you not see that my son has sneezed at all my words? Therefore shall certain death fall upon the suitors one and all, nor shall one of them escape death and the fates" (Murray trans.).

13. *Od.* 19.535–558.

14. Attempts to account for the illogicality are summarized by Saïd (*Homer and the Odyssey*, pp. 285–289) and Russo ("Books XVII–XX," pp. 104–105). My assertion that the illogicality has never been resolved echoes the latter's statement that "Penelope's decision ... is without evident motivation in our text and has never been successfully explained" ("Books XVII–XX," p. 7). See also Combellack, "Problems," pp. 32–40; Fenik, *Studies*, pp. 46–47; Kirk, *Songs*, pp. 246–247; Page, *Homeric Odyssey*, pp. 123–124; Rutherford, *Books*

XIX and XX, pp. 31–36; Steiner, *Books XVII and XVIII*, p. 27; Woodhouse, *Composition*, pp. 80–91.

15. Penelope's speech is actually her response to a compliment from Eurymachos. However, she has just dazzled all the suitors with her beauty (see quote 2.20), and we can be sure that all of them are paying the closest possible attention. In fact, it is Antinoös, the other leader of the suitors, who replies to her. Homer also makes it clear that Penelope's speech is heard by Odysseus (see quote 2.24), who is in the hall with the suitors disguised as a beggar.

16. I have omitted the words "you may" from the end of *Od.* 18.269 in Lattimore's translation to show that Odysseus is instructing Penelope to remarry when Telemachos has grown up, not giving her permission to do so. This revision is in accordance with other translations, including those of Cook, Fagles, Hammond, Huddleston, Murray, Rieu, and Shewring; see also Rutherford, *Books XIX and XX*, p. 32.

17. Hölscher, "Penelope," pp. 133–136. See also Erbse, *Beiträge*, pp. 81–87; Jones, *Homer's Odyssey*, pp. 164–165; Saïd, *Homer and the Odyssey*, p. 97; Thornton, *People and Themes*, pp. 96–108. For an overview, with references, of various interpretations of quote 2.2, see Steiner, *Books XVII and XVIII*, p. 196.

18. Although Penelope has not yet spoken with the beggar when she gives her speech to the suitors, she has heard from Eumaios the beggar's report that Odysseus is nearby and will be coming home with many treasures (*Od.* 17.525–527).

19. This point was also made by Combellack, "Problems," pp. 35–36, 38.

20. Some commentators believe that Odysseus really did give the instruction (Hölscher, "Penelope"; Thornton, *People and Themes*, pp. 96–108; Erbse, *Beiträge*, pp. 81–87; Jones, *Homer's Odyssey*, pp. 164–165; Combellack, "Problems," p. 35; Scodel, *Credible Impossibilities*, p. 62), while others assert that the genuineness of the instruction is neither confirmed nor denied elsewhere in the poem (Rutherford, *Books XIX and XX*, p. 32; Steiner, *Books XVII and XVIII*, p. 196). One scholar who shares my view is Büchner ("Penelopeszenen," pp. 139–140), who points to Odysseus's indignation at the wooing of Penelope (*Od.* 22.38, 321–325) as proof that he cannot have told her (or given her permission) to remarry.

Hölscher defends the genuineness of the instruction by citing numerous references in the *Odyssey* to Telemachos's coming of age. The existence of these references is hardly surprising, however, given the importance of the grown-up son to the poem (see section 5.6). Hölscher remains on shaky ground when he asserts that "Penelope herself in her conversation with Odysseus leaves no doubt that the recent maturing of her son is the decisive reason for her giving up on her husband's return" ("Penelope and the Suitors," p. 138). He supports this assertion by quoting Penelope at *Od.* 19.160–161 and 532, but the explanation that she gives in lines adjacent to these excerpts (19.159 and 533–534) is fully adequate, nicely consistent with the story line of the poem, and totally unrelated to Odysseus's supposed instruction.

21. *Od.* 19.158–161 and 524–534.

22. This is essentially the argument made by Woodhouse, *Composition*, pp. 86–87. See also Steiner, *Books XVII and XVIII*, p. 196.

23. *Od.* 19.137–158.

24. *Od.* 19.282–295.

25. There is still one more argument for the inauthenticity of the instruction. When Odysseus left for Troy, Halitherses predicted that he would not return for twenty years (*Od.* 2.171–176). If this prediction was communicated to Odysseus before he left, he clearly would not have told Penelope to remarry when Telemachos reached adulthood. Unfortunately, comparison of various translations shows that the Greek is ambiguous as to whether Halitherses communicated his prediction to Odysseus. Fortunately, the inauthenticity of the instruction has been adequately demonstrated by the arguments given in the main text. Note, however, that if the suitors believed that Halitherses shared his prediction with Odysseus (even if they did not believe the prediction itself), they would have reason to doubt that Odysseus actually gave Penelope that instruction. Since they apparently do not doubt the genuineness of the instruction, I prefer to assume that Halitherses does not say that he communicated his prediction to Odysseus.

26. One of the interpretations listed by Rutherford (*Books XIX and XX*, p. 32) and Steiner (*Books XVII and XVIII*, p. 196) is that Odysseus's instruction is fabricated by Penelope to explain a decision to remarry that she actually makes for other reasons.

27. Woodhouse, *Composition*, p. 165. All we are told about the swords worn by the suitors is that they are made of bronze and are sharpened on both sides (*Od.* 22.79–80), but Woodhouse is surely right to assume that they are not the heavy swords used in battle.

28. Quote 2.4 illustrates what Fenik (*Studies*, p. 107) calls "the interesting, if unsurprising, conclusion that the poet allows his characters the freedom of making plans that he presumably knows will not work out as they expect." Stated otherwise, "Homer must ... be granted the flexible realism of permitting changing circumstances to overrule his characters' earlier plans, especially when the original idea grows naturally out of the situation and is appropriate to the person conceiving it" (ibid., p. 109). Fenik (ibid., pp. 106–111) supports his conclusion with several examples, but he explicitly excludes the removal of the arms because he feels (for reasons I do not understand) that the plan stated in quote 2.4 does *not* arise naturally from the situation in which it is formulated (ibid., pp. 111–113). It may be noted that, although the scenario envisaged in the first lines of quote 2.4 never comes to pass, Odysseus does signal to Telemachos with a nod, or some similar gesture, in the run-up to the slaughter of the suitors: *Od.* 21.129–130, 431.

29. M. L. West (*Making of the Odyssey*, p. 249) believes that the middle part of quote 2.4, which implies that Telemachos is to remove the arms when the suitors are not present in the hall, is inconsistent with the first part, based on the implicit assumption that Odysseus will give the signal to remove the arms when everyone is in the hall. But this assumption is mistaken since the suitors routinely spend time amusing themselves in front of the palace (*Od.* 1.103–145; 4.625–674). Odysseus might not know the habits of the suitors, of course, but he would know how his grounds might reasonably be used.

30. When Odysseus uses the bow to kill the first suitor, the other suitors scan the walls of the hall and discover that all the arms are gone (*Od.* 22.21–

25). Shortly afterward, Telemachos rushes to the storeroom to get arms for his father, himself, and the two loyal slaves who will be fighting alongside them (*Od.* 22.101–112).

31. Combellack, "Problems," pp. 25–27; Woodhouse, *Composition*, pp. 158–168; Bowra, "Composition," pp. 50–51; Erbse, *Beiträge*, pp. 3–41; Kirk, *Songs*, pp. 243–244; Goold, "Removal of the Arms"; Page, *Homeric Odyssey*, pp. 92–98; Fenik, *Studies*, pp. 111–113; M. L. West, *Making of the Odyssey*, pp. 248–249. The last four of these critics are also disturbed by other departures from the original plan, even though these are easily explained. As for the crucial inconsistency, the fact that Odysseus and Telemachos do not leave arms in the hall for their own use, Page (*Homeric Odyssey*, p. 92) asserts that, when the battle with the suitors begins, "the poet makes it clear that it is a pity that nobody thought of taking this precaution." But the poet does no such thing. Telemachos simply tells his father that he is going to fetch arms for themselves and the loyal herdsmen and that "it is better for us to be armored" (*Od.* 22.101–104); this does *not* mean that it was an oversight or a mistake not to leave arms for themselves in the hall, as I explain in section 2.4. West's view that the poet "has muddled his preparations" for the battle (*Making of the Odyssey*, p. 138) is misguided for the same reason. Fenik (*Studies*, pp. 112, 113) asserts that Telemachos *forgets* to leave arms in the hall for himself and his father, but this ignores the fact that Odysseus and Telemachos remove the arms together and that Odysseus would also have to forget, which is unlikely given his concentrated attention described at the beginning and end of quote 2.3. More serious is the observation of Woodhouse (p. 161) that "the manner in which Odysseus now [in quote 2.3] speaks to his son about removal of the weapons of war seems to rule out any idea of previous discussion of the plan with him. The impression conveyed by the passage, taken by itself, is that the plan has flashed into his mind then and there, as the outcome of his silent pondering whilst waiting in the great hall for Penelopeia." In fact, I shall be arguing that Odysseus's final plan for dealing with the suitors, including the removal of the arms, *is* the outcome of his silent pondering while waiting in the great hall for Penelope (see section 2.4). This reading, together with the repetition characteristic of the oral style, may be a sufficient response to Woodhouse's remark.

Another inconsistency between quotes 2.3 and 2.4 concerns the fighting gear involved. Odysseus originally instructs Telemachos to leave behind a spear, a sword, and a shield for each of them (quote 2.4), but what father and son actually remove from the hall are spears, shields and helmets (quote 2.3; see also *Od.* 22.101–102, 108–111). As the mention of swords in quote 2.4 is odd (see Büchner, "Waffenbergung," p. 440), this inconsistency could be intentional, but the case for intentionality is not strong enough to be included in chapter 6.

32. I think this is a fair characterization even though the Greek is apparently less explicit about this than Lattimore's translation. Compare the last four lines of quote 2.4 with Murray's translation (which is equivalent to that of Hammond and to that given by Woodhouse, *Composition*, pp. 159–160): "But for us two alone leave behind two swords and two spears, and two oxhide shields for us to grasp, that we may rush up to them and seize them;

while as for the suitors, Pallas Athene and Zeus the counselor will beguile them."

33. Büchner, "Waffenbergung," pp. 440, 442; Erbse, *Beiträge*, p. 36.

34. According to one interpretation (Büchner, "Waffenbergung," p. 442), the realization that two panoplies left in the hall would arouse the suspicion of the suitors is itself sufficient to explain why Odysseus and Telemachos do not leave behind any arms for themselves. This interpretation requires us to believe that the hero who is famous for the quickness of his mind either does not see or does not appreciate the danger in leaving two panoplies in the hall when he first contemplates the removal of the arms (quote 2.4). It also leaves Odysseus without much of a plan for dealing with the suitors (Büchner asserts that it will be up to Telemachos to fetch arms for himself and his father when the battle is to begin).

35. *Od.* 18.344–345.

36. *Od.* 18.346–404.

37. The examples that I go on to cite refer to the following lines: *Od.* 17.465 (Antinoös), 17.491–492 (Telemachos), 14.110 (Eumaios), and 20.184 (Melanthios). See also *Od.* 17.27.

38. Russo, "Books XVII–XX," p. 77.

39. Rutherford, *Books XIX and XX*, p. 138.

40. *Od.* 21.1–82.

41. Rutherford, *Books XIX and XX*, p. 30; Rutherford, *Homer*, p. 69, n. 83; Steiner, *Books XVII and XVIII*, p. 182 (commentary on *Od.* 18.164–168). Some critics deny that Athene could influence Penelope to do something contrary to her own inclinations. For example, Felson-Rubin ("Penelope's Perspective," pp. 173–174) says, "We can assume that Athene could only influence Penelope in accord with Penelope's own character and disposition," while Silk ("Explorations," p. 40) says that "by the rules of 'double determination', divine initiative ... should be divine prompting for human impulse." However, there is no *rule* of double determination. It does often happen that divine intervention is aligned with human inclination, but this double causation of a human act is only one point in the spectrum of relationships between divine and human causation that are found in Homer (Lesky, "Causation," pp. 174, 187–193). In the present case, an opposition of divine and human wishes is clear from a comparison of *Od.* 18.178–179 (where Penelope rejects Eurynome's suggestion that she clean herself up before showing herself to the suitors) with 18.187–196 (where Athene puts Penelope to sleep and beautifies her). Even without this it is obvious from her constant longing for Odysseus and hatred of the suitors that, in the absence of Athene's intervention, Penelope would have no inclination to show herself to the suitors (see *Od.* 18.164–165). Her appearance before the suitors at *Od.* 16.409–451 is, of course, another matter entirely, for her purpose then is to insist that they stop plotting to murder her son.

42. Woodhouse (*Composition*, pp. 90–91) also likens Penelope's decision to hold the contest to her decision to show herself off to the suitors. For him these scenes show Homer resorting to a desperate measure inasmuch as the poet is unable to supply a human motivation for either decision. However, I go on to argue in section 2.5 that Odysseus, acting through Athene, supplies the human motivation for Penelope's decision to hold the contest.

43. E.g, *Od.* 14.178, 23.11–14. For justification of this belief see *Od.* 20.345–346 and quote 2.5. The most famous example, of course, is Agamemnon's "apology" at *Il.* 19.86–94.

44. *Od.* 19.476–479.

45. I take Murray's translation and the nearly identical rendering ("Athene had turned her thoughts elsewhere") in the translations of Hammond and Shewring to be equivalent to the literal translation "Athene had turned her mind" given by Cook or "Athena had turned her mind away" given by Griffin (*Odyssey*, p. 29) and Huddleston or "Athene hatte ihren Geist abgelenkt" given by Büchner ("Penelopeszenen," p. 147). I should note that Lattimore is not the only translator who fails to communicate that Athene was directing Penelope's thoughts; Merrill, for example, gives us "her perception Athena was turning aside."

46. In this interpretation, Penelope's distraction is natural since Athene begins to implant the idea of the contest in her mind as soon as she has brought the conversation to a (temporary) close by giving her attendants instructions for the care of the stranger. In the usual view, by contrast, Athene must anticipate Eurykleia's recognition of Odysseus's scar and have the foresight to divert Penelope's attention (Auerbach, *Mimesis*, p. 3).

47. *Od.* 19.505–509.

48. Penelope's decision to choose a new husband the next day, which comes as such a surprise after the first part of her conversation with the beggar, also leads Büchner to conclude that the idea of the contest comes to her while Eurykleia is washing the beggar's feet and she herself is lost in thought ("Penelopeszenen," pp. 147, 149). However, Büchner believes that it is Penelope who devises the contest and that she does so as a trick to put off the suitors once more, knowing that they will not be able to succeed with the bow. This theory has two serious problems. The first is Penelope's belief, expressed in the first lines of quote 2.1, that the contest will take her away from the house of Odysseus. To reconcile this apparent belief with his theory, Büchner (ibid., p. 148) is forced to postulate that Penelope, who has spoken quite openly with the beggar, is now hiding her intentions from him out of caution. This ad hoc postulate does not explain why she wakes up later in the night crying and wishing she were dead instead of facing the prospect of having "to please the mind of an inferior husband" (see *Od.* 20.57–83). The second problem is this: if Penelope refuses to take a new husband when no one wins the contest, she will be disobeying Odysseus's final instruction in quote 2.2, the suitors will know that she has been deceiving them again, and she will have accomplished nothing.

49. Athene: *Od.* 13.189–193; Odysseus: *Od.* 16.300–304.

50. This simple consideration, which goes back to Aristotle (see Scodel, *Credible Impossibilities*, p. 20, n. 46), eliminates the need for Murnaghan's awkward theory that Odysseus conceals his identity from Penelope owing to a general mistrust of women, even though he is well aware that she has remained faithful to him (Murnaghan, "Penelope's *Agnoia*," pp. 235–239). Her theory has difficulty in any case with the fact that Odysseus also doesn't want his father or the loyal swineherd to know that he has returned (*Od.* 16.301–302). The case of Telemachos is quite different. Although he becomes highly emotional when he is reunited with his father (*Od.* 16.213–220), he has the opportunity to receive the news and to compose himself while the two of them are alone at the steading of the swineherd. There will be no such opportunity for Penelope until the suitors are dead. (The case of the swineherd, to whom Odysseus eventually does reveal his identity, is analogous to that of Telemachos—see *Od.* 21.205–229.)

The simple explanation offered here for why Athene and Odysseus keep Penelope ignorant of the beggar's identity also undermines the suggestion of Emlyn-Jones that this is to be explained by Homer's wish to exploit the dramatic potential of a delayed recognition and to make this recognition a second climax (after the death of the suitors) that does justice to Penelope and her importance in the poem (Emlyn-Jones, "Reunion," pp. 215–221, 228; compare n. 3 on p. 209 of the same paper). The fact that the delayed recognition is a natural consequence of the dramatic situation in no way diminishes the benefits described by Emlyn-Jones.

51. Rutherford (*Books XIX and XX*, p. 35) remarks, "On Odysseus' side, his ingrained reluctance to trust others, his compulsive preference to delay and bide his time, make it practically impossible for him to reveal his identity at this stage, even if he were sure that his wife could contain her joy and keep his secret."

52. Calhoun ("Divine Entourage," p. 266, n. 27) remarks that "here the goddess may be little more than personification of the impulse to action, since Penelope had spoken of her intention the night before." If Penelope's intention was motivated by Athene, however, we can assume that the goddess actually intervenes in quote 2.6. Indeed, this assumption is sometimes made even without this justification (see, e.g., Jones, *Homer's Odyssey*, p. 195).

53. *Od.* 19.577–581 = 21.75–79.

54. Woodhouse, *Composition*, p. 88. The claim that these are the only examples of humanly unmotivated action in the *Odyssey* is debatable (see *Od.* 18.346–348, 20.284–286, and 20.345–349).

55. It is apparent from quote 2.7 that Penelope does not realize that her change of heart (her desire to show herself to the suitors) is due to the intervention of Athene. Similarly, at *Il.* 21.544–572 "the poet even gives us the thoughts of a hero who is in fact being driven to face Achilles by Apollo, but who, unaware of this, takes his own decision after a lengthy monologue" (Griffin, *Life and Death*, p. 42).

56. Erbse, *Beiträge*, pp. 36–37. Erbse cites the passages reproduced here in quotes 2.1, 2.5, and 2.6 when he credits Athene for the slaughter of the suitors, but leaves it to the reader to guess what her connection is with the first of these passages.

57. It is therefore worth noting that Homer's gods are not omniscient (see Clay, *Wrath*, p. 149). Ares does not know that his son Askalaphos has been killed until he hears this from Hera (*Il.* 13.516–525, 15.110–118); Poseidon does not realize that Odysseus has left Kalypso's island until he himself sees him sailing towards Scheria (*Od.* 5.282–289); and Helios does not know that his cattle have been killed by Odysseus's companions until he is told by his daughter Lampetia (*Od.* 12.374–376).

58. According to Erbse's interpretation (*Beiträge*, p. 37), the idea of using the bow has not entered Odysseus's head when he and Telemachos remove the arms from the hall. He decides not to leave behind arms for himself and his son simply because he realizes that his original plan will lead to disaster. He is able to remain calm despite this realization only thanks to his unshakable trust in his divine helper, Athene.

59. Hölscher, "Penelope," p. 136; Jones, *Homer's Odyssey*, pp. 164–165.

60. Suitors: *Od.* 22.255–259, 272–281, 297–309; Troy: *Od.* 8.514–520.

61. *Od.* 8.493.

62. Rutherford, *Books XIX and XX*, pp. 134, 198.

63. Erbse, *Beiträge*, pp. 36–37.

64. Indeed, Austin (*Archery*, p. 230) asserts that "the epithet receives emphasis from its unusual position."

65. *Od.* 14.486.

66. Fenik (*Studies*, p. 155) shows that the beggar's conversation with Penelope—a cornerstone and turning point of the *Odyssey*—is anticipated in its thematic elements and its emotional tone by his relatively inconsequential conversation with Eumaios in book 14.

67. *Od.* 20.28–30.

68. This interpretation is advocated by Woodhouse, *Composition*, pp. 110–112 and Jones, *Homer's Odyssey*, p. 174.

69. One might object to this interpretation on the basis of the obvious parallel between *Od.* 20.39–40 (see quote 2.9) and *Od.* 23.37–38 (the parallel is clear enough in Lattimore's translation, but it is clearer still in the translations of Cook, Hammond, and Murray). Since Penelope is certainly not thinking of the bow when she refers to Odysseus being "only one" in the latter passage, one is tempted to assume that Odysseus is not thinking of the bow when he refers to himself as "alone against many" in the former passage. However, the danger of extrapolating parallelism is illustrated by the comparison of quotes 5.31 and 5.36 that follows the latter passage.

70. A more concise statement of these points is made by Rutherford, *Books XIX and XX*, pp. 198–199.

71. Odysseus's new confidence can probably also be detected in the difference between how he reacts when Ktesippos throws an ox hoof at him and how he reacted the day before when Antinoös hit him with a footstool (*Od.* 20.301–302 and 17.465, respectively; cf. de Jong, "Between Word and Deed," p. 71).

72. Odysseus pondering alone: Lattimore and Shewring; Odysseus and Athene planning together: Merrill, Murray, and Fagles; ambiguous: Rieu ("plotting the destruction of the Suitors with Athene's aid"), Cook, Hammond, Goold ("Removal of the Arms," pp. 125–126), and Woodhouse (*Composition*, p. 160). Of these, Woodhouse's translation ("slaughter for suitors with Athene's aid devising") is notable for following the word order of the Greek.

73. *Od.* 20.384–386.

74. Woodhouse, *Composition*, p. 114.

75. Büchner, "Penelopeszenen," pp. 153–154. Some interesting points are also made by Tracy, *Story*, pp. 125–126.

76. *Od.* 21.102–105. The explanation of Telemachos's laughter suggested by Jones (*Homer's Odyssey*, p. 197) is, in my opinion, much less convincing that that of Büchner.

77. Büchner speaks of the moment when Telemachos first sees the weapon that can give Odysseus the upper hand: "Nun sieht er [Telemachos] plötzlich die Waffe vor sich, die jenem [Odysseus] die Überlegenheit verschaffen kann." If this means that Telemachos foresees his father's imminent triumph (so Fernández-Galiano, "Books XXI–XXII," p. 158), Büchner is clearly assuming too much, but this interpretation is unwarranted. Telemachos can see only that the bow would give his father the upper hand *in the right circumstances* (for example, Odysseus must get his hands on the bow), but even this is a great relief considering the apparently hopeless situation that Telemachos faced before his mother's announcement of the contest.

78. After Penelope declares her intention to hold the contest, Odysseus urges her to do so without delay (see quote 2.8), but this is certainly not what Amphimedon has in mind in quote 2.14.

79. On the subjectivity of Amphimedon's account, see Heubeck, "Books XXIII–XXIV," pp. 376–377. Amphimedon understandably neglects to mention how the suitors essentially took over the palace of Odysseus and even threatened the life of Telemachos. That he speaks from the point of view of the suitors is also clear when he says that an evil spirit brought Odysseus back to Ithaka (*Od.* 24.149–150). When he says that Penelope "was planning our death and black destruction" (*Od.* 24.127) with her ruse of the shroud for Laertes, he is simply referring to the eventual, indirect result of the ruse, which Penelope could not have known.

80. Odysseus: *Od.* 23.310–341; Amphimedon: *Od.* 24.125–185. The authenticity of Odysseus's summary is questioned by some (e.g., Tracy, *Story*, p. 138, n. 11), although not by others (e.g., Heubeck, "Books XXIII–XXIV," p. 346), on the grounds that it is given in indirect discourse, considered to be uncharacteristic of Homer. In my opinion, this objection is without merit: indirect discourse is demanded by the situation for parallelism with Penelope's contribution to the conversation (*Od.* 23.302–305) and because Odysseus has already twice described his experiences in direct speech, in his lengthy narrative to the Phaiakians (books 9–12) and during his conversation with Penelope in his disguise as a beggar (*Od.* 19.273–282).

81. Heubeck, "Books XXIII–XXIV," p. 378; Jones, *Homer's Odyssey*, p. 173; Kirk, *Songs*, p. 245; Page, *Homeric Odyssey*, p. 122; Rutherford, *Books XIX and XX*, pp. 35–36; Woodhouse, *Composition*, p. 117.

82. Some scholars have suggested that Penelope recognizes Odysseus during her conversation with the old beggar, but I follow Rutherford (*Books XIX and XX*, pp. 34–36) in rejecting this possibility. It is clear from her behavior after the slaughter (*Od.* 23.1–230) that she had no idea of the beggar's identity. In addition, her thoughts and tears when she wakes up during the night after telling the beggar of her decision to hold the contest for her hand in marriage (*Od.* 20.57–90) give no hint of the excitement we would expect if she has recognized her husband. On the contrary, she feels only dread at the prospect of having "to please the mind of an inferior husband," and prays that Artemis will slay her then and there. This prayer (*Od.* 20.60–63, 80) echoing the wish she expresses earlier in the day for a swift death from Artemis (*Od.* 18.202–205) shows that the meeting with her disguised husband has had no impact on her outlook, which is hardly believable even if she only suspects that the beggar might be Odysseus.

83. Hephaistos is called πολυμητις at *Il.* 21.355, πολυφρων at *Il.* 21.367 and *Od.* 8.297, 327. This comparison of Odysseus and Hephaistos is made by Clay (*Wrath*, p. 32) and Saïd (*Homer and the Odyssey*, p. 228); see also the relevant entries in Cunliffe's *Lexicon*.

84. Macleod, "Homer on Poetry," p. 304; Rutherford, "From the *Iliad*," p. 136; Burkert, "Ares and Aphrodite," p. 41; Jones, *Homer's Odyssey*, p. 73; Tracy, *Story*, p. 52.

85. Burkert, "Ares and Aphrodite."

86. *Od.* 23.35–38 (Lattimore's translation is not as clear as others).

87. *Od.* 23.256–284.

88. This problem is also mentioned by M. L. West (*Making of the Odyssey*, p. 295). Penelope actually displays no curiosity about the underworld, but this is just another unrealistic aspect of the narrative.

89. The generality of my claim may be unwarranted: Tracy (*Story*, p. 138) writes, "Before making love they embrace for a long time, and Odysseus shares with Penelope the one thing she really must in fairness know at once, namely that he must leave again soon." Similarly, Heubeck ("Books XXIII–XXIV," p. 340) says that "this is the best point at which to introduce an account of Tiresias' prophecy: if Penelope is to be told something of the future fate of her husband (which can hardly be avoided), then it is fitting that this should happen before the couple retire to bed."

90. *Od.* 23.300–343.

91. *Od.* 23.285–287.

92. Cf. *Od.* 23.342–343.

93. I have corrected Lattimore's translation by replacing "the gods" with "a god." The word θυμος which Lattimore here translates as "mind" is translated as "heart" by many other translators. The latter meaning is preferable more often than not, but I believe Lattimore's choice is appropriate in the present context.

94. Jones, *Homer's Odyssey*, p. 173; Kirk, *Songs*, pp. 246–247; Page, *Homeric Odyssey*, pp. 123–124.

95. Goold, "Removal of the Arms"; M. L. West, *Making of the Odyssey*, pp. 66, 248–249.

96. *Od.* 23.124–125 (Rieu, Jones, and Rieu). Compare Lattimore: "they say you have the best mind among men for craft."

97. *Od.* 3.120–122. See also *Od.* 4.240–289 and 16.240–242.

98. As emphasized by Clay (*Wrath*, pp. 123–124), Odysseus is telling himself in quote 2.17 that he must again exercise the endurance and self-restraint that were necessary in the Cyclops episode (if he had obeyed his impulse to kill Polyphemos, he and his men would have been trapped in the cave, unable to move the boulder from the entrance—*Od.* 9.299–305). It is not

necessarily implied, then, that he will defeat the suitors through his wits as he outsmarted the Cyclops. Furthermore, Odysseus reminds his men that his intelligence made possible the escape from the cave of the Cyclops in an episode where he has no opportunity to exercise his resourcefulness (*Od.* 12.208–212). In that episode, however, he is merely trying to reassure his men that he will be able to save them, as he eventually did in the cave of the Cyclops, even though he knows that his resourcefulness will be of no use in the approaching encounter with Skylla. In any case, by highlighting the role of Odysseus's cunning intelligence in the Cyclops episode, quote 2.17 puts Homer in an awkward position if his hero does not come up with a stratagem for dealing with the suitors.

99. I have taken the liberty of modifying Cook's translation by not capitalizing the first letter in each verse.

100. Jones, *Homer's Odyssey*, p. 120.

101. *Od.* 13.303 (Murray trans.).

102. *Od.* 13.386–387.

103. Contrary to Merrill's translation (*Od.* 13.303–304), Athene does not say (incorrectly) that she will help Odysseus weave a scheme and *then* hide his possessions.

104. *Od.* 13.307–310, 363–371, 372–373.

105. The fact that the instruction is a fabrication does not necessarily mean that Penelope's resignation is feigned. It is possible that she invents the instruction as a face-saving way to explain a genuine switch from resistance to acceptance (Steiner, *Books XVII and XVIII*, p. 196; Rutherford, *Books XIX and XX*, pp. 31–32). My view, however, is that Penelope only pretends to have surrendered at this point and does not actually capitulate until Athene instructs her to hold the contest.

106. Cf. Woodhouse, *Composition*, p. 90.

107. *Od.* 6.181.

108. Compare Odysseus's disbelief that he is back in Ithaka (*Od.* 13.324–334) with Penelope's resistance to believing that the "beggar" is Odysseus (*Od.* 23.97–103, 166–170).

109. *Od.* 23.177–204.

110. *Od.* 13.221–292 (note how Athene tries to use Odysseus's pride at 248–249). I owe this comparison of Athene and Penelope at the beginning and end of the Ithakan books to Rutherford, *Homer*, p. 90.

111. Woodhouse, *Composition*, p. 110.

112. This is one of the possible interpretations listed by Steiner, *Books XVII and XVIII*, p. 196.

113. Steiner, *Books XVII and XVIII*, p. 181. As it turns out, Penelope's speech does not prevent the suitors from plotting the murder of Telemachos one more time, but they are easily convinced to abandon this idea by an inauspicious bird sign (*Od.* 20.240–247; Büchner, "Penelopeszenen," p. 146).

114. *Od.* 15.28–35, 292–294; see also *Od.* 5.18–27, 13.425–428.

115. Wilamowitz, *Heimkehr*, pp. 19–20; Fenik, *Studies*, pp. 117–119.

116. *Od.* 17.489–492.

117. *Od.* 16.274–277.

118. Fenik, *Studies*, pp. 116–118; Rutherford, *Books XIX and XX*, p. 30.

119. Büchner ("Penelopeszenen," p. 144) and Jones (*Homer's Odyssey*, p. 168) agree with my reading of quote 2.23, although they do not share my interpretation of Telemachos's response.

120. The alternative view that Eurynome alludes to Odysseus's instruction (Russo, "Books XVII–XX," p. 61) cannot, of course, be correct if that instruction has been fabricated for this scene.

121. Odysseus must blind the Cyclops in order to survive, and he must slaughter the suitors in order to join his family and reclaim his rightful position in Ithaka. That Odysseus also wants revenge is made explicit at *Od.* 9.317 and 23.312–313 for the Cyclops and at *Od.* 5.24, 13.386, and 22.61–67 for the suitors.

122. *Od.* 9.316–317 (Murray trans.). This passage includes a Greek phrase (κακα βυσσοδομευων) that occurs also at *Od.* 17.465, 17.491, and 20.184. In section 2.4 I asserted that in its latter three occurrences this phrase (usually translated by Lattimore as "deeply devising evils") means only "wishing evil." But here (*Od.* 9.316) it refers to Odysseus's formulation of a detailed plan for blinding the Cyclops. There is no contradiction, however, because this occurrence of the phrase is accompanied by elaborating text ("if in any way I might take vengeance on him, and Athene grant me glory"), and I argued at the end of section 2.4 that descriptions that are more specific than "deeply devising evils" can indeed imply productive thinking and not merely a *wish* for revenge.

123. *Od.* 13.299–305, 314–323, 341–343.

124. *Od.* 1.48–62, 81–87; 5.7–17.

125. *Od.* 5.382–387, 427, 437.

126. Clay, *Wrath*, pp. 44–46; Calhoun, "Divine Entourage," pp. 268–269; Woodhouse, *Composition*, p. 38.

127. Note also that Athene's deference to Poseidon is described by the poet himself (that is, the omniscient narrator) at *Od.* 6.328–331.

128. See especially *Od.* 9.237–239, 336–339, and 420–466.

129. *Od.* 9.339 (Murray trans.). Odysseus sets up a similar dichotomy when he tells Arete and Alkinoös that Kalypso eventually urged him to leave her island, "either because of some message from Zeus, or because her own mind was turned" (*Od.* 7.262–263, Murray trans.). We know that Kalypso was moved by a message from Zeus conveyed by Hermes (*Od.* 5.28–115). I go on to argue that the divine-motivation alternative also applies in the case of Polyphemos.

130. *Od.* 9.507–516.

131. The conclusion that Athene helps Odysseus escape from the cave of the Cyclops is inconsistent with the thesis advanced by Clay in *The Wrath of Athena*. According to this thesis, Athene is angry at Odysseus and abandons him during the major part of his wanderings (ibid., pp. 43, 46, 51, 211) because he is too clever and "his intelligence calls into question the superiority of the gods themselves" (ibid., p. 209); she eventually drops her anger and helps Odysseus return home mainly so that he can fix what she considers to be an intolerable situation on Ithaka (ibid., p. 234). This thesis is implausible for several reasons, even if we ignore Athene's role in the Cyclops episode. First, Athene makes it clear in the two councils of the gods that her primary concern

is for the welfare of Odysseus (*Od.* 1.48–62, 5.5–20). Second, Athene delights in his cunning (see her reaction at *Od.* 13.287–295 to one of his deceptive tales) and feels an affinity towards him, not resentment, because they share this quality (quote 2.18). Clay does cite a passage from the *Odyssey* that seems to show Athene's supposed anger at Odysseus (ibid., pp. 49–50), but the deceptiveness of this passage (quote 6.32) will be demonstrated in section 6.6.

132. *Od.* 9.415–425.

133. *Od.* 13.344–354.

134. See *Od.* 13.412–419, especially the last two lines and the "too" in the penultimate line.

135. *Od.* 10.275–308.

136. *Od.* 10.281–286.

137. The intervention of Leukothea (*Od.* 5.333–353) does not pose a similar problem since it occurs after Zeus has assured the homecoming of Odysseus and has declared that Poseidon will have to give up his anger (*Od.* 1.76–79). It does not even bother Poseidon, who realizes that the other gods must have relented towards Odysseus but continues to harass him himself (*Od.* 5.282–381).

138. *Od.* 13.125–164.

139. *Il.* 8.1–40.

140. Athene says in the *Iliad* that Zeus often sent her to help Herakles (*Il.* 8.360–365; see also *Od.* 11.623–626).

141. Scott, "First Book," pp. 5–6.

142. *Od.* 1.82–87.

143. *Od.* 5.282–290.

144. *Od.* 13.132–133. The quotation is based on the translations of Cook and Lattimore.

145. *Od.* 1.76–77, 5.29–31.

146. *Il.* 24.331–468. Hermes also escorts Priam from the Greek ships after his meeting with Achilles, but this scene (*Il.* 24.679–694) has no parallel in the Circe episode.

147. My comparison of the Hermes scenes in *Il.* 24 and *Od.* 10 draws heavily on Groeger, "Kirke-Dichtung," p. 222. See also Usener, *Beobachtungen*, pp. 165–179.

148. *Il.* 24.465–467; *Od.* 10.292–301.

149. Jörgensen, "Auftreten," pp. 364–367. Exceptions to this rule are discussed by Calhoun, "Divine Entourage," pp. 270–272. Jörgensen shows that references to Zeus are not necessarily exceptions since "Zeus" is used as a generic term for the gods.

150. *Od.* 10.279 and *Il.* 24.348 are identical; the relevant parts of *Od.* 10.278 and *Il.* 24.347 are very similar in meaning, even though only the last word is the same in these two lines.

151. This reasonable inference is rejected implicitly by Jörgensen ("Auftreten," pp. 373–374), who argues that the duplicated description must reflect how Homer thought Hermes actually looked and that Odysseus recognizes the god from his undisguised appearance. Since Priam does not recognize Hermes, this position requires the awkward assumption that some people are better than others at recognizing the gods. Clay (*Wrath*, p. 24, n.

31) defends this assumption by quoting words of Hermes which seem to imply that he would be recognized if he were to enter the shelter of Achilles with Priam (*Il.* 24.462–464). But what Hermes actually suggests is simply that Achilles would realize that he was a god. This suggestion is justified (cf. *Il.* 24.563–567), but it does not require Achilles to be able to identify Hermes. In any case, Jörgensen's interpretation contradicts the more probable view that Hermes appears to Priam (and Odysseus) in disguise (*Il. Comm.* VI, p. 309; Macleod, *Iliad XXIV*, p. 116).

152. *Il.* 24.460–461.

153. Note the parallelism between Odysseus's account of how he was helped by the god Hermes and Menelaos's account of how *he* was helped by the goddess Eidothea. Menelaos does not recognize his helper (although he does realize that she must be a goddess: *Od.* 4.376), but she eventually reveals her identity (4.384–387), and this enables him to identify her at the beginning of his retrospective account (4.365). (Eidothea reveals her identity only by saying that her father is Proteus; how Menelaos knows her name as well is not explained.)

154. When Hermes identifies himself to Priam, he also reveals that he was sent by Zeus. In view of the parallels already established, we must consider the possibility that Hermes also tells Odysseus that he was sent by Zeus. For Odysseus to know that he was helped by Zeus would not be inconsistent with his belief that Zeus rejected his sacrificial offering at the end of the Cyclops episode (*Od.* 9.550–555): knowing all that was to happen before he reached Scheria, Odysseus believes that Zeus was planning the destruction of his ships and his companions, but this does not mean that Zeus could not help Odysseus himself.

155. Still another analogy deserves to be mentioned. In the proposed scenario, Zeus, owing to a commitment made to Athene, sends Hermes to prevent Circe from being able to put Odysseus under a spell. As reviewed in quote 2.25, Zeus, at the request of Athene, sends Hermes to instruct Kalypso to release Odysseus. Thus, if the proposed scenario is correct, Athene causes Zeus to send Hermes to save Odysseus from both Circe and Kalypso. This correspondence between the Circe and Kalypso episodes is an extension of the well-known parallel that Hermes "helps Odysseus escape the spell of both sorceresses" (Reinhardt, "Adventures," p. 96). Other well-known parallels between Circe and Kalypso will be reviewed in chapter 6 in connection with an altogether new correspondence between the two.

Although he does not invoke the Circe-Kalypso connection, Jörgensen ("Auftreten," p. 375) assumes that Hermes is sent to help Odysseus in the Circe episode as a result of a divine assembly like the one in which he is sent to tell Kalypso to release Odysseus (we know about the latter assembly because it is described by the omniscient poet, but not about the former because Odysseus does not know what takes place on Olympos).

156. The differences between the Hermes scenes in *Il.* 24 and *Od.* 10 were highlighted by Groeger, "Kirke-Dichtung," p. 222.

157. *Od.* 11.626; 24.1–10, 99–100.

158. Sentries: *Il.* 24.442–446; wand: *Il.* 24.343–344, *Od.* 5.47–48 (note that *Il.* 24.339–345 = *Od.* 5.43–49).

159. One of the obvious parallels, the closely similar descriptions of Hermes at *Il.* 24.347–348 and *Od.* 10.278–279, is also associated with a difference between the two scenes. The description of Hermes is well suited to its Iliadic context, but has no significance whatever in the Odyssean scene (Groeger, "Kirke-Dichtung," p. 222; Usener, *Beobachtungen*, p. 175). Hermes apparently adopts a disguise that suits his purposes in the Iliadic scene (*Il. Comm.* VI, p. 309; Macleod, *Iliad XXIV*, p. 116), but why does this disguise reappear in the Odyssean scene? In view of the large number of other parallels, it is tempting to say that the description of Hermes is repeated in order to underscore the connection between the two scenes. However, it is sufficient to note that verses are often reused in Homer without regard for their detailed applicability (e.g., M. L. West, *Making of the Odyssey*, pp. 70–79).

160. The only passage in the *Odyssey* that could pose a problem is *Od.* 10.330–332, where we learn that Hermes predicted to Circe that she would see Odysseus on his way back from Troy. This prediction raises the possibility that Hermes had a special interest in the Circe episode and that he came to Odysseus's aid on his own initiative. However, this passage could be just another expression of the poet's "fondness for the motif of a person realizing that an old prophecy is being fulfilled" (M. L. West, *Making of the Odyssey*, p. 192), also seen at 8.75–81, 9.507–512, and 13.172–178.

CHAPTER 3: The Humiliation of Agamemnon

1. Scodel, "Story-Teller," p. 51.
2. *Il.* 9.16–28.
3. *Il.* 9.96–113.
4. *Il.* 9.114–157.
5. *Il.* 9.158–161.
6. *Il.* 9.162–169.
7. *Il.* 9.264–299.
8. Cf. *Il.* 9.252–256.
9. *Il.* 9.300–306.
10. *Il.* 9.378–387.
11. *Il.* 11.790–802.
12. *Il.* 16.36–45, 64–70.
13. Similarly, when Achilles tells Patroklos that "it was not in my heart to be angry forever" (*Il.* 16.60–61), he is surely referring to how long he intended to stay out of the fighting in retaliation for Agamemnon's insult, not to how long he intended to experience anger (as if that were something he could control and decide in advance).
14. Achilles said essentially the same thing to his mother the day before (*Il.* 18.111–115; *Il.* 18.112–113 = 19.65–66 in the Greek). The statement "Still, we will let all this be a thing of the past" in 18.112 and 19.65 was first uttered by Achilles earlier on that day (at 16.60) when he was sending Patroklos to fight in his place.
15. *Il.* 19.74–75.
16. Compare: "[Achilles] regrets the quarrel with Agamemnon and its results. He is still angry—that emerges clearly from his words—but he will

curb his anger: he has a greater cause for anger now" (Knox, "Introduction," p. 54).

17. Willcock, *Companion*, p. 215.

18. *Il.* 13.105–114; 14.49–51, 128–132.

19. Arguing against the straightforward interpretation of quote 3.2 as a dishonest attempt by Agamemnon to evade responsibility for his maltreatment of Achilles, Dodds (*Irrational*, p. 3) cites quote 3.3 as evidence that Achilles agrees with Agamemnon's analysis (likewise Page, *Homeric Iliad*, p. 302). To exclude the possibility that Achilles is just pretending to agree, Dodds points out that Achilles has previously appealed to divine causation to explain Agamemnon's abusive behavior. Thus, in his reply to Odysseus's speech as Agamemnon's ambassador, Achilles says, "He cheated me and he did me hurt. Let him not beguile me with words again. This is enough for him. Let him of his own will be damned, since Zeus of the counsels has taken his wits away from him" (*Il.* 9.375–377). But here it is clear, despite the role attributed to Zeus, that Achilles blames Agamemnon, which is contrary to the thrust of quote 3.3. For further discussion, see Lesky, "Causation"; Mueller, *The Iliad*, pp. 119–122.

20. *Il.* 19.205–207.

21. *Il.* 19.233–237; cf. *Il. Comm.* V, p. 263.

22. Cf. Donlan, "Unequal Exchange" and "Reciprocities."

23. The interpretation of the so-called reconciliation of Achilles and Agamemnon that is assumed by Page (*Homeric Iliad*, pp. 311–315) is the antithesis of the analysis given in section 3.1. Page asserts that Agamemnon renews "his apology and his offer of compensation [made previously during the Embassy], at the very moment when the whole purpose of apology and compensation [to get Achilles to return to battle] has ceased to exist [because Achilles is now eager to return to battle to avenge the death of Patroklos]." Consequently, the (apparent) reconciliation is, for Page, "a flaw in the fabric of the Iliad." But Agamemnon does *not* apologize in any meaningful sense, and he does not *offer* compensation, but forces his gifts on Achilles. His purpose is not to secure Achilles' return to battle, for that is already guaranteed (as Page notes), but to assert his superior position. The Agamemnon of book 19 is the same as the Agamemnon of books 1 and 9.

24. The conventional view is expressed by Bassett, *Poetry*, pp. 175, 188, 197; Donlan, "Duelling," p. 170; Griffin, *Life and Death*, p. 71; Jones, *Homer's Iliad*, pp. 298, 299, 308; Kirk, *Songs*, p. 223; Macleod, *Iliad XXIV*, p. 31; Nagy, *Achaeans*, p. 32; Page, *Homeric Iliad*, p. 331, n. 20; *Il. Comm.* VI, pp. 165, 269–270, 271; Schein, *Hero*, p. 156; Sheppard, *Pattern*, pp. 201, 201–202; Taplin, *Soundings*, pp. 205, 258–259; M. L. West, *Making of the Iliad*, p. 410; Whitman, *Heroic Tradition*, p. 263; Willcock, *Companion*, p. 265 (still more references can be found in Postlethwaite, "Agamemnon"). While clearly holding the standard view, some of these authors note anomalies that will form part of my argument for an alternative interpretation. Taplin says, "It is a rather late and lowly 'curtain call' for Agamemnon. His prize is worth only one ox ([line] 886), and he makes no kind of direct response." Willcock says, "An awkwardness in the account of the spear-throwing event is that the prizes seem to be mentioned in reverse order in [line] 885 and that what turns out to be the second prize is in fact the weapon for the contest (but so was the first prize in the discus [weight throwing])"; he also notes that "Agamemnon can still find no words to reply to Achilleus."

25. The two exceptions are the armed combat and the weight throwing. In the latter (*Il.* 23.826–849), only the winner receives a prize; in the former, there are two prizes, but one of them is to be shared by the winner and the loser (*Il.* 23.804–810).

26. *Il.* 23.702–705.

27. In the chariot race, Achilles proposes to give the man presumed to be the best the prize actually won by Antilochos without asking the latter's permission (*Il.* 23.532–538). Given Antilochos' heated response (*Il.* 23.543–554), Achilles is not likely to risk a similar faux pas in the spear-throwing event.

28. At the beginning of the Quarrel, Achilles threatens to leave Troy, and Agamemnon replies, "Run away by all means if your heart drives you. I will not entreat you to stay here for my sake. There are others with me who will do me honor" (*Il.* 1.173–175).

29. *Il.* 23.647–649.

30. Griffin (*Life and Death*, p. 71), who believes that Achilles behaves magnanimously towards Agamemnon in the spear-throwing event, explains the latter's silence in terms of his inability to apologize with grace. But Agamemnon would be inclined not to apologize but to highlight the honor being bestowed upon him.

31. This plausible reasoning is evidently not airtight. For two authors who believe (without explaining the basis for their belief) that Achilles gives Agamemnon the loser's prize do not believe that any humiliation is intended. Dickie ("Fair and Foul Play," pp. 16–17) says that Achilles "willingly gives Agamemnon a prize and generously acknowledges his merits, while Agamemnon, for his part, willingly acquiesces in the first prize's going to another." According to Stanley (*Shield*, p. 230), "Achilleus is offering to Agamemnon the course of restraint that he has demonstrated in his own decision not to participate in the games."

32. Following Bassett ("The 'Αμαρτια of Achilles," p. 53), Postlethwaite questions Achilles' assertion that Agamemnon is the best spear-thrower (*Il.* 23.890–891). Achilles, he suggests, "is attempting to humiliate Agamemnon by making a statement which all know to be incorrect and thereby inviting him to acknowledge that the embarrassment of defeat is a very distinct possibility by accepting the prize without competition." Thus, "unlike the other competitions which make up the funeral games for Patroklos, Achilleus conducts the spear-throwing in a spirit not of magnanimity but rather of the same animosity which has characterized his dealings with Agamemnon throughout the poem" (Postlethwaite, "Agamemnon," p. 99). Postlethwaite's overall view of the spear-throwing event evidently coincides with mine, but his reasoning is quite different. His analysis quoted here implies that the prize Achilles gives Agamemnon is the one intended for the winner, whereas I claim that it is the one intended for the loser. More recently, he seems to accept the latter position on the basis of the order in which the prizes are listed (Postlethwaite, *Homer's Iliad*, p. 293). In any case, as I shall go on to argue,

Agamemnon's skill as a spear-thrower is irrelevant to his humiliation, and this irrelevance is the key to understanding and appreciating the artfulness of Achilles' revenge.

Allan and Cairns ("Conflict and Community," p. 136) see the antagonism pointed out by Postlethwaite manifested differently: "Achilles refuses to allow Agamemnon a chance to compete and thus prove his worth among the leaders, so that this exemption from competition ... can ... be regarded as a means of bolstering Achilles' own superiority." Kelly, who first endorsed Postlethwaite's position ("How to End," p. 383; see also Kelly, *Referential Commentary and Lexicon*, p. 240, n. 24), has since said, "It may be, perhaps, that this is less a case of active dishonouring of Agamemnon, and more a question of a certain agonothetic incompetence [on the part of Achilles]" ("Achilles in Control?," p. 107).

33. According to Cunliffe's lexicon, the Greek word used for "prize" in the context of the quarrel between Achilles and Agamemnon ($\gamma\varepsilon\rho\alpha\varsigma$) refers to a prize awarded to the king or a chief by the general consent or to a chief by the king; the word used in the context of the funeral games ($\alpha\varepsilon\theta\lambda o\nu$) refers to a prize for a victor in a contest. I do not think this difference weakens the connection I am trying to make.

34. *Il*. 9.328–336.

35. *Il*. 23.257–261.

36. The only exception is the weight-throwing contest, where only the winner is to receive a prize.

37. Where I see generosity, Kelly ("Achilles in Control?," pp. 96–98) sees Achilles' wish to show off his wealth. Regardless of his motivation, the point is that Achilles treats everyone very well until he gets to Agamemnon.

38. *Il*. 1.243–244, 355–356, 411–412; 16.55–59.

39. *Il*. 1.244, 412. Achilles also uses the term "best of the Achaians" for Agamemnon (*Il*. 1.90–91; cf. Nestor at *Il*. 2.82), but ironically.

40. Postlethwaite (*Homer's Iliad*, p. 293) concludes similarly that Achilles' treatment of Agamemnon "neatly reverses . . . Agamemnon's arrogant abuse of power in removing Achilleus' prize."

41. Bassett, "The $\text{'A}\mu\alpha\rho\tau\iota\alpha$ of Achilles," p. 53; Postlethwaite, "Agamemnon"; Postlethwaite, *Homer's Iliad*, p. 293.

42. *Il*. 23.288–538 together with 2.763–767.

43. To someone who is not familiar with Homer, the statement in line 895 of quote 3.4 that Agamemnon did not disobey Achilles could suggest that Agamemnon might have wanted to disobey the latter's proposal for the allocation of prizes. This inference would make my argument even stronger, but it would not be valid, as line 895 is formulaic (only the identity of the character changes) and carries no such connotation.

44. *Il. Comm.* VI, p. 271. I cite this authority because some translations (that of E. V. Rieu, before it was revised by Jones and D. C. H. Rieu, and that of Fagles) mistakenly state that Achilles gives the spear to Meriones.

45. *Il*. 1.188–222, esp. 194, 219–220.

46. Achilles does, of course, exercise restraint at the assembly where he is forced to accept Agamemnon's gifts, but this restraint is motivated solely by the desire to expedite his revenge against Hektor for the killing of Patroklos.

47. Jones, *Homer's* Iliad, pp. 294–296 (concerning *Il.* 22.262, 347, 396); *Il. Comm.* VI, p. 133 (concerning *Il.* 22. 260–272); Schein, *Hero*, pp. 152–153.

48. Bassett, *Poetry*, p. 198; Taplin, *Soundings*, pp. 62–63; Jones, *Homer's* Iliad, p. 47. Jones correctly cites *Il.* 16.16–18 as evidence that Achilles blames the army as a whole to some extent, but this does not mean that Agamemnon is not the focus of his wrath. Taplin calls attention to *Il.* 1.299, the sense of which Jones captures in his revision of Rieu's translation as follows: "You Greeks gave her to me, and now you take her back." But the focus of Achilles' wrath on Agamemnon is obvious in the continuation: "But there's much else by my swift black ship that is mine, and you will take none of that against my will. Come on, just try, so that everyone here can see what happens. Your black blood will soon be flowing down my spear." Achilles is clear at *Il.* 9.344, 367–369 that it is Agamemnon he blames for the seizure of his prize.

49. *Il.* 1.137–138.

50. Bassett, *Poetry*, pp. 176, 198.

51. *Il.* 1.231–232, as rendered in Jones' revision of Rieu's translation.

52. *Il.* 1.240–244, 407–412.

53. *Il.* 1.334–336.

54. *Il.* 9.196–204.

55. Fagles also leaves $\alpha\lambda\lambda\alpha$ untranslated, but extrapolates from the text to state explicitly what other translators only imply: "Take first prize and return to your hollow ships."

56. *Il. Comm.* VI, p. 270.

57. Richardson (*Il. Comm.* VI, pp. 164–165, 269) emphasizes the "marked sense of *diminuendo*" of the games that follow the funeral rites for Patroklos and points specifically to the spear-throwing event as the scene that brings the *diminuendo* to a close. In connection with this event, M. L. West (*Making of the Iliad*, p. 410) remarks, "We have the sense that P's stamina [P = the *Iliad* poet] is failing and that he is hastening to the end of the episode."

58. Some Greek manuscripts refer in *Od.* 24.87–89 to the funerals that had been attended by Achilles, not Agamemnon (Jones, *Homer's Odyssey*, p. 220), but this version would, if anything, only strengthen the point I am making.

59. The possibility that funeral games usually consisted of five events—a chariot race, boxing, wrestling, a foot race, and spear throwing—is suggested by *Il.* 23.621–623, 634–638 (Willcock, *Companion*, pp. 254, 262–263). If this is so, and if the additional three events in the *Iliad* are genuine (that is, not additions to Homer; cf. *Il. Comm.* VI, pp. 201–202, 258–259), these extra events would combine with the lavishness of the prizes offered by Achilles in establishing the splendidness of the games held in honor of Patroklos.

60. *Il.* 23.245–248.

61. Jones, *Homer's Odyssey*, p. 220; Rutherford, "From the *Iliad*," p. 130; Schein, *Hero*, p. 44; Usener, *Beobachtungen*, pp. 105, 108.

62. The parentheses I have inserted in quote 3.11 enclose material whose authenticity is suspect. To match the line division of the Greek, Lattimore's translation of *Il.* 23.91–92 would have to read something like this:

> "Therefore, let both our ashes be held in one single vessel,
> the golden two-handled urn the lady your mother gave you."

Line 92 is thought to have been added to the *Iliad* with *Od.* 24.73–74 in mind (*Il. Comm.* VI, p. 176), and is therefore ignored when I compare quotes 3.10 and 3.11. If the parenthesized material in quote 3.11 (or equivalent material elsewhere in the passage—cf. *Il. Comm.* VI, p. 174) is included in the comparison, the already significant correspondence between quotes 3.10 and 3.11 becomes even more striking. Although the two passages, as quoted in translation, describe somewhat differently the container for the remains of Achilles and Patroklos, the term used in the Greek is the same in both cases, translating directly to "golden amphora." Furthermore, these are the only passages in all of Homer that refer to a golden amphora, and in both cases the amphora was given by Achilles' mother. (The reader will note that quotes 3.10 and 3.11 justify a somewhat stronger statement: according to both passages, the amphora was given *to Achilles* by his mother. In the case of quote 3.10, however, Lattimore only assumes that Achilles was the recipient of the gift; this assumption is not explicitly supported by the Greek, and is not made by other translators.)

63. *Od.* 24.80–81.
64. *Il.* 23.96.
65. *Il.* 23.239–248; see also 252–254.
66. *Il.* 17.651–655, 679–692.
67. *Il.* 23.555–559, 794–797.
68. *Il.* 23.403–416, 543–554, 587–595, 787–792.
69. *Od.* 11.409–434, 451–453; 24.96–97, 199–202.
70. *Od.* 11.387–389; 24.19–22. Note that Achilles apparently knows the circumstances of Agamemnon's death before he hears about them from Agamemnon (*Od.* 24.28–34).
71. *Od.* 4.524–528; cf. Jones, *Homer's Odyssey*, p. 41.
72. Dowden, "Epic Tradition," p. 202; Mueller, *The Iliad*, p. 122; *Il. Comm.* VI, pp. 202–203, 220, 246, 249; Whitman, *Heroic Tradition*, pp. 263–264; Willcock, *Companion*, pp. 261, 285–287.
73. Heubeck ("Books XXIII–XXIV," p. 368) interprets quote 3.10 to mean that the bones of Antilochos are kept near those of Achilles and Patroklos, but slightly separated from them (perhaps in a separate vessel). The *Odyssey* also alludes to the friendship between Achilles and Antilochos by showing their shades, along with those of Patroklos and Aias, "hanging out" together in the underworld (*Od.* 11.467–469; 24.15–19).
74. *Od.* 11.543–564.
75. *Il.* 23.700–737; cf. *Il. Comm.* VI, p. 246, and Willcock, *Companion*, p. 261.
76. *Od.* 4.499–511; cf. *Il. Comm.* VI, p. 220.
77. *Il.* 23.473–481; cf. *Il. Comm.* VI, pp. 220, 222.
78. According to the *Little Iliad*, one of the poems of the Epic Cycle, the loss of Achilles' armor to Odysseus causes Aias to commit suicide (Burgess, *Tradition of the Trojan War*, p. 179; Dowden, "Epic Tradition," p. 199; M. L. West, *Greek Epic Fragments*, p. 121); the *Odyssey* clearly alludes to this suicide at 11.548–551 (Heubeck, "Books IX–XII," p. 110). Each of the post-Iliadic events I mention is therefore associated with the death of a Greek hero. The death of Agamemnon is obviously consistent with this pattern, but I do

not want to make too much of this, because one may wish to cite possible foreshadowing that departs from the pattern. For example, the Wooden Horse used in Odysseus's famous stratagem was made by Epeios (*Od.* 8.493; 11.524), who is mentioned in the *Iliad* only in connection with the funeral games for Patroklos (*Il.* 23.664–699, 836–840).

79. Clarke, *Art*, pp. 10–12; Heubeck, "General Introduction," pp. 16–17; Heubeck, "Books XXIII–XXIV," p. 380; S. West, "Books I–IV," p. 60.

80. In comparing the approaches to Achilles made by Priam and Agamemnon, I follow Taplin, *Soundings*, pp. 72–73, 269–270 (see also Rutherford, *Homer*, p. 52). That Homer wants us to make such a comparison is suggested by the parallelism noted by Macleod (*Iliad XXIV*, pp. 20–21) between *Il.* 9.378–387 and *Il.* 22.348–354. In the former passage, Achilles rejects Agamemnon's offer of gifts; in the latter, he rejects in very similar terms Hektor's dying request that he accept the ransom that Priam will offer for his son's body. (Macleod asserts that this parallelism is matched by a similarity in the final outcomes, that is, that Achilles eventually accepts Agamemnon's offer, just as he eventually allows Priam to ransom Hektor's body. As we have seen, however, Achilles never willingly accepts Agamemnon's gifts; they are essentially forced on him during the spurious reconciliation, when he will do anything to rejoin the fighting and avenge the death of Patroklos.)

81. *Il.* 21.97–105.

82. *Il.* 24.486–489, 503–506; cf. *Il.* 22.415–421 and Macleod, *Iliad XXIV*, p. 22.

83. *Il.* 24.519–521. Achilles' words echo those of Hekabe when she learns of Priam's intention to go to Achilles to ransom Hektor's body (*Il.* 24.203–205).

84. *Il.* 24.559–570, 583–586.

85. *Il.* 24.628–633. See the commentary on lines 629–632 in Macleod, *Iliad XXIV*, p. 142.

86. At *Il.* 24.650 Achilles addresses Priam as γερον φιλε, which has been translated as "aged sir and good friend" (Lattimore), "old friend" (Rieu, revised), and "dear old sir" (Murray, revised), of which the last may be the most accurate.

87. *Il.* 24.634–685.

88. *Il. Comm.* VI, pp. 165–166; see also, for example, Schein, *Hero*, p. 156.

89. I must take exception to the view that "the Achilles of the Lykaon scene is already in some sense the Achilles of the Priam scene" (Mueller, *The Iliad*, p. 71). For Achilles to see Priam as an individual with his own dignity, something inside him (his rage and the pride behind it) must first quiet down; no such transformation occurs in the Lykaon scene (see especially *Il.* 21.97–135), where Achilles is consumed by fury and self-assertion despite his awareness of the mortality he shares with his victim.

90. Postlethwaite, "Agamemnon," p. 102; Postlethwaite, *Homer's Iliad*, p. 307; *Il. Comm.* VI, p. 346.

91. *Il.* 23.156–157.

92. The relationship between Achilles and Agamemnon described in section 3.6 makes clear how we should understand the statement in *Il.* 24.649 that Achilles speaks sarcastically in quote 3.12: the sarcasm refers not to Achilles' dealings with Priam, which are quite harmonious at this point, but to his tone when speaking of Agamemnon. This is one of two possible interpretations attributed to Walter Leaf by Richardson (*Il. Comm.* VI, p. 344), and it is strongly endorsed by Postlethwaite (*Homer's Iliad*, p. 306).

93. A third dispute is also of interest thanks to an observation made by Kelly (*Referential Commentary and Lexicon*, pp. 84, 131; "Achilles in Control?," pp. 93–94) and by Allan and Cairns ("Conflict and Community," p. 136). When a quarrel between Idomeneus and the lesser Aias erupts during the chariot race, Achilles acts as a peacemaker (*Il.* 23.492–498), but only, note these authors, after Idomeneus has proposed to have the dispute arbitrated by Agamemnon (*Il.* 23.485–487). Allan and Cairns interpret this to mean that Achilles "continues to be acutely sensitive about his authority in relation to Agamemnon"; it is certainly true that he would not want Agamemnon to be given a position of respect in the games. Kelly first expressed a view similar to that of Allan and Cairns, but has since come to believe that Achilles must be reminded of his proper role; it is not clear though that someone who needed to be reminded would intervene as effectively as Achilles does. In any case, the way Achilles assumes the role proposed for Agamemnon prefigures the change in their relative positions on the scale of authority, as described in section 3.6.

94. This observation goes back to Eustathius (*Il. Comm.* VI, pp. 228–229).

95. *Il.* 23.293–295. For additional connections in the *Iliad* between Menelaos and Agamemnon, see Mueller, *The Iliad*, p. 167.

96. *Il.* 23.441.

97. *Il.* 1.152–168.

98. *Il.* 1.254–291. Agamemnon's arrogance is, of course, also evident in his original confrontation with Achilles (e.g., *Il.* 1.184–7).

99. Apparent allusions to the Quarrel in the disputes that follow the chariot race have often been pointed out (Macleod, *Iliad XXIV*, pp. 30–31; *Il. Comm.* VI, pp. 228–230; Sheppard, *Pattern*, p. 201; Taplin, *Soundings*, p. 255; Kelly, "Achilles in Control?," p. 98), but usually with no suggestion of a coherent pattern in these allusions. Macleod comes close to such a suggestion, however, and one of his arguments coincides with one of mine (the contrast between Menelaos's gratitude to Antilochos and Agamemnon's lack of gratitude to Achilles). As an adherent of the conventional interpretation of the spear-throwing event, Macleod naturally includes that event in the contrast between the funeral games and the Quarrel.

Although I have listed Taplin with those who relate a dispute after the chariot race to the Quarrel, he actually likens Antilochos's refusal to give up the mare (see quote 3.15) to Agamemnon's refusal to release the girl he has taken as a prize (*Il.* 1.29), the event that eventually triggers the Quarrel. This comparison is also made by some of the other authors mentioned, but in my opinion it is superficial: whereas Agamemnon intends to deprive a father of his daughter, Antilochos is justifiably indignant at the prospect of having the mare he won taken away from him.

100. Allan and Cairns, "Conflict and Community," pp. 133–135; Kelly, "Achilles in Control?," pp. 100–101.

101. The beginning and end of the funeral games are thus poles apart. The *Iliad* as a whole also has a polar structure (see Sheppard, *Pattern*, pp. 208–209; *Il. Comm.* VI, p. 5; Macleod, *Iliad XXIV*, p. 33, part (b); Schein, *Hero*, pp. 31–33; Schein, "Structure and Interpretation," pp. 345–348; Whitman, *Heroic Tradition*, pp. 256–257): The poem begins with the quarrel between Achilles and Agamemnon and ends with the reconciliation between Achilles and Priam; the cause of the quarrel can be traced to Agamemnon's rejection of a father's attempt to ransom his daughter, while the reconciliation is intimately connected with Achilles' acceptance of a father's attempt to ransom the body of his son. The well-known observation that a structural principle that is implemented on one scale in Homer is often implemented on other scales as well will be illustrated again in section 5.7.

CHAPTER 4: Inconsistency and the Homeric Question

1. The sentence that references this note draws on the eloquence of others; see Dodds, "Analysts," p. 1.

2. Horace, *Ars Poetica*, lines 358–360 (translation from Rutherford, *Homer*, p. 29, n. 92). Another ancient critic expressed a similar view: "I have myself cited a good many faults in Homer and the other greatest authors, and though these slips certainly offend my taste, yet I prefer to call them not wilful mistakes but careless oversights, let in casually almost and at random by the heedlessness of genius" ("Longinus," *On the Sublime* 33.4).

3. Aristotle (*Poetics*, chap. 25) treats contradictions separately from impossibilities because they can sometimes be resolved; contradictions that cannot be resolved—true inconsistencies—should evidently be considered impossibilities, although Aristotle does not explicitly include them in this category of problems.

4. Pope, *An Essay on Criticism*, lines 179–180 (see also lines 169–178).

5. S. West, "Books I–IV," p. 62. Similarly, Scodel's *Credible Impossibilities* is essentially Aristotelian in outlook. The explanation of Penelope's "surrender" proposed in chapter 2 provides a nice illustration of Pope's couplet (although one certainly not envisioned by Pope): the "error" is the surrender (a psychological impossibility for the reasons given in section 2.2), and the "stratagem" is the action that takes place below the surface of the poem.

6. M. L. West, "Homeric Question," p. 386.

7. Dodds, "Unitarians," p. 8.

8. Whitman, *Heroic Tradition*, p. 1.

9. See, for example, M. L. West, "Homeric Question"; A. Parry, "Have We Homer's *Iliad*?".

10. This succinct formulation is due to Fowler, "Homeric question," p. 220.

11. Clay, *Wrath*, pp. 3–4.

12. M. Parry, "Traditional Epithet" and "Oral Verse-Making," pp. 314–324.

13. Bowra, *Tradition and Design*, pp. 112–113; Bowra, *Heroic Poetry*, pp. 299–300.

14. Lord, "Huso," p. 441; see also Lord, *Singer of Tales*, pp. 94–95. An alleged example of this scenario cited by Lord ("Huso," p. 444) actually contains no inconsistency according to the interpretation suggested by Scott (*The Unity of Homer*, pp. 156–158). Scott greatly understated the number and seriousness of contradictions in Homer, but his rejection of this one was reasonable and was implicitly endorsed by A. Parry ("Introduction," pp. lvi–lvii).

15. Hansen, *Conference Sequence*.

16. Even if some inconsistencies are explained by the difficulties of oral improvisation, others might be better understood as signs of multiple authorship. Although this is certainly true in principle, Hansen argues in *The Conference Sequence* that scholars who continue to promote the viewpoint of the analysts while accepting the oral nature of the poems have not appreciated the full power of the explanation in terms of oral poetry.

17. See Janko, "Dictated Texts" (especially p. 7 on anomalies as signs of "the process of dictation at work in the texts"; on this see also *Il. Comm.* IV, p. 37). In my statement of the hypothesis I accept the argument of A. Parry ("Have We Homer's *Iliad*?", p. 201) that the name "Homer" "must be reserved for the poet who composed the *Iliad* at the time when it was put into writing."

18. A. Parry, "Introduction," p. lxi, n. 1. See also A. Parry, "Have We Homer's *Iliad*?", p. 178, n. 4, and pp. 214–216; Bowra, *Heroic Poetry*, pp. 240–241; Griffin, *Odyssey*, pp. 22–24; Rutherford, *Books XIX and XX*, pp. 44–46.

19. Mueller, *The Iliad*, p. 5. Heubeck ("General Introduction," p. 12) is more assertive: "The new concept of epic poetry, destined to create out of traditional methods and possibilities something that would both continue the tradition and yet surpass it, could only be realized by using the art of writing."

20. M. L. West, "Homeric Question," p. 391.

21. Thus, Heubeck, "General Introduction," pp. 11–12; A. Parry, "Have We Homer's *Iliad*?", pp. 190–201 on the greatness of the *Iliad*, together with pp. 212–216 (especially the last sentence) on the role of writing. The conviction that writing is necessary for grand design and powerful detail is attacked by Janko, "Dictated Texts," pp. 6–7.

22. Mueller, *The Iliad*, p. 176. Similarly, Goold, "Homeric Composition," p. 12: "[F]or some reason wholesale changes of the text were undesirable, an obstacle lay in the way, and alteration was kept to the absolute minimum."

23. Goold, "Homeric Composition"; Mueller, *The Iliad*, pp. 173–186; M. L. West, *Making of the Iliad*, chap. 5.

24. See S. West, "Transmission," p. 48.

25. Scodel (*Credible Impossibilities*, p. 14) makes explicit what other authors assume implicitly when she asserts that deliberate inconsistency (perverse inconsistency in my terminology) is not found in archaic Greek literature. Her examples of such inconsistency in later literature are outside the scope of this book; my *assumption* is that they have no bearing on the present discussion.

26. Gurdjieff first explained his ideas, including his ideas on art, to pupils around 1915. The ideas became generally available shortly after his death in 1949 with the publication of a record of his talks in Ouspensky's *In Search of the Miraculous: Fragments of an Unknown Teaching* and of his own *Beelzebub's Tales to His Grandson: An Objectively Impartial Criticism of the Life of Man*.

CHAPTER 5: The Relationship between the *Iliad* and the *Odyssey*

1. Burkert, "Ares and Aphrodite"; Doherty, "Introduction," pp. 6–7; Pucci, "Sirens"; Rutherford, "From the *Iliad*"; Usener, *Beobachtungen*; M. L. West, *Making of the Odyssey*, pp. 25–26, 70–76.

2. Cairns, "Introduction," p. 10; Rutherford, *Homer*, pp. 76–77. See also Knox, "Introduction," p. 23. Arguments for the priority of the *Iliad* were given in antiquity by "Longinus" (*On the Sublime* 9.12).

3. Rutherford, "From the *Iliad*," p. 121; Tracy, *Story*, pp. 149–150.

4. *Il. Comm.* IV, p. 14. Fowler ("Homeric question," p. 225) and M. L. West ("Homeric Question," p. 392) have expressed opposing opinions regarding the validity of Janko's conclusions. West's otherwise reasonable criticism ceases to apply to the relative chronology of the *Iliad* and the *Odyssey* if these two epics were composed by the same poet, a possibility consistent with Janko's results and with the thrust of the present volume.

5. The description in quote 3.10 of the jar containing the remains of Achilles and Patroklos is the most obvious allusion to the *Iliad* in the *Odyssey*. Other allusions are discussed by Burkert ("Ares and Aphrodite") and Pucci ("Sirens"). It should be noted that some authors (e.g., Nagy, *Achaeans*, p. 42) deny the possibility of such allusions; this position is rightly criticized by Rutherford ("From the *Iliad*," pp. 125–127) and is further undermined in chapter 5.

6. Rutherford, "From the *Iliad*"; Usener, *Beobachtungen*; M. L. West, *Making of the Odyssey*, pp. 25–26, 70–76.

7. *Il.* 22.440–441.

8. In Lattimore's translation, *Od.* 21.352 reads "ply their work also. The men shall have the bow in their keeping,"; I have modified this in quote 5.3 to preserve the strict parallelism with *Od.* 1.358 in quote 5.2 (and with *Il.* 6.492 in quote 5.1) that characterizes the Greek text.

9. Indeed, the absence of formulaic language in quotes 5.1–5.3 has been demonstrated by Usener (*Beobachtungen*, p. 56), who documents the rarity of the individual components of those passages (ibid., pp. 51–53). For example, both the first and second halves of *Il.* 6.490 (in quote 5.1) occur nowhere else in Homer except *Od.* 1.356 (in quote 5.2) and 21.350 (in quote 5.3).

10. *Od.* 2.93–110, 19.137–156, 24.129–148.

11. Rutherford, "From the *Iliad*," p. 141; Usener, *Beobachtungen*, p. 53. Note, in fact, that identical passages (*Od.* 1.332–335 = 21.63–66) are used to specify that Penelope is in the house at the time of quotes 5.2 and 5.3.

12. Cunliffe's lexicon on οικος and οικονδε. See also Usener, *Beobachtungen*, pp. 53–54, n. 18.

13. Cunliffe's lexicon on οικος.

14. Although Penelope's weaving and use of the distaff are mentioned briefly in other contexts (*Od.* 15.517, 17.97), the three tellings of the story of her ruse (*Od.* 2.93–110, 19.137–156, 24.129–148) create a much stronger impression.

15. S. West, "Books I–IV," p. 120.

16. Helen: *Od.* 4.135–146, 4.234–264; Arete: *Od.* 7.233–239, 11.335–341. Telemachos's remark is invalid even if the word that Lattimore translates as "discussion" is interpreted as "story-telling" (cf. Rutherford, "From the *Iliad*," p. 141), since one of Helen's contributions to the conversation is a story from the Trojan War.

17. Fernández-Galiano, "Books XXI–XXII," p. 190.

18. *Il.* 6.403, 22.56–57 and 104–107, 24.728–730.

19. Aristarchus athetized quote 5.2 (Fernández-Galiano, "Books XXI–XXII," p. 190; Usener, *Beobachtungen*, p. 53, n. 18; S. West, "Books I–IV," p. 120), meaning that he indicated doubt as to its authenticity but left it in the text (*Il. Comm.* IV, p. 23). Paradoxically, athetesis (as opposed to omission) by Aristarchus indicates that the athetized passage was well attested in the manuscripts known to him (*Il. Comm.* IV, p. 28).

West is inclined to follow Aristarchus in suspecting that quote 5.2 is an interpolation. While her observations on the strangeness of this passage are persuasive, I believe this strangeness was intentional on Homer's part, an aspect of what I will soon refer to (in the main text) as his perverseness.

20. This conclusion agrees with the views of most other commentators. Cf. Fernández-Galiano, "Books XXI–XXII," p. 190; *Il. Comm.* II, p. 224; Rutherford, "From the *Iliad*," pp. 140–141; Usener, *Beobachtungen*, p. 66 (see also the references cited by Usener in the continuation of n. 18 on p. 54); M. L. West, *Making of the Odyssey*, p. 70. However, on the basis of a single weak point in Usener's discussion, Griffin ("Relationship," p. 290) questions whether quote 5.1 was original to the *Iliad* and suggests instead that quotes 5.2 and 5.3 may have been derived from another source.

21. *Od.* 1.397–398.

22. The swineherd is following instructions given to him in secret by Odysseus at *Od.* 21.234–235; the signal for him to carry out the instructions is Odysseus's request at *Od.* 21.281–284.

23. Cf. Fernández-Galiano, "Books XXI–XXII," p. 194: Telemachos's "implicit confession of impotence is designed to lull the suitors into a sense of security." This interpretation is perfectly reasonable, but cannot account for Telemachos's claim to power in quote 5.3 (for which there is no logical explanation).

24. *Od.* 1.360–364 = *Od.* 21.354–358.

25. *Od.* 1.88–95. Athene gives the instructions to Telemachos at *Od.* 1.271–302.

26. *Od.* 2.6–145.

27. *Od.* 1.374–380 = *Od.* 2.139–145 except for the very beginning of the first line.

28. See Jones, *Homer's Odyssey*, p. 16; S. West, "Books I–IV," p. 121; Hansen, *Conference Sequence*, p. 31.

29. *Od.* 1.269–305.

30. *Od.* 1.320–324.

31. The last two lines of quote 5.6 have been modified from Lattimore's translation to preserve the parallelism with the corresponding lines of quotes 5.2 and 5.3 in the Greek text.

32. Usener, *Beobachtungen*, pp. 48–49; Rutherford, "From the *Iliad*," p. 141, n. 43; M. L. West, *Making of the Odyssey*, p. 70.

33. Both Nausikaa (the daughter of Alkinoös and Arete) and Athene tell Odysseus that Arete, not Alkinoös, decides whether the request of a suppliant is to be granted (*Od.* 6.310–315, 7.75–77), and Odysseus accordingly addresses his supplication to the queen (*Od.* 7.139–152). The fact that Alkinoös is the one who answers Odysseus's supplication merely reflects a difference between appearance and reality. The reality is that Arete holds the power, but Alkinoös wishes to maintain the appearance that the power is his (as we see in the last line of quote 5.6). He replies to the supplication in order to maintain this appearance, but his granting of Odysseus's request must be tentative until he can be sure that it will be backed by Arete. For this reason, he at first promises just to hold an assembly of elders in which the conveyance requested by Odysseus will be discussed (*Od.* 7.189–196). Not until Arete questions Odysseus and he gives her a most satisfactory response does Alkinoös unequivocally promise him the conveyance itself (*Od.* 7.317–328) and does Odysseus rejoice and express his gratitude (*Od.* 7.329–333).

Assistance in the keeping up of appearances is provided by the Phaiakian elder Echeneos, who diplomatically calls on Alkinoös whenever the attention of the court has come to be focused on Arete (*Od.* 7.155–166, 11.342–346). Finally, I would note that Odysseus's parting words to Arete form one component of a ring composition (Odysseus first addresses Arete at 7.146 and says farewell to her at 13.59; Alkinoös has Pontonoös serve wine at 7.179 and 13.50; Odysseus first addresses Alkinoös at 7.208 and says farewell to him at 13.38), and as such they conclude the Phaiakian section of the *Odyssey* with a reference to the hero's supplication of the queen (ring composition is discussed in section 5.7). For further discussion, see Fenik, *Studies*, pp. 105–106, 126–129 (Saïd [*Homer and the* Odyssey, pp. 264–266] ignores the crucial second part of Fenik's discussion, and when she states that Arete's proposal of gifts for Odysseus at 11.338–341 simply repeats the proposal made by Alkinoös at 8.387–397, she ignores the fact that Arete is proposing gifts in addition to those already collected by her husband).

34. *Od.* 24.23–97.

35. Another allusion to the *Iliad* can possibly be seen immediately after quote 3.10, in *Od.* 24.80–84, where Agamemnon describes the grave mound that was built for Achilles "by the wide Hellespont" so that it can be seen from the water by men yet to be born. The correspondence with Hektor's words at *Il.* 7.85–88 is especially persuasive if one considers his description of the Greek who might be buried in such a mound (*Il.* 7.73–75). This correspondence is discussed by Nagy (*Achaeans*, pp. 28–29), although this scholar on principle would not claim to have identified an allusion (ibid., p. 42).

36. Jones, *Homer's Odyssey*, p. 219.

37. Tracy, *Story*, p. 143. Tracy's statement that Achilles and Agamemnon are never reconciled in the *Iliad* can be interpreted in two ways. Either he adheres to the interpretation of the spear-throwing event advanced in chapter 3, or he means that the reconciliation assumed in the conventional interpretation of that event is only superficial. In any case, he goes on to say that the friendly conversation between Agamemnon and Achilles "shows that even the bitterest enemies can make it up and foreshadows the rapprochement between Odysseus and the families of the suitors." However, one crucial difference between the two scenes should be noted: the rapprochement between Odysseus and the families of the suitors requires forceful intervention by Zeus and Athene, but Homer gives no corresponding explanation for the apparently spontaneous reconciliation of Agamemnon and Achilles in the underworld.

38. *Od.* 11.543–564.

39. M. L. West, *Greek Epic Fragments*, p. 155; Burgess, *Tradition of the Trojan War*, p. 180; Dowden, "Epic Tradition," p. 200.

40. The most detailed accounts of Agamemnon's murder and related events are found at *Od.* 1.35–43, 3.261–275 and 303–312, 4.521–537, and 11.409–434, the last being the account of Agamemnon himself. It is worth noting that the shade of Achilles also alludes to the circumstances of Agamemnon's death (*Od.* 24.34).

41. *Od.* 4.521–537.

42. Although Homer is not known for the consistency of his eschatology, he does consistently reject the notion that a ghost, once admitted to the underworld, can visit the land of the living. In the *Little Iliad*, another poem from the Epic Cycle, the ghost of Achilles is said to appear to Neoptolemos (his son) at Troy (Burgess, *Tradition of the Trojan War*, p. 179; M. L. West, *Greek Epic Fragments*, p. 123; Dowden, "Epic Tradition," p. 199). But in the *Odyssey*, the shade of Achilles has to ask Odysseus (during the latter's visit to the underworld) whether Neoptolemos ever went to fight at Troy (*Od.* 11.492–493), despite the fact that "the *Odyssey* poet shows an extensive acquaintance with the subject matter of the *Little Iliad*" (M. L. West, *Greek Epic Fragments*, p. 16; cf. M. L. West, *Making of the Odyssey*, p. 28). As in the case of the warning of Agamemnon by the ghost of Achilles, it is as if the poet of the *Odyssey* wants to signal his rejection of a visitation by the ghost of Achilles that may have been traditional. The ghost of Patroklos does appear to Achilles in the *Iliad*, but only because he has not yet been buried and cannot enter the underworld; once he receives his "rite of burning," he says, he will never again "come back from death" (*Il.* 23.65–76).

43. One of the allusions to the *Iliad* discussed in section 3.3 is the statement at the end of quote 3.10 that Achilles prized Antilochos above the rest of his companions after the death of Patroklos. This statement contradicts a similar description in the *Iliad* of Achilles' attitude toward Automedon and Alkimos (*Il.* 24.574–575). I do not believe this contradiction is significant, however, since the close friendship between Achilles and Antilochos is well documented in the *Iliad* (see section 3.3). (In addition, the poem from the Epic Cycle known as the *Aithiopis* describes a relationship between Achilles and Antilochos that is analogous to the relationship between Achilles and

Patroklos in the *Iliad*: despite a warning from Thetis, Achilles kills Memnon after the latter kills Antilochos [Burgess, *Tradition of the Trojan War*, p. 179; M. L. West, *Greek Epic Fragments*, p. 113; Dowden, "Epic Tradition," p. 199; see also Willcock, *Companion*, p. 258].) Even if, despite this, we ignore the allusion to the *Iliad* in the last two lines of quote 3.10 (or regard these lines as inconsistent with the *Iliad*), we still have the undeniable allusion earlier in the passage to Patroklos's wish that his remains be buried with those of Achilles, and the relationship to the *Iliad* of the conversation between the shades of Achilles and Agamemnon remains essentially the same as I describe it in section 5.3.

44. The ABA structure reflected in the content of the three songs of Demodokos (as well as in Odysseus's reactions to them and in the time Homer devotes to them) is actually part of a more elaborate ring composition, for which see Whitman, *Heroic Tradition*, p. 289.

45. Lattimore is a little free in his translation of *Od.* 8.73–74. It is actually the song itself that is said to be famous (Segal, "*Kleos*," p. 207; see also the translations offered by Clay [*Wrath*, p. 98], Cook, Hammond, Merrill, Murray, Nagy [*Achaeans*, p. 22]), but of course the subject of the song (the quarrel between Odysseus and Achilles) must also be famous.

46. Clay, *Wrath*, p. 102; Knox, "Introduction," p. 23; Nagy, *Achaeans*, pp. 22–23.

47. Marg, "Das erste Lied," p. 24; Rüter, *Odysseeinterpretationen*, p. 248. The argument is rejected by Clay (*Wrath*, pp. 100–101) for reasons I do not understand, but Macleod ("Homer on Poetry," p. 303) and Rutherford ("From the *Iliad*," p. 136) agree that the quarrel of Demodokos's first song must be placed before the Quarrel of the *Iliad*.

Clay endorses the speculation of ancient commentators that the first song of Demodokos refers to a quarrel that occurred after the end of the *Iliad* over whether Troy would be taken by force or by guile. She points out that this interpretation allows us to connect the first song of Demodokos with the last one, inasmuch as the latter demonstrates the ultimate victory of guile by recounting the taking of Troy by means of Odysseus's stratagem of the Wooden Horse. But an equally cogent connection emerges if we assume that the supposed quarrel between Achilles and Odysseus took place not long after Agamemnon consulted the oracle concerning (presumably) the success of the upcoming expedition to Troy. For we can then say that the first song deals with the beginning of the Trojan War as the last one does with its end (Macleod, "Homer on Poetry," p. 305), a tidy arrangement indeed.

According to Clay, the quarrel between Achilles and Odysseus was a contest for supremacy between Achilles, unrivalled in might, and Odysseus, renowned for his cunning. But there would have been no basis for such a contest after the end of the *Iliad* (when, according to Clay, the quarrel took place). The indispensability of Achilles to the Greek cause had already been amply demonstrated by the deterioration in the Greek military position after his withdrawal from the fighting, as well as by the routing of the Trojan forces after his return. Furthermore, he had already won the greatest possible glory by his victory over the leading Trojan hero. By the end of the *Iliad*, Achilles surely had nothing to prove and no motivation to engage in a contest for supremacy with Odysseus. Equally, it would have been futile for Odysseus or anyone else to claim supremacy over Achilles. On the contrary, the stratagem of the Wooden Horse can be regarded as an homage to Achilles since it was based on the premise that the Trojans would believe that the Greeks had given up, a premise that became plausible only after the death of the supreme Greek warrior.

This argument obviously cannot be applied to the position of Rüter, who agrees with Clay and the ancient commentators regarding the subject of the quarrel (*Odysseeinterpretationen*, pp. 249–251) but places the quarrel before the time frame of the *Iliad*. In my opinion, however, all speculation regarding the subject of the quarrel between Achilles and Odysseus is pointless: what I argue in chapter 5 is that that quarrel is simply a device used by Homer in the *Odyssey* to elicit a certain kind of surprise as part of his strategy for defining the relationship between that poem and the *Iliad*.

48. Cf. *Il.* 1.91, 2.82.

49. *Il.* 2.1–71.

50. Hainsworth, "Books V–VIII," pp. 351–352 on *Od.* 8.79–82, 80; Jones, *Homer's Odyssey*, p. 71.

51. See Scodel, *Listening*, p. 164.

52. Phoinix says to Achilles that Agamemnon chose as his ambassadors to supplicate him "those who to yourself are the dearest of all the Argives" (*Il.* 9.520–522). Although Phoinix misrepresents the situation in some respects (Postlethwaite, *Homer's Iliad*, p. 140: it was Nestor, not Agamemnon, who selected the ambassadors, and Agamemnon's intention was not to *supplicate* Achilles), he cannot of course misrepresent to Achilles the latter's own feelings towards the ambassadors.

53. Clay, *Wrath*, p. 104; Nagy, *Achaeans*, pp. 51–53; Rüter, *Odysseeinterpretationen*, pp. 249–250; Rutherford, *Homer*, p. 78; Stanford, *Ulysses Theme*, p. 18.

54. In addition to the references in the preceding note, see *Il. Comm.* III, p. 102; Jones, *Homer's* Iliad, pp. 155–156; Postlethwaite, *Homer's Iliad*, p. 135; Scodel, *Listening*, p. 164; Taplin, *Soundings*, pp. 70–71; Willcock, *Companion*, pp. 101–102.

55. Nagy (*Achaeans*, pp. 52–55) attempts to reconcile quote 5.11 with a supposed enmity between Achilles and Odysseus by noting that the first two lines of the passage (lines 197 and 198) employ Greek grammatical forms ("duals") that refer to exactly two people and by asserting that the two whom Achilles calls "dearest of all the Achaians" must be Aias and Phoinix (the other two ambassadors besides Odysseus). Scodel (*Listening*, p. 164) argues convincingly that Achilles does *not* mean to exclude Odysseus by his use of duals: "Even if Achilles hated Odysseus, it would be very rude for him to greet the other two graciously and ignore Odysseus, who is clearly with them. If he did ignore Odysseus, could Odysseus ignore the snub and speak first, as if he had a chance to persuade him?" Moreover, Nagy's interpretation addresses only part of the famous problem of the duals in the Embassy scene. For example, it fails to account for the equally perplexing use of duals for the three ambassadors as they walk towards Achilles' shelter (line 182), pray for success in persuading him (line 183), and reach their destination (line 185).

The problem is so resistant to a convincing solution that Lattimore has suppressed the duals in the part of his translation reproduced in quote 5.11. I shall argue in chapter 6 that the problem's intractability supports a radically new interpretation that is also suggested by independent considerations.

56. Rüter (*Odysseeinterpretationen*, p. 250) sees a second cutting remark supposedly aimed at Odysseus in the speech of Achilles that contains quote 5.12. At *Il.* 9.345–347 Achilles says that, rather than trying in vain to persuade him to return to the fighting, Agamemnon should consider with Odysseus and the other kings how to prevent their ships from being set on fire by the Trojans. Any force this remark may have as an implied criticism of Odysseus is surely diminished by the mention of the other kings. Nevertheless, Rüter suggests that Achilles means to minimize the significance of Odysseus's cleverness and guile. This allows him to see a connection between Achilles' remark and the quarrel mentioned in the first song of Demodokos, which has been characterized as a dispute over whether Troy would be conquered by the guile of Odysseus or by the might of Achilles (see note 47 above). (As Rüter mentions, the connection he sees between Achilles' remark and the first song of Demodokos was also seen by Aristarchus; cf. Clay, *Wrath*, p. 104, n. 99.) Rüter claims that Odysseus refrains from making a rejoinder to Achilles' remark for fear of endangering the success of the Embassy. But Odysseus's participation in the Embassy is itself enough to put to rest the idea that he and Achilles are arguing over the relative merits of their respective strengths, for the mission of the Embassy is to recruit the might of Achilles to rescue the Greeks from a situation to which the guile of Odysseus offers no solution. (This straightforward observation is ignored by Nagy, who believes that the Embassy does contain evidence of the hostility between Achilles and Odysseus that is reflected in the first song of Demodokos. Instead, Nagy considers it ironic that "Odysseus is the one who is pleading for what the Achaeans most sorely need at this point, the might of Achilles" [Nagy, *Achaeans*, p. 48]. I regard this appeal to irony as simply a way to deal with inconvenient evidence.)

57. See Clay, *Wrath*, p. 103; Jones, *Homer's Odyssey*, p. 70; Macleod, "Homer on Poetry," p. 303; Marg, "Das erste Lied," pp. 24–26; Rüter, *Odysseeinterpretationen*, pp. 248–249; Rutherford, "From the *Iliad*," p. 136; Saïd, *Homer and the* Odyssey, p. 128; Tracy, *Story*, p. 51. A fascinating but highly speculative connection between the first song of Demodokos and the proem of the *Iliad* is described by Redfield, "Proem," pp. 472–473 (and attributed by Redfield to A. Pagliaro, "Il proemio dell' *Iliade*," *Nuovi saggi di critica semantica* [2nd ed., Messina and Florence, 1963], pp. 3–46).

Nagy (*Achaeans*, p. 43) acknowledges that in the first song of Demodokos "we do indeed see what amounts to an Iliadic overture in the thematic combination of Achilles, Agamemnon, grief for Trojans and Achaeans, involvement of Apollo, and the Will of Zeus." But he goes on to say, "Nevertheless, we may not infer that these themes were based specifically on the opening of our *Iliad*." The latter remark reflects his general stance that "when we are dealing with the traditional poetry of the Homeric (and Hesiodic) compositions, it is not justifiable to claim that a passage in any text can refer to another passage in another text" (Nagy, *Achaeans*, p. 42). This stance is contradicted by abundant evidence of Odyssean quotations from the *Iliad* (Usener *Beobachtungen*; M. L. West, *Making of the Odyssey*, pp. 25–26, 70–76; see also the general discussion in Rutherford, "From the *Iliad*," pp. 125–127), and it is incompatible with my analysis in chapter 5.

58. Tracy, *Story*, p. 51.
59. Jones, *Homer's Odyssey*, p. 70.
60. Clay, *Wrath*, p. 103.
61. Macleod, "Homer on Poetry," p. 303.
62. *Il.* 1.6–9.
63. *Il.* 1.8–53.
64. Zeus's plans entailing suffering for both sides are spelled out in some detail by Zeus himself at *Il.* 15.54–77.
65. Macleod, "Homer on Poetry," p. 303; Rutherford, "From the *Iliad*," p. 136. Nagy (*Achaeans*, pp. 64–65) also notes the parallels between the first song of Demodokos and Agamemnon's delusive dream, but believes that the song alludes not to the *Iliad* that has come down to us but to an alternative Iliadic tradition in which Odysseus took the place of Agamemnon as the adversary of Achilles. Nagy's theory has been criticized by Clay (*Wrath*, pp. 241–246) and is inconsistent with the thrust of my argument in chapter 5.
66. *Od.* 8.266–366.
67. Burkert, "Ares and Aphrodite," p. 32.
68. *Il.* 18.382–383.
69. Burkert, "Ares and Aphrodite," p. 33, n. 7.
70. *Il.* 24.601–603.
71. Willcock, *Companion*, p. 272.
72. *Il.* 5.355–363, 21.415–431; cf. Burkert, "Ares and Aphrodite," p. 38.
73. *Od.* 8.334–343.
74. Burkert, "Ares and Aphrodite," pp. 34–36. Burkert (ibid., pp. 36–39) shows that the second song of Demodokos actually alludes to divine passages in *Il.* 14 and *Il.* 21 in addition to the one in *Il.* 1 (see also Macleod, "Homer on Poetry," p. 304).
75. Although I maintain that the poet of the *Odyssey* fabricated the quarrel between Achilles and Odysseus, I only partially agree with Marg ("Das erste Lied," p. 21) when he characterizes the first song of Demodokos as an *Augenblickserfindung*—an invention of the moment. While it was certainly an invention of the *Odyssey* poet (see also Rüter, *Odysseeinterpretationen*, p. 247; Clay, *Wrath*, pp. 102, 241), I argue in sections 5.3 and 5.7 that it was designed not merely to serve the purposes of the moment (i.e., the particular place, or even the whole book, where the passage occurs) but also to correspond in certain respects to the other passages in the poem where Achilles plays an active role.
76. Hektor's preference for glory in death over shame in life (*Il.* 22.99–110) is not in quite the same category.
77. In addition to the Odyssean expressions of the Iliadic ethos that I go on to mention (quotes 5.7 and 5.21), consider *Od.* 1.236–240 and 24.30–33, where Telemachos and the shade of Achilles speak also of the inheritance of glory by the son of the man who won it (note that *Od.* 1.240 and 24.33 are essentially identical in the Greek).

78. See Usener, *Beobachtungen*, pp. 141–147.

79. Although Odysseus is dejected and longs for home when we see him near the end of his seven years (*Od.* 7.259–261) on the island of the nymph Kalypso (*Od.* 5.149–160; see also 1.48–59 and 5.13–17), Homer's statement that "the nymph was *no longer* pleasing to him" (*Od.* 5.153–154; italics added) shows that those seven years were not all spent in misery. In addition, we must not forget Odysseus's stay with the goddess Circe, which is so pleasant (if we ignore the brief rocky start) that his companions find it necessary after a year to persuade him to resume the journey home (*Od.* 10.467–475).

80. *Il.* 22.389.

81. *Od.* 11.152–153.

82. Page, *Homeric Odyssey*, p. 25 (referring to *Od.* 11.568–627).

83. Griffin, *Odyssey*, p. 92. Essentially the same interpretation of quote 5.25 is adopted by Hainsworth (*Il. Comm.* III, p. 116) and Mueller (*The Iliad*, pp. 37–38).

84. We have seen that the heroic ideal of the *Iliad* is also reaffirmed in the *Odyssey* by Agamemnon after he has been dead for ten years (quote 5.7). However, this affirmation is less relevant since it is found in a part of the poem where the dead are able to converse with each other without drinking blood from the land of the living.

85. Reinhardt ("Adventures," p. 119) takes the opposite view: "... the answer [quote 5.25] seems all the more like Achilleus for being unexpected. What would the dead Achilleus be like if not the reverse of the living one?"

86. The thesis that Achilles' reply to Odysseus repudiates the heroic ideal is usually based on his assertion in *Il.* 9.400–409 that his life is worth more than any quantity of possessions (*Il. Comm.* III, p. 102; Schein, *Hero*, p. 106; Willcock, *Companion*, p. 103). But "[h]eroes are not in pursuit of possessions as such, but of the honour which the possessions represent" (Postlethwaite, *Homer's Iliad*, p. 138), and Agamemnon does nothing to restore this honor in the offer communicated by Odysseus. Schein (*Hero*, pp. 105–106) also sees a "radical break from the heroic value system prevalent elsewhere in the poem" in *Il.* 9.318–320, apparently not recognizing that these lines must be read in the context provided by the two lines that precede them (cf. quote 5.26).

87. *Il.* 9.352–363.

88. Knox, "Introduction," p. 50.

89. In the translation by E. V. Rieu, as revised by Jones with D. C. H. Rieu, *Il.* 9.320 reads as follows: "The same death awaits the man who does much, and the man who does nothing." Given that Achilles is arguing that "the man who does much" is deprived of glory under Agamemnon's leadership, this rendering appears to refer to the role of glory as a compensation for death. (Not all students of Homer interpret *Il.* 9.320 in this way; compare, for example, Macleod, *Iliad XXIV*, p. 23, n. 1.)

90. Also see *Il.* 18.121, 22.393.

91. *Il.* 19.321–327.

92. The relation of quote 5.27 to quotes 5.28 and 5.29 has previously been pointed out by Macleod (*Iliad XXIV*, p. 128; "Homer on Poetry," p. 295) and Rutherford ("From the *Iliad*," p. 134).

93. There is one possible interaction involving Achilles that I ignore. Menelaos promised at Troy to give his daughter in marriage to Achilles' son Neoptolemos (*Od.* 4.4–7), and it is conceivable that the promise was made to Achilles even though he did not know whether his son was still alive (*Il.* 19.327). It seems more likely, however, that the promise was made to Neoptolemos, who reached Troy after the death of his father and became one of the foremost fighters for the Greek cause (*Od.* 11.492–493, 506–537).

94. These are all the interactions between *any* heroes from the *Iliad* that are described in the *Odyssey* and are inconsistent with the earlier poem. There is no inconsistency with the *Iliad* in Nestor's account of the quarrel between Agamemnon and Menelaos (*Od.* 3.130–150), in the conversation between Odysseus and the shade of Agamemnon (*Od.* 11.385–466), or in the interaction between Odysseus and the shade of Aias (*Od.* 11.543–564).

95. Brief notes from antiquity tell us that the Alexandrian scholars Aristophanes and Aristarchus considered *Od.* 23.296 to be the end of the *Odyssey* (Heubeck, "Books XXIII–XXIV," pp. 342–343; Page, *Homeric Odyssey*, p. 101; Rutherford, *Homer*, p. 98), but these notes do not explain what those scholars meant by "end" in this context. There is uncertainty because Aristarchus went on to question (via "athetesis") the authenticity of *Od.* 23.310–343 and 24.1–204, which makes no sense if he regarded *Od.* 23.297–24.548 as spurious in its entirety (Griffin, *Odyssey*, p. 73; Heubeck, "Books XXIII–XXIV," pp. 344, 356). The uncertainty is unimportant for my discussion since the conversation between the shades of Achilles and Agamemnon is part of one of the passages that was specifically athetized. It is also worth noting that athetesis, as opposed to deletion, by Aristarchus meant that the passage in question was suspect on internal grounds (linguistic oddity, impropriety, repetition, or inconsistency, only the last of which applies to the conversation between the shades of Achilles and Agamemnon [see Page, *Homeric Odyssey*, p. 119 on the linguistic normality of this passage]) but was well attested in the manuscripts available to him (*Il. Comm.* IV, pp. 27–28).

For modern discussion of the issue, see Griffin, *Odyssey*, pp. 73–74; Heubeck, "Books XXIII–XXIV," pp. 342–345, 353–354, 356–358, 361; Kelly, "How to End"; Kirk, *Songs*, pp. 248–251; Lord, *Singer of Tales*, pp. 177–185; Page, *Homeric Odyssey*, pp. 101–130; Rutherford, *Homer*, pp. 98–102; Tracy, *Story*, pp. 140–147. A corollary of Kelly's paper is that the "strange unevenness of style" emphasized by Rutherford (*Homer*, p. 101)—in particular, the contrast between the cursory treatment of the conflict with the suitors' relatives and the leisurely treatment of the episode at Laertes' farm—is easily explained if the last book of the *Odyssey* is authentic. Since I will be concerned primarily with the underworld conversation between Achilles and Agamemnon, it is also worth noting that Page's main argument against its authenticity (*Homeric Odyssey*, p. 119) is certainly wrong (see Heubeck, "Books XXIII–XXIV," p. 361).

96. It has been argued that Odysseus's visit to the underworld is a late addition to the *Odyssey* (e.g., Page, *Homeric Odyssey*, pp. 21–51), in which case the conversation between Odysseus and the shade of Achilles would not be authentic. However, neither this conversation nor any other passage from Odysseus's visit to the underworld that I discuss in this book is found in those

parts of the visit that are still considered suspect (*Od.* 11.225–332 and 565–627, according to Fowler, "Homeric question," p. 221, n. 7). For additional discussion, see Heubeck, "Books IX–XII," pp. 75–77 (and references given there) and section 6.8 of the present volume.

97. A full third of the *Iliad*: Mueller, *The Iliad*, p. 76.

98. Jones, *Homer's Odyssey*, pp. 203–204. See also Saïd, *Homer and the Odyssey*, pp. 213–214.

99. The similarity of *Od.* 22.61–64 to *Il.* 9.378–387 and *Il.* 22.348–354 was pointed out by Rutherford ("From the *Iliad*," pp. 129–130) and Schein ("Intertextuality," pp. 349, 352–356). A connection between the first two of these passages (they both describe the rejection of an offer of compensation) had previously been noted by Usener (*Beobachtungen*, p. 133, n. 9), while the similarity of the two passages from the *Iliad* was noted by Macleod (*Iliad XXIV*, pp. 20–21).

100. Rutherford, "From the *Iliad*," p. 130; Schein, "Intertextuality," pp. 349, 355–356.

101. Compare quote 5.30 with *Il.* 5.40–42, 5.55–58, 8.258–260, 11.446–449. Fernández-Galiano ("Books XXI–XXII," p. 238) focuses attention on the identical lines *Il.* 5.41, 5.57, 8.259, 11.448, and *Od.* 22.93.

102. Compare *Il.* 15.478–482 with *Od.* 22.120–125. The near identity of *Il.* 15.479–481 and *Od.* 22.122–124 is pointed out by Lattimore ("Introduction," p. 21) and Janko (*Il. Comm.* IV, p. 280), and a detailed discussion is provided by Usener (see following note).

103. Usener, *Beobachtungen*, pp. 95–103. Except for a brief reference (*Beobachtungen*, p. 102, n. 23), Usener does not consider one difference between the two re-arming scenes: one fighter (Odysseus) exchanges his bow for two spears (*Od.* 22.125), while the other (Teukros) acquires only one (*Il.* 15.482). It is interesting that the same difference is found between two scenes of ordinary arming (as opposed to re-arming) that are otherwise almost identical to each other, those of Paris (*Il.* 3.330–338) and Patroklos (*Il.* 16.131–139).

Usener (*Beobachtungen*, p. 97) points out that the two lines that relate to the helmet are formulaic, appearing not only in the re-arming scenes of Odysseus and Teukros, but also in the arming scenes of Paris and Patroklos. Although he tries to minimize the impact of this observation by illustrating the poet's freedom in the construction of arming scenes, it must be admitted that the formulaic nature of two of the lines common to the two re-arming scenes somewhat weakens the tie between them. Furthermore, one of the two lines may have found its way into one of the re-arming scenes only as a result of interpolation (see *Il. Comm.* IV, p. 280 on *Il.* 15.481). On the other hand, as Usener emphasizes, it is noteworthy that the word used to describe the shield in the two re-arming scenes (a word meaning "with four layers of hide" according to Cunliffe) appears nowhere else in all of Homer (*Beobachtungen*, pp. 97–98).

Given that the two re-arming scenes are connected, the significance of the connection may be illuminated by the fact that the scenes differ greatly in how well they are integrated into their respective contexts. The slaughter of the suitors must have both an archery phase and a spear-fighting phase, so the re-arming of Odysseus is essential. On the other hand, we never see Teukros fight after he has exchanged his bow for a spear, so his re-arming is poorly motivated (Wilamowitz, *Die Ilias und Homer*, p. 241). Teukros has already had an *aristeia* (a succession of victories by a single warrior) at *Il.* 8.266–315, so it is understandable if Homer does not want to give additional prominence to a hero not of the first rank. But then why does he bother to describe his re-arming? In section 5.6 I suggest that small changes to the *Iliad* may have been made during or after the composition of the *Odyssey*. If this is correct, the re-arming of Teukros could have been introduced to create the parallel with the re-arming of Odysseus. There are other possible explanations (see the commentary of Janko cited above and Usener, *Beobachtungen*, p. 99), but in my opinion they are very weak.

104. Jones, *Homer's Odyssey*, pp. 203–204. I would add that the Mnesterophonia includes an instance of vaunting over a slain enemy (*Od.* 22.285–291), something that is relatively common in the *Iliad*.

105. *Od.* 22.313–318.

106. *Od.* 21.146–147.

107. I paraphrase *Od.* 22.36–38. S. West ("Books I–IV," p. 57) observes that Odysseus leaves out the suitors' plot to murder Telemachos (*Od.* 4.660–673, 698–701) even though he is aware of it (*Od.* 13.425–426). Of the three grievances he does mention, he brings up only the last when he explains why Leodes must die (*Od.* 22.321–325).

108. *Od.* 22.319.

109. *Il.* 21.70–96. The similarity of the Lykaon scene and the Leodes scene that concludes the slaughter of the suitors is mentioned by Rutherford ("From the *Iliad*," p. 129) and discussed by Fenik (*Studies*, p. 197) and Usener (*Beobachtungen*, pp. 131–140).

110. Mueller, *The Iliad*, p. 89. See also Geddes, *Problem*, p. 156.

111. For example, when Zeus declares that he loved Hektor (*Il.* 24.68–70; cf. 22.168–172), he mentions that Hektor always honored him with sacrifices but ignores Hektor's boasting over the dying Patroklos at *Il.* 22.827–842.

112. *Il.* 22.391–394. The contrast between Odysseus's restraint of Eurykleia and Achilles' incitement of his comrades is often cited as evidence of a difference in values or outlook between the poet of the *Iliad* and the poet of the *Odyssey* (Griffin, *Odyssey*, p. 90; Jacoby, "Physiognomie," pp. 184–187; Usener, *Beobachtungen*, p. 206). However, this evidence should be reconsidered in the light of the discussion of quote 5.31 in part (*d*) of section 5.4.

113. The difficulty of reconciling quotes 5.31 and 5.32 is illustrated by a medieval commentator's desperate attempt in which he assigns a clearly inappropriate meaning to the verb that Lattimore translates as "glory" and others translate as "boast" (Geddes, *Problem*, p. 157, n. 15; Stanford, *Ulysses Theme*, p. 251, n. 20). Geddes believes that the two passages cannot be reconciled; Stanford believes that they can be. Stanford's argument is addressed in a note referenced after quote 5.33.

Surprisingly, Borthwick (*Odyssean Elements*, pp. 13–14) and Fernández-Galiano ("Books XXI–XXII," pp. 290–291 on *Od.* 22.411–416) see a parallel between the two passages instead of an inconsistency. Fernández-Galiano characterizes Odysseus's words over the body of Sokos as "humane and sympathetic" rather than boasting. This point of view is hard to swallow when one notes the similarities between Odysseus's words over Sokos and the vicious words that Achilles addresses to the dying Hektor at *Il.* 22.345–354. In any case, Homer states explicitly in quote 5.32 that Odysseus boasted over the body of Sokos (see the reference to *Il.* 11.449 in the entry for επευχομαι in Cunliffe's lexicon).

Borthwick draws attention to the term α δειλε ("poor wretch," or simply "wretch" in Lattimore's translation) that Odysseus uses to address Sokos, both in quote 5.32 and shortly before, and notes that this term "has compassionate overtones in Epic usage." According to Cunliffe's lexicon (entry for δειλος), however, α δειλε is "tinged with hostility or contempt" when Odysseus addresses Sokos (*Il.* 11.441 and 452) and when Hektor exults over Patroklos as he lies dying (*Il.* 16.837), the latter occasion being another of the instances of "the sympathetic α δειλε" that are cited by Borthwick.

Mueller (*The Iliad*, p. 89) classifies Odysseus's words over the body of Sokos as a gloating speech, but considers it "an unusually sombre and restrained instance of the genre." I believe that Hainsworth (*Il. Comm.* III, p. 273) gives the most accurate characterization when he remarks in connection with quote 5.32 that "Odysseus' boast sounds a mean, unpleasant note."

114. To help the reader judge the possible significance of the correspondence between Telemachos's killing of Amphinomos (quote 5.30) and Odysseus's killing of Sokos (quote 5.32), I note that 96 killings by spear are described in the *Iliad* in some detail, and 92 of these 96 do not conform to the pattern in quotes 5.30 and 5.32 (I base these counts on the list "Deaths in the Iliad" compiled by Johnston).

115. *Il.* 11.401–420.

116. Stanford (*Ulysses Theme*, p. 251, n. 21) characterizes quote 5.33 as "a taunt (with a definite incitement to boast)," and uses this characterization, together with the fact that Sokos wounds Odysseus before being killed by him, to argue that the Odysseus of the Sokos scene, like the Odysseus of the Eurykleia scene, believes that it is wrong to boast over a slain enemy, but nevertheless is driven to boast over Sokos by these provocations. However, quote 5.33 is no incitement to boast; it is merely a statement of a common practice to which no man or god objects in the *Iliad*, and it is also in perfect accord with Sarpedon's famous speech to Glaukos (see *Il.* 12.328).

117. Mueller, *The Iliad*, p. 109. See also *Il. Comm.* V, p. 34.

118. Jones, *Homer's Odyssey*, p. 209 on l. 384. See also Schein, *Hero*, p. 79.

119. *Il. Comm.* V, p. 114.

120. The similarity with the killing of Amphinomos by Telemachos (quote 5.30) and the killing of Sokos by Odysseus (quote 5.32) could conceivably be significant, but the spear throw by Euphorbos is not powerful enough to kill Patroklos outright.

121. It may be worth noting in addition that Menelaos is one of the fighters who delivers a gloating speech over the body of a victim (*Il.* 13.619–639).

122. Jones (*Homer's Odyssey*, p. 209) also calls attention to the connection between *Od.* 22.412 and *Il.* 17.19. However, his reference to *Od.* 23.59 is misplaced, in my opinion, because the subsequent lines make clear that Penelope tries to restrain Eurykleia's joy only because she does not believe the good news that has caused this joy.

123. This assertion can be verified by using *The Chicago Homer* (see bibliography under Kahane and Mueller) to check all the occurrences of the verbs Homer uses to refer to boasting: ευχομαι, επευχομαι, and ευχεταομαι.

124. The other verb Homer uses to refer to boasting in quote 5.35 (in the second boldfaced fragment) is the same verb he uses in quotes 5.32 and 5.33. Thus, the two verbs used to refer to boasting in quote 5.35 link the boldfaced part of quote 5.31 with the Sokos episode. However, this connection is much less convincing than the other connection via quote 5.35 that I go on to describe in section 5.4.

125. The connection that I claim between quote 5.35 and quote 5.31 is denied by Geddes (*Problem*, p. 156, n. 13) owing to the difference in the kind of boasting that is censured. But, as I pointed out, these are the only places in Homer where boasting of any kind is condemned, and both condemnations are contradicted by the conduct of the hero who voices the condemnation.

126. Fenik, "Stylization and Variety"; see also Mueller, *The Iliad*, p. 33.

127. As noted by Fenik ("Stylization and Variety," p. 70, n. 3), the line "Yet still, why does the heart within me debate on these things?" also appears at *Il.* 22.385. This fifth occurrence of the line is part of the victory speech Achilles delivers to the Greeks after he has killed Hektor, and may be intended to recall and balance Hektor's use of the line (*Il.* 22.122) in his deliberation at the beginning of his fatal encounter with Achilles—the last and most important of the four deliberation scenes and, in the words of Fenik (ibid., pp. 81–82), "the dramatic finale" to which the others build. The line "Deeply troubled, he spoke to his own great-hearted spirit:" also appears at *Il.* 18.5 and at *Od.* 5.298, 5.355, 5.407, and 5.464. Although both of the quoted lines can be found outside the deliberation scenes, these four scenes are the only places where the two lines occur in association with each other.

128. My discussion connecting the Odysseus-Sokos encounter with the Menelaos-Euphorbos encounter has made no use of the fact that the Greek hero who kills his Trojan counterpart has previously killed a brother of that Trojan. The reason is that "it is quite common in the *Iliad* for brothers to suffer death at the hands of one warrior" (Mueller, *The Iliad*, p. 88).

129. *Od.* 22.285–291. One author who considers Odysseus's declaration that "it is not piety to glory so over slain men" to be an authoritative statement of the moral verdict of the *Odyssey* (Geddes, *Problem*, pp. 155–156) regards the gloating speech of Philoitios as the exception that proves the rule (ibid., p. 156, n. 11). However, his reasons for this judgment (the gloating speech precedes Odysseus's declaration, Ktesippos is the most brutal suitor, Philoitios is a rustic herdsman) seem inadequate to me.

130. Jones, *Homer's Odyssey*, p. 209. Likewise, Jacoby ("Physiognomie," pp. 184–185) concludes that the winning of glory in the *Iliad* is replaced by divine punishment in the *Odyssey*.

131. That Odysseus would naturally seek revenge is self-evident. If textual support is desired, however, one need only observe that Menelaos (*Od.* 4.340–346), Helen (*Od.* 15.172–178), Halitherses (*Od.* 2.163–166), and Teiresias (*Od.* 11.114–120) all assume that Odysseus will kill the suitors without being prompted to do so by the gods. Erbse (*Beiträge*, p. 130) claims that Athene commands Odysseus to kill them at *Od.* 13.376 (see quote 6.42), but her words "consider how you can lay your hands on these shameless suitors" merely introduce her account of what has been going on in his palace and express what he will do anyway once he has heard this account—as is clear from his response (*Od.* 13.386–391 = quote 2.19). Athene does occasionally incite a suitor to insult Odysseus (*Od.* 18.346–364, 20.284–300), but she does this just to fan the flames of fury already raging inside him. During the slaughter, she exhorts Odysseus to show the strength and courage he possessed at Troy (*Od.* 22.224–238), but this is just what he asked her to do (*Od.* 13.387–391 in quote 2.19).

132. *Od.* 1.26–95, 5.1–42.

133. *Od.* 5.24.

134. *Od.* 24.478–481; note that 24.479–480 = 5.23–24.

135. *Od.* 2.139–145.

136. The parallel is discussed by Fenik (*Studies*, p. 210) and Jacoby ("Physiognomie," p. 186). Fenik and Jacoby (p. 188) note that the poet extends the parallel to the punishment of Odysseus's companions for slaughtering the cattle of Helios, but Fenik (pp. 212–215) argues persuasively that the punishment of the companions for this transgression is more similar to Poseidon's punishment of Odysseus for the blinding of the Cyclops Polyphemos.

137. *Od.* 1.28–43. The story of Aigisthos is also related at *Od.* 1.298–300, 3.193–198, 3.262–275, 3.303–310, 4.518–537, 11.409–426.

138. *Od.* 2.146–176. The suitors also receive other warnings (Fenik, *Studies*, p. 210), but the omen sent by Zeus and interpreted by Halitherses is the one most analogous to the warning received by Aigisthos (and as such is also emphasized by Erbse, *Beiträge*, p. 130).

139. *Od.* 1.40–41.

140. It is true that Athene sometimes incites the suitors to commit further outrages in order to intensify the suffering of Odysseus (*Od.* 18.346–348 and 20.284–286; see also 17.360–364), but she does this only to help him by stiffening his resolve.

141. *Od.* 1.29–30, 298–300; 3.193–205.

142. *Od.* 1.294–302. Nestor repeats Athene's advice (*Od.* 3.199–200 = 1.301–302), but the lines in which he does so are suspect (S. West, "Books I–IV," p. 172).

143. The glory that Odysseus is entitled to for having slaughtered the suitors receives no attention in the poem since it is necessary for the relatives of the suitors to forget the slaughter (cf. *Od.* 24.484–485). However, this has no bearing on whether Eurykleia should be able give a cry of triumph before the accommodation with the relatives has been arranged.

144. Heubeck ("Books XXIII–XXIV," p. 319) discusses the parallelism between quote 5.36 and the second half of quote 5.31, but overlooks the fact that in each passage Eurykleia is told not to express her jubilation.

145. Cf. *Od.* 23.36–38 and Heubeck, "Books XXIII–XXIV," p. 318.

146. Jones (*Homer's Odyssey*, p. 212) assumes that the "triumph" mentioned in quote 5.36 refers to the slaughter of the suitors. According to his interpretation, Penelope's rationale for telling Eurykleia not to "laugh aloud in triumph" is that "*human* triumphing is ... inappropriate" since (she believes) the suitors must have been killed by a god. This parallels exactly his interpretation of why Odysseus restrains Eurykleia in quote 5.31: "do not claim a human triumph when it is really a divine one" (ibid., p. 209). My position is that this agreement is misleading because both interpretations are erroneous.

147. In quote 5.37 Lattimore's translation of *Od.* 9.50 has been replaced by Murray's translation. The Greek text actually says "from horses" (αφ' 'ιππων) rather than "from chariots." At least in the *Iliad*, however, "horses" in the context of battle means "chariot" or "chariots" (Jones, *Homer's* Iliad, p. 41). Murray (along with many other translators) is almost certainly justified in translating αφ' 'ιππων as "from chariots." Even if he is not (as implied by Saïd, *Homer and the* Odyssey, p. 163), the main argument of section 5.5 remains valid, as no use is made of cavalry in the *Iliad*.

148. *Il.* 8.66–72, 11.84–91, 16.777–780. The italicized lines in quote 5.37 that specify the time of day are identical to lines in the Iliadic passages: *Od.* 9.56 = *Il.* 8.66 = *Il.* 11.84, and *Od.* 9.58 = *Il.* 16.779. Noting these and other correspondences, Heubeck ("Books IX–XII," p. 15) says, "The fighting is described in the language of the *Iliad*, thereby reinforcing the link with the events around Troy." Similarly, Jones (*Homer's Odyssey*, p. 81) observes that "the scene is notably Iliadic in flavour." Some scholars would see no significance in the repetition of evidently formulaic lines or even the repetition of the temporal structure (which could be regarded as a "type scene"). However, I am obliged to take seriously the Iliadic flavor of quote 5.37 because the results of sections 5.3 and 5.4 suggest that an Odyssean scene that is strongly linked to the *Iliad* should show some inconsistency with that poem, and this prediction needs to be checked.

149. The *Iliad*'s preference for fighting on foot is illustrated by the episode at 17.456–483. Alone in a chariot because Patroklos has been killed, Automedon chases Trojans but is unable to kill any because he cannot use his spear and manage the horses at the same time. When Alkimedon mounts the chariot to take charge of the horses, Automedon dismounts in order to fight. At 15.384–388 the Trojans do fight from chariots, but this is an exception that proves the rule, for they are fighting Greeks who are standing on the sterns of their beached ships.

150. *Il.* 2.846, 17.73.

151. *Il.* 5.12–17, 8.114–119. At 11.540–541 Hektor appears to be in his chariot when he fights with spear, sword, and stones, but the same verses are used at 11.264–265 for Agamemnon when he is not in his chariot (cf. *Il. Comm.* III, p. 282). At 16.404–414 Patroklos stabs someone with a spear from his chariot and then strikes someone else with a stone. Assuming that

Patroklos must be on foot to grab the stone, Janko (*Il. Comm.* IV, p. 369) observes that "Homer takes for granted that he often mounts and dismounts in rapid pursuit." Shortly afterwards, it should be noted, Patroklos and Sarpedon both dismount from their chariots (16.426–428) for their fateful encounter.

152. Borthwick, *Odyssean Elements*, p. 6; Goold, "Homeric Composition," p. 19; *Il. Comm.* VI, p. 24. The possibility of reciprocal influence of the two poems is also raised by Pucci, *Sirens*, pp. 84, 90, 96. The idea that the *Iliad* is in the main older than the *Odyssey* but contains younger parts that were influenced by the *Odyssey* was first proposed in the nineteenth century (see Usener, *Beobachtungen,* p. 2).

153. Jones, *Homer's Odyssey*, p. 19; S. West, "Books I–IV," p. 51.

154. Rutherford, *Homer*, p. 82, n. 23.

155. Griffin, *Odyssey*, p. 43.

156. Woodhouse, *Composition*, p. 249.

157. Scodel, *Listening*, pp. 15–16, 108–109. It is not entirely fair to say that Scodel's interpretation of quote 5.39 disregards the *Odyssey*, inasmuch as she admits that this passage "clearly has more power for a listener who knows the story of Odysseus's return."

158. Burgess, *Tradition of the Trojan War*, p. 178; M. L. West, *Greek Epic Fragments*, p. 71.

159. Willcock, *Companion*, p. 20; Scodel, *Listening*, p. 15. Rutherford (*Homer*, p. 82, n. 23) observes that Odysseus's description of himself as the father of Telemachos is "abnormal procedure" in the *Iliad*. Woodhouse (*Composition*, p. 249, n. 18) calls attention to the "curious emphasis" on Odysseus's son in quotes 5.39 and 5.40.

160. The pride in Telemachos which I believe is evident in quotes 5.39 and 5.40 is also seen by Kirk (*Il. Comm.* I, p. 366 on *Il.* 4.354) and M. L. West (*Making of the Iliad*, pp. 106–107; *Making of the Odyssey*, pp. 22, 98–99). However, Borthwick (*Odyssean Elements*, pp. 10, 11) and Willcock (*Companion*, p. 20) see only indications of Odysseus's strong family attachment.

161. Telemachos was just an infant when Odysseus left home to go to Troy: *Od.* 4.112, 144 ("newborn child" is more accurate than Lattimore's "young child" in both of these lines) and 11.447–449.

162. Borthwick (*Odyssean Elements*, pp. 6, 10, 11) and M. L. West (*Making of the Iliad*, pp. 106–107; *Making of the Odyssey*, pp. 22, 98–99) also answer in the negative. West maintains that quotes 5.39 and 5.40 presuppose a version of the *Odyssey* (the "proto-*Odyssey*") that predated the completion of the *Iliad*, and Borthwick seems to believe much the same. However, neither author, in my opinion, does justice to the strangeness of the passages which leads me to interpret them as intentional references or pointed allusions to the *Odyssey*.

163. Wilamowitz, *Heimkehr*, p. 186; Griffin, *Odyssey*, pp. 67–68; S. West, "Books I–IV," pp. 51, 91. Specifically, Τηλεμαχος = τηλε ("at a distance") + μαχ (cf. μαχη "fighting" or "a fight," μαχομαι "I fight") + ος (a noun ending). The interpretation in terms of archery is supported by the presence in *Il.* 4.354 (one of the verses where Odysseus refers to himself as the father of Telemachos) of the word προμαχος = προ ("in front") + μαχ + ος, which differs from Τηλεμαχος only in the prefix (we can ignore the case endings of the forms that actually appear in the verse) and refers to someone who, unlike an archer, fights in front or on the front line (Risch, "Namendeutungen," p. 87; Pucci, *Sirens*, p. 26; M. L. West, *Making of the Iliad*, pp. 145–146). The poet must have intentionally juxtaposed Τηλεμαχος and προμαχος, and I assume he would not have done this if the juxtaposition suggests a misleading interpretation of the name.

It has also been suggested that Telemachos's name reflects his father's fighting in a distant war (see references in M. L. West, *Making of the Odyssey*, p. 99, n. 12). Besides spoiling the contrast between Τηλεμαχος and προμαχος, this would imply that Telemachos was named for his father's participation in the Trojan War before he had even gone to Troy.

164. *Il. Comm.* III, p. 268 on *Il.* 11.385–395; Hainsworth, "Books V–VIII," p. 359 on *Od.* 8.215–218; Mueller, *The Iliad*, p. 77. Odysseus is given a bow to take on his nighttime spying expedition with Diomedes (even this has been interpreted an allusion to the *Odyssey*: *Il. Comm.* III, p. 179 on *Il.* 10.260), but he uses it only in place of a whip to strike horses.

165. *Od.* 8.215–228; 19.571–575; 21.393–426; 22.1–118.

166. Kirk (*Songs*, p. 290) characterizes the difference between the *Iliad* and the *Odyssey* in Odysseus's choice of weapon as a "marked inconsistency" which "strongly suggests that the tradition about Odysseus had developed separately in different poetical environments, for some time at least before the era of monumental composition" (similarly, see Page, *Homeric Odyssey*, pp. 157–158). While the inconsistency is undeniable, I am content to regard it as simply a practical choice by the poet, who assigned Odysseus whatever weapon was needed for each poem.

167. Griffin, *Odyssey*, p. 44; Lattimore, "Introduction," p. 5.

168. Goold, "Homeric Composition," pp. 20, 23; Lattimore, "Introduction," p. 4; S. West, "Books I–IV," pp. 52–53, 55. To be sure, the stature of Odysseus is established jointly by the journey of Telemachos, two songs of Demodokos, and the journey to the underworld.

169. S. West, "Books I–IV," p. 52.

170. Heubeck, "General Introduction," p. 17.

171. Clarke, *Art*, pp. 10–12; S. West, "Books I–IV," p. 60. Also see section 3.4.

172. Woodhouse, *Composition*, pp. 247–249.

173. As in *Od.* 17.489–491 (Telemachos suppresses a reaction to the abuse of his father) and 21.124–135 (upon a signal from his father, he pretends that he cannot string the bow).

174. *Od.* 24.504–515.

175. Stanford (*Ulysses Theme*, p. 44) has proposed another motivation for quotes 5.39 and 5.40. He suggests that in these passages Homer is concerned to show that "Odysseus's complete lack of intimate relationships among his comrades at arms ... was not due to any incapacity for affection on Odysseus's part." But Stanford's textual argument for the proposition that Odysseus had no close friend at Troy is weak and would apply just as well to other heroes; it is also contradicted by the sentiments of Menelaos at *Od.* 4.104–110, 169–180. Even if it were true that Odysseus had no close friend, having him refer to himself so strangely as the father of his son would seem a large price to pay for so little gain.

176. Instead of visualizing multiple rings, one for each pair of corresponding elements, we can think of a ring structure with any number of pairs of corresponding elements as a single ring with the elements placed in sequence around its circumference and spaced such that corresponding elements are represented by mirror-image points on either side of the ring. This approach is used, for example, by Mary Douglas in *Thinking in Circles*.

177. Gaisser, "Structural Analysis," p. 9; *Il. Comm.* V, p. 46; Schein, *Hero*, p. 33; Schein, "Structure and Interpretation," p. 347. For an interpretation involving four rings instead of three, see Willcock, *Companion*, p. 273 (but also see Macleod, *Iliad XXIV*, pp. 139–141 concerning the genuineness of lines 614–617 in quote 5.41).

178. For other examples, see the entries under "ring composition" in the index to Willcock's *Companion*.

179. The two types of ring structure that I go on to mention were discussed by Bassett (*Poetry*, pp. 121–122), and the examples I cite are taken from him. Bassett does not actually use the term "ring composition," which includes the case of a single ring (a simple framing or bookend structure: ABA), but instead calls attention to the important case of two rings by referring to the Homeric hysteron proteron ("latter first") or deuteron proteron ("second first") (ibid., pp. 119–128).

180. *Od.* 11.170–203, as summarized by Bassett, *Poetry*, p. 121. The seven-ring structure is not quite perfect (see *Od.* 11.197), but is nevertheless impressive; the three-ring analysis given by Heubeck ("Books IX–XII," p. 88) seems overly conservative.

181. For example, *Od.* 11.492–537 and 15.347–359.

182. Athene's plan: *Od.* 1.84–95; beginning of execution of second part of plan: *Od.* 1.96; beginning of execution of first part of plan: *Od.* 5.29. See Bassett, *Poetry*, p. 122; Jones, *Homer's Odyssey*, p. 4; S. West, "Books I–IV," p. 85 on lines 81–95. Bassett (*Poetry*, p. 251, n. 13) also cites more modest examples of this type of Homeric ring structure: *Od.* 6.209–250, 7.163–184, 8.389–445, 13.404–14.4, 15.75–119.

183. *Od.* 11.492–537.

184. The ring structure of the *Iliad* as a whole is discussed by Richardson (*Il. Comm.* VI, pp. 4–14) and Schein (*Hero*, pp. 30–33; "Structure and Interpretation," pp. 345–348). A large-scale ring structure in the *Odyssey* is described by Tracy (*Story*, p. 139).

185. *Il.* 23.534–538.

186. *Il.* 23.555–565.

187. *Il.* 23.615–623.

188. *Il. Comm.* VI, pp. 1–14; Schein, *Hero*, pp. 30–36; Schein, "Structure and Interpretation," pp. 345–352.

189. In each of the two conversations that constitute the second half of the corpus stack structure, the participants in the conversation appear to be friends and show no sign that they ever had a serious quarrel with each other. Since a friendly conversation is the opposite of a serious quarrel, act Y is the opposite of act X, as we expect in a stack structure. But we also expect something more: act X should be what makes act Y possible (a block cannot be removed from a stack until it has been added to the stack). This property is present in the small-scale stacks discussed in part (*a*) of section 5.7 (a question cannot be answered until it has been asked; a proposal cannot be carried out until it has been made) and in the Iliadic stack structure (it is not possible to take revenge for an outrage until the outrage has been perpetrated). However, this property is *not* present in the corpus stack structure since a serious quarrel is not a prerequisite for a friendly conversation. It would be possible to get around this difficulty if we could interpret the friendly conversations as implicit reconciliations (it is not possible for two parties to reconcile unless they have first quarreled), but this approach won't work in the case of the conversation between Odysseus and the shade of Achilles since (*a*) the quarrel between Achilles and Odysseus never actually occurred (it was invented for the first song of Demodokos) and (*b*) even if the quarrel occurred, Odysseus and Achilles would have to have reconciled before the Embassy (see part (*b*) of section 5.3). This imperfection will not stop me from using the term "corpus stack structure," but it does reveal a limitation of the terminology.

190. Since there are other passages that mention Achilles, it is perhaps more accurate to describe the set, as I have elsewhere, as the set of all the interactions between the protagonist of the *Iliad* and another individual that are related directly or indirectly in the *Odyssey*.

191. Tracy, *Story*, pp. 149–150.

192. *Il. Comm.* VI, pp. 21–24, 332; Rutherford, "From the *Iliad*," pp. 131–132.

193. *Il. Comm.* VI, p. 24.

194. Monro, *Homer's Odyssey*, p. 325. The observation made by Monro was also known in antiquity: see Clay, *Wrath*, p. 244, n. 8.

195. Page, *Homeric Odyssey*, pp. 158–159.

196. Rutherford, "From the *Iliad*," p. 120; Usener, *Beobachtungen*, p. 205; M. L. West, *Making of the Odyssey*, pp. 25, 70–77.

197. Cairns, "Introduction," pp. 10–11; Clay, *Wrath*, pp. 245–246; Kirk, *Songs*, pp. 299–300; Knox, "Introduction," p. 23; Lattimore, "Introduction," p. 20; Rutherford, "From the *Iliad*," p. 121; Schein, *Hero*, p. 38; Tracy, *Story*, p. 149, n. 2; Usener, *Beobachtungen*, p. 205; Whitehead, "Funeral," p. 120.

198. Nagy, *Achaeans*, pp. 20–21.

199. Clay, *Wrath*, p. 245.

200. As Achilles does in *Il*. 19.56–64.

201. There is a variation on Monro's Law that is relevant to the conversation between Odysseus and the shade of Achilles, though not to the part of the conversation that I discuss in chapter 5. According to Richmond Lattimore, "When the *Odyssey* recounts episodes from the tale of Troy, these episodes are never a part of the *Iliad*, but seem to fall outside, either before or after, the action of the *Iliad*" (Lattimore, "Introduction," p. 19; similarly: Knox, "Introduction," p. 23). This observation cannot be considered fundamental because it expresses the result of a variety of causes. Thus, some episodes related to the Trojan War that are found in the *Odyssey*, such as the death and burial of Achilles, the dispute between Odysseus and Aias over his armor, and the stratagem of the Wooden Horse, are only to be expected in a sequel to the *Iliad* (see section 5.1); the part of the conversation between Odysseus and the shade of Achilles that relates to Neoptolemos, Eurypylos, and Memnon (*Il.* 11.505-537, another of the passages cited by Lattimore in support of his observation) could be assigned to this category. Other Trojan episodes in the *Odyssey* have no Iliadic counterpart capable of serving the same function. For example, Helen's story of Odysseus's spying expedition in which he entered Troy disguised as a beggar (*Od.* 4.240-258) prefigures Odysseus's return to his palace in the same sort of disguise (cf. S. West, "Books I-IV," p. 209). Similarly, Odysseus's boast to the Phaiakians concerning his skill as an archer (*Od.* 8.215-220), which is phrased in such a way that it seems to prefigure the slaughter of the suitors (but cf. Hainsworth, "Books V-VIII," p. 359), cannot rely on the *Iliad* since Odysseus does not shoot a single arrow in that poem; presumably for this reason, it compares Odysseus as an archer with Philoktetes, who does not arrive in Troy until after the time frame of the *Iliad* (cf. *Il.* 2.716-725, which contains the only references to Philoktetes in the *Iliad*, and *Od.* 3.190). Note, however, that the assertion that only Philoktetes surpassed Odysseus in archery (*Od.* 8.219) appears to conflict with the *Iliad* since Meriones and Teukros are the archery contestants in the funeral games for Patroklos (*Il.* 23.850-883) and therefore presumably are also better archers than Odysseus (in addition, Idomeneus calls Teukros "best of all the Achaians in archery" at *Il.* 13.313-314). And of course the discussion in section 5.8 suggests that intentional inconsistency between the *Iliad* and the *Odyssey* is the motivating force behind some apparent manifestations of Monro's Law.

202. Schein, *Hero*, p. 44.

203. Nagy, *Achaeans*, p. 21; Cairns, "Introduction," p. 11.

204. Rutherford, "From the *Iliad*," p. 120. While true as far as it goes, this statement conflates two very different things: some passages in the *Odyssey* make one think of the Quarrel and feel the absence of any reference to it, but no passage begs for a reference to Hektor.

CHAPTER 6: Mysterious Inconsistency in the *Iliad* and the *Odyssey*

1. The selection of the ambassadors: *Il.* 9.168-169; the appeal of Odysseus and Achilles' reply: *Il.* 9.222-429; the appeal of Phoinix and Achilles' reply: *Il.* 9.432-619; the appeal of Aias and Achilles' reply: *Il.* 9.622-655; the passage bridging the interval from the planning of the embassy to the embassy itself: *Il.* 9.182-198.

2. The duals in question are found in *Il.* 9.182, 183, 185, 192, 196, 197, and 198, along with a plural (which may refer to two or more subjects) in line 186; the line numbers quoted here (from *Il. Comm.* III, p. 85) refer to the Greek, but should correspond closely with Lattimore's translation. Translators typically ignore most (or even all) of these duals since it is not clear how they are to be interpreted. Lattimore's translation, for example, shows only the duals in lines 182 and 192. Nagy (*Achaeans*, p. 52) provides a translation showing the duals in lines 196-198 because these particular duals support his theory that Achilles excludes Odysseus from the warm greeting in quote 5.11; my objections to this theory are found in the digression that follows quote 5.11.

3. See, for example, *Il. Comm.* III, pp. 85–87; *Il. Comm.* IV, p. 91 on *Il.* 13.346–348 and p. 363 on *Il.* 16.370–371; Goold, "Homeric Composition," pp. 10–11; Jones, *Homer's* Iliad, pp. 152–153; Mueller, *The Iliad*, p. 184; Nagy, *Achaeans*, pp. 49–55; Postlethwaite, *Homer's Iliad*, p. 133; Rutherford, *Homer*, pp. 108–110; Schein, *Hero*, pp. 125–126, n. 35; Scodel, "Pseudo-Intimacy" and *Listening*, pp. 160–172; Segal, "embassy and the duals"; M. L. West, *Making of the Iliad*, pp. 13–14; Whitman, *Heroic Tradition*, p. 344, n. 25; and Willcock, *Companion*, pp. 98–100. The most common explanation is that the duals were allowed to survive from a previous version where they were appropriate. The two envoys in the previous version are typically thought to be Odysseus and Aias, but there are significant objections to the addition of Phoinix unless other changes were also made (cf. Willcock). It has also been suggested that the duals are used appropriately, although ambiguously, to refer to Odysseus and Aias (Scodel), to Aias and Phoinix (Nagy), or sometimes to Odysseus and Aias and sometimes to the heralds (Segal). Rutherford speculates that a post-Homeric editor who believed that Phoinix must reside in Achilles' camp inserted duals referring to Odysseus and Aias but somehow overlooked the contrary indications at *Il.* 9.168, 426–429, 617–622, 658–659, and 688–690. Whitman favors an explanation in terms of a slip characteristic of oral poetry, in this case indicating a presumably once-familiar form of generic embassy scene with only two envoys; however, the Odyssean example he cites (*Od.* 8.48, to which could be added *Od.* 8.35 [Hainsworth, "Books V–VIII," pp. 347, 348]), in which a dual is used to refer to 52 crew members of a ship, is not likely to have originated in a precedent with only two men. Janko suggests that the inappropriate duals may be explained by certain peculiarities in linguistic usage, but these peculiarities relate only to dual verbs (see also Hainsworth, p. 87); dual verb forms are in fact used with plural nouns about a dozen times in the *Iliad*, but in the Embassy scene, Mueller points out, "dual pronouns and verbs reinforce each other ... to convey a strong vision of two delegates" (the dual pronoun τώ appears in lines 182, 192, and 196).

4. See Jones, *Homer's* Iliad, pp. 162–163.

5. *Il.* 9.690–692, where Odysseus reports to Agamemnon what Achilles said to him at *Il.* 9.426–429.

6. *Il.* 9.421–422, 617, 649, 657, 669.

7. For *Il.* 9.421–422, 617, and 657, see Nagy, *Achaeans*, p. 55; for *Il.* 9.649, 657, and 669, see *Il. Comm.* III, p. 85. In the passages which concern the delivery of a message to Agamemnon (*Il.* 9.421–422, 617, 649), the possibility that the plurals can be explained by the inclusion of the two heralds along with Odysseus and Aias is ruled out by 9.422, which states that the delivery of such a message is the privilege of councilors.

8. *Il. Comm.* III, p. 85.

9. Ibid.

10. The theory proposed by Scodel ("Pseudo-Intimacy," pp. 211–214; *Listening*, pp. 160–172) shares with the analysis offered in section 6.1 the notion that the notorious duals in the Embassy scene are intentional. In particular, she argues that these duals are used to heighten the mystery surrounding Phoinix, whose relationship with Achilles has not yet been revealed when he is selected to be one of the ambassadors. When this special

relationship is finally described in Phoinix's speech, it becomes apparent (according to Scodel) that the duals have always referred to Aias and Odysseus (and therefore have been used correctly). But if this is so, why does Homer replace the duals with plurals when he refers to Aias and Odysseus explicitly? This objection to the Aias-Odysseus interpretation of the duals was originally raised by Nagy (*Achaeans*, p. 55) before Scodel put forward her interpretation. It carries even more weight in the context of her theory since the explicit references to Aias and Odysseus first appear when the mystery of Phoinix has been (or is just about to be) cleared up by his speech, and continued use of duals would have supported the new understanding of the earlier, previously mysterious duals.

11. The illogicality of Phoinix's residence outside the Myrmidon camp is pointed out in *Il. Comm.* III, p. 82 and p. 118 on *Il.* 9.427. For points (*a*) and (*b*) see *Il.* 9.438–443 and 16.196, respectively.

12. That Homer gives no explanation for Phoinix's presence at the council is noted by Jones, *Homer's Iliad*, p. 152; Knox, "Introduction," p. 22; and Willcock, *Companion*, p. 98.

13. Compare *Il.* 9.252–259 and 9.438–443.

14. Although not without some resentment: *Il.* 9.613–615.

15. *Il.* 9.426–429.

16. *Il.* 11.790–802.

17. *Il.* 9.650–653. The fact that this vow was not communicated to Agamemnon, which I emphasized in section 6.1, is irrelevant in this new context: Achilles would assume that Odysseus and Aias had obeyed his instruction that Agamemnon be informed of his final decision, and, in any case, he had made this vow in the presence of the three ambassadors (as well as the two heralds and Patroklos).

18. With the formulaic style of oral poetry undoubtedly in mind, Page (*Homeric Iliad*, p. 330) declares in connection with *Il.* 9.648 = 16.59 that "nobody nowadays should suppose that the repetition of a line indicates interdependence of the two passages concerned." My opinion on this question is the same as that expressed by Rutherford ("From the *Iliad*," p. 119) in a slightly different context: "In this area as elsewhere, it seems likely that too much ground has been conceded to the oralists." The possibility of meaningful repetition in Homer is supported by Mueller, *The Iliad*, pp. 21–30. The discussion of quotes 5.2 and 5.3 in section 5.2 indicates that these passages are interdependent; other candidates for meaningful repetition are discussed in sections 6.3 and 9.2.

19. Jones, *Homer's Iliad*, p. 226; Mueller, *The Iliad*, p. 182; Postlethwaite, *Homer's Iliad*, p. 143; Schadewaldt, *Iliasstudien*, pp. 128–129; M. L. West, *Making of the Iliad*, p. 313; Willcock, *Companion*, pp. 111, 179.

20. Page, *Homeric Iliad*, pp. 329–330, n. 10; *Il. Comm.* IV, pp. 323–324. The rendering suggested by these scholars (or the equivalent "I thought") is implemented in the translations by Rieu et al. and Hammond.

21. *Il.* 9.649.

22. Janko (*Il. Comm.* IV, p. 322), while acknowledging that a reference to the Embassy was asserted in antiquity, prefers to see a reference to the prophecy (also voiced by Thetis) that Achilles will die soon after Hektor, even

though this prophecy does not appear until later in the poem (*Il.* 18.96) and, moreover, is not shared by Achilles with anyone else.

23. On one hand, we are told that the men in Agamemnon's shelter put questions to the ambassadors upon their return (*Il.* 9.669–671); on the other hand, we are told that Agamemnon was the first to pose a question and that each man retired to his own shelter when Odysseus had answered Agamemnon's question and Diomedes had uttered a response (*Il.* 9.672–713).

24. Willcock, *Companion*, pp. 103–104, 178. According to Willcock, the alternative explanation that Achilles "is not explicitly denying that he has received a warning from his mother but instead is saying that any such warning is not the reason for his refusal to fight" (e.g., Schadewaldt, *Iliasstudien*, p. 88, n. 3) "somewhat strains the Greek, although it is possible."

25. Postlethwaite, *Homer's Iliad*, p. 207.

26. A fragment from a play of Sophocles in which Odysseus accuses Achilles of cowardice (Marg, "Das erste Lied," pp. 18–19; Clay, *Wrath*, p. 99) is not relevant since it refers to an incident before the beginning of the Trojan War and thus before Achilles has had a chance to demonstrate his valor.

27. Kirk, *Songs*, pp. 214–215; Schadewaldt, *Iliasstudien*, p. 130.

28. Postlethwaite, *Homer's Iliad*, p. 208.

29. Consider the following interpretations of quote 6.3. Schadewaldt (*Iliasstudien*, p. 130) maintains that the return of Briseis is spoken of as a sign of the honor that Patroklos will create for Achilles by driving the enemy from the ships. Achilles, says Schadewaldt, wants Patroklos to create this honor for him but not to take away the highest honor for himself by completely defeating the Trojans. Similarly, Postlethwaite (*Homer's Iliad*, p. 208) says, "By fighting in his place Patroklos will win *time* [honor] for Achilleus as well as for himself, by showing how much the Achaians are missing their best warrior, but if he alone routs the Trojans, he will detract from Achilleus' *time* because the Achaians will not then be made aware of their dependence upon him; and so he encourages Patroklos to a limited victory only." It is not clear why, as Schadewaldt and Postlethwaite believe, Achilles would be honored for actions of Patroklos (and only if Patroklos does not accomplish too much). Sheppard (*Pattern*, p. 155) says that Achilles does not want Patroklos to drive the Trojans too far because then the Greeks might not feel the need for him and consequently might not restore Briseis and offer him gifts. According to Sheppard, in other words, the gifts and the return of Briseis are not to honor Achilles for the actions of Patroklos, but to entice him to return to the fighting. But why would the Greeks renew an offer that Achilles has already rejected in the most forceful terms possible, especially since, by sticking to the vow he made at the end of the Embassy, he has just demonstrated that he has no intention of relenting? Finally, Page (*Homeric Iliad*, p. 308) believes that Achilles is determined that the Greeks will restore Briseis to him and give him shining gifts in addition as a consequence of his eventual return to battle and the final defeat of the Trojans. This cannot be correct, however, since Achilles has asserted the primacy of his vow not to return to the fighting until it has reached his own ships, and a return under such circumstances would not win him gifts from the Greeks.

30. For multiple authorship, see, for example, Page, *Homeric Iliad*, pp. 304–310. For progressive fixation, see Goold, "Homeric Composition," pp. 10–11, 17; Mueller, *The Iliad*, pp. 181–183; M. L. West, *Making of the Iliad*, p. 54. Refer to chapter 4 for explanation of the terms "analyst," "unitarian," and "progressive fixation."

31. Of course, the theory can be saved if one assumes that references to the Embassy are late additions to the conversation (i.e., the conversation was not completely fixed before the Embassy was composed). As we shall see in a subsequent note, this is the position of M. L. West.

32. Schadewaldt, *Iliasstudien*, p. 129.

33. Martin Mueller and M. L. West are exceptions. Both scholars are advocates of progressive fixation, holding that the Embassy was added to the *Iliad* after the conversation between Achilles and Patroklos had already been fixed, but both admit that Achilles' words in *Il.* 16.61–63 allude to his vow to Aias in the Embassy (Mueller, *The Iliad*, p. 182; M. L. West, *Making of the Iliad*, p. 313). West (p. 312) interprets this allusion and other passages in *Il.* 16 that presuppose "later strata" of the poem as "brief insertions made for particular reasons."

34. *Il.* 16.71–73, with commentary from Page, *Homeric Iliad*, pp. 309–310.

35. Compare *Il.* 9.163–165 with 9.111–113.

36. In *Il.* 9.387 (the last line of quote 6.4), "Akhilleus appears to mean that he has 'paid' as it were a measure of humiliation to Agamemnon who must now 'pay' back an equivalent measure" (*Il. Comm.* III, p. 114). For me this implies something very like an apology.

37. Page, *Homeric Iliad*, pp. 305, 307; see also ibid., p. 330, n. 11.

38. In relation to quote 6.5, for example, Schadewaldt (*Iliasstudien*, p. 81) emphasizes that the Achaians have not begged Achilles, but rather have offered him a settlement. Kirk (*Songs*, p. 214) mentions as one possibility that the phraseology of the two passages that contain the disputed inconsistencies might be explicable as "a deliberate neglect by Achilles of offers which were unaccompanied by any frank admission of Agamemnon's highhandedness."

Hainsworth objects to Kirk's suggestion, noting in connection with quote 6.5 that "Akhilleus says nothing here about frank admissions on Agamemnon's part, Agamemnon being not so much as mentioned" (*Il. Comm.* III, p. 290). But this objection is surely inadequate, given the multiple occasions when Achilles does single out Agamemnon as the cause of his wrath—in the Quarrel, in the Embassy (e.g., quote 6.4), and in his conversation with Patroklos (e.g., quote 6.2). Even when Achilles wishes for massive Achaian losses (*Il.* 1.240–244, 408–412 [see part (*a*) of section 6.3]), it is because he wants Agamemnon to suffer for not having honored him. Since Agamemnon offers ample material compensation, Achilles' continued wrath can only be explained by the lack of what Kirk calls a frank admission of Agamemnon's high-handedness, i.e., an apology.

For further discussion see Postlethwaite, *Homer's Iliad*, p. 208; Willcock, *Companion*, pp. 177–179.

39. E. Bethe, quoted in Willcock, *Companion*, p. 178.

40. Rutherford, *Homer*, pp. 109–110; Schadewaldt, *Iliasstudien*, p. 137; Willcock, *Companion*, pp. 98, 178.

41. See, for example, Mueller, *The Iliad*, pp. 183–184.

42. I have inserted "far" into Lattimore's translation of *Il.* 2.82 on the basis of the translations by Nagy (*Achaeans*, pp. 26, 45) and Murray and Cunliffe's lexicon (which treats *Il.* 2.82 on p. 259).

43. Agamemnon's uncertainty as to whether the men will fight is perhaps even more apparent in Murray's translation of *Il.* 2.72: "But come, let us see if somehow we can arm the sons of the Achaeans" (the "somehow" inserted by Murray is, in fact, in the Greek). The same comment applies to Nestor's echo in quote 6.9 of Agamemnon in quote 6.8 (*Il.* 2.83 = 2.72).

44. Cf. Postlethwaite, *Homer's Iliad*, p. 51 on lines 134–137.

45. *Il.* 2.299–335.

46. Sheppard, *Pattern*, p. 26.

47. For example, see the response of Odysseus at *Il.* 14.95–102 to the suggestion of Agamemnon at *Il.* 14.74–79.

48. The bitterness of the Greek army aroused by Agamemnon's treatment of Achilles is made explicit by Poseidon at *Il.* 13.107–114 (see also Agamemnon at 14.49–51 and Diomedes at 14.131–132).

49. Note how Agamemnon transfers responsibility to Zeus when *Il.* 9.119–120 in quote 6.11 is transformed for public consumption into *Il.* 19.137–138 during the spurious reconciliation (also note that "mad" in 9.119 and "deluded" in 19.137 are alternative translations used by Lattimore for the same Greek word).

50. By saying that he was the first to be angry, Agamemnon also seems to be highlighting his exalted social position (as he does with the extravagant gifts offered to Achilles in the Embassy and forced on him in the spurious reconciliation), for that is what allows him to initiate a confrontation with the mighty Achilles.

51. Given his sensitivity regarding the Quarrel, it is natural to wonder why Agamemnon brings up the subject in the last speech of the Test episode. The answer probably lies in the speech given by Thersites when the army has settled down thanks to the intervention of Odysseus (*Il.* 2.225–242). This speech repeats the arguments made by Achilles in the Quarrel and strongly endorses his stance over that of Agamemnon (see Postlethwaite, *Homer's Iliad*, pp. 52–53 and especially Postlethwaite, "Thersites"). Thersites is humiliated by Odysseus, but not before he has brought into the open the "elephant in the room" which Agamemnon carefully ignored in quote 6.10. Knowing that Thersites' speech will have resonated with the men, even if they have been manipulated into submission by Odysseus, Agamemnon evidently feels compelled to defuse the subject, or at least to have the last word, and this is what we see in quote 6.12.

52. Some scholars consider the ill-conceived Test to be a symptom of unresolved inconsistencies between alternate story lines. For example: "Behind the paradoxes and confusions of the testing-motif in its present form one is probably right to detect other versions, in the earlier tradition or in the monumental poet's own repertoire, which omitted the test, or the test together with the council, or even the deceitful Dream itself" (*Il. Comm.* I, pp. 124–

125). In this interpretation, Agamemnon's use of the phrase "since it is the right way" (in Murray's translation: "as is customary") in *Il.* 2.73 (see quote 6.8) could signal Homer's attempt to disguise an awkward sequence of ideas (ibid., p. 122), but it could also reflect Agamemnon's own misgivings about the Test, which he does not want the princes to question (ibid.).

53. E.g., Taplin, *Soundings*, p. 93. Scodel (*Credible Impossibilities*, p. 50) points out that the comparison between the Test and the prelude to the embassy can be extended to include the contrasting responses to Agamemnon's speeches made by Thersites (*Il.* 2.225–242) and Diomedes (*Il.* 9.32–49).

54. The quotation is from the commentary on *Il.* 9.18–28 by Hainsworth (*Il. Comm.* III, pp. 61–62), who suggests that the verses in question may be a traditional characterization of Agamemnon or any despondent leader. For another scenario, see Mueller, *The Iliad*, pp. 176–177.

55. In counting the echoes of the Test later in the *Iliad*, I do not include the third passage in which Agamemnon proposes running away from Troy (*Il.* 14.65–81, in which he is speaking only to other leaders, not the entire army). Whereas the second such passage (9.17–28) is largely taken word for word from the first (2.110–141), the third passage repeats only two lines (14.69 = 2.116 = 9.23 and 14.74 = 2.139 = 9.26) and one of these (14.74) also appears in four other places in the *Iliad* (*Il. Comm.* IV, p. 157).

56. See, for example, Jones, *Homer's* Iliad, p. 68, and *Il. Comm.* I, p. 123 on *Il.* 2.76–83.

57. *Il.* 1.22–23.

58. *Il.* 1.275–291.

59. Sheppard, *Pattern*, p. 27.

60. *Il.* 2.84–86; Sheppard, *Pattern*, p. 28.

61. Reinhardt, *Die Ilias und ihr Dichter*, pp. 118–120.

62. *Il.* 4.14–19.

63. The quarrels in book 1 of the *Iliad* are compared by Rutherford, *Homer*, pp. 66–67.

64. *Il.* 1.545–550, 561–567.

65. *Il.* 1.589–594.

66. It may be noted that the Zeus's position of power derives to no small extent from his unmatched physical strength (*Il.* 1.565–567, 580–581; 8.10–27), while the Agamemnon's is purely political and is held in spite of the greater strength of Achilles (*Il.* 1.277–281); see Jones, *Homer's* Iliad, p. 60 on *Il.* 1.401. In addition, of course, Zeus is not subject to the self-delusion and weakness of spirit that often incapacitate Agamemnon.

67. Lattimore's translation of *Il.* 1.91 is "who now claims to be far the greatest of all the Achaians." The Greek word that is rendered here as "greatest" is often translated as "best" and is the same word that Lattimore himself translates as "best" in quotes 5.10 (*Od.* 8.78), 6.5 (*Il.* 1.244), 6.8 (*Il.* 2.82), and 6.17 (*Il.* 1.412), among other places. Besides substituting "best" for "greatest," I have deleted the word "all" for lack of support in the Greek text and to facilitate the comparison with *Il.* 2.82 (in quote 6.9) that I make later in section 6.3. In connection with that comparison, I should note that, according to the surviving manuscripts of the *Iliad*, the portion of *Il.* 1.91 translated as "far the best of the Achaians" in quote 6.16 should actually be translated as "far the best in the army." As Kirk (*Il. Comm.* I, p. 62 on *Il.* 1.91) points out, this is odd because the Alexandrian scholars agreed that the version shown in quote 6.16 is correct. Since the judgment of the ancients is favored by modern critics such as Kirk and Nagy (see *Achaeans*, pp. 26, 44), I shall accept it, noting that the essence of the comparison between 1.91 and 2.82 remains intact even if this judgment is incorrect.

68. Bassett (*Poetry*, p. 77) also regards quote 6.15 as a forward reference to the delusive dream sent by Zeus to Agamemnon. He believes, however, that this forward reference serves merely to prepare for that dream, whereas I will suggest that it has a deeper significance.

69. The treatment of dreams in the *Iliad* and the *Odyssey* is discussed by Dodds, *Irrational*, pp. 104–107 and the associated notes.

70. See Nagy, *Achaeans*, pp. 26–41.

71. The notion of "far" in "far the best" is expressed differently in the Greek of *Il.* 1.91 and 2.82, but Cunliffe's lexicon (pp. 259 and 336) specifically confirms its existence in these two lines. For a concern that is potentially more serious, see the note to *Il.* 1.91 referenced within quote 6.16. However, even if this concern should prove to be real, it is not fatal if we do not demand verbatim repetition but are satisfied with semantic equivalence (as in the case of "far the best").

72. As is well known, *Il.* 1.411–412 is repeated word for word at 16.273–274. The second occurrence, however, follows the usual pattern in which one character (Patroklos) is referring to another (Achilles) as "the best of the Achaians."

73. Indeed, the beginning of the Quarrel and Odysseus's speech concluding the episode of the Test are the only places in the *Iliad* where Kalchas is quoted (*Il.* 1.68–83, 92–100; 2.322–329). He is mentioned in one other passage (*Il.* 13.43–75), but only because Poseidon adopts his appearance and voice when encouraging the Greeks.

74. Sheppard, *Pattern*, pp. 29–30 (referring to *Il.* 1.188–218 and 2.155–184).

75. Two passages, *Il.* 4.64–104 and 5.711–909, are somewhat similar to the ones in question, but lack the important element of a crisis that must be averted at the last moment. In addition, Hera does not herself send Athene in the former but has Zeus send her (Athene) instead; in the latter (which admittedly contains some echoes of the Hera/Athene passage in the Test: 5.714 = 2.157; 5.719 = 2.166) Hera and Athene descend together to influence events in the mortal realm.

76. The four passages that make up the ring structure linking the Quarrel and the Test are not the only passages that connect the two episodes, but they are the only such passages where the connection is based on a shared peculiarity (a prophecy by Kalchas or a crisis averted at the last moment by Athene sent by Hera) rather than the substance of the Quarrel. This criterion eliminates from consideration passages that would spoil the ring structure: Agamemnon's speech excerpted in quote 6.12, the speech of Thersites (*Il.* 2.225–242; see Postlethwaite, "Thersites"), and the parts of the Quarrel to which these speeches refer.

77. Helenos: *Il.* 6.77–79; Ares: *Il.* 5.466–468; Automedon: *Il.* 17.512; Greeks flee: *Il.* 17.753–759.

78. On the duel between Hektor and Achilles in book 20 as an anticipation of their final encounter in book 22, see Fenik, *Battle Scenes*, p. 213, and *Il. Comm.* V, pp. 19, 336.

79. *Il.* 20.364–454.

80. *Il.* 20.79–352.

81. Edwards (*Il. Comm.* V, p. 325) remarks that "it is not clear ... how Poseidon knows that Apollo does not intend to help Aineias, or whether his words imply a threat to stop the junior god if he intervenes." The latter interpretation of the last line of quote 6.20 can be ruled out: Why would Poseidon prevent Apollo from rescuing Aineias if he himself wants Aineias to be saved?

82. Since Aineias is not a descendant of Laomedon (*Il.* 20.231–240), whose maltreatment of Poseidon aroused the latter's wrath against the Trojans (*Il.* 21.441–460), he does not belong to the group most hated by the god. However, he is an ally of that group, so Poseidon would not normally want to protect him (Scodel, *Credible Impossibilities*, p. 144).

83. Scodel, *Credible Impossibilities*, p. 143.

84. Fenik, *Battle Scenes*, p. 59.

85. *Il. Comm.* V, p. 302.

86. *Il.* 20.67–68; see also 21.435–469.

87. *Il.* 20.133–143.

88. Scheibner, *Aufbau*, p. 6; Nagy, *Achaeans*, p. 268; *Il. Comm.* V, p. 325; Scodel, *Credible Impossibilities*, p. 145. Scodel points out, however, that the poet could have just omitted Poseidon's threat to interfere if he wanted Apollo to rescue Aineias.

89. Critics have objected that, after saying he will intervene if Ares or Apollo hinders Achilles, Poseidon himself hinders him by covering his eyes with mist in order to rescue Aineias (Louis Erhardt, *Die Entstehung der homerischen Gedichte*, 1894, pp. 394–395 [cited by Scheibner, *Aufbau*, p. 7, n. 1]; Scodel, *Credible Impossibilities*, p. 145). This objection vanishes when one realizes that Poseidon's condition for intervening is designed just to protect Achilles.

90. The rescue of Aineias from Diomedes is begun by his mother Aphrodite (*Il.* 5.311ff.), but is taken over by Apollo (*Il.* 5.344–346, 432–446) when Aphrodite is wounded.

91. *Il.* 21.544–598.

92. Scheibner, *Aufbau*, p. 6.

93. This suggestion is motivated by Poseidon's prophecy that Aineias and his descendants will rule over the Trojans (*Il.* 20.302–308). See Willcock, *Companion*, pp. 222–223.

94. Scheibner, *Aufbau*, p. 7.

95. What I have in mind, of course, is not that Zeus would descend to rescue Aineias in person as Poseidon does, but that he would use thunder and lightening to stop the fighting (as at *Il.* 8.133–134) or to signal another god to remove Aineias from the scene.

96. *Il.* 20.300–308; see also 20.335–336.

97. Scodel, *Credible Impossibilities*, pp. 141–151. One of Scodel's points is that Zeus is the only god who acts to assist the fulfillment of fate (ibid., pp. 144–145); indeed, he does just this when, fearing that Achilles may storm Troy before this is fated, he tells the other gods to intervene in the war (*Il.* 20.23–30).

98. Sarpedon: *Il.* 16.433–438; Hektor: *Il.* 22.168–176. The thematic connection between these scenes is reinforced by the common lines in the responses of Hera and Athene (*Il.* 16.441–443 = 22.179–181). Concerning the fates of Sarpedon and Hektor, note that Zeus predicts their deaths at *Il.* 15.65–68.

99. *Il.* 20.293–299.

100. *Il.* 20.337–339.

101. Scheibner (*Aufbau*, pp. 87–88) remarks that the poet evidently intended Achilles' speech after the rescue of Hektor to be the counterpart of his speech after the rescue of Aineias.

102. *Il.* 20.108–109 (Murray trans.).

103. *Il.* 20.178–198.

104. *Il.* 20.200–202.

105. *Il.* 20.431–433 = 20.200–202.

106. *Il.* 20.429. For convenience I adopt the common view that Achilles' speech to Hektor consists only of this single line and that Achilles is speaking to himself in lines 425–427 (*Il. Comm.* V, pp. 336–337; Scheibner, *Aufbau*, p. 26; Scodel, *Credible Impossibilities*, p. 149). According to Lattimore's translation, however, the latter lines are actually addressed to Hektor. It is not clear to me that Lattimore is wrong, but it makes no difference for the present argument if he is right, since lines 425–427 are innocuous, containing neither taunts nor threats.

107. My view that the beginning of Hektor's reply, *Il.* 20.431–433, is not appropriate after Achilles' short, taunt-free speech and was just carried over from 20.200–202 echoes Scheibner (*Aufbau*, p. 26), who traces it to Karl Ludwig Kayser, *Homerische Abhandlungen* (1881), p. 21; Scodel (*Credible Impossibilities*, p. 149) seems to take a similar position. However, not all critics agree. Edwards (*Il. Comm.* V, p. 337) admits that the effect of 20.431–433 after the terse 20.429 "may seem to verge on the comic," but somehow manages a rationalization; Willcock (*Companion*, p. 231) is content to observe that the repeated verses (20.431–433 = 20.200–202) show the similarity between the Aineias and Hektor episodes.

108. *Il.* 20.81–82.

109. At *Il.* 3.332–333 Paris puts on a piece of armor that belongs to his half brother Lykaon.

110. *Il. Comm.* V, p. 302.

111. *Il.* 21.89–91.

112. *Il.* 20.407–418.

113. On the attempted supplication at *Il.* 20.463–472 as a compressed anticipation of Lykaon's supplication at 21.34–135, see Fenik, *Battle Scenes*, pp. 213–214; *Il. Comm.* V, pp. 20, 340; Postlethwaite, *Homer's Iliad*, pp. 256, 258. None of the other places in the *Iliad* where Trojans beg for their lives (always unsuccessfully) provides a close parallel with the Lykaon episode;

these other places are united with each other, however, by nearly identical lines: compare 6.47–50, 10.378–381, and 11.132–135.

114. *Il.* 20.213–241.

115. *Il. Comm.* V, p. 319.

116. *Il.* 20.460–472. Tros is killed immediately after a pair of brothers, one of whom is Dardanos. It may also be worth noting that Tros is the victim who attempts to supplicate Achilles in the anticipation of the Lykaon scene.

117. See *Il. Comm.* V, p. 339.

118. *Il.* 16.693–696.

119. *Il.* 20.300–308.

120. *Il.* 5.265–267. Note that this passage is connected with the scene in which Aineias is rescued by Aphrodite and then by Apollo.

121. *Il.* 20.233–235.

122. *Il.* 3.303, 5.159, 7.366, 13.376, 21.34, 22.351 (352 in the Greek), 24.171, 24.354, 24.629, 24.631.

123. Homer often refers to Skamandros as Xanthos, the name used by the gods (*Il.* 20.74), but I use only the former name for simplicity.

124. The pairs of opposed gods, ending with Hephaistos and Skamandros, are listed at *Il.* 20.67–74, shortly before the beginning of the Aineias episode at 20.79. The actual confrontation between Hephaistos and Skamandros occurs at 21.328–384; the remaining confrontations take place (or are defused) at 21.385–513.

125. A more elaborate ring structure based on different parallels has been proposed by Whitman (*Heroic Tradition*, p. 273). Neither Whitman's structure nor mine can account for two observations of Scheibner (*Aufbau*, p. 46): Just like Zeus at *Il.* 20.26–30, Skamandros at 21.308–310 is worried that Achilles will storm the city; Skamandros at 21.374–376 swears the same oath that was sworn by Hera and Athene, as described by Hera in the Aineias episode at 20.315–317.

126. *Il.* 20.130–131 in Rieu translation.

127. *Il.* 21.246–248 and quote 5.19.

128. *Il.* 21.304.

129. *Il.* 21.136–138, 145–147. Since the river god's motives are not in question, the fact that he does not save Asteropaios from Achilles cannot be used to infer any hostility against Asteropaios. Apollo's failure to save Aineias is another matter because Poseidon says that "Apollo will do nothing to keep grim death from him [Aineias]" (quote 6.20) and because he subsequently saves Hektor.

130. Forging of armor: *Il.* 18.468–614; shield decoration: *Il.* 18.483–607.

131. *Il.* 20.259–272.

132. *Il.* 18.481.

133. *Il. Comm.* V, pp. 202, 323. Scheibner (*Aufbau*, p. 80, n. 1) notes that a gold ring would be visible if the layers of the shield were concentric circles which decrease in radius from the innermost to the outermost layer, the configuration that is suspected for the oxhide layers of real shields (*Il. Comm.* V, p. 201). However, the bronze facing of such shields (i.e., the bronze layer atop the outermost layer of oxhide) extends over the full diameter of the shield. Furthermore, since Aineias's spear penetrated the two bronze layers of

Achilles' shield (*Il.* 20.269–272), it must have struck near the center of the shield if Scheibner's hypothesis is correct; this is a detail that one might expect the poet to mention since he mentions that Achilles' spear hits Aineias's shield near the rim. On the other hand, as Scheibner points out, the configuration he favors does correlate nicely with a plausible conjecture for the arrangement of decorative scenes on the shield (see Willcock, *Companion*, p. 210, chart 2).

134. *Il.* 20.269–272 was athetized by Aristarchus and is called "an uncomprehending addition to the text" by Edwards (*Il. Comm.* V, p. 202).

135. *Il.* 21.164–165 (note that 21.165 = 20.268 in the Greek). Achilles' shield also protects him from the spear thrown by Hektor in their final encounter (*Il.* 22.289–291), but the gold in the shield is not mentioned in this context.

136. That the poet gave significance to the stopping of a bronze-pointed spear by soft metal in the armor of Achilles is suggested by the existence of another instance of this phenomenon. At the end of book 21 a spear thrown by Agenor bounces off a tin greave made for Achilles by Hephaistos (*Il.* 21.592–594). This might be understandable if the spear made only glancing contact with the greave, but the indications are that it made a direct hit. Furthermore, it is difficult to solve this problem by postulating that metals change their properties in the hands of Hephaistos, inasmuch as the greaves are said to be made of "pliable tin" (*Il.* 18.612). Finally, it is worth noting that this is the only place in the *Iliad* where greaves are hit in battle (*Il. Comm.* VI, p. 102).

137. *Il.* 21.187–189.

138. *Il.* 21.140–142, 154–160, 186.

139. *Il.* 21.184–185.

140. *Il.* 20.105–107. See Fenik, *Battle Scenes*, p. 67.

141. When Zeus tells the other gods to interfere in the war as they see fit (*Il.* 20.23–25), he does not indicate that his order expires at the end of the day, as suggested in quote 6.23 (*Il. Comm.* VI, p. 72). However, the time limit agrees nicely with Hera's first speech in the Aineias episode (cf. *Il.* 20.125–127), reinforcing the connection between this episode and quote 6.23.

142. Scheibner (*Aufbau*, p. 99) likens quote 6.23 to *Il.* 21.308–323: in both passages Skamandros appeals for help to a power hostile to Achilles (Apollo or the river Simoeis, respectively), and in both cases the appeal has no result. If valid, this comparison would undermine my argument since it suggests a theme that provides another raison d'être for quote 6.23. However, even if we grant that quote 6.23 is a call for help (an interpretation that is open to question), the comparison is flawed because Simoeis has little chance to join forces with Skamandros before Hera has Hephaistos set fire to the Trojan plain. Scheibner acknowledges the justness of this observation when he says that Hera acts in the face of the imminent alliance of the two rivers (*Aufbau*, p. 100).

143. See quotation from Eduard Kammer in Scheibner, *Aufbau*, pp. 36–37.

144. *Il.* 7.337–343, 436–441.

145. *Il. Comm.* II, p. 316; *Il. Comm.* IV, p. 258.

146. The poet seems to indicate at *Il.* 12.118–121 that a warrior in his chariot can reach one of the gates in the wall without having to cross the ditch (*Il. Comm.* III, p. 330; Jones, *Homer's* Iliad, p. 173). The indication is ambiguous, however, and is best ignored since the Greeks themselves do not take advantage of any causeway elsewhere in the poem (see quotes 6.26–6.28).

147. If the Greeks were to leave their chariots at the ditch's edge when fleeing from the Trojans, they would lose their chariots to the Trojans and be at a disadvantage from then on. There is no indication in the *Iliad* that this happens.

148. M. L. West, *Making of the Iliad*, p. 265; *Il. Comm.* III, p. 325.

149. *Il.* 15.352–366. By making a path into the camp for the Trojans and their chariots, Apollo exposes them to the danger anticipated in the italicized part of quote 6.24. This does not mean that he is acting against the Trojans as in his treatment of Aineias discussed in section 6.4. On the contrary, he is being used by Zeus to assist the Trojans for a certain period (*Il.* 15.59–64, 229–235).

150. *Il. Comm.* IV, p. 363.

151. This problem is glossed over at *Il.* 8.253–255.

152. The Greek text is obscure (*Il. Comm.* III, p. 224; Schadewaldt, *Iliasstudien*, pp. 4–6; M. L. West, *Making of the Iliad*, pp. 248–249), but I believe the translations by Hammond and Rieu et al. convey the correct sense, that given by Schadewaldt (*Iliasstudien*, p. 40) and Jones (*Homer's* Iliad, p. 172). Other interpretations are assumed in Lattimore's translation and *Il. Comm.* I, p. 361.

153. In principle, it is possible that the ditch is more difficult to cross in one direction than the other, owing to a difference between the slopes of its two sides or to the location and orientation of the sharp stakes. If this is the case, the defensive purpose of the ditch suggests that it would be more difficult to cross when the Greeks return to the camp than when they leave it.

154. I have already observed that the retreat across the ditch that leaves the Greeks in their camp at the beginning of book 12 is not mentioned in the narrative. For the other Greek retreat across the ditch that goes unmentioned, see the discussion of *Il.* 8.213–214 in *Il. Comm.* II, p. 316. It should be noted that the crossing of the ditch is commonly ignored when the Greeks leave their camp, although crossings by Diomedes and Patroklos are described at 8.253–255 and 16.380–382, respectively.

155. *Il.* 8.343–345 = 15.1–3 except for necessary adjustments. Kirk infers from the closeness of this correspondence and the apparent nonformularity of the verses that one passage is probably derived from the other (*Il. Comm.* II, p. 326). After making a strong argument that points to the passage in book 8 as the original, he goes on to overrule this argument and to reach the opposite conclusion on the basis of a speculative scenario. Fortunately, the direction of the dependence is not important for the present discussion.

156. *Il.* 15.343, 346–347; *Il. Comm.* IV, p. 264.

157. *Il.* 17.760–761 (Hammond trans.).

158. *Od.* 12.39–141. Even Circe's account is incomplete. She does not mention Odysseus's second encounter with Charybdis, although she does mention the fig tree that will save his life during this encounter (*Od.* 12.103–104, 432–436). She also fails to mention Odysseus's detainment by Kalypso, but nothing she could have said would have prevented or shortened this detainment.

159. If the word "journey" in quote 6.29 is taken to refer to Odysseus's journey through life, not merely his journey to Ithaka (the second line of quote 6.29 notwithstanding), it can be argued that Teiresias *is* the one who tells Odysseus the stages of his journey (Dimock, *Unity*, p. 145; Reinhardt, "Adventures," p. 110; Tracy, *Story*, pp. 69–70). For Teiresias tells Odysseus about the insolent suitors he will find in his palace, what he must do after he has killed them, and how he himself will die, things he does not learn from Circe. However, this is not Odysseus's understanding of quote 6.29; he says to Achilles that "I came [to the underworld] for the need to consult Teiresias, if he might tell me some plan by which I might come back to rocky Ithaka" (*Od.* 11.479–480). If we nevertheless insist on accepting the questionable broad interpretation of the word "journey," we still cannot say that Teiresias will tell Odysseus how to make the journey, for it is unlikely that Odysseus would have made it even to Ithaka if he had not received Circe's warnings concerning the Sirens, Skylla, and Charybdis.

160. See, for example, Clay, *Wrath*, pp. 151–153; Fenik, *Studies*, pp. 120–126; Hansen, *Conference Sequence*, pp. 14–15; Heubeck, "Books IX–XII," pp. 72–73; Page, *Homeric Odyssey*, pp. 27–28, 32; Woodhouse, *Composition*, pp. 144–147.

161. On the unsuitability of quote 6.29 to Teiresias, see Reinhardt, "Adventures," p. 110.

162. Fenik, *Studies*, pp. 124–126.

163. *Od.* 1.13–15.

164. *Od.* 1.81–87, 5.29–31.

165. The attribution is surprising since Athene acts as Odysseus's helper in the *Odyssey* and is in fact responsible for Hermes' mission to rescue Odysseus from Kalypso's island. It is not entirely implausible, however, as Homer has previously referred to the bitter homecoming that Athene inflicted upon the Achaians (*Od.* 1.326–327; see also quote 6.34).

166. *Od.* 24.528–544.

167. A somewhat different perspective on the relationship between quotes 6.32 and 6.33 is presented by Dimock, *Unity*, pp. 65–66.

168. Odysseus relates the warnings of Teiresias and Circe in their proper chronological sequence (*Od.* 11.104–113 and 12.127–140, respectively), but he also refers to these warnings together when he describes the Thrinakian incident itself (both warnings are mentioned in *Od.* 12.266–269 and again in 12.271–276).

169. *Od.* 1.6–9. See also the accounts given by Odysseus to Penelope at *Od.* 19.273–279 (when Odysseus is disguised as a beggar and tactfully fails to mention Odysseus's stay with Kalypso) and *Od.* 23.329–337 (when the reunion of Odysseus and Penelope is complete and he gives an accurate summary of his journey). Odysseus neglects to mention the cattle of Helios when he first speaks with the king and queen of the Phaiakians (*Od.* 7.244–255), but this omission is no more consequential than that in quote 6.33; in fact, there is a close correspondence between the two passages (specifically, between *Od.* 7.249–251 and 5.131–133).

170. The cited evidence explains why an ancient commentator quoted by Clay (*Wrath*, p. 50) says in relation to quote 6.32 that "these verses are odd and at variance with the story" and why, as she also notes, "modern scholars question the soundness of the text although there are no solid grounds for doing so." Surprisingly, however, Clay herself believes that quote 6.32 is to be accepted at face value and that the wrath of Athene implicit in that passage is genuine. My objections to Clay's theory of the wrath of Athene are summarized in note 131 to chapter 2.

171. Note that the echo of the second part of the pattern (quote 6.33) at *Od.* 7.244–255 and the echoes of the third part of the pattern at *Od.* 19.273–279 and 23.329–337 do not change the succession of the reader's cognitive states since each echo repeats the most recent part of the pattern. It is perhaps worth noting also that the almost exact repetition of part of quote 6.33 in the first of these echoes (*Od.* 7.249–251 = 5.131–133 except for a change in person) is just one of a number of reuses of language from the Ogygian account of *Od.* 5 in Odysseus's response to Arete's questions in *Od.* 7 (see Apthorp, "The Language of *Odyssey* 5.7–20," p. 8).

172. Bassett, *Poetry*, p. 137. At the same time, Bassett, like many other authors (e.g., Clay, *Wrath*, pp. 24–25; Heubeck, "Books IX–XII," pp. 139, 140; Reinhardt, "Adventures," p. 101), points out that the last two lines of quote 6.35 perform the indispensable function of explaining how Odysseus knows about the exchange between Helios and Zeus recounted earlier in the passage, an exchange that took place "among the immortals" (i.e., on Olympos). But it could also be pointed out that only the details of this exchange (which are poetic and dramatic but not essential to the narrative) need to be filled in by Kalypso. The main facts are accessible to Odysseus without her help. The involvement of Helios in the destruction of his ship and the loss of his companions would have been obvious to him from the warnings of Teiresias and Circe; the involvement of Zeus would have been clear from the thunderbolt; and the existence of some sort of exchange between Helios and Zeus would therefore have been a natural inference. Indeed, it is reasonable to assume that Odysseus conveyed these inferences to Kalypso (not vice versa) when he arrived at Ogygia (this supposition offers a new perspective on the question "Why is Homer silent about the first encounter of Odysseus with Kalypso?"—a question raised and discussed by Woodhouse, *Composition*, pp. 48–53).

173. Although Hermes tells her that Zeus wants her to send Odysseus on his way home (*Od.* 5.112–115), Kalypso, when speaking with Odysseus, pretends that she does not know the will of the gods (*Od.* 5.165–170) and implies that she is helping him solely out of compassion (*Od.* 5.188–191). When he first speaks with the king and queen of the Phaiakians, Odysseus indicates that he does not know whether Kalypso released him on her own initiative or because she had received a message from Zeus (*Od.* 7.261–263).

Odysseus may have fabricated the last two lines of quote 6.35 as well as the details in the same passage that could be known only to the gods. However, this would not affect the triadic inconsistency, as the general correctness of his account is not in question (he knows about Helios from the warnings of Teiresias and Circe; Zeus's involvement is evident from the thunderbolt that destroyed his ship; and the role he assigns to Lampetia is at least plausible in view of what Circe told him at *Od.* 12.131–136).

174. Scodel ignores the contradictions and maintains that in quote 6.35 Odysseus merely supplements Homer's account of the conversation between Kalypso and Hermes: "Characters may expand on what the narrator has provided, so that an account which was apparently complete turns out to have had gaps" (*Credible Impossibilities*, p. 60). As another illustration of this alleged principle, Scodel (ibid., p. 59) points to the attacks on the wall of Troy that are mentioned by Andromache (*Il.* 6.435–439) but are never otherwise described by Homer even though they ostensibly took place during the time frame of the poem. The possibility that Homer omitted such significant attacks from his narrative of the war is so slight that Scodel's principle is called into question once again.

175. Compare *Od.* 10.135b–136 with 12.448b–449, 10.221–222 with 5.61–62, and 10.543–545 with 5.230–232. See also Austin, *Archery*, pp. 152–153; Reinhardt, "Adventures," pp. 95–97; Saïd, *Homer and the Odyssey*, pp. 171–174, 260–261; Scully, "Doubling," pp. 406–408; Tracy, *Story*, pp. 56–57; and Woodhouse, *Composition*, pp. 46–53. For differences between Circe and Kalypso see Stanford, *Ulysses Theme*, pp. 48–49.

176. Scholars differ in their interpretations of *Od.* 9.31–32: Scully ("Doubling," p. 407 [referring to p. 401]) appears to take these lines at face value, while Woodhouse (*Composition*, pp. 49–50) objects to the assertion that Circe forced Odysseus to stay with her and wanted him to be her husband. I am inclined to agree with Woodhouse, but I also believe that quote 6.36 merely distorts a similarity between Circe and Kalypso that is real enough: Homer's statement that Kalypso "was *no longer* pleasing to him" (*Od.* 5.153–154; italics added) suggests that Odysseus may have enjoyed the first year of his stay with Kalypso as much as he enjoyed his year-long stay with Circe. In any case, the important point is that Circe and Kalypso are linked together in the *Odyssey* both explicitly (in quote 6.36) and implicitly (by correspondences such as those cited in the preceding note).

177. The parallel roles of Circe and Kalypso are best appreciated in the wider context of the correspondences between the exotic adventures that precede and follow Odysseus's visit to the underworld, for which see the outline of the adventures provided by Tracy, *Story*, pp. 55–56.

178. Circe: *Od.* 12.39–141; Kalypso: *Od.* 5.276–277. That Circe and Kalypso both give Odysseus directions for his journey is pointed out by Scully, "Doubling," p. 407.

179. Circe: *Od.* 12.149–150 (= 11.7–8, but in the latter passage Circe is providing a wind for the trip to the underworld); Kalypso: *Od.* 5.268. This correspondence between Circe and Kalypso is noted by Jones, *Homer's Odyssey*, p. 116.

180. *Od.* 8.446–454. I say that the poet goes out of his way to mention Circe and Kalypso together in this passage because the knot that Circe taught Odysseus is an unnecessary invention.

181. This point has also been made by Hansen (*Conference Sequence*, p. 14) and Woodhouse (*Composition*, pp. 39–40). For the latter, it is absurd even to think that the journey inland and sacrifices to Poseidon advised by Teiresias have anything to do with expiation. Instead, Woodhouse would have us believe, Homer included the italicized passage at the end of quote 6.30 simply in order to explain the existence of a cult of Poseidon far from the sea.

182. *Od.* 1.20–21, 6.330–331; a further indication at 13.341–343 is implicit but just as clear. The only contrary indication is found in the prayer of Polyphemos to Poseidon (quote 6.45) discussed in section 6.8. Even if we accept the improbable notion that Poseidon might be responsible for the trouble with the suitors, the sacrifices recommended by Teiresias are still pointless since they are to be performed after Odysseus has killed the suitors.

183. In fact, this assumption underlies the remarks of Woodhouse (*Composition*, pp. 39–40) and Hansen (*Conference Sequence*, p. 14). The assumption is only a probability, however, not a rigorous requirement: Although Poseidon is the god of the sea, he can also act on land and shares dominion of the earth with Zeus and Hades (*Il.* 15.187–193). In the *Iliad* we see him intervening in the war and even creating an earthquake (*Il.* 20.57–65). In the *Odyssey* we see him act only at sea, but he is called the shaker of the earth in that poem, as he is in the *Iliad*.

184. Page, *Homeric Odyssey*, pp. 53–57; see also Kirk, *Songs*, pp. 229–230. The criticism of *Od.* 1.275 that Athene knows perfectly well that Penelope is not eager to remarry does not trouble me since in this scene she is disguised as a mortal and feigns ignorance (e.g., *Od.* 1.207, 225–226).

185. Appearance: *Od.* 4.141–150; strength: *Od.* 21.124–129. To the resemblance in appearance and strength could be added the resemblance in speech noticed by Nestor (*Od.* 3.124–125).

186. See Tracy, *Story*, pp. 29, 46–47, 89, 95.

187. Telemachos: *Od.* 3.14–20, 75–77; Odysseus: *Od.* 7.49–52. Athene also urges Penelope to take courage (*Od.* 4.825–829), but in a very different type of situation.

188. The lowly (Thersites): *Il.* 2.244–269; the exalted (Agamemnon and Achilles): *Il.* 4.349–355, 19.155–183. Nausicaa: *Od.* 6.141 ff.

189. Odysseus: *Od.* 16.206 (= 19.484, 21.208, 24.322; see also 23.101–102 = 23.169–170) in conjunction with *Od.* 5.107 (see also *Od.* 14.241 and *Il.* 2.329); Menelaos: *Od.* 4.82.

190. See Reinhardt, "Adventures," pp. 105–108; Lord, *Singer of Tales*, pp. 165–169; Hansen, *Conference Sequence*, pp. 8–19; and Plass, "Menelaus and Proteus," pp. 104–105.

191. *Od.* 4.389–390 = *Od.* 10.539–540. Note that *Od.* 4.390 is also duplicated (either exactly or essentially) at *Od.* 4.381, 424, 470.

192. Clay (*Wrath*, p. 152), Fenik (*Studies*, p. 125), and Heubeck ("Books IX–XII," p. 72) liken the information provided by Proteus to that provided by Teiresias, pointing out that neither seer specifies a route for the homeward journey. Reinhardt ("Adventures," p. 106), on the other hand, asserts that Proteus does show Menelaos the way home.

193. *Od.* 4.576–587.

194. For a detailed comparison of the missions of Athene and Hermes, see Hansen, *Conference Sequence*, pp. 28–33.

195. Athene on the plight of Odysseus: *Od.* 1.48–59 and 5.7–17.

196. Hermes' mission: *Od.* 1.84–87 (suggested by Athene) and 5.29–42 (commanded by Zeus).

197. For a perceptive comparison of the two divine assemblies, see Tracy, *Story*, p. 29.

198. Although not relevant to the present discussion, it is surely significant that the parallels between quotes 6.39 and 6.40 can be traced to a common source in the *Iliad* (Usener, *Beobachtungen*, pp. 169–172; M. L. West, *Making of the Odyssey*, p. 70): *Il.* 24.339–345 = *Od.* 5.43–49.

199. To avoid the inconsistency, Jones (*Homer's Odyssey*, p. 126) raises the possibility that Odysseus, not wanting to appear ungrateful to Athene, only speaks *as if* he has not already been warned by Teiresias. But such timidity would be out of character for Odysseus, even in his relationship with the goddess. Earlier in the same conversation, he has complained quite bluntly that she abandoned him during most of his journey home from Troy (*Od.* 13.316–323). One might argue that he is now compensating for having made that rather bitter complaint. Thus, Clay (*Wrath*, p. 205) maintains that Odysseus has changed his tune "from challenging and provoking the goddess to slightly obsequious flattery" with the aim of ensuring Athene's support in overcoming the suitors. But surely Athene's wish to help Odysseus is clear from what she says and does (*Od.* 13.361–371, not to mention quote 6.42) after she addresses his complaint and before he makes the supposedly obsequious remark in quote 6.43. And after that remark he makes it clear that he has not forgotten his complaint (note the word "too" in *Od.* 13.417–419) as he accuses her of also abandoning Telemachos.

200. *Od.* 11.405–434.

201. Compare *Od.* 13.342–343 with 11.102–103.

202. *Od.* 13.352–360 (compare 13.187–212; see also 13.248–252, 324–328).

203. *Od.* 7.317–328; 8.30–33, 555–566.

204. Page, Homeric Odyssey, pp. 41–42.

205. One might argue that the contradictions were not removed owing to a reluctance to delete anything that had been set in writing. However, I consider the scenario of progressive fixation to be discredited by observations made in sections 6.2 and 6.10.

206. Odysseus: *Od.* 11.100–103, 127–134; Menelaos: *Od.* 4.472–480, 583.

207. Proteus tells Menelaos about the homecoming of Agamemnon, his murder by Aigisthos, and the possibility that Orestes has already avenged his father's murder (*Od.* 4.512–547). With these things in mind, Fenik (*Studies*, p. 125) asserts that Proteus does tell Menelaos about the good and evil done in his palace while he has been away. This assertion is difficult to fathom since Agamemnon and Menelaos lived in different parts of Greece, and the Greek word translated as "palace" in quote 6.44 cannot refer to the family relationship of the two brothers (compare *Od.* 4.392 with *Od.* 23.56 and *Il.* 24.219).

208. Lord, *Singer of Tales*, pp. 165, 166; Hansen, *Conference Sequence*, p. 10.

209. Compare *Od.* 4.538–541 and 10.496–499 (Heubeck, "Books IX–XII," p. 72).

210. Reinhardt, "Adventures," p. 112.

211. Ibid.; see also ibid., p. 131.

212. The first of the two lines that are common to the prayer of Polyphemos and the prophecy of Teiresias is repeated by Circe (*Od.* 12.141 = 11.114). Since she does not repeat the second line (as noted by Hansen, *Conference Sequence*, p. 18), only Polyphemos and Eidothea allude to Teiresias's warning concerning the suitors.

213. Athene/Mentes: *Od.* 1.245–251; Nestor: 3.205–207; Menelaos: 4.316–321; Odysseus: 16.121–128; the assembly: 2.50–59 (quote 6.47); the suitors: 1.368–380.

214. Murray's translation; the translations given by A. Cook, Hammond, and Woodhouse (*Composition*, p. 159) are equivalent to Murray's. Cunliffe's lexicon defines the verb ($καταισχυνω$) as "to bring shame upon" or, in the context of *Od.* 19.12, "to mar the seemliness of."

215. When Woodhouse discusses the "excuse, lame as it might be, with which to parry awkward inquiries on the part of the suitors" (*Composition*, p. 165), one would think that he is referring to the second explanation in quote 6.46. In fact, he is referring to the combination of the two explanations, which he elsewhere calls "the elaborate excuse given at length in both passages [quotes 2.3 and 2.4]" (ibid., p. 161). When he goes on to say that "Homer's idea ... [in providing the "lame" excuse] was to show how besotted and fatuous were the suitors, how blind to every hint and warning of the coming storm," he appears to provide an alternative to my interpretation of the second explanation as an intentional inconsistency. However, Odysseus would never put his entire plan at risk by suggesting a pretext that the suitors might see through. In any case, the pretext is never used and therefore proves nothing about the suitors.

So far as I know, Rutherford (*Books XIX and XX*, p. 135 on *Od.* 19.12) is the only critic who singles out the second explanation for special comment: "But for him [Telemachos] and all the loyal household the very presence of the suitors already spoils the feast, so that the lines are both ironic and deceptive."

216. See Page, *Homeric Odyssey*, p. 99, n. 15. Combellack ("Problems," p. 24) claims there is no inconsistency: "I should think a group of young men without shields or missiles might well be eager to get some when faced with a careless fellow who has a deadly bow in his hands." But this point is valid only if the suitors think that the "careless fellow" is going to continue to shoot after having killed Antinoös, in which case he is not merely careless and the shooting of Antinoös was probably not accidental.

217. For an overview of various approaches to quote 6.48, see Fernández-Galiano, "Books XXI–XXII," pp. 223, 225.

218. Goold, "Removal of the Arms," pp. 127–128.

219. Büchner, "Waffenbergung," pp. 444–445. In fact, Büchner considers the entirety of the last three lines of quote 6.48 to be false. These lines were also rejected by Aristarchus.

220. This is the argument of Büchner: After everything Odysseus said and did before he shot Antinoös, and after Telemachos took his place at his father's side armed with his sword and spear (*Od.* 21.431–434), the suitors cannot doubt that he shot Antinoös intentionally and that they themselves are threatened (ibid., p. 444).

221. Fernández-Galiano, "Books XXI–XXII," p. 220.

222. *Od.* 17.468–476.

223. Büchner, "Waffenbergung," p. 445.

224. The scene I go on to analyze is found at *Od.* 17.336–488.

225. *Od.* 17.458–465 (Antinoös), 18.387–397 (Eurymachos), 20.287–301 (Ktesippos).

226. Since my argument for the intentionality of the inconsistency in quote 6.48 depends on Odysseus's declaration of his wish for death of Antinoös, I should mention that the verses containing this declaration (*Od.* 17.475–476) together with the verses containing Antinoös's response to it (*Od.* 17.477–480) were athetized by Aristarchus. The basis for the athetesis may have been the relative mildness of Antinoös's response: "For how could Antinous endure such curses, when he was so angered by smaller matters?" (Russo, "Books XVII–XX," p. 41). It is not obvious to me that the mildness of his response is unrealistic (perhaps he is calmer after venting his anger by throwing the footstool), but even if it is, this might just be a further indication of the lengths to which Homer was willing to go in order to include Odysseus's declaration.

227. What I am suggesting, just hypothetically, is that line 34 of *Od.* 22 could come right after line 25. Of course, line 34 would have to be modified so that it does not imply that Odysseus is replying to something said by the suitors. This is not a problem, since I believe that the passage was originally written in its present form, not that lines 26–33 were interpolated.

228. *Od.* 22.42–43.

229. Heubeck, "General Introduction," p. 7; Rutherford, "From the *Iliad*," p. 117; M. L. West, "Homeric Question," p. 388; M. L. West, *Making of the Iliad*, p. 7.

230. *Il. Comm.* IV, p. 14. The small linguistic gap that does exist is consistent with the standard view that the *Iliad* is (slightly) older than the *Odyssey*. Nevertheless, those who hold the currently popular view that the *Iliad* and the *Odyssey* were composed by different poets cite the linguistic gap between the poems as one of the main justifications for their opinion (M. L. West, "Homeric Question," p. 388).

231. The most thorough studies are those of Albert Gemoll ("Beziehungen") and Knut Usener (*Beobachtungen*) briefly summarized in M. L. West, *Making of the Odyssey*, pp. 25–26.

232. Indeed, the authors of two major studies of Iliadic quotations in the *Odyssey* believe in the separate authorship of the two epics (Rutherford, "From the *Iliad*," p. 120; Usener, *Beobachtungen*, pp. 205–206). On Usener's view that the *Odyssey*-poet was a rival of the *Iliad*-poet, see Jones, "Introduction," pp. 37–38.

233. M. L. West, *Making of the Iliad*, p. 71.

234. M. L. West (*Making of the Odyssey*, pp. 70–79) emphasizes that the *Odyssey* poet can be careless when he borrows lines from the *Iliad* or reuses lines of his own, but minimizes such carelessness on the part of the *Iliad* poet. This distinction supports his belief in separate authorship for the two poems. However, it is not difficult to find instances of careless reuse of lines in the *Iliad*. For example, Fenik (*Battle Scenes*, pp. 94–95) and Schadewaldt (*Iliasstudien*, p. 6) show that the lines *Il.* 11.362–367 = 20.449–454 fit their later context down to the last detail but are not well suited to their earlier context (the last line of the shared passage is ignored by these authors, but provides a nice confirmation of their assessment). Fenik concludes, "I think it must be admitted that we are faced with an example of the poet's carelessness, the causes of which we are not in a position to trace." Another example involves *Il.* 20.315–317 = 21.374–376: it is perfectly appropriate when Xanthos, the main river god of the Troad, swears under duress not to save the Trojans (21.373–376) but incongruous when the same oath is said to have been sworn by Hera and Athene (20.313–317), who would like nothing better than to annihilate Troy. West himself (p. 215) offers this example: *Il.* 9.18–22 refer naturally to recent events (the deceptive dream sent to Agamemnon by Zeus and the subsequent Greek losses on the battlefield), but the same lines at 2.111–115 have no clear reference.

235. See, for example, Rutherford, *Homer*, p. 82; Heubeck, "General Introduction," p. 17.

236. The idea that narrative strategies of the *Odyssey* reflect the character of its protagonist is not new: see Rutherford, *Books XIX and XX*, p. 7; Slatkin, "*Mētis* of the *Odyssey*"; Silk, "Explorations," p. 42.

237. The syntactic parallelism between the proem of the *Iliad* and that of the *Odyssey* (Bassett, "Proems," p. 340; S. West, "Books I–IV," p. 67; Pucci, *Sirens*, pp. 11–13) may be another manifestation, on a much smaller scale, of the poet's wish to forge a structural bond between the two epics.

238. Similarly, the one scene in the *Odyssey* in which the gods are portrayed in a light-hearted manner alludes through both language and content to all three such scenes in the *Iliad* (Burkert, "Ares and Aphrodite"). Another Odyssean scene, the song of the Sirens, alludes to the *Iliad* by its repeated use of specifically Iliadic diction (Pucci, "Sirens").

CHAPTER 7: Mysterious Inconsistency in the Writings of Gurdjieff

1. In the French edition of *Meetings with Remarkable Men* (based, like the English edition, on Gurdjieff's Russian text), the clause "our correspondence continued uninterruptedly for almost thirty-five years" in quote 7.2 is replaced by "our correspondence was never to stop" (Gurdjieff, *Rencontres*, p. 161), and the phrase "almost forty years" in quote 7.1 is replaced by "a very long time" (ibid., p. 158). Thus, the French translation eliminates both the "almost forty years" from quote 7.1 and the "almost thirty-five years" from quote 7.2. I argue that no translator would invent the thirty-five and forty-year periods, whereas a translator might have a reason for removing them from the text. The inference that the English translations shown in quotes 7.1 and 7.2 are more accurate than the corresponding French translations is confirmed by the Russian typescript of the Lubovedsky chapter kindly made available to me by Dr. Jon Thompson.

Why remove the references to the periods of forty and thirty-five years? One possible motivation would be to solve the following problem pointed out by Johnson, *Initiates*, p. 157. Gurdjieff's friend Soloviev was with him at the time of his last meeting with the prince (*RM*, pp. 149, 154–155), and the prince died three years after the meeting (*RM*, p. 163). Since Soloviev died in 1898 (*RM*, p. 165), the prince died in 1901 at the latest. The thirty-five year correspondence between Gurdjieff and the prince mentioned in quote 7.2 could therefore have begun no later than 1866. But that is the year of Gurdjieff's birth (Moore, *Gurdjieff*, pp. 339–340; see also Taylor, *America*, p. 16). (The year of his birth is actually not known with certainty, but 1866 is the earliest year for which there is evidence.) Removal of the references to the forty- and thirty-five-year periods eliminates this problem.

It is evident from this example and others that the French translators (as well as those responsible for the English translation of the First Series which first appeared in 1992) sometimes took it upon themselves to make what they thought were improvements to the text. The loss of information resulting from this aggressive approach has been documented elsewhere (*EWG*, pp. 6, 32–34, 135–137, 209–210 [n. 5], p. 227 [n. 2]).

2. The fact that the third element of the pattern discussed in section 7.1 consists of two mutually supporting components (quotes 7.3 and 7.4) is no reason to question its triadic structure or its similarity to the Odyssean patterns described in section 6.6. In that section we saw that the third element of the Circe triad likewise consists of two components (quote 6.31 and Circe's explanation to Odysseus of the stages of his journey home), and in a note referenced in that section I call attention to an echo of the second element of the Kalypso triad and to two echoes of the third element of that triad. As I mention in the note, each echo repeats the most recent part of the pattern, and therefore does not change the succession of cognitive states of the reader or the logical structure of the pattern.

3. See *BT*, pp. 530, 624–625, 626, 629.

4. *BT*, p. 387.

5. *BT*, p. 1177.

6. *RM*, p. 198.

7. The mentioned inconsistencies with specifically Gurdjieffian content are found in *Beelzebub's Tales*, while the ordinary narrative inconsistencies have been taken from *Meetings with Remarkable Men*. It is therefore important to note that *Beelzebub's Tales* also contains inconsistencies of the latter type. In the voyage of the spaceship *Karnak*, for example, the planet Deskaldino is called "a place of unforeseen stopping" (*BT*, p. 917), despite the fact that the visit to this planet was planned ahead of time (*BT*, pp. 657–659). This inconsistency has been mentioned elsewhere (*EWG*, p. 214, n. 31), but is worth bringing up again because of how it is treated in the French translation (and in the related English translation of 1992): Deskaldino is called "une planète sur laquelle il [le vaisseau *Karnak*] allait faire une halte imprévue au départ" (Gurdjieff, *Récits*, p. 876). The words "au départ" remove the inconsistency since the visit to Deskaldino was not planned until the voyage was well underway, but these words have no basis in the Russian text (Gurdjieff, *Rasskazy*, p. 909). As in the case of the Lubovedsky triad (see the first note to section 7.1), the French translators have taken it upon themselves to eliminate an inconsistency without realizing that it may have been intended by Gurdjieff.

8. One such inconsistency is discussed in *EWG*, pp. 4, 7, 71–72, and another in *EWG*, pp. 128–129. The first of these is an inconsistency presumably arranged by Gurdjieff between translations of his works into different languages (another such inconsistency is discussed in *EWG*, pp. 25–26). The second relates to a stratagem Gurdjieff employed as a writer and belongs to a class of inconsistencies that I plan to discuss in the last chapter of the second edition of *EWG*.

9. It should perhaps also be noted that there are inconsistencies between *Beelzebub's Tales* and *Meetings with Remarkable Men* (see section 9.5 and its first endnote), just as there are inconsistencies between the *Iliad* and the *Odyssey* (see sections 5.3–5.5).

10. See the entry for "Gurdjieff's writings, intentional inconsistency in" in the index to *EWG*.

CHAPTER 8: Allusions to Homer in *Meetings with Remarkable Men*

1. *Fragments*, p. 340.

2. *EWG*, pp. 147–149. The full significance of the allusion can be understood only if the cited pages are read in the broader context of the chapter in which they appear.

3. Lord, *Singer of Tales*, p. 3.

4. Ibid., p. 20.

5. Quoted by Mitchell and Nagy, "Introduction," p. xxiii.

6. *RM*, p. 36. The version sung by Gurdjieff's father of the mentioned excerpt from the Gilgamesh epic exhibits clear correspondences with and departures from modern translations. Unfortunately, it cannot be used to assess the reliability of oral transmission owing to the likelihood that Gurdjieff modified the song to create a certain structure (see *EWG*, pp. 102–105 and p. 222, n. 4).

7. M. Parry, "Traditional Epithet." Introductory treatments: Clark, "Formulas"; Kirk, *Songs*, pp. 59–68.

8. Bowra, *Heroic Poetry*, pp. 216, 217. See also Lord, *Singer of Tales*, pp. 5, 13, 17, etc.

9. On the nature of improvisation in oral poetry, see Janko, "Dictated Texts," p. 4.

10. Bowra, *Heroic Poetry*, pp. 216–217.

11. Lord, *Singer Resumes*, p. 102 (quoted in Janko, "Dictated Texts," p. 3).

12. Kirk, *Songs*, pp. 89–90, 96–101.

13. A. Parry, "Have We Homer's *Iliad*?"; the judgment that Parry refuted Kirk's theory of accurate oral transmission has been expressed by Fowler,

"Homeric question," p. 224, n. 15, and by Janko, "Dictated Texts," p. 12, n. 63.

14. Griffin, *Odyssey*, pp. 6–8; Rutherford, *Homer*, pp. 23–24.

15. Demodokos: *Od.* 8.43–45, 62–83, 254–369, 470–521. Phemios: *Od.* 1.153–155, 325–359; 17.261–263; 22.330–353. The theme of bardic performance is represented in book 17 not only by the reference to Phemios but also by the remarks of Eumaios in lines 518–521 (see quote 8.8) and 382–386. Another notable appearance of the theme is Alkinoös's complimentary comparison of Odysseus to a singer at 11.366–369.

16. *Iliad*: Burkert, "Ares and Aphrodite," pp. 34–39; Macleod, "Homer on Poetry," p. 304; see also my discussion of the second song of Demodokos at the end of part (*b*) of section 5.3. *Odyssey*: Rutherford, "From the *Iliad*," p. 136; Macleod, "Homer on Poetry," p. 304; see also section 2.10.

17. *RM*, pp. 167–173. In addition, the final chapter of the Second Series, entitled "The Material Question," describes Gurdjieff's resourcefulness in obtaining the money required to sustain his work (*EWG*, p. 136) and even mentions his resourcefulness explicitly (*RM*, pp. 251, 252). However, this chapter departs from Gurdjieff's intention that the Second Series should answer the question "What remarkable men have I met?" (*RM*, p. 30) since the remarkable man it describes is Gurdjieff himself. And in fact it can be shown that "The Material Question" does not belong to any of the three books of the Second Series (*EWG*, chap. 7). In the First Series, Beelzebub is said to have been known in his youth for his "extraordinarily resourceful intelligence" (*BT*, p. 52).

18. *Od.* 16.14–32.

19. *Od.* 16.213–219.

20. *Od.* 17.235–238. For other examples, see de Jong, "Between Word and Deed," pp. 67–72.

21. *Od.* 2.230–234 (Mentor); 5.8–12 (Athene); 4.690–693 (Penelope); see also 2.46–47 (Telemachos).

22. *Od.* 10.1–55; 12.260–419.

23. Odysseus himself acknowledges his powerlessness as only one man against many (*Od.* 12.297). In the second episode, there is actually a ringleader who could have been singled out for punishment (*Od.* 12.339–352), but we are not told whether Odysseus is aware of this fact (*Od.* 12.391–393). It makes little difference either way, since Odysseus knows from the warnings of Teiresias and Circe that his companions are doomed once they have harmed the cattle of Helios (see section 6.6).

24. Odysseus's determination to return home falters during his stay with Circe (cf. *Od.* 10.467–474), just as his self-restraint may be questioned when he reveals his identity to the Cyclops (cf. *Od.* 9.491–505), but these isolated incidents do little to lessen our overall impression of his firmness of purpose and self-control.

25. The characteristics of Odysseus noted by Lattimore ("Introduction," p. 19) are strength, courage, ingenuity, patience, self-control, and determination. Strength would clearly be out of place in a definition of a remarkable man, while courage and patience could both be considered elaborations of self-control and determination, which leaves us with ingenuity (or resourcefulness), self-control (or self-restraint), and determination.

26. *Od.* 14.29–31.
27. *RM*, pp. 34, 36, 40.
28. Traill, *Schliemann of Troy*, p. 47.
29. Hainsworth, "Odysseus and the Dogs."
30. Jones, *Homer's Odyssey*, p. 130.
31. Dimock, *Unity*, p. 191.
32. Commenting on *Od.* 14.30–31, Stanford (*Odyssey*, p. 217) says that Odysseus "is acting his part as a beggarman well, feigning fear." But the rest of his commentary on these verses is in line with the usual interpretation of Odysseus's reaction as an attempt to pacify the dogs. He quotes Rouse's translation ("But Odysseus knew the trick, sat on the ground and dropt his cudgel"), adds that "the maneuver was recognized in antiquity as a means of checking the ferocity of dogs" (while acknowledging that Homer did not seem to have much confidence in it), and gives linguistic support for the view that Odysseus's behavior would show the dogs that he was not hostile.
33. E. Cook, "Heroics," p. 129.
34. It should be noted that some translations avoid the inconsistency in quote 8.19 and are completely compatible with the interpretation of Dimock and Cook. For example, instead of "Odysseus prudently sat down on the ground" in quote 8.19, Albert Cook says that "Odysseus sat down in cunning," and Murray says much the same.
35. *Od.* 1.160–161, 374–378; 2.55–58, 75, 123; 3.315–316; 13.428; 14.92; 15.32; 17.378; 18.277–280; 19.159; 22.55–59.
36. *RM*, p. 40.
37. The relationship between quotes 8.24 and 8.25 also plays a role in a rather elaborate scheme in *Meetings with Remarkable Men* (*EWG*, pp. 162–163).
38. That the confirmation of a prediction made on the basis of a premise increases the credibility of that premise has been verified by Polya (*Plausible Reasoning*, vol. 2, chap. 15) within the framework of Bayesian probability theory for the special case in which the prediction is a necessary consequence of the premise. Polya's analysis can easily be generalized to the situation where the prediction is only a probable consequence of the premise. His discussion of the discovery of the planet Neptune (ibid., pp. 130–132) provides a very unconvincing illustration of the theory, one suggesting that probability formulas cannot be used to obtain even crude numerical estimates of credibility, but the unreasonable results he obtains for this example are caused by a careless error (a misidentification of a certain probability).
39. I have discussed elsewhere a possible allusion in Gurdjieff's writings to the Biblical account of the Creation (*EWG*, p. 196). This allusion is irrelevant to the present discussion because it is a phenomenon of an entirely different order. Whereas the allusions discussed in chapter 8 to Homer and the literature of ancient India are easily recognized by anyone familiar with the texts, the allusion to the Biblical Creation depends on an esoteric interpretation of its structure and can be seen only after a long and deep analysis of the writings of Gurdjieff.

40. Seymour-Smith, *Influential Books*, p. 448.

41. For example: Beke, *Digging Up The Dog: The Greek Roots of Gurdjieff's Esoteric Ideas*; Challenger, *Philosophy and Art in Gurdjieff's "Beelzebub": A Modern Sufi Odyssey*.

42. Peters, *Gurdjieff Remembered*, p. 122.

43. *Views*, p. 274.

44. *BT*, pp. 1192–1201. See also *Views*, pp. 96–100, 144–145, 221–223.

45. *Fragments*, p. 41.

46. Rosenblatt (*René Daumal*, p. 129) refers to the Vedas; Webb (*Harmonious Circle*, p. 144) mentions the Upanishads; and Sinclair (*Without Benefit*, p. 267) specifies the *Katha Upanishad*.

47. *BT*1992, p. 1090 (cf. *BT*, p. 1190).

48. See *Fragments*, p. 41, and *Views*, pp. 221–223; also, Gurdjieff identifies the horse as one's essence (*Views*, p. 144), which is purely emotional (*Views*, pp. 136, 137).

49. However, the correspondence between the carriage model and the chariot model does not extend to the reins that connect the horse(s) to the driver (compare quote 8.28 with *BT*, pp. 1200–1201).

50. *BT*, pp. 565–568 (or *BT*1992, pp. 516–519).

51. See also *Fragments*, p. 42.

52. Eliade, *Yoga*, pp. 36–37, 47–48, 66, and 118–120 (a discussion of yogic elements in the *Katha Upanishad*).

53. Eliade, *Yoga*, p. 114; Easwaran, *The Upanishads*, p. 38; Olivelle, *Upaniṣads*, p. lvi. My use of the form "Upanishads" is slightly inaccurate in the quotations from Eliade and Olivelle, as these authors use diacritical marks in their transliterations of Sanskrit words.

54. *BT*, pp. 765, 770; that the "higher being-body" referred to in these passages is the same as the soul is stated repeatedly (see *BT*, pp. 60–61, 695, 762, 796).

55. For example, the rider in the chariot model, called the self in quote 8.28, is identified as the soul in the well-regarded translation by Hume (*Principal Upanishads*, p. 351).

56. The Sanskrit word *ātman* is given two Gurdjieffian interpretations in section 8.7. When discussing the chariot model in the *Katha Upanishad*, I postulate a correspondence between the *ātman* in the model and what Gurdjieff calls "I." Then, in order to see quote 8.34 as relating *ātman* and *brahman*, I interpret the *ātman* as what Gurdjieff calls the soul. Strictly speaking, these interpretations are inconsistent with each other, as an "I" is not the same thing as a soul in Gurdjieff's teaching. However, the two are intimately connected: In order to create a soul in oneself, it is necessary first to create an "I"; the creation of the soul and the fixing in it of objective Reason then entail a further development of the "I" (the first assertion follows from *BT*, p. 1227, together with the fact that only a soul has "imperishable Being"; both assertions are justified by the voyage allegory discussed in chapter 3 and section 4.11 of *EWG* when one takes into account the connection between objective consciousness and the soul). Since section 8.7 is concerned only with allusions—and Gurdjieff even went so far as to completely change the significance of the horse in his carriage model in order to strengthen the

allusion to the chariot model—I do not think the inconsistency I have just acknowledged is of any importance.

57. *BT*, p. 245.

58. *Kaushītaki Upanishad* 2.1–2; *Brihadāranyaka Upanishad* 4.4.7. The statement that *brahman* is *prāna* is also found in *Brihadāranyaka Upanishad* 4.1.3 and 5.12, *Chāndogya Upanishad* 4.10.4–5, and *Taittirīya Upanishad* 3.1.3, but in these cases the statement is considered to be incomplete. In all six passages just cited, the Hume translation confirms that *prāna* is the word that Hume or Olivelle translates as breath, breathing spirit, lifebreath, breath of life, or life (depending on the passage and the translator). In addition, *Brihadāranyaka Upanishad* 3.9.9 says that the one irreducible god, which is called Brahman, is breath; this is extremely suggestive, but I have not seen explicit confirmation that the word here rendered as "breath" (by both Hume and Olivelle) is *prāna*. Finally, *Brihadāranyaka Upanishad* 1.6.3 equates *prāna* with the immortal, which is often associated with *brahman* (e.g., *Brihadāranyaka Upanishad* 2.5.1–14; *Chāndogya Upanishad* 4.15.1, 8.3.4, 8.7.4, 8.8.3, 8.10.1, 8.11.1, 8.14; *Katha Upanishad* 5.8, 6.1; *Mundaka Upanishad* 2.2.2).

59. Eliade, *Yoga*, p. 163.

60. For example: *Brihadāranyaka Upanishad* 2.5, 4.4.5, 4.4.17, 4.4.25; *Chāndogya Upanishad* 3.14, 4.15.1, 8.14, and the refrain common to 8.3.4, 8.7.4, 8.8.3, 8.10.1, and 8.11.1. For the chronology of the Upanishads, see Olivelle, *Upanisads*, pp. xxxvi–xxxvii.

61. Olivelle, *Upanisads*, pp. xli–xlv. The horse sacrifice was the most important animal sacrifice in ancient India (Hume, *Principal Upanishads*, p. 73, n. 2). The Soma sacrifice focused on the juice of Soma plants but included the sacrifice of a goat (Olivelle, *Upanisads*, p. xlv).

62. The 1950 translation of *Beelzebub's Tales* refers to Indian philosophy in the passage corresponding to quote 8.37, but the Russian edition shows that the 1992 translation is correct in specifying Hindu philosophy (Gurdjieff, *Rasskazy*, p. 252).

63. *BT*1992, p. 640 (cf. *BT*, p. 699).

64. My discussion of the religion chapter is based on *BT*, pp. 695–699, 724–725, 732. I should mention that the religion chapter does mention Brahmanists in passing (*BT*, p. 734).

65. This is not to say that there are no explicit references to Hinduism in the writings of Gurdjieff, but those that do exist are inconsequential (quote 8.37 is the most substantial; see also "the famous Hindu yogis" at *RM*, p. 138, "this Hindu" at *RM*, p. 158, and the reference to Brahmanists at *BT*, p. 734).

66. For the argument in section 8.7, it was unnecessary to mention that quote 8.34 and certain associated passages from the chapter of *Beelzebub's Tales* entitled "The First Visit of Beelzebub to India" are given a distinctly Gurdjieffian reformulation in the chapter entitled "The Holy Planet 'Purgatory'." Quote 8.34 essentially states that souls are formed in certain people from the "Most Great Foundation of the All-embracing of everything that exists" which "constantly emanates throughout the whole of the Universe." Similarly, the Purgatory chapter states that souls are formed in certain people from the "emanations issuing from the Most Most Holy Sun

Absolute into the space of the Universe" (*BT*, pp. 764–765, 768 together with pp. 138, 139, 756, 757, 760 on Theomertmalogos and pp. 60–61, 695, 762, 767, 796 on higher being-bodies). This parallel involving the Sun Absolute reinforces my identification of the "Most Great Foundation of the All-embracing of everything that exists" as the *brahman* since Gurdjieff himself states that the Absolute is "known in Hindu terminology as Brahman" (*Views*, p. 66). Other close parallels between the teaching attributed to the Buddha and its Gurdjieffian reformulation involve the purpose of souls in the Universe (compare *BT*, pp. 244–245 and 765, 797) and the transmigration of souls that have not yet been perfected at the time of death (compare *BT*, pp. 246 and 766–767). The key distinction between the teaching attributed to the Buddha and its Gurdjieffian reformulation is that, according to the latter, a soul can be formed only in someone who has already created in himself that which is sometimes called an astral body.

The connection between chapters 21 and 39 of *Beelzebub's Tales* that I have discussed in this note weakens, to some extent at least, one component of the argument in section 6.3 of *EWG*, namely, the component which asserts a uniquely close connection between chapters 16–18 and chapters 39–41.

67. In *EWG* I show that the division of *Meetings with Remarkable Men* into three books is based on the geometry of the enneagram, while the division of *Beelzebub's Tales* into three books is based on the dynamics of the symbol. Furthermore, the enneagrams that underlie the book divisions of the two works both represent Gurdjieff's conception of the path of spiritual development, but from complementary points of view. The idea that *Beelzebub's Tales* and *Meetings with Remarkable Men* complement each other can be reconciled with the fact that these two works are only the first two parts of a trilogy (*All and Everything*)—see *EWG*, pp. 5–6.

68. Challenger, *Philosophy and Art*, pp. 50–53, 66.

69. Ibid., pp. 48–50.

70. *RM*, pp. 35–36.

71. Cf. *Fragments*, pp. 61, 97, 144, 217.

72. The mythical healer Asclepius is mentioned six times in the *Iliad* (2.731; 4.194, 204; 11.613; 14.2; and most importantly at 11.518, where he is called "the great healer Asklepios" in Lattimore's translation) as the father of two doctors in the Greek army, Machaon and Podaleirios. In *Meetings with Remarkable Men*, Yelov refers to the doctor Dr. Sari-Ogli as "our esteemed Aesculapius [the latinized version of Asclepius]" (*RM*, p. 172). However, no significance can be attached to this reference since Asclepius is the subject of a significant mythology independent of the *Iliad*. Similarly, Makar, the first colonist of Lesbos according to myth (Macleod, *Iliad XXIV*, p. 135), is mentioned once in the *Iliad* and placed on Lesbos (*Il.* 24.544). Beelzebub is presumably referring to this Makar when he colorfully characterizes an undesirable situation as a place "where even 'Makar did not drive his goats'" (*BT*, p. 616). Again, this cannot reasonably be considered an allusion to the *Iliad* in view of the separate mythology surrounding Makar.

There is also the possibility of joint allusions to the *Iliad* and the *Odyssey*. Since antiquity each of these poems has been divided into 24 books. Could the 48 chapters of *Beelzebub's Tales* allude to the total number of books? This possibility is supported by Gurdjieff's reference to the "twenty-four subdivisions of the general totality of the exposition of my ideas" (*LIR*, pp. 81, 88), but it is undermined by his assertion elsewhere that he originally intended to write 36 books (*RM*, p. 6).

Beelzebub's Tales contains about 100 sayings attributed to Mullah Nassr Eddin. A small, but I believe significant, minority of these sayings (16) form a ring composition, a pattern of the form $A\ B\ C\ ...\ C^*\ B^*\ A^*$, where A and A^*, B and B^*, and so forth denote pairs of related sayings. The significance of this structure is underscored by the fact that Mullah Nassr Eddin himself makes his only appearance (*BT*, pp. 596–601) precisely at its middle, enclosing its innermost pair of related sayings. However, its purpose is a mystery. It conceivably alludes to ring composition in the Homeric epics, but such an allusion cannot be claimed with any confidence since ring composition is by no means exclusive to Homer.

In his second and third visits to the Earth, Beelzebub seeks to abolish, or at least to reduce, the practice of animal sacrifice. This emphasis on animal sacrifice could be regarded as a possible allusion both to the Homeric epics and to the Upanishads, although the practice was so widespread in the ancient world that this view seems too limited.

CHAPTER 9: Gurdjieff's Answer to the Homeric Question

1. *EWG*, pp. 9–10.

2. *Fragments*, pp. 26–27, 295–298.

3. Similarly, since Gurdjieff considers *The Thousand and One Nights* to be "literature in the full sense of the word" (*RM*, p. 18), it is tempting to infer (with Challenger, Philosophy and Art, pp. 38–39) that these tales must constitute a work of objective art. Regardless of whether this inference is correct, it is clear that *The Thousand and One Nights* cannot be the Eastern counterpart of the Homeric epics predicted in section 8.7, for the simple reason (in addition to its much later date) that Gurdjieff does not allude to these stories but mentions them explicitly. In section 9.7 we shall see that the Upanishads, the actual Eastern counterpart proposed in section 8.7, bear a relation to the ideas of Gurdjieff that is analogous to that of the Homeric epics.

4. *Fragments*, p. 297. See also *Views*, p. 35.

5. *Fragments*, p. 27.

6. *Fragments*, p. 296.

7. *Fragments*, p. 27.

8. Orage, *Commentaries*, p. 3.

9. *BT*, pp. 462, 464–465.

10. *BT*, pp. 451–452, 457, 492–493, 517–518.

11. The idea that knowledge could be encoded in a work of art that then would have to be deciphered pervades the art chapter of *Beelzebub's Tales*, but is expressed most explicitly on pp. 460, 488, and 521 of the original English translation and p. 421 of the 1992 translation (these references include only those places where the idea of decipherment is also most explicit in the original Russian). Decipherment is necessary to determine how the knowledge that is being transmitted is encoded in the unexpected and unusual experiences; the original plan was that it would be accomplished with the aid of a key (see section 9.3), but, according to Beelzebub, certain people have been able to decipher ancient art on their own, without the aid of a key (*BT*, pp. 520–522).

12. *BT*, pp. 466–467.

13. According to Orage (*Commentaries*, p. 17), Gurdjieff said that there are three "versions" of *Beelzebub's Tales*: "an outer, an inner, and an inmost"; I suggest that the inmost layer of meaning is encoded in the perverse inconsistencies.

14. Challenger, *Philosophy and Art*, chap. 3; Orage, *Commentaries*, pp. 3–4, 92–104; Tamdgidi, *Hypnosis*, pp. xvi, 91, 142–143, 184–185 (pp. 185–186 of Tamdgidi's book should be considered in the light of *EWG*, chap. 7).

15. *BT*, pp. 459–460.

16. Bowra, "Metre," pp. 23–24, and Kirk, *Songs*, pp. 119–120 (on dactylic hexameter); M. Parry, "Oral Verse-Making," p. 314 (on formulas); *Il. Comm.* IV, pp. 8–9 (on language); Rutherford, *Homer*, pp. 9–11, 26–27 (on formulas and language). Homer's dependence on a long tradition is also evident from his many references to other epic themes (Burgess, *Tradition of the Trojan War*, p. 209, n. 1; Cairns, "Introduction," pp. 36–38; Dowden, "Epic Tradition," pp. 196–197; Rutherford, *Homer*, pp. 6–9; M. L. West, *Making of the Iliad*, pp. 28–37).

17. *BT*, pp. 461–462. For a typical illustration, see *BT*, p. 465.

18. *BT*, p. 467.

19. *BT*, p. 522. Gurdjieff actually uses the term "lawful illogicality," but the modifier "lawful" is a complication that need not concern us. The word "illogicality" is a correct translation of Gurdjieff's Russian (Gurdjieff, *Rasskazy*, p. 519), but I cannot resist noting that the German translation of *Beelzebub's Tales*, which was completed in Gurdjieff's lifetime and approved by him, uses a word that is translated as "contradictions" or even "inconsistencies" (Gurdjieff, *Erzählungen*, p. 554).

20. *BT*, pp. 6–16.

21. *BT*, p. 455.

22. Iamblichus, *Life of Pythagoras*, p. 9. See also Bennett, *Gurdjieff: Making a New World*, p. 59.

23. *Views*, pp. 182–185.

24. I find it strange that the kind of objective art that does *not* transmit knowledge and does not require decipherment, examples of which are described in quote 9.3, is not mentioned in the art chapter of *Beelzebub's Tales*. Where such art is described in Gurdjieff's writings (e.g., *BT*, pp. 880–881; *RM*, pp. 128–133), it is possible to argue from the context that what is described is actually not a work of art but simply a demonstration of a scientific law which describes how external influences affect people (e.g., the law of Daivibrizkar mentioned in section 9.1). If this interpretation is correct, objective art would be limited to art which encodes knowledge in the automatic impressions created in accordance with such a law, as described in the art chapter of *Beelzebub's Tales*. My thesis regarding the Homeric epics would be unchanged if we were to adopt this more restrictive definition.

25. Mueller, *The Iliad*, p. 177 (see also p. 171). Macleod (*Iliad XXIV*, p. 43) is one reader who apparently does not find the echo disturbing.

26. Orage, *Commentaries*, p. 95.

27. Indeed, the routine reuse of verses is illustrated by clearly formulaic elements in the italicized parts of quotes 9.9 and 9.10. The verse *Il.* 4.163 = 6.447 is also used at *Od.* 15.211, and the verse *Il.* 4.165 = 6.449 (along with the phrase "sacred Ilion" which ends the preceding verse in the Greek) is also used at *Il.* 4.47 and 8.552. Of course, the existence of formulaic elements in a passage does not mean that the passage itself is formulaic.

28. *Il.* 16.855–858 = 22.361–364 except for the identity and epithet of the character named at the end of the fourth line. Mueller (*The Iliad*, pp. 28–30) gives a thorough discussion of these lines, the evidence for the meaningfulness of their repetition, and their connection with the third most important death in the *Iliad* (that of Sarpedon), while Fenik (*Battle Scenes*, p. 217) shows that these lines are part of a larger pattern that characterizes the death scenes of both Patroklos and Hektor.

29. Buxton, "Similes," p. 149.

30. In Lattimore's translation, the lion kills the doe as well as the fawns. While Lattimore is not alone, the lion kills only the fawns in the majority of translations I have consulted, and this interpretation makes more sense.

31. Another problem, of course, is that a deer is not likely to put its young in a lion's den (S. West, "Books I–IV," p. 213). However, it is not possible to have the lion kill the fawns in their own lair, as in the simile at *Il.* 11.113–119, since Odysseus will kill the suitors in his palace.

32. In connection with quote 9.13, some commentators discuss the less restrictive and therefore more common motif of a warrior who withdraws from the fighting out of anger at anyone for any reason (Fenik, *Battle Scenes*, pp. 121–122; Janko, *Il. Comm.* IV, pp. 105–106; Postlethwaite, *Homer's Iliad*, p. 179; Willcock, *Companion*, p. 150). Nagy (*Achaeans*, pp. 265–266) is one commentator who emphasizes the closer parallelism between quote 9.13 and the Quarrel that I consider to be of particular interest. However, he also claims a dictional correspondence that I find unconvincing (see Nagy, *Achaeans*, pp. 73–74 along with background in Redfield, "Proem," p. 459). A more modest correspondence, between *Il.* 13.460 and 18.257, is pointed out by Janko.

33. In *Il.* 20.178–183 Achilles accuses Aineias of challenging him in order to win honor and power from Priam, but says that Priam would not honor him with power even if he were to win their duel. Fenik (*Battle Scenes*, p. 122) sees this as an echo of the reason for the anger of Aineias in quote 9.13 (see also Postlethwaite, *Homer's Iliad*, p. 179). But there is no indication in the *Iliad* that Aineias is motivated by ambition or that he is aware that he is destined to become king of the Trojans (*Il.* 20.306–308). Achilles goes on to propose another explanation for Aineias's daring: perhaps the Trojans have offered to give him a fine estate if he kills Achilles (*Il.* 20.184–186). It is clear that Achilles is merely taunting Aineias and trying to undermine his confidence by suggesting that it is necessary to explain how he has the audacity to face him.

34. Fenik (*Battle Scenes*, p. 122) and Scodel (*Credible Impossibilities*, p. 36) find it odd that the poet feels obliged to explain why Aineias has been absent from the fighting. Hainsworth (*Il. Comm.* III, p. 327) suggests a possible reason: the poet, recalling that he had made Aineias the leader of one

of the five Trojan battalions in the assault on the Greek wall (*Il.* 12.88–104) but had never described the attack mounted by this battalion, feels that he owes the audience an explanation when Aineias makes his next appearance (quote 9.13). However, it is not believable that Aineias would have abandoned his command. Furthermore, the poet also failed to describe the attack mounted by the battalion headed by Paris, yet he provides no explanation when Paris makes *his* next appearance (*Il.* 13.490). I therefore agree with Fenik and Scodel.

35. Although Nagy does not connect quote 9.13 with the first song of Demodokos, he likewise interprets both passages in terms of *his* theoretical outlook: the former is assumed to derive from an epic tradition that featured Aineias instead of Achilles (Nagy, *Achaeans*, pp. 265–275), the latter from a tradition in which Achilles was offended by Odysseus instead of Agamemnon (ibid., p. 65).

36. The similes in quotes 9.11 and 9.14 are also linked together by Buxton ("Similes," pp. 149, 153), but he goes farther than I do.

37. Peleus: *Il.* 16.571–576 and 23.85–90 (supplication implied); Telemachos: *Od.* 15.272–281. Men who fled into exile after killing someone are also mentioned at *Il.* 2.661–670, 13.694–697 = 15.333–336, 15.430–439 and *Od.* 13.259–275, 14.380–381; however, these passages lack the element of supplication.

38. Priam is the only suppliant in Homer who also kisses the hands of the man he supplicates (*Il. Comm.* VI, pp. 322–323).

39. See, for example, Macleod, *Iliad XXIV*, p. 126; Postlethwaite, *Homer's Iliad*, p. 302; *Il. Comm.* VI, p. 323.

40. It is instructive to compare the repetition of the italicized lines in quotes 9.9 and 9.10 with the near repetition of the first three lines of quote 9.15 in quote 9.17. In each case the repeated lines are spoken by people who play opposing roles: (*a*) the chief defender of Troy and the leader of the army that threatens the city and (*b*) someone who is afraid that Priam will be killed and the man who might kill him. However, the second repetition has none of the dissonance that one feels in the first. The combination of astonishment and respect evoked in Achilles by the huge risk Priam is taking by visiting him harmonizes nicely with the combination of astonishment and dismay felt by Priam's wife. In quotes 9.9 and 9.10, by contrast, Hektor and Agamemnon use the same words to express discordant feelings, a fear of doom and a lust for revenge, so that the repetition of these words brings up by association a feeling opposed to the one currently being expressed. Thus, the use of the same lines by characters who play contrasting roles is like the simultaneous sounding of different musical notes in that it can produce an effect of either harmony or dissonance.

41. *Il.* 24.563–570, 585–586.

42. Macleod, *Iliad XXIV*, p. 126.

43. Macleod's explanation that the fugitive in the simile arouses wonder simply by virtue of the unexpectedness of his arrival is rejected as insufficient by Richardson (*Il. Comm.* VI, p. 323). Surprise caused by an unexpected visitor is common in Homer (see *Il. Comm.* VI, p. 324 on lines 482–484), but it is generally short-lived and not worthy of a simile.

Bowra (*Homer*, p. 64), on the other hand, considers the simile sound: "The comparison is surprising because Priam is compared to a murderer on the run, but it is entirely relevant, for Priam's arrival is as unexpected as that of a murderer, and the atmosphere is of bloodshed and death." There are two flaws in this statement. First, "murder" (both here and in quote 9.14) is too strong: the same verb κατακτείνω, meaning "I kill" or "I slay," is used in *Il.* 24.481 as in *Il.* 23.87, which refers to Patroklos's unintentional killing of a playmate as a child. Second, the killer who goes into exile is a fairly common motif in Homer (see note 37); the arrival of a fugitive killer at one's doorstep would probably cause some initial surprise but would not be fundamentally bewildering like the arrival of Priam at the dwelling of Achilles.

Taking an entirely different approach, Schlunk ("Suppliant-Exile," p. 208) attempts to justify the simile on the grounds that the image of the fugitive's presumably successful supplication serves "to introduce the 'humanitarian spirit' which pervades the close of the *Iliad*." However, this interpretation ignores the focus of the simile on the wonder evoked by Priam and the fugitive.

44. Macleod, *Iliad XXIV*, pp. 126–127.

45. Cunliffe's lexicon, referring to *Il.* 24.480–481 in the entry for ατη, asserts that "the homicide has been done under the impulse of the ατη." Hammond's translation is ambiguous.

46. Against my theory for why Lattimore translates ατη as "disaster" in *Il.* 24.480, I must note that, for no good reason (as far as I can judge from other translations), he translates ατη as "ruin" in *Il.* 9.504, 505, 512.

47. Macleod, *Iliad XXIV*, p. 127.

48. An instructive survey is given in Fenik, *Studies*, pp. 50–53. On inappropriate epithets, see also Clark, "Formulas," pp. 128–130, and the important observations in Rutherford, *Homer*, pp. 29–30, and Bowra, *Heroic Poetry*, pp. 239–240. Other dissonances not discussed here include unmetrical verses (Janko, "Dictated Texts," p. 7; M. L. West, *Making of the Odyssey*, pp. 81–82) and mismatches of rhythm and meaning (*Il. Comm.* I, pp. 23–24).

49. *BT*, pp. 349–351, 456, 458, 459.

50. This derivation, due to Dr. Anne Cotton, is more persuasive than the etymology proposed by Taylor (*Philosophy*, p. 87), who calls *legominism* "a transparent neologism constructed of *logos* 'word' and *mens* 'mind'."

51. *BT*, p. 459. See also *BT*, pp. 804–805.

52. Of the many authors who have called *Beelzebub's Tales* a legominism, some explicitly confuse a legominism with an objective work of art (Challenger, *Philosophy and Art*, p. 44; Henderson, *Hidden Meanings*, pp. 16–17; Orage, *Commentaries*, p. 104; Patterson, *Left Hand*, p. 9). Unlike a legominism, a work of art is not an oral communication and is not transmitted by initiates but passes automatically from generation to generation (*BT*, p. 460). In fact, as we go on to see in section 9.3, authentic art was conceived as an alternative to legominisms for the transmission of knowledge to future generations.

53. Pythagoras: *BT*, pp. 455–456; Aksharpanziar: *BT*, pp. 458–462.

54. I suggest that one initiate of art explains to another how information is encrypted in a work of art in the same way that the initiates who attended the conference that Pythagoras helped to organize explained this to each other, as described in *BT*, p. 463. In the field of architecture, for example, what would be passed from one initiate of art to another is a "minia-image" or model of a building. In the case of a dance or a ceremony, what would be passed on is a demonstration of various acts and manifestations. A potential problem with this interpretation is that a single initiate of art would not be able to duplicate those demonstrations by the conference attendees which involved more than one person (*BT*, pp. 482 ff.).

55. The English translation in quote 9.19 actually uses the singular "Legominism," but I have replaced "Legominism" with "Legominisms" since the plural is used in the Russian source (Gurdjieff, *Rasskazy*, p. 514). The plural is also used in the German translation of quote 9.19 (Gurdjieff, *Erzählungen*, p. 549); this is not the only place where the German translation of *Beelzebub's Tales* is more faithful to the Russian than either of the English translations even though it was largely based on the first English translation.

56. *BT*, p. 461.

57. *BT*, pp. 492–493.

58. *BT*, pp. 841–843.

59. In a second edition of *EWG*.

60. Inconsistencies between *Beelzebub's Tales* and *Meetings with Remarkable Men* are much less common than inconsistencies within either work. Besides the inconsistency discussed in section 9.5, I am aware of only the following. The assertion by one of the characters in *Meetings with Remarkable Men* that the ancient Chinese octave had only five notes (*RM*, p. 130) is strikingly inconsistent with the "history" of man's knowledge of the octave recounted in *Beelzebub's Tales*, which repeated refers to the "Chinese seven-toned subdivision of the octave" (*BT*, pp. 855, 856, 858, 865) and contrasts the seven-note octave of the Chinese with the five-note octave of the Greeks (*BT*, pp. 860–863).

61. *BT*, pp. 475–476, 519. The first of these passages is a little ambiguous because the dances that are called "sacred" in one place are called "religious" in another place (as well as on p. 464); the second passage, however, is perfectly clear.

62. *RM*, pp. 161–163.

63. *BT*, pp. 349, 350–351; the same idea appears on pp. 456, 458, and 459.

64. Past events: *BT*, pp. 458, 459; true knowledge: *BT*, p. 459.

65. *BT*, pp. 460, 461, and 461–462, respectively. Cf. quote 9.19, where Beelzebub uses the expression "information and various fragments of knowledge."

66. *BT*, p. 521.

67. *BT*, p. 519.

68. *RM*, p. 243.

69. Unlike the First Series, the Second Series does not actually give an account of the origin since knowledge may have been transmitted through works of art even before the creation of the sacred dances Gurdjieff witnessed in Central Asia. However, the Second Series does imply that this practice began at least two millennia before the origin assigned to it in the First Series.

70. A related inconsistency may be briefly noted: Beelzebub states that the method of legominism "is the sole means by which information about certain events that proceeded in times long past has accurately reached the beings of remote later generations" (*BT*, p. 351); this statement is inconsistent with, among other things, what Gurdjieff says about the sacred dances he witnessed in Central Asia (*RM*, pp. 161–163; see also *BT*, pp. 519–520).

71. *BT*, p. 465.

72. *BT*, p. 476; *RM*, pp. 161–162. See also *EWG*, pp. 58–59.

73. *BT*, p. 1202.

74. *Fragments*, p. 21.

75. Ibid., pp. 53, 59–60, 112–113.

76. Gurdjieff's assertion that a person has many "small I's" instead of a single permanent I is related to the modular conception of mind advocated by evolutionary psychologists (Pinker, *How the Mind Works*; Kurzban, *Why everyone (else) is a hypocrite*). But Gurdjieff also makes an assertion that these psychologists will find difficult to swallow, namely, that it is possible to develop a single permanent I (as I go on to discuss in section 9.6).

77. *Fragments*, p. 60. The "rolls" mentioned here are the recording apparatuses called "reels" in *BT*, pp. 1217–1218. The connection between the small I's and associations is made clearer in the French translation of *Fragments* (*Fragments d'un enseignement inconnu*, p. 97), thanks in part to an added footnote.

78. *BT*, pp. 1201–1202; *Fragments*, p. 142.

79. *Fragments*, p. 141.

80. *Views*, p. 70; de Salzmann, *Reality*, pp. 12, 15; *BT*, pp. 686, 770. As he himself emphasized, Gurdjieff was not the first to teach that our so-called waking existence is actually a kind of sleep (*Fragments*, p. 144).

81. *Fragments*, p. 145.

82. See also *Views*, p. 70.

83. My discussion of self-consciousness draws mainly on *Fragments*, pp. 141–142 but also on p. 188 of that work as well as *EWG*, pp. 21, 60–62. See also *Views*, pp. 79–80.

84. *Fragments*, p. 15.

85. *Fragments*, p. 278.

86. *Fragments*, pp. 145 (with the fourth state of consciousness defined as objective consciousness on p. 141), 278, 279; *BT*, pp. 814–818.

87. Quote 9.27 consists of remarks attributed to Gurdjieff in the story "Glimpses of Truth," written by one or two of his pupils with the aim of "giving an exposition of his ideas in a literary form" (*Fragments*, p. 10). Ouspensky connects the story with Gurdjieff's talks on art that he witnessed (ibid., p. 26), and says that the idea for the story originated with Gurdjieff himself (ibid., p. 10).

88. Brereton, "The Upanishads," pp. 118–135.

89. Hume, *Principal Upanishads*, p. 13.

90. *Fragments*, pp. 205, 214, 280; "Glimpses of Truth" in *Views*, pp. 14–16, 22.

91. The connection between microcosm and macrocosm is obscured in *Views*, p. 22, by a mistranslation ("Microcosmos" is mistakenly substituted for

"Macrocosmos") that is corrected in the excerpt from "Glimpses of Truth" in *Fragments*, p. 214.

92. *BT*, pp. 775, 777–780.

93. *Aitareya Upanishad* 1; *Brihadāranyaka Upanishad* 3.2.13 (see also 1.3.11–16). Regarding this set of correspondences, see Brereton, "The Upanishads," pp. 120–121; Hume, *Principal Upanishads*, p. 24; Olivelle, *Upanisads*, p. liii.

94. See Brereton, "The Upanishads," p. 119.

95. For a more complete review, see Brereton, "The Upanishads," pp. 118–135.

96. *Fragments*, p. 279.

97. *BT*, pp. 15–16.

98. Gurdjieff goes on to say that mentation by form in a given person depends on the conditions in which he or she has grown up (*BT*, pp. 15–16). This would mean that mentation by form, like mentation by thought, is subjective and therefore *not* suitable for ascertaining "the exact sense of all writing." This seems to be yet another inconsistency of the kind I last discussed in section 9.3.

99. *BT*, pp. 15, 88. See also *EWG*, p. 185.

100. *Fragments*, p. 27. Also note the unique emphasis on feelings and instinct in the chapter of the Second Series that represents the attainment of objective consciousness (*RM*, p. 226; cf. *EWG*, chap. 8, esp. p. 185).

Bibliography

When more than one publication is given for an article, the first one listed is the one that is used for page references in the present volume.

Allan, William, and Douglas Cairns. "Conflict and Community in the *Iliad*." In *Competition in the Ancient World*, edited by Nick Fisher and Hans van Wees, 113–146. Swansea: The Classical Press of Wales, 2011.

Apthorp, M. J. "The Language of *Odyssey* 5.7–20." *Classical Quarterly* 27 (1977): 1–9.

Auerbach, Erich. *Mimesis: The Representation of Reality in Western Literature* (trans. by Willard R. Trask). Princeton, NJ: Princeton University Press, 2003. First published 1953.

Austin, Norman. *Archery at the Dark of the Moon: Poetic Problems in Homer's Odyssey*. Berkeley and Los Angeles: University of California Press, 1975.

Bassett, Samuel Eliot. "The Ἁμαρτια of Achilles." *Transactions and Proceedings of the American Philological Association* 65 (1934): 47–69.

———. *The Poetry of Homer*. Lanham, MD: Lexington Books, 2003. First published 1938 by University of California Press.

———. "The Proems of the Iliad and the Odyssey." *American Journal of Philology* 44 (1923): 339–348.

Beke, George Latura. *Digging Up The Dog: The Greek Roots of Gurdjieff's Esoteric Ideas*. New York: Indications Press, 2005.

Bennett, J. G. *Gurdjieff: Making a New World*. New York: Harper & Row, 1973.

Besslich, Siegfried. *Schweigen—Verschweigen—Übergehen: Die Darstellung des Unausgesprochenen in der Odyssee*. Heidelberg: Carl Winter, 1966.

Borthwick, E. Kerr. *Odyssean Elements in the Iliad*. Inaug. lecture at Edinburgh University, 1983.

Bowra, C. M. "Composition." In *A Companion to Homer*, edited by Alan J. B. Wace and Frank H. Stubbings, 38–74. London: Macmillan, 1962.

———. *Heroic Poetry*. London: Macmillan, 1952.

———. *Homer*. London: Duckworth, 1972.

———. "Metre." In *A Companion to Homer*, edited by Alan J. B. Wace and Frank H. Stubbings, 19–25. London: Macmillan, 1962.

———. *Tradition and Design in the Iliad*. Oxford: Clarendon Press, 1930.

Brereton, Joel. "The Upanishads." In *Approaches to the Asian Classics*, edited by Wm. Theodore de Bary and Irene Bloom, 115–135. New York: Columbia University Press, 1990.

Büchner, Wilhelm. "Die Penelopeszenen in der Odyssee." *Hermes* 75 (1940): 129–167.

———. "Die Waffenbergung in der Odyssee." *Hermes* 67 (1932): 438–445.

Burgess, Jonathan S. *The Tradition of the Trojan War in Homer and the Epic Cycle*. Baltimore, MD: Johns Hopkins University Press, 2001.

Burkert, Walter. "The Song of Ares and Aphrodite: On the Relationship between the *Odyssey* and the *Iliad*" (trans. by G. M. Wright and P. V. Jones). In Doherty, *Oxford Readings*, 29–43. First published: *Rh. Mus.* 103 (1960): 130–144.

Buxton, Richard. "Similes and Other Likenesses." In Fowler, *Cambridge Companion*, 139–155.

Cairns, Douglas L. "Introduction." In Cairns, *Oxford Readings*, 117–146.

———, ed. *Oxford Readings in Homer's* Iliad. Oxford: Oxford University Press, 2001.

Calhoun, George M. "The Divine Entourage in Homer." *American Journal of Philology* 61 (1940): 257–277.

Challenger, Anna T. *Philosophy and Art in Gurdjieff's "Beelzebub": A Modern Sufi Odyssey*. Amsterdam: Rodopi, 2002.

Clark, Matthew. "Formulas, metre and type-scenes." In Fowler, *Cambridge Companion*, 117–138.

Clarke, Howard C. *The Art of the Odyssey*. London: Bristol Classical Press, 1989.

Clay, Jenny Strauss. *The Wrath of Athena*. Lanham, MD: Rowman and Littlefield, 1997. First published 1983 by Princeton University Press.

Combellack, Frederick M. "Three Odyssean Problems." *California Studies in Classical Antiquity* 6 (1973): 17–46.

Cook, Albert, trans. *Homer: The Odyssey*. 2nd ed. New York: W. W. Norton, 1993.

Cook, Erwin. "'Active' and 'Passive' Heroics in the *Odyssey*." In Doherty, *Oxford Readings*, 111–134. First published: *The Classical World* 93 (1999): 149–167.

Cunliffe, Richard John. *A Lexicon of the Homeric Dialect*. Norman, OK: University of Oklahoma Press, 1963. First published 1924 by Blackie and Son.

Defouw, Richard J. *The Enneagram in the Writings of Gurdjieff*. Indianapolis, IN: Dog Ear Publishing, 2011.

Dickie, Matthew W. "Fair and Foul Play in the Funeral Games in the *Iliad*." *Journal of Sport History* 11 (1984): 8–17.

Dimock, George E. *The Unity of the Odyssey*. Amherst, MA: University of Massachusetts Press, 1989.

Dodds, E. R. *The Greeks and the Irrational*. Berkeley and Los Angeles: University of California Press, 1951.

———. "Homer and the Analysts." In *Fifty Years (and Twelve) of Classical Scholarship*, edited by Maurice Platnauer, 1–8. Oxford: Basil Blackwell, 1968.

———. "Homer and the Unitarians." In *Fifty Years (and Twelve) of Classical Scholarship*, edited by Maurice Platnauer, 8–13. Oxford: Basil Blackwell, 1968.

Doherty, Lillian E. "Introduction." In Doherty, *Oxford Readings*, 1–17.

———, ed. *Oxford Readings in Classical Studies: Homer's* Odyssey. Oxford: Oxford University Press, 2009.

Donlan, Walter. "Duelling with Gifts in the *Iliad*: As the Audience Saw It." *Colby Quarterly* 29 (1993): 155–172.

———. "Reciprocities in Homer." *The Classical World* 75 (1981–1982): 137–175.

———. "The Unequal Exchange Between Glaucus and Diomedes in Light of the Homeric Gift-Economy." *Phoenix* 43 (1989): 1–15.

Douglas, Mary. *Thinking in Circles: An Essay on Ring Composition*. New Haven: Yale University Press, 2007.

Dowden, Ken. "The Epic Tradition in Greece." In Fowler, *Cambridge Companion*, 188–205.
Easwaran, Eknath, trans. *The Upanishads*. 2nd ed. Tomales, CA: Nilgiri Press, 2007.
Edwards, Mark W. *The Iliad: A Commentary*, vol. V: books 17–20. Cambridge: Cambridge University Press, 1991.
Eliade, Mircea. *Yoga: Immortality and Freedom* (trans. by Willard R. Trask). 2nd ed. Princeton, NJ: Princeton University Press, 1969. First published 1954 as *Le Yoga: Immortalité et Liberté*.
Emlyn-Jones, Chris. "The Reunion of Penelope and Odysseus." In Doherty, *Oxford Readings*, 208–230. First published: *Greece & Rome* 31 (1984): 1–18.
Erbse, Hartmut. *Beiträge zum Verständnis der Odyssee*. Berlin: Walter de Gruyter, 1972.
Fagles, Robert, trans. *Homer: The Iliad*. New York: Penguin, 1990.
———. *Homer: The Odyssey*. New York: Penguin, 1996.
Felson-Rubin, Nancy. "Penelope's Perspective: Character from Plot." In Schein, *Reading the* Odyssey, 163–183.
Fenik, Bernard. *Studies in the Odyssey*. Hermes Einzelschriften 30. Wiesbaden: Franz Steiner, 1974.
———. "Stylization and Variety: Four Monologues in the *Iliad*." In *Homer: Tradition and Invention*, edited by Bernard Fenik, 68–90. Leiden: Brill, 1978.
———. *Typical Battle Scenes in the Iliad: Studies in the Narrative Techniques of Homeric Battle Description*. Hermes Einzelschriften 21. Wiesbaden: Franz Steiner, 1968.
Fernández-Galiano, Manuel. "Books XXI–XXII." In *A Commentary on Homer's Odyssey*, vol. 3, by Joseph Russo, Manuel Fernández-Galiano, and Alfred Heubeck, 131–310. Oxford: Clarendon Press, 1992.
Foley, Helene P. "'Reverse Similes' and Sex Roles in the *Odyssey*." In Doherty, *Oxford Readings*, 189–207. First published: *Arethusa* 11 (1978): 7–26.
Fowler, Robert, ed. *The Cambridge Companion to Homer*. Cambridge: Cambridge University Press, 2004.
———. "The Homeric question." In Fowler, *Cambridge Companion*, 220–232.
Geddes, W. D. *The Problem of the Homeric Poems*. Ithaka, NY: Cornell University Library (digitized version available online), 2008. First published 1878 by Macmillan, London.
Gemoll, Albert. "Die Beziehungen zwischen *Ilias* und *Odyssee*." *Hermes* 18 (1883): 34–96.
Goold, G. P. "The Nature of Homeric Composition." *Illinois Classical Studies* 2 (1977): 1–34.
———. "The Removal of the Arms in the *Odyssey*." In *Studies in Honour of T. B. L. Webster*, vol. 1, 122–129. Bristol: Bristol University Press, 1986.
Griffin, Jasper. *Homer on Life and Death*. Oxford: Oxford University Press, 1980.
———. *Homer: The Odyssey*. 2nd ed. Cambridge: Cambridge University Press, 2004.
———. "The *Odyssey*'s Relationship to the *Iliad*" (review of Usener's *Beobachtungen zum Verhältnis der* Odyssee *zur* Ilias). *Classical Review* 41 (1991): 288–291.
Groeger, Max. "Die Kirke-Dichtung in der Odyssee." *Philologus* 59 (1900): 206–237.
Gurdjieff, G. I. *Beelzebub's Tales to His Grandson: An Objectively Impartial Criticism of the Life of Man*. New York: Penguin/Arkana, 1999. First published 1950 (as *All and Everything*) by Harcourt, Brace & World. A facsimile of the original edition with the title *All and Everything* is available (Aurora, OR: Two Rivers Press,

1993). An alternative translation published first in 1992 and later with minor refinements (New York: Jeremy P. Tarcher/Penguin, 2006) has both strengths and weaknesses relative to the original translation approved by Gurdjieff. The present volume usually quotes the 1950/1999 translation (referred to as *BT*), but occasionally quotes the 1992/2006 translation (referred to as *BT*1992).

———. *Beelzebubs Erzählungen für seinen Enkel: eine objektiv unparteiische Kritik des Lebens des Menschen*. Translated from the 1950 English translation of *Beelzebub's Tales* by Louise March. Basel: Sphinx, 1983. First published 1950. Revised ed. Triangle Editions, 2010.

———. *Rasskazy Velzevula svoemu vnuku: Obektivno-bespristrastnaya kritika zhizni lyudey*. Russian source for English translations of *Beelzebub's Tales*. Toronto: Traditional Studies Press, 2000.

———. *The Herald of Coming Good: First Appeal to Contemporary Humanity*. Translated from the Russian. Edmonds, WA: Holmes Publishing Group, Sure Fire Press, 1988; London: Book Studio, 2008. First published 1933 by La Société Anonyme des Éditions de l'Ouest, Paris and reprinted 1971 by Weiser.

———. *Life Is Real Only Then, When "I Am."* London: Penguin/Arkana, 1999. First published 1975 and 1978 (in an expanded edition) by E. P. Dutton.

———. *Meetings with Remarkable Men*. London: Penguin/Arkana, 1985. First published 1963 by E. P. Dutton.

———. *Rencontres avec des hommes remarquables*. Translated by Jeanne de Salzmann with Henri Tracol. Monaco: Éditions du Rocher, 2004. First published 1960 by Julliard.

———. *Transcripts of Gurdjieff's Meetings, 1941–1946*. London: Book Studio, 2008. First published in William Patrick Patterson, *Voices in the Dark: Esoteric, Occult & Secular Voices in Nazi-Occupied Paris 1940–44*, Fairfax, CA: Arete Communications, 2000.

———. *Views from the Real World: Early Talks of Gurdjieff in Moscow, Essentuki, Tiflis, Berlin, London, Paris, New York and Chicago as Recollected by His Pupils*. New York: Penguin Compass, 1984. First published 1973 by E. P. Dutton.

Hainsworth, J. B. "Books V–VIII." In *A Commentary on Homer's Odyssey*, vol. 1, by Alfred Heubeck, Stephanie West, and J. B. Hainsworth, 249–385. Oxford: Clarendon Press, 1988.

———. *The Iliad: A Commentary*, vol. III: books 9–12. Cambridge: Cambridge University Press, 1993.

———. "Odysseus and the Dogs." *Greece & Rome* 8 (1961): 122–125.

Hammond, Martin, trans. *Homer: The Iliad*. Penguin, 1987.

———. *Homer: The Odyssey*. New York and London: Bloomsbury, 2014 (first published 2000 by Duckworth).

Hansen, Wm. F. *The Conference Sequence: Patterned Narration and Narrative Inconsistency in the Odyssey*. Berkeley and Los Angeles: University of California Press, 1972.

Henderson, John. *Hidden Meanings and Picture-form Language in the Writings of G. I. Gurdjieff (Excavations of the Buried Dog)*. Bloomington, IN: AuthorHouse, 2007.

Heubeck, Alfred. "Books IX–XII." In *A Commentary on Homer's Odyssey*, vol. 2, by Alfred Heubeck and Arie Hoekstra, 3–143. Oxford: Clarendon Press, 1989.

———. "Books XXIII–XXIV." In *A Commentary on Homer's Odyssey*, vol. 3, by Joseph Russo, Manuel Fernández-Galiano, and Alfred Heubeck, 313–418. Oxford: Clarendon Press, 1992.

———. "General Introduction." In *A Commentary on Homer's Odyssey*, vol. 1, by Alfred Heubeck, Stephanie West, and J. B. Hainsworth, 3–23. Oxford: Clarendon Press, 1988.

Hölscher, Uvo. "Penelope and the Suitors" (trans. by Simon Richter). In Schein, *Reading the* Odyssey, 133–140. First published 1967 as "Penelope vor den Freiern" in *Lebende Antike: Symposium für Rudolph Sühnel* (edited by H. Meller and H.-J. Zimmermann; Berlin), 27–33.

Huddleston, James. Translation of the *Odyssey* used by Kahane and Mueller in *The Chicago Homer* at www.homer.library.northwestern.edu.

Hume, Robert Ernest, trans. *The Thirteen Principal Upanishads*. 2nd ed. New Delhi: Oxford University Press, 1983. First published in England 1921; 2nd ed. first published 1931 by Oxford University Press, London.

Iamblichus. *Iamblichus' Life of Pythagoras, or Pythagoric Life*. Translated by Thomas Taylor. Reprinted from 1818 ed. Rochester, VT: Inner Traditions International, 1986.

Jacoby, Felix. "Die geistige Physiognomie der Odyssee." *Die Antike* 9 (1933): 159–194. Reprinted in *Kleine philologishe Schriften* 1 (1961): 107–138.

Janko, Richard. "The Homeric Poems as Oral Dictated Texts." *Classical Quarterly* 48 (1998): 135–167. An online version of this paper, with pages numbered from 1 to 13, was used for the references to this paper in this book.

———. *The Iliad: A Commentary*, vol. IV: books 13–16. Cambridge: Cambridge University Press, 1994.

Johnson, K. Paul. *Initiates of Theosophical Masters*. Albany: State University of New York Press, 1995.

Johnston, Ian. "Deaths in the Iliad." http://records.viu.ca/~johnstoi/homer/Iliaddeaths.htm, 2001.

Jones, Peter. *Homer's Iliad: A Commentary on Three Translations*. London: Bristol Classical Press, 2003.

———. *Homer's Odyssey: A Commentary based on the English Translation of Richmond Lattimore*. London: Bristol Classical Press, 1988.

———. "Introduction." In *Homer: German Scholarship in Translation*, translated by G. M. Wright and P. V. Jones, 1–41. Oxford: Oxford University Press, 1997.

de Jong, Irene J. F. "Between Word and Deed: Hidden Thoughts in the *Odyssey*." In Doherty, *Oxford Readings*, 62–90. First published 1994 in *Modern Critical Theory and Classical Literature* (edited by Irene J. F. de Jong and J. P. Sullivan), Leiden: Brill, 27–50.

Jörgensen, Ove. "Das Auftreten der Götter in den Büchern ι–μ der Odyssee." *Hermes* 39 (1904): 357–382.

Kahane, Ahuvia, and Martin Mueller, eds. *The Chicago Homer*. www.homer.library.northwestern.edu.

Kelly, Adrian. "Achilles in Control? Managing Oneself and Others in the Funeral Games." In *Conflict and Consensus in Early Greek Hexameter Poetry*, edited by Paola Bassino, Lilah Grace Canevaro, and Barbara Graziosi, 87–108. Cambridge: Cambridge University Press, 2017.

———. "How to End an Orally-Derived Epic Poem." *Transactions of the American Philological Association* 137 (2007): 371–402.

———. *A Referential Commentary and Lexicon to* Iliad *VIII*. Oxford: Oxford University Press, 2007.

Kirk, G. S. *The Iliad: A Commentary*, vol. I: books 1–4. Cambridge: Cambridge University Press, 1985.

———. *The Iliad: A Commentary*, vol. II: books 5–8. Cambridge: Cambridge University Press, 1990.

———. *The Songs of Homer*. Cambridge: Cambridge University Press, 1962.

Knox, Bernard. "Introduction." In *The Iliad*, trans. by Robert Fagles. New York: Penguin Books, 1990.

Kurzban, Robert. *Why everyone (else) is a hypocrite: Evolution and the Modular Mind*. Princeton, NJ: Princeton University Press, 2010.

Lattimore, Richmond. "Introduction." In *The Odyssey of Homer*, trans. by Richmond Lattimore. New York: Harper & Row, 1967.

Lattimore, Richmond, trans. *The Iliad of Homer*. Chicago: University of Chicago Press, 2011. First published 1951. The 2011 edition includes an introduction and notes by Richard Martin.

———. *The Odyssey of Homer*. New York: Harper & Row, 1967.

Lesky, Albin. "Divine and Human Causation in Homeric Epic" (trans. by Leofranc Holford-Strevens). In Cairns, *Oxford Readings*, 170–202. Abridged from *Göttliche und menschliche Motivation im homerischen Epos*, Sitzungsberichte der Heidelberger Akademie der Wissenschaften, philosophische-historische Klasse, 1961, 4.

Longinus. *On the Sublime* (trans. by W. H. Fyfe, rev. by Donald Russell). In Loeb Classical Library 199. Cambridge, MA: Harvard University Press, 1999.

Lord, Albert B. "Homer and Huso II: Narrative Inconsistencies in Homer and Oral Poetry." *Transactions and Proceedings of the American Philological Association* 69 (1938): 439–445.

———. *The Singer of Tales*. 2nd ed. Cambridge, MA: Harvard University Press, 2000.

———. *The Singer Resumes the Tale*. Edited by M. L. Lord. Ithaca, NY, 1995.

Macleod, C. W. *Homer, Iliad Book XXIV*. Cambridge: Cambridge University Press, 1982.

———. "Homer on Poetry and the Poetry of Homer." In Cairns, *Oxford Readings*, 294–310. First published 1983 in his *Collected Essays*, Oxford: Oxford University Press.

Marg, Walter. "Das erste Lied des Demodocus." In *Navicula Chiloniensis: Festschrift für F. Jacoby*, 16–29. Leiden: Brill, 1956.

Merrill, Rodney, trans. *The Odyssey*. Ann Arbor, MI: University of Michigan Press, 2002.

Mitchell, Stephen, and Gregory Nagy. "Introduction." In *The Singer of Tales* by Albert B. Lord. 2nd ed. Cambridge, MA: Harvard University Press, 2000.

Monro, D. B. *Homer's Odyssey: Books XIII–XXIV*. Oxford, 1901.

Moore, James. *Gurdjieff: The Anatomy of a Myth*. Rockport, MA: Element, 1991.

Mueller, Martin. *The Iliad*. 2nd ed. London: Bristol Classical Press, 2009.

Mure, William. *Journal of a Tour in Greece and the Ionian Islands*. Edinburgh and London: William Blackwood and Sons, 1842.

Murnaghan, Sheila. "Penelope's *Agnoia*: Knowledge, Power, and Gender in the *Odyssey*." In Doherty, *Oxford Readings*, 231–246. First published: *Helios* NS 13 (1986): 103–115.

Murray, A. T., trans. *Homer: Iliad*. 2nd ed. Revised by William F. Wyatt. Loeb Classical Library 170 and 171. Cambridge, MA: Harvard University Press, 1999.

———. *Homer: Odyssey*. 2nd ed. Revised by George E. Dimock. Loeb Classical Library 104 and 105. Cambridge, MA: Harvard University Press, 1995 (reprinted with corrections 1998).

Nagy, Gregory. *The Best of the Achaeans: Concepts of the Hero in Archaic Greek Poetry*. Rev. ed. Baltimore, MD: Johns Hopkins University Press, 1999.

Nott, C. S. *Teachings of Gurdjieff: A Pupil's Journal*. New York: Weiser, 1962.

Olivelle, Patrick, trans. *Upanisads*. Oxford: Oxford University Press, 1996.

Orage, A. R. *A. R. Orage's Commentaries on G.I. Gurdjieff's "All and Everything: Beelzebub's Tales to His Grandson."* Edited by C. S. Nott, with an introduction by A. L. Staveley. Aurora, OR: Two Rivers Press, 1985. First published in Nott, *Teachings of Gurdjieff*, 125–215.

Ouspensky, P. D. *In Search of the Miraculous: Fragments of an Unknown Teaching*. New York: Harcourt, Brace & World, 1949. French translation by Philippe Lavastine: *Fragments d'un enseignement inconnu* (Paris: Éditions Stock).

Page, Denys L. *History and the Homeric Iliad*. Berkeley and Los Angeles: University of California Press, 1959.

———. *The Homeric Odyssey*. Oxford: Clarendon Press, 1955.

Parry, Adam. "Have We Homer's *Iliad*?". *Yale Classical Studies* 20 (1966): 175–216.

———. "Introduction." In *The Making of Homeric Verse: The Collected Papers of Milman Parry*, edited by Adam Parry, ix–lxii. Oxford: Oxford University Press, 1987. First published 1971.

Parry, Milman. "Studies in the Epic Technique of Oral Verse-Making. I. Homer and Homeric Style" (first publishing in *Harvard Studies in Classical Philology* 41 [1930]: 73–147). In *The Making of Homeric Verse: The Collected Papers of Milman Parry*, edited by Adam Parry, 266–324. Oxford: Oxford University Press, 1987 (first published 1971).

———. "The Traditional Epithet in Homer" (*L'Épithète traditionnelle dans Homère: Essai sur un problème de style homèrique*, one of Milman Parry's two 1928 doctoral dissertations at the University of Paris, trans. by Adam Parry). In *The Making of Homeric Verse: The Collected Papers of Milman Parry*, edited by Adam Parry, 1–190. Oxford: Oxford University Press, 1987 (first published 1971).

Patterson, William Patrick. *Taking with the Left Hand: Enneagram Craze, People of the Bookmark, & the Mouravieff 'Phenomenon'*. Fairfax, CA: Arete Communications, 1998.

Peters, Fritz. *Gurdjieff Remembered*. New York: Samuel Weiser, 1971. First published 1965 by Victor Gollancz.

Pinker, Steven. *How the Mind Works*. New York: W. W. Norton, 1997.

Plass, Paul. "Menelaus and Proteus." *Classical Journal* 65 (1969): 104–108.

Podlecki, Anthony J. "Some Odyssean Similes." *Greece & Rome* 18 (1971): 81–90.

Polya, G. *Mathematics and Plausible Reasoning*. Vol. 2, *Patterns of Plausible Inference*. 2nd ed. Princeton, NJ: Princeton University Press, 1968.

Postlethwaite, Norman. "Agamemnon, Best of Spearmen?". *Phoenix* 49 (1995): 95–103. [The punctuation in the title of the paper does not appear in the original publication, but is used when the paper is cited in the bibliography of Postlethwaite's commentary on the *Iliad*.]

———. *Homer's Iliad: A Commentary on the Translation of Richmond Lattimore*. Exeter, UK: University of Exeter Press, 2000.

———. "Thersites in the *Iliad*." *Greece & Rome* 35 (1988): 123–136.

Pucci, Pietro. *Odysseus Polutropos: Intertextual Readings in the* Odyssey *and the* Iliad. Ithaca, NY: Cornell University Press, 1987.

———. "The Song of the Sirens." In Schein, *Reading the* Odyssey, 191–199. First published: *Arethusa* 12 (1979): 121–132.

———. *The Song of the Sirens: Essays on Homer*. Lanham, MD: Rowman and Littlefield, 1998.

Redfield, James. "The Proem of the *Iliad*: Homer's Art." In Cairns, *Oxford Readings*, 456–477. First published: *Classical Philology* 74 (1979): 94–110.

Reinhardt, Karl. "The Adventures in the *Odyssey*" (trans. by Harriet I. Flower). In Schein, *Reading the* Odyssey, 63–132. First published 1948 as "Die Abenteuer der Odyssee" in Reinhardt's book *Von Werken und Formen* (Godesberg: Kupper), 52–162.

———. *Die Ilias und ihr Dichter*. Edited by Uvo Hölscher. Göttingen: Vandenhoeck und Ruprecht, 1961.

Richardson, Nicholas. *The Iliad: A Commentary*, vol. VI: books 21–24. Cambridge: Cambridge University Press, 1993.

Rieu, E. V., trans. *Homer: The Iliad*. Revised and updated by Peter Jones with D. C. H. Rieu. Penguin, 2003.

———. *Homer: The Odyssey*. Revised by D. C. H. Rieu. Penguin, 2003.

Risch, Ernst. "Namendeutungen und Wortererklärungen bei den ältesten griechischen Dictern." In *Eumusia: Festgabe für Ernst Howald*. Erlenbach: E. Rentsch, 1947.

Rosenblatt, Kathleen Ferrick. *René Daumal: The Life and Work of a Mystic Guide*. Albany, NY: State University of New York Press, 1999.

Russo, Joseph. "Books XVII–XX." In *A Commentary on Homer's Odyssey*, vol. 3, by Joseph Russo, Manuel Fernández-Galiano, and Alfred Heubeck, 3–127. Oxford: Clarendon Press, 1992.

Rüter, Klaus. *Odysseeinterpretationen: Untersuchungen zum ersten Buch und zur Phaiakis*. Edited by Kjeld Matthiessen. Göttingen: Vandenhoeck & Ruprecht, 1969.

Rutherford, Richard B. "From the *Iliad* to the *Odyssey*." In Cairns, *Oxford Readings*, 117–146. First published: *Bulletin of the Institute for Classical Studies* 38 (1991–1993): 47–54.

———. *Homer*. 2nd ed. Cambridge: Cambridge University Press, 2013.

———. *Homer, Odyssey Books XIX and XX*. Cambridge: Cambridge University Press, 1992.

———. "The Philosophy of the *Odyssey*." In Doherty, *Oxford Readings*, 155–188. First published: *Journal of Hellenic Studies* 106 (1986): 145–162.

Saïd, Suzanne. *Homer and the* Odyssey. Oxford: Oxford University Press, 2011.

de Salzmann, Jeanne. *The Reality of Being: The Fourth Way of Gurdjieff*. Boston: Shambhala, 2010.

Schadewaldt, Wolfgang. *Iliasstudien*. 3rd ed. Darmstadt: Wissenschaftliche Buchgesellschaft, 1966. Identical to 2nd ed. published 1943 in Leipzig.

Scheibner, Gerhard. *Der Aufbau des 20. und 21. Buches der Ilias*. Leipzig: Robert Noske, 1939.

Schein, Seth L. "Homeric Intertextuality: Two Examples." In *Euphrosyne: Studies in Ancient Epic and its Legacy in Honor of Dimitris N. Maronitis*, edited by John N. Kazazis and Antonios Rengakos, 349–356. Stuttgart: Franz Steiner, 1999.

———. "The *Iliad*: Structure and Interpretation." In *A New Companion to Homer*, edited by Ian Morris and Barry Powell, 345–359. Leiden: Brill, 1997.

———. *The Mortal Hero: An Introduction to Homer's* Iliad. Berkeley and Los Angeles: University of California Press, 1984.

———, ed. *Reading the* Odyssey: *Selected Interpretive Essays*. Princeton, NJ: Princeton University Press, 1996.

Schlunk, Robin R. "The Theme of the Suppliant-Exile in the *Iliad.*" *American Journal of Philology* 97 (1976): 199–209.

Scodel, Ruth. *Credible Impossibilities: Conventions and Strategies of Verisimilitude in Homer and Greek Tragedy*. Stuttgart: Teubner, 1999.

———. *Listening to Homer: Tradition, Narrative, and Audience*. Ann Arbor, MI: University of Michigan Press, 2009. First published 2002.

———. "Pseudo-Intimacy and the Prior Knowledge of the Homeric Audience." *Arethusa* 30 (1997): 201–219.

———. "The Story-Teller and His Audience." In Fowler, *Cambridge Companion*, 45–55.

Scott, John A. "The First Book of the Odyssey." *Transactions of the American Philological Association* 67 (1936): 1–6.

———. *The Unity of Homer*. Berkeley: University of California Press, 1921.

Scully, Stephen. "Doubling in the Tale of Odysseus." *The Classical World* 80 (1987): 401–417.

Segal, Charles. "The embassy and the duals of *Iliad* 9. 182–198." *Greek, Roman, and Byzantine Studies* 9 (1968): 101–114.

———. "*Kleos* and its Ironies in the *Odyssey*" (trans. by Harriet I. Flower). In Schein, *Reading the* Odyssey, 201–221. First published: *L'Antiquité Classique* 52 (1983), 22–47.

Seymour-Smith, Martin. *The 100 Most Influential Books Ever Written: The History of Thought from Ancient Times to Today*. New York: Citadel Press, 1998.

Sheppard, J. T. *The Pattern of the Iliad*. New York: Haskell House, 1966. First published 1922 in London.

Shewring, Walter, trans. *Homer:* The Odyssey. Oxford: Oxford University Press, 1980.

Silk, Michael. "The *Odyssey* and its Explorations." In Fowler, *Cambridge Companion*, 31–44.

Sinclair, Frank R. *Without Benefit of Clergy: Some Personal Footnotes to the Gurdjieff Teaching*. 2nd ed. Xlibris, 2009.

Slatkin, Laura M. "Composition by Theme and the *Mētis* of the *Odyssey*." In Schein, *Reading the* Odyssey, 223–237.

Stanford, W. B., ed. *The Odyssey of Homer*, vol. II. 2nd ed. New York: St. Martin's Press, 1965.

———. *The Ulysses Theme: A Study in the Adaptability of a Traditional Hero*. 2nd ed. Ann Arbor, MI: University of Michigan Press, 1968.

Stanley, Keith. *The Shield of Homer: Narrative Structure in the* Iliad. Princeton, NJ: Princeton University Press, 1993.

Steiner, Deborah. *Homer, Odyssey Books XVII and XVIII*. Cambridge: Cambridge University Press, 2010.

Tamdgidi, Mohammad H. *Gurdjieff and Hypnosis: A Hermeneutic Study*. New York: Palgrave Macmillan, 2009.

Taplin, Oliver. *Homeric Soundings: The Shaping of the* Iliad. Oxford: Clarendon Press, 1992.

Taylor, Paul Beekman. *Gurdjieff's Invention of America*. Utrecht: Eureka Editions, 2007.

———. *The Philosophy of G. I. Gurdjieff: Time, Word and Being in* All and Everything. Utrecht: Eureka Editions, 2007.

Thornton, Agathe. *People and Themes in Homer's Odyssey*. London: Methuen and University of Otago Press, 1970.

Tracy, Steven V. *The Story of the* Odyssey. Princeton, NJ: Princeton University Press, 1990.

Traill, David A. *Schliemann of Troy: Treasure and Deceit*. New York: St. Martin's Griffin, 1995.

Usener, Knut. *Beobachtungen zum Verhältnis der* Odyssee *zur* Ilias. Tübingen: Gunter Narr, 1990.

Waldock, A. J. A. *Sophocles the Dramatist*. Cambridge: Cambridge University Press, 1951.

Webb, James. *The Harmonious Circle: The Lives and Work of G. I. Gurdjieff, P. D. Ouspensky, and Their Followers*. New York: G. P. Putnam's Sons, 1980.

West, Martin L., ed. and trans. *Greek Epic Fragments: From the Seventh to the Fifth Centuries BC*. Loeb Classical Library 497. Cambridge, MA: Harvard University Press, 2003.

———. "The Homeric Question Today." *Proceedings of the American Philosophical Society* 155 (2011): 383–393.

———. *The Making of the Iliad: Disquisition and Analytical Commentary*. Oxford: Oxford University Press, 2011.

———. *The Making of the Odyssey*. Oxford: Oxford University Press, 2014.

West, Stephanie. "Books I–IV." In *A Commentary on Homer's Odyssey*, vol. 1, by Alfred Heubeck, Stephanie West, and J. B. Hainsworth, 51–245. Oxford: Clarendon Press, 1988.

———. "The Transmission of the Text." In *A Commentary on Homer's Odyssey*, vol. 1, by Alfred Heubeck, Stephanie West, and J. B. Hainsworth, 33–48. Oxford: Clarendon Press, 1988.

Whitehead, Oliver. "The Funeral of Achilles; an Epilogue to the *Iliad* in Book 24 of the *Odyssey*." *Greece & Rome* 31 (1984): 119–125.

Whitman, Cedric H. *Homer and the Heroic Tradition*. Cambridge, MA: Harvard University Press, 1958.

Wilamowitz-Moellendorff, Ulrich von. *Die Heimkehr des Odysseus*. Berlin: Weidmann, 1927.

———. *Die Ilias und Homer*. Berlin: Weidmann, 1916.

Willcock, Malcolm M. *A Companion to the* Iliad. Chicago: University of Chicago Press, 1976.

Woodhouse, W. J. *The Composition of Homer's Odyssey*. Oxford: Clarendon Press, 1930.

Index of Homeric Passages

The passages listed in this index are mainly those which appear in block quotations. Quote numbers are shown in bold in brackets following the verse numbers. References in chapters 7–9 to passages first discussed earlier in the book are not included, because they shed no light on the passages themselves.

Passages from the *Iliad*

1.59–64 [**6.15**]: 150–151, 308 (n. 68)
1.90–91 [**6.16**]: 150, 307 (n. 67)
1.106–108 [**6.17**]: 150, 152
1.161 [**3.16**]: 76
1.163–168 [**3.7**]: 64, 67
1.239–244 [**6.6**]: 143–145, 151
1.277–281 [**5.9**]: 93
1.298–303 [**3.17**]: 76
1.411–412 [**6.18**]: 151
2.26–30 [**6.7**]: 143–144, 151
2.35–40 [**5.15**]: 99, 143
2.72–75 [**6.8**]: 143–144, 147, 151, 306 (n. 43), 307 (n. 52)
2.79–83 [**6.9**]: 143–144, 147, 150–151, 306 (n. 43)
2.110–141 [**6.10**]: 144–147, 306 (n. 51)
2.259–260 [**5.39**]: 118–119, 297 (n. 157)
2.331–335 [**6.19**]: 152
2.375–378 [**6.12**]: 146, 148–149, 151, 306 (n. 51)
4.161–165 [**9.10**]: 234–236
4.303–309 [**5.38**]: 118
4.353–355 [**5.40**]: 118–119
6.447–456 [**9.9**]: 234–236
6.490–493 [**5.1**]: 85–88, 281 (n. 9), 282 (n. 20)
7.87–91 [**5.16**]: 101
8.335–345 [**6.27**]: 166
9.109–120 [**6.11**]: 145–146, 148, 306 (n. 49)
9.182–198: 132–135
9.197–204 [**5.11**]: 95, 97, 286–287 (n. 55), 301 (n. 2)
9.300–306 [**5.13**]: 96, 104, 139
9.308–317 [**5.12, 5.14**]: 96–97, 287 (n. 56)
9.316–322 [**5.26**]: 105, 289 (n. 86)
9.334–336 [**3.6**]: 63
9.378–387 [**6.4**]: 138–139, 141, 305 (nn. 36, 38)
9.411–416 [**5.18**]: 101, 104–105, 137
9.690–692: 133–134

11.47–52 [**6.26**]: 165
11.430–433 [**5.33**]: 110–111, 118, 293 (n. 116)
11.446–455 [**5.32**]: 110–113, 293 (nn. 113, 114, 120)
11.608–609 [**6.5**]: 141–142, 305 (n. 38)
12.49–86 [**6.24**]: 164–166, 313 (n. 149)
12.322–328 [**5.20**]: 101
13.459–461 [**9.13**]: 236–237, 331–332 (nn. 32–35)
15.343–345 [**6.28**]: 166
16.36–41 [**6.1**]: 136–137, 140
16.49–65 [**6.2**]: 136–140, 305 (n. 38)
16.52–4 [**3.5**]: 63
16.80–90 [**6.3**]: 138–139, 304 (n. 29)
16.369–371 [**6.25**]: 165
17.12–37 [**5.35**]: 112–113, 294 (nn. 124, 125)
17.536–542 [**5.34**]: 111
19.56–58 [**6.13**]: 148
19.65–70 [**3.1**]: 58–60, 65
19.83–92 [**3.2**]: 58, 148, 272 (n. 19)
19.139–144 [**3.8**]: 65
19.182–183 [**6.14**]: 149
19.270–275 [**3.3**]: 59, 272 (n. 19)
20.120–124 [**6.21**]: 161
20.293–296 [**6.20**]: 154, 309 (n. 81), 311 (n. 129)
21.229–232 [**6.23**]: 163, 312 (nn. 141, 142)
21.279–283 [**5.19**]: 101–102, 161
21.284–292 [**6.22**]: 161
22.304–305 [**5.17**]: 101
23.80–92 [**3.11**]: 69, 275–276 (n. 62)
23.492–495 [**5.42**]: 125
23.543–544 [**3.14**]: 75–76
23.553–554 [**3.15**]: 75–76, 278 (n. 99)
23.571–578 [**3.18**]: 76–77
23.606–611 [**3.19**]: 77
23.884–897 [**3.4**]: 61–68, 71–75, 78, 124, 274 (n. 43)
24.203–208 [**9.15**]: 237–238, 332 (n. 40)
24.224–227 [**9.16**]: 238
24.480–484 [**9.14, 9.18**]: 237–239, 333 (n. 43)
24.486–489 [**5.28**]: 106
24.519–521 [**9.17**]: 238, 332 (n. 40)
24.540–542 [**5.29**]: 106
24.599–620 [**5.41**]: 122, 299 (n. 177)
24.650–658 [**3.12**]: 74–75, 278 (n. 92)
24.669–670 [**3.13**]: 74–75

Passages from the *Odyssey*

1.96–102 [**6.39**]: 176
1.287–296 [**6.37**]: 173, 176
1.356–359 [**5.2**]: 85–90, 281 (n. 9), 282 (n. 19)
1.372–380 [**5.4**]: 89–90
2.50–59 [**6.47**]: 182
3.130–161 [**6.34**]: 170, 314 (n. 165)
4.335–340 [**9.12**]: 236

INDEX OF HOMERIC PASSAGES 349

4.389–393 [**6.44**]: 179–180
4.472–480 [**6.38**]: 175–176
5.29–42 [**2.25**]: 51–52
5.44–49 [**6.40**]: 176
5.105–111 [**6.32**]: 169–171, 269 (n. 131), 315 (n. 170)
5.129–134 [**6.33**]: 170–171, 314–315 (nn. 169, 171)
5.305–312 [**5.21**]: 102, 104
8.73–82 [**5.10**]: 94–95, 97–99
8.83–95 [**1.2**]: 4–6, 10, 255 (n. 39)
8.266–366: 34, 99–100
8.479–481 [**8.7**]: 204
8.521–531 [**9.11**]: 235–237
8.521–534 [**1.3**]: 4–7, 10–11, 253 (n. 14), 255 (n. 39)
9.12–15 [**1.8**]: 12
9.19–20 [**1.6**]: 7
9.29–32 [**6.36**]: 172, 316 (n. 176)
9.37–38 [**1.9**]: 12
9.40–43 [**1.4**]: 5, 254 (n. 16)
9.47–61 [**5.37**]: 117–118, 296 (nn. 147, 148)
9.528–535 [**6.45**]: 180, 317 (n. 182)
10.275–279 [**2.26**]: 52–54
10.302–306 [**2.27**]: 53
10.490–495 [**5.24**]: 103
10.539–540 [**6.29**]: 167–169, 175–176, 179, 314 (nn. 159, 161)
11.100–137 [**6.30**]: 168–169, 173, 177–178, 180, 317 (n. 181)
11.176–179 [**6.41**]: 177
11.350–353 [**5.6**]: 91, 283 (n. 33)
11.355–361 [**1.7**]: 8
11.473–476 [**5.22**]: 102, 104
11.482–486 [**5.23**]: 102–105
11.488–491 [**5.25**]: 104, 289 (nn. 83, 85)
11.494–503 [**5.27**]: 106, 289 (n. 92)
12.21–27 [**6.31**]: 168–169, 171
12.374–390 [**6.35**]: 170–171, 315–316 (nn. 172–174)
13.296–299 [**2.18**]: 39–41, 269 (n. 131)
13.375–381 [**6.42**]: 21, 39–40, 177, 295 (n. 131), 318 (n. 199)
13.383–385 [**6.43**]: 177–178, 318 (n. 199)
13.386–391 [**2.19**]: 40, 295 (n. 131)
14.29–38 [**8.19**]: 211–213, 325 (n. 34)
14.96–104 [**8.21**]: 214
14.276–283 [**8.20**]: 213
16.282–298 [**2.4**]: 20–22, 181, 183, 259–261 (nn. 28, 29, 31, 32, 34)
16.288–294 [**6.46**]: 181–182, 319 (n. 215)
17.496–497 [**2.22**]: 44–45
17.518–521 [**8.8**]: 205, 324 (n. 15)
18.158–162 [**2.5**]: 23–26, 41–44, 262 (n. 43)
18.163–168 [**2.7**]: 25–26, 43–44, 263 (n. 55)
18.169–176 [**2.21**]: 44–46
18.212–213 [**2.20**]: 41
18.221–225 [**2.23**]: 45, 268 (n. 119)
18.257–273 [**2.2**]: 17–18, 21, 26, 41–42, 46, 258 (n. 17), 262 (n. 48)
18.281–283 [**2.24**]: 42, 46, 258 (n. 15)
19.1–52 [**2.3, 6.46**]: 19–24, 31, 181–183, 260 (n. 31), 319 (n. 215)

19.204–212 [**1.5**]: 5–6, 11
19.571–581 [**2.1**]: 16–18, 24–26
19.583–587 [**2.8**]: 27–28, 37
20.9–13 [**2.10**]: 29–30
20.18–21 [**2.17**]: 38, 266–267 (n. 98)
20.38–43 [**2.9**]: 29–30, 264 (n. 69)
20.116–121 [**2.11**]: 29–30
20.229–234 [**2.13**]: 30
21.1–4 [**2.6**]: 25–26, 37, 263 (n. 52)
21.350–353 [**5.3**]: 86–91, 281 (n. 9), 282 (n. 23)
21.369–375 [**5.5**]: 89–91
21.412–415 [**2.12**]: 30
22.1–15 [**6.49**]: 184
22.21–33 [**6.48**]: 182–186, 319 (n. 217), 320 (nn. 219, 226)
22.91–94 [**5.30**]: 108, 110, 291 (n. 101), 293 (nn. 114, 120)
22.401–417 [**5.31**]: 109–116, 292 (n. 112), 294 (nn. 124, 125), 296 (nn. 144, 146)
23.59–68 [**5.36**]: 116, 296 (nn. 144, 146)
23.248–255 [**2.15**]: 35–37
23.260–261 [**2.16**]: 36–37
24.24–27 [**5.8**]: 92–94, 128
24.71–79 [**3.10**]: 69–71, 92, 129, 276 (nn. 62, 73), 281 (n. 5), 284–285 (n. 43)
24.85–92 [**3.9**]: 68–70, 92
24.93–94 [**5.7**]: 92, 102, 105, 289 (n. 84)
24.152–169 [**2.14**]: 33, 38, 265 (n. 78)

www.ingramcontent.com/pod-product-compliance
Lightning Source LLC
Chambersburg PA
CBHW071854290426
44110CB00013B/1135